Praise for
George Washington's Sur[

D1449317

"Tucker's account brims with colorful informati[ ]
episode in American history. Of most interest to military historians and
Revolutionary War buffs."

— *Kirkus Reviews*

"Pulls back the shroud of legend surrounding the battle of Trenton, revealing the
details of the turning point of the American Revolution. . . . Contrary to long-
standing theories that Washington won because of the incompetence of Hessian
leader Col. Johann Gottieb Rall, Tucker validates Rall's tenacity and deep military leadership. He also gives credit to unsung heroes in Washington's army."

— *Publishers Weekly*

"Tucker's book is less about myth-busting and more about re-creating . . . the
events of that day."

— *The Star-Ledger*

"A highly detailed and fairly balanced assessment not only of the Battle of
Trenton, but also of the Hessian commander Col. Rall. Phillip Thomas Tucker,
PhD, dispels many myths and legends that have been incorrectly told since the
end of the American Revolution. An enjoyable and scholarly read."

— Scott G. Rall, Descendant of Col. Johann G. Rall

"Transfers the meticulous details of American history into enduring reading.
Dr. Tucker's acknowledgment of the crucial role of those who are always mar-
ginalized is returned to the historical narrative."

— Mario Marcel Salas, Assistant Professor of Political Science (Ret.)

"Extensively researched and superbly argued in Tucker's compelling narrative,
this in-depth examination of George Washington's 'military miracle' at the battle of Trenton unquestionably confirms the vital importance of that stunning
victory.

— Jerry D. Morelock, PhD, Editor in Chief, *Armchair General* magazine

"Tucker combines a detailed analysis of Trenton as a brilliantly conceived and
executed military operation with a convincing argument for the battle as the
defining event of the American Revolution."

— Dennis Showalter, PhD, Professor of History, Colorado College

GEORGE WASHINGTON'S SURPRISE ATTACK

A NEW LOOK AT THE BATTLE THAT DECIDED THE FATE OF AMERICA

By Phillip Thomas Tucker, PhD

Foreword by David A. Hart, Trenton Historical Society

Skyhorse Publishing

Skyhorse Publishing books may be purchased in bulk at special discounts for sales promotion, corporate gifts, fund-raising, or educational purposes. Special editions can also be created to specifications. For details, contact the Special Sales Department, Skyhorse Publishing, 307 West 36th Street, 11th Floor, New York, NY 10018 or info@skyhorsepublishing.com.

Skyhorse® and Skyhorse Publishing® are registered trademarks of Skyhorse Publishing, Inc.®, a Delaware corporation.

Visit our website at www.skyhorsepublishing.com.

10 9 8 7 6 5 4 3 2 1

Cover design by Victoria Bellavia

Library of Congress Cataloging-in-Publication Data is available on file.

ISBN: 978-1-5107-0413-8
Ebook ISBN: 978-1-5107-1973-6

Printed in the United States of America

Dedication

To my father, Willard Thomas Tucker, 1924-2013.
He inspired this work in too many ways to count.
Most of all, his guiding hand, sage advice, and inspirational influence
made this book possible. As a true American patriot, he sincerely believed
in the inspirational value and importance of this work for today's America.

Contents

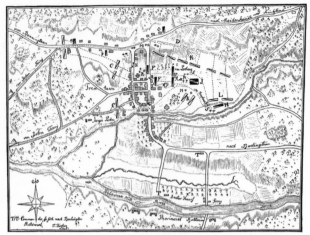

LIEUTENANT FISCHER'S MAP

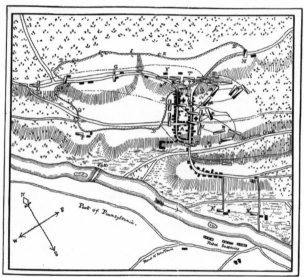

LIEUTENANT PIEL'S MAP

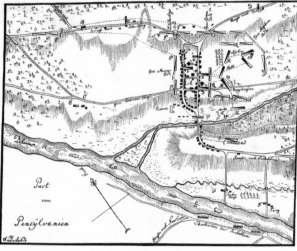

LIEUTENANT WIEDERHOLD'S MAP

Foreword

The revolution is on the ropes. Time and the enemy are poised to deliver the knockout blow.

Driven by defeat after defeat in New York and reeling from retreat after retreat across New Jersey, General George Washington and his ragtag army of largely peacetime farmers and humble shopkeepers finds itself in December 1776 encamped across the Delaware River. More dark days seem to loom on the horizon.

Cold, ill-equipped and demoralized—all that stands between Washington and an early exit from the War for Independence is the narrow meandering river nine miles north of Trenton at a place called McConkey's Ferry. Certain that the rebels have no stomach to fight on, Lord Cornwallis, the British field commander has closed down the campaign and headed for winter quarters, leaving a small garrison of hired Hessian mercenaries in Trenton to keep a wary eye on the beleaguered Continentals.

With winter coming on and enlistments due to expire at the end of the year Washington is desperate for action. He is anxious for even the slightest victory that might boost the morale of his dispirited troops, silence his critics in the Congress, and save face for the new nation.

His growing network of spies has advised him of an opportunity. Trenton, the burgeoning hamlet strategically located between New York and Philadelphia, is ripe for a surprise attack. But can the spies be trusted? Espionage is in its infancy and for the right price during these turbulent times a man might be tempted to trade his good name for a warm coat.

The weather forecast is foreboding. But the twenty-four hundred ill-clad soldiers do not need a weatherman to tell them the grim news. They can feel the chilling dampness gnawing at their bones and biting into the numb, bleeding toes of their rag-wrapped feet.

During a meeting of the war council, a daring plan is hatched. Trenton—with its stores of badly needed provisions—is the target. The goal will be a three-pronged dawn assault against the sleepy-eyed German garrison slumbering in their bedrolls following a night of Christmas cheer. At least that is the hope, if not the expectation.

All that remains is for the Continental troops to make the treacherous nighttime river crossing and brave the arduous march south in total darkness, along the rutted route to the unsuspecting town.

Casting shivering stares across from Pennsylvania, the men cannot see the Jersey embankment, which is cloaked in darkness and blanketed by snow. As men, horses, and canon are loaded onto the shallow draft Durham boats, sleet and freezing rain pelts the raw faces and unprotected hands of the weary troops. "Keep your powder dry, boys, " their commander cautions.

In the frosty night, air jagged ice floes the size of small boulders have choked the river, making the watery passage both tedious and tiring. The crossing takes longer than anticipated. Valuable time has been lost. Will they make it to Trenton before sunrise?

All down the line the battle cry goes out: "Victory or Death!" There is no turning back.

Thus begins one of the most bold and audacious maneuvers ever attempted in the annals of American military history. To say that in the minds of the Hessian officers stationed at Trenton that Washington's crossing of the ice-dammed Delaware in a blizzard on Christmas Night 1776 was as improbable as Hannibal's army crossing the Alps on the backs of elephants to face the Romans in 218 B.C., would not be an understatement. It's success set up the crucial "turning point" that changed the course of the war and the future of the world forever. In a prescient moment, acknowledgment as to the significance of the event comes fittingly passed down to history from Lord George Germain, the British colonial secretary at the time who is reported to have said: "All our hopes were blasted by that unhappy affair at Trenton."

—David A. Hart
Co-author of *Trenton: a novel*, and
Trustee for the Trenton Historical Society

Introduction

After securing victory at Yorktown, Virginia, in October 1781, with his soldiers of liberty and the troops of America's French ally, George Washington was celebrated as America's greatest conquering hero when he arrived with much fanfare in the prosperous Maryland state capital of Annapolis. Here, thankful city fathers, representing the American people's exuberance, presented a stirring city address to General Washington. However, they focused not on the recent Yorktown success, but on Washington's sparkling victory at Trenton, New Jersey, more than five years before. Emphasizing how Washington's December 26, 1776 miracle victory saved the revolution from an early death, the esteemed civic leaders of Annapolis declared, "We derive peculiar pleasure from the contemplation, that the successes [of Washington and his Continental Army] at Trenton and Princeton laid the corner stone of our freedom and independence."[1]

Articulating the sentiments of the American people, these heartfelt words of the Annapolis elite were right on target. Before Washington won his most improbable victory at Trenton on the snowy, bitterly cold morning of December 26, 1776, only a military miracle could have possibly saved the unprecedented egalitarian dream of America, a common people's revolution, and an audacious republican experiment. After having suffered one sharp military setback after another for months during America's darkest year of 1776, when the once-vibrant dream of nationhood had all but succumbed to an early, agonizing death, everything now depended upon a forty-five-year old former Virginia militia commander, who had yet to win a single battle in America's struggle for liberty after nearly a year and a half. Washington's military reputation and career lay in ruins. After the panicked members of the Continental Congress fled the new republic's capital of Philadelphia and with the British-Hessian Army drawing ever closer in early December, Washington was left with the sole responsibility to somehow do the impossible.

Therefore, the irrepressible Virginian, who proved to be at his best exactly when America's fortunes had fallen to their lowest ebb, took the greatest risk and gamble of his career. He decided to go for broke when the stakes could not have been higher for America. On Christmas night, which appeared to be the final Yuletide of the infant republic's short lifetime and a failed experiment in nationhood, Washington prepared to lead a stalwart band of ill-clad, often-defeated band of revolutionaries from across America into the cold depths of the dark unknown east of the Delaware River in a desperate bid to preserve a new, shining future for America.

Embarking upon what no one of either side imagined any sane military leader would attempt to even think about in the midst of winter's tight grip when eighteenth-century armies traditionally remained quietly in winter quarters, Washington sought to reverse the fortunes of war on one throw of the dice in what was literally America's last opportunity to do so. With Continental enlistments of almost all of his best troops about to expire at the year's end, Washington had little choice but to stake everything on his surprise attack on the Trenton garrison of the best professional soldiers in America, the Hessians.

By this time, America's resistance effort had fizzled miserably after a string of summer and autumn disasters. Without a late December victory from America's rustic revolutionaries, this struggle for America's possession, heart, and soul was over. If Washington lost the next battle, then the young American republic was fated to become nothing more than only an obscure footnote in history books. Washington fully realized that if he and what little remained of his Continental Army suffered yet another defeat during America's darkest hour, then the young American republic and dream was forever doomed to an ignominious end.

Consequently, undertaking what was truly a mission impossible, Washington planned to cross the swollen, ice-clogged Delaware River (like Julius Caesar who ferried his legionnaires across wide rivers to surprise his opponents in winter's depths) from eastern Pennsylvania to western New Jersey, conduct a lengthy night march south through uncharted territory to descend upon Trenton from the north, assault three veteran regiments (a full Hessian brigade) of well-trained troops, and capture the suddenly strategic Delaware river town of Trenton.

Quite simply, what Washington planned to embark upon was the most audacious offensive effort of the war. Because actual independence could only be achieved by winning victory on the battlefield, America's true creation story actually began *not* with the signing of the Declaration of Independence—"of but little importance" without military victory in Thomas Paine's insightful words—at Philadelphia, Pennsylvania, on July 4, 1776, but at Trenton on December 26, 1776 with the most improbable victory of the American Revolution. When the idealistic dream of a new people's republic had been transformed into a nightmare by early December 1776, the fortunes of war were miraculously reversed by Washington in what was his finest hour.

Clearly, the high-stakes showdown at Trenton was far more than the story of a typical battle of wasteful bloodletting because America's independence had to be won by the flintlock muskets and rifles of Washington's rough-hewn, illiterate common soldiers—mostly farmers and hunters—rather than by the pen of the erudite, aristocratic members of the well-educated colonial elite in Philadelphia. Therefore, this all-important clash of arms in the harsh environment of a swirling snowstorm resulted in the American Revolution's most dramatic reversal of fortunes in which the United States of America was truly born. With his one-sided December 26 success validating Thomas Jefferson's words in the Declaration of Independence, Washington's unexpected victory at Trenton earned a new lease of life for the American republic because the declaration's signing had been only a stillbirth that was more rhetorical, if not fanciful, than real. Therefore, Washington's victory at Trenton was in fact America's true creation story, rebirth, and original national *Illiad*.

All of the humiliating fiascos and defeats of 1776 during America's darkest period set the stage for Washington's Trenton miracle. Washington's improbable victory at Trenton provided a miraculous rebirth of the dying army and republic in the most dramatic reversal of America's fortunes at nearly the last possible moment. The stoic Virginian's remarkable December 26 success ensured that America's revolution against monarchy, imperialism, and empire was not just another doomed resistance effort, like so many ill-fated Celtic rebellions in Ireland and Scotland against the British Empire's might. Against all odds and when time was running out for America, the fortunes of war were miraculously reversed by Washington and his resilient "band of brothers" to shock the world in a hard-fought, urban battle that raged through Trenton's streets in the midst of a steady snowfall.

All in all, consequently, no single clash of arms was more either more timely or significant than Washington's first battlefield success of the American Revolution. Washington's seemingly impossible victory saved a dying revolution by only the narrowest of margins. Never in the annals of military history has a more maligned military leader, especially one without a formal military education or adequate military experience, achieved a victory with more significant long-term consequences and implications than Washington's dazzling success in the snows of Trenton.

Most importantly, America's great egalitarian dream and utopian vision of remaking the world anew were resurrected by Washington with the most surprising battlefield successes in American history. Defying traditional military axioms, Washington, whose command presence inspired his long-suffering citizen soldiers to rise to their supreme challenge in this most brutal of winter campaigns, stunned the day's leading military men on both sides of the Atlantic. Relying upon a brilliant battle-plan and an unprecedented synthesis of the elements of surprise, speed, stealth, and shock, Washington revered the hands of a cruel fate by orchestrating the most inventive, audacious, and innovative battleplan of the American Revolution: crossing the raging Delaware River at night, marching for nearly ten miles over difficult terrain in the inky blackness amid blizzard-like conditions, and then launching a simultaneous attack from two separate wings, or divisions, not long after the icy dawn of December 26, 1776 to catch a formidable opponent by surprise at Trenton. Washington's sparkling victory at Trenton was a tactical masterpiece second to none in the American Revolution.

However, Washington's victory at Trenton was only possible by his inspiring role in leading the way by example through the torrents of sleet, hail, snow, and blustery winds of a "blue norther" and then into the fiery forge of battle. Washington's strength of character, unshakable commitment to "the sacred Cause . . . of Liberty" (in his own words), his firm belief that God was guiding America's destiny, and sheer force of willpower fueled a relentless moral, physical, and spiritual drive to secure success at Trenton at any cost. Fortunately for America, the commander-in-chief's sterling qualities rose to the fore at Trenton in what was very much of a personal, psychological, and professional rebirth for Washington—not only as a military commander but also as a person. In a remarkable resurrection, Washington's finest traits as a commander emerged from the darkest depths of despair, adversity, and humiliation to reach an unprecedented zenith. Amid the greatest adversity and despite the longest odds for success, the dynamic Virginian inspired his often-defeated men to rise to their greatest challenge and reap their most surprising, unexpected victory. Exactly when the challenge was greatest, the combat prowess of the American fighting man rose magnificently to the fore during the desperate and close-quarter Dantesque struggle that raged fiercely from street to street covered in a thick layer of snow.

For more than two centuries, Washington's most unexpected battle-field success has been long shrouded in myth, legend, and romanticization. Consequently, a host of complexities, ironies, and contradictions about this major turning point in the course of American history have been overshadowed by stereotypes and romantic myths to grossly distort and obscure the truth. Despite the battle's vital importance, many of the most interesting aspects, realities, and perspectives about this legendary contest have been overlooked, ignored, or minimized by generations of Americans historians. Unfortunately, even leading scholars have preferred instead to cling to the many comfortable and familiar myths, traditional romance, and long-existing stereotypes.[2] Even revered Founding Father John Adams lamented how the American Revolution's truths were early transformed into little more than "melodramatic romance."[3] And highly respected historian Ray Raphael like-wise emphasized how the revolution's most famous episodes have been an "invention of history."[4] Likewise, Edward G. Lengel concluded how many so-called "truths" about the American Revolution simply "never actually happened."[5]

Therefore, long-deferred, seldom-asked questions will be explored more thoroughly than ever before in this work: just how much of the battle of Trenton's traditional, legendary, and long-accepted story has been distorted beyond recognition by the multiple layers of popular mythology, romance, and fiction? This book has been written to provide answers to such questions while presenting a host of new views, insights, and perspectives about the battle that turned the tide in America's darkest hour. By eliminating as much of the traditional romance, mythologies, distorted legends, and simplistic stereotypes as possible, a host of previously unexplored complexities and mysteries about what actually and really happened at the battle of Trenton and exactly why will be revealed in considerable detail for the first time in this work.

Therefore, the "real" story, warts and all, of the unforgettable saga of Trenton will be presented in full. Focused primarily on analyzing the hidden history of America's most pivotal battle during its struggle for existence, this book will explore the forgotten stories, mysteries, and legacies of the American Revolution's most dramatic confrontation. In addition, the lesser-known but key individuals, officers, and enlisted men on *both* sides who fought and died at Trenton for what they believed was right will be analyzed in great detail. Eclipsed by the giant shadow of "the father of the country," many of Washington's talented, resourceful top lieutenants, who made bold and timely independent tactical decisions that contributed to victory at Trenton, have been forgotten. Their story will be told.

Another especially overlooked but fascinating aspect of the tenacious struggle for the possession of Trenton was the forgotten bitter conflict between the German Hessians (the generic name for all Germans who served in the British Army in America) and hundreds of Washington's German American soldiers, including many German-born Continentals. In a fratricidal showdown that raged through Trenton's icy streets, Washington's German Regiment of Continentals played a key role in forcing the surrender of their fellow Teutonic countrymen.

Long overlooked by American historians, this tragic civil war among the German people on America soil was perhaps best represented by Colonel Johann Gottlieb Rall, the Hessian brigade's ill-fated commander whose reputation (and life) was destroyed by Trenton's loss. Not long after the battle, he encountered his own German cousin of Washington's Army, just before he died of wounds received leading a spirited counterattack into the embattled center of Trenton.[6]

The contradictions and complexities of the German experience in colonial America were also revealed by the fact that Colonel Rall's direct paternal descendant hailed from Maryland. German patriots on Rall's direct descendant's maternal side also fought at Trenton, Lieutenant Peter Weiser, First Pennsylvania Continental Regiment. His brother from Womelsdorf, Pennsylvania, Captain Benjamin Weiser served in Washington's German Regiment of Continental troops during the autumn of 1776.[7]

Clearly, by exploring such forgotten aspects of one of America's most famous battles, Trenton's story has proved to be far more revealing and fascinating than the simplistic, traditional morality play of righteous revolutionaries battling against merciless, evil mercenaries. The most popular Trenton myth has been that the Hessian garrison's alleged drunkenness in celebrating Christmas led to their ultimate downfall on the early morning of December 26. Unfortunately, this enduring stereotype and popular view has been only recently reinforced by the popular 2000 historical drama *The Crossing.*

Ironically, the *only* widespread drunkenness at Trenton resulted when Washington's soldiers celebrated their most improbable victory of the war. And contrary to the persistent stereotype of the savage, immoral, and Godless mercenary, Rall's Germans consisted mostly of a humble, pious soldiery of the Calvinist, or Reformed, faith, not unlike their revolutionary Protestant counterparts, who were less fundamentalist Calvinists, in Washington's ranks. As strict Calvinists, which was unrealized by Washington and his men at the time, the Hessians, on high alert, had not observed Christmas at Trenton in a festive, drunken manner, a celebration which they viewed as far too pagan and sacrilegious.[8]

Symbolically, given that so many German soldiers fought against each other at Trenton to reveal only one dimension of the many ironies and complexities of the German experience in America, it was perhaps appropriate that the famous 1851 painting *Washington Crossing the Delaware* was created by German American artist Emanuel Leutze. Merely an allegorical artistic representation rather an authentic historically correct depiction, one of America's most iconic paintings was ironically based upon a panoramic view of the Rhine River that was much wider than the Delaware, where Washington crossed the angry river to gain the New Jersey shore. Leutze's artistic masterpiece was also symbolic because some Germans who fought against each other at Trenton had once been neighbors in Germany's Rhine River region. Indeed, one central irony that revealed the horror of this Teutonic fratricidal conflict on American soil was the fact that soldiers from Germany, who faced each other in the swirling combat along Trenton's narrow, snow-covered streets, not only hailed from the same German communities and rural areas, including the Rhineland, but also were related by blood.

So many of the fundamental truths and realities of the battle of Trenton have been obscured by myths that even the most basic questions have been seldom asked. At least one historian William E. Woodward posed a most intriguing question that very few American historians have dared to investigate because of the sheer power of the iconic Washington mystique and the seemingly endless romantic mythology surrounding the battle of Trenton: "The short Trenton-Princeton campaign revealed a military mind of a high order [but] there is some doubt . . . as to whose plan it was."[9]

What has been overlooked was the fact that Washington had not formulated strategy and tactics on his own, especially in regard to the development of his brilliant Trenton tactical plan. He relied heavily upon the sound tactical advice of his talented team of experienced top lieutenants and "general officers," in Washington's words, in multiple December 1776 Councils of War, as required by the Continental Congress. Because the much-criticized American commander, who feared losing his job by dismissal from Congress for ample good reason, had lost a series of key battles on New York soil, Washington's most one-sided victory of his career shocked the English people and British Parliamentarians in London. Leading British politicians and strategists quite correctly "wondered, as many in Britain did, how [the] best soldiers in the world could be defeated by much smaller, generally untrained, and badly equipped forces, and how the most brilliant and seasoned generals in the Empire could be out-foxed by a wheat farmer?"[10]

For generations of Americans, Washington's own natural genius by itself has long served as the solitary, unquestioned explanation of his sparkling success at Trenton, while the alleged widespread Hessian drunkenness provided a secondary traditional explanation for Washington's most remarkable victory. German defeat has also been long explained by Colonel Rall's alleged incompetence and leadership failures at every level. However, the truth of the situation was far more complex and antithetical to the popular myths and stereotypes. His self-serving British and German superiors, who desperately needed a scapegoat for Trenton's disastrous loss to mask their own strategic miscalculations and tactical errors, widely condemned Rall, whose death at Trenton provided the golden opportunity to place all blame squarely on him.

Moral and religious factors have also provided traditional explanations for Washington's almost inexplicable success at Trenton. One popular story has emphasized how Washington was inspired by Old Testament's lessons about how ancient Hebrew zealots had vanquished Roman legionnaires in a holy war. One of the "best Washington fables" that developed from local New Jersey folklore focused on the alleged contributions of super spy John Honeyman. He supposedly provided Washington with vital intelligence about Trenton's vulnerabilities. Long accepted as gospel by even America's leading Revolutionary War historians and endlessly repeated in one book after another, such colorful stories like the popular Honeyman tale (another Trenton "legend") have little, if any, basis in fact.[11]

Only relatively recently have groundbreaking analytical studies explored tactical aspects of Revolutionary War battles in great detail. But, ironically, the far more crucial confrontation at Trenton has been overlooked and unexplored: a rather bizarre, almost inexplicable, omission in the historical record. The foremost of these "new military history" works has been Lawrence E. Babits's 1998 work, *A Devil of a Whipping: The Battle of Cowpens*. General Daniel Morgan's one-sided victory at Cowpens, South Carolina, on January 17, 1781, has been proclaimed as having resulted from the American Revolution's most brilliant battleplan. However, Washington's far more significant and critical success at

Trenton, reaped in the revolution's decisive "cockpit" theater of operations and at the struggle's most critical moment, was based upon a more innovative and enterprising battleplan that garnered more significant long-term results: saving the revolution and republic's life at the last minute. Indeed, in what was his master stroke of the war, Washington's skillful utilization of the classic tactical concept of the double envelopment led to the most improbable of victories to astound friend and foe alike. In essence, Washington repeated Hannibal's tactical masterpiece at Cannae in 216 BC at Trenton, eliminating an entire Hessian brigade of battle-hardened troops with the boldest of strokes and in relatively short order.[12]

Achieving the most difficult and rarest of tactical battlefield feats, Washington skillfully orchestrated a pincer movement (or double envelopment) at Trenton to reverse not only the American Revolution's course, but also America's destiny. In the highest stakes showdown of the war, Washington's brilliant orchestration of flexible, innovative tactics, based upon a well-balanced blend of mobility, surprise, and stealth, triumphed over the complex intricacies and formalities of conventional Eighteenth Century European warfare, especially those inspired by Prussian Frederick the Great. Washington reaped his remarkable success at Trenton by relying upon innovative asymmetrical tactics—born mostly of the frontier experience and Indian warfare (asymmetrical or guerrilla warfare) in which the element of surprise was paramount—of the stealthy pre-dawn surprise attack in wintertime, which was a rarity in the annals of traditional eighteenth-century European warfare. In overall terms, the true key to Washington's remarkable victory was the sudden emergence of a distinctive American way of waging war. Washington's success at Trenton, combined with his follow-up victory at Princeton, New Jersey, on January 3, 1777, would not have been possible without his timely and literally last-minute incorporation of fundamental axioms of the lessons of Indian warfare, especially the lightning-strike and surprise attack.

Even though the better-known battles of Saratoga, New York, and Yorktown have been the most celebrated of America's revolutionary victories, thanks to French weaponry in the former and the extensive benefits of the French Alliance in the latter (advantages only made possible by Washington's victory at Trenton), no battle of the Revolution was more purely and distinctly American or more important in overall terms (politically, morally, and psychologically) than the battle of Trenton. After all, successes at Saratoga (1777) or Yorktown (1781) would not have been possible without Washington's remarkable victory on December 26, 1776 to set the stage for those later victories. Quite simply, the battle of Trenton marked a turning point of not only the American Revolution, but also in world history.

By accomplishing the impossible in reaping victory at Trenton at the very lowest ebb of America's fortunes and darkest hour, Washington rejuvenated the fledgling republic's faith and spirit of resistance effort, restoring a new sense of optimism for ultimate success among the American people like no other single event in the war. Before the battle of Trenton, America's great republican dream and egalitarian vision had already all but suffered a premature death, except in the hearts and minds of very few resolute Americans, who never lost their religious-like faith in America's egalitarian promise, especially Washington's young men and boys who fought so magnificently at Trenton.[13]

Fortunately for America on December 26, 1776, the foremost fighting men among these precious few diehard revolutionaries, the truly "useful ones," who yet battled against a seemingly cruel fate and for a forlorn cause, were Washington and relatively few of his surviving citizen soldiers, who were mostly Continentals. Unlike so many other Americans who had lost faith, these soldiers refused to forsake the cherished dream of independence and the utopian vision of a new beginning for the common man. By refusing to allow the revolution to succumb to a premature death, Washington and his men saved the utopian, idealistic promise that the common people, regardless of class, family background, social rank, or birthplace, deserved equality. With musket, bayonet, and saber, Washington and his threadbare soldiers of liberty resurrected America's faith in the ultimate fulfillment of that egalitarian dream in one of the most surprising of victories in the military annals of world history.

Consequently, what Washington achieved at Trenton was a timely rescue of not only a people's revolution, but also the preservation of the very dream, vision, and essence of the very meaning of America. In this sense, the climactic showdown at Trenton was in fact a decisive struggle not only over the very heart and soul of America, but also about the possession of the North American continent. Indeed, what was later called Manifest Destiny was salvaged by Washington's victory at Trenton. Symbolically, Washington's crossing of the turbulent Delaware played a key role in setting the stage for America's westward expansion, ensuring the eventual crossing of the North American Continent and all the way to the Pacific in one of the great migrations in human history.

All in all, no single armed clash in American history was more important in determining America's future destiny than Washington's victory at Trenton, which resulted in a great symbolic philosophical, ideological, and spiritual regeneration of a new people, the Americans, and a new nation conceived in liberty. Quite simply, Washington's success on December saved the infant American nation from extinction and everlasting oblivion. Leading mostly farm boys of an army of homespun revolutionaries, who only rarely won a battle against better trained British and Hessian troops, the finest professional soldiers in the world, Washington's amazing triumph with his citizensoldier revolutionaries was not only over a veteran Hessian brigade, but also over the entrenched ancient concept of monarchy and autocratic rule of the Old World. Out of the lowest, darkest depths of America's misfortunes, the bright luminosity of Washington's remarkable victory at Trenton became a shining beacon of hope, pointing the way for America's eventual decisive victory and independence.

By any measure, this special place, where the American dream and republican experiment in nationhood were miraculously resurrected against the odds by Washington, who led his soldiers through a pitch-black, stormy night and to a rendezvous with a special destiny at Trenton like an Old Testament prophet and holy warrior, should be revered today as America's most sacred ground. Instead, Trenton has been scarred by a sad desecration while Gettysburg, Pennsylvania, thanks to commercial, tourist-oriented, and consumer culture excesses, has become America's most popular and iconic historical shrine only 150 miles to the west.

Today, the congested center of today's modern Trenton has been desecrated by a sad, if not tragic, scene of urban blight, impoverishment, drugs, and crime: a dark stain on this truly hallowed ground that represents a major turning point in American and world history. Here, on the most important single day in the American republic's young life, Washington and his men reached their full potential as both Americans and soldiers for the first time, having their finest day in a battle of notable firsts: the American Army's first urban battle and first use of "flying artillery."

Today, the United States military has focused on urban warfare challenges to counter global threats for the twenty-first century, but has continued to teach the military lessons of conventional battles, especially Gettysburg, to each new generation of young leaders, while overlooking America's first battle in an urban environment.

Although America's founding was nothing short of miraculous, no chapter of America's story was more miraculous than the most improbable victory in the annals of American military history at Trenton, where America's fast-fading life was resurrected to almost everyone's disbelief on a dark, stormy morning, when the stakes could not have been higher not only for America, but also for the world.

Most important, the unforgettable story of Trenton is truly a national epic saga, America's *Illiad*. In the annals of American history, never have so few Americans accomplished so much against the odds and chances for success to reap the most dramatic battlefield victory and the most important success in American military history, when "the fate of America" hung in the balance.[14]

Chapter I

Crossing the Rubicon: Washington's
Most Imposing Obstacle

December 1776 was the darkest and worst of times for the infant American republic and its often-defeated amateur army of ill-trained citizensoldiers. Consequently, the stakes could not have been higher not only for America, whose life hung by a mere thread, but also the world on Christmas Day 1776. In the unforgettable words of Thomas Paine: "The cause of America is in a great measure the cause of all mankind [and] we have it in our power to begin the world over again. The birthday of a new world is at hand."[14]

But by near the end of December, the golden, utopian dream of America was about to die. On the most bitterly cold Christmas evening that anyone could remember, George Washington stared in deep thought at the wide, menacing expanse of the ice-clogged and rain-swollen Delaware River with a deepening sense of foreboding. Not even his thick, woolen military cloak kept Washington, the only Founding Father to have gone to war, warm from the biting, cold winds that howled down the river. Now America's Rubicon, this raging river of destiny had suddenly become the most important in the fast-fading life of the infant American republic. For Washington, a successful crossing of the Delaware now amounted to nothing less than the saving of America.

Washington, therefore, was not deterred by the daunting prospect of his most risky and perilous undertaking of the war, despite the veil of darkness and stormy conditions. Born of the lowest depths of desperation, the cornerstone of Washington's most daring battleplan called for first crossing the Delaware with his relatively few remaining Continental soldiers, and a far lesser number of state troops: what little was left of a dying army. Quite simply, if Washington failed to cross the Delaware on Christmas night and then overwhelm the crack German garrison at Trenton, New Jersey, just before the dawn of December 26, then the United States of America was fated to succumb to an early death.

In consequence, Christmas Day 1776 was the bleakest day in the America's young life that was seemingly about to be extinguished forever. Inexperienced General Washington, the forty-five-year-old commander of the depleted Continental Army, had lost every battle in 1776, proving no match for experienced, professional British opponents. Independence had been declared in the previous summer during the zenith of American hopes and aspirations, but this bright optimism had faded away by late December.

But that hallowed declaration penned in Philadelphia no longer mattered because victory had to be won on the battlefield before America's independence truly became reality. While cornered on the Delaware River's west side and commanding a ragtag army, Washington had only a few days left in December to produce a military miracle to save the infant republic before the enlistments of most of his Continentals expired at year's end. With his back figuratively against the wall on Christmas Day, Washington was not contemplating peace on earth, good will to mankind, or the Yuletide. Instead, the determined Washington now possessed an obsession and burning resolve: "Victory or Death."

Indeed, America's fate, destiny, and future now lay in the boldest and most brilliant battleplan as well as the most audacious tactical movement of the American Revolution: crossing the wide Delaware River from eastern Pennsylvania to western New Jersey, and then marching around 2,400 ill-clad soldiers nearly ten miles in order to resume the offensive and catch the Hessian garrison at Trenton by surprise. During late summer and early days of autumn when the dense woodlands of the Delaware Valley were bright with glorious fall colors, the Delaware was a quiet, placid river. At that time, the wide river flowed lazily through a colorful patchwork of virgin forests, grassy meadows, and well-manicured farmlands. As since times immemorial, this majestic river ran gently south at its lowest stages in August and September, flowing toward the open expanse of Delaware Bay and then the Atlantic's cold waters. But now on Christmas Day and with the end of America's most traumatic year drawing to a close, the Delaware's usual tranquility and normal placid state had been altered dramatically.

Unlike when Washington's Army had last crossed this river during the fairer weather of early December at the end of its long, miserable retreat through New Jersey after the disastrous New York campaign, the Delaware was now an unpredictable, turbulent river that threatened to thwart Washington's desperate ambitions and America's last hopes. Whenever the heavy runoff of winter rains or snow poured into the Delaware and raised the water level, this untamed river became wild and unruly, overflowing its banks and flooding the surrounding low-lying countryside. Churning waters and swift currents carried huge logs, fallen trees, and other debris swiftly downstream, causing havoc among vessels on the Delaware. As an unkind fate would have it, Washington now planned his crossing at the exact time that the river was at its ugliest, highest, and most turbulent. Washington was now seemingly burdened with too many obstacles to possibly overcome. With time running out for America's most often-defeated general and his reeling Continental Army, Washington must first conquer the formidable natural elements and the tempestuous Delaware even before he had a chance to meet a full Hessian brigade, well-trained and disciplined German soldiers, at Trenton.

Fortunately, however, one defeat after another had already prepared not only Washington but also his main strike force (one of three columns desig-nated to cross the Delaware) of around 2,400 men for launching their most amphibious night operation before embarking upon a nearly ten-mile night-time march south upon Trenton. Now an experienced master at the intricate art of strategic retreats across wide, swift-flowing bodies of water, including this same river that he had recently gotten to know so intimately, Washington now benefitted from the hard lessons learned from repeated recent defeats in a stra-tegic theater of operations surrounded by interconnecting bodies of water. That most disadvantageous situation in the recent campaign around New York City ensured that Washington never won a single battle.

Significantly, in his most risky operation to date, Washington for the first time now employed a wide river to his tactical advantage because the over-confident Hessians at Trenton were convinced that the Americans could not possibly cross the angry and swollen Delaware in wintertime. Most impor-tantly, Washington had learned a host of invaluable lessons in regard to the distinct advantages of amphibious warfare and how to catch an opponent by surprise. After having retired across the Delaware with Washington's Army in early December, the cerebral but homespun Thomas Paine marveled at Washington's high level of competence in conducting a disciplined, organ-ized withdrawal of ill-trained troops across New Jersey, especially in regard to always-risky river crossings: "With a handful of men we sustained an orderly retreat . . . and had four rivers to cross."[15] But perhaps Lieutenant Samuel Blachley Webb, a Bunker Hill and Connecticut Line veteran who had been a former General Israel Putnam aide and now served as Washington's private secretary, said it best in a December 16 letter. With a wry sense of humor that revealed an inherent quality of his rustic revolutionaries that now worked to

Washington's benefit, Webb emphasized how: "Never was finer lads at a retreat than we are . . . ."[16] But at long last, Washington and his seasoned Continentals were going forward, not backward to escape an opponent, while employing the same well-honed skills that they had used in slipping across the Delaware and other eastern rivers to escape the eager clutches of Lieutenant General William Howe, the overall British commander in America.

Indeed, not only the men in the ranks but also Washington and his top lieutenant Henry Knox, who commanded the army's artillery, had become experts at the art of withdrawing this army and its weapons across a series of rivers. Washington had gained invaluable experience from the complex interplay in carefully coordinating delicate, stealthy movements between land and water forces—thanks in no small part to the abundant maritime skills of Colonel John Glover's hardy mariners mostly from Marblehead, Massachusetts—that had ensured the Continental Army's survival during the New York campaign.

Washington also now possessed the ability to transport his army across the Delaware once again because he had made doubly sure that he possessed a sufficient number of boats to cross the last natural obstacle that lay before Philadelphia, America's beleaguered capital, located barely thirty miles southwest of Trenton. Under the protective cover of the previous night, Christmas Eve, Washington had ordered a stealthy concentration of the previously gathered flotilla of boats, including flat-bottomed scows, for the perilous crossing. These vessels had been recently collected by four capable New Jersey militia commanders: Captains David Bray, who gathered twenty-five boats; Thomas Jones; and Jacob Gearhart—all of the Second Regiment, Hunterdon County, militia; and Colonel Philemon Dickinson, who commanded six regiments (each unit represented a specific county, either Burlington or Hunterdon) of his militia brigade. Hidden along the timbered Pennsylvania shore and in the midst of brown, dense thickets that covered low-lying, wooded islands near the shore above Sam McConkey's Ferry, where Washington planned to cross with his main force, the boats had been located close enough to now facilitate a quick concentration and a Christmas Day crossing.

Most of these invaluable vessels had been gathered by Continentals from multiple detachments as directed by Washington. But Rhode Islander General Nathanael Greene, Washington's "right arm," had also ordered General James Ewing and his rural Pennsylvania militiamen of a homespun brigade of five regiments, on December 10 to collect anything afloat on the Delaware to the south. During the last more than a week and a half on this cold December and as orchestrated with a deliberate, meticulous thoroughness by Washington, the relentless search for additional boats up and down the Delaware had been complete, including wide-ranging search parties that scoured the upper regions of not only the Delaware River but also the Lehigh Rivers, a 103-mile tributary of the Delaware in eastern Pennsylvania. Washington fully understood that the more boats he collected, the more quickly and effectively he would be able to transport his troops across the river from Pennsylvania to New Jersey when time was of the essence.

Therefore, Washington now possessed at least sixteen Durham boats, perhaps even more of these sturdy vessels that had long plied the Delaware's waters. The Durham boats were now the key to a successful crossing and the descent upon the Trenton garrison. Concealed for weeks in unmapped inlets, up narrow creeks, and on densely wooded (despite the absence of leaves), and reed-covered islands, the Durham boats had been securely guarded by the troops of Lord Stirling's Virginia, Pennsylvania, and Delaware brigades. Washington had earlier informed Lord Stirling (William Alexander) to move the fleet of boats downriver under cover of the inky darkness and concentrate this most unorthodox, odd-looking of flotillas at McConkey's Ferry.

Washington's wise precautions in having hidden the Durham boats under the cover of heavy timber, with dark-colored hulls blending in with brown, wintertime forests, immediately north of McConkey's ferry, proved most effective. The flotilla of boats had been quietly assembled under cover of the cold darkness just north of the ferry from where they were floated down with the surging current to where Washington's army planned to embark his force for the crossing. The boats were then brought down by Glover's able mariners from New England and hidden behind Taylor Island at McConkey's Ferry before a greater increase of ice floes filled the Delaware to hamper the laborious collection process.[17]

As early as December 22, an optimistic Colonel John Fitzgerald, a "warm hearted, brave and honest Irishman" of Washington's staff from Alexandria, Virginia, located on the west side of the Potomac just north of Mount Vernon, penned in his diary how "at McConkey's Ferry . . . A portion of the boats are there," after having been "brought downriver [with the current] to [Washington's] point of embarkation" across the Delaware.[18] Additional units of Washington's lengthy column, after having departed their Bucks County, Pennsylvania, encampments and assembled for an evening parade, converged on the main ferry crossing at McConkey's Ferry under the cold veil of the near-darkness to avoid detection as Washington had planned. Here, along a level shelf of bottomland located on the river's west side, hundreds of soldiers patiently awaited the order to board their assigned boats before embarking upon their risky journey across the overflowing Delaware that seemed to span endlessly to the New Jersey side of the river.

Washington's men maintained a perfect silence as directed by the commander-in-chief, even though the common soldiers yet had no idea of their ultimate destination or of Washington's exact plan on this frigid Christmas Day. Those young men and boys, almost all of whom were unable to swim, felt increasing apprehension, struggling to master their steadily mounting fears in the near-blackness beside the ice-coated Delaware. With sturdy .75 caliber Brown Bess flintlock muskets by the sides, Washington's soldiers were ready to do their duty, which now entailed considerably more risk than any previous mission. At McConkey's Ferry, even stoic Continentals without shoes, but with carefully wrapped feet, stood patiently in the thick mud, churned up by the gathering, that felt as cold as ice, without complaining as so often in the past.

An especially ambitious member of General Horatio Gates's staff, teenage Major James Wilkinson had just galloped all the way from Philadelphia for an opportunity to join Washington's main strike force. Gates kindly fulfilled Wilkinson's animated request to see action by writing a short note to Washington, providing a suitable excuse for the Marylander's unbridled zeal to see combat. A promising brigade leader despite his youthful impetuousness, Wilkinson reached Washington's forces just before the silent crowd of ill-clad revolutionaries began to embark upon the risky crossing of the icy Delaware. Riding past the lengthy column of soldiers wrapped in nervousness, anxiety, and too little clothing, Wilkinson delivered General Gates's letter to Washington, when he was "alone" and just as the commander-in-chief, with riding whip in hand and wearing his dark military cloak, was about to mount his horse and initiate the crossing of the Delaware.

Therefore, an incredulous Washington merely blurted out to the over-eager teenage staff officer, "What a time is this to hand me letters?" Wilkinson then informed the already overburdened and severely taxed Virginian that one sealed letter was from Gates, who had been pleading illness to skirt Washington's directives to assist him in his most hazardous operation to date. An irritated Washington responded, "Where is General Gates?" The young Marylander answered that the England-born Gates was in Philadelphia instead of located at the Delaware rivertown of Bristol, Bucks County, as Washington had ordered.

Despite already knowing the answer, Washington asked why the conniving Gates was yet in the nation's capital at such a crucial moment.

Young Wilkinson, who hailed from the rolling hills of southern Maryland tobacco country, then answered that the ever-ambitious Gates was conferring with Congress, scheming as usual behind Washington's back. Indeed, Gates was now on his way to Baltimore, where Congress had fled from the seemingly doomed Philadelphia, to confer with the president of Congress, John Hancock, in a shrewd attempt to gain political support and replace the much-maligned Washington. Here, along the windswept Delaware, Wilkinson was shocked by Washington's sudden but well-justified loss of temper, which he had long sought to control but never completely mastered, even toward his own mother.[19]

For ample good reason, Washington had slipped into a foul mood because so many things were already beginning to go awry, especially with the winter storm's arrival that now seemed to threaten all of his carefully laid plans and mock the commander-in-chief's quixotic ambitions. Knowing that time was not on his side, Washington now felt that his mostly farm boys moved too slowly to delay the crossing, threatening the fragile timetable. Worst of all and along with the descending "nor'easter," the river's high waters and the unexpected large ice floes that suddenly appeared on Christmas Day threatened not only the crossing timetable but also the entire battleplan. Washington never forgot how it had taken five days for his army to cross the Delaware in the fair weather conditions of early December during the recent retreat to escape Howe's pursuit.

Therefore, Washington was now haunted by the most torturous question of all: exactly how long would it now take for his army to cross the Delaware under such deplorable winter conditions? Not surprising, Washington's temper flashed more than once when slightly impertinent but well-meaning officers (certainly young staff officers but perhaps even general officers) suggested that he postpone the increasingly precarious river crossing until the following night, if the storm passed. But nothing could now shake Washington's firm resolve or determination to forge ahead, despite the increasing risks. Knowing that it was now or never, he continued to demonstrate steely nerves, will power, and strength of character at the most critical moment.[20]

Now nearly three hundred miles from his beloved Boston to the northeast, the irrepressible Colonel Henry Knox, one of Washington's most gifted top lieutenants despite his youth, never forgot on "that bitter night when the commander-in-chief had drawn up his little army to cross it, and had seen the powerful current bearing onward the floating masses of ice which threatened destruction to whosoever should venture upon its bosom [and] threatened to defeat the enterprise [an anxious Washington then made the urgent] demand, 'Who will lead us on?' [which was promptly answered by Glover and] the men of Marblehead and Marblehead alone, stood forward [and so] went the fishermen of Marblehead" to the flotilla of boats clustered along the icy shore."[21] And this crucial crossing of the Delaware was only possible by the efforts of the Massachusetts mariners under "Glover, about five and forty [age forty-four and a year younger than Washington], a little man, but active and a good soldier," wrote one officer.[22]

Indeed, at a time when veteran American officers doubted the wisdom of Washington's overambitious nighttime operation and risky strike across the Delaware to descend upon Trenton from the north, this was a turning point because it seemed that everything was now in jeopardy. Washington's complex battleplan now depended upon the contributions of only a relatively few New England soldiers—a mere thirty officers and 147 enlisted New England men, who now held the army's and the infant republic's lives in their hands. Fortunately for America, these hardy mariners of the Fourteenth Massachusetts Continental Regiment were elite members of Washington's combined amphibious, marine, and "ferrying command." For the formidable challenge of the most dangerous river crossing of the war, Washington now commanded some of the most experienced and durable men in all America. Glover's Massachusetts soldiers knew how to successfully cope with the harshest elements and rough waters, especially in cold, stormy weather. Most of all, these sturdy mariners from New England's leading ports could do the impossible in a crisis situation.

One fundamental reason that explained Washington's confidence lay in his faith in what these mariners could accomplish against the odds. Washington knew that he could rely completely on the scrappy and hard-driving but modest Colonel Glover and his seasoned Massachusetts men. After all, this present precarious situation was not the first time that everything hinged upon the seafaring capabilities, toughness, and experience of these Massachusetts mariners.

As highly respected members of America's first truly amphibious and marine regiment of ten companies of the so-called Marblehead Regiment, these Massachusetts Continentals were Washington's most versatile soldiers and the undisputed masters of amphibious operations. Occasionally causing headaches for generals but only when not engaged in battle or a risky operation, Glover's Massachusetts boys were high-spirited boatmen, fishermen, and sailors, who were "always full of fun and mischief." Although some of these New Englanders hailed from other fishing communities, like Salem, Beverly, and Lynn, along Massachusetts's rocky north shore beside cold, blue waters, the vast majority of these seafarers came straight from the picturesque port of Marblehead, situated just north of Boston.

To Washington's homespun farm boys of English descent from the Piedmont, tobacco-chewing, horse race-loving aristocratic planter's sons of the Virginia Tidewater, and roughhewn Scotch-Irish woodsmen from the western frontier, these Marbleheaders seemed almost like men from another world and time. First, Glover's men were foremost products of the sea. Most of all, these dependable mariners were immensely proud of their distinctive seafaring heritage and culture, insular, picturesque fishing community, and its magnificent sheltering harbor, nestled on the south side of a craggy Marblehead or "Great Neck" peninsula that jutted northeastward into the Atlantic.

Marblehead was located just southeast of the port of Salem. Settled around 1629 by free-thinking individualists and devout religious dissenters who had fled north from Boston's restrictive Puritan theocracy, Marblehead was situated in the southeast corner of Essex County. Marblehead boasted of one of New England's finest harbors, sheltered and almost landlocked, which was a precious gift from the blessings of nature to the seafaring community. Besides a sturdy work ethic, this excellent harbor explained the extent of Marblehead's longtime prosperity, after these enterprising people broke away from exploitative Boston and Salem merchants to sell their bountiful catches, mostly cod, directly to European and the Caribbean markets. Perched on a commanding, rocky ridge worn down by centuries of turbulent Atlantic coastal weather, this quaint fishing town of Marblehead presented a most disorderly yet scenic appearance. Reflecting their individualism and excessive democratic proclivities, Marblehead's residents had simply built their wooden houses of all sizes and shapes at every imaginable angle, erecting them anywhere precious space existed along the narrow, rock-strewn peninsula.

Along the Delaware River's west bank on this cold Christmas evening, Glover's seafaring men even now reflected their novel cultural, regional, and occupational distinctiveness in their own dissimilar appearances and unconventional attitudes that contrasted sharply with Washington's landlubber soldiers. Instead of standard Continental regulation uniforms of blue, Glover's men wore lightweight brown coats, trimmed in blue and with pewter buttons marked the numeral 14 on them. These standard New England fishing coats covered traditional seafaring garb, including fishing trousers, blue round jackets, some old waterproof leather buttons, and sailor's caps of thick wool that protected ears and heads on this stormy night. This traditional apparel had long warded off the bitter punishment of the north Atlantic's waters of the Labrador current and high, crashing waves of the Grand Banks. Here, along the turbulent Delaware on this Christmas evening so far from Marblehead, it looked almost as if Glover's mariners were yet working on their fishing boats at one of the world's greatest fisheries, the mist-shrouded Grand Banks situated on the Atlantic's sprawling Continental shelf. New England's leading fishing capital, Marblehead shipped more cod and other cold-water, bottom-feeding fish to the Caribbean sugar islands to feed the great mass of slaves necessary for sugar cane cultivation than any other New England fishing community.

Most importantly for the ultimate success of Washington's amphibious operation to cross the Delaware, Glover's Marblehead regiment was distinguished by its iron discipline, which even outmatched that of the legendary Hessian soldiers. In fact, these Bay State mariners were the most disciplined men in the Continental Army, immeasurably enhancing Washington's chances for success on this darkest and most tempestuous of nights. Quite simply, with Colonel Glover, a former daring sea captain of wide-ranging sloops and schooners, commanding his unique, multi-faceted regiment from Massachusetts as firmly on land as if yet facing dangers out at sea, this crack Continental unit was the army's best disciplined and most reliable regiment. The isolated environment of Marblehead's close-knit community and the crucial requirement for seamen to work closely together as a unit while fishing Newfoundland's lucrative but dangerous cod grounds created a teamwork-minded group of men. Therefore, they now performed as one in preparing for the perilous Delaware crossing. After all, far out in the rough waters of the north Atlantic, it was absolutely essential that everyone worked together closely and efficiently for survival. These special, unique qualities—especially among an amateur army of ever-independent-minded citizen soldiers—had early helped to transform Glover's command into one of the Continental Army's best units.

In addition, Colonel Glover's strict training and high standards forged an iron discipline that made the Marbleheaders into Washington's most efficient soldiers, regardless of the task or battlefield situation. Consequently, the Marbleheaders performed splendidly on any assignment, on land or water. Most of all, they were determined that England would never "enslave" America. Washington fully realized, the well-honed discipline, work ethic, and efficiency of Glover's men from years of service on the high seas were now critical for a successful Delaware crossing in stormy, winter conditions. These Marbleheaders had earlier taken orders without question, learning to immediately act upon a captain's orders when out at sea: a blind obedience that was absolutely necessary for a ship's and crew's efficiency and even survival at sea, especially during a raging storm. This process early instilled an iron-like discipline into these mariners.

Like Glover himself, the Marbleheaders looked back proudly to a humble ancestry of seafarers, who had also fished primarily for cod, and a vibrant, distinctive Celtic-Cornish culture that thrived along the scenic Cornish peninsula, bordering the Celtic Sea, and the rocky islands of Guernsey and Jersey in the English Channel. Spawned from a sea-toughened breed of Cornwall ancestors who hailed from a rugged land, where red sunsets dropped off the western horizon in America's direction, the Marbleheaders were extremely "vigorous and active." Drawing upon a rich cultural heritage and seafaring traditions, Glover's Massachusetts boys possessed those qualities were now exactly what was most of all required to meet the stiff challenges of Washington's dangerous nighttime crossing of the Delaware.

Most significantly, these Marblehead men, long accustomed to adversity and harsh winter conditions, were well-honed for the arduous task of man-handling boats across the roughest waters. Living in their isolated maritime world, Glover's men looked, thought, and talked very differently from their fellow Continentals who had never seen the ocean. Regardless of what class they hailed—from the lowest cabin boy to the more privileged members of the so-called codfish aristocracy—the Marbleheaders maintained their distinct, peculiar dialect, which contained idioms of speech that echoed the distant past of Elizabethan England. In their distinctive speech, therefore, Glover's men sounded not unlike cockney Englishmen, who they had faced in battle, but more like rural Cornwall fishermen.

From the beginning, Glover's men were natural, ideal revolutionaries with a do-or-die attitude. This longtime antagonism and distinct sense of rebellion against authority was in the Marbleheader's blood and part of their very being. Now a source of pride, the ancestors of Glover's men had long ago defied a strict Puritan and Boston's mindless theologic conformity that crushed the spirit of individualism and free-thinking. Like those distant ancestors who had thrived for generations in their little fishing villages along the rocky Cornish coast that looked so much like the rugged eastern

Massachusetts coastline, the Marbleheaders were long distinguished by a defiant sense of nonconformity.

For such sound reasons, Washington had based the launching of his ambitious Trenton battleplan of his main strike force on the absolute conviction that the Marbleheaders' ample abilities, skills, and peculiarities would once again rise to the fore when needed the most.[23] Washington's bold gamble in staking "everything on one final roll of the dice" and going for broke was based upon what Glover and his Marbleheaders could first perform with their own strong arms, work ethic, and combined civilian and military experience. These Marbleheaders had been long at odds with not only nature and the sea, but also with any hint of arbitrary and dictatorial authority, Puritan, colonial, or British. A lifelong struggle against adversity and hardship began early when the average Marblehead male went to sea as a pre-teen "cut-tail," sailing the more than one thousand-mile journey to the lucrative Grand Banks fisheries. Enduring unpredictable seas and harsh weather conditions, these hardy seamen engaged in the hardest work imaginable in the north Atlantic. Even though Grand Banks fishing was a summertime pursuit, weather conditions were often winter-like, when cold fronts and strong winds descended south with an icy vengeance from the Arctic. Life was dangerous, challenging, and hence often short for Marblehead seafarers during the months-long voyages to their ancestral fishing grounds.

In the Marbleheaders' unforgiving world, simply making a living from the sea often resulted in higher casualties than suffered by the typical eighteenth-century regiment in combat. During the fatal year of 1768, nine Marblehead sailing ships and their sizeable crews were lost to raging storms on the open seas: a tragic loss of more than 120 Marblehead sailors, who had sailed off during the summer fishing season and never returned to their beloved home port. Even on routine voyages to the Grand Banks, fathers, sons, and brothers had been swept over the ship's sides by sudden ocean swells, disappearing forever into the deep blue. So many open sea deaths left Marblehead with a disproportionate large percentage of widows and orphans. This brutally high attrition of hard-working seamen attempting to support families was followed by another fourteen lost vessels the following fatal year of 1769. But losses in 1771 were even higher for the long-suffering, stoic Marblehead community. So many ships were lost at sea that the town officially appealed directly to the Massachusetts government for relief to provide for the multitude of widows and orphans.

Paradoxically, Colonel Johann Rall's Hessians now stationed at Trenton had seen the Marbleheader's fishing grounds more recently than Glover's men, having sailed across the Grand Banks to America's shores during the third week of June 1776. Here, they had felt the same northeast winter-like gales as Glover's Marbleheaders had long experienced. Even more ironic, the Hessians had caught codfish—much-needed nourishment that Glover's hungry men would have now relished for a late dinner along the Delaware's west bank instead of their meager rations of salt pork and "firecakes" now carried in well-worn, leather knapsacks.

As if to compensate for notoriously short lives, the Marblehead mariners lived fast and hard. Either in wooden fishermen's cottages, built by ship's carpenters, or in the town's taverns, they socialized, smoked long clay pipes, and drank till the early morning hours. The Little Jugg Inn, Three Codds Tavern, The Foundation Inn, Aunty Bowen's Tavern on Gingerbread Hill, and the appropriately named The Bunch of Grapes, were Marblehead's most popular drinking establishments. After drinking too much rotgut rum, these experienced seafaring men often fought each other in Marblehead's dingy drinking houses, dark alleys, and crooked streets over real or imagined slights. Curving along the lengthy, rocky peninsula-ridge upon which perched Marblehead, these narrow, twisting dirt avenues had been christened with colorful names such as Frog Lane and Cradleskid Lane.[24]

Fortunately for Washington, these Marbleheaders were always at their best when the odds were the greatest. Glover's seamen were destined to play leading roles in overcoming three formidable opponents in the next twenty-four hours: the raging Delaware River, an angry Mother Nature, and an elite brigade of Hessians. As a confident Colonel John Fitzgerald, who knew that Washington's supreme faith placed in Glover and his mariners was well-founded, penned in his diary on December 25: "Colonel Glover's fishermen from Marblehead, Mass., are to manage the boats just as they did in the retreat from Long Island."[25]

Most importantly along the Delaware's west bank, the high quality of Glover's officers and men strengthened the overall sinews of Washington's ranks in terms of confidence and a sense of accomplishing the impossible. Personable, gregarious, and intelligent, Ireland-born Colonel Stephen Moylan, a polished Irish Catholic (like Colonel Fitzgerald from Alexandria, Virginia) and from a leading Irish merchant family of Philadelphia, matched Glover's men in determination. Like the large number of Gaelic warriors in Washington's ranks, this former Philadelphia merchant, who had been born in Cork and finely educated in Paris, had early advocated for America to embark upon "the glorious Cause" of independence, thanks in part to Ireland's own lengthy struggle for freedom against England's dominating might. In a September 27, 1776 letter to Congress, Moylan reflected upon the narrow, August 1776 escape to Manhattan Island from Long Island that saved thousands of troops by the seafaring skills of Glover's men. This last-minute salvation for so many of Washington's soldiers provided invaluable experience that was now about to pay high dividends for the arduous Delaware crossing. In Moylan's words: "Perhaps there does not occur in History a Sadder retreat, so well Concerted, So well executed, than was made from that Island." The "merry," good-natured Moylan, now a respected Washington aide and part of his revered "family" of young staff officers, had already made timely contributions in rushing supplies to Washington's Army and in hurrying Generals Lee and Gates' reinforcements south to join Washington in time to undertake the daring offensive against Trenton.[26]

Even the escalating winter northeaster seemed like a good omen to some of Washington's more optimistic soldiers, who saw the bright side of nature's wrath. Indeed, the wintery screen now provided Washington's task force was reminiscent of the army's good fortune when a thick layer of fog of late August had masked the stealthy withdrawal across the East River from Long Island to Manhattan Island, providing Glover's rescuers with a timely screen. Glover's men had saved thousands of Washington's soldiers from almost certain anni-hilation by utilizing muffled oars in rowing across the fog-shrouded East River during one of the war's most brilliant small-scale amphibious operations. And now the sinewy Marbleheaders busily prepared to ferry around 2,400 soldiers, horses for artillery, a company of Philadelphia cavalrymen, and all eighteen cannon across a swollen river at night for the first time in this war: a more daunting challenge. Back in more halcyon days than this Christmas evening, Washington had overseen the entire late August evacuation operation from Long Island to Manhattan Island, and then the crossing the Delaware from Trenton to the safety of eastern Pennsylvania only two weeks ago, gaining more valuable experience that he now put to good use.

Most importantly, the steady calm and confidence of Glover and his men had a significant psychological impact on Washington's troops at this key moment of heightened tension and anxiety. Just the mere sight of the stocky, self-assured Colonel Glover, the army's maritime operational master, inspired confidence. Here, at the muddy landing of McConkey's Ferry, he now wore a Scottish broadsword that the mid-April 1746 slaughter at Culloden, Scotland, survivor General Hugh Mercer, born in Scotland, certainly appreciated, and two finely crafted silver pistols. Glover and his lean, muscular soldiers now bolstered the can-do attitude of Washington's Continentals as never before. Most importantly, Glover's men now possessed a strong sense of team spirit, camaraderie, and esprit de corps, which prepared them for stern challenges posed by nature's harshest winter offerings and the Delaware's high waters.

By way of a strange osmosis, this calm, reassuring certitude of Glover and his hard-bitten mariners radiated a quiet outward confidence that lifted optimism among young Continental soldiers about to climb into the rain-soaked Durham boats. Just as Glover overcame his small stature and his humble origins by his own accomplishments and willpower to infuse a spunky fighting spirit that was a hallmark of his elite Massachusetts regiment, so he and his Marbleheaders, who carried the essence of the sea wherever they went, immeasurably fortified the determination of Washington's soldiers to cross the unruly Delaware. Around 2,400 young men and boys now depended solely upon what this resilient band of seasoned mariners could accomplish on the swirling, rain-swollen river that stretched around eight hundred feet.

Worst of all, the rampaging Delaware was now full of ice floes that promised to damage the hulls of wooden vessels if not skillfully handled by Glover's men. Below-freezing conditions of the recent thaws and the recent bright sunshine just before the nor'easter struck had broken up much of the ice lining the river banks upriver. These rapid temperature fluctuations now left the Delaware full of bobbing chunks of ice.

With an ominous will all their own, the ice floes moved unimpeded downstream with the surging, dark current, posing a serious threat to impede Washington's crossing and sabotage his delicate timetable. This more precarious situation on the Delaware could not have been fully anticipated by Washington. After all, such typical wintertime conditions on the Potomac around Mount Vernon, well below the fall line and tidal, were very different this time of year, with saltwater mixing with freshwater to negate such heavy ice floes as now carried by the dark currents which moved rapidly down the Delaware above the fall line.[27]

First and foremost, the discipline, teamwork, and sheer determination of Glover's experienced mariners had to overcome the serious threat posed by these ice floes during the seemingly endless hours of the long night that lay ahead. One aristocratic Pennsylvania officer, Alexander Graydon, of Irish descent from Philadelphia and a member of Colonel John Shee's Pennsylvania militia battalion, marveled at the discipline of Glover's ever-unorthodox New England regiment. He described how although "deficient perhaps, in polish [like their flinty, independent-minded commander, Glover], it possessed an apparent aptitude for the purpose of its institution, and gave a confidence that myriads of its meek and lowly brethren were incompetent to inspire."[28]

Long overlooked by traditional historians, yet another significant factor differentiated Glover's Massachusetts soldiers from the majority of their fellow Continental comrades: a rarer open-mindedness about race. After all, these seafarers and fishermen from Massachusetts's north shore had long served on sailing ships together with African Americans and Indians. This more liberal attitude among Glover's men reflected the longtime ethnic composition of New England's culturally diverse fishing communities that proportionately represented the ethnic diversity found on sailing vessels. Therefore, Marbleheaders of various races now served side by side in the ranks of America's first truly integrated military unit.

Therefore, on this blustery Christmas Day, Glover's regiment was Washington's most racially diverse command. What was most upsetting to the less tolerant Southern gentleman officers and elitist planter's sons from Virginia's upper-class world was the fact that so many black mariners now served as proud fighting men in Washington's most indispensable Continental outfit. In the summer of 1776 when Washington's Army first arrived in New York City, Alexander Graydon, who conveniently overlooked his own humble Irish immigrant roots, was shocked by the sight of "a number of negroes," who were treated as equals deserving of fair treatment and respect in Glover's ranks.[29]

Continuing a tradition of enlisting free blacks and Indians in New England units, including Rogers' Rangers, during the French and Indian War, African-American soldiers also either now, or had earlier, served in the other four New England regiments of Glover's mostly Massachusetts brigade of General John Sullivan's Division. Along with African-American comrades like Scipio Dodge, Nathaniel Small, Hannibal, and other black soldiers, Private Pompey Blackman, around age twenty, served in Colonel Loammi Baldwin's Twenty-Sixth Massachusetts Continental Regiment, which was now part of Washington's task force. Freed by his dying master, Nathan Wyman, of Woburn, Massachusetts, Blackman then settled down in Lexington, Massachusetts in 1773 as a free man. At Lexington, which sent eight other of her patriotic African-American sons to the front as fighting men, Blackman lived in the home of a white man who had "taken" him in. Blasting away with his trusty flintlock as a Massachusetts Minuteman,

Blackman had harassed the withdrawing British column on the road back to Boston's safety after the initial April 1775 clashes at Lexington and Concord.[30]

The Twenty-Sixth Massachusetts Continental Regiment had been raised in early 1776 and consisted of 113 men on this Christmas Day of destiny far from New England. They had been initially uniformed in brown coats, which served as a natural camouflage amid autumn's hues, in contrast to the traditional Continental blue. Ironically, these crack soldiers of the grenadier companies of Baldwin's veteran regiment wore tall miter caps, distinctive headgear comparable to Rall's Hessians. Because grenadiers were generally taller than other regimental members, these men stood out from their comrades of the Twenty-Sixth Massachusetts, which now served in Glover's New England brigade of four Massachusetts and one Connecticut regiment. The elevated brass front piece of this Hessian-style mitre cap worn by Baldwin's elite grenadiers was distinguished by the fancy scroll letters, "GW," which appropriately stood for George Washington. Baldwin's highly disciplined regiment, therefore, was known as the "George Washington Regiment." Even more ironic, these Bay State soldiers now carried English muskets, stamped with the royal crown, which had been captured by a wide-ranging Marblehead privateer, which had surprised a British ordnance store ship in November 1775.[31]

Most significantly, the highly motivated African-American soldiers of Glover's regiment were not slaves but free men. Last summer, both black and white seamen of Glover's ever-flexible command worked together, side by side to save Washington's forces during the risky evacuation off Long Island. When only an ambitious captain commanding "Company Nine," Glover, before becoming colonel of the Massachusetts state regiment before it evolved into the Fourteenth Massachusetts Continental Regiment, had served beside an African-American soldier named Romeo, who initially marched off to war with two of Glover's brothers: Samuel, a French and Indian War veteran, and Jonathan, who owned slaves, in the Marblehead company's ranks. And from Marblehead's neighboring port of Beverly, Massachusetts, the Seventh Company of Glover's Fourteenth Massachusetts Continental Regiment, now consisting of eight companies, under the command of Captain Moses Brown, a 1768 law graduate from Harvard College, included another African-American warrior, Esop Hale. But the vast majority of Glover's black soldiers hailed from Marblehead. Given mostly ancient Roman names from the annals of classical history like Caesar, Pomp, Coffee, Primus, and Pompey, these African-American patriots, both slave and free, were members of Marblehead's distinctive African-American community, located near the so-called Negro Burying Ground.

Because the fishing industry had long relied in part upon black labor, Marblehead's separate African-American community had evolved independently out of inclination rather than due to strict segregation as in the South. This small but vibrant black community located on a high point of the Marblehead peninsula had kept some vestiges of ancient West African cultural traditions, perhaps even religion, alive for generations. Consisting of around one hundred individuals of African descent by 1776, this black community was known for its liveliness, including good times at Black Joe's establishment perched atop the rocky Gingerbread Hill, which offered a wide, sweeping view of Marblehead and its bluish harbor filled with a throng of tall-masted sailing ships.

This merry place, where the rum, gin, and grog flowed like water, was owned by Joseph Brown. Brown's musical talents with the fiddle were unsurpassed and well-known along the Massachusetts coast. Like other members of the black community, Brown was proud of his African roots. He also possessed some Indian blood, extending back generations. When the exciting news of the Declaration of Independence's July 1776 signing in Philadelphia first reached Marblehead to cause the ringing church bells to echo across the rocky Marblehead peninsula, Joseph and his wife Lucretia were freed by their master to enjoy liberty's blessings. In gratitude to the prevailing Age of Enlightenment thought and desiring to fight for his country, Joseph joined the Continental Army, evidently serving in Glover's regiment.

For generations, free blacks worked as fisherman and sailors in New England's thriving fishing industry. Even slaves served as sailors and shipwrights on the high seas. White and black New Englanders had long served side by side not only on New England's fishing vessels but also on American privateers, including ships sailing out of Marblehead to raid French shipping during the French and Indian War. And New England's distinguished privateer tradition continued unabated during the American Revolution, with African American and Caucasian seamen from Marblehead serving together in strikes at the British Navy that had forcefully impressed many Marblehead citizens into English service.

Both slaves, including Africa-born Cato Prince, and freemen from Marblehead served in the Continental Army, continuing the deeply ingrained seafaring tradition of blacks and whites working, fighting, and dying together both on land and on the high seas. After having faced the same arctic gales and maritime hardships in laboring the cold, turbulent waters of the Grand Banks, black and white Marbleheaders were about to once again work closely together as a highly effective team in a comparable harsh environment in transporting

Washington's troops and cannons across the Delaware under the most adverse conditions. And then they would soon be fighting side by side against the Hessians in Trenton's snowy streets.

Significantly, the black Marbleheaders' seafaring tradition extended back for centuries to mother Africa, especially along the west African coast. Black seafaring traditions had early merged with the cultural Cornwall- and Massachusetts-derived seafaring traditions of white Marbleheaders to create New England's master seamen. Slavery existed in Marblehead, but in an overall relatively benign form (mostly house servants) compared to the South (mostly field hands). Colonel Glover owned slaves, including black teenagers Boston and Merrick Willson, who served in the Seventh Massachusetts Continental Regiment by 1781. But Boston and Merrick were privileged and somewhat pampered house servants, which was commonplace in New England's so-called codfish aristocracy. Here, in Mablehead, both free and slave black individuals, especially those African Americans owned by clergymen, received baptisms, got married, and sat as equals while worshiping the same God together in the wooden pews of Glover's church, First Church, or Old North Church. At their own choosing and perhaps in reverence to their west African ancestors, African Americans were laid to rest in their own "Negro burying place" in Marblehead's rocky soil. In Marblehead, like when working together far out at sea, a man was judged not as much by his color as how well he performed his seafaring duties, upon which the fate of the captain, the entire crew, and even the sailing ship itself often depended. Consequently, skin color was of relatively little significance in the seafarer's harsh world, where mutual survival depended upon ability, work ethic, and content of character, unlike on land where superficiality often reigned supreme.

At Cambridge, Massachusetts, during the winter of 1775-1776, the inevitable racial clash had occurred after Southern volunteers arrived in camp. Glover's men, including former slaves, and Daniel Morgan's Virginia riflemen, including slaveowners and their privileged sons, had brawled in a wild melee over the fundamental issue of race, until broken up by Washington himself. The mere presence of fully armed black soldiers who walked with pride and dignity, such as Romeo, Esop Hale, or other African Americans in the distinctive uniform of the Marblehead regiment, represented the ultimate racial threat and nightmare to slave-owning Virginians.[32]

Ironically, at this time, these Southerners, both western frontiersmen and city boys from towns like Williamsburg and Fredericksburg, might well have begun to alter their stereotypical concepts about race and the value of ebony Continental soldiers, because they now depended entirely upon Glover's men, including black mariners, to transport them safely across the Delaware. After all, the safety of the Old Dominion home state, homes, and families now depended upon what Glover's men accomplished against the odds. Therefore, in such a crisis situation, a pervasive Southern racism finally took a bad seat among Washington's ragged revolutionaries on this Christmas evening and night. As fate would have it, the stern demands of the Delaware crossing and the Trenton challenge now united black and white as one: the necessary emergency, high stakes, and winner-take-all situation that eventually assisted in forging an unprecedented unity. Along the Delaware, class and racial differences finally took a back seat among the members of this stratified, hierarchical society, thanks to the magnitude of the Trenton challenge. As never before, Washington's men of all colors now truly became a band of brothers united by the crucial mission of crossing the Delaware and capturing Trenton.

As Washington realized, Colonel Glover and his seafarers were just the kind of determined men who could be depended upon to keep the revolution's flickering flames alive in its darkest hour. Everything now depended upon the skill of Glover's men in deciphering the Delaware's tricky currents, nuances, and idiosyncrasies to successfully negotiate this treacherous river on an inky night in stormy conditions. Unknowingly bestowing a compliment, a Tory newspaperman of the *New York Gazette,* the first newspaper published in New York City, had severely lambasted Glover's fiery revolutionaries as early as 1774, deriding—and indirectly complimenting—them as "the mad-men of Marblehead [who already] are preparing for an early campaign against his Majesty's troops." But, ironically, to transport Washington's ragtag task force across the turbulent Delaware, nearly a quarter of a mile wide, during a severe winter storm at night in a desperate bid to catch some of the best troops in America by surprise was indeed a challenge only undertaken by absolute madmen, according to the conventional wisdom of leading military experts and graduates of military academies on both sides of the Atlantic.[33]

Another key factor also explained why Glover and his prized New Englanders were so highly motivated on December 25 and 26. Marblehead's close-knit community was even now in its death throes, and its people were suffering severely. With its able-bodied men no longer working out at sea to provide an income from fishing "the banks," Marblehead was now racked by backbreaking poverty that reduced its people to squalor. Living conditions became so dismal that impoverished citizens were forced to dig up roots and cut turf, as in Ireland, to fuel fires on this Christmas Day in Marblehead.

Infuriating Glover's men to no end and fueling the desire for revenge, this crushing poverty stemmed from the British Navy's closure of the Grand Banks, starting on July 20, 1775, to American vessels to economically destroy New England's fishing industry. Great Britain possessed the world's most powerful navy that enforced its harsh decree. As planned by London's calculating officials, who keenly knew how to wage economic warfare to shatter lives and families of rebels, the British blockade was now choking Marblehead to death. Clearly, stripped of their traditional livelihoods, the innocent families of Glover's hard-fighting Marblehead mariners continued to pay a high price for their undying patriotism, while their conscience-troubled menfolk along the faraway Delaware River now prepared to save the day for America.

Despite heartbreaking letters written from distressed family members that told of the terrible suffering back in Marblehead and fortunately for America at this crucial moment along the Delaware, Glover's regiment boasted proudly of one of the army's lowest desertion rates at a time when desertion had reached epic proportions in Washington's Army. However, this grim situation on the home front only inspired Glover's young men and boys to do their best on December 25 and 26. Great Britain's ruthless economic warfare against New England fishing communities especially Marblehead would shortly come back to haunt George III, England, and the legendary Rall brigade, which had never known defeat, in the climactic showdown at Trenton.[34] As temperatures plummeted and darkness deepened along the fast-moving river overflowing its icy banks, Connecticut's Lieutenant Elisha Bostwick described how Washington's hopeful army, "toward evining [sic] began to recross the Delaware" in the increasing cold.[35]

With blackness having descended so rapidly upon the Delaware's wind-swept valley, this inconspicuous setting might have well represented the final sunset for the young American nation if Washington's long-shot and high-stakes gamble was not won during the next twenty-four hours. Initial attempts by the Continental infantrymen to board the Durham boats were painstakingly slow, to Washington's endless irritation. The first soldiers to board the Durham boats were delayed because the river bank dropped sharply from the level flood plain—a flat shelf, or terrace, of bottom land—to the water's edge, where a sheet of ice covered the frozen river bank like a slippery blanket. Especially in the near-darkness, these dual obstacles resulted in hundreds of soldiers remaining motionless and massed close together in formation, waiting for their turn to cross the Delaware. Major Wilkinson, now serving as the trusty aide of Scotland-born General Arthur St. Clair who commanded one of Washington's brigades, wrote how the "Troops began to cross at sunset," which coincided with the rapidly-encroaching veil of blackness around 6:00 p.m.[36] All the while, masking his considerable anxiety, Washington displayed a calm command presence that steadied his men, reassuring them with his confident example and bold front. Even under these deplorable conditions and in a tense, crisis situation upon which everything hinged, Washington remained especially "self-collected." Most importantly, the common soldier's resolve was fortified by their commander-in-chief's appearance of steely determination. All the while, he exhibited an "invincible firmness and [a sense of] perseverance."[37]

As carefully planned by Washington, the Continental troops were to be relayed across the river by Glover's mariners in regular shifts: a methodical and systematic, but time-consuming, process. The frigid ground around the ferry landing where hundreds of awaiting Continental troops, with knapsacks and accouterments slung over too-thin apparel, were crowded under the tall syca-mores bare of leaves, had been churned into a slippery pulp, which additionally slowed the laborious embarkation process. Mud clung to soldier's shoes and pant legs like a sticky paste. Meanwhile, Washington's timetable for crossing began to fall further behind schedule. In only twelve hours, Washington had planned to have all his troops of two divisions, under the First Division under General John Sullivan and the Second Division under General Nathanael Greene, in advantageous positions on Trenton's outskirts to strike an hour before sunrise.[38]

Because the narrow, barge-like Durham boats were built to carry heavy freight instead of passengers in deep, sunken hulls, Washington's soldiers were forced to stand up during the precarious sojourn across the angry river. They were jammed close together in the crowded vessels, with men holding to the top of the boat's chest-high sides for balance, steadying themselves as best they could. Symbolically, not long after Captains William Washington and John Flahaven's vanguard of Virginia and New Jersey Continentals, respectively, pushed off and became the first soldiers to descend into the depths of the Durham boats, General Washington himself prepared to cross the around eight hundred-foot wide Delaware. He planned to accompany the foremost troops of General Adam Stephen's Virginia brigade, which were designated as the first infantry brigade to cross. Washington wanted to be one of the first Americans across the Delaware: a smart psychological and leadership decision calculated to inspire his troops during their most trying hour.

Clearly, Washington intentionally radiated confidence to his young soldiers, especially those men who could not swim and possessed ever-increasing doubts about the wisdom of this risky nighttime crossing. Meanwhile, Major William Raymond Lee, a fine tactician of the Fourteenth Massachusetts Continental Regiment with solid experience, worked hand in hand with Glover in managing the boat crews. He hailed from one of Marblehead's leading and wealthiest families. While Glover, although a brigade commander, orchestrated the efforts of the Marbleheader crews during the crossing, Major Lee commanded the Fourteenth Massachusetts Continental Regiment.

To ensure the presence of an authority figure to make sure everything went well, Glover prudently assigned a respected officer, either a captain or lieutenant, to manage the rowing and steering crews of from four to five enlisted Marbleheaders in each Durham boat. In successfully navigating the ice-encumbered currents, these veteran officers ensured that the strong-armed crews rowed together in unison and performed smoothly like a well-oiled team, as if yet navigating the tricky waters of the Grand Banks, where the lashings of frigid, high winds and swollen waves had long conditioned them for the arduous task of crossing the Delaware. The river's swirling, black waters proved especially challenging for Glover's swarthy seamen, because the rain-swollen water level was higher, the currents faster, and the night darker than anticipated.

Each of these highly maneuverable Durham boats, looking almost like giant canoes except that they were flat-bottomed, had been designed by Robert Durham in the 1750s to carry hefty cargoes of timber, ore and pigiron, timber, and natural produce from upriver down to the Philadelphia market. Most iron ore was mined from the hills of upper Bucks County, Pennsylvania, where the Durham Iron Furnace or Works, located just two miles south of the Northampton County line and ten miles south of Easton, Pennsylvania, had been established in 1727. Since the mid-1750s, Declaration of Independence signer Ireland-born George Taylor and his partner leased and operated the Durham Iron Works.

Ironically, for Glover's black mariners now manning the Durham boats, these vessels had long transported iron ore mined more cheaply in Pennsylvania for higher profits to undercut England's manufacturers because of black slave labor. For America's war effort, the Durham Furnace now produced a steady flow of cannonballs, grapeshot, and cannons. However, this precious iron ore came not only from Pennsylvania's hills to the north in a wild region known as the Upper Bucks, but also from the Delaware's other side, where the Oxford Furnace produced war munitions. Iron was New Jersey's most significant nonagricultural export, and it was transported in sizeable quantities down the Delaware from the northwest New Jersey Highlands.

Enterprising civilian boatmen, most likely Robert Durham himself, of the Durham Iron Works located on the Delaware only several miles below Easton, Pennsylvania, had first created this extremely sturdy Durham boat for shipping tons of iron ore to Philadelphia. Varying from forty- to sixty-six feet in length, eight feet wide, and pointed at each end, the largest Durham boats transported a maximum capacity load of around fifteen tons, including cargoes of primarily pig iron and ore, but also timber, grain, and even whisky down the Delaware to Philadelphia, from where America's rich natural bounty was then shipped to Europe's cities and the highly profitable sugar plantations of the Caribbean Islands. But during this perilous crossing of an untamed river that seemed to span forever in the blackness, the Durham boat's length now became an unexpected liability. The sharp, repeated impact of ice chunks and the heavy current pushed the boats off course and farther downstream. Therefore, more strenuous physical efforts were required from Glover's hardworking men to get the Durham boats back on proper course and heading directly east toward Garret Johnson's Ferry yet far away on the blackened Jersey shore lined with tall trees draped in winter's hue.

However, for Washington's purposes, these Durham boats were ideal—even down to the black-painted hulls that provided greater concealment in the night just in case enemy scouts lurked nearby—for the task for transporting hundreds of nervous, young infantrymen across the wide river: oversized vessels with the twin, seemingly contradictory advantages of shallow, light drafts (for passing over the fall line's rapids) combined with an impressive 30,000-pound load capacity. Even though the steering oars on each pointed end of the vessel were manned by the muscular Massachusetts mariners, maneuvering the Durham boats was difficult for Glover's Marbleheaders with the high water, the darkness, and winter storm. In fair weather conditions, lengthy poles manned by experienced river-men allowed these light-weighing crafts, when unloaded after returning from Philadelphia, to be "poled" back upriver (after the boat had been oared downriver), if the wind was not in their favor to utilize the mast by raising and inflating the canvas of two sails against the current along the river's most shallow side.

Initially upon pushing off from the Pennsylvania shore and to counter the combined effect of the strong current and contrary winds sweeping south, Glover's mariners relied more upon eighteen-foot long oars in their laborious efforts to row their boats across the stormy Delaware. After shoving away from the icy Pennsylvania shore, two Massachusetts mariners of the five-man crews walked to and fro along the slick running boards, or footboards (also called walking rails), along the gunwales on each side of the heavily loaded vessel, pushing the lengthy poles against the river bottom. Despite the rough waters and the risk of losing their balance and falling headfirst into churning waters, the sweating Marbleheaders, with their long hair queued in the tradition of seamen, muscled the Durham boat against the swirling currents by pushing and applying full body pressure against the long eighteen-foot poles. With quiet business-like efficiency, the Durham boats were first poled (an entirely new kind of labor for the versatile Marblehead Mariners) and then rowed upon reaching deeper water beyond the Pennsylvania shore.

Then, making another hurried final adjustment after the closely synchronized rowing with oars, the task of poling was once again resumed by Glover's men upon reaching more shallow waters near the Jersey shore. With such a light weight and shallow draft of less than two feet even when fully loaded, the Durham boats now made ideal landing craft for Washington's infantrymen. Now the Durham boats were able to land about forty American fighting men on a distant shore. With their usual ingenuity and skill, the dynamic leadership team of Colonels Henry Knox and Glover carefully supervised the initial loading of troops, while Washington, mounted on his splendid chestnut sorrel at the windswept riverbank, initially surveyed the hectic activity to make sure that the crossing progressed smoothly. Then, when General Adam Stephen's Virginians began to cross the Delaware, the commander-in-chief gingerly stepped into a Durham boat in a classic demonstration of leading by example to instill confidence for a safe crossing, especially to anxious soldiers who could not swim if a boat suddenly capsized. Washington left his "noble horse," in the words of Private John Howland, of Providence, Rhode Island, on the river's west bank with a trusty aide. The Virginian's favorite charger was later brought across the river, most likely in a ferry boat that was larger than a Durham boat.

One of Colonel Glover's most trusted Massachusetts officers received the coveted assignment and "honor" of transporting Washington with special care across the Delaware. Captain William Blackler, Jr. was tasked with the all-important mission of escorting Washington across the Delaware because he and the Marbleheaders of his veteran company "were the most knowledgeable about how to cross" the river. A successful merchant and shipper, Blackler owned Marblehead's second wide-ranging privateer, armed with a dozen cannon, which had first set sail in September 1776 to raid British shipping. Blackler had served with Glover on Marblehead's patriot committee of inspection to enforce the non-importation of British goods in 1775. Age thirty-six and baptized at a Marblehead Church on May 18, 1740 on the day of his birth, Captain Blackler possessed considerable military experience and seafaring expertise. Therefore, he could be depended on to make sure that Washington was transported safely across the swollen Delaware in the most adverse conditions. Blackler had married Rebekah Chipman, and his first son, John Chipman Blackler, was born in January 1771. After having raised a Marblehead militia company as early as 1773, he spent his fortune in equipping his command of zealous volunteers. Then, based upon merit and ability, Blackler was appointed captain in late June 1775. Blackler now must have wondered if he would survive this winter campaign and live long enough to see his wedding anniversary, December 27, or his young son again back in his beloved Marblehead nestled on the picturesque harbor. Glover's most reliable captain survived the Trenton challenge, but Blackler was destined to be crippled from serious wounds suffered at Saratoga in the fall of 1777.

With a piece of white paper pinned to his hat, like other Continental officers as Washington had specified to designate rank that could be seen in the darkness, Blackler commanded the sturdy Durham boat that carried Washington into the very vortex of the Delaware's swirling, dark waters. One experienced seaman who manned one of the perfectly synchronized oars of the Durham boat during Washington's delicate passage was Private John Johns Russell. He was born in his beloved port of Marblehead on November 2, 1755. Joseph Widger, who was fated to die in an August 1812 naval battle during the War of 1812, was another hardy Marbleheader who manned the fast-moving oars of Blackler's Durham boat. All the while, humble Massachusetts enlisted men and their esteemed commander-in-chief alike shivered from the same icy blasts of arctic gales sweeping down the river's wide, open expanse from the northeast to additionally churn up the already rough waters.

Each Durham boat was carefully navigated with a veteran seaman's refined skill against the currents, the ice floes, and the blustery winds, which were funneled between the tree-lined river banks to cut like a knife. All the while, Glover's soldiers, cursing, struggling, and sweating, worked long and hard (which at least kept them warmer than their half-frozen passengers, including Washington) in passing boatload after boatload of Continentals across the river in the most nightmarish conditions. During the perilous, nerve-racking journey through the wet darkness and wintry gales, cold-numbed soldiers, from teenagers to graybeards, hunkered low to escape the icy winds that pierced their thin layers of clothing better suited for summer campaigning.

Thanks to the tireless, energetic efforts of the imposing Knox, a giant in girth and height, and the diminutive "maritime wizard" Glover, the seemingly impossible task of transporting the hundreds of Washington's troops across the Delaware initially flowed smoothly once underway. However, the progress of Washington's main strike force was not matched by the other two forces attempting to cross the Delaware at two points below McConkey's Ferry. Colonel John Cadwalader, who had turned down a Continental commission offered by Washington to remain in command of his beloved Philadelphians and his large middle-class militia (a Philadelphia Associator brigade) column of around 1,200 men and a six hundred-man brigade of New England Continentals, under Rhode Islander Colonel Daniel Hitchcock, age thirty-six, ran into trouble. Here, a dozen miles south of McConkey's Ferry at Neshaminy Ferry near Bristol, Pennsylvania, Cadwalader's assigned crossing point (the southernmost) was located below the middle crossing point of General James Ewing and his Pennsylvania militia. All three of Washington's designated crossing points were located almost at an equal distance from each other. Washington's and Cadwalader's crossing points far outflanked Trenton to the north and south, respectively, while Ewing had been positioned almost directly across from Trenton. Ewing and his task force, consisting of York, Cumberland, Lancaster, and Bucks County boys, had been ordered to cross at the South Trenton Ferry, just to Trenton's south, to strike Trenton from the south while Washington attacked from the north. Despite the best efforts of the specialized rowing soldiers of Major Jehu Eyre's Second Company of the City and Liberties of Philadelphia, Philadelphia Artillery battalion (a militia rather than a Continental unit), the imposing challenge of crossing the Delaware during a winter storm proved too daunting for Cadwalader's attempt to land at Burlington, New Jersey.

Ironically, just before he had entered Captain Blackler's Durham boat to embark upon his passage of the Delaware, Washington had written a brief message around 6:00 p.m. to General Cadwalader. He expressed the strongest hope that Cadwalader's Philadelphians downriver and opposite Burlington would "create as great a diversion [to the south] as possible," to enhance his own bid to catch Colonel Rall and his garrison by surprise by attack from the north.[39]

Assigned to the column of Cadwalader's Philadelphians, including militiamen who wore distinctive "PB" (Philadelphia Battalion) brass buttons with their specific numerical designation displayed, situated around twenty miles below McConkey's Ferry and as he penned in his diary about the situation upon crossing at Dunk's Ferry, south of Neshaminy Ferry, and after having been initially thwarted at Neshaminy Ferry, Captain Thomas Rodney recorded the extent of the challenge, while never forgetting the night. Now serving with a Dover, Delaware, volunteer company, Rodney described how "the wind blew very hard and there was much rain and sleet, and there was so much floating ice in the River that we had the greatest difficulty" in crossing the angry river in the haunting December blackness.[40] However, in truth and despite the formidable obstacles, but a "single file of Colonel Glover's regiment of military mariners would have given them [Cadwalader's Philadelphia column] the proper time for crossing, and shown the way in which it could most easily be accomplished."[41]

Indicating why the two ferries—McConkey's Ferry on the Pennsylvania side and Garret Johnson's Ferry, proper, on the New Jersey shore were linked together as a common watery passageway and what was essentially the McConkey-Johnson Ferry—had been established on the west bank at this point, the river narrowed during its gradual descent south toward Trenton to around eight hundred feet in width. But this more restrictive natural configuration only made the river's currents, already higher than usual thanks to swollen waters from rain and melting ice, run even swifter and with more turbulence at this relatively narrower point.

After the initial crossing of the Delaware began at around 6:00 p.m., an ever-increasing level of difficulties was encountered by the hard-working Marbleheaders, coinciding with more gusty winds, rougher and yet-rising waters, and a heavier sheet of snow and snow. With the almost full winter moon (waning gibbous just a few days after a full moon) on the rise—beginning at 5:31 p.m.—in a high winter arc, and now hidden by clouds, young Major Wilkinson, the enterprising southern Marylander of the planter class, and whose grandfather had migrated from England in 1729, described how "the force of the current, the sharpness of the frost, the darkness of the night, the ice [floes] and a high wind rendered the passage of the river extremely difficult."[42]

As the nasty northeaster howled with greater intensity and chilled Washington's men to the bone, the ever-vigorous Colonel Knox, the son of Scotch-Irish immigrants from northern Ireland, continued to orchestrate this precarious movement of nervous troops to the east bank of the raging river with consummate skill. Under the cold, wet deluge, Stirling's Delaware, Pennsylvania, and Virginia brigade, leading the veteran infantry of Greene's Second Division, prepared to embark and cross the most formidable natural obstacle that these men had ever faced, following Stephen's Virginia vanguard brigade. Spirits among the less determined leaders and enlisted men plummeted, falling in proportion to the increasing wrath unleashed by the angry winter storm. To some religious and superstitious-minded soldiers, mirroring the cultural belief system of the ancient Romans, the intensifying storm seemed like an ill omen, a harbinger of certain disaster. In consequence, a tense silence pervaded in the ranks, along with the growing conviction that the winter storm had already wrecked Washington's slim chances for success. Struggling against a seemingly vengeful Mother Nature, Knox was nagged by doubts about getting everyone safely across in time with so much floating ice from upriver cascading down to repeatedly slam into the vulnerable sides of the Durham boats, now filled with increasingly anxious infantrymen, all crammed together like sardines.

From a distance to the sight of Glover's mariners, especially in the omnipresent darkness, the descending ice floes were imperceptible. And then when they were suddenly close to the Durham boat, these chunks of ice, with only a fraction bobbing above the surface, appeared deceptively insignificant until they suddenly slammed violently into wooden hulls with a thud and a sharp jolt. These violent jolts to the hull's left, or northern, side forced some Durham boats slightly off course, pushing them a short distance downstream with the strong, onrushing current until Glover's seamen mastered the situation and regained control. Knowing their mission's supreme importance that even surpassed the stealthy withdrawal from Long Island on that hot August night, the Marblehead boys muscled their Durham boats back on course and in line with Johnson's Ferry on the distant east bank that was yet unseen in the blackness. However, through the deluge, a distant flaming torch, lamp, or light from the fireplaces of an illuminated Johnson Ferry House was eventually barely seen when Glover's mariners neared the east bank, serving as a dim beacon to guide the Marbleheaders to their final objective.

Although only in his mid-twenties and hardly looking the part, America's most dynamic artillery commander Colonel Knox considered the Delaware crossing a task that "seemed impossible," as he soon candidly admitted to wife Lucy Flucker Knox, the pampered daughter of a former Massachusetts former. However, Knox concealed his growing fears from his nerve-racked troops, especially the scrawny, ill-nourished teenagers from America's hardscrabble small farms on the western frontier and in the South. These soaked, cold-numbed youngsters looked up to not only Washington, but also Knox like a father for guidance during this hellish night on the Delaware. If anyone could accomplish the impossible in getting Washington's main task force across the Delaware, Knox was that energetic, resourceful officer, as Washington fully appreciated.

After all, crossing the around eight hundred foot-wide Delaware was even more daunting than Knox's amazing feat of transporting around sixty cannon, including large siege pieces and mortars—weighing 119,000 pounds—on oxen-drawn sleds from Fort Ticonderoga, New York, and more than three hundred miles in six weeks across New England's frozen countryside, including the heavily timbered mountains of western Massachusetts, the Berkshires, to Washington's Army during the 1775-1776 siege of Boston. Most importantly, Knox's tireless efforts forced Howe's evacuation of Boston in March 1776 to bestow Washington with his first success as the army's commander. But now Knox's seemingly impossible mission was even more formidable, requiring the safe transportation of nearly four hundred tons of ordinance across the Delaware as quickly as possible and without incident.[43]

Thankfully, Glover's exhausted mariners, as ragged as Washington's other men, received some timely assistance when most needed, thanks to Washington's and Knox's efforts to speed up their most hazardous operation to date. To add much-needed extra muscle to the herculean effort in what was already becoming a losing race with time that continued to slip away, a contingent of eighty-five cannoneers from Captain Joseph Moulder's Associator company of Knox's Regiment of Continental Artillery was assigned to assist Glover's mariners in their monumental undertaking.

Under the command of capable, twenty-five-year-old Lieutenant Anthony Cuthbert, who was one of Philadelphia's shipbuilders and had once enjoyed a peaceful existence in a comfortable brick house on fashionable Penn Street with wife Sarah, these hardy Pennsylvania artillerymen were a perfect fit for this crucial assignment. Cuthbert's young gunners consisted of durable sailors, long-shoremen, riggers, seamen, ship's carpenters, shipwrights, and other comparable experienced hands from the dingy wharves and docks situated for two miles along the Delaware, especially Penn's Landing, in east Philadelphia. Moulder's independent company, which had been formed as an Associator artillery unit of the City and Liberties of Philadelphia, was heavily Irish and Scotch-Irish. However, this fine artillery company also included Germans, Dutch, and other ethnic groups who had sided with America's cause in which men were considered equal, regardless of place of birth or origin.

And more timely assistance for Glover's overworked seamen was forthcoming from a small contingent of civilian volunteers, veteran Pennsylvania and New Jersey boatmen and ferrymen, who had suddenly appeared at exactly the right time and place. Having served under Glover in the past, John Blunt, an experienced ship captain who had long sailed the Delaware's tricky waters, provided his navigational expertise in helping to get the bobbing fleet of Durham boats back and forth across the churning river. Most important, these experienced freshwater boatmen understood intimately the Delaware's treacherous currents and its often-unfathomable inherent characteristics, especially during winter and high water conditions, than Glover's Atlantic seafarers.[44]

In orchestrating the nightmarish crossing and attempting to get everyone across without the loss of a single man, meanwhile, Knox remained a constant swirl of nonstop activity. To make sure that all was proceeding as planned and that his men followed his orders to the letter, the erudite Bostonite, whose massive size made his voice sound like a bellowing bull in the New England woods, shouted out precise instructions, sharp criticisms, and inspiring encouragement in "a deep bass heard above the crash of the ice which filled the river." Knox's directives echoed out of the inky darkness and across the Delaware like the blaring war trumpet of the Hebrew "Mighty Warrior" Gideon (the "Destroyer") of the Old Testament.[45]

All the while, additional Continental troops from Pennsylvania, Delaware, New York, Virginia, Maryland, and New England piled quietly into the wet, wooden bottoms of the Durham boats. With an icy rain and light snow tumbling down, these grim-faced soldiers wearily descended into the slippery, black hulls as if entering a cold, dark tomb from which they feared that they would never emerge. Wrapped in old, lice-covered blankets to cover threadbare summer uniforms, now full of holes where not patched, many soldiers were understandably consumed by their own gloomy thoughts and anxieties that surrounded them like the sting of the biting cold, fearing the worst before their Durham boats were even launched in the blackness on this most haunting of nights. For good reason, these Continentals grew more apprehensive, if not deeply troubled, not only about the ever-increasing risks inherent with this perilous river crossing, but also about what the sunrise of December 26 might bring for them on the mysterious New Jersey side of the river, when they faced an elite brigade of crack German soldiers known for their ruthlessness in battle. While the merciless northeast wind cut their thin clothing and carried the reverberating sound of barking officer's orders across river like unearthly directives from angry Roman gods of war, Mars, Glover, and Knox shouted themselves hoarse in issuing orders to ensure that everything flowed like clockwork as much as possible under the most appalling conditions.

Rather than standing fully erect to receive the full force of a wintery blast hurtling down the river, half-frozen soldiers huddled low and close together for warmth in the boat's water-soaked hull. Acting on instinct, they crounched behind the high, wooden gunwales to provide some slight protection against the harsh elements. Looking more like hungry beggars or homeless refugees from London's dirty streets than Continental soldiers about to meet some of Europe's finest troops at Trenton, Washington's cargoes of hunkered-down Continentals were ferried slowly over what seemed like a vast watery expanse and toward the tree-lined New Jersey shore, masked in an eerie, blackened silence, that seemed to portent disaster up ahead. Meanwhile, the relentless orchestration of the continuous crossing of troops, with around thirty-five to forty men per Durham boat, by Knox and Glover only fell further behind Washington's overly optimistic (and entirely unrealistic) timetable of transporting everyone across by midnight.

Perhaps some of Washington's more aristocratic officers, proud young blue-bloods, schooled in the ancient classics, like the intellectual Virginian Lieutenant James Monroe, had read Homer's *The Iliad* in which Achilles and his Myrmidon warrior companions, who accompanied the Greek war fleet, had sailed across the deep-blue Aegean Sea with colorful war banners flying to conquer mighty Troy in their "black boats" that each contained around fifty warriors. If so, then such college-educated Continental officers versed in the timeless lessons of *The Illiad* (ironically actually the West's first anti-war narrative) might have thought back to that ancient time of around 1200 BC, when courageous Greek warriors slaughtered their fellow man, the hated Trojans, as fiercely as fighting men now engaged in the struggle for America's heart and soul in 1776, but also yet simultaneously longed to return home to loving families, almost as if nothing had changed across the intervening centuries. This central tragedy of the human experience—the curse of incessant warfare with all its surreal horrors—linked Washington's Continentals to the cherished western legacy of ancient Greek warriors, who fought and died far from home: mankind's timeless burden and tragic fate—whether at Troy or Trenton—in which human beings are seemingly destined to endlessly destroy each other from either an uncontrollable biological urge, or a monumental genetic defect and, ironically, for reasons often forgotten in time.[46]

Utilizing their extensive knowledge and experience of handling boats in windy and icy conditions from long Atlantic voyages that had lasted for months, the Marbleheaders skillfully employed their lengthy, wooden oars and "shad poles" to head off floating ice, bobbing up and down in dark waters and almost impossible to see in the inky blackness. Such desperate, last-second efforts prevented some larger ice chunks from damaging the vulnerable wooden hulls of the Durham boats. Most of all, the closely coordinated, smooth rhythms of the Marbleheaders and ceaseless laboring of Glover's men in unison as a well-trained team were vital for a successful crossing of the cantankerous river. Therefore, Glover, the former experienced sea captain who knew that survival on the ever-hostile Atlantic depended upon close teamwork, made sure that his mariners at the oars of the Durham boats, as lengthy as nearly seventy feet, labored effectively as one. Glover's soaked men knew exactly what was required of them to transport an ad hoc force of revolutionaries all the way to the Jersey shore. They now worked with an obsessive zeal, realizing that there was no tomorrow if they failed in their crucial role.

For Glover's Continentals, the stiff challenge of the Delaware itself was not a new experience. After all, Marblehead schooners had long taken these same seamen to the Grand Banks, where they were dropped off in small dories which they then rowed in the steady rhythm of close synchronization to reap the bountiful harvest from the world's most fertile fishing grounds. Luckily for Washington during his final desperate bid to reverse America's sagging fortunes before it was too late, Glover's high-spirited soldier-sailors were experienced dorymen, whose coordinated rowing skills were second to none. In fact, the daring "bravo of dorymen [was] legendary," and this can-do attitude, well-honed skill, and high level of experience once again now emerged in timely fashion on the Delaware on the most crucial night in America's existence.[47]

Even beardless drummer boys and fifers of Glover's regiment put down their instruments, wet and ice-covered, to assist in the arduous task of rowing the big Durham boats across the choppy river. Providing a much-needed respite, these mere boys, including bright-eyed teenagers, gave the older, grizzled mariners a brief rest in the crowded boats overflowing with a huddled mass of half-frozen, miserable soldiers, who wondered if they would safely or even ever reach the elusive east bank. Glover's young musicians included drummers Benjamin and John Thompson, who were brothers, Hugh Raynor, and John Anthoine.

Another musician of the Fourteenth Massachusetts Continental Regiment was fifer Thomas Grant, Jr., the son of Captain Thomas Grant, Sr. He had just celebrated his fifteenth birthday only a dozen days before on December 13. A pious member of the Second Congregationalist Church, Captain Grant commanded the Marblehead company in which his son served as a fifer. Before America embarked upon its bold bid for liberty, Grant was Marblehead's most gifted silversmith. He operated his own Marblehead shop, where his son worked by his side. Grant created some of New England's most elegant masterpieces in high-grade silver, demonstrating a creative skill that he now applied to the art of war and in killing his fellow man. Most, if not all, of these young musicians of Glover's regiment very likely contributed in the time-consuming crossing of the unruly Delaware that seemed to have no end.[48]

As a sad fate would have it, the ranks of Glover's musicians had not been immune to a recent cruel decimation. Glover's regiment lost one fine drummer, Philip Follett, who was captured at the battle of Long Island. He was part of an inseparable father-son team, which was fully prepared to sacrifice their all for America's freedom. Philip was the beloved son of Thomas Follett, Sr., who died of disease when the regiment was stationed at Cambridge where Washington first took command in July 1775. The other son, Thomas Follett, Jr., was released by Glover to attend to the welfare of his impoverished family and grieving mother in long-suffering Marblehead. But never forsaking the struggle for liberty, the young man soon went out to sea aboard a privateer to wage war against British shipping. He was determined to avenge his father's death, eager to play his patriotic part at sea while Glover's regiment fought on land. Clearly, fortunately for Washington and his ragtag army, the commitment of such dedicated young men in Glover's Bay State regiment was very much of a personal and family affair, revealing yet another reason why this close-knit elite command, the pride of Marblehead, functioned so efficiently on land and water on December 25–26.[49]

Amid the pelting mixture of rain, snow, and sleet that continued to pour down upon poorly protected heads, some Continental officers drew their sabers to employ them in desperate attempts to keep ice chunks from ramming into the sides of the Durham boats. Each jarring thump that shook vessels reminded the nervous, half-frozen occupants of the omnipresent danger that so suddenly struck out of the blackness. Most of Washington's city boys and farm lads could not swim, which naturally heightened concerns about a boat's sinking. Consequently, heightened tension and fear consumed even the most tried Continental veteran, who had already risked his life at Harlem Heights, Pell's Point, or White Plains, throughout the long, nerve-racking journey across the turbulent river. On this darkest of nights, a Durham boat's sinking, especially in icy, rough waters with strong currents, was now a certain death sentence even for a strong swimmer, of which there were few. In desperation, therefore, agile Massachusetts oarsmen and strong-armed pole-men attempted to wardoff the largest ice floes from striking fragile hulls, but such efforts were usually too late.

Such desperate attempts resulted in some lost swords, or the tips of officer's swords breaking off in chunks of ice.

In later years, one elegant, decorative sword, without a tip, was fished out of the Delaware's waters at McConkey's Ferry, which revealed one such frantic effort. Because of the sword's high quality and obvious expensive quality, some historians speculated that the saber might have belonged to Washington himself, who was one of the first to cross over America's river of destiny. Or perhaps this sword came from one of Washington's faithful band of staff officers, such as Lieutenant Tench Tilghman (Maryland), Colonels Stephen Moylan (Pennsylvania), John Fitzgerald (Virginia), and Joseph Trumbull (Connecticut), and Lieutenant Colonels Samuel Blachley Webb (Connecticut) and Richard Carey, Jr. (Massachusetts).

These highly esteemed members of Washington's "family" most likely also crossed the Delaware with Washington in Captain Blackler's Durham boat. This exquisite saber of a high-ranking officer was later allegedly positively "identified" as Washington's own. It was, therefore, speculated that "when a large piece of floating ice bore down upon them [the soldiers in Washington's boat under Captain Blackler were already] engaged in keeping the ice clear of the other parts of the boat, and, seeing no help from them, General Washington plunged his sword into the frozen mass and pushed it from the boat. In doing so, however, he found that the weapon had stuck fast, and in endeavoring to pull it out the point broke off in the ice and the other part fell from the General's frozen fingers into the water."[50]

A seasoned Continental soldier named Oliver Cromwell was one African American who crossed the Delaware on this hellish night that no one would ever forget. He was not a slave but a free man. A diligent farmer, Cromwell tilled New Jersey soil to earn the fruits of his own labor. Born on May 23, 1752 in the village of Black Horse, now Columbus, Burlington County, Cromwell hailed from the pine-covered lands of south New Jersey. This area was distinguished by a relatively large free black population, thanks to past abolitionist Quaker influences and activities. The famous Emanuel Leutze painting entitled *Washington Crossing the Delaware* has been often criticized by modern historians and scholars for the abundance of its historical inaccuracies. But in fact, the African-American soldier, wearing a short, blue sailor's jacket typically worn by New England seamen, depicted by Leutze in Washington's Durham boat (more correctly that of Captain Blackler) was actually quite accurate, representing one of Glover's black mariners. Leutze's soldier of African descent has been most often misidentified as Prince Whipple, who was a slave owned by

Declaration of Independence signer William Whipple. However, he was with his master on December 26, 1776 and not in the Trenton-Princeton Campaign. Prince Whipple only later served with Washington's Army at Saratoga.[51]

Meanwhile, around forty of Captain Flahaven's soldiers of the First New Jersey Continental Regiment, Eastern Battalion, from such eastern New Jersey counties as Essex, Morris, Bergen, Somerset, Middlesex, and Monmouth, reached the east bank in one of the first Durham boats. The poorly shod feet of Captains Flahaven and Washington's vanguard troops were already wet after struggling to get ashore in the blackness. With the darkness and the storm's intensity concealing where the water ended and land began, the first soldiers to gain the east bank sloshed through shallow, cold water before gaining firm ground at Johnson's Ferry. Here, a solid sheet of ice lined the bank. These men, consequently, underwent "the greatest fatigue" in the "breaking [of] a passage" through the frozen mass clogging the river's east bank. However, the vanguard Virginians and New Jersey men, mostly Scotch-Irish soldiers of the Presbyterian faith like the majority of New Jersey Continentals, shortly trudged inland across higher ground than they had just left on Pennsylvania side, pushing deeper into western New Jersey to fulfill General Washington's orders. Here, the overall topography consisted of rolling hills and high plateaus: terrain that briefly reminded Captain Washington's Old Dominion men of their own homeland in northern and western Virginia.

After gaining the windswept east bank upon disembarking from Captain Blackler's Durham boat, Washington began to busily supervise the landing of additional troops, just as he had overseen his army's embarkation during the stealthy escape from Long Island at the East River ferry less than four months before. Playing another psychological high card, the commander-in-chief remained in the forefront at the busy Garret Johnson's landing site, well within sight of unloading soldiers to inspire resolve and instill a sense of calm. With his horse yet attended by a trusty soldier on the Pennsylvania side, Washington stood tall for all to see on the New Jersey shore.

Here, by the glare of flashing torchlight half-dimmed by the dropping sheets of the sleet and snow, Washington spent an extended period personally supervising the landing of hundreds of Continentals, who poured inland with each new boatload of cold-numbed soldiers. Later, once the operation was progressing smoothly and as additional groups of Continentals poured ashore, he finally sat down on an empty wooden beehive, which served as his ad hoc command post and offered no protection from the harsh elements. But Washington was shortly back on his feet. While his long, dark military cloak flapped in the wind and with his hair tied and pulled back in a stylish queue, Washington exhorted his newly disembarked troops to bear up to the severe hardship and then to get ready to fight like men, when the decisive moment came. With a benign expression despite the freezing cold that stung faces, Washington watched the hushed files of ill-clothed troops, who yet maintained a disciplined silence as ordered, steadily disembarking in the narrow river bottoms of level ground immediately situated below a slight, wooded bluff located just west of the small, wood-frame Garret Johnson Ferry House.

Encouraged by the sight of enhanced discipline in the ranks that brought a sense of relief, Washington had never seen so many of his soldiers so quiet as he had specifically ordered: a good sign for future success at Trenton. All the while he maintained a confident manner that was noticed by the common soldiers. Washington's dignified command presence, quiet authority, and assuring words continued to radiate a calm confidence, if not a slight hint of an air of invincibility, that emanated from his inspiring physical presence and moral authority. Proving to be an accomplished master at masking his mounting apprehensions with his timetable of reaching Trenton just before dawn shattered, Washington hid his increasing doubts to present a stoic appearance that preserved morale and fueled confidence among his men. All the while, the former planter from Mount Vernon felt the heavy burden of command responsibility for having undertaken the war's most daring gamble, and one that would determine if a revolutionary army and a young republic would live or die in the hours ahead.[52]

Meanwhile, just the mere sight of Washington posturing and talking with confidence to his troops along the east bank lifted the spirits of each new arriving group of soldiers. These Continentals appreciated the fact that their commander-in-chief, unlike Howe or thirty-seven-year-old Lord Charles Cornwallis, Howe's top lieutenant who had already retired to New York City, was now in the forefront, sharing the same dangers and enduring the same deprivations as the lowest private. In consequence, Washington was already seen as a father figure to the men in the ranks, long before he was viewed as the "father of his country" by his nation.

Ever-optimistic Colonel William "Billy" Tudor, a Boston-born intellectual and lawyer who possessed a prestigious Harvard College degree (Class of 1769) and was well-read on the day's leading military works, now served as legal councilor to the commander-in-chief and the army's Judge Advocate General. He looked unkindly upon the lower-class Irish, especially the immigrants, who served in the Continental Army's ranks. In an informative Christmas Eve letter penned to his future wife, Delia Jarvis, back in Boston, the twenty-six-year-old Tudor explained Washington's all-important moral and psychological impact on the men, who looked to him for not only for guidance, but also for deliverance: "I cannot desert a man [Washington] who has deserted everything to defend his country, and whose chief misfortune . . . is that a large part of [the infant nation lacks the necessary] spirit to defend itself."[53] Indeed, at the most critical moment in the war, Washington continued to demonstrate a most remarkable ability to inspire others by his mere presence and actions. To one and all, the commander-in-chief, in his desperate bid to secure America's salvation, revealed a rare leadership quality, because he now "attained his greatest nobility at times of crisis."[54]

While standing erect just below the small Johnson Ferry House which was distinguished by a gambrel roof, Washington supervised the landing of hundreds of additional troops with a steady, reassuring hand. Knox continued to efficiently manage the time-consuming task of a disciplined and carefully orchestrated embarkation from the river's west side. Now separated by the Delaware, a flotilla of Durham boats, and pitch blackness, Washington and Greene continued to perform as a highly effective leadership team at their respective ends of the crossing point during the most audacious river crossing of the war.

From the river's level flood plain on the blustery New Jersey shore, the wooded terrain rose sharply a short distance east of the ferry landing and up to the small, one-story Johnson Ferry House. Small and quaint, this Dutch-influenced frame farmhouse, built around 1740, overlooked the wide river and ferry landing. Serving as a tavern and inn, this white-washed, wooden house was where weary passengers, traveling along the dusty road to Philadelphia, had long stopped to eat and lodge for the night. Only a short distance away from the diminutive Johnson House and standing on the lower ground near the river, Washington shouted additional instructions in the night, while newly arriving bands of stiff, half-frozen soldiers climbed out of the big Durham boats with cramped legs and wet feet. Once on solid New Jersey ground, they began to feel more confident. One American never forgot the inspiring sight of Washington, who "stands on the bank of the river, wrapped in his cloak, superintending the landing of the troops."[55]

Like feisty Scotch-Irishman Sam McConkey on the west bank, so James Slack, also a patriotic Presbyterian of Scotch-Irish descent, which almost always equated to the most ardent of revolutionaries, now operated Johnson's Ferry. Located about ten miles upriver and north of Trenton, this ferry had been formerly known as Palmer's or Parmer's Ferry. Bringing some peace of mind in this regard, Washington could now safely rely upon McConkey and Slack, two trusty Scotch-Irishmen, for what was now yet vital for the success of this risky operation: absolute secrecy.

After all, a party of Continental scouts and a small Hessian patrol had skirmished at this exact location on Christmas Eve. Fulfilling his patriotic duty, Slack also personally assisted with the hectic crossing just below his small house, now covered in a blanket of newly fallen snow, situated on its elevated perch among the tall hardwood trees lining the slope. Named after Garret Johnson, the father of Robert and Rutt, who began ferry operations in 1761, this relatively little-known ferry was now leased from Rutt Johnson. However, the ferry had been operated by the enterprising team of James and Richard Slack since 1767.[56]

Meanwhile, additional cold-numbed soldiers poured ashore in increasing numbers to Washington's absolute delight. Most important, these Continentals, especially high-ranking officers, were no ordinary fighting men. Fortunately for Washington, he could count on a brilliant constellation of promising, mostly young, leaders. A good many of these officers were destined to emerge as major players and national leaders in America's story in the future: the first, Washington, and fifth, James Monroe, presidents of the United States, and the nation's future war and treasury secretaries, the gregarious Knox and handsome Alexander Hamilton, respectively, were always at the forefront.

In addition, future leaders of states, both from existing states (former colonies) and those yet to be formed west of the Appalachians, also now served in Washington's ranks, including Colonel Charles Scott, Kentucky's future governor who commanded the Fifth Virginia Continental Regiment, Stephen's Virginia brigade, which was the first infantry brigade to reach the frozen New Jersey soil and Captain William Hull, Nineteenth Connecticut Continental Regiment, Glover's brigade, who became the future governor of the Michigan Territory. All of these gifted leaders and men of distinction were now fully prepared to do or die at Trenton in a desperate bid to save the fast-fading life of their dying nation. These relatively faithful few, both officers and enlisted men, were among what little remained of this fledgling republic's most die-hard revolutionaries, after thousands of less resolved patriots had already deserted in droves during the disastrous New York Campaign and long, miserable retreat through New Jersey. Without any normal complaining or cursing of their commanders and politicians, these most resolute of rebels in arms against the king were now "patiently bearing the fatigues and hardships of a winter's campaign, rather than suffer their country to be exposed to the further ravages of a barbarous [and] vindictive foe."[57]

Meanwhile, the trusty vanguard of veteran Continentals from Virginia and New Jersey continued to push farther inland beyond the ferry to gain the higher ground that lay immediately beyond, or east of, the river bottom. Here, where the ground rose sharply—essentially a slight river bluff located just beyond the river's east bank—a short distance to the Johnson Ferry House and farther up the heavily timbered slope, Captain Flahaven's New Jersey boys and Captain Washington's Virginians continued to move inland with firm discipline. Seasoned fighting men, they eased across the snowy ground like ghosts in the night, fanning out during their advance to create a wide protective screen. After pushing uphill and east through the dark woodlands and once atop the level ground of a high plateau that overlooked the broad river behind them, these vanguard New Jersey and Virginia troops then quickly fanned out and took defensive positions on this high ground perch to protect the low-lying crossing point immediately to the west, just in case any nearby enemy mounted a counterattack.

Meanwhile, the seasoned New Jersey Continentals, along with Captain Washington's Virginia vanguard, strained eyes toward dark treelines before them to the east. Despite low visibility, they searched for glimpses of any Hessians, whose dark blue uniforms would blend in with the eerie blackness. The driving ice and snow eliminated any pale light of the cloud-screened moon, despite its near fullness, limiting visibility to almost zero. If a Hessian force was in the vicinity and drove the Americans from their yet precarious toehold on the Jersey shore, then Washington's vulnerable task force, of which only a fraction had reached the east side by this time, would never know what had hit them, wrecking the commander-in-chief's masterplan for reversing the revolution's tide with one bold stroke.

Meanwhile, across the river at McConkey's Ferry, even more Durham boats, slowly but surely, were rowed by Glover's men out into the river's maelstrom. Stacked up on the Pennsylvania frozen shore, additional Continental soldiers, now looking more like scarecrows in a Virginia Piedmont cornfield than regular fighting men, without proper winter uniformsor warm greatcoats, filed quietly into the slippery Durham boats, which dipped lower into the water with the added weight. Without fanfare or much noise, these overloaded boats were pushed offshore and then poled by Glover's Massachusetts boys, while apprehensive Continental soldiers prayed that they would survive the risky journey in the night and winter storm.

During the time-consuming passage over the turbulent river that seemed as much of a foe as any British or Hessian regiment, the Durham boats pitched and swayed in the swift current and blustery, northeastern winds. All the while, the Marbleheaders gamely struggled against the rising tide to keep their vessels on a straight course. Rowing relentlessly against the current's surging strength in the icy cold that felt like New England in February, the hands of Glover's hard-working men grew numb, after becoming wet by the river's waters and from the steady deluge from the skies.

Following behind Captain Flahaven's band of New Jersey Continentals and Captain Washington's Virginians, the next infantry unit to gain their footing on New Jersey soil were troops of General Stephen's brigade, the Fourth, Fifth, and Sixth Virginia Continental Regiments. Most important, Washington had personally selected these three crack Virginia regiments to serve as the vigilant vanguard brigade to lead the lengthy advance on Trenton from the north. These veteran Virginians of Stephen's vanguard brigade were ordered inland by Washington on the double. Their assignment was to secure the high ground, now held only by the thin screen of Flahaven's New Jersey men and Captain Washington's Virginia soldiers, amid the thick hardwood timber standing just beyond the yet-vulnerable landing site to ensure that the entire strike force could assemble on solid ground unimpeded. With clanging gear that rang hauntingly through the dark woodlands, Stephen's seasoned troops pushed uphill to make the landing site more secure. Once atop the plateau after traversing the slippery slope, the experienced Virginia general, whose stately limestone mansion, built in 1774, stood on a hill overlooking Tuscarora Creek in western Virginia (today's Martinsburg, West Virginia), then deployed his Old Dominion troops in a wide screen amid the timber in protective fashion.

Fortunately, no Hessian infantry pickets or British cavalrymen, of the Sixteenth Light Horse, from the Trenton garrison had been stationed anywhere near Johnson's Ferry. Ironically, these mounted Britons could have served as an ideal mobile task force if stationed on the east bank at Johnson's Ferry to give early warning to the Trenton garrison at the first sign of Washington's crossing.

Meanwhile, departing the high ground plateau in a hurry with the sudden arrival of Stephen's Virginians, Captain Flahaven's New Jersey Continentals then pushed farther inland on their prearranged assignment: to eventually gain the northern end of the River Road, which paralleled the north-south flowing Delaware and led to Trenton's southwest edge, far to the southeast at its intersection with the Bear Tavern Road. Knowing this rolling countryside of mixed forests and scattered farmlands quite well, these New Jersey Continentals were also on a key assignment to gain an advanced position about three miles northwest of Trenton to intercept any civilians or enemy scouts or patrols, which might sound a timely warning to the Trenton garrison. Likewise moving ahead at a fairly good pace despite the falling snow, Captain Washington's invigorated Virginians possessed a comparable mission north of Trenton roughly parallel, to the east, of Flahaven's key River Road assignment.

Upon reaching the low-lying eastern shore where the high waters lapped at the icy river bank, larger numbers of troops continued to pour out of their cramped quarters. As if thankful to escape their harrowing confines, they quickly emerged from the water-slick Durham boats that made ideal landing craft for infantrymen, almost as if these durable vessels had been specially designed for this express purpose. Much to their relief, ever-larger numbers of Washington's troops, stiff and sore, swarmed inland to gain solid ground. Incredibly, Washington's ad hoc flotilla of boats was unleashing hundreds of troops without losing a man. Safely reaching the New Jersey shore brought an instant sense of relief among these young men and boys, while heightening expectations for a successful enterprise on this freezing morning in a wilderness-like region that they had never seen before.

After gaining solid ground, the Continentals quickly assembled on the Jersey side, instantly falling into formation. They then shouldered muskets with a surprising measure of discipline, as if on a parade ground in Philadelphia, Williamsburg, or Boston on a calm summer day instead of now caught amid an escalating snowstorm on a hostile shore. Moving briskly from the low ground at Johnson's Ferry and uphill past the little ferry house was not enough exertion to warm these men, barely working out numbness and stiffness from joints and legs. All the while, the incessant showers of snow and ice continued to tumble down, spraying the column to impede the ascent up the slope. Attempting to stay warm and dry amid the bone-numbing cold and omnipresent wetness remained a chief concern for Washington's men. Almost like Canadian geese instinctively drying off for self-preservation, especially if a nearby predator suddenly approached, some Continental soldiers flapped arms against bodies. Meanwhile, other half-frozen men rubbed their hands together and stamped feet in place on the snowy ground to increase circulation after the freezing ride across the Delaware.

Hour after hour in the frigid blackness and despite worsening weather, Glover's mariners somehow managed to keep a steady flow of Durham boats relentlessly moving back and forth from bank to bank, with the smoothness of an automated conveyorbelt. Indeed, after Adam Stephen's vanguard brigade crossed over to the east side, the troops of Greene's Division, Hugh Mercer's, Lord Stirling's, and Matthias de Roche Fermoy's brigades, respectively, were ferried across the swollen river. Then, John Sullivan's Division, consisting of Colonel Paul Sargent's brigade, John Glover's New England brigade, and Arthur St. Clair's New Hampshire and Massachusetts brigade, respectively, passed over.

Washington's only New York infantrymen, the soaked soldiers of the First and Third New York Continental Regiments, of Sargent's brigade, probably had no idea that the Delaware's waters originated in their home state. For Moulder's hard-working Philadelphians, under the finely educated Lieutenant Cuthbert, and Glover's rawboned mariners, the laborious effort in getting so many boats repeatedly across the river and as quickly as possible in the stormy blackness was a seemingly endless struggle against the water, cold, and wind. Sweaty Marbleheaders were exhausted from the strenuous exertions and back-breaking labor that strained muscles and sapped physical endurance, but not one Massachusetts mariner stopped the endless rowing that had to be continued without a break in Washington's desperate race against time. To this day, no one knows exactly how many trips were made by the Durham boats across the Delaware on that awful night. But whatever the total, that number was far too many for Glover's overworked, worn men, who pushed themselves ever harder to the point of collapse to fulfill their vital mission upon which Washington and the army depended.

All the while, Washington's soldiers were lashed by an even heavier deluge of rain, wind, ice, and snow by 11:00 p.m., when the near full moon, fully obscured by banks of black clouds, was about two-thirds of the way to its high point in the winter sky and the storm's full wrath swept the Delaware valley with greater fury. A thin layer of ice formed on the edges of wooden oars, poles, and boats, and created a brittle crust on soldier's wool coats and cotton shirt sleeves during the repetitious journeys across the Delaware. Muscles hurt from the steady rowing and backs ached as if they had been plowing the rocky fields of New England all day, but the arm-weary Marblehead boys kept dutifully at their arduous task.

With a determination that made Glover most proud of his men, the New Englanders continued to labor hour after hour in the depths of the horrendous storm that made them feel so "crimmy" in their own peculiar dialect from a distinctive seafaring people and culture of the faraway rocky shores of picturesque Cornwall, where green rolling hills of green offered breathtaking vistas that overlooked the Atlantic. With the storm only intensifying and unleashing more misery upon Washington's men, the Marbleheaders' well-honed skills as seamen and fishermen in the north Atlantic's rough waters continued to expedite the relentless ferrying of troops across the Delaware. With his soaked Connecticut comrades, Lieutenant Elisha Bostwick recorded how hundreds of Continental soldiers, including men who were bundled up in all manner of clothing and looking like rag dolls, passed safely across the river, "but by the obstructions of ice in the river [we would] not get all across till quite late in the evening & all the time a constant fall of Snow and Some rain . . . ."[58]

In his journal, Sergeant Thomas McCarty, of Irish heritage, who fought for the honor of the Old Dominion and his Eighth Virginia Continental Regiment, described how this was "the worst day of sleet rain that could be."[59] The articulate, well-educated Major Wilkinson, who hailed from the high-yield tobacco country of southern Maryland, described how the "force of the current, the sharpness of the frost, the darkness of the night, the ice which made during the operation and the high wind, rendered the passage of the river extremely difficult."[60]

To ward off nature's bitterest wrath, unlike the rest of Washington's men who were not as fortunate, some of Glover's mariners wore seamen's hats of thick brown woolen yarn. On such a miserable night that tested a man's physical endurance and mental toughness to the upmost, this traditional seafaring headgear, along with loose-fitting seamen's trousers, was invaluable in allowing the Marbleheaders to more effectively ward off the elements than their non-seafaring comrades and perform more smoothly in their exertions. Like no other head apparel worn in Washington's Army, the distinctive headgear of Glover's men had been made waterproof with tar and other resistant substances to provide protection against harsh Grand Banks weather. Therefore, compared to Washington's other Continentals, the heads of Massachusetts fishermen and seafarers, who already wore waterproof leather buttons for the same reasons, were better protected from the snow, rain, and sleet.[61]

Hour after hour, the vast majority of Washington's men remained wet, soaked to the skin, and very cold, shaking and suffering in the intensifying stormy conditions. Insidiously, the biting cold steadily sapped the strength of bodies already worn down by the rigors of a grueling summer and autumn campaign, the long New Jersey retreat, low nutrition diets, and the ravages of disease. Men who should have been hospitalized instead shouldered muskets and gamely crossed over the Delaware. The popular, "fife-major" of the Fifteenth Massachusetts Continental Regiment, St. Clair's brigade, now designated as a reserve unit of Sullivan's Division, and one of the last infantry units to cross the Delaware, teenage Private Johnny Greenwood described how: "Over the river we then went in a flat-bottomed scow, and . . . I was with the first that crossed" the river at the head of his veteran regiment.[62]

Continuing to work together throughout this most miserable of nights as a highly effective team, Colonels Glover and Knox were in the process of performing a miracle that would have astounded the military experts, especially the recently captured General Charles Lee, the self-proclaimed military genius. An incredulous Lee, ironically, had recently criticized Washington's seemingly inexplicable, mysterious obsession in having gathered all the vessels, including the Durham boats, along a seventy-mile stretch of the Delaware, asking "for heaven's sake what use can they be of?"[63]

Like the aristocratic Howe and seemingly everyone in the British Army, especially the Hessians at Trenton, Cornwallis could not have possibly imagined that Washington and his troops might dare stir from their dreary, eastern Pennsylvania encampments this winter and attempt to do the unthinkable on Christmas Day, especially during an intense winter storm, when Lee's probing question was about to be convincingly answered by the resourceful and suddenly unpredictable Washington once and for all. Most importantly, what the military experts, leaders, and strategists on both sides of the Atlantic failed to realize that Washington, thanks to Glover's and his versatile Bay State regiment's invaluable contributions, was now about to engage in his first battle in which he had finally controlled the main waterway and gained the initiative.

The Crossing's Greatest Challenge, Artillery

Midnight had already come and gone, and much faster than Washington had hoped. Although the perilous crossing was now hours behind schedule (Washington had planned to have all his forces in New Jersey by midnight) with far more difficulties having been encountered than anyone had originally imagined, nevertheless, Washington now possessed reason to feel a bit more optimistic for the first time. After all, no Hessians or British soldiers had been encountered or seen at either the crossing point or beyond, ensuring that Washington's stealthy movements north of Trenton yet went undetected.

Meanwhile, Captain Flahaven's New Jersey vanguard and Captain Washington's Virginia vanguard continued to move unimpeded farther inland, trudging over the snowy landscape. They advanced straight east through the blackened forests from Johnson's Ferry on the initial mission of securing the strategic crossroads on the Bear Tavern Road and the Scotch Road several miles inland.

As if their previous task in transporting around 2,400 troops across the menacing river was only a warm-up exercise, Glover and Knox yet faced their greatest challenge during the entire crossing: the army's outsized, but vital artillery arm now had to be ferried to the Jersey shore. Ironically, this over-achieving orphaned son of a hard-driving ship captain named Knox now needed to utilize some of his Bostonian father's old seafaring skills to transport all of Washington's artillery safely across the volatile Delaware. The near impossibility of this supreme challenge of simultaneously overcoming high water, strong northeast winds, and an ever-increasing number of ice floes in the pitch-blackness amid a raging storm had already caused considerable havoc to Washington's delicate, overlycomplex battleplan.

South of McConkey's Ferry, Cadwalader's belated effort of attempting to cross at Dunk's Ferry, after having been earlier thwarted by a heavy concentration of ice at Neshaminy Ferry just to the north, was way behind schedule. With the storm intensifying and the unruly river now dominated by a turbulence seldom seen, the popular Philadelphian, in charge of the southernmost crossing point, simply could not get the cumbersome guns and frightened artillery horses, and ammunition supplies of his militia brigade and a mostly New England Continental brigade across the river at Dunk's Ferry, opposite Burlington. In addition, Ewing and his Pennsylvania militia, north of Cadwalader at the middle crossing point below McConkey's Ferry, were experiencing even more trouble in attempting to cross at the South Trenton Ferry.

All of Washington's artillery and horses, both cavalry and artillery animals, around 150 horses, which were in anything but good shape after the lengthy withdrawal across New Jersey and because of the lack of forage in eastern Pennsylvania this winter, now required Knox's maximum effort and skill in successfully transporting his heaviest loads across the river. Washington's main column's eighteen cannon, artillery ammunition, and horses amounted to around a staggering four hundred tons in weight. And all of this had to be brought across the Delaware as quickly as possible: the most formidable challenge ever faced by Knox, who had already confronted a good many tough assignments. Quite simply, Washington's greatest firepower, tactical asset, and advantage in weaponry had to be safety transported across the river if victory was to be secured at Trenton on December 26.

Indeed, everything now depended upon getting Washington's sole remaining eighteen cannon, which were now even more precious after the loss of almost all of the Continental Army's artillery during the past campaign, across the Delaware. Most of all, Knox fully realized the stern challenge of overwhelming Washington's principal objective, knowing that Trenton was "the most considerable" of Howe's winter cantonments. However, the harsh weather only continued to worsen, pushing Washington's fragile timetable of attacking Trenton just before dawn even further behind schedule in the stormy early morning hours.

Thoroughly exhausted after their maximum effort, the Marbleheaders now faced even more hard work ahead under worsening conditions. No doubt, Glover's worn seamen cursed their hard luck and fate, as when caught in an angry tempest when far out in the Atlantic. Perhaps in weak moments under such severe adversity, some of Glover's young fishermen and sailors now wished to have been back in a warm, cozy Marblehead tavern, where the rum flowed freely into the morning's wee hours on such stormy winter nights, when everyone with an ounce of sense remained inside near warm fireplaces.

Fortunately, Washington now possessed a number of sturdy ferry boats and at least one "flat-bottomed scow" for transporting a massed array of cannon, artillery horses, and ammunition carts across a treacherous river. As Washington fully realized, Knox's seven three-pounders, three four-pounders, six six-pounders, and two five and a half-inch howitzers were the key to any chance of securing victory over a full Hessian brigade at Trenton. To face this disproportionate amount of American firepower that included some cannon that had been transported by oxen-drawn sleds over the New England's snow-covered hills by the ever-resourceful Knox from Fort Ticonderoga to Cambridge last year, all that Colonel Rall, even if he managed to get his cannon into position in time to confront Washington's planned surprise attack just before dawn, possessed were six little three-pounders: Washington's much coveted mismatch. Luckily for Washington, the Hessians' heavy artillery, big eighteen-pounders from New York City, yet lingered rearward and far from Trenton, thanks to Howe's rapid pursuit of Washington through New Jersey.

Most importantly, Washington was determined to possess not only more cannon but also larger caliber guns than his Hessian opponents at the most decisive moment. For the final showdown at Trenton, the "long-arm" savvy of a much-criticized former Virginia militia colonel and enthusiastic fox hunter of Virginia's fields and meadows was destined to prevail and not that of the respected professional, highly educated German leaders, who had more thoroughly learned the most important Frederickan "long-arm" lessons from Frederick the Great, who was the Prussian master of massed firepower and the employment of larger caliber cannon, especially the howitzer and twelve-pounder. Even more, Washington now utilized some of the most cherished axioms later adopted so effectively by Napoleon, especially the golden rule that any infantry deficiencies, or limitations—either in quality, spirit, or quantity—could be best compensated for by an over-abundance of artillery. However, and fortunately for the upcoming battle's outcome along the Delaware, Washington violated Napoleon's axiom that too much artillery, especially large six-pounders, was theoretically detrimental for an infantry force in conducting a stealthy, long-distance raid, not to mention a river crossing amid a snowstorm, because too much speed, mobility, and flexibility would be sacrificed in consequence. Quite simply, the unorthodox Washington, acting on his natural instincts and well-honed experience from a meticulous management of Mount Vernon's lands with a military-like precision, and a hefty dose of good American common sense instead of dry, scholarly military textbooks, was about to accomplish what even Napoleon would dare not attempt to do.

Nearly an impossibility, what Colonel Glover and his exhausted seamen now had to accomplish against the odds was to transport all of Washington's remaining artillery of Knox's Regiment of Continental Artillery across the Delaware as quickly as possible. Fortunately, after the Continental Army had lost nearly 150 cannons during the disastrous New York Campaign, primarily at Forts Washington and Lee, the army's remaining artillery consisted of some of the best guns: Captain Alexander Hamilton's two six-pounders of the New York State Company Continental Artillery; two six-pounders and two five and a half-inch howitzers of Captain Thomas Forrest's Second Company, Pennsylvania State Artillery, which was Knox's largest battery in number of guns; Captain Winthrop Sargent's two six-pounders of the Massachusetts Company of Continental Artillery; Captain Sebastian Baumann's three three-pounders of the New York Company of Continental Artillery; Captain Daniel Neil's two three-pounders of the Eastern Company, New Jersey State Artillery; Captain Samuel Hugg's two three-pounders of the Western Company, New Jersey State Artillery; and Captain Joseph Moulder's three long French four-pounders of the Second Company of Artillery, Philadelphia Associators, which possessed the largest number of cannoneers at eighty-five.[64]

Because Washington's artillery was so heavy, ungainly, and took up so much room, especially the teams of nervous horses assigned to each gun, Knox now benefitted from the relative luxury of Washington having utilized considerable foresight by collecting a flotilla of flat-bottomed ferry boats—much larger than the Durham boats and, more importantly, with level, relatively wide wooden surfaces—to transport the bulky guns and teams of horses, in full harness, across the river. Along with at least one ferry boat from McConkey's Ferry, at least three other ferry boats from Johnson's Ferry and Coryell's Ferry, to the north, where Cornwallis had been frustrated earlier in December (when first reaching Trenton after Washington had just narrowly slipped across the Delaware to escape to the eastern Pennsylvania shore) in his attempt to find boats because of Washington's prior orders to collect all boats, were now utilized to maximum benefit. Fortunately, Glover's mariners already possessed solid experience with handling ferry boats, having employed these ungainly crafts in saving so many of Washington's troops and artillery during the narrow escape across the East River from Long Island to safety on Manhattan Island.

Meanwhile, as part of his three-pronged crossing of the Delaware at three different points, Washington's other two columns, under the Scotch-Irish Pennsylvania commanders Ewing and Cadwalader, continued to encounter more trouble in attempting to cross at two ferries, South Trenton and Dunk's, respectively, from north to south. Ewing and Cadwalader also employed ferry boats, but even the use of these crafts was not sufficient in accomplishing their respective tasks, which were simply overwhelming. Because Cadwalader could not transport his artillery and frightened horses across at Dunk's Ferry, he cancelled the risky operation because of the intensifying storm. Assuming that Washington had also cancelled operations under such appalling conditions, Cadwalader ordered around six hundred of his light troops, who had already reached the opposite shore, back to the safety of the Pennsylvania shore, just after midnight. Meanwhile Ewing, whose primary mission was to secure the Assunpink bridge in southern Trenton to cut off the Rall brigade's escape south by the time that Washington attack from the north and then to link with Washington's main force, likewise aborted his own efforts without a single soldier ever reaching the New Jersey shore.

Because the Americans had earlier taken possession of a number of Delaware River ferries along as much as a seventy-five mile stretch of the river that had been thoroughly scoured for boats on Washington's orders, they had already secured a sufficient number of ferry boats for the transport of all of Knox's artillery across the river. In addition, at least one, flat-bottomed scow, but very likely additional such vessels that hauled heavy freight, was also utilized for carrying horses, cannon, and artillery powder carts over the Delaware. Before the later-day standard use of artillery caissons and limber chests, Knox possessed at least eighteen powder carts, one for each gun. Whereas the individual infantryman carried sixty musket cartridges, tons of artillery ammunition had to be transported across the Delaware. Some artillery ammunition supplies was stored in the twin side boxes located in a bracket wooden carriage located on each side and just below the cannon's barrel.

With more than a sufficient number of wide, flat-bottomed ferry boats at Glover's disposal from McConkey's and Johnson's Ferries as well as those ferries located farther north up the Delaware, all eighteen of Knox's cannon, teams, and ammunition carts now could be easily accommodated. Thoroughly soaked, ill-clad artillerymen pushed, grunted, and cursed in the arduous labor of pushing artillery pieces aboard the ferry boats safe and sound, while the icy rain and snow poured down to make hard work even more miserable. The iron and bronze guns were heavy and awkward, requiring the most strenuous efforts just in pushing cannon from the shore and onto the ferry boats. Footing for the poorly-shod loaders was slippery along the muddy bank and then the wooden floor of the ferry boats in the wet blackness. No doubt some of Knox's artillerymen of his Continental regiment (wearing distinctive artillery buttons— with an exquisite cannon and flag design—made by a Concord, Massachusetts, manufacturer, as a result of Knox's early 1776 purchase order), slipped or fell while pushing the heavy cannon to the ferry landings, and then manhandling the guns onto the water- and ice-slick ferry boats.

If Washington had not possessed the luxury of so many sturdy ferry boats at this time, then the Durham boats would have been only able to take one gun across at a time, or one per boat, at most, because of the vessel's relatively narrow, steep, and canoe-shaped hulls. Therefore, eighteen separate trips would have been required for transporting each gun—a single six-pounder with ammunition stored in wooden boxes mounted on the gun carriage weighed more than a ton—across in Durham boats, promising to waste more precious time. Clearly, the Durham boats were entirely unsuitable for carrying cannon and ammunition carts, because of their overall narrowness, deep hulls, and cross support eight-foot wooden beams stretching from side to side across the hull's rim.

In addition, eighteen teams of artillery horses for each gun—nearly seventy-two horses (four per artillery piece) in total—had to be transported across the river, which would have been impossible, if only Durham boats were available. Thanks to Washington's prior farsighted decisions, the ferry boats, at forty-feet long and about twelve feet wide, were now ideal for transporting so many iron and bronze cannon, horses, and ammunition carts across the river. A French officer noted how the ferries of America's eastern waters were nothing more than "a flat boat with oars." After all, these much-used ferries usually transported local farmer's large Conestoga wagons, with heavy loads, and their four-horse teams in harness and small herds of cattle or sheep to market. As important, the ferry boat's width, which bestowed greater stability in rough waters along with the flat bottom, could not only easily accommodate Knox's artillery pieces, but also a good many skittish horses, especially if they balked or became frightened on choppy waters filled with chunks of ice.

Always eager to accept a new challenge–seemingly the more arduous the better—young Colonel Knox, at only age twenty-six, was the perfect choice for the task of orchestrating the hazardous crossing of so much artillery. Of large stature and weighing around 280 pounds, Knox possessed not only tireless energy but also a powerful will to succeed, regardless of the obstacles. Knox's sense of optimism proved an invaluable asset in this crisis situation. And despite his hulking size, he was "very active, and of a gay and amiable character." On this darkest and most miserable of all nights, teenage Major Wilkinson never forgot the unmistakable sound of Knox's "stentorian lungs" in directing the complex movements and intricacies of the tricky river crossing.

Knox's "great booming voice" continued to serve as a "public address system" that echoed across the river, while carefully orchestrating the crossing in the hope of getting all of the artillery across as quickly as possible. The bulky, intellectual Bostonian looked as affectionately upon his remaining eighteen cannon as his artillerymen's welfare, fretting over their safety and well-being. Knox had already commanded Washington's artillery for a year and a half, and he knew more about artillery than any officer in the army. If anyone could get all of Washington's artillery safety across the Delaware, and especially when assisted by Glover and his hardworking mariners, it was Knox, who stood more than six feet in height to tower over most of his smaller, wiry cannoneers, especially the many beardless teenagers in the ranks.

Growing doubts had earlier risen about the wisdom of transporting so many artillery pieces across the river with the storm's increased fury, until Knox had personally assured the anxious commander-in-chief that the task could be accomplished against the odds. Washington needed to hear no more. With time of the essence, Knox's good-natured, gregarious disposition was transformed by the stormy crossing into a strict efficiency and business-like focus of getting the job done as soon as possible.

In part because of his youth and lack of a military education, Knox had much to prove at this time, fueling his determination to succeed in his toughest mission. He had proposed the formation of an entire "Corps of Continental Army" instead of only a single artillery regiment, with himself at the helm, to Washington on December 18. Knowing well the supreme importance of a more powerful artillery corps, Washington had readily agreed with Knox's wise concept.

Washington had already requested a timely enlargement of Knox's artillery regiment on November 14, and Knox's proposal significantly bolstered his case. When Congress granted Washington almost complete power as a military commander without civilian interference on November 12 thanks to sagging American fortunes, Washington had smartly ordered the recruitment of "three Battalions of Artillery," taking full advantage of this unprecedented opportunity to strengthen his army.

For the arduous task of transporting all of Washington's artillery and its horses and ammunition carts across the river, the dynamic team of Knox, the large-sized "beachmaster," and small-sized Glover, the gifted son but humble descendant of carpenters, exceeded even Washington's lofty expectations. Most of all, Washington was determined that his main strike force possessed a high ratio of guns per the total number of infantry that was unprecedented. Indeed, the usual ratio was only two or three cannon per every thousand soldiers. To support his around 2,400 infantrymen, Washington's eighteen guns equated to more than three times the normal ratio. This ratio was closer than the equation utilized with remarkable success by Frederick the Great. The legendary Prussian leader's faith in the accompaniment of six cannon per every one thousand Prussians during the Seven Years' War had paid handsome dividends on one battlefield after another: an exceptionally high ratio unmatched even by the greatest of all artillery masters, Napoleon. By comparison, Napoleon attempted, and often failed, to achieve a much-coveted artillery ratio of five guns for every thousand soldiers. As he envisioned, consequently, Washington now planned to out-gun the Trenton garrison by three-to-one.[65] Significantly, Washington was faithfully adhering to one principal secret of Napoleon's amazing successes on hard-fought battlefields across Europe: a commander "could never have too many guns" on the field of strife.[66]

With tactical clarity and considerable insight, Washington already envisioned how the outcome of the upcoming showdown at Trenton could be determined mostly by the proper employment of artillery, especially if carefully placed on high ground. While the blustery winter wind whistled down the Delaware and through the thin apparel of Washington's men, Knox's guns, ammunition, and horses continued to be loaded as fast as possible yet gingerly on at least four sturdy ferry boats. Impeding the grueling work of loading cumbersome artillery pieces, the snow and temperatures, dipping below thirty degrees in the early morning hours, continued to plummet upon Washington's men. Compared to the task of transporting hundreds of infantrymen across the river in the Durham boats, the formidable job of getting all of Washington's artillery—or nearly four hundred tons in total weight—across the watery expanse was far more challenging. Almost as if yet reposing at his comfortable Massachusetts home beside his independent-minded wife Lucy, who believed in sharing a sense of equality with her husband, the composed Knox was now "no more perturbed in a nocturnal blizzard on the Delaware River than he would have been in a warm tavern after closing his bookshop" in fashionable Boston.[67]

One at a time, each artillery piece was rolled carefully onto the approximately twelve-foot wide, wooden decks of the ferry boats with vigorous effort. The cannon were then made as securely as possible in place by the gunners. Evidently, the artillery pieces were lashed to wooden railings on the ferry boat's raised sides to keep Washington's most precious "long-arm" cargoes from rolling during the harrowing passage over the river. Very likely, heavy wooden blocks were also placed at the base of artillery wheels to prevent excessive movement once underway.

After the cannon were finally hauled aboard, nervous artillery horses were then led onto ferry boats in the eerie blackness. Washington's artillerymen, meanwhile, did all that they could to keep artillery horses calm in the tension-filled darkness, so that they would not rearup, buck, or cause a panic among other animals to shift weight during the crossing. Once the guns and horses were secured and the ferry boat finally lurched out into dark waters, experienced ferrymen and boatmen, like James Slack and other capable watermen, and Knox's veteran gunners worked closely together in pulling the lengthy rope, or cable, that extended to the opposite bank that must have seemed like miles away. As part of an extensive pulley system and likewise propelled by men working oars, the large ferry boats were muscled against the rushing currents and through the steady flow of ice chunks, despite those that crashed into the thin, wooden sides of the lumbering, slow-moving ferry boats with loud thuds.

Then, after what seemed like an eternity, the first ferry boats disgorged their invaluable "long-arm" contents on the New Jersey side. Overall, the unloading process was easier than imagined because of the openings on either end of the ferry boat consisted of large ramps that had been made for securely landing of wagons, cattle, and teams of horses. In addition, the landing site at Johnson's Ferry was excellent for wheeling cumbersome artillery pieces ashore because the shelf of bottom ground, part of the diminutive flood plain, was level and situated just west of where the ground began to rise up sharply to the snow-covered Johnson Ferry House. With a distinctive architectural design—even for western New Jersey—of having two fireplaces located in the house's middle as opposed to the ends as usual, the bright lights inside illuminated the Johnson Ferry House. Therefore, this small house now stood like a shiny beacon on higher ground for the busy boatmen yet struggling across the river and the lengthy formation of Continentals toiling uphill at a snail's pace along the slippery slope and through the falling snow.

However, this laborious process of loading and unloading artillery, neighing horses, and heavy ammunition carts and the methodical passage back and forth across the river took longer than anyone expected. And, of course, the ferry boats, around forty feet in length, presented larger targets than the Durham boats to the ice floes unhinged upriver by the recent thaw. Suddenly out of the blackness, large chucks of ice struck the wide sides of the ferry boats, pushing them a bit downriver with the current, stretching the rope cable linking them from shore to shore. Besides experienced ferryman Slack, other civilian volunteers from Hopewell, New Jersey, also provided timely assistance during Washington's tortuous crossing. Meanwhile, this hellish night became even colder with the northeaster growing more severe during the bleak, early morning hours. Such deplorable climactic conditions now made the unenviable job of transporting so much artillery across the river seemingly an even more "impossible" task, in Knox's estimation, while Washington's delicate timetable—he had planned for all of *both* his infantry and cannon to cross by midnight—continued to fall apart in the mud and snow.

All the while, Knox's cannon continued to be unloaded one by one, thanks to at least four ferry boats in full operation. At long last, the final field piece was rolled by exhausted artillerymen onto New Jersey soil to complete a task that could only be described as nightmarish. Almost certainly, the wet, mud-splattered men who had struggled mightily with these heavy guns for what seemed like infinity breathed a sign of relief, while resting to regain their strength. For most of the night, Glover's mariners, assisted by Captain Moulder's Philadelphia boys who now served under one of the battery's best lieutenants, Lieutenant Cuthbert, had poled, rowed, guided, and steered the flotilla of Durham boats and then ferried them successfully through the gales, sleet, and snow. In total, they ferried twenty-nine infantry regiments and battalions; one small light cavalry company from Philadelphia; and more than two hundred artillery and cavalry horses (of the officer corps, including Washington's staff, and the Philadelphia company) and seven complete artillery units, representing four states, across the most temperamental river that any of these men had ever seen.

Incredibly, Glover's Marbleheaders performed their crucial mission of transporting around 2,400 soldiers, about thirty-five to forty men (therefore perhaps as many as nearly seventy trips across the river by the Durham boats based on an average of thirty-five men per boat) at a time in each Durham boat, across an eight hundred-foot stretch of water so efficiently that not a soldier or horse was lost. Most importantly, no artillery pieces were lost, even at the snowstorm's height, to the utter amazement of one and all. Thanks to the broad, lengthy ferry boats and Knox and Glover's tireless efforts to inspire their men to do the impossible in the storm's depths, Washington's entire artillery arm was now in a position to advance on Trenton.

All in all, Washington's audacious nighttime crossing had taken eight hours in what was a freezing nightmare that was almost surreal to the men in the ranks. However, against all odds, this seemingly impossible mission was finally accomplished, but three hours late. Clearly, Washington's timetable had been as unrealistic as it was overly optimistic. In the end, even Knox was surprised (and proud of course) at his amazing crossing success after eight hours of the most intensive, arduous effort yet put forth by any American soldiers in this war. As Knox penned in his letter: "About two o'clock the troops were all on the Jersey side [and] we then were about nine miles from the object."[68]

Born in County Derry, amid the rolling hills of northern Ireland, Colonel John Haslet and his crack First Delaware Continental Regiment, now reduced to only 108 men, was assigned as the rear-guard at McConkey's Ferry, because of their discipline, toughness, and reliability. The Delaware regiment was the last infantry unit to cross the Delaware, after the final artillery piece reached the New Jersey side. As Haslet penned in a letter to his friend Caesar Rodney: "On Christmas, at 3 o'clock we recrossed the river" of no return, at least until a victory was won by Washington's ragged revolutionaries at Trenton.[69] Summarizing the most risky of operations that he had so skillfully managed with typical personal finesse and traditional New England efficiency, Colonel Knox concluded with justifiable satisfaction in a letter to wife Lucy how: "Accordingly a part of the army, consisting of about 2,500 or 3,000 [2,400] passed the river on Christmas night, with almost infinite difficulty, with eighteen pieces of artillery [and] The floating ice in the river made the labor almost incredible. However, perseverance accomplished what at first seemed impossible."[70]

Never one to exaggerate, especially when it came to his own personal accomplishments, Knox's unprecedented use of the word "incredible" was not hyperbole because not a single artillery piece or cannoneer found a watery grave in the swirling Delaware. Despite the harsh arctic gales, ice floes, high waters, pitch blackness, and the heaviest punishment from a mixture of snow, hail, and sleet, and just an ever-optimistic Glover had first promised Washington with a self-assured confidence not questioned by anyone in this army, the most audacious river crossing of the war succeeded in the end.

Without all that Knox and Glover had accomplished in a seemingly impossible situation, the entire "expedition would no doubt have failed," when America could no longer afford such a sharp setback. Glover's experienced mariners had even surpassed their remarkable performance in evacuating Washington's stranded forces off Long Island and away from Howe's greedy clutches. At that time, the "war might have ended months ago on Long Island if Glover's regiment had not saved the beat army and its equipment" near the end of August 1776. And now Glover had succeeded in keeping the very heart and pulse of America's primary resistance effort alive by what he and his mariners had achieved by bestowing upon Washington the opportunity to fulfill his tactical ambitious and masterful battle plan. In the end, Colonel Glover made good his almost cocky, but solemn, promise to Washington: that he and his Marblehead mariners could do the impossible and succeed in transporting the entire army, including artillery, across the Delaware without incident or loss. "You need not be troubled [as] my boys can manage it."[71]

The full extent of the difficulties in crossing the Delaware at the storm's peak was best seen in the dismal fate of Cadwalader and Ewing's columns that met with frustration to the south. The thwarted commanders of both assault columns simply concluded that it was "impossible" to cross the Delaware and fulfill their key missions as assigned by Washington. Washington's overly ambitious undertaking of a simultaneous three-pronged crossing along such a lengthy stretch of the Delaware was a flat failure, except in regard to the main assault column.

Ironically, however, Washington's primary assault column had been wisely disproportionately bolstered by artillery, which in part compensated for such a dire eventuality that would seem to have sabotaged all chances for success: clearly, a result of Washington's wisdom rather than a mere stroke of good fortune. In the end, Cadwalader's diversionary effort—which targeted Burlington—with his Pennsylvania militia and New England Continentals and militia to Trenton's south at Dunk's Ferry was aborted, while Ewing's troops (who were to have linked with Washington at Trenton) never crossed at South Trenton Ferry just below Trenton, Assunpink Creek, and Trenton Falls (the fall line located immediately north of Trenton), because of "the Quantity of Ice ["tidal ice jams"] was so great" on the Delaware. The overall situation became so precarious that an overwhelmed Ewing failed to even attempt a crossing because of the concentration of ice flows, backed up by Trenton Falls, that made the river's sharp elbow turn impassible.

Even though Cadwalader crossed at Dunk's Ferry after aborting his crossing at Bristol just to the north as originally planned, with his mostly Philadelphia Associators, or militia, and more than five hundred New Englanders, he simply concluded around 4:00 a.m. that his artillery pieces could not be taken across because of the storm's severity, ice floes, and the "heavy ice pack" that covered the river's east bank. Mistakenly assuming that Washington's main column had likewise been similarly frustrated in crossing the Delaware, therefore, Cadwalader returned to the Pennsylvania shore. Displaying little of Washington's iron determination, Cadwalader gave up the attempt because he "imagine[d] the badness of the night must have prevented you from passing over as you intended." Fortunately, for America's fortunes, Washington, Knox, and Glover had been more persistent and resolute in completing the first phase of their crucial mission upon which America's hopes now hinged. Determined not to be thwarted from crossing the Delaware by anything unleashed by man or Mother Nature, this dynamic trio of America's finest military leaders succeeded in doing the impossible on the night of December 25–26.[72]

Most importantly, the systematic falling apart of Washington's three-pronged assault plan—already around three hours behind schedule by

3:00 a.m.—only indicated the wisdom of Washington's farsighted decision that all of Knox's artillery should accompany the main column, which now packed the disproportionate might of "long-arm" firepower. Clearly, in the end, Washington's faith in what the experience, skill, and esprit de corps of Glover's mariner command could accomplish on the Delaware's waters was well-rewarded.[73] With his timetable in shambles, a frustrated, if not angry, Washington lamented how the vast "quantity of Ice, made that Night, impeded the passage of Boats so much, that it was three Oclock [a.m.] before the Artillery could all be got over" the Delaware.[74] This significant setback "made me despair of surprizing [sic] the Town, as I well knew we could not reach it before the day fairly broke . . . ."[75]

But there was a silver lining. Fortunately, Washington's wise decision to bring all of his artillery—seven three-pounders, three four-pounders, six six-pounders, and two five and a half-inch howitzers—with him was perhaps his most important decision of the campaign. This disproportionate, massive amount of artillery firepower—far exceeding the normal ratio of cannon per the number of troops—was exactly what was needed to stack the odds in Washington's favor in the upcoming showdown at Trenton, especially now that two of three columns had failed to cross the Delaware. Fully convinced that his eighteen guns would decide the day at Trenton on December 26, Washington's wisdom and foresight now dramatically maximized his chances for success.

Clearly, thanks to the crisis situation, the forty-five-year-old Washington had now evolved into a first class tactical visionary, who planned to utilize his artillery arm for maximum effect in an offensive role more thoroughly than ever before. Indeed, Washington planned to not only surprise but also to overwhelm the Hessian brigade with massive artillery firepower as early as possible. Such a well-calculated tactical decision, as much as any other made by the resolute Virginian in his finest hour, demonstrated the depth of Washington's tactical reasoning and wisdom that had risen to the fore. In part because he felt that he had nothing to lose with America's life on the brink of an early death, Washington was now on a winning streak in regard to having already made a host of smart, well-conceived command and tactical decisions long before meeting his Trenton opponent in the dramatic showdown to decide America's fate.

Meanwhile, Washington's infantrymen continued to move inland. After each Durham boatload of troops reached the frozen New Jersey side and the Continentals jumped overboard to wade through freezing water up to their knees in some cases, Washington's soldiers had then assembled on the river bottom's level ground at the foot of the slight, but sharp, river bluff, covered with thick stands of hardwood timber. Then, the cold-numbed Continentals, thankful for a safe passage over the angriest river that they had ever crossed, moved in a silent column up the heavily timbered slope, easing along the snow-covered road that ran beside the Johnson Ferry House. From the elevated perch of the Johnson Ferry House, the forested terrain rose around three hundred yards until a fairly level plateau of high ground above the river was reached by Washington's soldiers of liberty.

Here, on the windswept plateau, in perhaps an open apple or peach orchard which abounded on this splendid 490-acre New Jersey farm, Washington's seven Continental brigades assembled amid the falling snow and icy winds that swept through their ranks with a vengeance. Washington's soldiers, wet and weary, formed up in line, coughing, sneezing, and shivering in the biting cold. But the Continentals yet remained quiet as sternly ordered by Washington, maintaining discipline. For once, none of the usual talking or complaining was heard among the men in the inky blackness.

Half-frozen Continentals stomped up and down to keep circulation flowing, trying hard to warm. Seeing his ill-clothed troops suffering so severely, Washington then once again gambled. Many soldiers had gotten their feet wet from either standing in the Durham boat's bottom or by jumping out of the boat and into shallow water upon nearing the Jersey shore, or both. And a good many of Washington's men were already in bad shape, having been ill on the Pennsylvania side in recent weeks. In fact, many Continentals should have been in an infirmary instead of active campaigning, especially on a freezing winter night amid a snowstorm. Therefore, Washington ordered bonfires built to warm up his suffering men, who were shivering in the heartless winds and soaked from their knees down in some cases. All the while and without mercy, the icy wind "cuts like a knife," wrote one half-frozen soldier.

Washington's decision to allow his troops, thanks to their trusty pieces of flint and steel from knapsacks and wet pockets, to build fires was yet a risky one, because Hessian scouts or patrols might be roaming in the vicinity. But he felt it was absolutely necessary to get his troops in better condition for any chance of successfully meeting the many stiff challenges that lay ahead. Washington gambled that the little fires on the high ground would not be seen by any advanced Hessian scouts or British cavalry, because of the blinding tempest. Here, atop the little plateau that loomed above the Delaware, Washington's weary infantrymen gained some much-needed rest and warmth, before the inevitable order to move out into the stormy depths of the unmapped New Jersey countryside.

Washington possessed another good and as significant reason to call a halt out of absolute necessity. In fact, the hard work of Washington's 416 artillerymen had only begun during this most daring of offensive thrusts, with no rest for the weary. Knox's veteran cannoneers had to get all eighteen cannon up the slippery, snow-covered slope. Now situated in the level river bottoms just below the Johnson Ferry House, the bundled-up artillerymen of Knox's guns tightened wet leather and rope harnesses to skittish artillery horses in preparation for pulling the guns uphill.

Working efficiently, the gunners then hooked up gun carriages to teams of horses, before moving up the snowy bluff to the top of the windswept plateau. Artillery horses struggled to pull the guns, now seemingly weighing more than ever before, up the slope along the snow-covered artery that more resembled a mere trail hewn through tall, virgin oaks by pioneers long ago than a well-traveled road. Artillery horses strained in hauling their heavy loads past the small Johnson ferry house, draped in a fresh shroud of white. Finally, Washington's artillery pieces gained the high ground after another arduous struggle of exhausted gunners against a seeming conspiracy of geography, stubborn animals, and the harsh elements: no small accomplishment along slippery and unfamiliar ascending terrain under a ceaseless deluge from the skies. Here, atop the commanding plateau and after so much effort that had begun more than nine hours before on the Delaware's west bank, Knox's eighteen guns were now in an advanced position in preparation for Washington's final order to begin their descent deeper into western New Jersey and the dark unknown of an almost trackless wilderness region lying north of Trenton.[76]

All eighteen field pieces, with iron and bronze barrels and wooden wheels partially encrusted in ice from the incessant sleet falling, of Knox's Regiment of Artillery were placed in a relatively neat line for the lengthy descent upon Trenton nearly ten miles to the south. Indicating the supreme importance of artillery's role in his overall tactical plan to overwhelm the entire Rall brigade of three veteran regiments with massed long-arm firepower, Washington was very careful and circumspect about the specific placement of his artillery in column. Washington's decisions were well-thought-out, guaranteeing that Knox's guns would be "ready to go into action at a moment's notice" once Trenton was finally reached.

Most significant, the precision of the commander-in-chief's orders revealed the extent of the high degree of his tactical clarity, vision, and insight, providing a formula for future success: "Four pieces [will be] at the head of each Column [designated as Sullivan's First Division and Greene's Second Division], three pieces at the head of the second Brigade of each Division, and two pieces with each of the Reserves." Washington's well-conceived instructions resulted in the judicious placement of Captain Samuel Forrest's four Pennsylvania cannon positioned at the head of the first brigade in line, Mercer's Maryland, Connecticut, and Massachusetts brigade of 833 men (Washington's third largest brigade after Glover's brigade and Sargent's brigade, respectively), which served as the lead brigade of Greene's Second Division column proper, while General Stephen's Virginia brigade (consisting of 549 soldiers) served as the light, highly mobile vanguard, after Captain Washington's Virginians splintered off to advance on their independent mission, before the main column.

In maintaining his clear tactical vision in regard to early maximizing his artillery arm's capabilities in the upcoming confrontation, Washington wisely planned to have his artillery firepower positioned at the head of not only the main column, but also at the head of each brigade, seamlessly mixing the strength of artillery with veteran infantry muscle to pack the greatest punch—to guarantee a concentrated firepower—at the battle's opening. As Napoleon fully understood by assigning two artillery pieces to each French regiment (1809) not only to increase each unit's firepower, but also to bolster his soldier's morale, especially young non-veterans, to enhance overall combat capabilities of both arms. Equally important if Washington caught Colonel Rall and his brigade by surprise as planned, he also now realized that once his artillery was setup on the high ground just north of Trenton, then the winter storm would then be at his veteran cannoneer's backs, while the town's German defenders would be looking into the wrath of the nor'easter wrath driven by a stiff wind: another key advantage, especially at an important battle's beginning.[77]

Meanwhile, the storm raging over the quiet Delaware Valley continued unabated throughout the early morning hours, as if mocking Washington's hopes of reaching and surprising Rall at Trenton. Young Johnny Greenwood described the average Continental soldier's sad plight, including a good many men "without even shoes." With the respite, the cold-numbed troops of Greenwood's Massachusetts regiment, St. Clair's New England brigade of around five hundred men, (Sullivan's reserve command), "began to pull down the [rail] fences and make fires to warm ourselves, for the storm was increasing rapidly . . . it rained, hailed, snowed, and froze, and at the same time blew a perfect hurricane [for] after putting the rails on to burn, the wind and the fire would cut them in two in a moment, and when I turned my face toward the fire my back would be freezing [but] by turning round and round I kept myself from perishing before the large bonfire."[78]

By the flickering light of wet wood that of course burned with more difficulty than dry wood, Washington felt pity at the sight of his soldiers in threadbare uniforms that were now thoroughly soaked. Woolen and silk scarves were wrapped around heads and worn under old, dirty slouch hats that no respectable, upper-class Virginia planter back home would wear on his sprawling Tidewater plantation. Washington must have wondered how these young men and boys could possibly succeed in making the difficult trek of nearly ten miles march on this freezing night all the way to Trenton. After all, many of Washington's finest soldiers now only wore "but parts of shoes [now wet] to their feet."[79]

Some of Washington's men were wrapped in dirty, grease-covered blankets—essentially makeshift ponchos—that badly needed cleaning and patching. But even these rudely fashioned, ad hoc garments were precious few. Before crossing the Delaware, Washington's Continentals had felt a growing sense of discouragement with the haunting knowledge that Philadelphia newspapers had recently carried appeals for citizens to donate blankets, but relatively few were forthcoming.

Most of all, Washington realized that he needed to get his troops in the best shape possible by warming them up and allowing them some rest before the inevitable combat upon which so much hinged. He walked among his shivering band of motley soldiers, instilling confidence with his presence and inspiring words. Appealing to pride as well as patriotism, Washington presented a very personal challenge to his young, unsophisticated farmer-soldiers that not only revolved around patriotism but also around the time-honored concept of manhood: "I hope you will all fight like men" on this day of destiny.[80]

Unknown to him in the deepening storm, Washington actually possessed far less reason to worry about his troop's fighting resolve by this time. An unexpected development was already stealthy in the process of occurring to fulfill exactly what Washington had long worked so hard to create in attempting to transform amateur troops into a hardcore, close-knit band of brothers who were ready to die for each other. Significantly, this almost inexplicable phenomenon occurred just after the common soldier's spirits had plummeted to a new all-time low, thanks to the combined negative effect of the crossing delays,

Washington's shattered timetable, and the storm's escalating severity. Instead of resulting in a shattered morale as so often in the past, something unusual and unexpected happened among the men of Washington's isolated task force amid the falling snow and blustery gales of winter.

In a strange way, it was almost as if the Delaware's successful crossing and an unprecedented measure of adversity had somehow bestowed a renewed faith among the common soldiers from across America, with this notable development in itself becoming viewed by these men as a harbinger of an upcoming victory on New Jersey soil. Indeed, in purely psychological terms, the sheer fortitude, courage, and nerve required by Washington's homespun soldiers, mostly yeomen farmers unable to swim, to faithfully follow an aristocratic Virginia general with losing ways and embark upon the perilous passage over a wide, ice-clogged river at night was in essence a significant moral and psychological victory in itself. Therefore, this tangible success now bolstered spirits and faith to an unprecedented degree, boding well for future success at Trenton.

After the gloomy sense of defeatism that had long gripped this often-losing army like an ever-tightening vise from which there was no escape, the ever-perceptive Private Greenwood felt this refreshingly new pulsating surge of a moral rejuvenation and renewal of optimism, that lay just below the surface, which suddenly fueled greater resolve among Washington's long-suffering rank and file in a crisis situation: "The noise of the solders coming over [the river] and clearing away the ice, the rattling of the cannon wheels on the frozen ground, and the cheerfulness of my fellow-comrades encouraged me beyond expression, and . . . I felt great pleasure" and a new burning sense of optimism and expectation of success.[81] With Washington's leadership ability reaching a new height, more of these often-defeated Continental soldiers began to believe in themselves and in what their commander-in-chief could achieve east of the Delaware. They were becoming increasingly convinced that in Washington "we had the right man to lead the cause of American liberty," in the words of General Sullivan's perceptive brother.[82]

But, ironically, even Washington, at least not until the fighting for Trenton's possession began, was not yet fully aware of this stealthy and subtle, almost subconscious, transformation that was quietly taking place among his long-suffering troops even now. Instead the commander-in-chief, yet felt a nagging sense of foreboding, expecting the worst because of his thoroughly shattered timetable. Washington now realized he would be unable to launch his attack an hour before daylight to catch the Hessians by surprise. Again playing the master psychologist, Washington bolstered the resolve among the common soldiery by emphasizing his watchword, "Victory or Death," which reminded everyone what was truly now at stake. The relatively small number of troops at Washington's disposal continued to trouble the over-burdened commander-in-chief, with once robust Continental regiments so severely decimated by the ravages of disease, death, and desertions. As Washington had earlier revealed in a letter to Colonel Joseph Reed, however, the depleted ranks of his finest Continental regiments had failed to diminish his determination: ". . . our numbers, I am sorry to say, being less than [hoped] Yet nothing but dire necessity will, nay must, justify an attack."[83]

II

Turning Point: Washington's Audacious Decision to Forge Ahead

Upon first accepting command of the Continental Army, the inexperienced Washington had solemnly written to a confidential letter to his brother, "I am embarked on a wide ocean . . . in which, perhaps, no safe harbor is to be found."[1] Ironically, Washington's anguished words more directly applied to the seemingly no-win situation in which he now found himself and more than at any other time in the revolutionary struggle.

Indeed, because of the lengthy delay in transporting all eighteen pieces of Knox's artillery across the river and with his overly optimistic schedule more than three hours behind schedule after the final boat crossed around 3:00 a.m. instead of by midnight as planned, Washington faced not only his own personal crisis but also a major decision in the cold darkness between 3:00 a.m. and to "near" 4:00 a.m. Nothing was now more vital to success than time, because Washington's plan was based upon reaching Trenton's outskirts and attacking an hour before dawn at around 5:00 a.m. And now too much precious time had been lost, slipping away along with the fast-fading chances for success. Therefore, in his own words, Washington was overwhelmed with a sense of absolute "despair of surprizing [sic]" Trenton, because he and his men now could not reach it before the dawn of Thursday, December 26.

This key turning point moment came during the crucial hour that his troops needed to regroup and gain a much-needed respite on the river's east side. With so many recent setbacks yet weighing heavily on his mind, Washington now faced his greatest dilemma: given the rapidly deteriorating situation, worsening weather conditions, and disintegrated timetable, should the march and attack on Trenton, yet nearly ten miles to the south, be aborted now that he was entirely unable to strike an hour before dawn as planned? And Cadwalader and Ewing had aborted their own offensive operations for these same reasons, assuming that Washington had done the same. As he penned, Washington now faced the crucial turning point situation that "made me despair of surprizing [sic] the Town, as I well knew we could not reach it before the day was fairly broke, but as I was certain there was no making a Retreat without being discovered, and harassed on repassing the River, I determined to push on at all Events."[2]

With this audacious decision, Washington continued to demonstrate remarkable strength of will and character well-honed by abundant past adversity. He, therefore, was completely "undismayed by disaster, unchanged by change of fortune," at a time when an unkind fate had seemingly turned against his best laid plains and ambitions.[3] Most of all, Washington was consumed by the obsession that because "we are contending for our Liberty," Trenton must be attacked regardless of the odds, costs, or sacrifice.[4] Washington's bold decision to faithfully adhere to his original plan and forge on to Trenton was especially bold for a variety of reasons, including the fact that increasing numbers of his men and officers, including high-ranking ones, believed that it now would be wise to abort the entire operation.[5] All the while, consequently, Washington went to great efforts to lift spirits with encouraging words, fortifying resolve and morale for the stiff challenges that lay ahead.[6]

Although he realized that his soldiers were in overall bad shape and his delicate timetable had been shattered beyond recognition, Washington knew from recent intelligence that the Hessians at Trenton were equally weary and vulnerable. Fortunately to additionally embolden Washington at this time, no Hessian soldiers had been posted along the river north of Trenton to ascertain the rebel's crossing of the Delaware, and sound a warning at Trenton. Therefore, because the element of surprise was fully intact, the opportunity yet existed for the ragged Americans to score a remarkable victory, when least expected. And, most of all, Washington had lost too many battles to allow such a golden opportunity pass by when the life of his army and nation was at stake.

Despite his own overly ambitious plans having gone awry, a strong-willed Washington kept his poise and offensive-mindedness. With a Virginia planter's stubbornness, he remained firm in his resolve to keep going and pushing ahead to Trenton, regardless of the situation or circumstances. Unlike a good many other commanders, Washington was undaunted. He maintained his firm determination to carry through with his original tactical plan, regardless of all that had gone wrong. For Washington, there was now no turning back. In making his final fateful decision amid the biting cold and howling winds, Washington reached down deeply and drew greater strength from his strong religious faith, perhaps including one of his favorite Bible passages, the 101st Psalm that now applied perfectly to this nerve-racking situation and to Colonel Rall's three Hessian regiments in regard to a righteous sense of morality: "I will early destroy all the wicked of the land." In addition, Washington felt that his "chosen people" (Americans) and their infant republic possessed the special destiny of creating a new world (the shining "city upon a hill"), and this nascent nationalistic faith fueled a burning desire to continue onward into the dark depths of "the lion's den." Combing his strong religious faith and a nascent American nationalism, Washington had learned his moral lessons well at Pohick Church, west of Mount Vernon, where he had long sat in pew twenty-eight.

Keenly noticed by his men, who felt encouraged by the inspiring sight, Washington remained "a study in quiet resolve," calmness, and steely determination, regardless of the seemingly dramatically reduced combat capabilities and overall chances for success because of the storm's intensity and shattered timetable. Clearly, Washington had just made not only "the most momentous decision" of his career in deciding to continue to push onward to Trenton in a raging storm, as if it were a bright Sunday day in springtime and everything was yet progressing smoothly and right ontime, but also the most important decision in America's young life. Instead of giving up hope or forsaking his clear vision of what it took to reap a dramatic victory against the odds at Trenton to rejuvenate America's "righteous Cause," in his own words, Washington was only fueled with a greater determination to succeed at any cost.[7]

Most significant at this crucial moment, the die-hard Virginian felt that he was not alone in his desperate bid to reverse America's fate, having written on December 23 how if "we are successful, which Heaven grant" to America.[8] And most important for Washington, the audacious decision to continue leading the advance upon Trenton was also very much about something much larger than even his troops realized. Most of all, Washington was determined to continue his advance upon Trenton "for America's future [because] He was, in a sense, the first believer in Manifest Destiny."[9]

As he had written to dignified Robert Morris on Christmas Day and just before crossing the Delaware, Washington was determined that for a beleaguered America, whose fortunes had sunk to her lowest depths, "the next Christmas [1777] will prove happier than the present" one.[10] And this was now only possible by marching on and overwhelming Trenton. Ironically, at the war's beginning in a letter, he had promised wife Martha Custis Washington (their eighteenth wedding anniversary was next month) at Mount Vernon that he would be home by Christmas 1775, believing that the conflict would be short.[11] But the war's harsh realities had changed Washington's hopes and ambitions, and had even brought the nagging fear that the British planned on "seizing Mrs. Washington by way of revenge upon me."[12]

Like some ghostly aberration appearing suddenly out of the sheet of snow and sleet, the commander-in-chief rode among his troops, speaking encouraging words to lift sagging spirits. As never before, Washington inspired his band of soldiers, who keenly felt the gnawing cold, by his dominant commanding presence and indomitability of his single-minded, if not stubborn, purpose to see the job through to the end. He now readied his troops for their greatest challenge to date in a classic case of do or die. More than ever before, Washington was determined out of "dire necessity" to proceed onward through the eye of the raging storm, and toward the potential promised land of Trenton to reverse his infant republic's fate. Most of all, he was determined that the British would never "put Shackles upon Freeman," in his own defiant words that he was now determined to back up with desperate action. As throughout this campaign, Washington continued to be resilient, adaptive, and creative.

Fortunately, Washington had already benefitted immensely from British and Hessian leadership failures on multiple levels, increasing his overall chances for success. Ironically, Washington had gained the Delaware's east bank undetected in part because Colonel Rall's repeated appeals to his superiors had been ignored. Rall had wisely requested General Alexander Leslie, on December 20, to garrison the hamlet of Maidenhead (today's Lawrenceville, New Jersey), on the Princeton Road just northeast Trenton, with a small force, but more importantly to patrol Johnson's Ferry, and Howell's Ferry, to the south and located about half-way between Johnson's Ferry and Trenton: an advanced warning system for the Trenton garrison.

Other experienced Hessian officers at Trenton likewise had early understood the urgent need to guard Johnson's Ferry. Major Johann Jost, or Justus, Matthaeus, Rall Regiment, had informed Rall that Pennington, northeast of Johnson's Ferry but located closer to the ferry than Maidenhead, should be "held by a detachment from which there could be detailed scouts to John's [Johnson's] ferry and in this manner they could watch the movements of the enemy." However, Rall's request to occupy Maidenhead was not only not acted upon, but also was openly mocked by General Leslie, at Princeton, for his timely, on-target strategic insights.

An experienced commander, Rall had been so firmly convinced of the urgent need to guard Johnson's Ferry that he had even gone over the heads of Leslie and thirty-six-year-old Colonel Carl Emilius Ulrich von Donop, a wealthy German aristocrat of ability, by again requesting, also on December 20 but this time to General James Grant at New Brunswick, that reliable guardians should be positioned at this strategic location. Once again, Rall was not only ignored but also ridiculed. A member of England's upper class and a career soldier, Grant was convinced that Washington possessed neither leadership skill nor offensive capabilities. Therefore, Johnson's Ferry and the Delaware's east bank was left entirely unguarded, without so much as a single mounted picket who could have sounded an early warning of Washington's movements to the Trenton garrison.

In preparation for the march of nearly ten miles ahead in utter darkness, meanwhile, Washington hoped that his troops had now gained some extra warmth and vitality for the upcoming arduous demands. After all, to fulfill Washington's demanding requirements, these soldiers now had to march onward for the night's remainder in a raging storm. Therefore, the remaining reserves of strength of these ragtag revolutionaries needed to be conserved. Fortunately, Washington's decision for his men to warmup by erecting bonfires paid dividends in the hours ahead. After the soldiers rested for about an hour and braced for an unprecedented degree of adversity and challenges, Washington ordered his sleepless troops into column just before 4:00 a.m.

It was nearly a full hour since the last of Knox's artillery had been ferried across the river at around 3:00 a.m. By this time, Washington's timetable was already nearly four hours behind schedule. He had originally planned to strike Trenton an hour before daylight at around 5:00 a.m. And he was yet nearly ten miles from his objective, while the energy-sapping northeaster had yet to reach its full fury. Consequently, Washington's key to victory, the element of surprise, seemed to have been lost for good, but relatively few individuals, especially the determined commander-in-chief, thought about turning back.

Galloping up and down the lengthy column and through the snow flakes gently falling upon his dark military cloak, Washington "formed my Detachment into two divisions." He then carefully checked his infantry and artillery units, making sure that everything was in its proper place and ready for the long march to Trenton. In a hurry to resume the march, Washington bestowed last-minute advice and instructions, before ordering the column to move out. After having made sure that heavy knapsacks and packs fit snugly

to backs, Washington's troops finally began to lurch forward through the cascading snow. With Stephen's 549-man brigade of three Virginia regiments
leading the way, Greene's lengthy column of Second Division troops began to
push east from the high ground plateau just above the Johnson Ferry House,
marching through the driving showers of sleet and snow around 4:00 p.m.
Consisting of veterans, Mercer's Maryland, Connecticut, and Massachusetts
brigade advanced just behind Stephen's Virginians, while Stirling's brigade, of
four regiments, followed the Scotland-born Mercer, the former Jacobite rebel
now in his second revolt against British rule and domination.

As carefully arranged by Washington, Greene's Second Division was followed by Sullivan's First Division. Meanwhile, Brigadier General Matthias-
Alexis Roche de Fermoy's brigade of two regiments (638 men) brought up the
rear of Greene's Division. All the while, the omnipresent blackness and the
biting cold wrapped up the slowly marching troops in a wintry shroud that
seemed almost like an eternal tomb. As if pulled onward by some unseen, irresistible force, Washington's soldiers were drawn deeper into the night's haunting
darkness amid winter's icy grip, surging toward the enticing, but elusive, vision
of a brighter day for America's fortunes in the future. With well-worn flintlock
muskets on shoulders, the veteran Continentals ventured farther into an alien
countryside of dense woodlands engulfed in a snowy blackness, marching farther away from that nightmarish river known as the Delaware.[13]

Washington had just concluded an impromptu commander's conference
with his top lieutenants right before 4:00 a.m. inside the cozy Johnson Ferry
House, where yellow flames from stone fireplaces warmed the small, plain
wooden structure, with snow-covered roof, that retained the heat. Here, as
an added precaution, Washington went over his final plans one last time to
clarify missions in order to avoid any possible confusion about specific assignments and responsibilities. For Washington's daring battle-plan to succeed this
morning, the commander-in-chief's top officers must now all be thinking the
same way, with exact details firmly set in place and mind. After all, this little
vagabond army could no longer afford any mistakes, bungling, or confusion as
had occurred so often in the past.

To enhance the probability of his two columns striking Trenton simultaneously in a pincer movement from two different directions an hour before daylight, Washington ordered his leading officers to set their pocketwatches by his
own watch. From the tiny village of Derby (named for a river and market town
in England), Connecticut and founded in 1642 at the site of an Indian trading

post in the Lower Naugatuck Valley and whose lofty legal ambitions had ended abruptly with the "shots heard around the world" at Lexington, after recently having been admitted to the bar, the enterprising Captain William Hull served in Glover's Brigade. Having attended Yale University with Nathan Hale—and who had earlier served in the ranks beside the promising young man—Hull was a respected officer of the Nineteenth Connecticut Continental Regiment. To ensure a synchronized offensive effort from Washington's two divisions, the New Englander wrote how: "The General gave orders that every Officer's Watch should be set by his, and the Moment of Attack was fixed."[14]

Meanwhile, the two advanced parties of around forty dependable soldiers each of Captains Washington and Flahaven's companies from two widely separated states that represented north and south, New Jersey and Virginia, continued to lead the way. Out in front of the head of Greene's Second Division column, both contingents advanced in single file on opposite sides of the narrow road. Given dual key independent assignments by Washington, each advanced party continued to act independently ahead of the main column with instructions to establish secure points about three miles from Trenton and setup roadblocks on the two main roads leading to Trenton from the north. Armed with trusty hunting rifles, the battle-hardened westerners of Captain Washington's contingent of Third Virginia Continental Regiment soldiers pushed east from the windswept plateau with the initial objective of first gaining the Bear Tavern Road, before turning and then moving south in the hope of securing blocking points north of Trenton.

Meanwhile, Captain Flahaven's Jersey men, who were rookies, but \highly-motivated soldiers and knew Hunterdon County well, trudged through the undisturbed snow with the equally important mission of eventually gaining the head of the River Road, where it met the Bear Tavern Road. Each advanced band of Continental soldiers surged onward at a steady pace to fulfill their orders and confirm Washington's confidence in them.

Washington's choice to assign a raw detachment of New Jersey men, under Captain Flahaven, on such a vital mission seemed like a questionable decision at first glance. However, what especially comforted Washington was the fact that these Jersey Continentals were eager to redeem their home state from enemy occupation, and that they were now led a most reliable captain, John Flahaven. In his late forties, Flahaven was proud of his Irish roots that included a revolutionary legacy against the hated English. His widowed father, Roger Flahaven, had migrated from Ireland's green shores to Philadelphia with his six children, including young John, in 1728.

His devout Catholic family faithfully worshiped God and Ireland's patron saint, St. Patrick, at St. Mary's Catholic Church, located on Fourth Street between Spruce and Walnut, Philadelphia, and not far from where the Declaration of Independence had been signed at Carpenter's Hall, when America's fortunes were so much brighter. Here, at the city's first Catholic cathedral, built in 1763, many of Philadelphia's leading Catholics worshiped with a quiet devotion. John's father remarried a woman, perhaps an Irish immigrant as well, named Catherine in 1768, and their daughter Bridget, John's half sister, was born in 1771, while John prospered as a thrifty Philadelphia merchant. With his Irish Catholicism faith having long thrived among family and neighbors at St. Mary's Church, Captain Flahaven was now a holy warrior. As fate would have it, this promising Ireland-born Continental officer would be captured by British troops not long after the battle of Trenton.[15]

Meanwhile, Washington's most rearward troops began to move out, following the foremost men in the silent ranks of America's most faithful, resilient soldiers. After all their intense labor in rowing and poling the lumbering Durham boats across the Delaware for most of the night, Glover and his exhausted mariners received little rest. Worn-out Massachusetts officers barked out "Shoulder your firelocks," and the weary Marbleheaders of Glover's brigade (Washington's largest brigade with 1,259 men) formed in line with their comrades just behind Colonel Sargent's New York, Connecticut, and Massachusetts brigade and before St. Clair's New England brigade amid Sullivan's lengthy divisional column with well-honed precision, as if performing maneuvers on the town's training ground of Windmill Hill, which overlooked Marblehead harbor's sparkling waters of blue. With Colonel Glover at the regiment's head, the Fourteenth Massachusetts Continental Regiment's soldiers, stiff and sore, moved off within the cramped column of Sullivan's First Division. With leather cartridge-boxes full of sixty rounds, Major Lee's versatile Marbleheaders were prepared to fight on land as infantrymen now that their back-breaking amphibious mariner duties were finally over, much to their relief.

Exhausted from assisting Glover's seamen in the hours-long crossing, Lieutenant Cuthbert's contingent of young Philadelphia artillerymen of Captain Moulder's company, consisting of a number of urban dandies with fine uniforms and fancy educations, but far more tough Scotch-Irishmen from the city's seedy, rough-and-tumble waterfront district, moved out with their fellow Pennsylvania artillerymen. Delighted to be reunited with their four-pounders imported from France and Moulder's other cannoneers, the Pennsylvania artillerymen now pushed forward with their "four long French" guns not far from Glover's Massachusetts regiment, when the troops of Sullivan's First Division column lurched ahead through the falling snow.

From their strenuous crossing efforts, the backs, arms, and shoulders of Glover's mariners, like Cuthbert's Philadelphia gunners, were racked by pain and soreness. Despite their mind-numbing weariness and aching muscles, the Marbleheaders marched over the frozen ground with a slightly different step from the landlubbers, without whistling merrily or singing traditional sea-faring songs on this night of sheer misery. To the astonishment of one and all, Washington's order for complete silence was respected and faithfully maintained hour after hour. Amid the cold gloom of Hunterdon County's dark woodlands covered in a white, wintry blanket that was impenetrable, some of Glover's men no doubt thought of the comforting memories of the beloved Marblehead, now three hundred miles away, which was one of the most beautiful ports in all New England, especially in the summer and early fall.[16]

Descending across gently sloping ground and initially straight east from the high plateau above Johnson's Ferry, Washington's troops continued to inch onward across unfamiliar terrain. In a December 27 letter, one of Washington's officers described the suffering of the men in the ranks, from the highest ranking officer to the lowest private: "That night was sleety and cold and the roads slippery" in the darkness, resulting a slow, tedious march, while more precious time was lost to Washington.[17]

To avoid confusion in the blackened New Jersey woodlands through which the little road ran, Washington assigned a number of reliable guides, including trusty, local volunteers, who had recently joined his strike force upon learning of the river crossing, not only at the column's head but also before each brigade, as an added precaution. Almost as if Washington was anticipating even more of the worst weather yet seen this winter in the Delaware River Valley, his farsighted calculation guaranteed that no combat brigade would wander off course, take the wrong road, or get lost amid the dense, uncharted woodlands in the storm's limited visibility and the pitch blackness.

These reliable, local New Jersey men, such as John Muirhead, John Mott, an enterprising officer from Gates's northern army who had been recruiting in this part of the Garden State for the New Jersey Continental Line, David Laning, and John Guild volunteered their services at considerable risk to themselves and their families, especially if Washington lost his risky gamble at Trenton. Out in front of the slogging troops who almost looked more like snowmen than soldiers, these knowledgeable mounted guides, whose well-shod horses, evidently with icehorseshoes to cope with icy conditions, galloped down the road, leading Washington's soldiers northeast and ever-deeper into the stormy woodlands.[18]

From the plateau just east of the Johnson Ferry House, Washington's troops marched first east and then mostly northeast along the barely discernable Johnson's Ferry Road. Now covered in a sheet of ice and snow, this narrow artery, sometimes known as the Pennington Road because it led toward through the hardwood forests and to the small agricultural community—located about four and a half miles to the northeast—of that same name, led northeast to the Bear Tavern Road and then eventually to the Pennington Road proper. Washington hoped to eventually gain the Pennington Road, which led straight south to the northern edge of Trenton, located just south of Pennington.

From the plateau, the road from the ferry led over terrain that dipped slightly and then rose again amid a dense forest of mostly oaks and hickories. Only a relatively few evergreens, a mere scattering of cedars and pines, could be readily seen against a white background by the most alert and observant soldiers when marching by. Already the march's pace was excruciatingly slow, causing Washington even greater cause for concern. Private Greenwood, the feisty New England teenager, described the difficulty in toiling up the slippery slope from the ferry and the painfully slow marching along the ferry road that passed through tangled woodlands, now bathed in pitch blackness and freezing cold: "After our men had all crossed—and there were not, as I could see, more than 200 of us—we began [to] march, not advancing faster than a child ten years old could walk . . . . "[19]

With the nearly full winter moon completely obscured by heavy clouds, the only visibility during the slow march across mostly ascended gradually terrain now came from a handful of blazing torches. In the hope of preventing a mishap, these flaming torches had been wedged by Knox's veteran artillerymen on the wooden carriages of field pieces. Offering only slight illumination, these torches now jolted up and down with each rut encountered by the gunners along the road. In the ranks of Colonel Charles Webb's Nineteenth Connecticut Continental Regiment, Glover's brigade, that included hardy soldiers from New London, Fairfield, Litchfield, and New Haven Counties, which were all (except for Litchfield) located along the Atlantic coast, Lieutenant Elisha Bostwick described how the improvised "torches of our field pieces [were] Stuck in the Exhalters [which] sparkled & blazed in the Storm all night."[20]

It was a wise precaution that this relatively faint illumination from these flickering torches bestowed some light around Washington's precious field pieces to make sure that these invaluable guns were safely transported, because of the importance of their upcoming role in battle. In addition, Knox's experienced artillerymen, at the head of each infantry brigade, needed to make sure that the tompions—or bore plugs—and vent plugs protecting vents, by which the black powder was charged to fire these guns, on iron and bronze barrels remained firmly in place, while the cannon labored slowly along the bumpy road leading northeast from Johnson's Ferry and toward the ferry road's intersection with Bear Tavern Road. If a vent plug was suddenly jarred loose or fell out, then the heavy deluge promised that ice, snow, and water would seep inside the cannon's barrel.

On foot and trudging through the snow like everyone else, Knox's seasoned gunners also made sure that delicate wooden artillery wheels, already made brittle by the freezing weather, did not crack on fallen tree limbs or road ruts worn down by heavy farmer's wagons transporting goods to market. Therefore, because of the fragility of the slender artillery wheels, these rough spots along the road were spotted beforehand by sharp-eyed cannoneers in the flickering torchlight, and then prudently avoided as much as possible. However, even some wooden gun carriages became increasingly weak by the ordeal of moving over rough terrain. Meanwhile, as the grueling march lengthened and the ground dipped gently once again and then rose to the high ground upon which the Bear Tavern, to the northeast, was perched, the eyes of Washington's soldiers grew more acclimated to the night's blackness. Therefore, visibility was slightly enhanced for the slogging men in the ranks, while the lengthy column of solemn-faced Americans eased northeast through the wintry, New Jersey woodlands of late December.

Some, if not all, of Knox's artillery horses were as unprepared for a winter campaign as Washington's soldiers, however. Revealing one of the few mistakes that were made by Washington in regard to his otherwise thorough and careful operational preparations during what was certainly his best-planned campaign to date, most artillery horses were entirely "without shoes," or "ice-shoes." In consequence, these laboring animals, in pulling their heavy loads, often lost their footing and slid on the ice and snow, especially on rugged terrain. Therefore, the over-worked artillery horses, already ill-fed, cold, and weak, had to be closely watched by shivering cannoneers throughout the more than nine-mile trek to Trenton.[21]

At this time, a special, close bond existed between Knox's gunners and their cherished cannon; a feeling not unlike even the most cynical and battle-hardened cavalryman for his favorite horse. Captain Alexander Hamilton, the intellectual soldier-scholar who now commanded his own New York battery of two six-pounders with a sense of pride and authority that helped to mask his lowly background in the West Indies, had been often seen walking beside his favorite cannon, while "absent-mindedly patting it from time to time, as if it were a favorite horse or plaything."[22] Advancing at the head of Mercer's brigade, Sergeant Joseph White, a member of Captain Forrest's Second Company of the Pennsylvania State Artillery, possessed a special love for his "favorite" artillery piece, which he admired fondly as "the best in the regiment." Orderly Sergeant White "loved" this field piece like no other gun with a passion not completely understandable to the average foot-slogging infantryman, who maintained a healthy rivalry with Knox's gunners. Unknown to the busy gun crew at this time, the wooden support system of the heavy gun barrel of White's cannon, creaking slowly over the snow and ice, was now already fatally compromised by the combined rigors of the crossing and moving inland over rough ground.[23]

Most of all, none of Knox's artillerymen wanted to see their faithful cannon left behind, which was not unlike abandoning a lover or family member. On this terrible night seemingly in the middle of nowhere, therefore, Knox's artillerymen paid closer attention to their field piece's welfare, because Washington's cannoneers almost instinctively knew that the artillery's upcoming performance at Trenton would separate winner from loser.

Meanwhile, Washington continued to worry and fret, and for ample good reason. His overly optimistic schedule and ambitious timetable to launch the attack an hour before sunrise around 5:00 a.m., which had been based upon a rosy scenario of everyone and everything safely getting across the Delaware by midnight, was now even more of an impossibility, as more time slipped away in the blinding woodlands and cold darkness. Washington worried if the Hessian brigade at Trenton was now on high alert, especially with so many Tories, who might have informed the garrison, living in this Hunterdon County country-side? On Saturday December 14, a worried Washington had written with exasperation how, "I do not doubt but they are well informed of everything we do." Had British or Hessian scouts spied Washington's time-consuming crossing of the Delaware and warned the entire Trenton garrison by this time? No one, especially Washington, could be sure. But Washington knew full well that if his movements were discovered, then it would be "prove fatal to us," as he penned to Colonel Joseph Reed.

Pushing onward into the night's biting cold, hundreds of Continentals from the Blue Ridge Mountains to the Tidewater and from New England to the South continued to march generally northeast to gain the Bear Tavern Road as soon as possible. However, Washington's column now seemed to have been practically swallowed up by the storm's dark intensity that showed no signs of letting up. Moving across the frigid landscape and farther away from their muddy Pennsylvania encampments, Washington's men eased deeper into the frozen blackness of New Jersey while trying hard to stay alert and awake. But the going was slow in part because so much of the narrow road gradually rose from the river, requiring the struggling men to trudge up a slippery slope, which was more challenging ascent because of creeping weariness.

Meanwhile, the concentration of Continental troops in the column's rear, the reserve brigades, were more encumbered than Washington's lead brigades, which had churned up the roadbed into a slippery, muddy slush by the time that the latecomers marched by. Therefore, as if limited visibility was not enough of a severe handicap on this hellish march, the most rearward troops were forced to slog along the sides of the mud-slick road in thin files of ill-clad soldiers along the black woodline to escape the quagmire. All the while additional precious time was lost, slipping away into the cold New Jersey night like Washington's opportunity to surprise the Hessians, or so it seemed. Not long after 4:00 a.m., the column of Greene's and Sullivan's Divisions stretched out for hundreds of yards in the cheerless, frozen darkness, with men struggling through the clinging mess that seemed to suck up and spitout not only more time, but also Washington's fast-fading chances for success.

After pushing generally northeast for a little more than a mile for what seemed like an eternity, Washington's troops toiled up the final stretch of gradually ascending terrain to gain their next key objective: the obscure, little crossroads at the plain-looking Bear Tavern, blanketed in a fresh layer of snow, that stood out prominently like a beacon in the middle of nowhere. Now half-hidden amid a snowy expanse, this two-story wood-frame tavern, with a sturdy stone foundation and a wide front porch running across the length of the inn's front, stood at the northeast corner of the barely discernable crossroads covered in white. Here, just northeast of Johnson's Ferry and northwest of Trenton and at the intersection of the east-west running ferry road with the north-south

Bear Tavern Road, the slow-moving head of Washington's column suddenly appeared out of the blinding snowfall like some ghostly winter aberration.

Mounted out in front as usual in leading the way, Washington then directed his troops, with flintlocks on shoulders and burdened with extra ammunition and rations, to turn sharply to the right, or south, onto the Bear Tavern Road. From the relative high ground of this little crossroads nestled amid the silent woodlands, this narrow road led straight south toward Trenton. Thankfully, for the exhausted common soldiers with sore, half-frozen feet, the Bear Tavern Road led down gradually sloping terrain that made movement a bit easier for worn soldiers, horses, and Knox's eighteen artillery pieces that were keeping up with the slogging infantrymen. However, the barely visible road, a mere path hewn through the hardwood wilderness, remained difficult to see for the soldiers (fortunately the New Jersey guides knew the area) caught amid the storm's intensity. All the while, Captain Washington's and Flahaven's advance parties continued to push south as best they could, moving with firm resolution through the snow on opposite sides of the "slippery" Bear Tavern Road.[24]

The Nightmarish March South To Trenton

Meanwhile, with high hopes even though the storm continued to wreck havoc on Washington's already badly fractured timetable, the toughened Continentals moved relentlessly down slightly descending ground from the snowy crossroads. With the nine-pound weight of muskets feeling heavier than usual, hundreds of young men and boys from New York to Virginia now headed south in the tempest. Then, Washington's soldiers reached terrain that gradually rose, while maintaining discipline and silence as ordered. Veterans felt added confidence, because they now possessed leather pouches and cartridge-boxes, which initially kept cartridges dry, overflowing with sixty rounds per man.

Reflecting the grim situation that seemingly bode ill for American fortunes, the usual joking, laughter, light-hearted banter, and nervous talk that had always distinguished this amateurish, ever-individualistic army of citizen soldiers whenever they were on the move were now eerily absent. Meanwhile, exhausted artillery horses continued to struggle onward through the heavy blanket of snow, growing wearier and steadily losing strength like Washington's men in the ranks. Keeping pace with the trudging infantrymen in the inky blackness, Captain Forrest's four artillery pieces from Philadelphia rumbled over the frozen ground at the column's head, as Washington had directed in no uncertain terms.[25]

Meanwhile, the howling nor'easter continued to unleash a menacing blend of ice and snow, mixed in with an occasional hard rain, despite freezing temperatures. However, at least the mere physical act of placing one foot in front of the other in marching south down the Bear Tavern Road increased circulation to make the bodies of fagged soldiers a bit warmer. But nothing could stop the cold from stinging faces, noses, hands, and ears. Veterans of the battles of Long Island, Harlem Heights, and White Plains that were fought under clear, blue skies, Washington's soldiers of summer possessed neither gloves nor mittens in the dead of winter. But the feet of Washington's men suffered the most severely from the combined effect of the omnipresent wetness, snow-covered ground, and the bitter cold. The icy mud and freezing slush which had been churned up by hundreds of marching feet that now filled the roadbed could not be avoided by exhausted men unable to see hardly anything before them. Already in bad shape even before the march began, worn-out leather shoes, if not falling apart by this time, became thoroughly soaked, along with thin socks and half-frozen feet of the common soldiers. All along the route, makeshift shoes on feet began to fall apart as the march lengthened into the night.

But Washington's hopeful revolutionaries had much more to worry about than just cold feet, faces, and hands on the most exhausting march of their lives. Most important, the Continentals had to somehow do the seemingly impossible in keeping firing pans, flints, and black powder dry amid the steady deluge. The winter warfare experience of the most savvy veterans, including those fortunate men who had survived the doomed attack through the cobblestone streets of Quebec last December and veteran New Englanders, especially those older individuals who had served in hard-hitting ranger companies, including Rogers' Rangers, who were masters of winter campaigns against the French, Indians and Canadians in the previous war, now paid off.

More so than in the case of the average farm boys in the ranks who had not fought in wilderness regions, these French and Indian War veterans of winter warfare's rigors understood the importance—literally life-or-death—of keeping firing mechanisms water-free. Savvy frontiersmen had long protected their firing mechanisms from water, snow, and dirt with greased deerskin stock scabbards, known to westerners as "cow knees." But relatively few of Washington's men now possessed these invaluable protective coverings because they were not issued by Continental quartermasters, who distributed only standardized equipment based upon European models and knew nothing of the stern challenges of winter warfare.

However, to counter the wetness and snowfall, some experienced common soldiers began to wrap firing mechanisms with the edge of their thin, woolen blankets, but even these precious commodities, dirty and torn, were in short supply. Reflecting the rapid rise of apathy, defeatism, and Loyalist sentiment, only a mere 113 blankets had been donated to Washington's Army from America's civilian population, despite the Pennsylvania Committee of Safety and Robert Morris's best efforts. Philadelphia's citizens also sent only a trickle of blankets to Cadwalader's Philadelphia militiamen, who gained additional coveted blankets only a few days before because these troops were their own local boys, while Washington's Continentals hailed from faraway regions, especially Virginia and New England. Therefore, the majority of the Continentals went without blankets when needed the most.

However, a few Continentals rejoiced at having been issued a number of "woolen blankets"—sent by the hard-working, dedicated Morris, "very simple in his manners, but his mind is subtle and acute," wrote one observer, in Philadelphia and to "his everlasting credit"—just before the Delaware crossing. Ireland-born Colonel Edward Hand, one of the commander-in-chief's favorites, had recently complained to Washington that many of his crack Pennsylvania riflemen, the army's best marksmen, were entirely shoeless and without blankets. Therefore, Washington had dispatched details of soldiers to scour Bucks County, Pennsylvania, to beg, borrow, or confiscate blankets for his elite riflemen of the First Pennsylvania Continental Regiment. Not ordered to do so by officers, however, a good many soldiers, especially novices unfamiliar with the demands of winter campaigning, failed to sling their around five-foot-long muskets facing down so that no water seeped down musketbarrels.[26]

Meanwhile, from the Piedmont's rolling hills and the lower-lying Tidewater to the east, mostly yeomen, who knew more about growing profitable crops of corn and wheat than the hard-learned lessons of frontier and winter warfare, possessed relatively little knowledge of the urgent necessity of protecting muskets in winter. Captain John Mott, from Gates's northern army and now one of Washington's trusty guides, whose own home stood on the River Road near the Delaware's east bank just northwest of Trenton, was now forced to improvise out of dire necessity. Without a blanket to use as a cover, Mott tried to keep a thin handkerchief, perhaps made of silk, over the firing mechanism and priming pan of his fusil, a light flintlock musket carried by fusiliers, in a futile bid to keep his weapon and powder dry.[27]

Meanwhile, many of Washington's young soldiers were nagged by dark thoughts, falling prey to equally pessimistic doubts about what lay in store for them at Trenton. If killed in the upcoming battle with the much-dreaded Hessians, whose combat prowess was legendary, they knew that Congress, now exiled in Baltimore after fleeing Philadelphia, had not passed a single act to support widows and families, who would have to fend for themselves in hard times. Even worse, the frontiersmen in Washington's ranks, including Hand's crack riflemen, also felt concern for their families' welfare because they were isolated on the western frontier of Pennsylvania, New York, and Maryland, which were now vulnerable to Indian attack, while their menfolk marched toward a rendevous with destiny at a river community of which they had never heard, Trenton.[28]

Leading the Twenty-Sixth Massachusetts Continental Regiment, Glover's brigade, Colonel Loammi Baldwin, who lamented that he was "without any great coat" like the rest of his Bay State soldiers, suffered severely from the bone-chilling cold that now felt more severe than winter in his native New England. With a dark premonition of what might happen to him in the upcoming battle upon which so much depended, Baldwin had recently promised his wife in a letter how, "I must return" to you and their young son, "if I live through this [winter] campaign" so far from home."[29]

Perhaps a worried Washington now thought about the last time that American troops had mounted a winter offensive effort against garrison troops defending an urban area. Ironically, this desperate attack occurred at the end of last December, when Ireland-born General Richard Montgomery led an ambitious winter offensive. Montgomery's ragtag forces had advanced through an intense snowstorm in multiple assault columns, meeting a bloody repulse amid Quebec's narrow streets and the greatest disaster to American arms to date. During America's first invasion of foreign soil, the thirty-eight-year-old Montgomery was killed, becoming America's first national hero.

Now hoping for the best with a badly shattered timetable, Washington almost certainly reflected on that earlier snowy fiasco in Canada, while leading his troops south down the white-shrouded Bear Tavern Road, ever-closer to Trenton. On this frigid, early Thursday morning, Washington knew that he now had only five more days left, before that ever-encroaching fateful Tuesday would come when most of his Continental soldier's enlistments expired on December 31. At that time, Washington's army would practically disappear before his eyes.

Clearly, for Washington, the army, and America, it was now or never. But what almost certainly now haunted Washington during the difficult and agonizingly slow march down the Bear Tavern Road, swept by bone-chilling northeast winds, was the haunting memory of his own lengthy, personal losing streak. Seemingly nothing had ever gone quite right tactically for this Virginia planter on the battlefield against professional opponents, stemming all the way back since his very first days as a young soldier in the service of Virginia. As a newspaperman had summarized what seemed to be a most ill-fated destiny stemming as far back as the French and Indian War, Washington possessed "a high Reputation for Military Skill, Integrity, and Valor; tho' Success has not always attended his Undertakings."[30] Even his own mother, the quite formidable Mary Ball Washington, with an iron will all her own, yet regretted that her son had ever engaged in military pursuits, looking down upon him in consequence.[31]

Clearly, achieving a success in the hours ahead at Trenton was all about resurrecting the will to resist among the American people, because the darkest of moods now dominated America, whose fortunes had reached their lowest point. Fortunately and most important, neither Washington or his ragged followers, slogging with stoic fortitude and grim determination through the swirling snow in the lengthening column of suffering troops, believed that they were now "vanquished," however. At this crucial time in the dark New Jersey woodlands north of Trenton, Washington's strike force of around 2,400 men, the cream of the Continental Army, now represented the largest contingent of American soldiers in any one place. Most important and mirroring the views of their commander who practically stood alone among leadership in his determination to reverse America's fortunes, these men yet believed in themselves and that they could accomplish against the odds.[32] Among these relatively few remaining Continentals were troops who Washington had first proudly designated on July 3, 1775 upon taking command at Cambridge as "the American Army," which was the first official use of the term in American history.[33]

During this most exhausting of marches through the swirling snow and impenetrable darkness, Colonel John Stark, commanding a hard-hitting New Hampshire Regiment in St. Clair's brigade, Sullivan's Division, possessed extensive knowledge about winter warfare's challenges, necessary requirements, and elusive mysteries. As second only to legendary Major Robert Rogers as the foremost partisan leader of Rogers' Rangers during the brutal northern frontier fighting of the French and Indian War, Stark was early recognized for his tactical skill, coolness under fire, and leadership ability. Most important, he was familiar with winter warfare's unique demands, including the tactical advantages of moving swiftly on sleds and snowshoes across snowy terrain.[34]

When large flakes of snow were not tumbling down, a cold rain, mixed with sleet, also fell silently on the lengthy, quiet column of meagerly clad soldiers, who continued to fully rely on Washington's much-ridiculed tactical skill to rise to the fore while they trudged south along the Bear Tavern Road. In an eerie, haunting rhythm that provided the only sound in the surreal silence, the faint platter of heavy droplets of icy water hitting the snow-covered ground was heard, while heavier sleet made a sharper sound in striking nearby tree branches hanging over the long column. But nothing could break the strange, wintry stillness of the New Jersey hardwood forests during this nightmarish ordeal. Indeed, much like America's soldiers in their silent suffering, even the surrounding natural world and its nocturnal creatures remained perfectly quiet in the early morning darkness, as if transfixed in viewing what might well be Washington's greatest folly.

The relentless, steady rhythm of ice dropping upon the slow-moving ranks and the ground mixed with the plodding sound of marching feet of hundreds of soldiers were the only muffled sounds along the route. Washington's Continentals, numbed by the cold and sleep deprivation, continued to demonstrate a remarkable degree of discipline, obeying the commander-in-chief's strict orders to maintain "a profound silence."[35] Consequently, Washington was encouraged by such positive signs which revealed that his men were determined, and that, in the Virginian's words, "Americans will fight for their Liberties and property" to the very end.[36] More than ever before, Washington was beginning to see another dream fulfilled on the arduous march to Trenton: "The General hopes and trusts, that every officer and man, will endeavour so to live, and act, as becomes a Christian Soldier defending the dearest Rights and Liberties of his country."[37]

All the while, Washington's formations inched ever-southward in this most haunting of nights, heading farther into an unknown countryside draped in crystalline white. With the situation now especially critical because of the pressing need to makeup as much lost time as possible with the shattered timetable, it now seemed to an anxious Washington that his troops were only moving only at a snail's pace.

However, the march's overall slowness that could not be prevented allowed the foremost cannoneers to keep their guns up front as ordered by Washington, while pushing south down the Bear Tavern Road. Among Knox's "youthful gunners" were members of a sprightly artillery company hailing from Philadelphia's busy docks and wharves. Commanded by Captain Moulder and eager to unleash devastation from their three French four-pounders against the Teutonic invaders of America, these tough city boys of the Second Company of Artillery, Philadelphia Associators, had caused Washington headaches in the past, but not on this all-important night when this inherent toughness was put to good use for once. With a determination to reach Trenton in unison with the veteran infantrymen, these high-spirited Philadelphia gunners advanced at the head of one of Sullivan's leading infantry brigades. For these hard-bitten cannoneers who seldom ever acted like they were actually from the "City of Brotherly Love," Washington's upcoming strike on Trenton was also very much about protecting their own city, homes, and families located just to the southwest and farther down the Delaware River.[38]

The eerie silence that dominated the woodlands lining the road continued to accompany Washington's sprawling column, whose length seemed to have no end, casting a strange pall over this nighttime march that seemed most ominous. All the while, Washington's soldiers pushed ever-south through the tempest, toiling across a relatively high, relatively flat tract of tableland. South of, and below, the small log tavern that bore its name, the Bear Tavern Road was yet little more than a mere path that had been cut through the virgin forests of Hunterdon County, which was yet largely a wilderness area, especially along the Delaware that flowed in the valley to the column's right, or west. With the storm blowing from the northeast to their backs, Washington's veterans steadily trudged up gradually ascending ground to a high plateau known today as Kerr Ridge.

Here, the Bear Tavern Road continued to run straight south through the dense, New Jersey woodlands. This higher and more level ground allowed for the column of Washington's snow trekkers to pick up the pace, making up for some lost time, but not enough. And now the windy blasts sweeping from the northeast raged more fiercely across the higher ground to cut more keenly through thin civilian clothes and uniforms of shivering men, who had never been so cold in their lives. Each soldier, suffering, praying in silence and thinking of the home that he might never see again, endured his own private hell on his frigid morning.

On such a nightmarish night, this narrow roadway remained especially treacherous to the footing of Washington's men. The increasing weariness that only deepened as the night lengthened, the early stages of hypothermia setting-in because of wet (from the crossing) and half-frozen feet helped to make footing difficult for ill-shod soldiers floundering south with increasing weariness, especially in the column's rear. Clearly, despite their best efforts, not enough time could be made up by the slogging Continentals, with muskets on shoulders now feeling even more like heavy leaden weights, to come even remotely close in salvaging Washington's shattered timetable of reaching Trenton's outskirts for unleashing an attack an hour before dawn.[39] Nevertheless, Washington was determined to succeed at any cost to reverse the war's course, because of a simple equation that he had emphasized in the conflict's beginning: "the once happy and peaceful plains of America are either to be drenched with Blood, or Inhabited by Slaves."[40]

Covered in a sheet of ice and snow, the slick roadbed, balking artillery horses, the overall lack of visibility in blizzard-like conditions, and the seemingly endless other inevitable problems of a large strike force moving at night over unfamiliar ground caused Washington's column to repeatedly halt. Therefore, even more precious time was lost by Washington, whose optimistic plans continued to crumble around him. In the Fifteenth Massachusetts Continental Regiment's ranks and not yet knowing of Washington's ultimate objective, Private Greenwood, the enthusiastic New Englander who had yet to shave, was perplexed by this frustrating and "apparently circuitous march . . . and stopping frequently, though for what purpose I know not [and] During the whole of the march it alternately hailed, rained, snowed, and blew tremendously."[41]

But then thankfully, the agonizing march was about to become more steady in its overall general progression, gaining even an yet unseen measure of momentum in the night's cold tranquillity. Rising gradually from the heavily timbered valley of the Delaware River to the west, the commanding plateau, the Kerr Ridge area, gained by Washington's troops was good ground—level, fertile, and uneroded—for agriculture. This elevated terrain had been early cleared and made productive by industrious farmers in consequence. On the top of this flat plateau through which the Bear Tavern Road now ran south in generally a straight line, a commanding view—if not for the night or stormy weather—would have been offered to the south, because the land was so relatively high, dropping on every side in this distance. To the right, or west, the terrain plunged into the Delaware Valley's depths. This high ground atop windswept Kerr Ridge was open and relatively good for marching soldiers to finally bring some minor relief to weary legs that had grown steadily heavier because the plateau, upon which the road ran generally straight and true, was generally level. At a better and fairly good pace, therefore, the slogging men of Washington's column, continued to move south across Kerr Ridge along Bear Tavern Road, which then turned slightly southeast imperceptibly, with relative ease, despite the storm's fury that seemed to hold a special grudge against rustic revolutionaries, who had rebelled against their king in London.

However, Washington's veteran soldiers, especially former hunters, trappers, and other woodsmen, who could almost instinctively read even an unfamiliar landscape's most reclusive secrets, based upon the nuanced complexity of topographical intricacies, knew that at some point this lofty high ground perch, commanding the entire area, had to eventually descend sharply because of its sheer height, because Trenton was low-lying in the river bottom to the south. Even the name of this little, forgotten road, that continued to curve gently southeastward through an untamed region, had been christened by a long-forgotten, early pioneer, who had killed a black bear near it, indicated that this sparsely settled region was black bear country. And the veteran hunters in Washington's ranks knew that only the roughest terrain and deepest wilderness were the black bear's favorite haunts. Indeed, for less astute, backwoods-savvy soldiers, especially city and farm boys, the relatively easy marching terrain along the high, windswept plateau of Kerr Ridge was actually deceiving, because the greatest challenge, after the Delaware crossing, on this time-consuming march south to Trenton lay just ahead: "a deep chasm" in this remote wilderness that was about to present Washington with his most serious natural obstacle on the long trek to Trenton.

So far, Washington and his men had been relatively fortunate in having encountered generally and relatively favorable terrain in pushing east along first the Johnson's Ferry Road and then south down the Bear Tavern Road, both of which were relatively straight except when the troops first gained the Bear Tavern Road, which caused them to turn sharply to the right, or south, off the ferry road. The roughest spot that Washington's men had encountered during the march had come almost immediately when the troops struggled from the river valley's depths and up the small, but sharp, bluff and past the Johnson's Ferry House to reach the plateau's top just east of the quaint ferry house. Then, all the way to remote Bear Tavern, seemingly secure in its isolation so far north of Trenton, and along the roughhewn road of the same name, Washington's Continentals had pushed across generally accommodating terrain along the just more than a mile and a half stretch of road running south and then slightly southeast from where they had first gained the Bear Tavern Road.

But all of that relatively good fortune was about to quite suddenly change for Washington's trekkers, who were ill-prepared for the upcoming challenge that was about to catch them by surprise. Swept by a merciless frigid wind, the high ground of the Kerr Ridge plateau and the snowy Bear Tavern Road were about to plunge dramatically downward, as the road continued southeast from this snowy high ground perch to descend into the most densely wooded, deepest, and roughest terrain yet encountered by them on the grueling march to Washington's ultimate objective, Trenton.

Jacob's Creek Crossing

Meanwhile, Washington's thin column of troops continued to move relentlessly onward along the level stretches of the Bear Tavern Road. Washington hoped for the best despite seemingly little chance for success. In a resistance effort gone terribly wrong, Washington's men pushed steadily through the frozen woodlands, masked in an inky blackness, with an almost blind faith that kept them driving onward. This most bitter of nights was darker because of the storm's intensification and sheer force. Driven by blustery northeast winds, the ceaseless bands of rain, sleet, and snow lashed Washington's troops without mercy. All the while, an eerie quiet yet hung heavy over the dark-hued column, now stretched out across the white-shrouded Kerr Ridge in a mostly southeastward curve stretching more than a mile, like a funeral shroud. Almost as if a premonition of yet another upcoming defeat at the Hessians' hands as during the New York Campaign, the northeaster's unbridled fury and the black woodlands, of mostly hickory and oak, had seemingly wrapped up the toiling column, mocking Washington's grandiose ambition of ever reaching Trenton in time.

The pace of these determined but bone-weary Continentals along the road that had been hewn through the pristine Hunterdon County forests remained much too slow for Washington who feared the worst. The march was already several hours behind schedule. Washington realized that no surprise attack on Trenton would be forthcoming just before dawn as planned. And this lag time only increased much to the consternation, if not anger, of Washington, who rode near the column's head, attempting to hurry everyone onward through the snow. Washington was also increasingly concerned about the column's ever-expanding length, growing like a cancer with each passing mile.

Unlike the recent trek over the generally high, level of the plateau, Washington and his cold-numbed soldiers, with Stephen's three seasoned regiments—the Fourth, Fifth, and Sixth Virginia Continental Regiments—leading the way, now approached the last and most formidable natural obstacle that lay between them and Trenton, the heavily timbered, gorge-like depression of Jacob's Creek. Thanks to geography's contours, this serious natural impediment explained why the narrow road had turned ever so slightly southeastward to reach that portion of the creek which was the narrowest, and hence the most fordable for travelers and especially the overloaded farm wagons that had long transported tons of produce to market in Trenton.

All of a sudden to Washington's foremost soldiers from the Old Dominion, the ground dipped sharply to the south, and the ice- and snow-slick road plunged downward off the Kerr Ridge plateau. Therefore, Washington's lengthy column, like a giant brown snake, suddenly eased up tentatively, almost by way of some primeval instinct, upon encountering such a formidable obstacle before entering into the mysterious heavily wooded environs of low-lying Jacob's Creek and embarking upon its deepest descent of the night. To Washington, who might not have even known of the existence of this most forbidding natural obstacle, and his worn troops, it must have almost like the Bear Tavern Road had simply disappeared, because of the steep, sudden descent, into a deep, black recess that loomed before them. In the pitch blackness and rather ominously, the land sharply dropped from atop plateau into the uncharted, densely timbered depths of Jacob's Creek, which was much darker than when the troops had been atop the plateau just left behind to the north.

Strung out for more than a mile, Washington's column of half-frozen soldiers were forced to come to an abrupt halt because no bridge along Bear Tavern Road, which plunged down into the deep ravine of the heavily wooded creek bottom, ever had been built over Jacob's Creek. No wooden bridge had been constructed in part because of the unpredictability of this often turbulent watercourse, whose relatively small size masked its inherent tempestuousness, which so often rapidly rose with torrential spring and summer rains or the winter runoff, swelling angrily beyond its banks. Over the centuries, this seasonal flooding of Jacob's Creek, including rainwater running off the Kerr Ridge plateau just to the north, but primarily from the heavier runoff farther east down more elevated terrain in the descent toward the Delaware, had cut a deep ravine through the relatively soft soil.

Only learned belatedly by Washington, the Delaware River was hardly the only formidable natural barrier that lay between the main task force and his coveted objective. Jacob's Creek presented the most serious natural obstacle, especially on such a horrendous night and for worn soldiers, who felt like they could not possibly go any farther, on the New Jersey side. Not only the creek's high waters, swollen by recent rains, but also the steep descent into a narrow gorge-like ravine, where the flooded creek flowed in a southwest direction to eventually enter the Delaware about two miles below, or south, of McConkey's Ferry, now offered a far more considerable challenge to the already behind schedule advance on Trenton than Washington had previously imagined.

For the foot-weary Continentals, just attempting to ease down the icy slope—a steep descent of more than one hundred feet along a narrow path cut through the forest—without falling was difficult enough. Deteriorating ground conditions worsened after the first soldiers, Stephen's Virginia Continentals, gingerly eased down the snow-covered slope of the deeply cut ravine, descending laboriously into the blackened depths of the heavily wooded creek bottom. Sore feet of the first ranks of marching men quickly uncovered the initial layer of snow and ice, tearing up the topsoil to leave only a sheet of slush and mud that was as slippery as ice. Ironically, providing an unexpected boon, soldiers with feet wrapped in rags and pieces of cloth now discovered that they had slightly better footing than upper class, educated Continental officers in expensive leather boots, which had shrunk and grew tighter from wetness, bought at fancy boot-making shops in Boston, Williamsburg, or Philadelphia.

Feeling the ground drop before them, hundreds of Washington's anxious troops, with ice-coated and wet, cold flintlocks on shoulders, struggled down the sloping ground, attempting to keep their balance and footing. Ever so slowly, they moved toward the creek bottom, which was situated amid a wide hollow filled with virgin hardwood timber, mostly tall sycamores, whose large, white trunks blended in perfectly with the snowy landscape. Along the creek's heavily wooded banks, the sycamore's broad limbs towered above the fast-moving creek, draping over it in a natural canopy now bare of leaves. As first discovered by Washington's most advanced scouts, Jacob's Creek was now overflowing its banks from recent rains, and its waters were boiling with sufficient speed so that it was not frozen over, except along its ice-crusted banks.[42] Fortunately, Washington now benefitted immeasurably from the influence of capable officers, from lieutenants to generals, who steadied the men in the ranks, verifying his earlier wisdom that because "the War must be carried on systematically [we] must have good Officers" of all grades.[43]

Weary infantrymen, from drummer boys not yet out of their teens to grizzled veterans in their fifties and with gray hair on chins, shortly began to lose their footing on the slippery, descending ground. But the steep slope, that plunged downward a hundred feet, was even precarious for the relatively few mounted officers. Washington, mounted on his big "chestnut sorrel charger," was no exception. In fact, Washington was at even greater risk, because he was riding up and down the lengthy column to encourage his men down the steep slope that had reduced the march's pace to a crawl. Marching beside his freezing Connecticut comrades who forged ahead toward the blackened depths of the raging creek and its heavily-timbered environs, Lieutenant Elisha Bostwick never forgot Washington's close call. When "passing a Slanting Slippery bank [of Jacob's Creek] his excellency's horse['s] hind feet both slip'd from under him."[44]

When the hind legs of Washington's war horse, without its feet properly shod for winter weather with "ice-shoes," buckled on the snowy slope, the frightened animal started to slide rearward. It now seemed that Washington was just about to pitch forward over the horse's head and be thrown headlong onto the frozen ground to very likely break his neck. However, the commander-in-chief, a "splendid horseman," demonstrated his masterful equestrian skill and easy agility.

Fortunately, the brawny Washington was of sufficient size (six foot, three inches) and strength to quickly shift his weight with an experienced horseman's natural graceful ease. With inordinately large hands, the powerful Virginian, therefore, literally manhandled the skittish, panicked animal to salvage the precarious situation. Acting on instinct and well-honed skill, Washington instantly "Siez'd his horses Mane [to jerk its head upright] & the horse recovered" its balance at the last second. Demonstrating superior equestrian ability, he had adroitly shifted his weight just in time, allowing the frightened horse to regain its balance on the icy slope.

A master fox-hunter who had long roamed Virginia's fields, woodlands, and meadows during the excitement of the chase, Washington had handled horses for most of his life. And now these finely honed skills suddenly reappeared and fortunately for this struggling army and America's struggle for liberty, when needed the most at a remote place in Hunterdon County, New Jersey, called Jacob's Creek. Belatedly, some nearby soldiers grabbed Washington's horse in an attempt to stabilize the panicked animal, but by then it was too late. Almost certainly, the horse would have fallen over and very likely crushed its rider without the Virginian's "equestrian tour de force" that revealed not only his master horsemanship, but also nerves of steel in a crucial situation.[45] One officer later marveled at Washington's mastery of horses, writing how "it is the general himself who breaks all his own horses; and he is a very excellent and bold horseman, leaping the highest fences, and going extremely quickly, without standing upon his stirrups, bearing on the bridle, or letting his horse run wild."[46]

Here, at rain-swollen Jacob's Creek, therefore, the commander-in-chief's own considerable horsemen skills saved him from a serious, perhaps fatal, injury that might well have sabotaged any chances for success at Trenton. Only recently on the Pennsylvania shore, Brigade Major Daniel Box had received a severe compound fracture to his left arm, leaving him crippled thereafter, when his horse slipped on the ice and fell hard. Washington possessed a well-deserved reputation as one of the best equestrians not only in the army, but also in Tidewater Virginia. This close brush with disaster on the slippery slope of Jacob's Creek reconfirmed that lofty reputation. Had Washington fallen and had been seriously hurt, the psychological and moral blow on his young troops almost certainly would been devastating at this time.[47]

Seemingly always on target with his analysis, Captain Hamilton fully realized as much, writing how Washington was "essential to the safety of America."[48] Once again and as written earlier in a letter, Washington could now admit that "providence . . . has been more bountiful to me than I deserve" in this struggle for liberty.[49]

All the while, this cyclonic northeaster continued to unleash successive, unrelenting bands of rain, sleet, and snow, propelled by high northeast winds, upon the thin column that stretched out along the Bear Tavern Road, while additional units piled up upon entering the heavily timbered ravine of Jacob's Creek. Supposedly two of Washington's officers allegedly froze to death on this march, but this was only a popular tale and romantic embellishment of the mythical revolution. Indeed, this enduring story of the two soldiers freezing to death cannot be verified, nor the names of the two alleged victims. But the storm's harshness certainly possessed the potential to take lives. Young Captain William Hull, a scholarly Connecticut friend of Nathan Hale now serving in Glover's brigade, and even though familiar with New England's severe winters, scribbled in a January 1, 1777 letter to Andrew Adams how what he now experienced was "as violent a storm as I ever felt."[50]

Fortunately, Washington's soldiers were now less exposed to the raging storm, after they descended from higher ground and into the deep ravine of Jacob's Creek. The ravine's deepness provided some slight protection from the storm's worst punishment, especially from the full force of icy northeast winds that cut like a knife. As in crossing the Delaware, the greatest challenge posed by the sharp descent into Jacob's Creek was for the passage of Knox's artillery.

Colonel Knox now faced yet another severe crisis and a quandary of how to get all eighteen cannon down the steep slope of more than one hundred feet along a narrow slope, across the rain-swollen creek, and then up the other side of the deep gorge of Jacob's Creek without serious mishap.

At the head of Greene's main column, proper, before Mercer's brigade that moved just behind Stephen's Virginian vanguard of three regiments, the foremost battery, which had rushed from Philadelphia to reach Trenton on December 4 after receiving urgent orders to join Washington's Army three days before, that now approached Jacob's Creek's valley was Captain Thomas Forrest's Second Company of the Philadelphia State Artillery. Forrest's company consisted of two big six-pounders and two five and one half-inch howitzers. Captain Forrest and his fifty-two Pennsylvania cannoneers now gained the assistance of a good many strong-armed infantrymen to help in the laborious task of safety transporting across treacherous Jacob's Creek.

It was most appropriate and not an accident that Forrest's battery of four guns was now positioned at the head of Greene's column and, therefore, the first battery to be hauled down into the deep, timber-filled ravine of Jacob's Creek. This fine artillery unit could be counted on in a pitch. In fact, Captain Forrest's battery was one of the few "long-arm" commands in Knox's Artillery that possessed a good deal of solid pre-war militia experience, extending back to the Associators of Pennsylvania. Forrest's artillery command was an extralegal paramilitary organization, or a so-called association, that was in essence only a militia unit because the Quakers had refused to organize armed forces for Pennsylvania's protection since they were pacifists. Pennsylvania's Associators of Philadelphia had been first formed in 1747 for self-defense outside the apathetic Quaker-dominated government. Therefore, Forrest's artillery company was a state unit, which proudly represented Pennsylvania longer than most commands, infantry or artillery, which transferred from state to Continental service. Consisting of more than fifty rough-and-ready Philadelphians who possessed solid training and high motivation, Forrest's artillery unit had been first organized for the defense of America's largest city and its waterway approaches in mid-October 1776.

Captain Forrest, born in Philadelphia in 1747, the same year that the Associatiors (militia) had been founded in Philadelphia, and despite only in his twenties, was an excellent artillery commander. He was just the kind of bold, imaginative, and tactically flexible "long-arm" officer with aggressive instincts, who Washington needed to play a key role in the upcoming showdown at

Trenton. With solid experience as an Associator, Forrest was commissioned captain by Pennsylvania authorities in Ireland-born Colonel Thomas Procter's Pennsylvania State Artillery Battalion on October 5, 1776. Forrest's Second Company of Procter's Battalion had departed the Delaware River defenses of Fort Island, before proceeding northeast up this river of destiny to join Washington's Army. For the upcoming showdown at Trenton, Forrest depended upon capable top lieutenants, such as Irishman Lieutenant Patrick Duffy, who was every inch a Celtic-Gaelic fighter. Now Captain Forrest's best lieutenant, this feisty Irish officer hated the Hessians for a variety of reasons, describing them as nothing more than "Savages." Most importantly, this Philadelphia artillery company was in much better shape than Washington's other artillery units by this time, because it had been thankfully spared the New York Campaign's brutal decimation, and Forrest's unit had been bolstered by recent recruitment.[51]

Clearly, it was no coincidence that this excellent Pennsylvania State artillery command and its resourceful, dependable commander had been selected to head Washington's main column (Second Division) under Greene, leading the way for the foremost infantry brigade under Mercer, just behind Stephen's Virginia vanguard of soldiers in their trademark hunting shirts under extra layers of other clothing. In a key tactical decision that was destined to pay off at Trenton, Washington demonstrated considerable tactical insight by having placed the best-trained and most-disciplined artillery units at the column's head. Relying on keen "long-arm" insights and sage judgment that revealed his full appreciation of his artillery's previously untapped capabilities and potential, Washington knew that the prowess of Forrest's Pennsylvania cannoneers would be vital at the battle's very beginning at a time, when there could be no margin for error, ensuring that he early gained the upper hand as soon as possible once the contest opened.

Therefore, only the most experienced artillery commanders and most disciplined gunners had been placed at the column's van by Washington. But yet another key factor explained why Washington and Knox had assigned Forrest's four cannon to the head of Greene's column. Just from Philadelphia and unlike most of Knox's other artillery units which had either lost or depleted much of their ammunition during the arduous New York Campaign and its futile battles of summer and fall, Captain Forrest's company possessed an abundant supply of powder and shot, if the Hessian troops counterattacked with their usual aggressiveness and most lethal offensive asset in the manner of Frederick the Great, the bayonet.

And most importantly, as Washington and Knox fully realized, Forrest's artillerymen also now carried more grapeshot and canister, which was smaller than grapeshot, than any other artillery unit in the main strike force. Both grapeshot and canister were the gunner's premier anti-personnel ammunition that essentially transformed cannon into giant shotguns: an advantage that would prove especially valuable at Trenton. Scores of large (grapeshot) and small (canister) iron balls inflicted terrible damage upon dense ranks of infantry, especially at close range, knocking down footsoldiers like tenpins and breaking up even the most determined assault, including those launched with the bayonet.

While the small wooden artillery ammunition carts and ammunition side boxes, firmly fitted on gun carriages, of Forrest's company contained only 132 six-pounder round shot, the confident Philadelphia captain now possessed a disproportionate supply of canister, 467 loads, and "Grape," at 161 loads for his two six-pounders and two five and a half-inch howitzers. Thanks to having retreated so close to Philadelphia by early December, Washington was most fortunate to have gained the city's premier battery, especially since its combat capabilities were enhanced by such a disproportionate share of canister and grape—destined to be Washington's most devastating secret weapon at Trenton—only because these guns had been principally supplied with this latter type of ammunition best calculated to rip apart the sails and rigging of attacking British warships in defense of Philadelphia's water approaches.

Washington's foresight guaranteed that his most lethal artillery unit was positioned at the head of his main attack column, where he himself rode in the forefront, which then followed by Captain Hamilton's two New York six-pounders at the front of Stirling's Delaware, Pennsylvania, and Virginia brigade. Such key factors explained why this single artillery company of all Captain Proctor's Philadelphia Artillery Battalion had been pulled from Philadelphia's defenses to assist Washington in his greatest hour of need.

Indeed, Knox's best artillery unit and most reliable "long-arm" commander, Forrest, who was destined to gain a major's rank only days after his upcoming sparkling Trenton performance, and his able top lieutenants, Emerald Islander Duffy and Lieutenant Worley Emes, continued to occupy the most advanced artillery position in Washington's column. In fact, Forrest was a better choice for his key mission at the head of Greene's Second Division than the ever-cantankerous Captain Procter, who was known for his ultra-independent ways, hot Irish temper, and quarrelsome nature. For the upcoming stern challenge at Trenton, Washington needed everyone, especially his top officers and unit commanders, both infantry and artillery, to work closely together and in harmony as a team and to obey his orders without question.

As Washington fully realized, Forrest's state artillery command from the cosmopolitan, heavily ethnic environment of Philadelphia was a most dependable unit in a crisis situation. At this time, Forrest's command consisted of many foreign-born gunners, especially Irish, including cannoneers, who had gained artillery experience aboard British ships before the American Revolution. But the lofty level of training, experience, and discipline of Forrest's Philadelphia cannoneers was unable to makeup for what they now lacked in clothing, especially footwear, during the march on Trenton. In a letter, Lieutenant Duffy recently described how his urbanite young artillerymen from Philadelphia were "very much Nonplus'd for Shoes and Watch Coats." Likewise, Captain Forrest complained how his Pennsylvania boys suffered severely from the "want of Shoes and Watch Coats," and lacked "Regimental Coats."[52] Unfortunately, for Washington's men, it was "as if they [Congress] thought Men were made of Stocks or Stones and equally insensible of frost and Snow," in the general's own frustrated words.[53]

But in truth, Forrest's gunners were most fortunate compared to so many fellow Pennsylvanians of Washington's Army. More than three thousand Pennsylvania and Philadelphia soldiers, consisting of the state's best troops, had been captured, primarily at Fort Washington, while another 1,500 captive men of the Pennsylvania Flying Camp had died of disease, primarily from the ravages of typhoid fever. With white-tailed deer tails and turkey feathers in tricorn and slouch hats, these young men and boys from Pennsylvania had naively marched off to war with delusions of glory, as if embarking upon a romantic adventure in a bygone age. Instead, these innocents had only found the ugly reality of a seemingly endless series of disasters and tragic deaths across New York and New Jersey, while Pennsylvania failed to galvanize an effective home state defense, especially on the threatened western frontier which faced Indian attacks.[54]

Captain Forrest and his Pennsylvania state artillerymen now served with a heightened determination not only to protect their vulnerable home city at the head of Delaware Bay, but also to avenge the loss of so many fallen and imprisoned comrades, many who were now rapidly dying of disease in and around New York City. While Washington's infantrymen rested in line in the bone-numbing cold before entering the deep ravine of Jacob's Creek, the young artillerymen from Philadelphia went to work with zeal. A long way from his Connecticut home where even those Canadian-like bitter winters seldom seemed as cold as during this storm that now so tightly gripped the Delaware Valley, Lieutenant Elisha Bostwick described the preparations for getting all of Knox's artillery down the precarious, icy slope to cross Jacob's Creek, "Our [artillery] horses were then unharness'd & the artillerymen prepared" for yet another stern challenge.[55]

With scores of men employing a lengthy artillery rope in yet another strenuous undertaking, field pieces began to be carefully hauled down the snow-slick slope leading to Jacob's Creek. Sturdy oak and hickory trees served as firm mooring posts by which leverage and muscle could be best utilized by both cannoneers and infantrymen to gingerly lower field pieces down the ravine's steep slope. This time-consuming task was especially daunting because the barrel and carriage of just one of Forrest's six-pounders weighed more than a thousand pounds. Along with Washington, anxious artillery officers watched closely, shouting orders and supervising the delicate operation. As he fully realized, Washington could not afford to lose a single field piece, especially after having been so laboriously brought across the Delaware and so far down the Bear Tavern Road, when he was about to face a full Hessian brigade that had never lost a battle.

Only a slight fracture, especially if clogged with ice, in a fragile, slender wooden artillery wheel or gun carriage could render a light field piece immobile and inoperable. Therefore, all eighteen cannon of Knox's cannon had to be carefully manhandled down the steep slope by already exhausted men and then pulled across the swirling, dark waters rushing over the banks. And then the entire time-consuming process—beginning with Forrest's Pennsylvania guns—had to be repeated up the northern edge of the equally steep slope on the opposite, or southern, side of the fast-moving creek, which flowed west and descended toward the Delaware along a steady, but very gradual, drop in terrain.

Already emaciated, underfed, and not yet recovered from the long retreat across New Jersey, exhausted artillery horses proved too weak to pull the iron and bronze cannon out of the muddy creek bottom, and then uphill on the creek's other side. Therefore, soldier manpower, despite already worn-down by the crossing's and march's rigors, completed the arduous task of pulling the cumbersome field pieces, whose wheels cut deeply in the muddy bottoms, up the snowy slope.

While the road dropped sharply from the high ground almost to the creek's north bank, where only a relatively narrow level section of wooded bottom ground bordered Jacob's Creek at this point, the artillerymen's work was somewhat easier because a broader stretch of level ground, or creek bottom, stood immediately on the creek's south side. Here, the wet, exhausted artillerymen briefly rested, before the imposing task of pushing up and pulling the guns up the sloping ground on the creek's other side. However, by this time, much of the creek bottoms, especially on the more level south side, was partially flooded by the creek's overflowing waters.

Therefore, even more precious time was lost in the snowy, densely timbered depths of Jacob's Creek, with Washington's unrealistic timetable continuing to fall apart beyond all recognition. But at last, Knox's final artillery piece, the eighteenth gun, was taken across the high, brown waters of Jacob's Creek by thoroughly soaked artillerymen, after more backbreaking labor. As in the Delaware crossing, not a single artillery piece was lost in traversing the gorge-like depression of Jacob's Creek. Fortunately, small rocks, generally flat and worn smooth by water erosion, along the creek bottoms helped to ensure that none of Washington's cannon became permanently mired in the mud, and that no slender artillery wheels splintered into pieces.

In addition, the crossing of such a relatively smooth creek bottom of mostly flat rocks also meant that none of Washington's men broke ankles or legs on a pitch-black night, when few soldiers could see their own hands before their faces in the storm. By this time, the hard-working artillerymen, wet and muddy from the creek crossing, were now thoroughly exhausted, but their challenges were only beginning on this unforgettable morning in Hunterdon County. Once finally across the imposing obstacle of Jacob's Creek, Captain Forrest and his Philadelphia artillerymen again took their assigned places at the head of Greene's column to resume the trek down the Bear Tavern Road, nestled in the midst of a primeval wilderness that continued to slow Washington's progress and ambition of reaching Trenton as soon as possible.[56] With no margin for error and racing the clock, Washington had embarked upon the kind of desperate venture that he had cautioned John Hancock about only recently in September: "We should on all occasions avoid a general action or put anything to the risque [risk], unless compelled by a necessity, into which we ought never to be drawn."[57]

Fortunately for Washington's exhausted men, the Bear Tavern Road now turned sharply to the right, or west, almost immediately upon reaching the creek's other side to follow the creek bottom's mostly level ground, instead of ascending all the way up a small, wooded hill before them to the south, or directly opposite from where they had crossed the raging watercourse. Here, the road turned abruptly to follow the more favorable lay of the land, with Washington's troops trudging west down the slightly plunging wooded hollow of the creek bottoms, sandwiched between forested hills to the north and south, which gently dropped toward the Delaware to the west.

Because the flooded creek flowed straight west toward the Delaware, so the road now ran in the same direction in following the easiest topography, with both the creek and the road running parallel and dipping slightly westward through the timbered hollow, now filled with a crowd of marching men with muskets on shoulders. All the while, the stoic Continentals, never more wet and miserable, yet remained quiet as ordered by Washington, moving onward with a firm determination to reach Trenton before it was too late. Washington continued to play an essential role in keeping the winding column pushing forward, despite all the obstacles and impediments met along the way.

Not long after the painfully slow crossing of the troublesome Jacob's Creek, yet another east-west flowing watercourse (like Jacob's Creek), that ran through its own wooded ravine, was shortly encountered by Stephen's three regiments of seasoned Virginians at the head of Washington's column. Known as Ewing Creek, this smaller, but equally rain-swollen, watercourse flowed slightly perpendicular, by the time it entered Jacob's Creek from the east, to the Jacob's Creek ravine that ran generally east-west at this point. With a rapid rush of water overlapping its banks, this formerly inconsequential, peaceful creek was now confronted by Washington's tired men not long after they pushed only a short distance down Bear Tavern Road, after turning sharply west through the blackened woodlands draped in snow.

Now consumed by a fast-flowing torrent, Ewing Creek was a tributary of Jacob's Creek, and was located just south of the first crossing point. Presenting yet another nasty surprise for Washington and his soldiers this morning, this overflowing tributary entered the main creek just east, or a short distance down Jacob's Creek, of where the main strike force had already passed over. Even though the bottoms of both Jacob's and Ewing Creeks merged into one where they intersected amid the dish-shaped timbered hollow, this challenging feature of topography ensured that Washington's soldiers now encountered yet another deep ravine amid a thick virgin woodlands by which the entire laborious process of the combined efforts of both artillerymen and infantrymen in hauling the artillery across high waters had to be repeated: an exhausting task that continued to cost more precious time. Finally, after another difficult struggle against the triumvirate of nature, weariness, and the harsh elements, the second ravine carved out by the waters of Jacob's Creek, or its flooded southern tributary, was likewise overcome, after Washington's troops had additionally exerted themselves on a hellish night that no one would ever forget, and seemed to have no end.

After safely crossing to Ewing Creek's timbered southwest side, the Bear Tavern Road then turned sharply to the left, or south, from its westerly direction parallel to Jacob's Creek, and the terrain ascended sharply out of the heavily wooded, dual depths of Jacob's Creek and Ewing Creek bottoms now covered in a thick blanket of ice and snow. While trusty flintlocks on shoulders and under the uncomfortable weight of packs, knapsacks, weapons, sixty rounds of ammunition and rations for three days, the foremost of Washington's men began to lurch up the slippery slope, finally leaving the troublesome wooded lowlands of the twin creeks behind. With nothing but their will and the last, ever-diminishing reserves of strength pushing them relentlessly onward through the falling snow, the Continentals once again struggled up another steep slope to reach higher ground: another generally level plateau of this alien wilderness region. Finally escaping the depths of the creek bottoms and rugged forested ravines, Washington's troops felt a small measure of relief upon gaining the more level ground that provided for easier marching for sore legs and feet, after the grueling crossings of the twin obstacles of Jacob's and Ewing Creeks.

At long last straightening out like an arrow, the Bear Tavern Road now ran in a southeastward direction, just like it had before the column's deep descent into the gorge-like ravine of Jacob's Creek. At this point just south of Jacob's Creek, the key intersection of the Bear Tavern Road and the Upper Ferry Road, that led to Howell's Ferry on the Delaware to the southwest, was located barely two miles distant and farther down this snowy road just to the southeast.

Finally, with the entire infantry column and all eighteen artillery pieces having emerged unscathed almost miraculously out of the deep, timbered hollow of both Jacob's Creek and Ewing Creek, Washington's march proceeded steadily south over the whitish landscape and down the Bear Tavern Road toward Trenton. Leaving no details overlooked in their micro-management style, both Washington and Knox made sure that the carefully chosen artillery, the two six-pounders and two five and a half-inch howitzers, continued to advance at the column's head proper, or Mercer's Connecticut, Maryland, and Massachusetts brigade, and before each following brigade of Continental troops with an ever-decreasing number of cannon.

Fortunately for Washington's exhausted men, the torturous march down the Bear Tavern Road now became somewhat easier. Toiling onward through the snow, Washington's troops continued south to enter the northern edge of yet another plateau, where the land leveled out once again. Thankfully for the foot-sloggers, the terrain and the road continued to gently rise, leveled out again, and then dipped slightly, before again ascending over ever-rising ground that led south. Better time was now made by the marching troops because the column proceeded across favorable terrain that gradually now rose higher to a wind-swept elevation of around 250 feet. Here, at this high point, the winds howled more fiercely, sweeping the thin column of long-suffering men and sending a deeper chill through Washington's sojourners, who continued to stumble onward in the bitter night in the hopeful of salvaging something positive out of this New Jersey ordeal.

Most importantly and fortunately for Washington, this generally more level terrain allowed for Knox's artillery, especially Captain Forrest's Pennsylvania guns, to keep up at the column's head (Mercer's brigade), and each following Continental brigade, with exhausted horses straining harder in pulling the creaking artillery pieces over a snowy landscape drenched in an omnipresent blackness. Clearly, with artillery pieces now moving forward at the head of columns and brigades, the dynamic team of Washington and Knox, who both fully appreciated artillery's decisiveness on the battlefield, were setting the stage for placing their guns in the most advantageous position and then utilizing them in an aggressive manner once the fighting erupted.

In the December 18, 1776 words of Colonel Knox, who had learned his artillery lessons well during the New York Campaign, which emphasized how it was now time to take a page out of the military manual of the British, who utilized the most effective artillery arm in America: "They scarcely or ever detach a single Regiment without two or three field pieces; the regulations of their artillery are founded upon the most convincing experience of their utility, & we shall have no reason to blush by imitating them in those particulars."[58]

Meanwhile, most of Washington's common soldiers knew not yet exactly where they were headed in the cold darkness or their exact mission, thanks to their commander's penchant for secrecy. Consequently, this exhaustive march deeper into an unknown country of virgin wilderness and the New Jersey blackness remained a mystery. Young men and boys from across America, therefore, continued to place a blind, almost religious-like faith in Washington's leadership and ability, despite him having been at the head of so many recent defeats and fiascos: a rather remarkable vote of confidence under the circumstances. In purely logical terms, the common soldier's faith in the commander-in-chief was hardly fully justified at this time, however.

Consequently, these relatively few Continental and state soldiers who remained with Washington were now the staunchest believers in what their commander-in-chief could achieve against the odds, when few others possessed any faith in the Virginian's tactical abilities. Many people sincerely believed that Washington was entirely unfit to command even a sergeant's guard. Knowing that the stoic Virginian was trapped in a no-win situation, General Anthony Wayne wrote how "My heart bleeds for poor Washington," but relatively few others in America were so sympathetic.

Fueling their faith and strengthening badly frayed belief systems, these resolute fighting men were convinced that America possessed a special destiny and held a promising future for a free people. Most of all, they were convinced that God yet supported America in its life-and-death struggle, because this higher moral law superseded the arbitrary rule of George III and Parliament. Almost instinctively, teenage Private Greenwood, who now carried both a musket and his favorite fife, knew that this blind reliance in Washington's highly questionable leadership ability was somewhat a risky gamble in itself, but an absolutely necessary vote of confidence, if an important victory was to be secured for America. Therefore, he waxed philosophically: "None of the officers knew where we were going or what we were going about, for it was a secret expedition, and we, the bulk of the men [knew] anything about the country [of western New Jersey but] This was not unusual, however, as I never heard soldiers say anything, nor ever saw them trouble themselves, as to where they were or where they were led. It was enough for them to know that wherever the officers commanded they must go, be it through fire and water, for it was all the same owing to the impossibility of being in a worse condition than their present one, and therefore the men always liked to be kept moving in expectation of bettering themselves" and their country's sinking fortunes.[59] Under such severe adversity on the torturous march to Trenton, perhaps some of Washington's men recalled the inspiring lyrics of a popular song ("Chester"), which emphasized, "Let tyrants shake their iron rod, And slavery clank her galling chains . . . We fear them not; we trust in God."[60] Washington's soldiers also felt the heavy responsibility of literally carrying America's fate and future with them on the trek to Trenton, because, in Sam Adams' words, they were "now the guardians of [our] own liberties."[61]

For such reasons, Washington looked with a sense of admiration upon these young men and boys, who "act from the noblest of all Principles, Love of Freedom and their Country."[62] But the iron discipline now displayed in the ranks was what most of all impressed Washington, who had long believed that "it is Subordination and Discipline (the Life and Soul of an Army), which next under Providence, is to make us formidable to our enemies, honourable in ourselves, and respected in the world."[63]

Perhaps some of Greenwood's Fifteenth Massachusetts comrades, including a good many Continental soldiers from the picturesque Connecticut community of Litchfield, which "was situated on a large plain more elevated than the surrounding terrain," wrote one officer, realized that whatever they now endured, it was far worse for their unfortunate friends, relatives, and neighbors captured at Long Island and Fort Washington. Such harsh realities only made Washington's troops more determined to succeed this morning at all costs. Therefore, a pent-up longing for revenge was another factor that also motivated Washington's soldiers to keep moving through the blowing snow and toward whatever unknown fate lay in store for them to the south. Of the thirty-two Litchfield soldiers captured at Fort Washington, for instance, twenty had already died in the disease-ridden New York prisons and death ships, while another half dozen of Litchfield's sons eventually succumbed on the death march journey back home to their same agricultural community of "about fifty houses pretty near each other, with a large square . . . in the middle," after their release from a prison hell. Counting the four men killed in Fort Washington's ill-advised defense at Manhattan Island's north end in mid-November, only six soldiers, out of the original thirty-six, ever returned to see their homes and families at Litchfield, nested in a little valley in northwest Connecticut, or Litchfield Hills, again.[64]

On this frigid night amid the windswept forests north of Trenton, Washington's soldiers, without gloves or mittens and some without socks or shoes, suffered the early stages of hypothermia. The night's cold had thoroughly numbed limbs, especially lower extremities, and faces while hypothermia sapped moral, awareness, and motor skills. As the march progressed south along the ascending ground of the windswept plateau of the unfamiliar countryside, except to the handful of Hunterdon County guides and Flahaven's New Jersey Continentals, conditions only became worse. Additional feeling went out of hands and feet of an ever-increasing number of soldiers, who continued to gamely trudge ahead. Many of Washington's men no longer felt the cold's bitter sting, which was an early sign of frostbite: a gradually deteriorating physical condition not fully realized by the victim at this time, including such faithful soldiers as Ireland-born Private William McCarty. This veteran Irish soldier of Lieutenant Francis Ware's First Maryland Continental Infantry, Mercer's brigade, suffered frostbite on both feet, paying a high price for his patriotism on this terrible night.

Colonel William Smallwood's Maryland Continentals were recruited primarily from the thriving ports of Baltimore, which the exiled Congress now called home, Annapolis, and the lucrative Tidewater tobacco plantations situated among the gently rolling hills of the Maryland Piedmont. These crack Marylanders had once worn such resplendent uniforms that envious New Englanders and middle state soldiers, especially Pennsylvanians from the western frontier, openly mocked. Taunts and insults were promptly returned by the spunky Maryland boys, who were always ready for a fight. Westerners, especially the Virginians, derisively called the finely uniformed Marylanders "Maccaronies"—a popular sobriquet for dandy—not only because they wore "macaroni cocked hats," but also because they were mostly city slickers. These high-spirited "Maccaronies" consisted of a diverse ethnic mix, which included Irish, Germans, French, Scots, English, and Dutch soldiers, reflecting the varied urban and ethnic compositions of the bustling ports of Baltimore and Annapolis. But those resplendent uniforms, created by the best tailors in Baltimore and Annapolis and once worn so proudly by these planter's sons, lawyers, artisans, and merchants, were no more by this time.

On the miserable sojourn to Trenton, the majority of Washington's common soldiers now wore old slouch hats of wool or felt, like those of everyday lower- and middle-class American farmers who raised mostly hogs and corn for market and consumption, while Continental officers primarily wore the more stylish tricorn hats with decorative cockades, green-colored for junior officers and white-colored for captains: a color difference that mirrored class and economic divisions between officers and enlisted men. But no headgear now adequately protected the necks, faces, and ears of Washington's men of any rank from the searing cold of late December that made this the most nightmarish marches in the army's history.[65]

All the while, Washington was tormented not as much by the cold as by a painful "despair of surprizing [sic] the Town" of Trenton, upon which America's fortunes now hinged.[66] After pushing across the plateau's high ground, where the howling winds swept through the lengthy column like "a perfect hurricane" in one private's words, that rose to around 250 feet, the land generally leveled out. All the while, Washington's troops were unprotected from this bone-chilling force of nature, making the few blankets and coats wrapped around them flap in the gales like new leaves of a birch tree on a windy April morning. However, the excruciating march of the long column of Continentals now became a bit easier for the foot-weary, sleep-deprived soldiers, as they finally approached the little hamlet of Birmingham, now wrapped in a cocoon of snow, blackness, and silence that dominated a landscape of white as far as the eye could see.[67]

A Lonely, Frozen Crossroads in the Middle of Nowhere

Fortunately, for Washington's seemingly lost trekkers who continued to trudge ever-southward, the storm finally began to somewhat abate, but only slightly. At long last, the omnipresent mixture of rain, sleet, and snow started to lessen, increasing ever so slightly degree of visibility as Washington's troops neared the frozen crossroads, which was about half-way to Trenton. But this was only a brief lull—like another cruel practical trick played by a vengeful Mother Nature that seemed to have sided with Great Britain in this war—before the arrival of another round of even more severe weather. After pushing slightly southeast down the snowy Bear Tavern Roadand with the ground yet gently ascending, Washington's foremost soldiers at long last reached the frozen crossroads of Birmingham, which was nestled amid a twisted maze of black oak and hickory thickets, with a few scattered cedars and pines of dark green.

After the weary Americans had already trudged about five miles from the river landing site, the tiny village of Birmingham was the proverbial fork in the road for Washington and his men. Here, at yet another relative high point, where the Bear Tavern Road intersected the road that led southwest about a mile and a quarter to Howell's Ferry on the Delaware, some of Washington's exhausted soldiers felt that they could go no farther by this time. Closely monitoring his troops under the steady deluge, Washington ordered a halt for his men to rest and gain strength. While trying in vain to stay warm, worn-out Continentals rested on the snow-covered ground around the little crossroads cloaked in snow, while the howling wind whistled through the bare, swaying trees overhead, causing branches to crack and squeak in the eerie silence that griped Hunterdon County like a frozen vise.

Especially now and more needed than any previous point on the arduous march, this halt at the obscure Birmingham crossroads provided a timely respite, as the number of stragglers had increased dramatically. They now needed time to catch up to the column. Even an anxious Washington, whose stamina was legendary, was worn down—as much mentally and psychologically as physically—by "an agonizing ride" in leading his revolutionary army ever-southward on a nerve-racking march to either a rare victory or yet another disaster.

With only division and brigade commanders and staff officers mounted on war horses, most Continental officers remained on foot, suffering the same misery as the ragged privates in the ranks. No wonder, wrote Major Wilkinson, that many officers "gloomy and despondent" by the taxing ordeal. So far, young officers like Lieutenant Elisha Bostwick, who had yet to fully recover from a serious bout of sickness, had struggled to keep up his comrades of the Nineteenth Continental Infantry Regiment, under Colonel Webb. Never forgetting the sight, Bostwick described how "a halt was made at which time his Excellency & Aids came near to front on the Side of the Patch where the Soldiers Stood [to stay out of the mud and slush filling the narrow roadway and] I heard his Excellency as he was comeing [sic] on Speaking to & Encouraging the Soldiers. The words he Spoke as he pass'd by where I stood & in my hearing were these ["] Soldiers keep by your officers for Gods Sake[,] keep by your officers [which was] Spoke in a deep & Solemn voice."[68]

Throughout the past, Washington's extensive efforts in having created a capable officer corps continued to pay dividends on the weary march to Trenton. As he explained one secret of his success as a commander-in-chief, whose orders were now obeyed to the letter: "Be easy and condescending to your officers, but not too familiar, lest you subject yourself to a want of that respect which is necessary to support a proper command," especially during just such a challenging ordeal as on this miserable night.[69] As never before, Washington inspired his men, who were "engaged in the Cause of Liberty and their Country," wrote the commander-in-chief, to do the impossible.[70]

Washington's advice was sound, because officers were essential in keeping the column together and formations tight in the freezing darkness. Feeling an instinctive need to replenish bodily systems, weakened by hypothermia, worn down by the river crossing and the frigid march and perhaps believing that nourishment might somehow warm up their thoroughly chilled bodies, soldiers with half-frozen fingers removed pre-cooked rations from stiff, ice-caked haversack and knapsacks with difficulty. Then, while snow continued to drop over the isolated Birmington crossroads, hungry men eagerly took bites of their salt pork and doughy "firecake" rations. After gobbling down their cold meal, some soldiers sipped from wooden canteens, especially if they contained a much-needed mixture of water and local applejack, called "Jersey lightning" by the men—that would not freeze like plain water—to ward off the bone-numbing cold, provide stimulation, fight off hypothermia, and fortify the body and its loss of circulation against winter storm's harshness.

While the Hessians continued to sleep peacefully in Trenton's warm houses in ignorant bliss about what was happening to the north, Washington's men gobbled down a meager early morning breakfast on a seemingly ill-fated morning upon which every ounce of strength was needed. Making sure that everything was in order, Washington was too busy to eat. He held a hasty impromptu commander's conference with his generals and staff officers, reconfirming his tactical plan and last-minute requirements to his top lieutenants for the final descent upon Trenton around five miles to the south.

Earning a much-needed respite on the most demanding and longest night of their lives, young soldiers rested at this snowy hamlet of only a few little wooden houses seemingly located in the middle of nowhere. These precious moments of a sweet respite were savored, because the men knew that there would be no more breaks during these fast-fading early morning hours. Sleepless Marblehead soldiers, even more tired than Washington's other men because of their efforts in the laborious Delaware River crossing, very likely now wished that they were enjoying a warm meal of their home town's dried cod or flounder to provide nourishment instead of tasteless firecakes, and foul-tasting salt port—the staple of poor western frontier landlubbers, who had never seen the ocean before. As ordered by Washington, no fires were kindled to warm up the half-froze bodies for fear of alerting the enemy. Clearly, now that he was close to Trenton, Washington continued to take no unnecessary risks at a time when none could be afforded for America's fortunes.

Nearing 6:00 a.m. with the first breaking of a cold dawn drawing ever-nearer and now situated at the Birmingham crossroads about five miles from Trenton and an hour after his original time to have launched his attack, Washington made his last dispositions for the final descent upon Trenton. Knowing that precious time was slipping away, Washington hurriedly prepared his strike force to now operate separately as two separate divisions. Around 1,200 soldiers, mostly armed with the .75 caliber Brown Bess musket of ten and half pounds, were assigned to each column. Commanded by Generals Sullivan and Greene, each column consisted of three infantry brigades. Each column of the First (Sullivan) and Second (Greene) Divisions was composed of a lead first brigade, a middle second brigade, and finally, a third, or the so-called "reserve" brigade.

Now designated as the right wing of Washington's strike force, Sullivan and his newly designated First Division of three brigades, under Sargent, Glover, and St. Clair, respectively, were issued orders to take the southern, or lower, road that continued straight south from Birmingham before veering slightly to the right, or west. Merely a continuation of the Bear Tavern Road, this so-called River Road led first straight south and then southeast to run parallel to the river, which would allow Sullivan's First Division to advance upon Trenton and enter the town's lower end from the southwest: the southern arm of Washington's pincer movement.

Meanwhile, Greene's Second Division column was designated as the left wing, consisting of Stephen's, Mercer's, Stirling's, and Fermoy's Brigades, the reserve brigade, respectively. This left wing contingent was the main strike force of four brigades, under Washington's personal command, which planned to eventually advance upon Trenton from the northwest by way of the upper, or northern, road on the left, the Pennington Road: the northern arm of the pincer movement, or double envelopment. But first before descending south toward Trenton, Greene's column had to push more than a mile through the snow-covered woodlands to the left, or east, from the relative high ground of the Birmingham crossroads, and then down gently sloping terrain along the Upper Ferry Road, east of the crossroads. This challenging route would take the Washington-Greene column first to the Scotch Road, nearly a mile to the east through more unmapped territory. Then, from this intersection, the Scotch Road flowed south through the forests and eventually led to the Pennington Road, which ran parallel to the Scotch Road and linked Pennington, northeast of Johnson's Ferry, to Trenton, to the southeast: the more direct route that led straight south and into Trenton's northwestern edge.

Compared to Sullivan and his three First Division brigades that Washington ordered to shortly push south from Birmingham along a generally straight line down the River Road that was essentially a mere continuation of the Bear Tavern Road, Greene's assignment was the much more difficult and demanding, especially in such stormy conditions. Greene's march involved a longer route and required a greater effort in first pushing nearly a mile farther east to gain the Scotch Road before turning sharply south, or to the right. Meanwhile, east of Greene's Second Division column, Sullivan's First Division column would march straight south by a shorter parallel route along gently descending terrain by way of the River Road that sloped downhill toward the ever-troublesome river across even lower ground and all the way nearly to the Delaware's east bank.

Because Greene's route was longer, including first a march east and parallel to Trenton, and more demanding because of its longer length, Washington's orders called for Greene to proceed first, while Sullivan's troops, mostly New Englanders, rested on their arms in a tense formation amid the incessant snow flurries and blowing snow. Here, at windswept Birmingham, Sullivan's New Englanders awaited the belated signal to begin the march straight south down the River Road: a most imprecise coordination of two widely separated divisions for Washington's planned simultaneous tactical strike on Trenton from two directions. Checking every detail and making all precautions, Washington, therefore, continued to make sure that he and his officers operated by synchronized watches to coordinate the two widely separated arms of the pincer movement calculated to hit Trenton from two directions at the same time.

Significantly, Washington provided more muscle for Greene's Second Division column, with an extra Continental brigade in contrast to Sullivan's more diminutive column, because he planned to secure the commanding heights at the northern end of town—the key to the upcoming struggle for possession of Trenton. Greene's column consisted of mostly seasoned Continentals from Virginia, Pennsylvania, Delaware, Maryland, Massachusetts, and Connecticut troops, and they could be counted upon by Washington. After experiencing a series of defeats, they had endured the anguish of the humiliating retreat across New Jersey. Consequently, these men now eagerly awaited an opportunity to strike back at those yet unbeaten troops, who had pursed them in an almost festive delight. General Sullivan, meanwhile, commanded soldiers mostly from General Gates's and Lee's forces, consisting of two Massachusetts, Connecticut, New Hampshire, and New York infantry regiments.

Finding some solace in the frigid blackness while experiencing the usual pre-battle nervous apprehension with America's most important battle to date drawing near, the thirty-two-year-old General Greene, the army's mathematically minded rising star who lamented the sad realities of "this unhappy war," might have now thought about what the future might hold for his pregnant wife, pretty Caty. She was about to have her second child back at their two story wooden home, modest and plain that reflected his Quaker antecedents, which was nestled in a majestic bend of the Pawtuxet River, in Coventry, Rhode Island. During the lengthy march on Trenton, Greene very likely thought back upon what would become of his yet unnamed child, if he failed to survive Washington's most audacious gamble.[71]

In a striking paradox that revealed the extent of how this struggle was as much of a civil war as a people's revolution, the two leading Celtic commanders of each respective assault column understood this grim reality from insights gleamed from the Emerald Isle's tortured history and England's subjugation, especially so many failed uprisings of the common people. The robust but ever-energetic Knox was the son-in-law of a Loyalist, who had fled to England to escape America's internal turmoil. And Sullivan's own beloved brother, William, who was fated to be killed in this war, now wore the resplendent uniform of a British colonel.[72]

Most importantly, the eighteen guns of Knox's Regiment of Continental Artillery were divided almost equally between the two columns to bestow considerable "long-arm" strength to each pincer arm. Clearly, this was one of Washington's most significant decisions of the campaign. Washington's well-thought-out decision revealed that he fully appreciated the fact that for his double-pronged attack and double envelopment to have any real chance of succeeding, each strike column had to be significantly bolstered by an ample number of artillery pieces, especially now that wetness would certainly make a good many infantrymen's flintlocks inoperable during the storm. In fact, Washington's equitable, judicious division of artillery between Greene's and Sullivan's assault columns was a decision that the ever-artillery-minded Napoleon himself would have certainly appreciated.

Washington ordered the guns of Captains Forrest's, Hamilton's, and Baumann's commands, respectively, to accompany Greene's Second Division column, a total of nine cannon. The other nine guns of Captains Neil's, Moulder's, and Sargent's artillery units were ordered advance down the River Road with Sullivan's First Division. An exacting Washington, knowing that precision and meticulousness might spell the difference between winner and loser, continued to make sure that four artillery pieces would advance at each column's head, with three guns at the head of the next, or second, brigade in the center of each separate column, and two cannon with the final brigade, or reserves. Such careful placement of these iron and bronze guns ensured the early deployment of artillery to guarantee a disproportionate, if not decisive, impact by massing heavy firepower at the most decisive point in the earliest stage of the upcoming contest for Trenton's possession.

Consequently, Captain Forrest's four guns, the big six-pounders and two five and a half-inch howitzers, would continue to advance at the head of Greene's main column, proper just before Mercer's brigade, just behind Stephen's van-guard brigade of Virginians. Washington's insightful decision—Napoleonic in concept—was as unorthodox as it was tactically sound and vital. Such forward artillery placement guaranteed not only early firepower superiority over his

Hessian opponent once the battle opened, but also bestowed tactical flexibility. Washington, therefore, planned to possess a considerably enhanced tactical flexibility to maneuver and shift his artillery to the most advantageous and strategic positions to either support the initial attack with overwhelming firepower, or to parry any emerging threat, especially a German counterattack: a maximum and highly flexible utilization of artillery firepower, which if combined with the element of surprise, was calculated by the visionary Washington to deliver a powerful one-two punch to the Rall brigade.

However, the careful placement of the four pieces of artillery with the lead brigade at the column's head was yet a risky gamble. After all, if Washington's surprise attack was early detected or faltered in the very beginning, and the Hessians quickly employed their favorite tactic of counterattacking with the bayonet, then Washington's most advanced artillery would be in jeopardy. But remaining positive and optimistic despite the series of setbacks, a resolute Washington was not thinking about losing the initiative or suffering a reversal. Most of all, in a well-calculated gamble, the former Virginia militia colonel was now going for broke, winner take all. By stacking the odds in his favor as much as possible and in relying upon a brilliant battleplan, Washington increased his chances for success, because neither his nation or army could now afford another setback of any kind.

All in all, Washington was about to undertake what was actually a most prudent gamble with so much at stake. By relying upon stealth and the element of surprise, Washington, consequently, planned to completely overpower Rall's brigade as swiftly as possible, before these elite German troops had a chance to counterattack with their customary aggressiveness. And this most vital of tactical objectives could best be secured by an early application of an overwhelming amount of massed artillery firepower concentrated along the high ground north of Trenton to hit the Hessian garrison early and as hard as possible and then to unleash infantry assaults from multiple directions simultaneously.

Washington, consequently, had gathered every available gun and brought all of his artillery across the river not just to support the upcoming attack, but also to blast neatly aligned Hessian formation to pieces before they could launch a counterstroke. With such hard-hitting tactical views in mind, both Washington and Knox, his artillery commander par excellence, wanted to unleash even more firepower than the available eighteen cannon, however. Therefore, a specially picked detachment of seasoned artillerymen advanced near the head of both assault columns. These well-trained cannoneers, not assigned artillery pieces, now carried extra artillery equipment to man any captured Hessian three-pounders. In fact, Washington's farsighted desire to secure additional cannon on the battlefield played an early role in his decision to attack Trenton. After all, by capturing all the artillery (half a dozen guns) of the Rall brigade, then the commander-in-chief would be able to provide his artillery-short army with more than 30 percent more guns to raise the total strength of Knox's artillery arm from eighteen to twenty-four field pieces.

Captains Hamilton's and Baumann's artillery units—now at the head of Mercer's and Stirling's brigade, respectively—had been originally raised by New York to defend the strategic Hudson Highlands, located north of New York City and nestled between that cosmopolitan city and Albany, New York. But now these two New York artillery units were assigned to Greene's Second Division column so that these well-served guns would be engaged sidebyside once the battle opened. At this time, Baumann's artillery command, in which a German-born commander led primarily non-German cannoneers, was Knox's second largest artillery unit with eighty gunners. Meanwhile, Captain Moulder's Philadelphia unit of three four-pounders possessed the largest number of cannoneers, with eighty-five artillerymen. However, by this time, Lieutenant Cuthbert's artillerymen of Moulder's company, whose members hailed from the gritty east Philadelphia waterfront, were the most worn-out of any of Washington's gunners, after their efforts in assisting Glover's Marblehead mariners ferrying hundreds of troops during the nightmarish Delaware crossing.

What was also tactically significant was the fact that the forward-thinking Washington retained the smallest artillery units, or lightest, in terms of manpower for the main attack column to ensure greater mobility and tactical flexibility, once the battle at Trenton erupted in all its fury. Indeed, Captain Hamilton's command possessed the least number of artillerymen with only thirty-six cannoneers but perhaps as low as thirty-two, while the next smallest artillery command was Forrest's "long-arm" company with fifty-two gunners. Clearly, as revealed by his careful placement of artillery with each column, Washington fully appreciated how the key to determine the forthcoming engagement's outcome called for the simple equation and tactical requirement that meant getting his largest and best cannon to the front and deployed as quickly as possible on the high ground just north of Trenton to command the entire town.

With a keen eye for topography after having earlier passed through Trenton during the early December withdrawal, Washington had kept the important topographical knowledge of the exact location of the best and most advantageous high ground situated north of Trenton in his mind. He knew that this lofty perch on the town's northern outskirts was about to become the battlefield's key if he could catch the Hessians by surprise and first place Knox's artillery atop the commanding heights to dominate the entire town and the river valley below. Therefore, only the most reliable, flexible, and maneuverable artillery unit, with the largest size guns—Captain Forrest's six-pounders and the five and a half-inch howitzers—were employed at the head of Greene's main column, proper, so that it would be the first to unleash this formidable firepower from a high ground perch as soon as possible at the battle's beginning.[73]

Amid the bitter cold and oppressive pall of apprehension surrounding the frozen crossroads at Birmingham, while the snow continued to softly cascade down in silence and the winter winds blew unceasingly to make blankets now covering soldiers flap, Washington made other final last-minute preparations and adjustments. Knowing that no detail could be overlooked, he now seemed to be everywhere at once, while his men now either rested on muskets or tried to force back some feeling to cold-numbed feet in the frigid darkness.

By this time, the early stages of frostbite was setting in and affecting outermost extremities of a good many soldiers. Blood veins in limbs narrowed, with blood flowing from hands and feet to the heart for protecting the body from the intense cold, leaving human tissue vulnerable to actual freezing. Washington's long-suffering troops were now tired almost beyond endurance. Some soldiers thought about little but sleep, after mind-numbing fatigue had slowly eaten away at the morale and stamina.

From high-ranking general to lowly private, these young men and boys found no answer about how to stay warm. Here, at the darkened, obscure crossroads of Birmingham consumed by the storm's wrath and heightened apprehension, Washington's soldiers mustered their last ounces of strength and stamina for the many stiff challenges yet ahead. Some soldiers, most likely Glover's seamen because of their strenuous crossing efforts that had spanned too many hours to remember, perhaps now catnapped on the cold ground around the Birmingham crossroads, ignoring the steadily piling up of the snow around them in their mind-numbing fatigue.

Never more alert or vigilant despite the cold and misery, Washington continued to leave nothing to chance. He made sure that at least two mounted guides, local "farmers," but also including Hunterdon County militiamen, would continue to lead the advance at the head of each column, once he gave the final order to move out into more unknown countryside north of Trenton bathed in white. All the while, young soldiers became increasingly more anxious, not knowing what to expect in the hours ahead. They thought of God and far-away homes and families, who had just celebrated Christmas, in these frozen moments at the lonely Birmingham crossroads.

Much had to be on Captain John Mott's anxiety-ridden mind while he continued to serve as a knowledgeable guide because he knew the Trenton area so well. A member of Gates's northern army, he had been recently scouring Hunterdon County to recruit men for the New Jersey Line. Mott lived near the Hermitage, the stately home of Philemon Dickinson situated on the river bottoms and located just south of the River Road, northwest of Trenton and about two-thirds of the way down the River Road from Birmingham to Trenton. Much like General Greene, Mott had forsaken the core pacifist beliefs of his Quaker roots to engage in America's struggle for liberty. Like so many other New Jersey soldiers, he had some very personal scores to settle with the Hessians. Now haunted by those searing memories of the hated invaders, he had only recently defended his home and family against a forging party of half a dozen Hessians. Mott had killed two Teutonic intruders with his family under threat on Sunday December 22. However, Mott's spirited defense of home and family came at a high price. Mott had been forced to flee for his life to escape the inevitable retaliation. He then rejoined Washington's Army to avenge his family's suffering.

While the dropping snow and whipping winds swirled around the forlorn hamlet of Birmingham, Washington continued to make last-minute precautions at the crossroads amid the seemingly haunted forests—silent, eerie, and blackened in the night—northwest of Trenton. Washington ordered that all flaming torches, which had been set up on artillery carriages to enhance visibility for gunners in transporting the artillery pieces, be extinguished to ensure that the final descent upon Trenton would not be betrayed to any advanced enemy scouts or patrols. As throughout the night, no single detail was too small for Washington's careful calculation or meticulous consideration. Stemming from his experience in managing the vast acreage of Mount Vernon, Washington's eye for minutiae and exact detail was absolutely essential for any future tactical success, and the commander-in-chief was excelling in this crucial regard. But more important and seemingly for the first time on this early December 26 that seemed preordained for yet another American fiasco, the gods of war, luck, or fortune now began to smile upon Washington, because no such formidable natural obstacles, as Jacob's Creek or Ewing's Creek, now lay threateningly before either Greene's or Sullivan's columns for the remainder of the march to Trenton.[74]

Far ahead to the southeast and north of Trenton, meanwhile, Captain Washington's advance party of Virginians gained possession of the Pennington Road and an advanced point along the Princeton Road, setting up blocking positions. In Lieutenant Monroe's words: "Captain Washington executed his orders faithfully. He soon took possession of the point to which he was ordered, and holding it through the night, intercepted and made prisoners of many who were passing in directions to and from Trenton."[75]

Meanwhile, after having already established a blocking force on the River Road, Captain Flahaven's New Jersey Continentals were reassigned to the head of Sullivan's column to lead the advance down the River Road. Despite their weariness, Flahaven's half-frozen New Jersey boys once again headed off through the falling snow on their own, disappearing into the cold darkness while venturing down the River Road, before Sullivan's First Division advanced. Both column's advance parties—seasoned Virginians under Captain Washington and less experienced, but capable, New Jersey boys under Captain Flahaven—accomplished their key missions of keeping Trenton effectively cut off from the outside world on three sides, north, west, and east, until only the town's southern end (which Ewing's Pennsylvania militia was to have closed) remained open thanks to the stone bridge across the Assunpink. Eventually, both advanced detachments, consisting of around forty men apiece, eventually reunited with each of Washington's columns below, or south of, the village of Birmingham, to lead Greene's and Sullivan's late-comers, from east to west, down their respective roads leading to Trenton and a rendezvous with destiny.[76]

Finally, after his soldiers rested in the swirling snow at the silent Birmingham crossroads, about halfway to their ultimate strategic objective, in preparation for the final descent upon Trenton, Washington barked out the long-awaited order for the troops of both columns, or divisions, to prepare to move out. Despite being sick, worn-out, or hoarse, young and middle-aged Continental officers shouted orders for all to hear. In a manner not seen in the British Army, Washington's officers then walked among their men to make sure that everyone was up and in their assigned place in column, while snowflakes tumbled down.

For the final push to Trenton, these experienced leaders, who voiced Washington's no-nonsense directive, now reminded their ragged soldiers that "no man is to quit his Ranks on pain of instant punishment." Some sleeping soldiers, curled up on the snowy ground to stay as warm as possible in what almost appeared to be fetal positions, were awakened by their officers only with some difficulty. These men finally emerged from deep sleeps, induced by the intoxicating effect of cold and weariness, from which they would not have otherwise awakened. Private Johnny Greenwood was one such lucky soldier, but he experienced a close call. The teenager had almost fallen into what could have been a fatal sleep, feeling an illusionary sense of well-being, warmth, and comfort that was a lethal as a Hessian bullet or bayonet, after: "we halted on the road, I sat down on the stump of a tree and was so benumbed with cold that I wanted to go to sleep; had I been passed unnoticed I should have frozen to death without knowing it; but as good luck always attended me, Sergeant Madden came and, rousing me up, made me walk about. We then began to march against, just in the old slow way" into the freezing blackness of the windswept woodlands, leafless and cloaked in winter's brown drabness, that seemed to have no end north of Trenton. Perhaps Private Greenwood's decision to sit down on a snowy stump rather than on the colder ground saved his life.[77]

Meanwhile, Washington, just relatively refreshed by a hasty, light breakfast, perhaps including even a few sips of coffee—rather than English tea—to reinvigorate his body, thanks to the generosity of Benjamin Moore at his small dwelling at the Birmingham crossroads, gave final pep talks to his silent troops amid the cascade of snow. Washington and his top lieutenants reminded their scarecrow looking-like soldiers that the situation was crucial, and one that was now one of "Victory or Death." In addition, it was time for America's most stalwart fighting men to avenge the disgrace of so many past fiascos and defeats, including New York City's loss, and to prove the British wrong about their earlier boast that the American soldiers were nothing but "raw, undisciplined, cowardly men," who could not win a victory.

Finally, when it seemed that all available Continental troops were aroused and hustled into their assigned places in column, Washington ordered his Second Division troops forward at about the same time that the northeaster increased its fury, as if to thwart the final bid to reach Trenton. With "a most violent storm" unleashing a steady, driving "Rain Hail and Snow intermixed," Washington directed Greene's column of Second Division soldiers to move out to the left, and toward the east to gain the Scotch Road.

To provide encouragement to his exhausted troops lashed by winter's harshest offerings, a mounted Washington rode up and down the column to ensure that everyone was moving out and everything was going according to plan. Then, leading by example, Washington galloped to the head of the lengthy column, which pushed toward where the sun would soon rise. Commanding reliable veterans, Brigadier General Stephen's small Virginia brigade of three regiments once again led the way, lurching forward with grim resolve. Advancing before Greene's main column in its vanguard role, this hard-fighting Old Dominion brigade now consisted of barely four hundred soldiers, after nearly an equal number sick men had been left on the Delaware's other side. Stephen's Fourth, Fifth, and Sixth Virginia Continental Regiments, under Lieutenant Colonel Robert Lawson, and Colonels Charles Scott, and Mordecai Buckner, respectively, pushed east through the drifting snow and toward an unknown fate in the frigid blackness. Selected by Washington in a vote of confidence that boasted their pride and can-do attitude as intended, these Old Dominion veterans served as a trusty, tactically flexible vanguard. Under Washington's orders to hurl aside any advanced Hessian pickets or any picket posts that they might encounter along the way, these hardened Virginia Continentals surged east with a heightened sense of determination.

Indeed, proving himself a master at matching exactly the right men with the proper missions, Washington fully realized that these Stephen's seasoned Virginia soldiers, his own home state boys, now operated with an especially "sharp edge"—as the commander-in-chief had fully anticipated—for this key assignment of overwhelming any initial resistance met along the way. Indeed, these Virginia Continental units consisted of some of Washington's most reliable troops. Conversely, however, these same sterling characteristics, especially a high esprit de corps, warrior ethos, and outright aggressiveness, also explained why the Virginian's ranks had been so thoroughly depleted, resulting in the exacting of a high price on the battlefield.[78]

On August 1, 1776, Sam Adams described a key factor that also now motivated Washington's men in their upcoming showdown against the Hessians: "The hearts of [our] soldiers beat high wit the spirit of freedom; they are animated with the justice of their cause, and while the grasp their swords can look up to Heaven for assistance [and our] adversaries are composed of wretches who laugh at the rights of humanity, who turn religion into derision, and would for high wagers, direct their swords against their leaders or their country."[79]

With Stephen's three Virginia regiments of his crack vanguard brigade leading the advance of the main strike column, Greene's Second Division under Washington's personal leadership, the commander-in-chief had placed much faith in the leadership abilities of the hard-nosed General Stephen, and his brigade's experienced regimental commanders. His faith was well-founded. However, historians have long incorrectly viewed Stephen as little more than a drunken buffoon and incompetent backwoods rustic of little ability. General Stephen's image has suffered because he was the consummate outsider—a raw-boned westerner from Virginia's Shenandoah Valley, Scottish immigrant who was not connected to the privileged planter elite by aristocratic antecedents, without influential Congressional supporters, and not linked by marriage to any ruling family of Virginia. Additionally Stephen was a close friend to Washington's greatest rival, England-born General Gates. In fact, Stephen had even advised Gates to purchase the Virginia property where he made his home, Traveller's Rest. Like Washington at Mount Vernon, Stephen found his greatest peace at his sprawling Bower plantation amid the fertile farmlands of the lower Shenandoah Valley in Frederick County, Virginia. While Washington, as Braddock's aide-de-camp escaped unscathed, Stephen had been "shot through the body" during the decimation of Braddock's ill-fated expedition in the Ohio country in July 1755.

While Washington earned his pre-revolution military reputation primarily from commanding the Virginia Regiment as mostly a distant commander during the French and Indian War, Stephen had played a more direct role in actually leading the Virginia Regiment in the field. As second-in-command, this former British Army officer—unlike Washington—had served as the First Virginia Regiment's acting commander for longer extended periods than Washington. Therefore, Stephen evolved into one of Virginia's most effective Indian fighters. He had learned how to defeat the ever-elusive Indians on their own terms. An expert at wilderness warfare, Stephen also knew how to "roast them" with par-tisan-like tactics that were hard-hitting, as he confidently informed Virginia's governor in 1756.

Stephen's hands-on role in molding the First Virginia Regiment during the French and Indian War were impressive, after Washington retired in 1759 to marry Martha Custiss. Stephens boasted how his disciplined Virginia soldiers could "parade as well as prussians [ironically as if writing about Colonel Rall's troops now stationed at Trenton], and the fighting in a Close Country as well as Tartars." With aggressive tactics, Stephen had helped to save the Ohio County and Fort Pitt, the future site of Pittsburgh. Stephen, a Renaissance man, earned a Master of Arts Degree from King's College of the University of Aberdeen, Scotland. He then excelled in medical school at the University of Edinburgh for three years. Imbued with liberal Age of Enlightenment thought gained from the inspirational writings of leading Scottish intellectuals, Stephen served on early revolutionary committees established by the Second Virginia Convention in March 1775, where he sat with Washington and Thomas Jefferson.

Ironically, Washington was now able to launch his strike upon Trenton in part because Stephen had already played a vital role in neutralizing the troublesome Ohio Valley tribes by playing a key role in convincing them to declare neutrality instead of allying with the British, and then ravaging the Virginia, Maryland, and Pennsylvania frontier—a dangerous second front that would have forced Washington to simultaneously face enemies both in front and behind at this crucial time—as during the French and Indian War. Stephens had been instrumental in the signing of the Treaty of Pittsburgh with the Ohio Valley tribes in October 1775. This treaty was yet holding firm on December 26, 1776: a most fortunate development for America.

On the march to Trenton, therefore, Washington needed the hard-bitten Stephen, his leadership expertise, and considerable tactical ability, which had been well-honed after more than two decades of commendable service and nearly a dozen military campaigns. Stephen had even survived the Fort Necessity July 1754 debacle by Washington's side, seemingly leading a charmed life. Indeed, if anyone could effectively lead the way for Greene's Second Division column to overwhelm any initial Hessian resistance standing before Trenton, it was this consummate frontier warrior named Stephen. After all, he even carved a road over the untamed Allegheny Mountains for a British-American expedition to push deep into the Ohio Country to attack New France's most easternmost outpost known as Fort Duquesne, today's Pittsburgh. As he had penned, Stephens demonstrated that he could "Hurl Mountains out of their Seat," in leading veteran Virginia troops, who were "Capable to do anything." Yet a relative newcomer to the New World, Stephen had journeyed to America as a hopeful immigrant from Aberdeenshire, Scotland, in 1748.[80]

Most importantly and as Washington fully realized, General Stephen was now backed up by some very good top lieutenants, who now led the three Virginia regiments of his small brigade onward through the snow and east toward the Pennington Road. Charles Scott was the foremost among these dependable Old Dominion colonels. An experienced soldier at age thirty-eight, he was known as Charley Scott by his admiring troops, who would follow him to hell and back if necessary. Scott's rise, from a private's rank, had been meteoritic. Life's hard experiences had well prepared the ambitious Scott, a future general and Kentucky governor despite little education, for the upcoming Trenton challenge.

Colonel Scott hailed from the Virginia planter class and a once-prosperous family that owned Tidewater tobacco plantations along the muddy James River near Richmond. His family traced its Virginia roots back to the mid-1600s. Forsaking a dreary future as a carpenter when Virginia faced a host of new threats during the French and Indian War, the independent-minded Scott enlisted in Washington's First Virginia Regiment at age sixteen, before the Cumberland County court officially assigned him a guardian, after his father's 1755 death. Therefore, Washington's regiment early became the young man's surrogate home.

With black hair and eyes, Scott was distinguished by a dark and swarthy appearance. But Scott was not as dark as one First Virginia Regimental comrade, Moses Johnson, who was a product of a black-white union, a white father and black slave mother. Like Stephen, Scott had served in the military, including under Washington, for more than twenty years before the dramatic showdown at Trenton. Therefore, Stephen and Scott knew Washington very well and vice versa, explaining in no small part why they were primary leaders of his vanguard and a most effective leadership team, leading the way for Greene's Second Division.

Scott affectionately referred to the autocratic Washington as "the old boss," which delighted his homespun Fifth Virginia soldiers. Like Stephen, Scott had also early excelled as an Indian fighter on the western frontier, possessing invaluable qualities that rose to the fore during this winter campaign on New Jersey soil. Early highly esteemed by Washington for his abilities, Sergeant Scott had capably led small parties that scouted Indian and French movements deep in hostile country, including around strategic Fort Duquesne. These frontier Virginians took the scalps of both Indians and Frenchmen during the bitter wilderness struggle for possession of the Ohio Valley. Because of Scott's contributions as the finest scout, woodsman, and sergeant of the First Virginia Regiment, Washington had personally promoted the promising young man to an officer's rank.

Then in 1760, Scott served as a hard-hitting captain in the southern campaign against the troublesome Cherokee, earning additional acclaim, including from his new regimental commander, Stephen, after Washington's retirement. Scott's precarious existence as a daring frontier scout ended when he married a pretty Irish girl, Francs Sweeney, on February 22, 1762, on Washington's thirtieth birthday. Scott and his beloved Frankey, who brought nearly a dozen slaves with her to the union, lived together on Scott's Muddy

Creek farm near the James River around thirty miles upriver from the bustling tobacco port of Richmond. Here, he built a gristmill on Muddy Creek, and then acquired additional fertile land for growing wheat and tobacco. Benefitting from 650 acres in the James River country, the Scott family grew rapidly. Scott's first daughter was born around 1763, followed by four sons before the American Revolution.

After the "shots heard around the world" at Lexington Green, Scott early organized a company of young volunteers from the Tidewater's Cumberland County, located just west of Richmond, to defend the land he loved. Anticipating a British invasion by sea, Virginia concentrated its troops at Williamsburg, Virginia's capital. Here, Scott was elected overall commander-in-chief and the first commander of Virginia's forces, because of his "great reputation" and ability. From the beginning, Scott was one of the most diehard, radical revolutionaries in all Virginia. He early advocated not only independence but also in taking the initiative against the Old Dominion's enemies.

After the battle of Bunker Hill, Scott became the second in command of the Second Virginia Regiment, while his younger brother, Joseph, served in the same regiment as a lieutenant. Scott also played a key role in leading Virginians to victory over Lord John Murray Dunmore, the royal governor, his loyalists, and recently liberated Virginia slaves of his "Ethiopian" regiment, including at the battle—the first engagement in Virginia—of Great Bridge on December 9, 1775. Not dwelling upon a paradox's complexities and America's early contradictions, this freedom-loving owner of slaves fought against armed African Americans in uniforms on Virginia soil.

After the sharp clash at Great Bridge, Scott then took command of all Virginia troops in the lower Tidewater region. In February 1776, he gained a lieutenant colonel's rank in the Second Virginia Continental Regiment, and then served as the Fifth Virginia Continental Regiment's colonel in early May. This veteran regiment, now one of Washington's best, was composed of soldiers from Henrico, Spotsylvania, Bedford, Loudoun, Richmond, Bedford, Lancaster, Northumberland, Chesterfield, and Hanover Counties. Scott had then led his regiment north with the other Old Dominion regiments of Stephen's brigade—now Washington's vanguard—to join the main army just in time for the Trenton challenge, while wife Frankey deftly managed not only their five children, four boys and one girl, but also the Muddy Creek farm and slaves in Scott's long absence.[81] During "This most Horrid War," Colonel Scott's sense of determination to succeed on December 26 can perhaps be best seen in his own words from a letter: "I set little value upon my health when put in competition with my duty to my country and the glorious cause we are engaged in."[82]

General Stephen's other capable regiment commander on the march to Trenton was Colonel Mondecai Buckner. He likewise bolstered the Virginia vanguard's overall quality and combat capabilities under Stephen's steady hand and leadership. Buckner also possessed extensive experience during the French and Indian War on Virginia's western frontier. Now ably leading the Sixth Virginia Continental Regiment, which consisted of zealous volunteers from New Kent, Prince George, Spotsylvania, Charles City, Amherst, Pittsylvania, Buckingham, Dinwiddie, and Lunenburg Counties, Virginia, Buckner had served as a captain under Stephen in his First Virginia Regiment beginning in 1758, or nearly two decades ago. He married the wealthy Elizabeth Stanard in 1768, and then settled down in the fertile Piedmont of Spotsylvania County, where he was elected judge in 1742 and justice of the county. In mid-February 1776, Buckner was appointed the Sixth Virginia Continental Regiment's colonel.[83]

Lieutenant Colonel Robert Lawson now served as Stephen's remaining regimental commander of Washington's vanguard, after having been promoted from major since mid-August 1776. Destined to eventually gain a general's rank in the Virginia militia by the time of the Yorktown Campaign in 1781, he now led the Fourth Virginia Continental Regiment ever-closer to Trenton. Lawson, age twenty-eight and the youngest of Stephen's top lieutenants, hailed from Prince Edward County, in central Virginia's Piedmont in the Appomattox River country. Only recently on December 13, 1776, he had barely missed his seventh anniversary of his marriage to pretty Sarah Meriwether Pierce, who presented him with his first child, Sarah Meriwether Lawson, on September 13, 1770. The child's sudden death on April 19, 1771 sent Lawson into a spiral of deep grief. Lawson named his next child, who would be conceived this coming spring, in honor of that great republican dream and struggle for liberty that now motivated him in the early hours of December 26 during the descent upon Trenton: America Lawson.

All the while as Stephen and his trusty top Virginia lieutenants, Scott, Buckner, and Lawson, continued to lead the vanguard onward through the snow and deeper into the storm-lashed night, Washington also rode to the left, or east, with Greene's lumbering column. Washington once again continued to demonstrate more of his legendary equestrian skill in riding down the column's length, as if on a summer day in Tidewater Virginia. Indeed, the commander-in-chief was continuing to prove that he was one of the "the greatest horseman of his age," especially on this bone-chilling night in Hunterdon County. Pushing east and farther away from the icy Birmingham crossroads, Washington led Greene's Second Division through the incessant shower of snow flakes that gently tumbled down upon the lengthy column. The entire battleplan now hinged upon the dynamic team of the paternal Washington and young Greene quickly gaining the Scotch Road, which was buried up ahead in the blackness under the freshly fallen snow amid this unfamiliar terrain to the east.

Meanwhile, in contrast to Greene's column, Sullivan's First Division only had to advance straight south along the River Road, a mere continuation of the Bear Tavern Road that led south from Birmingham. On his trusty steed, Washington encouraged Greene's soldiers onward into the night's and storm's depths in the hope of gaining the Scotch Road, which lay somewhere in the blackness to the east, according to his knowledgeable Hunterdon County scouts. Fortunately, this seemingly endless march for Greene's Second Division troops was made slightly easier because the terrain now gently slope downward almost all the way, although leveling out for a lengthy stretch at one point, along the Upper Ferry Road to the Scotch Road, a distance of just more than a mile. Once again and like the intersection of the Johnson's Ferry Road and the Bear Tavern Road and then the Bear Tavern Road and the Upper Ferry Road because the area's narrow roads—former game trails that had then evolved into Indian trails before becoming pot-holed wagon roads for New Jersey farmers—generally followed high ground or ridge-tops, this was also the case with the Upper Ferry Road that led the pitch-black forests to the Scotch Road. With time of the essence, Washington's most pressing immediate objective was for Greene's column to reach the strategic intersection of the Upper Ferry Road and the Scotch Road as soon as possible, as more precious time was running out. All the while, Washington's men continued to slog onward on little more than a hope and a prayer.

Upon finally reaching the vital intersection of the Upper Ferry and the Scotch Road, which was nearly four miles southeast of the two-story Bear Tavern where the lengthy march south had first begun, Washington conferred with his most knowledgeable Hunterdon County guides. They informed Washington that this snow-covered trail cutting through the thick woodlands was indeed the coveted Scotch Road during a brief, hasty conference on horse-back. With the ground covered in a thick sheet of white and with visibility near zero in the stormy darkness, the anxious commander-in-chief had to make absolutely sure that the proper road was taken by Greene's column for the final descent upon Trenton. To be sure, no error could be made in this regard at this crucial moment.

Indeed, everything now hinged upon the lengthy column of Greene's exhausted soldiers of the First Division not missing this last critical turn for the final push south on Trenton. Having been assured with conviction, Washington then signaled for the column to turn right, and Stephen's hardened Virginia Continentals were the first troops to shift south. Now facing his troops in the proper direction and feeling more confident for eventual success, the determined commander-in-chief continued to lead Greene's Second Division column, which lurched forward once again. Going down the right road, Greene's troops marched straight south and down the gently sloping ground that led toward Washington's long-sought objective of Trenton.

As Washington and other veteran soldiers, especially the woodsmen, trappers, and hunters in the ranks, now sensed by the gradually dropping terrain, this was indeed now a final descent toward the silent valley of the Delaware, after the river curved gradually eastward from McConkey's Ferry to form a sharp elbow at Trenton. Despite the near-zero visibility and without maps, Washington had managed to get the main strike column on the proper road during the raging snowstorm after marching Greene's Second Division just more than a mile east through the blinding darkness and dense forest. Below both the remote Birmingham crossroads and the Scotch Road-Upper Ferry Road crossroads, the land now dropped gradually toward Trenton, because the Delaware had turned to flow more southeastward to curve toward the town's southern end. Just south of the relatively high ground of the Upper Ferry Road and its intersection with the Scotch Road, this sudden change of topography also indicated to Washington, blessed with well-honed frontier instincts, that he was finally now on the correct course for the final descent off the last high ground before Trenton, and down gently descending terrain that led south.

Likewise, Washington's Continentals, especially the western frontiersmen in the ranks, whose lives had often depended upon accurately understanding and instantly interpreting the land's and forest's many hidden nuances, now realized that their strategic objective was looming ever-closer, because the descending ground eventually ended along the low-lying river bottoms at the southern end of Trenton. Most importantly, not a single Hessian scout, picket, or patrol, had been seen or encountered by Washington's troops at any point during the long march. Therefore, the prospects for future success at Trenton brightened the spirits of the savviest veterans, who now deciphered an increasing number of positive signs and omens. In consequence, the overall pace of Washington's march south down the descending ground of the rough-hewn Scotch Road picked up, fueling more hopeful expectations among the common soldiery. Trenton now lay a little more than three miles to the southeast, the Promised Land, if everything went right for Washington's men.

While this "most violent storm" increased its fury in the night and Greene's column surged south down the Scotch Road, Colonel John Stark and his New Hampshire Regiment led the advance of Sullivan's column south. Captain Flahaven's and his New Jersey soldiers, who had rejoined the main column of Sullivan's First Division by this time, likewise pushed forward with the foremost New Hampshire veterans trudging through the snow. In slogging down the River Road from the Birmingham crossroads and compared to Greene's Second Division troops to the east, the movement was now relatively easy for Sullivan's soldiers because of the gently sloping ground leading to the Delaware.

With hope in their hearts and well-worn flintlocks on shoulders, the New England and New York infantrymen of the First Division moved down the slippery River Road in a slightly southeast direction. Sullivan's lengthy column inched across the whitish landscape that contrasted sharply with the dark, hard-wood forests under churning skies. While a bitterly cold wind whistled through the tall trees lining both sides of the road, General Sullivan rode down the River Road to inspire confidence and to make sure that everyone was trudging onward. All the while, he encouraged his First Division troops of the western column like Washington and Greene in the eastern column, now moving on a parallel course down the Scotch Road.

In protective fashion similar to the ancient Praetorian Guard, Washington was escorted down the ice-covered Scotch Road by Captain Samuel Morris's twenty-five cavalrymen of the First Troop of Philadelphia Light Horse. Nearly half of these young horse-soldiers were either Ireland-born or descendants of Irish immigrants, including many members of the Friendly Sons of St. Patrick. Especially from the cynical viewpoint of Washington's western frontiersmen, this diminutive cavalry command was an ostentatious unit, consisting of young men from wealthy families and established individuals of "independent means." After having ridden out of Philadelphia in colorful uniforms, that they had purchased themselves at considerable expense from the capital's best tailors, on Sunday December 1, 1776, to a cheering crowd, this band of cavalrymen had first linked with Washington at Trenton during the recent withdrawal.

Private George Fullerton, an Irish member of the Friendly Sons of St. Patrick, was one such finely uniformed trooper from Philadelphia. As a sad fate would have it, he would be fatally cut down in battling for liberty during this winter campaign. Private Benjamin Randolph, a skilled cabinet maker who lived in a stately brick house on fashionable Chesnut Street, where Martha Washington had stayed during the New York Campaign, galloped down the snowy Scotch Road with the First Troops of the Philadelphia Light Horse. The trustworthy color bearer of these confident "gentleman-rebels" now carried a fine yellow silk battleflag, decorated with the colorful, hand-painted image of a holy angel blowing a brass trumpet and a dignified-looking American Indian facing each other in the banner's center. Carried with pride and reflecting how this struggle was a religious-like crusade for freedom, the Philadelphian's fancy battle flag was designed by artist John Folwell and hand-painted by James Claypoole in September 1775.

Washington also now possessed reliable infantry guardians of a special pro-tective unit which was created in March 1776. With the mission of guarding Washington and his headquarters, this elite command consisted of 75 care-fully selected, battle-tested soldiers, who were "the flower and pick of the army." At this time, the Commander-in-Chief Guards, unofficially known as the Life Guard, protected the commander-in-chief with their lives. Born in Newport, Rhode Island, in late February 1748 and a former member of Glover's Regiment, Captain Caleb Gibbs, who was now part of Washington's close-knit "family" of staff officers and soon destined for a major's rank, had been chosen by Washington to command his diehard protectors and personal guardians in early March 1776. Washington, therefore, affectionately called his Life Guard troops "my regiment" with an unconcealed fondness.[84]

Also galloping south in the mounted cavalcade down the slick Scotch Road with Washington and his cocky, if not slightly pretentious, Philadelphia troopers were the young, gifted members of his own personal staff, whom he affectionately called "my family." Wearing his hair long and tied together in a queue behind his back—ironically like the Hessian enlisted men at Trenton—slender Lieutenant Tench Tilghman was one of the most respected members of Washington's staff. The privileged son of a wealthy Philadelphia merchant, he was a smart, energetic volunteer aide-de-camp from the Pennsylvania battalion of the Flying Camp. The popular Tench (a family name from his mother's side of the family) Tilghman now served as Washington's indispensable secretary:

a coveted, prestigious position in which he served faithfully all the way to the siege of Yorktown in October 1781.

This young man of promise had been born thirty-two years before on this very day, making him older than most of Washington's staff members, who were mostly in their twenties. Born on his father's tobacco plantation, known as "Fausley," in Talbot County on Maryland's fertile eastern shore, southeast of Baltimore on Chesapeake Bay's east side, Tilghman was one of Washington's most indispensable men this morning. Like so many other Celtic-Gaelic soldiers in Washington's Army, Tilghman was proud of his distinctive Irish heritage and antecedents on his mother's side. Without hesitation, he had liquidated his assets and given up a lucrative profession as a Philadelphia merchant just to serve as a low-level officer in a Philadelphia militia company to fight for American freedom. Tench was also motivated to wipe a stain from the family name. His father, James Tilghman, who had been a prewar friend of Washington who occasionally had been a guest at the Marylander's eastern shore home, had been a patriotic during the initial protest against England's arbitrary highhandedness, until independence was declared, which was a step too far for him but not his son.

Without an active officer's commission and refusing to receive any pay for his entire period of service—nearly five years—because of his "determination to share the fate of my country," Tilghman's seemingly limitless abilities, thanks to a fine education from today's University of Pennsylvania, writing skills, and natural intelligence, had first earned him a permanent place on Washington's staff in August 1776. Handsome, dashing, and a stylish dresser of the upper class, he was somewhat of a dandy. Blessed with winning ways, Tilghman was also an incorrigible ladies' man. During the summer of 1775, he had eagerly eyed General Philip Schuyler's enchanting daughter. She "was the finest tempered Girl in the World" to the smitten Tilghman, who only saw her best qualities from a distance. Betsy Schuyler later became the wife of another one of Washington's young rising stars and future indispensable staff member, who now commanded a well-disciplined New York artillery company at the head of Stirling's brigade in Greene's Second Division column: Captain Alexander Hamilton.

While flirting with the attractive, captivating Betsy, Tilghman had served as a secretary to the new nation's commissioners, who signed a treaty with the Onondaga tribe of the Iroquois Confederacy from northern New York to keep them from siding with the British. Tilghman learned to respect the Indians like few whites. Not blinded by race, culture, or upper class status, the young Marylander from the eastern shore admired Indian values, especially their stoicism, wisdom, and strength of character. In consequence, he was adopted into the Onondaga tribe, earning the affectionate name Teahokalonde.

Most of all, the gregarious Tilghman was a social creature, and even before the beautiful Betsy was about to depart with her father after the treaty signing, he had already turned his romantic sights upon not only the readily available Onondaga girls, but also on the more attractive—in a true connoisseur's elevated opinion—Stockbridge Indian maidens. By December 1776, the capable Lieutenant Tilghman was highly esteemed throughout the army, and by no one more than Washington. This contrarian, complex Marylander openly disdained selfish concerns and the only too-frequent behind-the-scenes scheming for personal advancement like so many other officers, desiring only to perform his patriotic duties to the best of his ability.

Like many families across America in what was in essence a civil war, the revolution had torn apart the Tilghman family. This independent-minded planter's son hailed from one of Maryland's leading Tidewater families that was mostly Loyalist, including his father and his brother, Philemon, who now served in the British Navy. Tilghman would fall dangerously ill at Valley Force next winter, which eventually led to an untimely death in 1786.

As Washington's longest serving aide, Tilghman would be dispatched by Washington to inform Congress of America's 1781 victory at Yorktown. Although they were technically enemies, this distinguished graduate (1761) of the College of Philadelphia continued to write letters to his loyalist, but "honored father," James. However, this delicate correspondence was continued only under the mutually agreed condition that they broach nothing on "the score of politics" that might permanently sever ties between father and son. In his letter describing the march down the Scotch Road and through the wind-whipped snow, Tilghman marveled at the common soldier's stoicism and iron discipline, writing how: "the Night was excessively severe, both cold and snowey [sic], which the Men bore without the least murmur [after] We were . . . Much delayed in crossing the River," on such a terrible night.[85]

As revealed in a letter, young Colonel Knox was also amazed at the combination of discipline and hardy fortitude of Washington's infantrymen, who kept trudging onward with a resolve not previously seen in this war. He described how: "The night was cold and stormy; it hailed with great violence [but] the troops marched with the most profound silence and good order."[86] The firm resolution and silent suffering of Washington's men now verified the words of Sam Adams, who emphasized in an August 1, 1776 letter how, "The hand of Heaven appears to have led us on to be, perhaps humble instruments and means in the great providential dispensation which is completing," and could be only now fulfilled by victory at Trenton.[87]

During their silent march down the Scotch Road, Washington's troops of Greene's left wing (Second Division) very likely contemplated many things, while caught in the icy grip of the bitter nor'eastern. For the large percentage of Irish soldiers, both Catholic and especially Scotch-Irish Prostestants from Ulster Province in the ranks, they might have now reflected on Ireland's long-time tragic fate, because the repeated people's uprisings had been crushed by British might. So many Irish fighting men from the "Old Country," and mostly from the Middle Colonies, especially Pennsylvania, served in Washington's Army that this common people's struggle in America was viewed by London's officials as little more than just another Presbyterian or Ulster Rebellion.

Hundreds of Washington's soldiers yet retained their distinct Celtic-Gaelic cultural values, pride, belief systems, and characteristics, including even some men yet speaking ancient Gaelic. All in all, around 40 percent of Washington's main strike force now consisted of seasoned Irish and Scotch-Irish soldiers, whose hatred of England knew no bounds. No doubt some Emerald Islanders on the march to Trenton almost certainly thought of the new American nation's first martyr and fellow countryman, General Richard Montgomery. So that Americans "Might Live and yet be free," as one popular song went, the Irishman had been killed on a snow-covered Quebec street on a comparable December morning only last December.

Perhaps Washington's Ulstermen from northern Ireland also drew moral strength from the 1,646 words—that yet applied to the stern Trenton challenge—of a liberty-loving Scotch-Irish freedom fighter, who had spoken encouraging words to his Irish warriors before launching a headlong attack upon the English to reap a dramatic victory against the odds: "Know that those that stand before you ready to fight are [your oppressors and] Now you have Arms in your hands as good as they have, and you are Gentlemen as good as they are. You are the Flower of Ulster, descended from an Ancient and Honourable a Stock of People as any in Europe."[88]

Throughout America's struggle for liberty, a high percentage of Irish and Scotch-Irish soldiers served disproportionately as the hard-hitting "shock troops of Independence." And symbolically an equally high percentage of

Celtic-Gaelic soldiers now served as the "shock" troops of Washington's main strike force in both divisions, while moving relentlessly south on a parallel course toward Trenton and a full Hessian brigade, whose combat prowess was unmatched.[89] Washington's ranks now overflowed with never-say-die Irish, including large numbers of immigrants, who were now fighting America's battles. Indeed, the "fiercest and most ardent Americans of all, however, were the Presbyterian Irish settlers and their descendants."[90] Even while the falling snow continued to pile up and the blustery gales cut through the ranks like a knife, Washington's Irish and Scotch-Irish marched on Trenton in what was essentially a resurrection of "The Spirit of the truly brave/From thy obscure Sequestered grave/Montgomery arise."[91]

And Washington's Scottish soldiers, who perhaps noted the irony of trudging south toward Trenton down the Scotch Road that had been named after some early Celtic settler, might have now reflected upon the painful lessons Scotland's bloody wars of independence. However, Washington's Scots now had no idea that their strategic objective on December 26 had been named for a fellow Scotsman, William Trent, whose stylish, two-story brick mansion stood near the river on Trenton's south side. Symbolically, Trent hailed from the picturesque Scottish Highlands, whose freedom-loving people had long resisted English oppression. In a strange twist of fate, some of Washington's Irish, Scotch-Irish, and Scottish men, or their immigrant ancestors, had been first brought to America's shores by Trent's sailing ships that had carried large numbers of indentured servants and immigrants to Philadelphia.

Washington's Scotsmen had never forgotten how their Celtic homeland so far away had been so ruthlessly conquered by the English, despite heroic resistance from fiery Scottish leaders like William Wallace, of Elderslie, Scotland, who led a popular uprising when Scotland's own future had been as dark as America's own on December 26, 1776: a deep-seated revolutionary source of inspiration for Washington's Scotland-born and Scotch-Irish troops, because the humble Wallace had led the common people to one victory after another over superior English forces. Like Washington's Scots, Wallace had fought with the heart, waging a holy war "to do or die." He was a famed Scottish nationalist and holy warrior, who quoted Psalms and spoke Gaelic, and led his popular uprising when it appeared "Scotland was lost" (now the exact situation in regard to America) to the English.

Consequently, even in the windswept snows of Hunterdon County, the enduring revolutionary example of two thousand years of heroic Celtic defiance

and armed resistance against foreign invaders yet inspired Washington's revolutionaries, especially the Scots, during an equally dark hour of America's desperate struggle for life. In many ways, the Scottish Wars of Independence were
comparable to America's own struggle in 1776, with a free people attempting to
remain free of foreign domination and to determine their own destiny.

Besides Generals Mercer, Stephen, who was described as "a Scotchsman,"
and St. Clair, the most respected Scottish general in Washington's ranks was
Lord Stirling, the son of a Scottish immigrant. He described the Scotch Road
"so slippery" that footing was maintained only with great difficulty. Although
he gained his lofty military appointment primarily because of powerful New
Jersey political connections, this Scotsman was anything but a typical political general. In fact, he was one of Washington's hardest fighting commanders.
Although an aristocratic, wealthy native New Yorker married to the sister of
New Jersey's governor, Stirling was every inch the authentic Scottish warrior
determined to make America free.

Ironically, Lord Stirling, who hailed from a lowland Scotland family,
had early envisioned the distinct possibilities of attacking not only Trenton,
but also very likely the main British base at Brunswick (Washington's early
January 1777 ambition after capturing Trenton), where General Grant served
as the overall commander of Hessian and British forces in New Jersey, in part
because Grant was a fellow Scotsman: another case of a civil war between
Scots on American soil. The portly Grant had been born in wealth and privilege, basking in his elevated social status as the privileged lord of Ballindalloch
Castle. Finely educated at private schools in New York, where he had been
born, and a principal founder of the first lending library, the New York
Literary Society, in New York, Stirling was the proud owner of a considerable
estate, including slaves, at Basking Ridge, New Jersey. He had early gained
military experience by serving as the aide to General William Shirley during
the French and Indian War, leading to his 1775 appointment by Congress to
a general's rank.[92]

But why so many Americans had honored Stirling's dubious title of lord
has remained somewhat of a mystery. An amused, sardonic French aristocrat in
the service of America simply wrote how Stirling's "birth, his titles and pretty
extensive property have given him more importance in America, than his talents could ever have acquired him. The title of *Lord*, which was refused him in
England, is not here contested with him: he claimed this title from inheritance
. . . he is accused of liking the table and bottle, full as much as becomes a lord
[but] He is brave" as a general.[93]

Despite his lofty title of "Lord," this New Jersey aristocrat now commanded one of Washington's finest combat brigades, and he handled it with consummate skill. Forged in the fire of battle, Stirling's seasoned brigade consisted of durable Pennsylvania, Virginia, and Delaware troops. They had served as Washington's dependable rear-guard on more than one occasion during the long, cheerless withdrawal through New Jersey. Beginning at Princeton before crossing into eastern Pennsylvania, Washington had assigned Stirling's and Stephen's brigades—significantly five of seven regiments consisted of Virginians—as his rearguard to face Lord Cornwallis' dogged pursuit.

One of Stirling's best regiments was the crack Third Virginia, now leading the brigade's advance, consisting battle-hardened men. These well-trained Third Virginia Continentals were led by Colonel George Weedon, who was extremely popular with the rank and file. He had been the merry innkeeper who had long operated the town's most lively tavern, located on main street, today's Caroline Street, in Fredericksburg, Virginia. Weedon was also Mercer's neighbor, and a friend of Washington, Jefferson, and Patrick Henry of "Give Me Liberty or Give Me Death" fame. These Virginia Founding Fathers had often patronized Weedon's popular meeting place, the Rising Sun Tavern, which he had owned since 1766. Here, with other members of his rarified gentleman's dining "Club," Washington had often drank rum, discussed race horses—Weedon's favorite topic after damning Great Britain—and played cards so recklessly that he complained of losing "as usual" in his diary.

Weedon was also the Tidewater town's postmaster who conveniently worked out of his tavern, and also the respected colonel of Virginia troops. At the Rising Sun Tavern before the war's beginning, Washington had met with other Virginia officers, including Weedon, who one patriot-hating Englishman condemned as "very active and zealous in blowing the flames of sedition." Weedon and Washington had long made a good natural team, both in regard to revolutionary politics and insurrection hatched out over potent drinks at Weedon's tavern, which was now reunited on the eve of America's most important battle to date. Symbolically, Washington, Mercer, and Weedon's destines had been long intertwined in war and peace. Upon relocating from western Pennsylvania to the Virginia Tidewater on Washington's recommendations, the Scotland-born Mercer had first stayed at Weedon's busy Fredericksburg tavern, where he and Washington had early and often talked about the remarkable concept of an independent American nation. Mercer then married a sweet, young Virginia girl named Isabella, Weedon's sister. Therefore, the Scotsman named his fourth son George Weedon Mercer in honor of his close friend.

Though somewhat portly and easygoing that were obvious legacies of his more carefree innkeeper days and thanks to ample French and War experience that included solid service under General Stephen, Weedon had taken command of the Third Virginia Continental Regiment in mid-August 1776. On September 12, he had then linked up with Washington's Army, after a dusty four hundred mile-march to New York City with slightly more than six hundred men from mostly western and northern Virginia. But now trudging through the blowing snow along the Scotch Road, those six hundred zealous Old Dominion volunteers had been culled by the brutal Darwinian-like process of a war of attrition to only around 140 men by this time.[94]

The Scotland-born Mercer had organized the Third Virginia Continental Regiment, but then took command of the Flying Camp upon gaining a well-deserved general's rank. Mercer's departure allowed Weedon, who was affectionately known as "Old Joe Gourd" to his boys because of his endearing penchant for having served over-generous amounts of spiked punch with an out-sized gourd ladle, to take command of this versatile infantry command that was as adept at "true Bush-fighting way" as with conventional tactics. Young James Monroe, the future United States president, had first joined this revered Old Dominion regiment. The Third Virginia Continental Regiment's antecedent unit, the Culpeper Minute Battalion from the western frontier, had once terrorized the more genteel, refined citizens of Williamsburg, Virginia, at the war's beginning by their fierce, war-like looks alone. These minute men from along the wild, picturesque Blue Ridge country presented western frontier appearances that shocked Williamsburg's good citizens. After all, the rambunctious Old Dominion volunteers were distinguished by long hair, fringed hunting shirts, scalping knives, Long Rifles, tomahawks, deerskin moccasins, Indian leggings, and a devil-may-care attitude. In addition, they had proudly worn the patriot slogan "Liberty or Death" across their fringed buckskin hunting shirts.

Most of all, these resourceful Virginia Continentals now under Weedon's command were hard as nails. Now an ambitious lieutenant, Monroe's first captain, John Thornton, of Culpeper County, Virginia, had roughly hurled a "Tory" preacher out of his own church in Fredericksburg, when his sermon even hinted to a peaceful submission to England. The high confidence, can-do attitude, and jaunty air of these rough-hewn Virginia Continentals were evident from their wartime-fashionable wearing of hats "cocked on one side," and by Washington's repeated reliance on them in key combat situations. These Old Dominion boys had guarded the army's vulnerable rear, along with the three regiments of Stephen's brigade and the other Virginia command, the First Virginia Continental Regiment, of Stirling's brigade, of which the Third Virginia Continental Regiment was apart, during the dismal withdrawal through New Jersey.

Despite its frontier ways and rustic appearances, the Third Virginia Continental Regiment was in fact an elite unit. Weedon's regiment had been trained and drilled to exceptionally high standards by the celebrated victor at the October 10, 1774 battle of Point Pleasant over the Ohio Valley Indians, Ireland-born Andrew Lewis. On a hot late summer day at Harlem Heights, New York, when the Americans forced the enemy to turn and run for the first time, Colonel Weedon bragged how the famed Scottish Highlanders, the Black Watch Regiment, "got cursedly thrashed." The former Fredericksburg innkeeper had a close call on that memorable September 16, 1776, when his saber's hilt was shot away by a British bullet. Most important for Washington, the Third Virginia Continental Regiment was now filled with a good many of his own friends, former comrades, and acquaintances. He knew these men intimately and to be reliable, having socialized with them across Virginia, including at Weedon's tavern and the Raleigh Tavern in Williamsburg.[95]

As repeatedly demonstrated in the past, Washington's confidence in his Virginia boys was well-placed. Upon first reaching Washington's Army, Captain John Chilton, Third Virginia Continental Regiment, described in a letter to his father-in-law of a common feeling among the army's ranks in regard to these sharpshooting Virginia frontiersmen and tobacco planter sons: "great things are expected from the Virginians." Washington was never disappointed in his own high expectations placed upon Weedon's high-spirited soldiers, who fought with their hearts and well-honed skills to excel on the battlefield.[96]

The widely accepted view about the superiority of the combat prowess of Virginia troops was backed up by at least one Pennsylvania general, Anthony Wayne. Of Scotch-Irish antecedents, General Wayne lamented the regional differences in the Continental Army that sapped overall cohesion: "Had [Washington] but Southern troops he would not be necessitated so often to fly before an enemy . . . ."[97]

Even amid Hunterdon County's snowy depths and despite knowing that if killed on December 26, then they could not be buried because of the frozen ground, the fighting spirit among Washington's Southern troops remained exceptionally high, stemming from past accomplishments and a distinct sense of regional pride. However, provincialism had long fueled an intense sectional rivalry, which caused New Englanders, or "Yankees," and Southerners, or "Buckskins" that included Pennsylvanians from the western frontier. Even Washington, reflecting Virginia planter class prejudices, had denounced New Englanders, especially the "lower class of these people," in his own words, but also including officers, as "an exceedingly dirty and nasty people." However, this healthy rivalry between northern and southern soldiers also spurred an intense competition to win battlefield laurels and would rise to the fore during the upcoming showdown at Trenton.

At this time when so many members of Colonel Weedon's regiment were "bare of clothes," the irrepressible Captain Chilton, a thirty-six-year-old planter from Fauquier County, described how the Third Virginia soldiers were "very willing to fight them on any terms." While "fighting for Liberty," this devoted father of five was fated to be killed at the battle of Brandywine on September 11, 1777. This heated regional rivalry between North and South explained in part why Washington decided to place all the Southerners in Greene's Second Division column, while Sullivan's First Division column consisted of New Englanders, except for two New York Continental regiments (the First and Third) of Sargent's brigade and the three non-New England artillery units, two Jersey commands and one Philadelphia "long-arm" unit. As planned by Washington, the two divisions would vie with each other for reaping the most battlefield laurels in the upcoming clash at Trenton that loomed just ahead.[98]

Especially for Scotland-born veterans like Mercer, the slow, stumbling march of Washington's troops south down the icy Scotch Road and ever-closer to Trenton might have reminded them of those long-lost Jacobite glory days of 1745 and 1746, when thousands of Scottish Highland warriors had followed the ill-starred destiny of twenty-four-year-old Bonny Prince Charley, the last heir to the Stuart throne, during his ambitious attempt to capture London and restore Scotland autonomy. At war against Protestantism and foreign domination, these Jacobite Highlanders, including even fanatical Celtic chaplains, who carried sharp broadswords and an abiding hatred of the English, had terrified all England by challenging George III's rule by winning dramatic victories at places like Falkirk, Scotland (on January 17, 1746 and ironically where William Wallace was decisively defeated in July 1298), and pushing within one hundred miles of their greatest prize, London.[99]

Meanwhile, time was running out for Washington and his much-hampered pursuit of his great prize, Trenton. Daylight was approaching, and the possibility of unleashing the planned 5:00 a.m. attack had evaporated long ago. In a letter, Washington had once referred to the "Womb of Time," that ironically was now not about a birth but all about the ever-increasing odds for America's early death, if victory was not soon reaped at Trenton.[100] Back in September 1758, Washington had written how time was "that never failing expositor of all things," and that sage, old adage was never more true than in regard to the situation for his two columns struggling through the snows north of Trenton.[101]

Inching through the swirling tempest that stubbornly refused to diminish, Washington's two columns—Greene, the left wing, along the Scotch Road and Sullivan, the right wing, pushing down the River Road—continued to move relentlessly ever-southward over a snow-shrouded landscape and farther into the blinding darkness. Communications between the two drawn-out columns, now separated by pitch blackness and more than a mile and a dense tangle of wintery woodlands, were nonexistent. Therefore, Washington could only hope that both assault columns of his ever-optimistic pincer movement were proceeding as planned and at roughly the same pace south along two parallel roads that pointed south like two twin daggers toward Trenton's heart. Most of all, Washington feared that the two separated columns, lurching ahead blindly in the cold darkness and across unfamiliar terrain, would never reach the town's outskirts in a timely fashion for a simultaneous attack on Trenton to fulfill his lofty tactical vision of a double envelopment.

While the snow and ice poured down to cause more havoc upon the commander-in-chief's already shattered plans and timetable, the march of Greene's and Sullivan's columns continued to ease down gently sloping terrain as they neared the Delaware that curved slightly east eventually to where Washington's troops would again meet it at Trenton. Fortunately, along both the River and Scotch Roads below the tiny village of Birmingham, the terrain dropped away in a gradual descent south and toward Trenton, allowing relatively easier marching for weary men, who had been up all night. But because Sullivan's route paralleled and lay closer to the river, the land fell more sharply than on the generally higher terrain encountered by Greene's Second Division troops to the east. However, the farther that Sullivan's troops pushed south, the closer the First Division's column neared the Delaware, where the ground sloped more gradually.

When Sullivan's division first proceeded south from the Birmingham crossroads, the Delaware lay just more than a mile and a half to the west. But after Sullivan's troops trudged almost directly south, but slightly southeast, for just more than a mile from Birmingham, the yet unseen Delaware lay only three-quarters of a mile to the west. Meanwhile, during the relentless push ever-southward, the snow-covered terrain to Sullivan's right, between the river and the lengthy column of mostly New England troops remained generally high, revealing little indication to Sullivan's men that the river flowed just to the west. Although the ground continued to slope downward ever since the right wing column had departed the Birmingham crossroads, the terrain was yet gently rolling and relatively high for easier marching to Sullivan's leg-weary soldiers, while they plodded wearily onward and down the River Road over gradually descending ground.

Then, at a point just more than a mile south of Birmingham, the troops of Sullivan's column descended down a sharper slope to encounter the first natural obstacle during the gradual descent south toward the river and Trenton: Heath Creek, or today's Gold Run, which was located about three miles south of Jacob's Creek. Running in a southwest direction toward the Delaware and parallel to Jacob's Creek far to the north, this small creek crossed the road upon which Sullivan's First Division soldiers trudged, barely able to put one foot before the other.

But fortunately and unlike Jacob's Creek, this smaller creek had not cut a deep ravine in its descent toward the river because of less top soil and more bed-rock just below the surface. Therefore, unlike at Jacob's Creek, Sullivan's rather easy crossing of Heath Creek only resulted in a relatively short delay. Here, as earlier at Jacob's Creek, Sullivan's soldiers continued to get their feet, already cold and half-numb, wet, however. Nevertheless, these half-frozen scarecrows stumbled onward with undiminished determination, pushing forward toward where their officers now led them forward into the dark unknown in a supreme leap of faith.

Just after crossing Heath Creek, Sullivan's First Division troops continued to slog a short distance south down the River Road to finally gain the barely dis-cernable Lower Ferry Road, which paralleled the ice-laced creek in its descent southwest toward the Delaware to Beatty's Ferry, just under a quarter mile away. Here, and thanks to intimate knowledge about his own home area from guide Captain John Mott, a mounted Sullivan signaled for his half-frozen troops to turn sharply to the right, and march southwest and parallel to the little creek flowing toward the Delaware. The Lower Ferry Road led west to the River Road proper, which more closely paralleled the river, following close to its east bank. Just as Heath Creek fell more sharply in cutting southwest and roughly per-pendicular to the north-south flowing Delaware, so the Lower Ferry Road also descended in a like manner toward the river.

However, unlike the gorge-like obstacle at the Jacob's Creek crossing to the north, the topography now proved far more favorable for Sullivan's weary foot-sloggers, because the creek descended through a wide, timbered hollow, which was sandwiched by higher ground on each side to the north and south. For the steadily marching First Division troops, this was a relatively easy access point leading southwest from higher to lower ground along the river, while the steeper, bluff-like terrain farther south and closer to Trenton would have impeded a comparable march west from the relatively high ground to the river bottom below.

Much to the relief of Sullivan's New Jersey, Massachusetts, and Philadelphia artillerymen, who dreaded the prospect of encountering another nightmarish Jacob's Creek-like ravine, what was now presented to the First Division's worn soldiers was a natural avenue leading straight to the river along a comparatively easy route. Therefore, after shifting their ranks, Sullivan's Continentals now marched mostly southeast through the steady deluge of snow to ease down gradually descending terrain that dropped toward the river, and fell more sharply, although along terrain that yet made relatively easy marching for infantry and accompanying artillery, as they pushed ever-nearer to the Delaware. By this time, clothing and uniforms of these exhausted soldiers, who had never felt colder, were heavier, sodden with wetness and snow. And, worst of all, there was no shelter from the storm and no rest in the inky blackness.

After trudging wearily around half a mile southwest parallel to Heath Creek, Sullivan's threadbare soldiers finally reached the River Road, proper, that lay along the river's east bank. Here, the lengthy column, consisting of Sargent, Glover, and St. Clair's brigades, respectively, turned sharply left off the Lower Ferry Road and onto the snow-covered main River Road running southeast and leading straight into Trenton's southwestern end. Therefore, Sullivan's troops must have felt a sense of relief upon gaining the river's firm bottom ground—which made for easier marching—and finally having gotten off the high ground, where the wind gusts cut through uniforms and the snow had piled up, and in reaching close to the river's east bank without great difficulty, or significantly slowing up the march's progress. Indeed, just to the right and beside the dark belt of winter's leafless oaks, hickories, and sycamores lining the east bank, the Delaware's swift, brown waters flowed south toward Trenton and Sullivan's ultimate objective that had to be reached as soon as possible.

But in fact not everything was going well in Sullivan's First Division column, even though it had finally reached the River Road proper for the final descent upon Trenton. Numbed by a combination of freezing cold, hypothermia, and an unprecedented weariness, some men moved onward like ice-caked Zombies through the snow and howling winds. During the march southeast down the slippery River Road, one determined officer in Glover's regiment, Lieutenant Joshua Orne, who was Glover's old business associate back in Marblehead, suddenly found himself in serious trouble. He was completely worn down by the ravages of the cold and hypothermia from the combined effects of the seemingly endless rowing of a Durham boat across the river, and then the seemingly endless struggle of marching through the drifting snow mile after weary mile. Therefore, with his strength and energy thoroughly sapped and suffering severely, Lieutenant Orne simply could go no farther down the River Road. Far from his fine mansion and close friends back at his picturesque home port, the aristocratic lieutenant hailed from a leading Marblehead merchant family, which could not help him now. Orne was one of the best officers in the experienced company commanded by Colonel Glover's son. With his stamina failing him and his luck running out, Lieutenant Orne staggered out of the shuffling column of Glover's Massachusetts regiment in the blinding snowstorm. Orne's dilemma in the darkness and the raging storm's intensity was life-threatening.

Neither Captain John Glover, Jr., and the company's other lieutenant, Marston Watson, Ensign William Hawks, or their enlisted men saw Orne's sad plight. With the first signs of hypothermia setting in, including the loss of feeling in his lower extremities, and weakened from the strenuous exertions in crossing the Delaware and marching all night, Orne fell hard in the snow. He tumbled down by the side of the River Road, and then lay in a hump in the snow. With everyone else just focused on simply putting one foot before the other, the Massachusetts soldiers marched past Orne's prostrate form that no longer betrayed movement or any sign of life. No doubt believing that he would never again see his father, Colonel Azor Orne, who had served on key revolutionary committees of Marblehead, or his merchant family of the so-called codfish aristocracy, Lieutenant Orne lay comatose beside the road, as a soft veil of dropping snow began to slowly cover his motionless body.

Meanwhile, Fourteenth Massachusetts Continental Regiment soldiers continued to struggle slowly onward down the River Road with Colonel Glover, as usual, at the head of his mostly Massachusetts brigade. Fortunately, one of the last stragglers, evidently of St. Clair's brigade to Glover's rear, stumbled accidently upon the perfectly still lieutenant beside the road. He aroused Orne and helped the groggy officer to his feet. Once revived and awakened from a deep, comforting sleep that would have proved fatal, Orne again shouldered his musket, which now felt as heavy as lead, and continued slogging down the River Road. He even later picked up the pace, hoping to catch up to Glover's Bay State regiment, before it was too late. Clearly, it was a close call for Lieutenant Orne.[102]

Amid the blinding snow flurries and as best he could, young Greenwood likewise struggled onward against mind-numbing weariness amid the lengthy column of St. Clair's brigade in reserve. He described how the worn soldiers, stumbling and sliding along the slick road surface, after hundreds of marching feet had already churned up the initial layer of snow, were "nearly half dead with cold for the want of clothing, as, putting the storm to one side, many of our soldiers had not a shoe to their feet and their clothes were ragged as those of a beggar."[103]

Perhaps no soldiers in Sullivan's column were colder than the African Americans of the First Division, which contained more blacks than Greene's Second Division. In regard to Washington's New England units, wrote one officer, "no regiment is seen in which there are not negroes in abundance, and among them there are able-bodied, strong and brave fellows" fighting for America.[104] And another soldier penned how there was "a lot of Negroes" in every Massachusetts regiment.[105] On the torturous march to Trenton, black and white soldiers struggled onward together, assisting each other in continuing ever-southward through the snow and freezing cold.

Then, as if he didn't have enough to worry about, Washington received even more reason for concern about the wisdom of having decided to continue marching upon Trenton with the arrival of the most disturbing news from Colonel Glover's son. A vigilant Captain John Glover, Jr., who was the favorite, not just because he was firstborn of eleven children, child of his father-colonel, conducted a brief inspection of his tough Marblehead Continentals, while his suffering troops labored by in a badly stretched-out First Division column that seemed to have no end. To his horror, Captain Glover now discovered that a good many flintlocks of his Third Company Marbleheaders were completely soaked and inoperable, with wet ammunition as well. Because so many cartridges (sixty rounds) had been issued, Washington's Continentals had insufficient room for all of their rounds in leather cartridge-boxes that protected paper cartridges against rain and snow.

Therefore, the common soldiers had placed the extra twenty cartridges in their pockets which then became thoroughly soaked during their long ordeal. For the first time and compared to those New Englanders, especially Rogers' Rangers, who had long battled against a resourceful opponent in winter campaigns during the French and Indian War, the seafarer's lack of western frontier experience now came back to haunt the Marbleheaders at this crucial moment. Glover's Massachusetts men, who had long praised "Nature [for] the formation of our harbor" at Marblehead, now cursed a seemingly spiteful Mother Nature who seemed to have sided with Colonel Rall on this most tempestuous of early winter mornings.

Captain Glover's unit was the Marblehead colonel's favorite company, and the regiment's best drilled command. Therefore, this Grenadier Guard-like company of the Fourteenth Massachusetts Continental Regiment was destined to play a key role in the fighting that lay ahead at Trenton. Thanks to the heightened concern of the colonel's meticulous son, who was proving as capable as a leader as his father during this relentless march, the twenty-one-year-old captain immediately reported the disturbing news to his father, who then quickly dispatched word to General Sullivan.

The resilient son of hopeful immigrants from Ireland, Sullivan and his hard-working aides then checked their soldier's weapons to verify the validity of Glover's alarming report, which proved only too true. Every inch a fighter and even though the snow was falling heavier than ever, Sullivan then barked out, "Well, boys, we must fight them with the bayonets!" Then Sullivan dispatched a courier, or most likely a trusty aide, on a fast horse not back up the River Road and then back to Birmingham and onto the Scotch Road to alert Washington, but by way of some unnamed perpendicular road (a mere trail through the woodlands), about a mile south, or below, the Birmingham crossroads, that connected the River Road and the Scotch Road.

When Washington finally received the grim news that might have caused a less determined commander to suddenly abort this already most risky of operations after so many things had gone afoul, he continued to maintain his calm composure and firm resolution in the face of this new crisis, while the snow and sleet fell around him as if it would never stop. He shouted out orders that were transmitted to Sullivan and the First Division soldiers along the ice-slick River Road by his aide and private secretary, Lieutenant Colonel Samuel Blatchley Webb, born in Wethersfield, Connecticut in 1753, who had been wounded at the battle of Bunker Hill, or Breed's Hill: "Then tell the general to use the bayonet and penetrate into the town; for the town must be taken and I am resolved to take it." With no choice remaining, Washington now planned to rely upon the bayonet, the last-ditch conventional tactic that had brought so much past successes to the Hessians and British. To fuel resolve, Washington responded to this latest set-back by riding up and down the column's length, shouting orders and increasing the pace of his marching men, who forged ahead through the snow.

Clearly, Glover's son had made a most timely contribution, and one of his last. In barely six months, Captain John Glover, Jr., would be dead. He was fated to be lost at sea while serving aboard a privateer schooner. With flags flying in the salty air, these wide-ranging privateers sailed out of Marblehead to wage war on British warships to break up their death grip on the prime fishing grounds of the Grand Banks, Marblehead's economy, and the port's primary maritime industry, so that fishing could once again provide a living for a destitute people: a ruthless war of attrition on yet another front for Colonel Glover and his Bay State mariners, whose struggle this morning in Hunterdon County was as much about hard economic realities as lofty Age of Enlightenment ideology and idealism.[106]

Thanks to Captain Glover's timely warning, Sullivan immediately ordered his First Division men to clean their flintlocks as best they could, while the wind howled through the swaying trees, that cast no shadows on this most miserable of nights, surrounding the sheet-pelted column strung-out along the River Road. With the moon yet covered by dark clouds and casting no light to seemingly dim Washington's fortunes, the mostly New Englanders began frantically wiping and blowing away snow and ice encrusted on firing mechanisms. As Washington and Sullivan had ordered, what relatively few soldiers who possessed bayonets now fixed them to smoothbore flintlock barrels. Glover's men were among the relatively few troops in Sullivan's Division, and in the entire Continental Army, who could now count on the trusty cold steel of bayonets and only because Marblehead privateers had earlier captured British ships that provided invaluable war supplies. Therefore, Colonel Glover's boys now marched down the River Road with added confidence because they possessed fine bayonets, made in England, and knew how to use them as expertly as a wooden oar of a Durham boat on the Delaware's choppy waters.[107]

Wondering what else could possibly go wrong this seemingly ill-destined morning which might have reminded of when he, at age twenty-two, had written in April 1755 how "surely no man ever made a worse beginning" in regard to his initial military service, Washington hurriedly issued the same order to clean off weapons to all soldiers of Greene's Second Division column. A flurry of hectic activity rippled down the tattered ranks, with Washington's timely order awakening some half-asleep men about to fall by the snowy wayside. Besides

Lieutenant Orne's timely warning, other members of Sullivan's column also discovered that the snow and ice had made their weapons inoperable.

In leading the advance toward his own house situated along the River Road while serving as a sharp-eyed advanced guide for Sullivan's Division, Captain John Mott was one soldier who likewise made this shocking discovery that caused so much consternation. Clearly, in breaking military tradition, Washington's troops were unprepared for initiating a winter campaign even of short duration, and especially during an intense snowstorm. In serving as a guide for Sullivan's column laboring down the River Road, Mott had earlier attempted in vain to protect the black priming powder in his firing pan of a trusty fusil, or "fuzee," which was a shorter, lighter-weight version of the smoothbore musket and usually carried by American officers, with only a thin handkerchief.[108]

Also in the slow-moving ranks of Sullivan's column that were spread-out along the River Road like a long, black snake crawling over a white-colored landscape and cutting through heavy woodlands, Greenwood also felt an initial panic of uncertainly upon realizing that his Massachusetts regiment's combat capabilities, especially with so few bayonets, had been seriously eroded because: "As we had been in the storm all night we were not only wet through and through ourselves, but our guns and powder were wet also, so that I do not believe one would go off" if fired.[109]

Amid the predawn wintry stillness, that was so surreal that there seemed to be no more war, and heightened anxiety that hung over the head of Greene's column like a cloud, Washington's doubts about not only catching the Hessians by surprise but also about exactly how many of his soldier's weapons would fire once the battle opened in full fury continued to be a nagging concern. A less determined commander than Washington might well have yet aborted what seemed to be a doomed march of folly, which now possessed all the self-defeating ingredients of yet another inevitable American disaster in the making. But much like Napoleon, the enduring strength and weight of Washington's moral, spiritual, and physical drive kept his resolve firm and faith unshaken, despite—or perhaps because of—each new setback. Most of all, he remained firmly focused on fulfilling his single-minded vision and his primary goal of securing victory at Trenton at any cost. Even though the weather conditions worsened and setbacks continued to pile up like a spiraling of bad gambling debts, Washington's ambitious vision, firm resolve, and initial plan never waved.

At the head of his Delaware, Pennsylvania, Maryland, Virginia, Massachusetts, and Connecticut infantrymen pushing down the Scotch Road with muskets on shoulders, General Greene also naturally felt greater concern. This bright, gifted Rhode Islander of almost limitless potential worried because Washington now only possessed what was most of all "a very pitiful army to trust the liberties of America," and one whose already limited combat capabilities had been even additionally dramatically reduced by the weather on the eve of its most important battle to date.[110] Washington could only hope and pray that his men would rise to the Trenton challenge, as during the ambush of Braddock expedition and the resulting disaster, when the "Virginia companies behav'd like Men and died like Soldiers," as penned in a letter.[111]

Fortunately, for America, what relatively few soldiers who now remained trudging onward in Washington's ranks were incredibly tough, resilient, and durable, including the commander-in-chief's own supporting cast of top lieutenants. And perhaps no one at the senior leadership level was tougher than General Mercer himself. During the daring September 1756 raid on the Indian village of Kittanning, Captain Mercer had been badly wounded with a broken right arm, and then became separated from the raiding party in the wilderness of the Ohio country during its long withdrawal back east across the parallel, north-south running ridges of the Allegheny Mountains.

Now riding at the head of his own veteran infantry brigade of Maryland, Connecticut, and Massachusetts troops surging down the windblown Scotch Road with high hopes for reaping a sparkling success at Trenton, Mercer might have reflected upon that harrowing experience. As revealed by an article in the *Pennsylvania Gazette*, Mercer had successfully evaded Indians during "14 days in getting [safely on his own] to Fort Littleton [and] He had a miraculous Escape, living ten Days on two dried Clams and a Rattle Snake, with the Assistance of a few Berries."[112]

Most importantly, Washington could count on such resourceful men to the very end. The determined Virginian now rode forward at the column's head with the army's two rising stars, Colonel Knox, the former bookseller from Boston, and General Greene, a former militia private from a Quaker family, both of whom he had early groomed after recognizing their outstanding leadership abilities even though neither men possessed ample military experience or educations that qualified them for such high placement in the army's hierarchy. Clearly, unlike the British military system, this revolutionary army of free men and mostly yeomen farmers was an unprecedented place where a man of talent could rise up through his own abilities rather than aristocratic bloodlines and elevated upper class status.[113]

Meanwhile, Washington continued to encourage Greene's First Division troops south through the incessant flurries of snow and sleet, pushing down the Scotch Road, and ever-closer to the all-important Pennington Road, which paralleled and intersected the Scotch Road from the north, where the little town of Pennington lay just northeast of Bear Tavern. With more precious time slipping away and knowing that his nation's life was now hanging by a mere thread, Washington galloped down the column and implored at a loud voice, "Press on, press on, boys!" Once they gained the Pennington Road, just north of Trenton, at the advanced point now held by the half-frozen soldiers of Captain Washington's and Lieutenant Monroe's little advance guard of trusty Virginia soldiers, Greene's Second Division column would have an open avenue, although slick with ice and snow covered, into the northern end of town.[114]

While the snow descended heavier upon the twin columns of Washington's right and left wings and the biting cold never seemed more severe, no music was played by the young regimental fifers to lift the men's spirits as in comparable miserable situations, because of Washington's directive to maintain perfect silence. Marching in Sullivan's column of quiet soldiers, Boston-born Johnny Greenwood had long bolstered his comrade's morale by his lively fife playing. Greenwood had grown up in a fine Salem Street house, because his father, a Boston dentist and merchant, was engaged in the lucrative ivory trade with Africa. The grandson of a distinguished Harvard professional, Greenwood was also inspired by a distinguished warrior ancestor, who had served as an officer-chaplain in the conquering Puritan Army of diehard Protestants under Oliver Cromwell.

When only nine or ten years of age, Greenwood had found an old fife and quickly learned to play. Therefore, he early became a fifer in a Boston militia company which served under an "English" flag. At age thirteen, Greenwood was sent to live with his uncle in Falmouth, today's Portland, Maine, before the escalating crisis with Great Britain changed everything. He then became the much-pampered "boy" fifer of the local militia company known as "the Cadets" in which his uncle served as an officer. When the war erupted at Lexington and Concord when the famous "shot heard 'round the world" was fired in anger, Greenwood ran away from his uncle's command because he feared his family "would all be killed" by the British, who occupied Boston. He consequently had gone forth with a determination "to fight for my country."

Upon reaching Boston, Greenwood promptly enlisted, while basking in the British's derogatory name for New England rebels, the "Yankees." Despite his father having paid for a substitute to take his son's place in the ranks, Greenwood remained faithfully with his Massachusetts Regiment. Despite the spoiled pet of the older soldiers and looking too small for his age, Greenwood was a fighter. He knew how to use a tomahawk, sword, and musket, the last of which he now carried with him down the icy River Road and toward an unknown fate at Trenton. Like other soldiers, Private Greenwood was now fueled by a sense of revenge, after having learned in the recent Canadian Campaign, that the "Indians and the English acted very much alike, that is, without principle." For such reasons, Johnny now struggled onward through the snow with Sullivan's column, despite a recent illness that had ravished Colonel John Patterson's regiment until scores of his comrades and friends "died like rotten sheep," in his embittered words.

On such an awful night in western New Jersey when this little "fife-major," who was the "favorite" of the entire New England regiment, could not play his spirited martial tunes—his hands were too cold and he obeyed Washington's strict orders for silence—that had so often cheered his comrades, perhaps Johnny Greenwood yet recalled his mother's final words to him before he marched off to war: "hope [that] you will behave like a soldier." And now his mother's "hope" also ensured that Greenwood continued to march silently beside his equally determined Fifteenth Massachusetts comrades.[115]

Teenage Major Wilkinson, serving with St. Clair's staff, was one of the relatively few Americans who was now riding a horse south toward Trenton. Benefitting from a fine classical education and possessing a distinct taste for music, art, and fine living, Wilkinson was a Maryland cavalier and a proper Southern gentleman. He was very much of a product of the planter class. Wilkinson benefitted from his privileged upbringing in the South's northeastern edge and amid southern Maryland's tobacco country of fertile river and creek valley and rolling hills. His grandfather, Joseph, had been an enterprising English tobacco merchant, before deciding to settle in Calvert County, Maryland, at Stoakling Manor, the family's tobacco plantation.

But life was not easy for young James, because of falling tobacco prices, spiraling debts, and his father's early death, before his mid-thirties, when he was only six. Stoakling Manor had to be sold to pay off spiraling debts and taxes. Wilkinson then attended the same school in Baltimore, Maryland, as Washington's stepson, John Custiss. Here, far away from the Calvert County tobacco plantation, Wilkinson grew to relish the vibrancy of city life, basking in its cultured sophistication. His soaring ambitions led him to attend medical school in Philadelphia at only age sixteen. In less than two years, Wilkinson left medical school in April 1775 to open up a medical practice on the western frontier at Monocacy, Maryland, which had been settled primarily by German immigrants.

Then, while visiting Philadelphia, he discovered his true calling, when the revolution erupted to present new opportunities. After only practicing medicine for less than three months, the impetuous young man joined the army, following his "strongest inclination." He shortly gained an appointment as a captain of the Second Continental Regiment. Looking younger than his age of eighteen, Wilkinson evolved into a fine officer. Wilkinson had felt considerable shock—like Washington—on first discovering the ultra-democratic sentiment among the New Englanders, who openly violated traditional Southern planter class social values and protocol. Although Wilkinson was considered "more nice than wise" by an equally ambitious Benedict Arnold, he now rode down the River Road with the Scotland-born General St. Clair and staff at the head of the New Hampshire and Massachusetts Continental brigade.[116]

Meanwhile, Washington steadily led his Second Division troops farther down the Scotch Road, easing ever-closer to Trenton while whatever light might have been normally forthcoming from the high moon was yet obscured by storm clouds. Riding back and forth on his chestnut sorrel with its distinctive copper-red color, Washington encouraged his footsore troops, whose faces, hands, and feet were numb from the cold, onward like Moses leading the Children of Israel from the horrors of a cruel Egyptian bondage. Most of all, Washington now relied on God's favor and the "astonishing interpositions of providence" to bring him victory in America's greatest hour of need. With so many doubts yet lingering in his mind, he reached down into the depths of his soul to implore God's assistance when needed the most. As he had written to Colonel Reed, who had once called Trenton home, on December 23, Washington knew that "if we are successful [then it would be something] which heaven grant."[117]

In fact and as penned in a letter, a thankful Washington, after narrowly surviving the slaughter of the Braddock disaster, was fully convinced how, "I now exist and appear in the land of the living by the miraculous Care of Providence, that protected me beyond all human expectation [because] I had 4 bullets through my Coat, and two Horses shot under me, and yet escaped unhurt . . . ."[118]

Symbolically, the forward movements of both Greene's and Sullivan's columns of sickly, hopeful, and weakened soldiers actually represented a holy pilgrimage of sorts, presenting almost something out of the Book of Exodus, because their unshakable belief in God, or "Providence" in Washington's terminology, bestowing an eventual victory over the much-feared Hessians. This powerful belief continued to drive these ragtag soldiers of liberty onward through the foulest and most brutal weather than they had ever seen. No coincidence, the most religious men, even while the mind-numbing exhaustion and the omnipresent cold gnawed at them with a vengeance, were also the most faithful in believing that this dying revolution could be yet resurrected, relying upon the power of faith and their own deep personal religious convictions precisely because it seemed as if nothing else could be depended upon in this war.

After all, Washington's New Englanders were the descendants of the Puritans, God's natural rebels, who had broken away from the Church of England to "purify" (hence their name) it and start the world anew in America. And after having gone to war under colorful war banners emblazoned with Biblically inspired slogans such as "Resistance to Tyrans is Obedience to God," and "An Appeal to God,", these battle-hardened soldiers from Massachusetts, Connecticut, and New Hampshire of Sullivan's First Division—along with the New Yorkers—were now fortified by a strong religious belief system based on the Old Testament, including a lengthy heritage of antinomianism, or the willful moral right to break artificial manmade bonds because of God's higher moral laws. Bolstering their endurance in this crisis situation in the desire to reach Trenton as soon as possible, these young men and boys now carried their unique belief system with them through the biting winds and snows of Hunterdon County.

In this sense, the moral motivations of Sullivan's First Division, of mostly New Englanders, was now not unlike that of Oliver Cromwell's Puritan Army, which had waged a holy war against England's enemies like Christian Crusaders invading the Holy Land. Most of all, Washington's Continentals fully convinced that their struggle was a righteous one, and fundamentally "the cause of heaven against hell," in the words of one patriot preacher. Clearly, Washington and his men had much to inspire and drive them onward on this most bleak of late December mornings.

By this time, there was no turning back for either Washington or his worn-out soldiers, who just kept pushing—more like machines than mortal men—through the snow and ever-farther south, almost as if being drawn by some unseen gravitational force toward Trenton and an uncertain fate. Crossing the Delaware in essence had been America's Rubicon, or symbolically not unlike the Old Testament's Jordan River. And on December 26, Washington's soldiers seemed to instinctively sense as much, which was a realization that motivated them to keep moving on this darkest, coldest, and stormiest of nights. All the while, the cutting wind chilled the bones of America's most stalwart revolutionaries to the very marrow.

Indeed, the possibilities for moral, physical, and spiritual redemption for this often-beaten revolutionary army and a faltering fledgling republic yet lay for the taking on the Delaware's east side, and whatever Washington and his soldiers could accomplish against a full Hessian brigade at Trenton. In a letter to Washington, Declaration of Independence signer Edward, or "Ned," Rutledge, of South Carolina, emphasized exactly where the most and last remaining faith for the dream of America was now firmly placed: "Our reliance continues, therefore, to be, under God, on your wisdom and fortitude and that of your forces." Washington's troops, consequently, realized that they must keep trudging with a relentless determination toward the seemingly unattainable goal of Trenton in a desperate bid to resurrect America's life, until no more strength or energy remained in tired, half-froze bodies racked by malnutrition, disease, and bitter cold.

Most of all, these hardened American soldiers, the most committed and determined of America's remaining band of defenders, knew that they must overcome every single obstacle placed in their path this seemingly ill-fated morning by bad luck, the unmerciful winter storm, obstacles of geography, and plain old bad luck, while ignoring the cold misery, creeping hypothermia, and bone-numbing weariness that racked bodies, including those soldiers who now should have been hospitalized. Consequently, these young men and boys from New England to Virginia, who were saddled with an awesome responsibility and burden of keeping the flicking flame of this new experiment in nationhood and republicanisn alive against the odds, continued to struggle ever-southward like frigid ghosts out of a dream. And all the while, they marched relentlessly ever-southward without ever knowing if a cruel fate or God's helping hand was now directing them toward an uncertain destiny, either a great victory or another fiasco.

With anxious faces, now numb from the first sign of flesh freezing, and a hard-earned stoicism created like tough calluses by the series of past defeats, Washington's Continentals, toughened month after month seemingly for this very challenge, continued to wage their own private war against the driving snow, biting cold, and ice. Washington's ranks had been cruelly culled for months, but what was now left for the attack on a full German brigade was an experienced, highly motivated team of warriors, who were bonded tightly together by adversity and suffering. By this time, many soldiers were suffering from frostbite, and no doubt from the first hallucinations brought about by hypothermia, with all sensation first leaving fingers and toes, and then feet and hands. In gamely forging ahead, therefore, Washington's soldiers were pushing beyond what was beyond normal endurance and almost what was humanly possible, because they realized that everything now depended upon them going onward in the night's harshness. But how were more than one thousand ill-clad, undernourished soldiers of America able to overcome so much adversity?

First and foremost, despite all the recent setbacks, Washington and his men nevertheless believed that God was yet on America's side. As if bestowed by providence, a thick fog had masked the escape of much of Washington's Army, thanks to Glover's mariners, across the East River from Long Island to the southern end of Manhattan Island in late August. And now in a providential way, Washington had been once again bestowed with a raging storm that screened his final approach to Trenton.

Coughing, freezing, and sneezing, Washington's common soldiers continued to push onward with firm, if not grim, resolution that had only intensified with the recent order to fix bayonets with so many flintlocks inoperable. But if nothing else, these resilient fighting men from across America could at least depend upon the sharp point of a steel bayonet while doing little more than placing their last ounces of hope in a much-needed miracle from God and in the hope that Washington might finally succeed in his tactical design. A blind faith and destiny itself now seemed to be drawing Washington and his men, including many soldiers with numb half-frozen feet and hands that had lost feeling hours ago, onward through the pitiless winds and swirling snow of a little known wilderness area in which they were now seemingly lost, as if only wanting to find their way out of the blinding storm to escape nature's most bitter wrath.

But in continuing to march down the barely recognizable Scotch Road blanketed in snow, these Continental soldiers, understanding the full implications of Washington's motto "Victory or Death" that revealed the commander-in-chief's unshakeable resolution to do or die, were marching onward in a final bid to revitalize an old utopian dream that seemed to have died: the real meaning of America as an almost magical land of moral, spiritual, and physical rebirth for people from distant shores. And this much-needed rejuvenation of a people, a new nation, and a special destiny had to be won with a victory in the next few hours, because this was the last chance to do so for America. In essence, Washington and men were now trudging south in search of moral redemption and the rejuvenation of a dying revolutionary struggle that could only be achieved by reaping a dramatic success at Trenton.

Therefore, in their darkest, most bleak, and coldest hour of December 26, Washington's soldiers, including men of all ages who freely quoted the Bible from memory to motivate themselves and their freezing comrades on this tortuous march, prayed for deliverance from two storms—one man-made and the other from nature. All the while, the eerie silence of a cold tranquillity dominated the grueling trek, and nothing could be heard by Washington's men but the soft, plodding tread of hundreds of feet on snow. Washington prayed, "May that Being, who is powerful to save, and in whose hands is the fate of nations, look down with an eye of tender pity and compassion upon" America's struggle and cause to make the world anew. Washington and his men found an inspirational analogy in the spiritual words of the Old Testament: Joshua leading his small band of determined Jewish holy warriors across the Jordan River to vanquish Israel's mortal enemies, the Canaanites, to create a new moral kingdom of God and "righteous commonwealth" in the Land of Canaan.

A former Loudon County, Virginia, preacher now serving as the highly respected chaplain of the Third Virginia Continental Regiment, David Griffith, who had been ordained by the Bishop of London, and who often conducted religious services at Washington's own headquarters, had recently provided inspiring spiritual council to fortify Washington's already strong religious faith and that of his men. For Washington and his religious-minded soldiers, who now saw themselves and their cause as now being sternly tested by God to test the validity and strength of their faith, Trenton indeed now represented another ancient Jericho for these homespun New World soldiers, who were revolutionary idealists motivated by lofty ideals of the Age of Enlightenment. And this new symbolic Jericho—Trenton—had to be now overwhelmed by a new generation of righteous, God-fearing holy warriors for a new spiritual and moral resurrection of this beleaguered land, now known as the United States of America, as in Canaan as long ago.

And for Washington's final desperate bid for deliverance and redemption with the revolutionary struggle now at its lowest ebb, a good many far-flung

American units, some new and some veteran, had come together at almost the last minute and for the first time to now perform with an amazing efficiency during Washington's most audacious undertaking. Even unknown to them at this time, Washington's troops were even now in the process of being forged into a much determined soldiery by a steely synthesis of adversity and sheer desperation born of the greatest crisis ever faced by the young nation conceived in liberty: the painful, difficult, and slow evolution that resulted in the creation of a truly nationalistic and first "American Army," as emphasized the commander-in-chief.

In his mid-thirties, General Greene, the philosophical "fighting Quaker" and genteel Rhode Island anchorsmith, who early sensed this quiet evolution of such subtle developments in the army's ranks, despite their thorough depletion through a cruel attrition: "We bear beating very well . . . the more we are beat the better we grow." Indeed, although they hardly looked like real fighting men in either appearances, maneuvers, or manners, Washington's common soldiers were now motivated by an unprecedented high level of determination to succeed at any cost, thanks in no small part to their commander-in-chief's inspirational words and actions that had fueled this new fighting spirit to fever pitch, when they were about to descend upon Trenton from two directions.

Against all predictions, these Americans continued to maintain firm discipline and a "profound silence," as ordered by Washington, displaying an unprecedented sense of determination, almost as if they were British or Hessian professionals instead of only ragged, untrained citizensoldiers, mostly rawboned farm boys, imbued with idealistic notions about America's endless promise and potential, which were yet nothing more than a starry-eyed dream. Therefore and despite commanding a force so greatly "reduced by Sickness, Desertion, & Political Deaths," in his own words, Washington now actually possessed a much more mature, toughened, and determined soldiery than ever before. Fortunately for America, he finally had this highly motivated force of hardened veterans moving forward with confidence, fortified resolve, and a good chance to secure a rare victory in a win-all or lose-all situation.[119] Captain William Hull described in a letter how Washington's men slogged onward through the whipping winter winds and snow with an unprecedented degree of "Resolution and Firmness" that was truly a sight to behold, after so many past disasters for American arms.[120]

Only now on this most challenging, darkest, and stormiest of nights was Washington beginning to fully realize what had been happening right before his eyes: a remarkable but quiet and subtle transformation, born of severe adversity and a heightened sense of desperation, that was now occurring almost inexplicably, if not magically and certainly quite mysteriously, among the often-inscrutable common soldiery, until crossing the Delaware. In amazement about what he now felt and sensed developing around him, an astounded Washington described how something quite remarkable was happening among his followers during the long trek to Trenton, because unlike so often in the past: "The difficulty of passing the River in a very severe Night, and their March thro' a violent Storm of Snow and Hail, did not in the least abate their Ardour."[121]

Chapter III

All Quiet at Trenton

Quite suddenly and if only ever so slightly, America's fortunes were finally beginning to look up, because Washington was now presented with an even better opportunity than he originally thought. Trenton as well as the Rall brigade, the group that had "incontestably suffered the most of any" brigade in the British Army, had never been so vulnerable before.[1]

Additionally, one of Washington's best allies continued to be the extremely low esteem held by Colonel Rall's Germans, yet to lose a battle, for American soldiers in general. Washington's so-called American "Rebeller" was widely denounced by the Hessians for his lack of soldierly qualities, including courage. Lieutenant Jakob Piel, a skilled map maker who was now stationed at Trenton with his von Lossberg Regiment, concluded with pride how "the rebels" had "never on any occasion been able to withstand us."[2]

As class conscious as other highly professional German officers, Colonel Henrich Anton von Heringen, who had commanded the von Lossberg Regiment until dying of dysentery in September 1776 and finding a lonely grave in Brooklyn, had viewed the long lines of captured American prisoners at Long Island in absolute astonishment and unmasked disgust: "We found no professional soldiers [as] Among the prisoners are many so-called colonels, lieutenant colonels, majors, and other officers, who however [before the conflict] are nothing but mechanics, tailors, shoemakers, wigmakers, barbers, etc."[3] A close look at Washington's vanquished soldiers had brought not only utter dismay but also open laughter from the well-trained, smartly uniformed German and British victors, who hardly could believe their eyes. Irish Captain Frederick Mackenzie never forgot the close sight of Washington's captured men at Fort Washington: "A great many of these were lads under fifteen, and old men . . . Their odd figures frequently excited the laughter of our soldiers."[4]

But no more American solider was now held in greater contempt by Hessian and British alike than Washington himself. Expressing a view shared by so many others on both sides of the Atlantic, Ambrose Serle, Sir Howe's civilian personal secretary, described the often-defeated commander-in-chief as nothing more than "a little paltry colonel of a militia of bandits."[5] In September 1776, Hessian adjutant general Karl Leopold Baurmeister analyzed with considerable insight how Washington was doomed to defeat because "whatever knowledge [he had] of the science of war will be useless to organize the raw rabble of conscripted men" under his command.[6]

Most of all, the confident Hessian troops garrisoned at Trenton still basked in their recent successes on American soil that had already garnered the "greatest honor," in one Hessian officer's words, to German arms. They had played the leading role in overwhelming Fort Washington, a seemingly impregnable fortress, by assault, inflicting yet another defeat after Washington made the mistake of attempting to hold onto the only remaining position on Manhattan Island.[7] In fact, most of these cocky German soldiers, perhaps Colonel Rall himself, had only recently believed that Christmas 25, 1776 would be the war's last Yuletide. After all, the Hessians had so often seen that whenever Washington's men were attacked, as one young Hessian lieutenant wrote, "they ran, as all mobs do."[8]

Therefore, these German professional soldiers at Trenton now believed that they would soon return to Germany to be reunited with friends and family. But instead of the much-anticipated reunion, Rall's men were now stuck at dreary, cheerless Trenton and badly in need of rest. After the New York Campaign, Rall's fusiliers and grenadiers were sick and tired of battling homespun revolutionaries in a strange land far from home. They found little glory in fighting a people, mostly farmers like themselves, struggling for their own freedom. During their own personal odyssey on the Atlantic's other side, the average German soldier on American soil was little more than a clog in the long-accepted mercenary system that exploited the young and rural poor of various German states, such as Hesse-Cassel, Brunswick, Hesse-Hanau and a trio of small states.

This time-honored Teutonic practice was increasingly condemned by European humanitarians and liberals as a corrupt, immoral soldier trade. Money-hungry monarchies of Christian Europe had traditionally benefitted from hiring out their fighting men, including against Islam, throughout the seventeenth and eighteenth Centuries. No one knew exactly how many sons of impoverished German farming families, especially lowly peasants, had been impressed into regular army service, marched off to distant wars, and never returned to their homelands along the Rhine and Weser Rivers, while greedy rulers grew rich.

More than half of the nearly thirty thousand German soldiers who served in America hailed from the landlocked, mid-sized German kingdom known as Hesse-Cassel, or Hessen-Kassel, in today's west central Germany: hence, the generalized name and popular generic appellation of Hessians for all German troops who fought in America. Here, ruling his domain from the "beautiful town" of Cassel that had been recently rebuilt by skilled architects, the Landgrave Frederick II, the cousin of King George III who was also the king of Hanover, gained vast profits by hiring out his subjects as cannon fodder. Half a dozen minor German states contributed soldiers to England's bid to subjugate America.

All in all, these well-trained Hessian troops filled a large void in the British war effort because of the conflict's unpopularity in England and the diminutive British Army already being overextended by global commitments. Because of pressing economic and global considerations, Great Britain had long been the best customer of lower class German cannon fodder, securing at the lowest price, from the small north German principality of Hesse-Cassel. Hessian troops had even been earlier utilized for the Albion island's defense against anticipated Jacobite French and Scottish invasions. Hessians had also served in stemming the surging Jacobite rebel tide at Culloden in 1746. England's successful utilization of ready-made German military units of a professional standing army had not only permitted the British to tie down the troublesome French in Europe but also allowed for the bolstering of a military machine for imperial adventures and overseas expansion far from the mainland.

And now an entire Hessian brigade of hardened professional soldiers was stationed at Trenton primarily because they were essentially pawns in the strategic chessboard game of England's imperial ambitions to retain control of their sprawling North American empire to counter its chief international rival France. Contrary to conventional wisdom, the British government's controversial decision to dispatch thousands of German soldiers to wage war against its own subjects was far less morally offensive to many European intellectuals than the Landgrave's crass sale of his own soldiers' services.

But more importantly, the sending of thousands of Hessian troops to America had helped to fuel greater moral outrage in America that in part led to the signing of the Declaration of Independence in Philadelphia on July 4, 1776. In fact, America's direct "answer to the treaty with the Landgrave was the Declaration of Independence." In a strange case of the revolutionary struggle now having come full circle in regard to the impending showdown at Trenton, therefore, the very fighting men whom Washington was about to attack had already played an unintentional early role in the establishment of the new American nation.[9]

Colonel Johann Gottlieb Rall, age fifty, was anything but the worst of all possible commanders: one of the most persistent myths of the battle of Trenton. By December 1776, this hard-fighting Hesse-Cassel colonel possessed not only thirty-six years of solid military experience, but also a most distinguished record and a lengthy list of battlefield accomplishments that earned him the well-deserved sobriquet of "The Lion." In truth, Rall was destined to become a victim at Trenton principally because of a cancerous hubris at higher leadership levels rather than inherent military deficiencies.[10]

Like almost everyone else in the British Army, Rall was confident this December when hopes of smashing the rebellion were never higher. Vanquishing Washington's amateurs at war had been so relatively easy that it even became a source of some embarrassment among the German victors at Trenton by this time. This well-deserved contempt for America's ragtag revolutionaries in dirty farmer's and hunter's clothes caused Donop's adjutant to lament with disgust how "what we have seen so far brings us little honour to fight against these" Americans in rebellion against their own king for reasons not readily understood by Germans not privy to Age of Enlightenment thought and ideology.[11]

But in fact Colonel Rall was neither complacent or entirely a victim of his own hubris as so commonly alleged by his distractors. He had received timely intelligence from three different sources on December 23 that Washington's troops had been issued three day's rations and were making vigorous preparations for an offensive operation. On December 24, therefore, Rall had dispatched two strong parties on reconnaissance missions north of Trenton: one marched all the way to Pennington and the other one, under Captain Adam Christoph, or Christian, Steding, of the von Lossberg Regiment, pushed up the River Road to Johnson's Ferry and then on to Pennington.

Nevertheless, generations of American historians have long embraced the popular image and stereotype that Colonel Rall was the most incompetent and befuddled of commanders of the American Revolution. But like so many other experienced men and officers in the British Army *before* the battle of Trenton, Lieutenant Jacob Piel viewed Rall as a highly capable commander of outstanding military ability. To shatter another popular stereotype that has long endured to become gospel, Lieutenant Andreas Wiederhold, Knyphausen Regiment, described Rall as "all too easy-going," which was very much the anthesis of the stereotypical mindless martinet and despotic Teutonic officer.

At the head of his men, Rall had known nothing but one victory after another in America, beginning with the battle of Long Island. Here, he captured one of the first American battle flags, embroidered with the word "Liberty." Instead of the incompetent buffoon so long alleged by historians, Rall was in truth one of the hardest fighting, most tactically astute, and aggressive German colonels in America. Unlike so many fellow German officers of high rank, he had advanced not by way of politics, noble blood, or currying the favor of the Landgrave, but by demonstrating outstanding ability on one battlefield after another.

Indeed, by December 1776, Rall was a proven winner on every battlefield upon which he led troops. And his admiring men of the enlisted ranks loved him for leading them to so many victories. As usual in a typical hierarchy military setting where inflated egos and vanity dominated the ranks of the upper echelon, than as today, he engendered considerable jealousy among his superiors for his winning ways. Unlike Howe's officers, who were almost exclusively of the privileged ruling class aristocracy, especially the British who Captain Alexander Hamilton acidly denounced as "effeminate striplings," Rall possessed common roots: the anthesis of an officer and a gentleman. Unlike his more aristocratic peers, the hard-fighting colonel forged surprisingly close bonds with the common soldier in the ranks: the first sign of a good commander and a key to success on multiple levels.

Born in Hesse-Cassel, Rall was the son of a middle-class officer who spent his entire life in the military. He had first enlisted in his father's regiment as a serious-minded, ambitious young cadet. Rall rose from cadet to a second lieutenant's rank in 1745 and then major in 1760 on his own merit. To secure greater career opportunities like so many other foreign officers who served in Russia's Imperial Armies during the eighteenth century, Rall fought under Catherine the Great's banner from 1771 to 1772. He demonstrated leadership ability under Count Gregory Orlov against the Islamic Turks of the Ottoman Empire during the Russo-Turkish War on Russia's southeastern frontier, defending Christianity of the Orthodox faith and Mother Russia, which had been victimized by invaders, including the Mongols, for centuries.

Rall has been long condemned by American historians for not erecting earthworks to defend Trenton. However, in truth, the town of Trenton was simply too sprawling and too vulnerable on three sides to be defended, even by a full brigade. In addition, relinquishing the initiative by cowering behind defenses and awaiting an attack was simply not part of the military traditions and ethos of offensive-minded and professional German soldiers and quite unlike some other European militaries, especially the defensive-oriented Russians. The experienced Rall knew better than to waste a great deal of time and extensive efforts, especially in regard to wearing out his men, in erecting defenses that could be easily outflanked by attackers. He allegedly mocked Major Friedrich von Dechow, commanding the Knyphausen Regiment at Trenton, who had advocated the creation of fortifications, declaring, "Works!-pooh-pooh."[12]

Most Hessian officers, such as thirty-year-old Lieutenant Ernst Christian Schwabe who had served for sixteen years in the von Lossberg Regiment, were entirely unconcerned about any unpleasant surprises stemming from Washington's generalship, which had been long mocked. After all, the rebellious Americans were now widely considered to be little more than a disorganized body of "half-starved, half-clothed, half-armed, discontented, ungovernable, undisciplined wretches."[13]

Of course, at this time, Colonel Rall had no way of knowing that among this despised rabble of revolutionaries was his own cousin, a middle-class cobbler from Maryland and a Continental captain of Washington's German Regiment. He was now advancing toward Trenton along with hundreds of his Teutonic comrades in Greene's Second Division column. Interestingly, Colonel Glover had started out life as a lowly shoemaker before becoming a successful merchant and ship captain of Marblehead, demonstrating that social mobility for a bright, industrious man was possible in New England.[14]

Although deserted by most inhabitants, Trenton meant something very special to Rall and his men, promising that they would put up a stiff fight in defending their newfound winter home. Because of his excellent battlefield performances throughout the New York Campaign, especially at Fort Washington and White Plains, Rall had been awarded the assignment of occupying Trenton by Howe himself.[15] He now commanded Trenton and its environs from his modest quarters at the two-story house of Stacy Potts on King Street near the town's center. Potts had grown wealthy from profits generated by his nearby tannery and a small iron works on Petty's Run on Trenton's northern and western outskirts. Rall's acting King Street headquarters, located on the street's west side, was strategically located near the heart of Trenton and just across the street from the Anglican, or English, Church.[16]

On this stormy Christmas night, Potts's roaring stone fireplaces in his wood-frame house provided ample warmth to Rall's cozy headquarters. Earlier near sunset on Christmas Day, the alarm had been sounded when Hessian pickets on the town's northwestern outskirts were fired upon by a band of Americans lurking in the dark New Jersey forests. A small raiding party under Captain George Wallis's Fourth Virginia Continental Regiment, Stephen's brigade—which Rall assumed was the force that General Grant had earlier warned him about in a message written late on the night of December 24 to reach Trenton on Christmas morning—proved of little concern. These Virginia riflemen had only briefly harassed Corporal William Hartung's picket post on the Pennington Road northwest of Trenton with long-range gunfire.

Half a dozen Hessians were hit by the Virginian's accurate gunfire from deadly Long Rifles erupting from a belt of black woodlands, however. Like a prudent commander, Rall had turned out his entire brigade on the double to meet the sudden threat. But the troublemaking band of around thirty Virginians soon slipped away into the night, vanishing like ghosts. Entirely unknown to Washington, this daring raid by his fellow staters had been launched across the Delaware by his brigade commander General Stephen. Washington's former top lieutenant of his Virginia Regiment during the French and Indian War had been actively waging his own personal war in typical guerrilla fashion. As written just before midnight on Christmas Eve, Grant's warning—about an attack from Washington's Army instead of only a company-sized raiding party—had been grossly overexaggerated, or so it seemed to Rall and his top lieutenants, who dismissed the threat and its implications.

Like other officers at Trenton, therefore, Rall experienced considerable relief by Christmas evening after the pesky Virginia sharpshooters faded away into the night. After all, Trenton's northern approaches were now well guarded, after Rall prudently strengthened them by pickets with trusty veteran officers in timely fashion. He had significantly upgraded his advanced warning system around Trenton's immediate outskirts in case any new threat from roving rebels suddenly emerged along the Pennington Road. In fact, Rall had done every-thing right and by the book.

On this stormy night, not taking any chances, he even made sure that his own grenadier regiment remained under arms and in a state of full alert at their previously specified alarm houses along King Street. In fact, based on Rall's wise precautions, the entire Rall Brigade, now well honed from the practice of responding to recent alarms, was ready to quickly assemble at three predesignated points—one for each regiment—to defend Trenton. Besides the Rall Regiment, hundreds of troops of the brigade's other two regiments also slept in uniform, with cartridge-boxes strapped on. As a result, Rall and his garrison were not guilty of what was later described as "fanciful security," as so long assumed. In truth, the garrison was on full and "high alert," as the German "troops have lain on their arms every night," penned one Hessian in a letter.[17]

Meanwhile, the omnipresent legacy of Frederick the Great, who was even admired by Washington's officers, was alive and well at Trenton. The notable battlefield achievements of this dynamic Prussian king and prince-elector of the sprawling Holy Roman Empire yet inspired the tough fighting men of Rall brigade. In a strange irony and like members of the Rall Brigade, some of Washington's soldiers, including the general himself, now carried copies of Frederick the Great's *Instructions*. By winning so many sparkling victories over Prussia's enemies, especially Austria, he had transformed Prussia, despite being landlocked and surrounded by hostile neighbors, into a major European power. His remarkable successes stemmed in part from the creation of a superior officer corps and an elite military caste system, based upon the ruling nobility and a professional standing army, of which Frederick the Great was the revered father.

As part of this omnipresent martial legacy, highly efficient Rall Brigade officers had been educated at the West Point-like Collegium Carolinum in Cassel. Here, they had learned about the mysteries of engineering, tactics, cartography, foreign languages, mathematics, and logistics. Like Rall's officers, the common Hessian soldiers also were the disciplined products of Frederick the Great's professional standing army tradition. This enduring memory of the blue-uniformed master of war (nicknamed "Old Fritz"), especially among Rall's veterans who had served under Frederick the Great, yet lingered with vibrance among the crack soldiers stationed at Trenton.[18]

Barely six months earlier on June 18, 1776, ironically, Frederick the Great had written a letter to Voltaire, one of the greatest French Enlightenment thinkers, writers, and philosophers. He lamented the sad fate of so many of his Teutonic countrymen, especially lower-class members, who had become nothing more than manipulated pawns of the ruling elite when their princes "sold his subjects to the English as one sells cattle to be dragged to the shambles [and] I pity the poor Hessians who end their lives unhappily and useless in America."[19]

Frederick the Great had been prophetic about the future disasters awaiting German troops—nearly thirty thousand in total—sent to faraway America, including Colonel Rall and his crack brigade, which had been molded by the omnipresent Frederickan legacy. Symbolically, Hesse-Cassel's ruler, Langraf Frederick II, who signed the contract with Great Britain for fifteen regiments to serve in North America in mid-January 1776, had been named after the Prussian military genius. The Hessians' tactics, drill, and values were copied from those of the Prussian Army. Even more, the very weapons, including muskets, of the Hessians had been made in Prussia. And the blue uniforms of the Knyphausen and Rall Regiments stationed at Trenton were modeled after Prussian Army uniforms. The Hessians also hailed from other Germanic states besides Hesse-Cassel, such as Brunswick, Waldeck, Anspach-Beyreuth, Hesse Hanau, and Anhalt Zerbst. Soldiers from these diverve regions possessed different faiths (Catholic and Protestant), dialects and community values.

But unfortunately for Rall and his isolated brigade at Trenton, senior British and Hessian leadership in America possessed few of Frederick the Great's sterling qualities that had made him legendary. By this time, consequently, Rall's greatest obstacles to Trenton's successful defense were not his owncomplacency or hubris, but most of all the failings of his own senior commanders, both British and Hessian. These senior leaders lacked his lofty level of experience—some thirty-six years—and repeated success as a combat commander. With keen tactical instincts, therefore, Rall had sensed earlier that trouble was brewing outside Trenton. Rall drew careful conclusions that were entirely different from those of most of his aristocratic, elitist superiors in regard to Trenton's vulnerability.

General Howe, writing to Lord Germain on December 20, described how his defensive positions, including Trenton, and winter quarters in New Jersey, stretching nearly to headquarters at New York City, were secure. He felt that there was nothing to worry about because of "the strength of the corps placed in the advanced posts [including Trenton and therefore] I conclude the troops will be in perfect security."[20] Lord Cornwallis had initially convinced Howe, who might have been in part swayed by his top lieutenant's royal connections in having served as an aide-de-camp to King George III himself, to retain possession of Trenton. Even though Howe had earlier complained that he had too few troops for pursuing Washington all the way to the Delaware, he nevertheless had then paradoxically concluded that in regard to Trenton, "I apprehended no danger."[21]

A long-existing sense of "perfect security" among the British high command, especially in faraway New York City, now presented an ideal opportunity that Washington had envisioned with tactical clarity and was about to exploit to the fullest. Like Howe, Cornwallis, and other top leaders, both British and Hessian, General Grant was equally complacent until it was too late on Christmas Eve. Despite having overall responsibility of the British-Hessian defensive line stretching from central New Jersey to western New Jersey, Grant had never set foot in Trenton to inspect this advanced outpost. In regard to the possibility that Washington might strike across the Delaware, Grant had been long convinced that, "I own I did not think them equal to the attempt." Despite many years of sound military experience, Grant was a high-living epicure who was now more concerned about the fine culinary dishes placed on his dinner table by his personal chief and servants than Trenton's safety until it was far too late. From beginning to end, General Grant and his British superiors were far more complacent and negligent than Colonel Rall.[22]

Even sexual dynamics played a large role in presenting Washington with a golden opportunity at Trenton, in his own confident words, "to clip their wings, while they are so spread" out across so much of New Jersey in winter quarters. No one was more negligent than Colonel Donop, Rall's immediate superior, except Howe, Cornwallis, and Grant. Waging war like feudal lords, Howe and Grant enjoyed living in grand style, including with readily available pretty women, both married and unmarried, who served as mistresses. When Trenton was about to be attacked by Washington's much-despised rebels, Donop was only emulating Howe's rakish ways that were legendary. While Howe thoroughly "enjoyed Madam" Betsy Loring in New York City, the commander of Hessian troops who manned the posts at Trenton and Bordentown, both located on the Delaware, likewise engaged in his own sexual escapades on these cold December nights. Donop had also lost his head to this "exceedingly beautiful young widow" of a doctor of Mount Holly, New Jersey, only around twenty miles south of Trenton and below Bordentown.

Leading his 450 South New Jersey militia, Colonel Samuel Griffin, a capable Son of Erin from Virginia, had succeeded in his vital December 22–23 diversion on the Delaware's east side. He had boldly captured Mount Holly, which was located almost directly below Trenton and east of Philadelphia. As planned by Washington, the ever-aggressive Donop took the bait provided by Griffin's diversion, moving almost his entire corps of around two thousand troops from his Bordentown headquarters south to Mount Holly. According to

Washington's well-conceived plan, Griffin then withdrew his militiamen in true partisan fashion, avoiding an unwinnable open field fight with battle-hardened regulars. Griffin's withdrawal bestowed even more overconfidence and complacency to additionally dull Donop's aggressive instincts and tactical perception, thanks to the sight of even more untrained New Jersey militiamen on the run as usual.

Instead of prudently retiring back north to Bordentown, located on the Delaware around a dozen miles north of Mount Holly and much closer to Trenton, Donop made the ill-fated decision to remain securely in place at Mount Holly in order to romp with his promiscuous New Jersey girl, who was young widow of a physician, when far from his Bordenstown headquarters. After all, Donop felt nothing but contempt for his bumbling opponents. He repeatedly denounced them as "the rascals," as if they were little more than naughty children in need of harsh discipline. As hoped by Washington and instead of retiring back north to Bordentown, Donop was now well beyond adequate supporting distance—around twenty miles—of Trenton at Mount Holly, when Washington was about to strike Trenton. As if he were a rookie commander instead of a seasoned leader, Donop had been brilliantly drawn by Washington's diversion more than half a dozen miles farther south, helping to seal Rall's fate at Trenton on December 26.

With a discerning eye for beauty and carnal opportunities that revealed his aristocratic background, meanwhile, Donop thoroughly joyed himself at Mount Holly on Christmas Eve. He was making love to the pretty widow and a woman of a much lower class (as he was of noble blood) precisely when Washington was about to deliver his masterstroke. For three days and all the way to Christmas Day, Donop acted much like a lovesick school boy who had indulged in too much good sex after having moved the alluring young woman into his own personal headquarters. The passionate lovemaking from long pent-up lust effectively took Donop's mind, perhaps also addled by alcohol, and tactical instincts off Rall's increasingly precarious situation at Trenton until it was too late. Also ensuring the lack of future cooperation for Trenton's defense, Donop and Rall were at odds in part because they were direct opposites: the forty-three-year-old Donop was a Hesse-Cassel blueblood from a distinguished Castle Woebbel noble family of the principality of Lippe, while Rall hailed from middle class antecedents. In fact, they had been quarreling since December 14. Donop was especially upset because Rall had already gone over his head to secure the coveted Trenton assignment. Rall had appealed directly to Grant, committing the sin of what the by-the-book Donop deemed as "improper ambition." Consequently, Donop had refused to inspect Trenton while occupied by Rall and his three-regiment brigade, leaving his troublesome, lower-born colonel on his own to do his best under difficult circumstances.

Clearly, the combination of Griffin's effective tactical diversion below Trenton as ordered by Washington, a dysfunctional Hessian command structure, and the attractive, alluring widow—perhaps an American spy—at Mount Holly helped to set the stage for Washington's upcoming success at Trenton. As Washington so fondly wished and hoped, Donop remained far away from his Bordentown headquarters and around twenty miles south of Trenton for four crucial days. Fortunately for Washington, this sexy American widow's carnal skills ensured that a couple thousand Hessian troops and Rall's immediate superior remained far beyond supporting distance of Trenton at the most critical moment. On December 23, Donop only warned Rall "to be on our guard" instead of prudently sending reinforcements to Trenton: another way of saying that the isolated Rall was left alone and out on a limb, while washing his own hands of the upcoming debacle that sent shock rippling on both sides of the Atlantic. All of these diverse, but closely related, factors ensured that three thousand German and British soldiers, a force larger than Washington's main strike force, played no role in Trenton's defense when they were needed the most.[23]

Washington's Forgotten Warriors, the Germans

While Dunop was making passionate love to the pretty American widow in a large, warm feather bed beside a warm, roaring fireplace at Mount Holly, Colonel Rall could hardly realize that around 2,400 Americans under the much-maligned Washington were now relentlessly headed his way across a snow-covered landscape with an unprecedented determination to succeed at any cost. After all, European armies, even Prussian, seldom fought at night, or in inclement weather, especially during wintertime: clear violations of traditional military axioms and the time-honored rules of waging conventional warfare. And to the foreign occupier's way of thinking, an even more unimaginable thought was that the Americans might possibly be capable of launching an offensive strike, especially with Washington yet in command after the easy capture by British cavalry of England-born General Charles Lee, who was generally considered

America's finest military leader, at White's Tavern at Basking Ridge, New Jersey, on December 12.

But even more inconceivable to Rall was the fact that around 370 German Americans, including his own Maryland cousin and many highly motivated soldiers who had been born in Germany, including from his own native Hesse Cassel, were now advancing with overflowing cartridge-boxes toward Trenton in the bulging ranks of Washington's German Regiment. Even more paradoxical, Washington's troops, especially his Teutonic soldiers, were also partly inspired by Frederick the Great's martial legacies and lessons like the Hessians themselves. Having been only recently dispatched from Philadelphia by Congress to reinforce Washington's Army, an entire German American regiment, Washington's largest, now marched south toward Trenton in Greene's Second Division column with the burning desire to wreck havoc on their own countrymen. Only a relatively handful of Irish and Scotch-Irish soldiers in the ranks made this not a Continental infantry regiment composed of entirely Germans, born across the Atlantic, and German Americans, who had been born in America. Almost certainly, German soldiers of this command had informed Washington, who in part based his strategy on the belief that Hessians celebrated Christmas not just on December 25 but also on December 26 during a two-day holiday, of traditional German customs from the distant homeland.

As fate would have it, the German Regiment was the only unit in Washington's Army officially designated by its distinctive ethnic composition. Authorized by the Continental Congress to counter the British Government's decision to employ German troops to subjugate America, Washington's Teutonic regiment consisted of five companies composed of Germans from eastern Pennsylvania, while the remaining four companies were filled with Maryland soldiers like Colonel Rall's own cousin.

This Germanic Continental command had made a timely recent addition to the army, becoming Washington's largest regiment with 374 men. However, despite yet to face its baptismal fire, the German Regiment was well trained. Most importantly, this command was led by so many excellent officers, mostly from Pennsylvania and Maryland, such as Lieutenant Colonel George Stricker of Frederick County, Maryland. Stricker possessed solid experience as a captain in Colonel William Smallwood's elite First Maryland Battalion, which had been cut to pieces in a series of charges launched against Cornwallis's troops at Long Island on August 27, 1776. In the shivering ranks of Greene's lengthy column of Second Division troops, the lieutenant colonel's young son, Cadet John Stricker, now marched south toward Trenton near his officer father.

Colonel Stricker was blessed with a solid officer corps which ensured that he led the German Regiment most effectively this morning: Major Ludwig Weltner, a "britchesmaker" who lived with wife Mary in the northwest Maryland town of Frederick on the Monocacy River; Captain Daniel Burhardt whose stepson, Private Henry Magg, now served in the ranks; Captain George Hubley of Lancaster, Pennsylvania, who was fated to die in this war; and Captains Jacob Bunner; Benjamin Weiser from the town of Womelsdorf, Northumberland County, Pennsylvania; John David Woelpper; William Heyser, of Hagerstown, Maryland, who was born in Germany in 1737, migrated to America in 1765, and then became a proud naturalized American citizen at Annapolis, Maryland, in September 1772; Henry Fister of Frederick County; and George Keeports of the port of Baltimore, Maryland. Most of these Pennsylvania Germans, especially the officers, hailed from Philadelphia. Many officers from Maryland and Pennsylvania were bilingual, speaking both German and English. During the long trek through the snow while moving ever-closer to Trenton, they well might have hummed or thought of the mocking, but inspirational, words of a popular German song, distinguished by an especially memorable line and a distinct taste of Teutonic humor:

> "England's Georgie, Emperor, King,
> Is for God and us too small a thing."

Entirely unknown to the troops garrisoned at Trenton, Colonel Rall's fellow countrymen in Washington's German Regiment advanced steadily southward as part of General Matthias Alexis de Roche Fermoy's Brigade, Greene's Second Division. Along the slick Scotch Road, these Teutonic soldiers now marched relentlessly toward a bloody rendezvous with their fellow countrymen, including perhaps relatives from their same ancestral regions of Germany. Eight companies—four from Maryland and four from Pennsylvania—of the German Regiment had been initially authorized on June 27, 1776, when the Continental Congress attempted to tap into the abundant manpower of the new republic's second largest ethnic group after the Irish.

The German Regiment's size had been increased by yet another company (one from Pennsylvania) that was authorized in mid-July 1776. The four companies of Maryland Germans were composed of both rural and urban soldiers of mostly middle-class origins, with four companies consisting of volunteers from Baltimore and four companies made up of soldiers from Frederick County on the western frontier. Meanwhile, the Germans from the four Pennsylvania companies hailed from areas where German Lutheran and Reformed congregations were the most heavily concentrated, as in Philadelphia, the Pennsylvania towns of Kensington and Germantown, and the Susquehanna River settlements in Lancaster County, like Lebanon, as opposed to pacifist German communities of the Amish, Dunkards, and Mennonites.

These Teutonic warriors from Maryland and Pennsylvania—a rare dual-state regiment in Washington's Army whose units were almost always designated by state—were now commanded by German-born Colonel Nicholas Haussegger. He hailed from near the town of Lebanon, situated on Quittapahilla Creek, in fertile Lancaster County, Pennsylvania. Haussegger was a native of the ancient city of Hanover, in northern Germany, on the Leine River. Drained by the Susquehanna River, Haussegger's adopted homeland was a picturesque region of rich farmlands, first settled by German immigrants, nestled in the central Lebanon Valley. He possessed solid military experience as an exacting officer during the French and Indian War, and then as a Fourth Pennsylvania battalion major during the disastrous Canadian Campaign under hard-fighting Anthony Wayne, before taking command of the German Regiment in July 1776.[24]

Significantly, Haussegger's German-American troops were in overall better condition and better uniformed than any other infantry in Washington's strike force at this time. Unlike Washington's soldiers who had endured the series of crushing defeats around New York City and the gloomy retreat through New Jersey, the German Regiment's soldiers had spent the fall 1776 months garrisoned at their comfortable barracks in Philadelphia. This sophisticated capital city's seemingly endless lures—taverns, gambling dens, painted ladies, cheap rotgut whisky, and rows of dingy whorehouses—proved a strong temptation for young men, like Thomas Rose, who were away from home for the first time. An "incomparably good drummer" with large, brown eyes, and long black hair tied in a queue under a plain "old wool hat," Rose deserted on September 4, 1776.[25]

Haussegger's German Continentals had been yet quartered at their Philadelphia barracks by the end of November, awaiting the arrival of additional equipment before taking the field. After only a relatively short march northeast from Philadelphia, the first contingent of Haussegger's regiment had joined Washington's Army at Trenton on December 5. Therefore, the German Regiment was far less depleted than Washington's other regiments:

a key advantage that would result in the command's disproportionate contribution to victory at Trenton. By this time, Washington's Germanic unit contained a whopping total of 374 men—thirty-five officers, forty noncommissioned officers, five staff officers, and 294 rank and file—which was more than double the manpower of Washington's badly decimated regiments, such as the diminutive Fifth Virginia Continental Regiment, Stephen's Brigade, of only 129 men. The German Regiment's ranks were now full of relatively fresh, healthy Teutonic warriors, from western frontier farmers of German peasant stock to classically educated burghers, primarily of the officer's ranks, from Philadelphia's and Baltimore's cobblestone streets. As a strange fate would have it to reveal the complexities of the German experience in America, Washington's German Regiment was now about to engage in its first battle and against their fellow countrymen.[26]

Although only recently formed, the German Regiment was not only Washington's largest and best-preserved regiment, but also contained soldiers with solid military experience from service in combat-tested units, including Smallwood's elite battalion of Marylanders. Some of Haussegger's soldiers had marched with Maryland's Flying Camp and in the Associator units of Pennsylvania. A former cadet, Captain John Weidman was one such veteran ex-Associator officer. He hailed from Lancaster County, Pennsylvania. Major Ludwig, or William, Weltner, who migrated from Germany to Philadelphia by way of Europe's largest port city, Rotterdam, Netherlands, in 1751, had served as a Frederick County Militia major. Major John David Woelpper, a Virginian German, knew Washington well, having campaigned as a sergeant under him when the austere Mount Vernon planter commanded the highly touted Virginia Regiment during the French and Indian War. Like Major Weltner, Woelpper was born in Germany. He reached America's shores in October 1749 via bustling Rotterdam, from where he departed for the New World with high hopes and bright dreams.

Many of the German Regiment's officers and men, including those with high rank, had served in prewar militia units in both rural and urban areas and in Maryland and Pennsylvania. Captain Benjamin Weiser, born in Pennsylvania in 1744 and the son of German-born Conrad Weiser, who had negotiated peace treaties between the Iroquois and the Pennsylvania Colony and led the Pennsylvania Regiment with skill during the French and Indian War, had served as an officer in the Northumberland County, Pennsylvania, militia battalion. Other German Regiment officers had been members of the well-trained

Baltimore Mechanical Company of Militia, the Baltimore Town Militia Battalion, the Baltimore Artillery, and the Frederick County Militia. Some of Haussegger's more seasoned officers also benefitted from prior European military experience, such as Adjutant Louis Van Linkensdorf of Pennsylvania. He had served as an officer in an elite Swiss Regiment on the Mediterranean island of Sardinia. All in all, therefore, Washington's German Regiment benefitted from an exceptionally wide-ranging, high level of military experiences from both sides of the Atlantic because so many officers had served in European armies, during the French and Indian War, and in militia and Continental service.[27]

And a good many experienced soldiers also solidified the German Regiment's enlisted ranks for the Trenton challenge. Twenty-three-year-old Private Thomas Wenick was known as an excellent marksman. Standing more than five foot, six inches, he was a veteran hunter, or jaeger, from the dark, evergreen forests of his Teutonic homeland. "A talkative fellow," Wenick loved playing cards.[28] Another common German soldier of Washington's German Regiment was a young man born in Hesse-Cassel, thirty-two-year-old Private John Man Flicket. Hailing from the rich farm lands of his transplanted, adopted homeland near Maytown, in the Susquehanna River country of Lancaster County, Pennsylvania, he was "tall [with], long black hair, much given to smoking & drinking."[29]

Washington also now possessed experienced German-born leaders in his main strike force beyond the German Regiment's ranks. Lieutenant Colonel Baron Friedrich von Weisenfels now led around eighty soldiers of the Third New York Continental Regiment, Sargent's Brigade, which advanced down the windswept River Road with Sullivan's First Division.[30] And two veteran companies of Samuel John Atlee's Pennsylvania Battalion (regiment), which had been hard-hit at the battle of Long Island and its survivors were now attached to Stirling's Brigade, consisted of large numbers of German American patriots. The unit's commander, Samuel John Atlee, a hardened French and Indian War veteran who had been born in Trenton, was captured during the battle.[31] In battling against the odds under Stirling's command after the Long Island fiasco, Atlee's Battalion of Pennsylvania State troops then lost more good men at Fort Washington. Less than three months apart, these twin disasters resulted in a merger of the fortunate survivors of three battalions of Pennsylvania State troops, who now marched in Stirling's Brigade at the head of Greene's column, just behind Mercer's brigade.[32]

Likewise, capable German artillery officers also led their cannoneers forward down parallel roads beside their slow-moving field pieces in both Greene's and

Sullivan's columns. Captain Sebastian Baumann was the foremost commander among these Teutonic artillery leaders. He now commanded eighty artillerymen of the New York Company Continental Artillery in Greene's advancing First Division. Captain Baumann was born in the ancient city of Frankfort-on-the-Main, Hesse-Cassel, on April 6, 1739. He was one of Washington's most educated and well-trained artillery commanders in Greene's Second Division column. Smart, versatile, and talented, Baumann had received an excellent education as a military engineer at Heidelberg University, Germany, on the Neckar River.

He first migrated with his family to America as an idealistic young man, settling in New York. Here, Baumann had made his American dream come true, thriving as a thrifty merchant. He was commissioned as an artillery officer with a major's rank in Colonel John Lamb's New York Artillery in early 1776. Representing a solid vote of confidence, Baumann had been entrusted by Knox to remove the last American cannon from New York City during the evacuation. He was the last artillery officer to leave the doomed city, with all of his guns in tow: no small accomplishment under trying circumstances. Clearly, Captain Baumann was a well-trained officer and just the kind of artillery commander that Washington could rely on the morning of December 26, when everything was at stake for America. Most symbolically, this exceptional Germany-born artillery commander was destined to be yet firing his well-aimed cannon upon a cornered opponent, Cornwallis, who had just recently chased Baumann's unit across the Delaware in the New Jersey withdrawal, during the siege of Yorktown in October 1781.[33]

In addition, German American soldiers of the Lutheran and Reformed faiths, Protestants, Catholics, and even Hebrew, were scattered in lesser numbers in virtually every regiment in Washington's Army, except for those commands raised in areas, which were relatively few, entirely devoid of German populations. Both Protestant Germans and German Jews served in Maryland units from Baltimore, where a large and prosperous German and German Jewish community thrived and where many of these men had been leading merchants. These German American soldiers possessed a deep-seated love for liberty that extended back to Old World Germanic roots.

Indeed, such nascent republican Germans had early opposed autocratic rule of centralized government, which explained in part why they had first migrated to America. In the June 2, 1775 words of one such revolutionary-minded German, motivated by the enlightened concepts of Freiheit von (the uplifting from oppression in order to become *vogelfrei*, or "free as a bird"), who fled to America's friendly shores to escape religious persecution, high taxes, ruling elites, government corruption, and autocratic abuses of central Europe: "We cherish civil and religious liberty as a precious gift vouchsafed to us by God." Therefore, combined with the inspirational words of Chaplain John Conrad, a Reformed pastor of Lancaster County and now serving as the German Regiment's faithful chaplain, lofty Age of Enlightenment idealism burned brightly in the hearts and minds of the Continental soldiers of Washington's forgotten Teutonic Regiment and other units and was especially so on the freezing morning of December 26.

Washington's German Americans were also highly motivated by the desire to defend their Pennsylvania home communities. These Germanic Continentals hoped that Washington's desperate offensive gamble would deliver a devastating preemptive blow so that the Hessians and British would be less likely to invade, pillage, and burn down their own Pennsylvania homes and make their families homeless in wintertime, including for many German Americans from the appropriately named Heidelberg township in Berks County, Pennsylvania. The township of rolling farmlands in the Schuylkill River country of southeast Pennsylvania had been named after the cultured city, distinguished by Heidelberg Castle that overlooked ancient Heidelberg and one of Europe's oldest universities, nestled along the Neckar River in southwest Germany. One such determined Teutonic soldier from Pennsylvania who now marched toward Trenton in Washington's German Regiment was Sergeant John Kredelbach. As a sad fate would have it, he was destined to be "hanged by the [British] regulars" in October 1777.[34]

However, the many contradictions, ironies, and complexities of the German experience in America ran exceptionally deep and were closely intertwined, defying long-existing stereotypes and simplistic generalizations. Consequently, some of Washington's Germans possessed second thoughts—like some of Rall's Hessians who had already faced German American soldiers, such as Pennsylvania brothers Lieutenant Henry Bedinger and fifteen-year-old Daniel Bedinger, who had helped to decimate the charging Hessian formations with blistering fire from their deadly Long Rifles at Fort Washington—about attacking their fellow countrymen, who after all might have been their own relatives and who were mostly common tillers of the soil back in Germany like themselves.

In general, officers of both Washington's German Regiment and the Rall brigade at Trenton belonged to a class more elevated than the lowly privates in the ranks. Ironically, some identical divisions that separated Hessian officers, including those men of lower nobility, from the common Hessian soldiers and middle class noncommissioned and officers of common background also separated officers of Haussegger's Regiment, including members of a New World aristocracy, from the enlisted ranks of mostly yeomen farmers of middle-class status.

But, of course, the average American fighting man in Haussegger's command was better off economically and possessed a far more promising future than the common Hessian soldier from impoverished Hesse-Cassel. Rall's enlisted men in service were little more than exploited pawns, who hailed primarily from lowly peasant families that barely scratched out a meager existence on the poor soil of Hesse-Cassel. While many of Rall's common soldiers had been struggling members of economically ruined communities yet to recover from the widespread devastation of the Thirty Years War, some of Rall's top officers hailed from some of the best families in Germany. As could be expected in representing an Old World environment and hierarchical society, class differences and divisions between officers and enlisted men were wider in Rall's brigade than in Washington's German Regiment, where more enlightened egalitarian thought existed. However, many of Rall's and Washington's officers also shared comparable common middle-class backgrounds, and even humble origins in some cases.

Two Teutonic soldiers of the German Regiment from Maryland, Privates David Barringer and Michael Beiker, deserted Washington's German Regiment on Christmas Eve. Almost certainly, these two soldiers were the two mysterious American deserters who reached Trenton to inform Rall and other top German officers, who could not speak English, in their native language that rations for three days had been cooked by the Americans and that an attack from Washington was soon forthcoming on Trenton.[35]

Commanding the well-trained German Regiment, Colonel Haussengger was one of Washington's German-born soldiers who were beginning to have serious misgivings about fighting against his countrymen. He had narrowly survived the disastrous Canadian invasion when Montgomery's desperate assault on snowy Quebec ended in a bloody fiasco in late December 1775. For such reasons, Haussegger, a hat maker by profession who possessed a nice house, a hatter shop in the market town of Lebanon, and a five-acre farm located just outside the agrarian community, was becoming more of a reluctant revolutionary by this time. In a case of history coming full circle, a good many of

Haussegger's Germans had originally migrated to America for freedom, and now that liberty was threatened not only by the British, but also by the Teutonic soldiers garrisoned at Trenton.[36] All the while during blizzard-like conditions of December 26, the young men and boys of Washington's German Regiment continued to trudge south toward Trenton while an eerie silence, hanging heavy like the ever-diminishing chances for Washington's success at Trenton, yet dominated Greene's lengthy Second Division column to reflect the solemn mood in the ranks of hundreds of German Continentals, who were about to engage in battle for the first time on American soil.

Late Night Celebration at Abraham Hunt's House

Postmaster Abraham Hunt was one of Trenton's most respected merchants and leading citizens. And like the equally opportunistic Stacy Potts, Hunt had grown wealthier by trading freely with both sides in a war that brought new economic opportunities. Clearly, Trenton's leading commercial and businessmen knew not only how to preserve their gains, but also how to profit from the foreign occupation of their home town.

A festive Yuletide gathering was held on Christmas evening in Hunt's finely furnished parlor at his two-story, brick home located on the northwest corner of King and Second Streets. As one of Trenton's wealthiest merchants who possessed a well-stocked cellar filled with only the finest liquors and wines, like richly flavored Madeira and even heavily fortified beer so favored by Germans, Hunt was well liked by the Hessian officers. Known as much for his hospitality as for his high-grade Virginia tobacco (perhaps even Washington's own Mount Vernon tobacco at some point) that was made readily available to Hessian visitors, Hunt was not a Tory, however. Therefore, Hunt's property was never confiscated by American forces at anytime during the war years.

Playing a risky, high stakes game but one at which he was skilled, Hunt merely feigned loyalty to the Crown to preserve his considerable wealth and high community status. In truth, Hunt was a lieutenant colonel of the Hunterdon County, New Jersey, militia regiment commanded by Isaac Smith. And on this snowy Christmas night, he provided invaluable service to Washington by throwing a lavish supper party well supplied with good food, freshly killed local fare, such as turkey and thick venison (white-tailed deer) steaks, and, of course, unlimited amounts of alcoholic drink. Instead of retiring to his headquarters at the white-painted Stacy Potts's house, a wooden structure unlike the Hunt

House, for a good night's sleep, Rall attended the Christmas party. Here, he enjoyed himself thoroughly, drinking alcohol, smoking only the best tobacco from a long-stemmed clay pipe, and playing card games in the parlor. Partaking in a common diversion that took his mind off the war's horrors and the deaths of old friends, Rall especially enjoyed gambling at the old French game called Pharaoh (shortened to Faro) that was now at its height of popularity in Europe. Faro was not embraced by the American public until the nineteenth century.

When Rall finally returned to his King Street headquarters in the early morning hours, he carried in his pocket a handwritten note from a Tory farmer, a German named Mohl from Bucks County, Pennsylvania, which warned of Washington's impending attack. He had seen Washington's men forming up for the Delaware crossing, and immediately made his way to Trenton. A black servant had played an unintentional role in helping Washington to achieve surprise on December 26 by having refused to allow the homespun Pennsylvania farmer to step into Hunt's well-heated parlor filled with finely dressed merry makers of a higher class than the lowly agriculturalist. Therefore, the Loyalist farmer had hastily scribbled a brief note containing vital intelligence about Washington's impending attack on Trenton. Engrossed in his gambling and the good times away from the war's vexations and without anyone present who could translate English to German, Rall merely placed the little note in his vest pocket without reading it after the vital message had been handed to him by the "negro waiter."[37]

But this popular chapter of the Trenton story has been endlessly overemphasized by historians in order to demonstrate the folly of the Hessian commander and by Americans to reemphasize the failings of a truly "Contemptible Enemy" of America, which succeeded in shifting blame from his high-ranking British, including Howe, and German superiors, who had repeatedly ignored Rall's desperate calls for reinforcements. By this time, Rall had already received sufficient warnings from spies and British intelligence and he had responded accordingly. After having received Grant's Christmas Eve warning of Washington's impending attack, Rall had dutifully taken precautions and even sent out patrols, including one bolstered by a field piece, and kept hundreds of his best troops ready for action.

Therefore, while Rall celebrated Christmas in the soothing warmth and mirth of the Hunt mansion, he was very likely the only German in Trenton doing so on this miserable Yuletide. Everyone else in Rall's garrison maintained firm discipline by obeying orders, following specific assignments, and getting much-needed rest after the constant alarms, mostly false, over the last few days that left consecutive sleepless nights for the Hessians. Now working to Washington's favor, Rall's entire garrison had been aroused and turned out on December 22, 23, and 25 to meet either real or imagined threats. In fact, this Yuletide was the least festive and most sober of Christmas seasons in the lives of Rall's young men and boys now so far from home.

However, the most fatal flaw that now dominated German thinking at Trenton was that so many recent warnings had been sounded that the Hessians now had already become the victims of the crying wolf. Indeed, after having responded to the fire of Captain Wallis's small raiding party of Virginians on the late evening of Christmas Day, the Hessians had returned to their warm quarters, which provided a most comforting shelter from the storm. Rall felt secure that this latest threat from the accurate Virginia sharpshooters was the one that he had been warned about by Grant, whose letter arrived on Christmas morning.

With the storm raging with new intensity in the predawn darkness that convinced Rall that Trenton was entirely secure from any attack, Major Dechow, commanding the Knyphausen Regiment, basked in the Christmas spirit in his loneliness. He took pity on his young soldiers, who were now near their wits' end and utterly exhausted from so many past alarms and seemingly endless duties. Dechow, therefore, decided to cancel the usual predawn patrol for December 26 that would have placed 125 men and two cannon at the ferry house picket post just below the Assunpink, where the now-thwarted Ewing and his Pennsylvania militia had planned to cross the Delaware at the South Trenton Ferry just below the town. After all, everyone knew that these ragtag rebels, so often humiliated and vanquished so easily for months on one battle-field after another, were led by the "Poor Devils as the rebel generals are," and that their undisciplined soldiers were nothing but a "cowardly banditti." Most of all, British leadership believed that the American soldiers simply lacked the moral courage to fight like true, professional fighting men, especially in regard to launching an offensive strike.

In keeping with the American longtime stereotypical image of Hessian soldiers as Old World barbarians (which was as distorted as the common view of the British soldier as nothing more than an unthinking robot by American propagandists and then later-day historians), one of the most enduring myths of the Trenton story was that the Hessians were roaring drunk in wild celebration of Christmas, almost as if still in the port of Bermerlehe—from where the

Germans had first embarked for America—on the North Sea, or in a noisy Rotterdam tavern or a favorite bordello: the condition that has long allegedly made them vulnerable to Washington's attack on the morning of December 26. Of course, most Hessians certainly favored good German lager beer, but very little of this popular beverage existed among the Trenton garrison. And the fine wines for sale by Trenton's gouging American merchants, selling to patriot and loyalist alike, were much too expensive not only for the average common soldier, but also even for Rall's officers.

In truth and in a compliment to superior discipline for occupation troops in enemy countryside, the only vice among the Hessian soldiers for the Yuletide was the joyous experience of smoking tobacco from long-stemmed clay pipes, as back home in Germany with family and friends. Actually at this time, of course, far more American soldiers in Washington's two advancing columns were almost certainly taking an occasional cold mouthful of rum and whiskey, diluted and mixed in with creek or river water, from ice-crusted wooden canteens to warm themselves against the storm's harshest offerings during the final push toward Trenton.

Indeed, as Washington's two columns of half-frozen soldiers relentlessly approached Trenton from the north and yet undetected by the Trenton garrison, hundreds of highly disciplined Hessians of Rall's own grenadier regiment were sleeping in their quarters in the hours before daylight. However, they wore full uniforms with accouterments strapped on and with weapons, in excellent condition as prescribed by regulations, stacked in neat rows nearby. The Hessian regiment, therefore, was well prepared to rapidly assemble at Rall's previously assigned points in Trenton at the first sound of an alarm.

The fact that Washington had partly based his offensive strategy upon the belief that the Germans were wildly celebrating Christmas was in fact a dangerous assumption and a serious miscalculation. Instead on this cheerless Yultide in a silent, snow-shrouded Trenton, the Hessians, most of whom were deeply religious and strict Calvinists, had been only thinking of home, observing religious aspects of the Yuletide, and praying to survive this miserable war, which they wanted to end to be reunited with friends and families once again.

While Washington's troops drew closer, they now either rested or slept around their little decorated Christmas trees, according to German Yuletide tradition, set up in their quarters. Most of all, these German fighting men respected their faith and their dedicated chaplains, primarily of the Lutheran faith. As if still worshiping in a beautiful, towering Gothic Cathedral back in the old medieval towns of Marburg, Wetzlar or Eisenbach in Hesse-Cassel, they had often knelt before these revered men of God at their nightly vespers while quartered in Trenton. A favorite hymn of these battle-hardened Teutonic warriors from their respective Calvinist principalities was entitled "A Mighty Fortress Is Our God." Even during Howe's amphibious landing at Kip's Bay on September 15, 1776, the Hessians, who had been as nervous as when Washington's men crossed the Delaware because so few knew how to swim, believed that they were about to be slaughtered in a frontal attack because light defenses, with an unknown number of Americans, stood before them. Therefore, on that hot Sunday that had rang over Kip's Bay's sparkling waters to the amazement of Washington's troops waiting in the sweltering trenches, these strict German Calvinists had sung their favorite Calvinist hymns in preparation for meeting their Maker.[38]

One of the greatest misconceptions about the story of Trenton was that Rall's Hessians were entirely unready to respond quickly to an attack and practically unable to defend themselves because of the alleged excessive intoxication from the Yuletide celebration, and that one "of the turning points, therefore, of American history is fixed in the decanter of Col. Abram Hunt . . . ."[39] However, in truth, this overemphasized traditional explanation of Hessian surprise and defeat at Trenton was just another part of the mythical revolution, ignoring that fact of how close the Rall brigade came to nearly turning the tide of battle. This popular anti-German stereotype of excessive drunkenness and heathen-like unrestraint was first created by a highly effective American propaganda machine—and then was mimicked by generations of American historians—to demonstrate an alleged decadence and immorality in the natural process of demonizing the enemy to rally support against the invaders.

Ironically, Washington and his men now failed to realize how a devout Calvinism ensured that these Hessians at Trenton never observed this Yuletide Season in the manner of the debauched, ancient Roman ruling class at a drunken orgy or annual festive to celebrate and pay homage to the gods. In fact, unlike the Brunswickers from north Germany (mostly Catholic), Rall's soldiers were mostly of a strict Calvinist faith, and they did not celebrate the Christmas Holiday. Emphasizing the drunken Hessian stereotypical perspective that has endured to this day, Colonel Fitzgerald, of Washington's staff, penned in his diary how the Germans "make a great deal of Christmas in Germany, and no doubt the Hessians will drink a great deal of beer and have a dance to-night. They will be sleepy to-morrow morning. Washington will set the tune for them about daybreak."[40] In truth, a far greater liability for the Rall garrison was not the effects from drunken and unrestrained celebration, but a host of cardinal violations of Frederick the Great's central axioms of war, which condemned "wars of position" and relied instead upon mobility and flexibility to reap decisive victories across Europe: essentially Washington's brilliant tactical formula for success on December 26.[41]

By this time, the Hessian garrison at a quiet, serene Trenton, now seemingly entombed in blizzard-like conditions, were indeed vulnerable, but not from excessive Yuletide drinking. Almost all sound was muffled by the softly cascading snow, casting a comforting spell, while an eerie silence pervaded over Trenton. Starting on December 22, Rall's troops were worn down by the monotonous series of alarms and threats, both real and imaginary, emitting hauntingly from the dark woodlands of the hostile, mysterious New Jersey countryside that looked so unlike their native homeland across the sea.

While Rall's men were indeed the undisputed masters of Trenton, the western New Jersey countryside was an entirely different matter and situation altogether. By late December, this ever-rising tide of insurrection mocked Howe's overconfident December 20 words to Lord George Sackville Germain, King George III's powerful Secretary of the State for the Colonies, that New Jersey was in "almost general submission." Ironically, Germain had grown up in Ireland and helped to smash yet a new generation of Scottish rebels, among them was Washington's friend General Mercer, at bloody Culloden in 1746.

As in most guerrilla wars with foreign invaders deep in hostile territory and occupying stationary, defensive positions during active insurgencies, effective Hessian control of their environment ended at the town's limits. Therefore, new, aggressive tactics of insurgency warfare initiated by the roving bands of New Jersey militia had recently ensured that the Trenton garrison was almost constantly on alert while facing an increasingly hostile environment on consecutive days before Washington struck. Conducting surprise mini-raids and intelligence-gathering missions in the brown-hued countryside both north and south of Trenton to draw attention away from Washington's selected multiple crossing points along the Delaware, these wide-ranging New Jersey and Pennsylvania militia strikes, both dispatched by Washington and with aggressive independent officers acting on their own initiative to strike on their own, helped to pave the way to the Hessian brigade's doom in the end. Consequently in overall tactical terms, Colonel Rall and his troops were blind and bottled up in their cozy, winter quarters in Trenton on December 25 and 26, while Washington's two columns—Sullivan's First and Greene's Second Divisions—steadily approached from the north with an unexpected blend of stealth and audacity not previously seen on this scale with American troops in this war.

By this time, even Rall's small detachment of British light cavalry had been cowed into remaining safely in Trenton rather than out on the necessary long-distance reconnaissance assignments to ascertain any new developments, especially at McConkey's Ferry, and sound early warning of Washington's approach across country. Commanding the New Jersey militia brigade of Hunterdon County soldier-farmers, who fought by day and then went home to families and firesides by night in true guerrilla fashion, Colonel Philemon Dickinson, who was stationed on Pennsylvania soil just across the river from Trenton, had repeatedly launched small-scale strikes this December.

Even though these were mere pinpricks, they proved highly effective in harassing the beleaguered Trenton garrison, wearing down even the best troops, who were not accustomed to the inscrutable ways of insurgency. Acting on well-honed instincts and a high level of experience, Rall had always taken the bait, overreacting to perceived threats in an aggressive manner. Rall had repeatedly sent out detachments to meet the expected attack that never came because the savvy New Jersey militiamen, in classic guerrilla style, simply melted away into the thick forests along the Delaware or retired back across the river to the Pennsylvania shore before late-arriving Hessians came to grips with their most persistent irritant (and one that was growing) this winter.

Therefore, Washington benefitted from the prior actions of Ewing's Pennsylvania militia, just below Trenton, which had played its part in harassing the Rall garrison. This December, the beleaguered Trenton garrison had been seemingly sandwiched between Dickinson's threats from the north and Ewing's activities from the south, with each commander having utilized their wide-ranging militiamen, New Jersey (mostly Hunterdon County boys) and Pennsylvania, respectively, to cross the river at almost any time to unleash roving bands of partisans. Attempting in vain to confront the baffling fine art of asymmetrical warfare for which they were neither prepared nor trained, the Hessians had understandably become disillusioned, disgruntled, and mentally exhausted by Christmas Day. Therefore, a deep feeling of frustration, combined with anxiety, infiltrated the mindset of the young Hessian soldiers, eroding the recent sky-high morale that had already peaked with the series of New York Campaign victories. In a completely unexpected development, the Hessian's one-sided victories at Long Island, White Plains, and Fort Washington had only built up an overblown confidence that had been easily deflated in short order by a new, fast-moving type of unconventional warfare that was unfamiliar to them, thanks to an escalating insurgency that seemed to have no end.[42]

Another forgotten advantage now possessed by Washington lay not as much in Rall's alleged incompetence, drunkenness, and negligence as a commander as in his ambition that had served him well in the past. What historians have most often overlooked was the simple fact that explained some of Rall's seemingly wrongheaded decisions, especially in regard to not erecting defenses to protect the town, since arriving with his brigade at Trenton on December 14; quite simply, he never planned to spend the winter on the Delaware's east side with his brigade.

In truth, Rall's greatest failing at Trenton was that he in fact possessed not too little, but too broad of a strategic vision that was as bold as it was right on target. Like Washington, he was planning to unleash his own masterstroke that might end the war. Therefore, from Howe, Colonel Rall had early requested not only his own regiment, but also two other regiments to be stationed at Trenton, while Donop had initially planned for the garrisoning of only a single regiment at Trenton. Donop viewed Trenton as little more than an isolated picket outpost of relatively little strategic importance and just another winter quarters. Howe gave Rall all that he had asked for—the ordering of the entire brigade to be stationed at Trenton—not simply as a reward for his past battlefield accomplishments, but more importantly to fulfill a most ambitious plan to yet capture Philadelphia this winter.

Explaining in large part why he in fact had ignored the seemingly prudent orders from Donop and suggestions from his subordinate officers, like the respected Major Dechow, to fortify the town, the strategic-minded Rall was in fact merely biding his time at Trenton. As he advised his top lieutenants, Rall was only waiting for the arrival of colder winter weather to freeze the Delaware so that he could lead his three regiments and artillery across the river and capture America's vulnerable capital. Besides driving another nail into the coffin of rebellion and achieving a significant political and strategic coup, Rall also wanted to gain better winter quarters for his well-deserving troops in Philadelphia compared to the small, mostly vacant, houses of Trenton.

Therefore, Washington was correct in his obsessive fear of the Delaware freezing to permit the British-Hessian Army to resume offensive operations: a key factor that fueled his decision to launch his bold preemptive strike on Trenton because he knew that he could not possibly stop such an operation.

Indeed, on December 20, Howe wrote to Lord Germain in London to inform him that he was only awaiting the Delaware's freezing to resume the advance, spearheaded by the crack Rall brigade, upon Philadelphia. What the ever-aggressive Rall had in mind, with Howe's blessings and full support, was the boldest of strokes that could not possibly fail under the circumstances unless Washington launched his own preemptive strike.

Rall, therefore, never planned to defend Trenton or to remain idle along the Delaware's east bank for the entire winter: a forgotten factor that fully explained why he erected no defenses. In consequence, no vast amount of supplies, "or no stores of any Consequence," as a surprised Washington later wrote much to his disappointment after the town's capture, had been stored in Trenton for the long winter, because Philadelphia was still Howe's and Rall's strategic objective during this winter of opportunity.

Thanks to the ambitious Howe-Rall plan to push on to Philadelphia once the Delaware froze, the six artillery pieces of the Rall brigade were not placed at any point on the town's outskirts in a defensive stance or behind any newly built earthworks. Ideally, two guns seemingly should have been situated in the engineer's recommended redoubt at the head of King and Queen Streets as advocated by Donop's knowledgeable engineer, but they would have been easily outflanked on both sides and early overwhelmed by Greene's Second Division vanguard Virginians and the hundreds of men who followed close behind. On this cold night, consequently, these German light bronze guns now remained "uselessly" in rearward positions—close to Rall's headquarters near in the town's center—rather than in defense of the town's northern perimeter.

Yet planning to soon push southwest on America's undefended capital, Hessian soldiers had previously boasted that they would shortly celebrate Christmas in a captured Philadelphia. A German officer assigned to Howe's headquarters described how Rall had already requested permission to continue the advance on Philadelphia once the Delaware froze over. Therefore, by way of verbal rather than written orders, Howe had ordered for the Rall brigade to remain in readiness at Trenton in preparation for the final push to Philadelphia once the Delaware sufficiently froze. Howe later admitted after his return to England that Rall and his three regiments were situated "so near to Philadelphia [so] that we might possibly have taken possession of it in the course of the winter," after the Delaware froze over. In this regard, Howe could not have chosen a better or experienced commander in a more advanced position to gain his politically vital objective, America's capital. Howe's heavy reliance on Rall's aggressiveness and tactical skill had been repeatedly demonstrated in the past, and it was now no different in regard to the tantalizing prospect of capturing Philadelphia, America's most important city. After all, Rall now commanded the most lethal warriors in America, whose reputations had preceded them for ample good reason.

In fact, Colonel Rall's tough, disciplined grenadiers had already killed more Americans than any regiment in Howe's victorious army. However, the Rall Regiment was a Landgrenadiere command, or a militia-like unit, consisting mostly of young farm boys, or peasants in European terminology, from the infertile, rocky land of Hesse-Cassel. Launching a final drive upon the virtually undefended capital and America's largest city would be a most audacious stroke calculated by Howe to end the rebellion with one blow while bestowing ever-lasting glory to Rall and his German soldiers and, of course, their British commander in New York City. Even if Washington attempted to defend the capital, such a guaranteed feeble, if not disastrous, effort in a stand up fight would be just another mismatch and inevitable defeat, as so often in the past.

Therefore, fortunately for Washington and his bold preemptive strike to reverse the war's disastrous course, Trenton was now ripe for the taking, because Philadelphia yet remained Howe's and Rall's most pressing strategic objective. In a desperate race in which the stakes could not possibly have been higher for both sides, Washington's surprise attack on Trenton was calculated to catch Rall and his Hessian brigade by surprise before they themselves could catch the Americans by surprise by launching their own strike upon Philadelphia once the Delaware froze over.[43]

In response to Rall's growing concerns about escalating guerrilla activities, especially from Dickinson's New Jersey and Ewing's Pennsylvania emboldened militiamen, an apathetic Grant remained comatose, basking in the comfort of faraway New Brunswick on the Raritan River. Rall's desperate messages for assistance had to be written out in French, as Rall knew little English. Then these urgent pleas were translated into English for Grant by an English regiment commander: yet another liability that additionally slowed the already laborious flow of communications, relayed by mounted courier, between Rall and his incompetent superiors.

Despite Rall's repeated messages for assistance, Grant continued to be dismissive of threats to Trenton, partly because of his jealousy toward Rall's winning ways and an almost xenophobic contempt for German soldiers, especially

Colonel Rall, in the tradition of British career officers. Blinded by a dangerous blend of national and cultural arrogance, the high-ranking Briton viewed Rall as needlessly concerned about his own safety and only exaggerating his vulnerability. Unfortunately for Rall and his isolated brigade, General Grant failed to perform his duty in protecting Trenton.

Grant's fatal flaws had been long covered up by friends in high places: one weakness of an entrenched military system that led to the steady erosion of the overall quality of British leadership that risked fossilization, especially when far from London. Grant had responded to Rall's increasing concerns on December 17—nearly ten days before Washington's attack on Trenton—by writing how, "I can hardly believe that Washington would venture at this season of the year to pass the Delaware."[44] Before America's bid for liberty when he displayed the same blind arrogance, Grant had confidently informed Parliament how the colonists would "never dare to face an English army and didn't possess any of the qualifications necessary to make a good soldier."[45]

But now these most ridiculed soldiers in all America were relentlessly descending upon Trenton from the north, while performing and obeying orders with a discipline fitting the finest professional fighting men on the continent. Most importantly by this time, the average fighting man in Washington's ranks, in one soldier's words, were determined to demonstrate once and for all that American "[b]oys can fight."[46] Unknown to British and German leadership, the war was even now in the process of changing, along with a heightened resolve that had suddenly emerged among Washington's soldiers, who had long been the butt of so many jokes on both sides of the Atlantic.

In encouraging his Second Division troops southward down the snowy Scotch Road and just before the first faint hint of dawn appeared on the frozen eastern horizon, Washington remained vigilant just in case the Hessians dispatched a sortie north from Trenton. After all, Washington's command was now divided into two divisions and widely separated: a cardinal sin according to the axioms of war and all the great captains, especially if the alerted enemy suddenly attacked from Trenton. Meanwhile, Washington's ragged soldiers, including a good many men, such as Captain Alexander Hamilton, not yet fully recovered from illnesses and who should have been recuperating in hospitals, gamely kept up with their plodding units during the arduous trek southward. While northeastern winds swept over the column without pity and young and old Continentals continued to lose strength with each weary mile, cold-numbed men blew hot breath on half-frozen fingers in a futile effort to warm themselves in the tempest. The added weight of snow clinging to shoes and boots made every step more difficult and laborious.

Hauling their cannon through the icy gales while the meager clothing flapped around them, Washington's hardworking artillerymen of both Greene's and Sullivan's columns continued to hurry their guns onward over the snowy landscape. Most importantly, these veteran gunners from across America somehow managed to keep up with the infantrymen's pace. Incredibly and against the odds, none of Knox's artillery crews fell behind during the exhaustive odyssey in the blackness. By this time as they neared the north of Trenton, the wooden wheels of the artillery pieces and lumbering ammunition carts of Forrest, Hamilton, and Baumann's guns were very likely wrapped in old blankets and cloth to muffle the creaking noise. As Washington and Knox fully realized, it was all important that the most expertly served and largest cannon remained at the head of the column as these guns would become the first engaged in combat.

Consequently, while yet mounted and as if surveying the progress of work in the sprawling fields of Mount Vernon, a vigilant Washington continued to carefully make sure that Captain Forrest's artillery pieces did not fall behind the head of Mercer's seasoned brigade because these guns, the two long six-pounders and two five and a half-inch howitzers, would become paramount at the battle's opening that loomed just ahead. He also displayed the same concern in regard to the field pieces of Hamilton's New York battery, which was one of the finest disciplined artillery units in Washington's Army, thanks to the West Indian-born captain's tireless efforts.[47]

Galloping back and forth along the column's sprawling length, Washington seemed to be everywhere at once despite the falling sleet and snow, speaking words of encouragement and making sure everything was in order. Like a man possessed on a morning seemingly tailor-made to thwart his best efforts, Washington was determined in part to prove himself and extinguish the prevalent conviction on both sides of the Atlantic that he was "not fit to command a sergeant's guard," as charged General Lee, who was so widely respected by both sides, unlike himself. With the burden of saving America weighing more heavily upon him than any other man in America, this much-maligned Virginia planter knew that this was now a do or die situation for himself and his infant nation, which seemed destined for an early, untimely, and tragic death. Most of all, this was Washington's last chance and final gamble in which the winner would take all at a time when very few people believed that a former militia colonel could possibly pull off a tactical miracle by doing what was so rare for him, prevailing in a battle, especially one of supreme importance.[48]

In regard to the upcoming, much-belated attack on Trenton, all that Washington could now do was to hope and pray that he and his long-suffering Continentals were not fated to suffer the much-dreaded "Fatal Day," as he described it in a letter, similar to Braddock's fiasco in which the mounted Virginian had narrowly escaped with his life.[49]

Pale Dawn Over a Sleepy Trenton

With his bone-weary troops advancing steadily down the ice-covered Scotch Road to gain the Pennington Road as rapidly as possible, Washington's desperate, high-stakes race with the sunrise to reach Trenton's northwestern outskirts with Greene's Second Division continued unabated. Often losing their footing along the slippery roadbed that had been long ago hewn through Hunterdon County's dense forests that must have reminded the Hessians of the Black and Teutoburg Forests, where three entire Roman Legions were destroyed by fierce German tribes in 9 AD, back home, Greene's troops felt a mounting sense of nervousness as they neared Trenton. A wave of growing apprehension about approaching Trenton and the inevitable battle with the always-victorious Hessians swept through the ranks of these young men and boys so far from home, thanks to so many past defeats. As if knowing as much, meanwhile, Washington and his fellow officers encouraged everyone to keep moving onward through the howling northeaster while steadying their men as best they could before meeting their greatest challenge. Washington continued to inspire his generally unsophisticated (but yet commonsense smart), homespun farm boys, the large number of immigrant Irish and Scots, and beardless teenagers who had never received proper educations. These stalwart souls moved onward with legs weary, when flintlocks on shoulders never felt heavier, and they never felt colder.

At long last after the lengthy descent south and down the gently sloping Scotch Road, Greene's Second Division troops finally neared the strategic intersection with the Pennington Road. Here, just before reaching the Scotch Road-Pennington Road intersection, Stephen's Virginia vanguard, positioned at the head of Greene's column, finally met the stationary, half-frozen soldiers of Captain Washington's foremost vanguard, which had accomplished its mission of guarding the main road that led into Trenton from the northwest. Like a protective mother hen taking in her lost young, Stephen's Virginia boys united with the soldiers of Captain Washington and Lieutenant Monroe's vanguard, which emerged into the Old Dominion fold at another obscure place in the trackless New Jersey countryside. After having successfully completed their mission, the little band of cold-numbed Virginia riflemen felt considerable relief upon joining an entire brigade of their fellow Virginia Continental soldiers after having been on their own and vulnerable before the main column for so long.

Realizing that they were on the last leg of their arduous journey to reach Trenton, Washington's troops moved onward with renewed vitality and higher spirits down the Pennington Road, into which the Scotch-Road had smoothly merged almost without anyone noticing the stealthy transition along the snow-covered ground and amid the stormy night. After the local New Jersey guides had informed him that Trenton was just ahead, Washington rode forward. Symbolically, he was determined to lead the way toward what would be either a great victory or a monumental fiasco, or perhaps even a battlefield death.

But Washington was emboldened as never before. After having so many close brushes with death going back to the French and Indian War, he sincerely believed that a kind providence now protected him, sparing him for a special purpose, which was now securing victory at Trenton to save America before it was too late. As throughout this most bitter of nights and with a confident assurance as if only riding forth on a spring morning to survey his extensive holdings of his Virginia plantation along the Potomac, the commander-in-chief's calming presence at the front continued to fortify his soldier's resolve, bolster spirits, and steady frayed nerves before meeting the much-touted Hessian Brigade in a climactic showdown.

Obeying orders to remain silent and close to their officers, the common soldiers kept slogging southward in Greene's Second Division column. From across America, these young Continentals were partly fueled to continue pushing down the Pennington Road by the knowledge that the frozen dawn of December 26 was drawing closer and would come near at 7:21 a.m. But with the punishing northeaster showing no signs of letting up, the first hint of a muted, pale sunrise on the eastern horizon could not be easily determined except for the snow on the ground gradually becoming a bit lighter to the eye. After not following his early preordained course in life as once preached by his Quaker parents' pacifist faith, although he sympathized with Quaker principles, even while he wore a sharp sword by his side, the plainspoken General Greene might have now longed for happy times and the warm, reassuring comfort of his favorite Bunch of Grapes Tavern, owned by Elisha Doane, on King Street (now State Street) near the waterfront in the heart of Boston.

Meanwhile, the heavy, moisture-laden skies over Hunterdon County on the eastern horizon retained a nighttime blackness, made even darker by dense storm clouds. Fortunately, by this time, the strong, high winds of the Jet Stream began to push the northeaster farther east and toward the Atlantic, instead of hovering with its former intensity over western New Jersey and the hard-hit Delaware Valley. Washington's troops, consequently, now moved and operated farther away from the eye of the storm, which had already unleashed a couple feet of snow in Virginia and Washington's Mount Vernon.

At long last at around twenty minutes after 7:00 a.m., and slowly but surely, the sky began to lighten faintly when the day's first light finally began to force it belabored way through the thick cloud cover that hovered over eastern horizon. This first dull simmer of light of the palest of dawns started to appear on the eastern horizon. However, this slight illumination revealed to Washington how far Greene's column of weary soldiers was yet strung out down the Pennington Road, which seemed smothered under an endless white blanket as far as the eye could see. In a most revealing December 27 letter, one of Washington's officers estimated how, "it was day break when we were two miles from Trenton, but happily the enemy were not apprised of our design . . . ."[50]

Neither Washington, even though his plan to strike at 5:00 a.m. was shattered, nor his men could believe their good fortune. As during the risky evacuation from Long Island and even while the storm continued to swirl around him, Washington's luck in stealthy maneuvers in close proximity of the enemy remained firmly intact. The silence among the ranks of his ever-individualistic men continued to be profound, indicating to Washington that discipline among his troops remained firmly intact. Hence, despite all of their suffering, he now knew that these resilient soldiers were ready for action. Most incredible of all, Washington had already won a major victory, having succeeded in convincing his weary men that they could accomplish what even they had believed impossible only a few hours before.

The late December day's growing light around 7:30 a.m. also revealed what perhaps many soldiers certainly thought would be impossible throughout this most nightmarish of marches, after having struggled across troublesome Jacob's Creek and its rugged, heavily wooded environs, especially raging Ewing Creek, and the season's most fierce winter storm: Washington's Second Division column now remained as cohesive as when it had first marched to McConkey's

Ferry more than twelve hours before, without his relatively few Continentals units getting lost, entangled, or reduced extensively by straggling or even desertion under the army's most arduous undertaking of the war.

Even more astounding and despite their bone-weariness, the spirits of Washington's troops remained surprisingly high, in part because they had survived the worst night of their lives. Especially after having finally reached the Pennington Road, a new sense of optimism for success soared through the ranks, almost as if these soldiers somehow instinctively knew that they were getting closer to the most elusive of all things in the history of this revolutionary army, an amazing victory that would astound the world. Ironically, the storm's harshness continued to work to Washington's favor on this terrible night in part because the common soldiers realized that straggling behind the main column was virtually a death sentence. The fact that Hunderton County was Tory country, despite Dickinson's zealous rebels, also ensured that large numbers of Continental soldiers had not fallen out of Washington's column to be left behind to the Loyalists' wrath.[51]

Amid the relative shelter of the dark woodlands, which acted as a breaker against the furious northeast winds, lining the rutted artery known as Scotch Road just northwest of Trenton, the first light of this frozen Thursday in western New Jersey also revealed just how pathetic Washington's men appeared at this time. After the long, arduous march, Washington's best Continental troops looked even more like forlorn scarecrows—with wet, stubbledfaces, in tattered clothing, wrapped in blankets, and mud-smeared—than real soldiers, who now held America's fate and future destiny squarely in their hands. As revealed in a letter, Ireland-born Colonel Moylan marveled how "what a morning [it] was for men clad as ours are, to march nine miles to attack an enemy provided with every necessary and elated with a succession of advantages over our handful of men whom they were accustomed to see retreating before them."[52]

But more importantly in regard to shortly meeting the famed Rall brigade in its own cozy nest of Trenton, where "everyone [now] lay in pleasant quarters," wrote Lieutenant Wiederhold in his diary, Washington's common soldiers were only able to reach the Pennington Road in relatively good shape primarily because they were a hardened, enthusiastic cadre of young, experienced soldiers now led by capable officers, who were as determined to succeed as the men in the enlisted ranks, and had been inspired by Washington's herculean efforts.

This unexpected and improbable development in a crisis situation was one benefit of the brutal Darwinian-like process of the New York Campaign and

New Jersey retreat that had so unmercifully culled Washington's ranks to now leave only the most physically robust, morally committed, and resilient patriots in what little was left of Washington's Army. Thousands of once-enthusiastic patriots, when the war was going so well for America, were no more, having deserted and vanished long ago. Consequently, what had been left—the toughest and most durable chaff—for Washington to undertake his most audacious gamble was an exceptionally highly motivated and toughened soldiery. This brutal evolutionary-like process of attrition that had left only on the best, brightest, and most die-hard soldiers explained the sudden appearance of an unprecedented amount of superior discipline and elevated sense of sheer determination that now dominated Washington's ranks: maintaining perfect silence, keeping up with the column, and staying close to officers as ordered during the marathon trek of nearly ten miles through a blustery winter storm, which, fortunately, was yet at their backs, over unmapped country during a pitch-black night and the worst possible conditions for an offensive operation.

Equally important, Washington's men were yet supremely idealistic, motivated by the desire to preserve their newly declared independence and save their dying nation before it was too late, knowing that Trenton offered the last chance to accomplish these feats. Silently leading Greene's Second Division steadily south down the Pennington Road in protective fashion, General Stephen's vanguard of veteran Virginians consisted of especially highly durable soldiers. Hardened by both the frontier experience and the war's rigors, these steadfast Virginians were well known to the Indians, who had felt the sharp sting and lethality of their blazing Long Rifles. Indeed, Stephen's Virginia boys "can march and shoot with any in the known world," bragged the fiery Stephen, whose words proved prophetic in the upcoming showdown at Trenton.

And among Washington's lieutenants, no Virginia commander was tougher or more resourceful than Stephen himself. The outspoken Scotsman had been one of the first Virginia leaders to advocate open revolt against Great Britain's might so that America could go its own way and fulfill its boundless potential. Now engaged in the last-ditch offensive effort to prove his point, he had once proclaimed with unbridled confidence: "Let us be provided with arms and ammunition [and] the gates of hell cannot prevail against America." The hard-bitten Stephen was Washington's "old tempestuous old comrade," and he remained indispensable in demanding combat situations of importance, as the commander-in-chief fully realized. Neither time, this fierce storm, nor the freezing night had dimmed Stephen's martial ardor, feistiness, or fighting spirit. During the withdrawal through New Jersey, he had warned New Jersey's governor that if the Tories, who had been captured by his men, were released for whatever reason, then his own Old Dominion "soldiery will put them to death."[53] And in a display of western frontier toughness that had once again risen to the fore on the march to Trenton, Stephens had meant every word of the grisly threat.

Despite the severe disruptions of Washington's delicate timetable that had been shattered beyond all recognition, Stephen remained optimistic for eventual success at Trenton largely because he fully appreciated the yet untapped, latent potential of America's fighting men, despite having been vanquished so often in the recent past. In a prophetic warning to the British government before the American Revolution, he had emphasized how American soldiers could rise magnificently to even the most daunting challenge, as now posed at Trenton: with only "a few Brave men, on the Conclusion of Harvest, laid down their Sickles, & Pitch forks, took up their Rifles & Tomahawks, march[ed] 300 miles without Noise or parade, took position in the Enemy's Country, chastised them [and] imposed on them more humiliating Terms, than before could be done by all the Kings forces ever employd [sic] against them [consequently] let the Enemies of America hear this & Tremble!"[54]

And now on the morning of December 26, Washington's Virginia soldiers now "were determined to fight to the last for their country," and never were these young men and boys more resolute than on this sleety morning in Hunterdon County's depths.[55] Having grown steadily since crossing the angry Delaware, this representative heightened sense of optimism, elan, and fighting spirit had glowed unseen, but ever-so-brightly even on this darkest of nights in the hearts and minds of the surviving soldiers of Washington's thinned ranks. This development was early expressed by Lieutenant Samuel Blachley Webb, Washington's private secretary and respected staff member, who confidently penned in a prophetic December letter: "we shall drub the dogs."[56]

But no one in this little, ragged force of diehard revolutionaries was now more determined to reap a success against the odds this morning than Washington himself. Washington demonstrated that he was at his best when seemingly everything else was at its worst and against him. As never before in this war, he was now "prepared to die," if necessary, to secure victory. Washington, therefore, had already made peace with his Maker, trusting in God during his greatest personal crisis of his life. During "this dangerous undertaking, justified by the deplorable state of our affairs and worthy [of] the chief who projected it [,] I have never doubted that he had resolved to stake his life on the issue" of capturing Trenton at any cost, wrote the analytical Major Wilkinson. An immensely complex, intriguing person on multiple levels and not unlike Washington himself, teenage Wilkinson was a walking contradiction. He was blessed with winning ways that masked a darker side that was decidedly Machiavellian. Less than two decades before, he had been born on a typical Southern tobacco plantation, just south of the slow-moving dark waters of Hunting Creek, nestled in the tobacco country of Calvert County in southern Maryland, located just three miles northeast of the picturesque little town of Benedict on the majestic Patuxent River, a tributary of the Chesapeake Bay.[57]

Mile after mile of pushing relentlessly toward Trenton and either glory or yet another fiasco, the desperate commander-in-chief felt the heightened burden and almost unbearable pressure in knowing that everything was now at stake for his ragtag army and America during this cold early morning. If Washington now suffered any kind of reversal at Trenton, not only Philadelphia but also this much-depleted Continental Army, especially with a swollen river to its back, and the American cause would be doomed. And any defeat suffered by Washington at Trenton would ensure a virtually unopposed march of Howe's legions to the defenseless American capital to destroy the last lingering hope of French intervention that represented America's salvation, delivering a certain death stroke to this people's revolution.[58] Consequently, as never before, the long-suffering Washington now relied and placed his faith upon the "interposition of Providence" to bring America her most badly needed victory of the war.[59]

With heightened resolve and an iron determination unwavering, Washington ignored the haunting realization of an ugly, disturbing reality: "We could not reach [Trenton] before the day was fairly broke, but as I was certain there was no making a Retreat without being discovered, and harassed on repassing the River, I determined to push on at all Events."[60] Therefore, with the stakes so high for America's destiny, a heightened degree of pre-battle apprehension and just plain nerves consumed the very fiber of Greene's Second Division troops, with failed battles and fiascos yet fresh in mind while they pushed through the ice and snow showers just north of Trenton. Some of Washington's soldiers might have now recalled the Old Testament words that had inspired faith among the God-fearing Israelite warriors to conquer the fierce Canaanites after the ancient Hebrew warriors crossed over their own strategic river of destiny, the legendary Jordan, which also ran north-south like the Delaware, for America: "Be strong and courageous [and] Do not be afraid or terrified because of them for the Lord your God goes with you" during their desperate bid to conquer Jericho.

Precious time continued to slip away during Washington's relentless march south down the windswept Pennington Road, while Greene's grim-faced Continentals, with limbs sore and numb from the cold, trudged steadily through the blowing winds and swirling snow in a last-ditch effort to conquer or be conquered. Most important, the Hessians at Trenton were not yet alerted to Washington's stealthy, improbable approach on such a horrendous night in western New Jersey that no one would ever forget.

No Continental soldier of either division had heard a single bugle blast, drumbeat, or signal gun to shatter the stillness from the lower ground around Trenton, and hardly anyone, especially Washington, who rode forward at the column's head with Greene, the stocky, former Quaker who was likewise wrapped in a military cloak, could believe that their good fortune for both divisions had lasted all the way to the day's first faint light at around half past 7:00 a.m. Indeed, by this time, few members of the yet-comatose Trenton garrison's more than 1,500 troops were up and stirring, as would have been the case if no severe storm had descended with such an unbridled fury upon the Delaware Valley.

Meanwhile, along the empty streets hidden under a new layer of freshly fallen snow, the approximate one hundred wooden houses of Trenton remained dark and silent, as if deserted. Assigned to quarters in civilian homes located in the middle and southern part of the northern end—near the corner of King and Second Street—of King Street, also known as High Street, the grenadiers of the four Rall Regiment companies continued to sleep peacefully while the large flakes of snow tumbled down in silence on wooden rooftops. Trenton possessed two main streets, King and Queen Streets, which ran north-south through the town. Leading up from the lower ground along the river where the two parallel roads crossed Front (nearest to the river), First, and Second Streets, from south to north, these two primary arteries extended completely through the town to meet on high ground at the town's north end to create a narrow wedge, spanning from lower to high ground.

Meanwhile, to the east on the parallel street to King Street, the experienced troops of the four fusilier companies of the Knyphausen Regiment slept in the relative warmth of private houses along Queen Street, sometimes called Bridge Street that led to the stone bridge across Assunpink Creek, in the town's southern, or lower town, and also in some little wooden houses situated below the creek, before continuing to Bordentown on the Delaware. And stationed above Rall's grenadiers, the fusiliers of four von Lossberg Regiment companies rested in bliss in the Anglican Church and in darkened houses located along both sides of the north end of King Street—including in the Micajah How house on the east side and in the Thomas Barnes, Rebecca Coxe, and Isaac Smith Houses on the street's west side. Since most of Trenton's largest houses, including brick structures, were situated along King Street, Hessians quartered along this main artery benefitted from more relative comfort than their comrades now sleeping in the smaller wooden houses off King and Queen Streets. Taverns and even the town's jail also provided quarters for Rall's troops. Appropriately, Rall's headquarters, the two-story Stacy Potts's house, was located on King Street in the heart of Trenton.

However, thanks to Rall's previous precautions, one fusilier company, under Captain Ernst von Altenbockum, was situated in small structures along the Pennington Road, guarding this vital artery on Trenton's northwest. Rall brigade dispositions in part reflected the fact that the von Lossberg Regiment had been the last regiment of the command to arrive in Trenton, after the Rall and Knyphausen Regiments had already secured most of the finest houses as sleeping quarters.

Meanwhile, Washington's sudden good fortune, which had been so abysmal for so long, continued to hold up surprisingly well, longer than he had a right to expect. Despite the night's long, torturous ordeal, things were shaping up for the distinct possibility of the forty-five-year-old Virginian, who was yet looking for his first true battlefield victory, exploiting what he now considered his long-awaited "lucky Chance" against a seemingly invincible opponent. Therefore, Washington continued to implore his troops, tired beyond endurance and on rubbery legs, onward down the Pennington Road, while bitter winds and falling snow accompanied them as their constant, heartless companions that seemed determined to deny them success. All the while, Washington was nagged by the grim prospect and distinct possibly of meeting another abject failure in "surprising the Town" and overwhelming the Hessian brigade.[61]

Numb with cold and tired from a long, sleepless night, Washington's common soldiers were equally concerned as each hour had slipped away, along with the already slim chances for success at Trenton. Young Johnny Greenwood could hardly image how a complete surprise of Trenton could possibly be achieved by Washington, but "if we did, they must have been a lazy, indolent set of rascals, which is nothing to the credit of a regular army . . . But any who would even suppose such a thing must indeed be ignorant, when it is well known that our whole country was filled with timid, designing tories and informers of all descriptions and our march so slow that it was impossible but that they should be apprised of it."[62]

However, all of Washington's good luck suddenly seemed to have burst when he was shocked to suddenly see a small American patrol headed his way, moving north through the falling snow! This bundled-up party of nondescript Continentals had approached close to the head of Greene's Second Division column without having been seen because of limited visibility, returning lazily up the Pennington Road from Trenton's direction. Incredibly, now going the wrong way, these soldiers never had been part of the army's forward movement, even though they were from one of Washington's own regiments now leading the Second Division's advance, the Fourth Virginia Continental Regiment, under Lieutenant Colonel Robert Lawson, of Stephen's brigade.

This motley group of around thirty Continentals, with a handful of company officers, had crossed the Delaware on Christmas Day's afternoon. They had done so not on their own initiative, but on General Stephen's direct orders, issued from the Pennsylvania side of the river, to strike Trenton's advanced pickets. These Virginians had attacked the advanced Hessian picket detachment, under the immediate command of twenty-six-year-old Corporal Wilhelm Hartung, who had been born in Elbingerode in the Harz Mountains, of Lieutenant Andreas Weiderhold's advanced force on the Pennington Road just to the southeast. In true guerrilla fashion, this Indian-like strike by these adventuresome Virginia Continentals had resulted in the hot, but brief, firefight northwest of Trenton on the previous evening.

Washington was completely unaware of this rather remarkable development of a top lieutenant waging his own personal war on New Jersey soil that threatened to sabotage his best-laid plans of gaining the element of surprise. Before Washington's orders were issued for the Trenton operation to begin, the ever-independently minded General Stephen had been fighting the hated Hessians on his own hook and with a typical unbridled Celtic enthusiasm. To avenge the recent death of one of his beloved Virginia boys to a fatal German bullet, Stephen had ordered this small, highly mobile task force on its unsupported raid to strike Trenton's advanced outposts: an audacious decision considering that Rall possessed not only a full brigade but also a readily available, experienced British cavalry detachment that could have cut such a small party of infantrymen, especially when stranded on the river's wrong, or east, side, to pieces.

Gaining a measure of pride and self-respect lost in the disastrous New York Campaign, these sharpshooting Virginians of Captain George Wallis's company had inflicted a disproportionate amount of damage on the Hessian pickets on Christmas night. With skillful shooting from their barking Long Rifles as if hunting deer or turkey back home, they systematically cut down half a dozen soldiers of Hartung's advanced force at long range with a ruthless efficiency. Now, after a job well done and after having been only belatedly pursued by the thoroughly aroused Germans, the Virginia boys had then returned wearily up the snowy Pennington Road to eventually recross the Delaware to the safety of Pennsylvania soil. They had inflicted yet another psychological blow to the increasingly nervous Trenton garrison. Amid the blinding snowstorm and cold that cut to the bone, they now ran straight into General Washington himself and Greene's column descending relentlessly down the Scotch Road quite by accident.

Revealing his heightened tension, taut nerves, and anxiety about not now being able to surprise the Rall Brigade after the Virginia riflemen's ill-timed harassment, Washington's legendary self-control and self-discipline momentarily vanished in thin air. He now snapped angrily for the first time during the harrowing ordeal of the march on Trenton: a long overdue, if not necessary, release of pent-up anxiety and frustration after his considerable mastery of self-control that had held up for so long since crossing the Delaware. An exasperated Washington immediately turned his wrath on a much surprised General Stephen, an old French and Indian War regimental superior who rode nearby the commander-in-chief.

Clearly, Stephen was guilty of no simple breach of protocol, but a serious violation: he had not bothered to ask permission from Washington for his raiding party to cross the river and harass the Trenton garrison. Believing that the element of surprise had been lost, consequently, the commander-in-chief's little remaining optimism for surprising Rall now sank to a new low. Washington feared that the entire Trenton garrison was now alerted, preparing to meet his advance, thanks to Captain Wallis's ill-timed raid that had caused considerable excitement among the Trenton garrison the previous night.

However, Washington was again most fortunate. He had no idea that Trenton was now even more vulnerable precisely because of the fact that this little raiding party of Virginia boys had been mistaken by the Germans for the main force attack that Donop, who spoke French fluently to reveal his fine education and upper class roots, had recently warned Rall about. As if still battling

Indians along Virginia's Blue Ridge or the Ohio Valley on his own, Stephen was certainly at fault for fighting his own personal war of vengeance. But to be perfectly fair, Stephen was correct in waging guerrilla war and wearing down his opponent on his own because he had not known about Washington's decision to attack Trenton when he had ordered Wallis's company to cross the river and reap sweet "revenge." Despite his shortcomings that were more temperamental than tactical, Stephen was exactly the type of no-nonsense, almost fanatical, hard-hitting brigade commander who Washington now needed to lead the advance of Greene's Second Division column just behind Captain Washington's vanguard of Virginians when the battle opened in full fury.[63]

But despite all his escalating concerns, Washington had no need to worry about the Trenton garrison's alertness or preparedness this momentous morning that was destined to decide America's fate. A snow-shrouded and undisturbed Trenton yet lay bathed in a frigid, eerie silence, presenting a serene appearance. In truth, what had settled over the little town was literally a great lull just before Washington's man-made storm descended upon the quiet town with a vengeance seldom seen in this war. With fighting instincts and senses dulled by a sense of deepening complacency after the Virginia sharpshooter's strike faded away and with the arrival of nature's tempest, hundreds of worn Hessian soldiers reposed in deep sleep on this stormy night, forgetting all about threats, both real and imagined, to Trenton.

All in all, these Germans were utterly exhausted from the combined effect of the New York Campaign's rigors, the lengthy pursuit of Washington's ghost army across New Jersey's flatlands, and the escalating harassment from the resurgent New Jersey militia, which had repeatedly lashed out at targets of opportunity when least expected. So far from home on this sad and sullen Yuletide, Rall's young soldiers, in frayed, dirty uniforms of summer, were now thoroughly tired of the nasty game of war while racked by illness, the horrors of guerilla warfare, and disillusionment. For brutal winter weather, the Hessians lacked almost everything that was necessary to cope because the Rall brigade was now at nearly the end of an overly extended supply line that stretched northeast and all the way to New York City. Rall's men now slept soundly in part to forget their weariness, the nightmare of a growing insurgency, the pain of being far away from home and family, and the war's escalating brutality. In the words of one exasperated and weary Hessian officer at Trenton: "We have not slept one night in peace since we came to this place [and] The troops have lain on their arms every night, but they can endure it no longer."[64]

Because he was unaware of the true situation at Trenton, an even more apprehensive Washington, expecting the worst because of his wrecked time-table of having wanted to attack at 5:00 a.m., continued to hurry his soldiers down the Pennington Road. All the while, the snow and sleet continued to pelt the lengthy column of mostly Continentals, as if attempting to thwart Washington's renewed attempt to hasten his soldier's pace to reach Trenton as soon as possible. Trenton's peaceful setting was about to be shattered by thousands of fast-approaching American soldiers, who were now fueled by a potent mixture of adrenaline, desperation, and revenge. Most of all, they were now motivated to fulfill Washington's desperate, but supremely motivating, motto of "Victory or Death" at any cost. All the while, Washington's inspiring leadership ensured that his men would follow him to hell and back, and in undertaking the greatest challenge of their lives.

Additionally, Washington's Continentals yet recalled Tom Paine's inspiring words from the pages of *The American Crisis,* having taken them to heart: "These are the times that try men's souls. The summer soldier and the sunshine patriot will, in this crisis, shrink from the service of their country; but he that stands it now, deserves the loves and thanks of man and woman. Tyranny, like hell, is not easily conquered; yet we have this consolation with us, that the harder the conflict, the more glorious the triumph"; an invigorating promise of achieving a sparkling success at Trenton that only fueled a more rapid push of Washington's troops, of both divisions, down both the snowbound parallel arteries, the Pennington and River Roads. Now the most popular inspirational voice of the common people, the transplanted Englishman's idealistic rhetoric fortified the resolve of Washington and his faithful followers to do or die this morning. Most of all, "I [was] determined," wrote Washington, to now succeed at any cost. At this crucial moment for America's fortunes, Washington and his men's determination to reap victory at Trenton had evolved into what might be described as almost a viable, innate force of nature, much like the howling nor'easter itself, that had been pent-up for so long from the seemingly endless series of defeats and humiliating withdrawals, after so many self-inflicted wounds, incompetence, internal divisions, and even cowardice. And now this reenergized force of will that now fueled Washington's troops was finally about to break loose in full fury upon Trenton and the unprepared Rall brigade.

Fueled by a heightened determination to emerge victorious this morning that had only steadily increased since crossing the Delaware, Greene's troops, despite in rags, torn blankets, and almost barefoot, continued to surge down the Pennington Road at an increased pace and with greater confidence. All the while, the homespun revolutionaries yet maintained their discipline and silence that matched the haunting quiet of the falling snow, which muffled the sound of thousands of marching feet. In an amazing, unprecedented display of discipline, Washington's strict orders that "a profound silence is to be observed, both by officers and men," was yet obeyed to the letter.[65]

However, anxiety and mental anguish were high among a good many American officers, including Washington, because of the knowledge that they were hours behind schedule and shortly would have to face a full Hessian brigade of crack troops in broad daylight. In the strange quiet in which the only sound was that of the treading of hundreds of feet in the snow, perhaps some of Greene's New Englanders, contemplating the upcoming battle with the dreaded Hessians, recalled the words of a fiery Massachusetts preacher who strengthened the soldier's resolve by emphasizing "May we take to ourselves the whole armour of God," from the book of Ephesians.[66]

All of a sudden breathless New Jersey scouts, including the local strong-armed blacksmith and miller named David Lanning, came running back through the falling snow with the latest intelligence, breaking the monotony of seemingly endless marching southward. Upon reaching a mounted Washington at the column's head, these local New Jersey men excitedly reported in low tones that they had ascertained the exact location of the first Hessian pickets on the Pennington Road about a mile from Trenton's center. Of all places, these foremost Hessian pickets were garrisoned at a little cooper shop, where Richard Howell and son Arthur (two other sons, John and Elias, were apprenticed elsewhere) along the road northwest of Trenton. This well-known shop had been previously seen by Lanning when passing down the Pennington Road. And Washington had previously heard about the use of the cooper shop by the Hessians from his New Jersey informants. Most importantly, Washington fully realized that the Hessians had not been alerted at all, bringing a great sigh of relief and a sense of elation to the troubled Virginian.

Before meeting the Rall brigade in the final showdown at Trenton, Washington called a brief halt so that his weary, sleepless troops could briefly rest on muskets and catch their breath, while his strung-out units closed up during the respite. He also had to allow more time for Sullivan's First Division, to the southwest along the River Road, to ease closer to Trenton for any possibility of a simultaneous attack of both divisions before Greene's Second Division column could strike as one.

Fortunately, and besides the storm, a thick belt of dark woodlands now screened Greene's lengthy column, stretched out along the Pennington Road for hundreds of yards, from view of the advanced Hessian picket outposts. Almost incredibly, after all that had gone wrong with Washington's plan and timetable, an entire Hessian brigade could yet be caught by surprise at Trenton. Therefore, this brief respite for the Second Division troops just outside a completely quiet Trenton was much-needed for the exhausted common soldiery, who had been up all night.

One of Stephen's top lieutenants, Major George Johnston, Fifth Virginia Regiment, checked his watch. He realized that much more precious time had slipped away than he thought. While standing at the head of his half-frozen soldiers, with the other two regiments (the Fourth and Sixth Virginia) of Stephen's Virginia vanguard, now poised on the Pennington Road just northwest of Trenton in the gathering yet faint, early morning light, dulled by the dense, low-hanging cloud cover and dropping snow, he estimated the time and wrote how: "At 7, we halted within 500 yds of their advanced guard [at the little frame cooper house of Arthur and Richard Howell] until the until the Right wing, commanded by General Sullivan [who led the First Division] could get within the same distance of another of the Guards, posted on the River road" to the southwest.[67]

By way of careful tactical calculation, Washington was attempting to do whatever and all that he could to ensure a simultaneous attack from two different directions, the ever-elusive double envelopment. Unlike in the past, everything now had to go exactly right and according to Washington's intricate tactical design if an impressive victory was to be achieved at Trenton. In a strange way, all of the many past defeats and miscalculations now had made Washington even more exceptionally meticulous, exacting, and a stickler for all details during this most desperate of bids to reverse the war's course before it was too late. Washington early realized that he could only succeed if all aspects of the advance and upcoming attack were closely scrutinized with unprecedented precision and micromanaged to the last detail.

With the level of tension rising among the silent column of bedraggled, winter soldiers, the 7:20 a.m. dawn had quickly passed by almost without much notice or contemplation because everyone was simply too exhausted. Cottony plumes of breath hung in the cold air before fading silently away like Washington's chances for success, or so it seemed. However, as yet not a shot had been fired from a single Hessian picket or Gefreiter (private) to sound the alarm. Not a single early morning songbird, after having found shelter from the storm in oak thickets, clumps of darkgreen cedars, and thorny bushes, had heralded the dawn's arrival with a melody. Like a late Christmas gift presented to Washington, a vulnerable Trenton yet lay in the quiet serenity of a false security, hubris, and complacency. Hardly believing his good fortune after all had been seemingly lost with so many delays in crossing the Delaware and during the long, agonizing march on Trenton, Washington ordered the advance to move faster down the road during the final approach.

After pushing out of the black woodlands northwest of Trenton and with open ground, blanketed in snow, bordering each side of the Pennington Road, Washington then quickly deployed Greene's Second Division into three separate assault columns. Mercer's brigade, the lead brigade just before Stirling and to Stephen's rear, formed in a column on the right and Stephen's Virginia vanguard brigade, while Lord Stirling's brigade moved ahead and formed a center column. Most importantly, the farsighted Washington issued orders for Fermoy's 638-man Pennsylvania brigade, a third assault column on the left, on a vital mission: to eventually shift east to gain the strategic Princeton-Trenton Road northeast of town. Around 8:00 a.m. the three columns of Greene's Second Division were set firmly in place across the snow-covered landscape, and prepared for their respective assignments as deemed by Washington.

On Washington's eagerly awaited signal, lengthy files of Continental soldiers then pushed off on the double with a new bounce in their step and in high spirits. The usual clattering of gear of large numbers of troops was now muffled by multiple layers of winter clothing and blankets wrapped around bodies of young men and boys fortunate enough to have even this meager extra covering. On the double and with flintlocks on shoulders, hundreds of soldiers of the German Regiment and Colonel Edward Hand's Pennsylvania rifle regiment pushed across the snowy fields to the east. Fermoy's Pennsylvanians, and also Marylanders in the German Regiment's ranks, of these two fine Continental regiments raced over the wintery landscape in the hope of gaining their key tactical objective of aligning aside the Princeton-Trenton Road to the east. Determined men with plenty of combat savvy, the 254 sharpshooters of Hand's First Pennsylvania Continental Regiment provided the combat experience that the German Regiment lacked.

Not far from the busy commander-in-chief, meanwhile, Captain Washington's and Lieutenant Monroe's Virginians, the vanguard, surged forward with their Long Rifles in hand before the advance of Stephen's Virginia vanguard brigade, swarming down the Pennington Road at the center column's head. Shouting and out in front as usual, an animated Washington encouraged his troops of the center column onward at the long trot. As long trained as if just for this moment, hundreds of Continentals, with trusty smoothbore flintlocks on shoulders, raced through the snow on the double, knowing that no additional precious time could be wasted on this cold New Jersey morning.

Leading the way in company with his young staff officers like a Moses leading his people to a new day, Washington rode forward on his "noble horse" in the forefront of Stephen's surging Virginians, who basked in having been at last unleashed to demonstrate their worth. With a tight discipline seldom seen in this war, hundreds of American soldiers pushed forward on the double and with enthusiasm, heading toward their preassigned objectives with alacrity, while adrenaline pumped through their bodies and warded off the terrible cold.

Less than an hour after the first signs of dawn on this ill-lit morning and with the wrath of the snow storm yet to their backs, Washington's reinvigorated troops surged toward Trenton's northwestern outskirts with renewed confidence in broad daylight. Fortunately, omnipresent dark skies and a light ground fog, hugging the terrain as far as the eye could see, compensated for the suddenly increased visibility from the faint winter light of early morning, providing a lingering measure of concealment for Washington's fast-advancing Continentals. With his troops already having exceeded even his high expectations, Washington was encouraged by the sight of his energized soldiers swarming onward with a renewed vigor and enthusiasm. Marveling at the encouraging spectacle that bestowed greater hope for the success of "his brilliant encircling movement," the Virginian never forgot how his resurgent men now "seemed to vie with the other in pressing forward" in a bid to reap the desperately needed victory that might just save an infant republic from a premature death.

All the while, the three Hessian regiments of the Rall brigade were not yet aroused, and Colonel Rall remained in a comfortable, deep sleep at Stacy Potts's large, white frame house near Trenton's center. Then, while Trenton yet remained perfectly quiet, the foremost Virginians, panting and breathless, under Captain Washington, who led the way, finally reached Trenton's northwestern outskirts. General Washington galloped forward on his large chestnut sorrel, staying much closer to the front ranks than was prudent for safety's sake. In surging down the snowy Pennington Road, the fast-moving vanguard of the foremost Virginia Continentals reached the vicinity of an isolated, lone house wrapped in solitude and a wintry shroud. Here, ignoring the nasty weather but knowing he needed more fuel, an early-rising civilian was outside chopping wood for a morning fire to cook breakfast and to warm his house. Fortunately for Washington and his men, he was not a Tory.

Washington knew that in order to achieve a complete surprise, the foremost German pickets guarding Trenton's northwestern outskirts needed to be captured or eliminated before they spread the alarm to arouse the garrison. Fortunately, the commander-in-chief now possessed sound intelligence from the vigilant Lanning as to the presence of the Hessian Pennington Road picket post about a half mile before the town. Realizing that he had not yet reached the most advanced Hessian picket post and in order to confirm the prior intelligence, Washington boldly rode right up to the man and asked, "Can you tell me where the Hessian picket is?" Amazingly, in continuing to seemingly do everything on his own, Washington was now performing much like a low-ranking reconnaissance or staff officer in gathering accurate information verified by his own eyes and ears that he could trust unfailingly.

Thinking that this approaching force was a British column dispatched to reinforce Trenton, the civilian was initially hesitant to reply to the towering figure of obvious authority on horseback. Then Captain Thomas Forrest, who had managed to keep his six-pounders and howitzers in their assigned place at the Second Division column's head after much effort and as Washington had ordered, said: "You may speak for that is General Washington." With his face suddenly brightening, the farmer was now eager to assist the liberators of his own hometown. He pointed to the nearby cooper house of Richard Howell, where the most advanced Hessian pickets were located.

In the pale winter light of early morning when all hell was about to break loose just northwest of Trenton, even though unrealized by him at the time, Lieutenant Andreas Wiederhold felt an inexplicable sense of uneasiness. A fine officer of ability, Wiederhold had been commended for gallantry on the battlefield as early as fourteen years before. He now trusted his veteran's instincts. Even though the experienced lieutenant was an intellectual scholar-solder of the Knyphausen Regiment, Wiederhold had never quite lost either his common touch or common sense. Although holding no bitterness, he had been unfairly denied a captain's rank because he, like Colonel Rall, lacked noble blood and priviledged background that meant everything in his hierarchical eighteenth-century society.

Wiederhold was a commoner of humble origins like his enlisted men, and every blueblood officer, in the proud tradition of the Prussian officer corps, was aware of that fact and never allowed him to forget it. Because this atypical German lieutenant so closely identified with his men, including the lowest private in the ranks, and led his troops by example, they in turn respected him. Partly reflecting his common roots, Wiederhold was also a man of compassion and faith, duly writing "God be praised" in his diary. Therefore, as a true Christian who was color blind, Wiederhold felt a deep, Quaker-like sympathy toward African Americans in bondage, lamenting their sad plight, while their owners, including men in Washington's Virginia regiments, paradoxically now fought for the liberty of whites, not blacks.

Here, at Howell's cooper house, located just south of the icy intersection of the Pennington and Scotch Road about a half mile northwest of Trenton, Wiederhold's creeping sense of uneasiness grew even stronger: a sixth sense well-honed and heightened in this hardened veteran whose instincts could not have been sharper this early morning. After having been dispatched on the previous evening, or Christmas Day, in answering the alarm upon the outburst of firing from the strike of Captain Wallis's Virginia patrol on the most advanced Hessian pickets located on the Pennington Road, having been up half the night in organizing his defensive ring of pickets, and after having sent out patrols for added security, Wiederhold now commanded Trenton's most advanced picket post. This duty-minded lieutenant felt a solemn responsibility in commanding "my little picket house," which was located along "the road to John's [Johnson's] Ferry]," in Wiederhold's words.

As the senior officer in overall command of seven advanced picket posts on both the Pennington Road and the River Road, to the south and upon which Sullivan's First Division now marched, and in the intervening ground between the two snow-bound roads, he recalled how so many past successes had bestowed an abundant amount of "Hessian glory which could be shared by every good man with honor" in the Rall brigade. And Wiederhold had won his own fair share of this coveted glory during the New York Campaign.

For instance, to gain the American's exposed right flank, he had won widespread recognition for leading the cheering Knyphausen Regiment soldiers across the Bronx River while a hail of American bullets splashed around him. Lieutenant Wiederhold had then encouraged his attacking troops up Chatterton Hill to help win the day at White Plains only last October. Then, in mid-November, he had commanded the regiment's vanguard in the "very spearhead" during the "suicidal" attack up the open slopes of Mount Washington, "a hard nut to crack," in his own words. Here, at Fort Washington, he took over the leadership of his fusilier company when all senior officers had been cut down by the deadly rifle fire of Colonel Moses Rawlings's Maryland marksmen.

Demonstrating those sterling qualities that had allowed him to rise from private to sergeant major in 1760 and to earn an officer's rank for distinguished service during the Seven Years' War, Wiederhold now ventured forth from the warmth of the wooden cooper's house to verify for himself that all was safe and sound along the eerily quiet Pennington Road. He also now eagerly looked for the return of his early morning picket patrol with "bright daylight" having now begun to illuminate the snowy landscape. The conscientious lieutenant now half-expected to see his last patrol of weary men come trudging down the Pennington Road in returning through the snow.

However, Wiederhold was not completely trusting of what the cold-numbed, young members of his first returning patrols had told him—that everything was perfectly quiet—when they had staggered back to his snowy picket outpost about an hour before dawn. Born in Spangenberg, Hesse-Cassel, Wiederhold was one of the Knyphausen Regiment's best officers at age forty-four. He possessed more than a quarter century of solid military experience, including years of service as a tough sergeant major who brooked no indiscipline. Most importantly, as a seasoned warrior, he was now once again relying upon his own well-honed instincts, which sometimes had caused him to boldly question his superiors to their dismay and endless irritation.

Wiederhold suspected that the returning members of his early morning patrol had been lax in their duties—understandable given the soldiers' weariness, the Christmas season, and stormy weather—, failing to complete a thorough, proper reconnaissance along the Pennington Road. Who could have blamed these young men for having only hunkered down in shelter to warm and protect themselves from winter's harshest offerings this morning, especially on the Christmas holiday when they were thinking about their faraway homes, wives, families, and children instead of killing American rebels, who were mostly farmers like themselves and only battling for their personal freedom?

Acting on a gut instinct, although exhausted after an anxious night spent worrying about ghost-like American raiders suddenly emerging out of the blackness to reap revenge on their tormentors, Wiederhold sought to investigate the situation for himself. Upon peering north toward more elevated terrain, upon which the Pennington Road ran, and through the heavy fall of snow flakes cascading down, the seasoned Knyphausen Regiment lieutenant was shocked by what he suddenly saw: in the distance, around sixty men, looking like ghostly apparitions, pouring out from the blackened woodlands to the northwest, and moving forward at a good pace, despite the thick snow cover. Straining his eyes at the unbelievable sight that took his breath away, Wiederhold soon realized that these men possessed firearms and the discipline of tried soldiers. Indeed, these men advanced south at the "long trot" through the open fields of snow around the Pennington Road, after having spilled from the dark forests only about two hundred yards distant. What these attackers gave the veteran lieutenant was an early morning shock at the sight of the most improbable development, especially given the storm's intensity and the overwhelming contempt held by the Hessans for American soldiers.

Wiederhold now realized that his most advanced Pennington Road sentries were not sufficiently alert. He knew where to lay blame for this unexpected and rare breach in discipline "because it was a holiday." At first, the fusilier lieutenant mistakenly thought that this advancing force was just "merely a roaming party" on yet another small raid, like Wallis's Virginians, to harass Trenton's most advanced pickets as in the past.

Wiederhold began to shout out the alarm at the top of his voice. The already uniformed fusiliers grabbed their dry weapons from a nearby row of muskets and prepared to meet the fast-moving interlopers. Not yet realizing that he was facing Washington's main force of veteran Continentals, Wiederhold and his disciplined Knyphausen Regiment soldiers were quickly under arms. They were determined to put up a good fight and maintain their lofty reputations. With shiny muskets already loaded just in case of such a surprise, thanks to Rall's wisdom, the aroused Hessians poured like a flood from Howell's cooper house, located just below, or south of, the snowy intersection of the Scotch and Pennington Roads, rushing out into the biting cold and the harsh northeast wind. Lieutenant Wiederhold, in his own words, was now determined "to give the enemy a firm challenge," believing that he was confronting only a small raiding party of ragtag militia.

However, Wiederhold soon realized that these rebels continued to move forward without any hint of tentativeness. Most alarming to the lieutenant, they were surging onward as if they meant business. All in all, these Americans were simply acting much too boldly, heading directly toward Trenton and a full Hessian brigade with far too much confidence for a relatively small body of men. Lieutenant Wiederhold now understood that these onrushing soldiers, even though they looked more like New Jersey farmers than professional fighting men, represented a far more serious threat than a small band of raiders: obviously a fast-moving vanguard, which was leading a much larger body of soldiers—the main American force—advancing not far behind them.

Confirming his conviction that far more attackers had to be advancing just behind this vanguard, Wiederhold then saw larger numbers of American soldiers pouring from the blackened belt of woodlands and surging through the open fields covered in snow. In fact, it soon seemed as if the Americans were swarming everywhere. This vanguard of seasoned Virginians, displaying a level of discipline matching that of the Hessians to the surprise of all who saw the sight, quickly formed into a neat firing line on Pennington Road, standing tall before Wiederhold's thin formation of slightly shorter men. Aligning with a precision that revealed that these unsoldierly looking Americans were battle-hardened veterans, Captain Washington's Virginia Continentals then unleashed the morning's first volley that erupted from both sides of the road. Breaking the morning stillness, the American volley crashed and rang across the open fields, which had been overflowing with crops of corn, oats, and wheat only a few months before. Echoing through the crisp, early morning air, this resounding volley announced the sudden arrival of Washington's main strike force just outside and northwest of Trenton.

But in the Virginia Continental's sense of elation, excitement in catching the enemy by surprise, and an overeagerness to hit tempting Hessian targets, including Wiederhold himself, they unleashed their first fire when the range was yet too great for the volley to strike home. Therefore, no damage was inflicted upon the small line of eighteen exposed Hessian pickets and their sword-wielding commander, who stood before them to present an ideal, tempting target. Nevertheless, the Germans boldly held not only their ground but also their fire. They also maintained their composure and discipline even as the first hail of bullets whistled close by. Then, while Captain Washington's soldiers hurriedly reloaded their flintlocks, the foremost company of Stephen's Virginia men, advancing rapidly behind the vanguard, then aligned in a neat rank and opened fire.

Still upset that his picket patrol had been "not alert enough" this morning to now place him and his men in such a bad fix, the veteran fusilier lieutenant thought clearly in this crisis situation and quickly developed a plan of action. Displaying considerable nerve, he calmly waited for Captain Washington's and Stephen's Virginians to swarm even closer after they unleashed their initial volleys before ordering his men to return fire. After the third volley exploded from the overeager Virginians, out of breath and panting, who continued to miss their targets, Wiederhold finally screamed for his pickets to open up with the first Hessian fire of the day.

Meanwhile, more of Washington's attackers continued to emerge out of the blinding snowstorm like wintry demons from some Arctic region heading toward Lieutenant Wiederhold's band of isolated men. An unstoppable tide, the Americans advanced swiftly through the fallow fields and open meadows, bathed in a fresh sheet of snow, until Wiederhold and his band of Knyphausen fusiliers were "almost surrounded by several battalions." With lengthy lines of Greene's Second Division troops overlapping his flanks like an ocean wave, Wiederhold finally ordered his handful of men rearward.

He now planned to fall back to the next, and main, advanced picket post held by von Lossberg fusiliers. In a final act of defiance and feeling the shame of running before the most despicable of foes, two Knyphausen Regiment fusiliers quickly reloaded while falling back, frantically jamming bullets into musket barrels with long wooden ramrods. Then, in a show of bravado, they suddenly spun around and turned to gamely face the onslaught of Old Dominion attackers. The two Hessian pickets then calmly took aim and fired at their onrushing opponent. Near the mounted General Washington at the front as usual, Colonel Fitzgerald wrote in his diary how, "Two of them fired on us, but the bullets whistled over our heads."[68]

This hot exchange of initial volleys delivered along the Pennington Road resulted in no casualties on either side. The lack of casualties revealed the high degree of nervous excitement, weariness, and overeagerness of the Virginians, which was only natural at an important engagement's opening. However, on the town's northwest outskirts, this fight was only beginning for the seventeen Hessian pickets under Lieutenant Wiederhold's command. Even though "I was passed by several [of Greene's] battalions" on the flanks, especially to the south where the Maryland, Connecticut, and Massachusetts troops of Mercer's brigade swarmed forward from the west, Wiederhold ordered his band of Knyphausen pickets to continue to offer resistance while falling back toward Trenton "under a steady fire." Previously chosen for the key assignment "to attack and force the enemies Guards and seize such posts as may prevent them from forming in the streets" of Trenton, Captain Washington's foremost vanguard and Stephen's lead brigade of Virginia Continentals fulfilled their mission with skill and alacrity.[69]

With the chase through the snow now on toward Trenton, Washington ordered Captain Washington and his elite contingent of Third Virginia Continental Regiment soldiers, of Stirling's brigade, who had only recently rejoined the army just north of the intersection of the Pennington and Scotch Roads from their independent advanced assignment, down the snowy roadway in pursuit. Eager to strike a blow and push all the way to Trenton, these Virginia soldiers were now "determined to fight to the last for their country," wrote Captain Chilton. With a resounding cheer that echoed through the air, Captain Washington's Virginians dashed down the Pennington Road in an attempt to capture the Hessian pickets before they escaped to Trenton and sounded the alarm. After having already demonstrated spunk in defying the odds, the two especially belligerent Germans of Wiederhold's advanced picket detachment were finally overwhelmed by the onrushing Virginians, who took mercy on their exhausted captives. There was no killing of prisoners on this post-Yuletide morning because this war between cousins had not yet degenerated to that horrific point.

Meanwhile, "under constant fire," Wiederhold's survivors continued to withdraw at a steady pace toward the main picket headquarters, just northwest of town, about a half mile to the east. Captain Ernst Eberhard von Altenbockum commanded this picket headquarters. At age forty, he was an unmarried officer with twenty-two years of hard-earned experience in the von Lossberg Regiment. Located at the Alexander Calhoun House that also served as a little general store on the Pennington Road, the picket headquarters now became Washington's next target. Born in Courland, a Baltic Sea region of rolling hills, dense forests, and medieval towns in western Lativa where many ethnic Germans lived, in 1736, Altenbockum was a most enterprising officer. He had taken command of the 170-man detachment of the advanced guard of the right column during the steamrolling assault on Fort Washington, when Major Dechow was cut down in leading the Knyphausen Regiment up the commanding heights to a mid-November 1776 victory.

Here, at the picket headquarters, sleepy Hessians had already poured from the house when they heard the first outburst of firing. These weary von Lossbergers had been under arms for three consecutive nights and sleeping in uniforms, with leather cartridge-boxes strapped on, and had been ready for action on a moment's notice for the last eight days like other regimental members. These advanced Hessians northwest of town had been caught off guard in no small part because of sheer exhaustion from having answered so many recent alarms and previous threats, both real and imaginary.

Barking out orders in the frigid cold, Captain Altenbockum rallied around twenty of his seasoned fusiliers in record time. With what appeared to be a robotic ease, Altenbockum's pickets then formed a straight line astride the Pennington Road before the snow-covered Calhoun house, as long practiced on drill fields, on both sides of the Atlantic, so often in the past. In facing northwest and looking up the road through the falling snow, they made their defensive stand against the raging American tide that had so suddenly emerged out of the dark woodlands. To protect his flank and his exposed Pennington Road position, Altenbockum "formed a right angle across the street before the captain's quarters." At last, a sweeping volley erupted from a concentration of Hessian muskets, thundering across the high ground northwest of Trenton.

Despite facing overwhelming odds, the Hessians continued to demonstrate that they yet possessed plenty of feistiness and fighting spirit that surprised the foremost Americans, including even hardened veterans. Here, before the wood-frame Calhoun House and standing astride the Pennington Road in guardian fashion to buy time for the yet-unassembling men of the Rall brigade situated in the river valley below in Trenton, Altenbrockum's little formation was bolstered when Lieutenant Wiederhold and his withdrawing pickets suddenly raced up. They hurriedly formed up beside Altenbockum's soldiers, extending their right to the street's other side. Captain Altenbockum now felt more confident with the arrival of Wiederhold's veterans, knowing that he had to buy time in order to give the Rall brigade, on lower ground to the southeast, time to rally.

The united band of Knyphausen and von Lossberg Regimental members now stood side by side, defying Washington's Virginia vanguard. But now even more American troops were seen swarming southeast toward Trenton and across the open fields of a harsh New Jersey winter, disturbing the freshly fallen snow and Altenbockum's chances of holding firm. After firing a ragged volley, Altenbockum ordered his fusiliers of the Fifth Company, von Lossberg Regiment, to reload in a hurry.

But the luxury of sufficient time no longer remained with Captain Washington and his Third Virginia troops already practically right on top of the badly outnumbered fusiliers, charging down the Pennington Road as if nothing could stop these Old Dominion veterans. Nevertheless, most Germans of the two united picket outposts refused to flee southeast to join their comrades in Trenton. Instead, the Hessians continued to hold their ground, standing firm to buy precious time for the Rall brigade. With time rapidly running out, Altenbockum hoped that the main picket detail of von Lossbergers retiring from the Princeton-Trenton Road might yet reinforce him. However, as fate would have it, these eagerly awaited reinforcements failed to reach the hard-pressed captain's position in time.[70]

One of Washington's elated attackers was surprised at the spunky fighting spirit demonstrated by these outnumbered Hessians, of two picket outposts, who were now united under the experienced leadership team of Altenbockum and Wiederhold. During one of the day's most spirited delaying actions, the advanced pickets, who represented two regiments, stood their ground with defiance. Demonstrating courage and sheer nerve in the face of the American onslaught, the foremost Hessians before Trenton now fought back in a defensive position before Captain Altenbockum's headquarters. These Germans no longer fired volleys as ordered by officers. Instead, they blasted away at will, loading and firing rapidly. Bestowing a compliment, one of Washington's soldiers, described in a letter how "Their advance guard gave our advance guard several smart fires" this morning.[71]

Buying additional precious time for the Rall brigade, Captain Altenbockum and Lieutenant Wiederhold stood firm in the snowy street with their pickets, even while Captain Washington's fast-moving Virginians, tall, lanky western men with Long Rifles, closed in for the kill. Large-sized and burly like Lieutenant Monroe who advanced beside him, Captain Washington now demonstrated how thoroughly he had been transformed from the quiet, pious divinity student to a model warrior. With a florid complication, placid face, and the gentlemanly manners of a typical Virginia Tidewater aristocrat of the planter class, Captain Washington had once believed with all his heart that killing his fellow man was the worst of all sins during a more innocent time that was no more. Only a year ago a fresh-faced sophomore attending classes at the prestigious College of William and Mary in Williamsburg, Lieutenant Monroe described with admiration how "Captain Washington moved forward with the vanguard in front, attacked the enemy's picket, shot down [an] officer. . . ."[72]

Indeed, by this time, the Virginian's fire was not only closer but also more concentrated and accurate, inflicting an escalating amount of damage on the spunky Hessians, including the fallen lieutenant cut down by a single shot from the sharp-eyed Captain Washington. Captain Altenbockum, far from his Courland homeland on the Atlantic's other side, now faced a howling tide of attackers led by the cousin, Captain Washington, of the commander-in-chief, while the German American cousin of Trenton's commander was among the troops now swiftly descending upon Trenton. All the while, Altenbockum and his band of pickets continued to face the brunt of Washington's vanguard surging down the Pennington Road. Along with the fallen von Lossberg lieutenant, a sergeant and several privates were also hit by the Virginians' rifle fire that swept through the Hessians' ranks.

Presenting a most encouraging sight before his troops, meanwhile, Washington hurried Stephen's Virginia brigade onward through the snow flurries behind his cousin's onrushing vanguard. Major George Johnston, the third highest ranking officer of Colonel Charles Scott's Fifth Virginian Continental Regiment in Stephen's vanguard brigade, marveled at Washington's inspiring, dynamic leadership, writing how, "Our noble countryman [from Mount Vernon] at the head of the Virginia brigades, exposed to the utmost danger, bid us [to] follow [and] We cheerfully did so in a long trot" toward the head of King Street at Trenton's northern edge.[73]

After having witnessed so many American soldiers panicking, fleeing, and surrendering throughout the New York Campaign, Washington was elated by this novel sight of elite Hessian soldiers fleeing for their lives down the Pennington Road. Perhaps as an old fox hunter of the Virginia Tidewater's forests, meadows, and murky swamps, he recalled that especially dark September day on Harlem Heights when he had felt the humiliating sting of the blaring notes of a contemptuous British bugler, who mocked the withdrawing Americans by playing a traditional fox hunting call.

That searing taunt had infuriated Washington and fueled a desire for revenge: the ultimate insult on the American character that he now planned to erase with the most unexpected of victories at Trenton. Exorcising an old demon and humiliating stereotype that had become accepted as fact on both sides of the Atlantic, Washington was relieved by the sight of his onrushing troops now thoroughly dispelling at least one persistent stereotype (Americans always run from Hessians) that had long stained the fighting qualities of Washington and his men.

Mounted on his splendid charger before his surging ranks of cheering Continentals, Washington also briefly admired the discipline of the Hessian pickets, who had been well trained by Altenbockum and Wiederhold. Even in this crisis situation, the Germans continued to follow their officer's orders and maintain discipline under Washington's onslaught. Although having been surprised this morning and now facing overwhelming numbers, the Hessian pickets continued to resist Captain Washington's advance down the Pennington Road with a fighting spirit that stirred a measure of respect among the attackers. At this time, the commander-in-chief felt an unexpected sense of admiration for these crack fighting men. As he later informed the Continental Congress with ample justification, these German pickets "behaved very well."[74]

To the hard-hit Hessian pickets, the situation became more precarious with each passing minute, with hundreds of Continentals charging out of a blinding snowstorm and screaming like Indians from the Ohio Valley. The fact that any Hessian soldiers now offered even the slightest resistance whatsoever was truly remarkable under these circumstances. Without orders or reinforcements while fighting a losing battle, these advanced Hessians gamely fought back. A perplexed Wiederhold grew frustrated because "no one came to see what was happening, or to reinforce and assist us. But [the pickets] did their duty" to the end.[75]

However, Lieutenant Wiederhold also felt fortunate to some degree. He knew that if "I had not stepped out of the picket hut and seen the enemy, they would possibly have been upon me before I could take up arms" and buy time for the Rall brigade to form for action.[76] But the relentless pressure and sheer weight applied by Captain Washington's and Stephen's Virginians was too much to bear. Captain Altenbockum and Lieutenant Wiederhold no longer had any choice. As written in his diary, Wiederhold described how it was now "necessary, in order not to be cut off from the garrison, to retreat toward the garrison as no one came . . . to reinforce and assist us, even though the Rall Regiment was the duty watch on this night."[77]

In the end, Lieutenant Wiederhold's and Altenbockum's pickets barely escaped Washington's surging tide lapping at their flanks, threatening encirclement and entrapment. One fallen Hessian officer was left behind near the road. Lieutenant Georg Christoph, or Christian, Kimm, age thirty-three, was that unfortunate Hessian officer. He had been cut down by Captain Washington, a good shot with a Long Rifle, within fifty yards of the Calhoun House to rise no more. The mortally wounded Kimm lay prostrate in the snow with his life ebbing away in a pool of red. Meanwhile, Captain Washington's elated Virginians surged past the fallen Hessian officer with victory cheers echoing through the cold, December air. Altenbockum and Wielderhold's retreating pickets had no time to report the disastrous tactical situation to Colonel Rall because the foremost onrushing Virginians under Captain Washington "entered the [northwestern edge of] town with them pell-mell," wrote Colonel Knox in a letter.[78]

By this time, many of Greene's Second Division troops already began to sense victory, especially with the intoxicating sight of Hessians fleeing before them. As if caught in a footrace beyond their control, both Americans and Germans now headed southeast for Trenton on the double. Captain Hull never forgot how "the first sound of the musquetry [sic] and the retreat of the guards animated the men and they pushed on with resolution and firmness" across the snowy ground. All the while, Washington led the way, waving his sword, shouting encouragement for his fast-moving boys, and imploring them to keep up the chase to apply an unrelenting pressure that equated to victory.[79]

During the relentless pursuit southeast down the Pennington Road, a mounted Captain Samuel Morris, leading the Philadelphia upper class dandies and mostly former members of the Gloucester Fox Hunting Club of his hard-riding light horse company, was deeply moved by the sad sight of the dying Lieutenant Kimm. The handsome Hessian officer, only recently promoted to an officer's rank, was sprawled out on the ground just beyond the Calhoun House. Here, he lay in a widening puddle of blood that stained the snow with a bright red. Swayed by the tragic sight, Morris suddenly departed the head of his mounted light horse company, cantering over to Lieutenant Kimm.

In the time-honored cavalier tradition of warriors who still cherished old-fashioned concepts of honor and chivalry that were almost medieval, the Philadelphia-born Morris dismounted to offer assistance. Meanwhile, the captain's troopers, such as Lieutenant James Budden, Cornet John Dunlap, and his own brother Ensign Anthony Morris, who would be shortly killed at Princeton, looked on in disbelief. The forty-two-year-old Morris then approached Kimm, who needed urgent medical assistance. With the Philadelphia cavalry company consisting of nearly one-half of Irish troopers, Morris's young Celtic-Gaelic horsemen, who had paid for their fancy uniforms, arms, and equipment out of their own monies, also felt some empathy toward the fallen German officer.

But the ever-practical General Greene, ignoring all of the lessons that he had been taught while growing up as a Quaker, would have none of it. With America's most important battle having only fairly begun, this was no time for such humanitarian and chivalric niceties. Therefore, Greene shouted in a harsh tone to the aristocratic, forty-two-year-old cavalry captain, "No time for that, get back on your horse!" Clearly, the often-demonstrated etiquette of war was not to be played out at Trenton, where so much was at stake. As Greene fully realized, Morris's valuable leadership was now needed because these young Philadelphia horsemen, including twenty members of the Gloucester Fox Hunting Club founded by Morris, were now engaged in their first engagement as a unit, even though they had been organized in 1774.

Hoping to erase the rebuke by daring action and more clearly aware that he was no longer playing a game as when leading young Philadelphians on fox hunts through Pennsylvania's farms and fields, Captain Morris then led his young troopers of the Philadelphia Light Horse in a thundering gallop down the icy Pennington Road. All the while, the company's beautiful yellow flag of fine silk flapped at the head of the little column of fox hunting cavaliers, who were in the process of learning about the ugly realities of war. While the elated Americans continued to rush by, the Hessian lieutenant, who received no medical attention, lay helpless in the snow. Fated to die this evening, Lieutenant Kimm was the first man on either side to suffer a mortal wound at the battle of Trenton.[80]

In the face of Washington's relentless onslaught that was the anthesis of the fiasco at Kip's Bay, the Hessian picket's withdrawal never degenerated into a wild flight down the road, however. With plenty of fight left and unwilling to concede anything to American rebels, these Hessian veterans continued to turn and face their attackers, "keeping up a constant retreating fire from behind houses" along the embattled Pennington Road. In what seemed like an eternity, the panting German pickets under Altenbockum and Wiederhold finally reached the head of King Street, where Rall had been advised by Donop's well-educated engineer to erect an artillery redoubt at this high point: sound advice that had been ignored. Especially at this time, these two enterprising officers now lamented Rall's failure to follow these sage recommendations.[81]

Under heavy pressure from the onrushing Virginians, Captain Altenbockum and his men turned to the right, or south, to gain King Street. With the ground sloping south through the town and all the way to the river, they then headed down the snowy slope, but only for a short distance, in the direction of their own regiment. These breathless von Lossbergers, with their energy expended but not their fighting spirit, smartly took cover in the town's northernmost houses, modest wooden structures, just north of where their von Lossberg Regiment comrades were located. Meanwhile, Lieutenant Wiederhold and his pickets continued to retire farther east across the high ground and past King Street's head. From this high ground perch, Wiederhold then yelled for his men to turn south and retire down Queen Street, which paralleled King Street. But exhausted from their long withdrawal and delaying action, they did not proceed all the way down Queen Street to rejoin their Knyphausen Regiment near the street's southern end.[82]

While Altenbockum and his men withdrew down King Street that descended the slope toward the heart of Trenton, Lieutenant Wiederhold, just to the east, was not finishing fighting, however. Knowing the importance of attempting to hold the dual heads of King and Queen Streets, vital high ground that yet must be contested because Colonel Rall needed to regain this perch and the most strategic crossroads in Trenton and in the hope of buying more time for the Rall brigade to organize, Wiederhold and his stubborn pickets "took a position in front of one of the first houses of the town and fired at the enemy who were forming in battle order on the upper side of town." He then ordered his picket detachment to make yet another defensive stand in the wooden houses that stood on lower ground just below the northern end of Queen Street.[83]

In his diary, the hard-fighting Knyhausen Regiment lieutenant described the setting for America's most important armed clash to date: "Trenton is a small place, lying on the left bank of the Delaware River [and] is divided into two parts, the upper and lower city, by [Assunpink] creek [and] the parts are joined together however, by a stone bridge. It has nearly 100 houses, which had been abandoned by most of the residents."[84] A vital gateway leading to Philadelphia just to the southwest, this little but prosperous commercial community was about to become the very vortex of the storm in the upcoming struggle that would determine America's fate and future destiny.

Unknown to the Rall brigade troops, something entirely new was about to descend upon Trenton with a vengeance. A new kind of warfare, largely home-grown, highly irregular, and borrowed in no small part from Indian warfare and the western frontier experience, was about to suddenly envelope a well-trained conventional soldiery, whose traditional concepts for waging war were fast-becoming outdated and obsolete in America.

Despite the Hessian's legendary ferocity in combat, lengthy winning streak, overall military superiority, and iron discipline, nothing in the past military experiences of these orthodox European fighting men adequately prepared them for what they least expected at this time: a steamrolling tide of a large number of angry rebels suddenly descending upon them from the surrounding wooded countryside and a raging storm at a time when they believed that the war was all but over. Nothing could have possibly have readied Rall's troops for what was about to happen to one of the best combat brigades, on either side, in America.

So far, Washington's battleplan was working to perfection in regard to the First and Second Division's simultaneous advance, ensuring that the Trenton garrison was caught by surprise by a mere motley collection of "country clowns," in Colonel Rall's words. Rall's professional arrogance was understandable because this highly respected commander from Hesse-Cassel had served with distinction in the War of the Austrian Succession, the Seven Years War, and with the Russian Army with General Alexis Orloff and for Catherine the Great during the fourth Russo-Turkish War in 1771 to1772, reaping success everywhere he had fought. But never in all of his vast military experience had Rall ever been the victim of a greater surprise than at Trenton.

Absolutely nothing in Rall's more than thirty years of military experience had prepared this hardened career officer for Washington's unexpected asymmetrical challenge. In battling against the Islamic-inspired imperialism of the Ottoman Turks as a younger man, Rall had faithfully continued a German holy warrior tradition, extending back to the Crusades, of waging war against Islam's relentless, dogged advance to spread the Koran by the sword. But now Rall was about to confront a sudden surprise attack from fellow Christians, who were imbued with the republican faith and belief that God was on their side, which combined to make them almost as fanatical this early Thursday morning as those Islamic holy warriors inspired by the Koran's words to destroy the hated infidel.[85]

As so carefully planned by Washington and relying on what became Napoleon's primary means of reaping victory across Europe, the amount of shock delivered by a surprise blitzkrieg attack upon the Trenton garrison was considerable. In a letter to his wife Sarah, Lieutenant Joseph Hodgkins, a thirty-two-year old cobbler from the coastal fishing village of Ipswich in northeast Massachusetts, wrote how Washington's sudden attack seemingly out of nowhere "gave the Enemy a grate [sic] shock."[86] This thorough shock delivered by Washington when least expected had not resulted primarily from a rude awakening from drunkenness or late night Yuletide revelry, but from the shattering of conventional wisdom to reveal the fallacy of the universal Hessian certitude (shared by the British), as recently expressed by Ireland-born and Oxford-educated Lord Francis Rawdon, who hailed from a ruling Anglo-Irish noble family, "that their army [Washington's] is all broken to pieces."[87]

Unknown to the Hessians at this time, something subtle, but very significant, had changed since Washington's string of humiliating setbacks and defeats. An unseen, stealthy transformation had taken place among the American soldiery in the cold darkness during the Delaware crossing and the arduous march on Trenton. Now emboldened as never before, Washington's battle-hardened soldiers of the two assault columns were now exceptionally "in fine spirits." And, most of all, these "Continental troops are really well disciplined" by the time of their greatest challenge to date. Therefore, they "will fight bravely," accurately predicted one visionary Connecticut soldier, whose bold prophecy was now coming true at long last to the Hessians' utter disbelief and shock.[88]

In Washington's words that described the sweetest sound that he had ever heard, "The upper Division [Second] arrived at the Enemys advance Post, exactly at Eight O'clock, and in three Minutes after, I found, from the fire on the lower Road, that that [First] Division had also got up."[89] Washington's masterstroke of a double envelopment was becoming an amazing tactical reality as he had previously envisioned with clarity at his headquarters west of the Delaware. Therefore, Washington's spirits soared to new, if not dizzying, heights, when he finally realized that his bold tactical plan of a "brilliant encircling movement" had succeeded when Sullivan's First Division to the southwest suddenly struck.

Fulfilling his fondest expectations, Washington now knew that he had won his audacious tactical gamble of launching a pincer movement with two divisions even amid a fierce northeaster by what he happily heard suddenly erupting to the southwest. Only three minutes after Stephen's Virginians attacked the picket outpost at the Howell's cooper house along the Pennington Road at 8:00 a.m. and although this eagerly awaited sound near the river was a bit muffled by the howling wind and veil of falling snow, Washington, mounted on the high ground north of Trenton, felt a surging, intoxicating sense of elation when he first heard firing from the direction of the River Road about a quarter mile to the southwest at 8:03 a.m.

Sounding to Washington like the harbinger of the sweetest of successes and bestowing immeasurable relief to the anxious commander-in-chief long consumed with worry, this most joyous sound yet heard by Washington was a single cannon shot fired from thirty-one-year-old Colonel Paul Dudley Sargent's mostly New England brigade, which surged down the River Road at the head of Sullivan's column just behind Flahaven's onrushing New Jersey vanguard.

Booming over the wintery landscape like a distant thunder storm on a hot August afternoon, the First Division's first shot echoing to the southwest was unleashed from a three-pounder from Captain Daniel Neil's New Jersey artillery company. Most importantly, these Garden State gunners symbolically initiated the struggle for the liberation of a subjugated New Jersey town on Washington's right wing. The New Jersey cannon of the Eastern Company of New Jersey State Artillery might have been fired from the young, handsome captain himself or one of his top lieutenants, either John Coughty, of Irish heritage, or Thomas Vandyke, of Dutch ancestry.

At this most exhilarating of moments for the often-vanquished Washington, Sullivan's fast-moving column of First Division troops continued to be led by Captain Flahaven's New Jersey Continentals while Colonel John Stark's hard-hitting New Hampshire regiment of rawboned New England veterans, Sargent's brigade, followed close behind. Because of level terrain and adrenaline pulsated through their systems, Sullivan's troops advanced at a good pace southeast along the River Road. Now unleashed, Sullivan's men headed toward the town's southwestern end. Most importantly, the vanguard of Sullivan's First Division column rushed toward Trenton's lower end at the exact time as planned by Washington, revealing a remarkably close coordination of multiple attack columns, especially under such adverse conditions that made footing treacherous. As indicated by the rattle of musketry from both divisions, Washington's strike force were now attacking simultaneously, and exactly as originally envisioned by the commander-in-chief with a farsighted tactical clarity back in eastern Pennsylvania.

In a timeliness that was almost miraculous under the circumstances, both assault columns of Washington's right and left wings (the First and Second Divisions, respectively) of his well-designed pincer movement struck hard at almost exactly the same time. The gods of war, perhaps even Mars himself of the Roman people, now seemed to be on the American's side this morning, smiling benignly on Washington and his ragamuffin revolutionaries, if only because they had persevered for so long against all manner of adversity. Clearly, even more than the precarious Delaware crossing, this was now Washington's finest hour, and an unprecedented measure of personal and professional redemption.

Waking up to a snowy nightmare in which he suddenly saw far more attacking Americans than ever imagined, the most advanced Hessian picket on the River Road and the farthest south of Captain Altenbockum's string of pickets fired a belated return shot at the swarm of howling soldiers of Sullivan's vanguard charging toward him. Frightened out of his wits, this lone Hessian picket then fled down the road and toward the picket headquarters. Here, duplicating the success of Captain Washington's Virginia vanguard in sweeping aside Wielderhold and Altenbockum's advanced pickets to the northeast, Captain Flahaven's band of First New Jersey Continental Regiment soldiers, who were especially eager to liberate this occupied New Jersey town and its downtrodden patriotic citizens, poured down the River Road with loud cheers.

Most likely now carrying antiquated Wilson-contract flintlocks marked "New Jersey" from the days of the French and Indian War, the hard-charging New Jersey Continentals surged through the snow flurries toward the main Hessian picket post at Philemon Dickinson's home located about a half mile beyond Trenton's southwestern outskirts, the Hermitage. Now leading the local New Jersey militia on the river's west side, Colonel Dickinson was fortunate that this fine mansion had not been already burned down in retaliation for his guerrilla activities: an unexpected benefit of winter's arrival since the Hessian occupiers had needed warm quarters, sparing the stately mansion.

Overlooking the Delaware's turbid waters now filled with bobbing chunks of ice, this sprawling country estate of the wealthy Dickinson, who had purchased this property on July 30, 1776, was situated on the low ground of the river's floodplain. The Hermitage was the home of this hard-fighting New Jersey militia general, delegate to the New Jersey provincial congress, and former Hunterdon County militia colonel, who had been raised as a Quaker. Most recently, Dickinson led the New Jersey militia brigade, consisting mostly of Hunterdon County men but also Burlington County soldiers, in unleashing guerrilla strikes that one modern historian has appropriately called "Dickinson's Hunterdon uprising," which helped to weaken the Trenton garrison.

In yet another example of the tragedy of America's first civil war, Philemon's brother, John Dickinson, had refused to sign the Declaration of Independence as a conservative Pennsylvania delegate, which in part reflected his Quaker upbringing. Nevertheless, placing himself on the right side of history, John later led a militia brigade with a brigadier's commission against his homeland's invaders. As demonstrated repeatedly in those dark days before Christmas 1776, in waging his own personal guerrilla war much like General Stephen without Washington's knowledge, Dickinson had enjoyed nothing more than harassing the stationary Trenton garrison this December. He had earlier driven Colonel Rall and his men, who viewed these guerrilla fighters as contemptible "peasant canaille," to distraction, helping to wear down the Trenton garrison and make them more vulnerable to Washington's surprise attack.

With prior knowledge of exactly where the foremost Hessian pickets were quartered, Captain Flahaven's first focus was directed at overwhelming the first Hessian picket position near the River Road, located just southwest of the River Road, and roughly parallel to Lieutenant Wiederhold's Pennington Road picket outpost to the northeast. By this time, the Hessian picket headquarters on the snowbound River Road was more vulnerable than usual. The routine morning patrol of three jaegers, or light troops, had only proceeded as far north up the river as the John Mott (now at the head of Sullivan's column) house, or "the rebel captain's house" as it was known to the Germans, before retiring back to the Dickinson House with the report that all was well this morning, thanks to the storm's intensity and the pervasive lax Yuletide mood.

Like their stubborn picket comrades who fought gamely along the Pennington Road, Lieutenant Friedrich von Grothausen likewise attempted to make a defensive stand to buy precious time for the Rall brigade in town to rally. The veteran lieutenant rushed out of the Hermitage headquarters when the first crackle of gunfire erupted to the northeast on the Pennington Road at 8:00 a.m. Alerted jaegers then poured forth from their quarters at the Dickinson House, the dreary log cabin slave quarters that were certainly not unnoticed by the black soldiers in Sullivan's ranks and two wooden barns that had provided shelter from the storm.

Grothausen posted some of his well-trained men in good defensive positions, taking necessary precautions. Shouting orders while the crackle of musketry echoed in the Pennington Road sector, Lieutenant Grothausen then led a detachment of his jaegers northeast on the double with the intention of reinforcing Altenbockum's pickets on the Pennington Road. Having no idea that Washington's force had crossed the Delaware and assuming that only another Captain Wallis-like raid was now in progress, he acted aggressively toward the sudden threat, pushing north of the River Road. But Groththausen soon spied the lengthy lines of Sullivan's Continentals pouring across the snowy landscape as far as the eye could see.

Likewise, Ewing's Pennsylvania artillery unleashed ten shots from the river's other side upon the Hessian picket position at his own residence, causing more havoc in the lower town. Groththausen, therefore, wisely turned his picket detachment around, and the Hessians hurriedly backtracked through the snow. The fast-thinking lieutenant then formed his lithe, green-uniformed jaegers, the best marksmen of the Rall brigade, into a thin defensive line astride the River Road. Like Wiederhold and Altenbockum along the Pennington Road, Grothausen continued to perform admirably under pressure, especially in responding quickly to fast-paced tactical developments on the River Road.

But for Grothausen and his elite jaegers, it was already too late to defend the River Road, the main artery leading into Trenton's southwest edge and the Rall brigade's left-rear. This band of Hessians now faced Flahaven's New Jersey Continentals, whose fighting blood was up. And Colonel Stark and his

New Hampshire troops surged immediately behind the New Jersey soldiers in steamrolling down the River Road in the hard-fighting frontier tradition of the rough-and-tumble Green Mountain Boys. With more of Washington's First Division soldiers pouring through the flat river bottoms below the River Road, Grothausen's isolated picket position was first outflanked on its vulnerable left by Sullivan's lengthy line of onrushing New Englanders that extended west and almost to the swollen river. Astounded, if not a bit unnerved, by the incredible sight, Corporal Franz Bauer saw that "the rebels were coming in strong force [and] with bayonets fixed" and increasing momentum.

With a shout and a flurry of well-aimed shots, Flahaven's New Jersey boys descended upon Grothausen's green-coated jaegers at the main picket post headquarters on the snow-covered River Road. Grothausen, facing far too many onrushing Continentals before him to count and knowing that he was about to be outflanked, ordered his outgunned band of pickets to retreat off the two hundred-acre Dickinson property and southeast down the River Road toward Trenton before it was too late. Clearly, Sullivan's confident First Division attackers moved onward in an unstoppable tide, surging with confidence through the falling snow "towards the town firing."

Described as a "gallant" officer, Captain Flahaven now made the most of the tactical opportunity, exploiting his initial gains to the fullest. Shouting encouragement and waving his sword, Flahaven led his band of around forty New Jersey soldiers, who were engaged in their first battle, across the fertile lands of the Dickinson estate and down the icy River Road on the double. Viewing firsthand how this once-prosperous estate had been plundered by both the British and Hessians only reminded these New Jersey soldiers of the sad fate of their own homes and families in occupied territory. Such disturbing knowledge fueled the determination of Flahaven's swift-moving attackers to continue to apply pressure on the Hessians, who fled from these Schnellentruppen, or fast troops. After having been forced out of their cozy river manor with its exquisite English gardens and greenhouses and stylish outbuildings now covered in snow, Lieutenant Grothhausen and his green-uniformed pickets fled southeast down the River Road under a hail of bullets. Never before defeated until this bitterly cold Thursday morning, the jaegers headed toward Trenton on the double, with the howling New Jersey Continentals close behind.

Hundreds of First Division troops, loading and firing on the run, continued to push toward Trenton at a brisk pace behind Flahaven's troops: first Stark's New Hampshire regiment of veterans and then Sargent's New York,

Massachusetts, and Connecticut brigade, which was followed by two full brigades—Glover and St. Clair, respectively—of mostly New Englanders, advanced behind the New Hampshire boys. The bundled-up soldiers of Sullivan's surging ranks swept onward on both sides of the River Road, pouring closer to their long-coveted objective of Trenton with cheers that pierced the frigid air.

Amid the white landscape tinged with an occasional scattered patch of brown stands of skeleton-like timber devoid of leaves, additional iron and bronze artillery pieces of Sullivan's First Division were deployed on open ground near the road. Quickly loaded and primed by expert cannoneers, these guns of Knox's Regiment then opened fire to additionally shatter Grothausen's futile hope for making another defensive stand to buy time for the Rall brigade to rally.

Most importantly by this time, the reassuring echo of the First Division's cannon booming southwest of Trenton told Washington that all was going well in Sullivan's attack, which served as the southern arm and right wing of his pincer movement. Basking in the glow of realizing that his most audacious battle plan of the war had worked to perfection so far, the elated commander-in-chief now sensed the kill with his onrushing troops of both columns were making good progress in surging closer to Trenton.

After the most advanced Hessians were hurled aside like chaff before the wind, the way was now wide open for Sullivan's assault to continue unabated down the River Road and into Trenton's southwestern end. As Washington had originally envisioned, his two separate columns were striking hard in unison from multiple directions in a near perfect double envelopment: the dual advance of Sullivan's First Division, sweeping toward the town's southwest edge, and Greene's Second Division, descending upon Trenton from the northwest. Most significantly, these dual steamrolling advances were not only pushing aside all initial resistance, but also simultaneously gaining more ground and momentum that went entirely unchecked.

Against all the odds and expectations of even the most optimistic soldiers, Washington's two widely separated divisions managed to strike simultaneously. Near the head of the Second Division, Colonel Fitzgerald, one of the most respected members of Washington's staff and a native of County Wicklow, Ireland, never forgot the dramatic moment, which lifted the spirits of Washington's attackers all along the line: "The next moment we heard [Hessian] drums beat and a bugle sound [to the south to arouse the Trenton garrison], and then from the west came the boom of a cannon [a three-pounder of Captain

Neil's Eastern Company, New Jersey State Artillery and] General Washington's face lighted up instantly, for he knew that it was one of Sullivan's guns."[90]

As revealed in a most informative letter, Colonel Knox also described the dramatic moment when American spirits and fortunes skyrocketed to an unprecedented height not believed possible only a short time before, with the knowledge that Washington's onrushing troops, despite the endless exertions and deprivations and a miserable, sleepless night that was the longest of their lives, successfully "arrived by two routes at the same time, about half an hour after daylight, within one mile of the town."[91]

Indeed, the sharp, crackling gunfire echoing over the snow-covered landscape from two different directions signaled the "remarkable" realization of Washington's complex battleplan that had seemed totally unworkable only a short time before. With his Connecticut comrades of Glover's mostly Massachusetts brigade advancing behind the foremost brigade under Sargent, Lieutenant Elisha Bostwick, Nineteenth Connecticut Continental Regiment, recalled the fulfillment of Washington's closely coordinated offensive tactics of a "brilliant encircling movement" that were so rarely achieved in unison by even the most experienced commanders, especially during the rigors of wintertime, when two separated columns struck simultaneously in a successful pincer movement: "it was not long before we heard the out Centries [sic] of the Enemy both on the road we were in and the Eastern road & their out gards [sic] retreated fireing [sic]" in return.[92]

Like an electric current, consequently, a greater sense of confidence surged through Washington's ranks in both sectors with the almost unbelievable realization, energizing everyone to continue charging to keep up unrelenting pressure on the fleeing opponent. Major James Wilkinson, the young Marylander of so much promise, never forget how Greene's "attack . . . on the left [now] was immediately answered by Colonel Stark in our front, who forced the enemy's picket" from the Hermitage and the surrounding area along the snowy River Road.[93]

In describing this much-anticipated moment just after 8:00 a.m. (around forty minutes after daybreak) and the timely, close synchronization of twin widely separated movements of two divisions upon which decisive success hinged this morning, Major George Johnston, leading the Fifth Virginia Continental Regiment, Stephen's vanguard brigade, perhaps said it best when he wrote how "Here our two Major Gen'ls, Green . . . and Sullivan, exhibited the greatest proof of generalship by getting to their respective posts within five minutes of each other, tho' they had parted 4 miles from Town, and took different Routes."[94]

Indeed, with his two wings striking simultaneously, Washington had now achieved the most elusive and difficult of all tactical accomplishments by any commander in the complex art of war: the double envelopment. Washington's intricate and masterful battle plan was based upon the time-proven concept of divide and conquer, with his two assault columns simultaneously striking opposite ends of town to ensure that the Rall brigade's three regiments could not unite as one on this day. What Washington had now duplicated was in fact a classic double envelopment reminiscent of Hannibal's tactical masterpiece at Cannae in 216 BC during the Second Punic War, when he and his Carthaginians, who were North Africans, annihilated a powerful, overconfident Roman Army and its allies.

Washington's dual simultaneous assaults of two separate wings in a brilliantly conceived pincer movement were working to perfection and as successfully as Washington had originally envisioned. That seemingly almost impossible dream—the most difficult and elusive tactical achievement on the battlefield—of catching a formidable opponent by surprise with a simultaneous, well-coordinated, and perfectly timed strike with multiple assault columns now became an almost unbelievable tactical reality for Washington. Perhaps in the end, only these militarily uneducated members, especially Washington, of a ragamuffin revolutionary army would have even considered for a moment the utter impracticality of even attempting such a seemingly impossible nighttime crossing of a swollen river and striking simultaneously with multiple assault columns, especially on such a stormy night, after a lengthy nighttime march of two separate wings across unfamiliar terrain. Indeed, these rustic amateurs in rebellion had known so little about warfare's conventional rules that they simply had not known enough to realize that such an utter impractical and overly ambitious offensive effort should never have been launched in the first place.

Fortunately, for America, neither Washington nor his top lieutenants had been professional soldiers or schooled in the art of the traditional axioms of war and European ways of waging conventional warfare. And, ironically, perhaps no one in this ragtag American army was more surprised by this remarkable tactical achievement of a double envelopment, so rarely obtained in wartime, especially after so much had gone wrong the previous night and then morning than Washington.[95]

Major Wilkinson, who possessed solid experience as an esteemed member of Generals Greene, Benedict Arnold, Gates staffs, and most recently St. Clair's staffs, recorded the initial success of Sullivan's southern arm of Washington's pincer movement: "in our front, [when Flahaven] forced the enemy's picket and pressed it [toward] the town, our columns being close on [their] heels" of the Captain Grothausen's fleeing jaegers, who now sought only to escape the sudden onslaught.[96]

However, the capable Colonel Rall had yet to make his first tactical move in attempting to checkmate Washington's masterful tactical design. Colonel Fitzgerald, the enterprising Irish Catholic who had migrated from just south of Dublin in 1769, marveled at the sight presented to the entrepreneurial Alexandrian, General Washington, and Captain Washington's vanguard from the commanding heights overlooking Trenton from the north when he viewed the Rall and the von Lossberg Regiments in the process of attempting to organize on the lower ground of King Street to the south: "We could see a great commotion down toward the meeting-house [St. Michael's Episcopal Church, which was Trenton's first Anglican Church of England and known simply as the English Church], men running here and there, officers swinging their swords . . . .."[97]

Stunned by the surprise attack that had burst so suddenly out of the blinding snowstorm and wintry New Jersey forests, the Germans gamely attempted to rally at their predesignated regimental points of assembly. Already uniformed grenadiers of Rall Regiment, the best-prepared unit—the "regiment du jour," or the "regiment of the day"—continued to pour out of the dark rows of private houses. Indeed, making one of his most forward-thinking leadership decisions, Colonel Rall had his own grenadier regiment—each separate regiment took rotating shifts for this assignment—on full alert in their King Street "alarm houses," sleeping under arms with cartridge-boxes on and in full uniform, just in case the Americans pulled off the miracle of a surprise. Long minimized by historians, Rall's wisdom, insight, and prudence meant that leather cartridge-boxes and other equipment remained strapped to sleeping soldiers to save precious time in assembling, which now paid dividends in meeting Washington's sudden threat.[98]

Despite the blinding storm, meanwhile, the two-pronged attack of Washington's two divisions continued to gain more momentum with each passing minute. For the first time in this war of seemingly endless tragedies, frustrations, and disappointments, Washington's tactical plan was working to perfection and ever so smoothly. Most significant, the resolute commander from Mount Vernon was now in the process of doing what almost everyone believed was impossible for him—or anyone else for that matter—to accomplish in such a crisis situation: catching a full Hessian brigade by surprise and finally breaking a disastrous, seemingly endless chain of personal tactical failures and fiascos that went all the way back to the French and Indian War, when he had doomed his own Virginia regiment by foolishly attempting to defend a "death-trap" at Fort Necessity in western Pennsylvania.[99]

As never before seen in this war, Washington was now maintaining the initiative, advantage, and the momentum in a new kind of waging war, based on stealth, rapid movement, and hard-hitting offensive capabilities for him. After unleashing what was a brilliant pincer movement to confound his opponent, he now sought to exploit the element of surprise to the fullest. Because Washington realized that Rall's troops never had been caught by a surprise attack in wintertime and in an urban environment, he hoped that these legendary professional soldiers, who had never lost a battle, would be so confused that they would not have sufficient time to form in neat lines to either resist his attack from two directions simultaneously or to launch their own counterattack with the bayonet.[100]

A Natural Bowl and Trap

From the snow-covered head of King Street where the bone-numbing winter gales swept off the heights, Washington viewed the swirling chaos of Trenton that lay before him on lower ground to the south. Feeling an intoxicating sense of exhilaration in having caught the Hessians by surprise to fulfill the coveted requirements of the most elusive and coveted tactical movement in the art of war, Washington almost certainly now felt less of the biting cold. Instead, he was warmed by the soothing glow of having achieved a most impressive initial tactical success by catching the Rall brigade by surprise with a masterful double envelopment maneuver.

At the top of his lungs, an ecstatic Washington shouted to his onrushing troops who had never acted with more confidence, Captain Washington and Stephen's Virginians, respectively, who led the way, for all to hear: "There, my brave fellows, are the enemies of your country. Remember now what you are about to fight for!" Washington's soldiers in the forefront of Greene's fast-moving column felt reinvigorated by the inspiring sight and the words of their animated commander, who had finally placed his troops in excellent positions with a decided tactical advantage while bestowing them with the opportunity to reap a remarkable tactical success.[101]

Clearly, as planned, Washington now possessed a host of distinct and unprecedented tactical advantages, which had absolutely nothing to do with alleged drunken state of the Rall garrison and now could be exploited to the fullest. Once again as in escaping Cornwallis's grasp earlier in December by crossing the Delaware that provided a timely natural barrier, so favorable geography once again now bestowed Washington with key advantages: Trenton and the entire Hessian brigade were situated not only on open ground but also on lower terrain, which was dominated by Washington's newly secured advanced position on the heights overlooking the town on the north. Only around fifty feet above sea level at the town's southern end in the Delaware's bottoms, Trenton, which was the northernmost city in the broad Delaware Valley, was dominated by the high ground, now teeming with invigorated Americans, on the north.

Washington easily gained his most important tactical advantage by taking full possession of the heights above Trenton after the stubborn Hessian pickets had been pushed aside. All in all, the Hessian brigade could not have been assigned to a more ill-suited place—first known as "Trent-towne" by William Trent—in all Hopewell Township, New Jersey, to defend. An important communications hub on the King's Highway, or the Old Post Road, that stretched from New York City to Philadelphia and where four roads intersected, Trenton was a strategic crossroads in the fertile Piedmont.

Situated between the pine barrens of southern New Jersey and northern New Jersey's Highlands and west of the state's central plains, this attractive (at least before the war) commercial town had long been a key trading center and relatively prosperous for its small size because of its key location at the head of navigation for merchant ships plying the Delaware. Thanks in part to geography and the town's size, and fortunately for Washington, Rall's garrison of around 1,500 troops was much too small to defend all of Trenton and its sprawling environs.

Washington's reliance upon the well-honed abilities of experienced officers, who could make their own tactical decisions in the confusion and heat of battle, continued to pay off. Like Captain Washington's accomplishment in in clearing Hessians off the strategic Pennington Road, Flahaven also continued to push some very good opposing troops, the jaegers, down the River Road while leading the attack of Sullivan's First Division down the River Road. Also known as chausseurs, or light troops, these tough jaegers were primarily the sons of foresters and gamekeepers of vast royal estates owned by wealthy German aristocrats. Unlike the Pennsylvania and Maryland riflemen who placed their faith in the Long Rifle and dry black powder, the German jaegers carried well-balanced, beautifully crafted short rifles known for their deadly accuracy, which were far superior to the large caliber Brown Bess smoothbore muskets carried by British soldiers.

In serving as highly mobile light infantry, the jaegers had early struck fear into American soldiers because of their deadly sharpshooting skills, which had been well honed from former occupations as foresters and hunters in the moun-tainous region of the evergreen-dominated Black Forest of Bavaria in south-west Germany. Therefore, they had rightly earned the respectful reputation among Washington's men as the deadly "foresters from Hell." But at Trenton the German jaegers (hunters) now found themselves caught amid what was becoming a fast-paced urban battle: the ultimate conundrum and nightmare scenario for these men, who fought best in thick woodlands. The jaeger's dark green uniform coats blended well with America's forests, but these elite German soldiers were now exposed in the open on a white landscape, ideal targets for Washington's marksmen.

Worst of all for Colonel Rall's troops, who were trained to face a con-ventional opponent in open, level fields that resembled the finely trimmed parade grounds back in faraway Hanover or Heidelberg, were now situated in a snow-covered urban environment in a bowl-like depression, especially at the low-lying foot of King and Queen Streets near the river, surrounded by high ground on the town's outskirts, especially on the north. In addition, Trenton was generally an open town and not overly congested, which was to the attacker's advantage, thanks also to the two parallel avenues that passed through the town.

Also to Rall's tactical detriment in mounting a sturdy defense, Trenton was nestled in a blind corner confined by two deep watercourses, the Delaware River and Assunpink Creek, a tributary now swollen by winter rains and runoff. The Assunpink's brownish waters flowed southwest into the Delaware at Trenton's southern end. Once Washington's troops secured all of the high ground north of town, then the Rall brigade would have to make the best of it in attempting to fight back from lower ground and with the Assunpink to its back. Quite simply, the Rall brigade had no man-made or natural defenses from which to make a defensive stand.[102] As if to signify that the commander-in-chief's luck had finally come full circle, Rall's disadvantageous tactical, psychological, and geographical situation was eerily almost identical to Washington's disastrous decision to defend low-lying Fort Necessity, the French and Indian War fiasco. Washington must have basked in the fact that he now controlled the strategic high ground, placing him for once on the right side of the ever-elusive tactical formula for success.[103]

Equally significant in bestowing yet another distinct advantage to Washington this early morning was the fact that not only the Hessian garrison but also its six bronze cannon were not in advantageous positions to defend the town's outskirts, especially on the north. Instead, the brigade's cannon were located in the town's center and a good distance (nearly a quarter mile directly south) from the heights north of town.

The Rall Regiment's bronze guns were now positioned in front of the King Street guardhouse near Rall's headquarters near the town's center, while the von Lossberg Regiment and Knyphausen Regiment's cannon were situated just southeast in the Anglican Church's rear. And by the time that Washington gained the heights above town, the Rall Regiment's two guns—now under Lieutenant Friedrich Fischer who was second-in-command—were not ready for action, thanks to Dechow's cancellation of the usual 4:00 a.m. morning patrol. The fact that two guns were assigned to each Hessian regiment instead of a single artillery corps went against the wise tactical philosophy of the importance of artillery concentration—Napoleon always placed supreme importance on massing artillery—at all times to reduce "long-arm" capabilities, especially the possibility of a solid defense of Trenton.

Because the available housing in Trenton was inadequate to house an entire brigade, Rall's infantry were widely scattered throughout the town on the night of December 25. Except for the old French and Indian War-period barracks, which was located at the town's southwest edge between Front Street, an east-west running street that was closest to the river, and the parallel Second Street a block north, the Trenton garrison was not concentrated in military-like sleeping quarters. Instead, the Rall brigade's soldiers were housed primarily in private homes, mostly deserted, from Trenton's northern end, where the von Lossbergers were quartered on King Street, to the southern end of town, especially around the lower end, or foot, of Queen Street, where the Knyphausen Regiment was quartered east of King Street.

In addition, the Knyphausen troops were also assigned in houses on the south side of Assunpink Creek. Ensuring a lengthier assembly time to meet the surprise attack, the Knyphausen Regiment soldiers were divided by the swollen creek when Sullivan's First Division struck with a vengeance. Occupying small, modest houses on both sides of King Street in the town's center and lower end, therefore, the Rall Regiment of grenadiers were sandwiched between its two sister regiments.

When Washington attacked in the pale winter light of early morning and much to his advantage, the garrison's sleeping quarters were widely scattered in the majority of the hundred private homes, mostly small, wood-frame structures, located throughout the town. Befitting their higher status and upper class antecedents, Hessian officers had taken up residence in the best houses, especially large brick structures, and separate from the enlisted men: another liability for rapidly organizing an adequate defense of the vital river town by an entire brigade. Sheer exhaustion also played a role in reducing the Rall brigade's response time and overall defensive capabilities due to so many recent sleepless nights from answering alarms and mounting patrols that resulted in soldiers not having taken their cartridge-boxes "off for eight days," wrote Rall on December 20. For a variety of reasons, consequently, Rall's scattered brigade would neither unite nor fight as one this morning to confront Washington's attackers of either division.[104]

Additionally, Lieutenant Jakob Piel, an experienced von Lossberg officer and Rall's capable adjutant who detested the "so called Jankees" and was aware that the enlistments of so many Continental soldiers expired on January 1, 1777, revealed one of Washington's most invaluable psychological advantages that ensured maximum shock on this morning, "In truth I must confess we have universally thought too little of the rebels . . . ."[105] General Grant, therefore, had refused to send Rall his repeatedly requested reinforcements—including to guard Washington's crossing point at Johnson's Ferry— and even three separate appeals in one day, December 20, and as revealed in his missive to General Alexander Leslie, who commanded British troops at the pretty college town of Princeton, just northeast of Trenton and on the King's Road to New York City: "I do not believe [Washington] will attempt it."[106]

Equally important, Washington was fortunate in other ways this Thursday morning, which so much was at stake. Dechow's cancellation of the early morning patrol, with Lieutenant Fischer's two cannon of the Rall Regiment, to the "Doctor House"—situated along the river just north of the South

Trenton Ferry immediately below Trenton and where Ewing's Pennsylvania Militia brigade was to have crossed to gain the New Jersey side of the Delaware—to watch this key ferry located just below the turbid Assunpink, was a godsend, because this usual morning patrol of grenadiers and artillerymen, both of the Rall Regiment, would have early detected Ewing's attempt to cross the river.

Consequently, the Rall brigade's six bronze three-pounders, with two field pieces assigned to each of the three regiments, were now located far inside the town's depths. They should have been positioned on the town's outskirts, especially on the north, along the high ground perimeter. Instead Rall's half dozen cannon were disadvantageously situated in a relatively low-lying area in contrast to the heights north of town. This ill-advised placement made the brigade's artillery incapable of "immediate use in the event of an attack [with] them parked, first, in the graveyard back of the English [Anglican] church." Near the town's center, the Rall brigade's half dozen cannon were now in relatively useless positions by the time that Washington struck and possessed the luxury of deploying his troops at will.[107]

Most of all, the Rall brigade was not only completely surprised but also in overall poor shape when Washington unleashed his pent-up fury from two directions. Not only were the German troops more vulnerable because they were worn out—physically and mentally—from constant patrols, alarms, and extra duties, but also because they were not prepared for winter combat. Without warm winter uniforms, especially the traditional woolen greatcoats long worn by European soldiers, the Hessians now possessed only thin summer uniforms. Expressing bitterness in his diary about his brigade's thorough unpreparedness for winter combat and hence Washington's early morning onslaught, a frustrated Lieutenant Wiederhold complained: "Our army's exhausted and destitute of small clothes [and] whether the soldiers were wearing pants, shoes, shirt, etc."[108]

Immensely benefitting Washington's plan, Wiederhold also explained the Rall brigade's central dilemma of the boy who cried wolf syndrome: "Where the enemy always caused us false alarms, [we] sent more than enough troops, and where the actual attacks were to be expected and actually did occur, [we] gave little consideration."[109] Given a host of such key advantages, Washington had placed himself in the best position to succeed. He had gained a host of key advantages from a masterful, imaginative, and flexible tactical plan of a daring double envelopment, especially when combined with effective diversions, an effective intelligence network, and just good fortune.

Washington's most important diversion was in having ordered fellow Virginian Samuel Griffin to capture Mount Holly to ensure that Donop and his Hessian reinforcements remained too far from Trenton to assist Rall when under attack. Most of all, Rall had been victimized by Washington's brilliant surprise attack from two directions because of the lack of support, organizational and command structure limitations, failures at regimental, brigade and headquarters levels, an overabundance of contradictory and confusing intelligence, and the firm conviction that the optimal time for the ragtag Americans, if they dared to stir which seemed most unlikely, to unleash a possible surprise attack had already passed.[110]

Chapter IV

Washington Pouncing Like
"An Eagle Upon a Hen"

On this sleety New Jersey morning, meanwhile, Washington's onrushing troops of Greene's Second Division continued to converge on Trenton en masse from the northwest. A mounted Washington shouted encouragement and orders, infusing even more confidence among the Continentals surging forward with fixed bayonets. All morning, he had been effectively "Encourageing [sic] the Soldiers" of all ranks, and exactly when his half-frozen men had most needed inspiration. For the upcoming battle in blizzard-like conditions and low visibility in a restricted urban area that was guaranteed to be confusing, Washington emphasized that his "Soldiers keep by your officers."[1]

Twenty-six-year-old Colonel Clement Biddle hailed from a leading Quaker family. The Biddle family had migrated to the Pennsylvania Colony in 1681, during the first wave of migration of this pious Puritan sect that embraced "covenant theology" and broke away from the Anglican, or Church of England, because they considered it too restrictive and Catholic-like. Now serving as the army's deputy quartermaster-general, he had early formed a volunteer company that he proudly named the Quaker Blues. Biddle was the privileged son of a wealthy Philadelphia importer and shipper who also owned the imposing three-story Indian King Tavern and Inn in Philadelphia. Biddle and his gracious wife were known for their "gracious hospitality" in operating the popular tavern.

However, Biddle was fated to lose his beloved tavern when the British captured Philadelphia in1777 and promptly renamed the establishment the British Tavern. Amid the cascading snow flakes, this devoted staff officer now rode beside Scottish General St. Clair, who led his New Hampshire and Massachusetts brigade, in Sullivan's column now advancing rapidly south along the River Road and toward southwest Trenton.

The debonair Major Wilkinson married Biddle's very attractive sister, Ann, who was known by friends and family as Nancy, in Philadelphia in 1778. Watching in amazement while Washington's soldiers surged onward, he long remembered how he "never could conceive that one spirit should so universally animate both officers and men to rush forward into action" as on this cold morning when the stakes could not have been higher.[2]

Like Washington, the contemplative Greene was now enjoying his finest day, leading his Second Division with skill into the fray and encouraging his men onward through the snow flurries. Colonel Biddle and General Greene were second generation Quakers (the sons of Quakers) who had become thoroughly radicalized—or Americanized in this case by the Age of Enlightenment ideology—to forsake their pacifist upbringing and Quaker leaders' advice to remain neutral to become some of Washington's most fiery revolutionaries. They were now leading hundreds of American soldiers upon this suddenly strategic mercantile town that had been established by Quakers just barely a century before, while inspired by the nationalistic words of Thomas Paine, whose father was a Quaker.

And now after having "left the Friends [Quakers]" with a clear conscience to cast his fate with America's sacred cause of liberty, General Greene possessed a double motivation to strike a devastating blow this morning. This reflective man was haunted by his own responsibility for Fort Washington's devastating loss. With convincing arguments, he had swayed a reluctant Washington, who later graciously took full responsibility for the disaster in his report to Congress, to commit the folly of attempting to hold the indefensible fort. Therefore, by this time, this former lowly blacksmith and merchant from Rhode Island was very much a troubled soul. Greene yet felt "mad, sick and sorry" for the most grievous tactical mistake of his military career, thanks largely to that pervasive tactical disease known as Bunkerhillism. Consequently, no senior commander in Washington's Army was now more motivated to redeem himself at Trenton this early Thursday morning than Greene.

Appropriately for Greene's bid for personal and professional redemption, the very enemy troops who were most responsible for the considerable feat of capturing Fort Washington—the Rall, Knyphausen, and von Lossberg Regiments—were now garrisoned at Trenton. As penned in a letter to wife Kitty, who was fourteen years his junior, Greene was most of all determined to reap a victory at Trenton to sever forever "the chains of slavery forging for posterity [and] to defend our common rights, and repel the bold invaders of freedom [as] The cause is the cause of God and man."[3]

All of Trenton now lay invitingly before the onrushing troops of the Second Division, lifting Greene's spirits and those of his eager men, who had old scores to settle this morning. From the high ground above Trenton and looking south through the falling snow, Washington could see much of the length of prosperous commercial town located at the intersection of the Delaware and Assunpink Creek. Here, at the most unlikely of places, the fate of America was about to be decided.

As a native Rhode Islander whose bright potential was limitless, Greene possessed no prior knowledge that Trenton had been established in 1679 by Quakers, who had idealistically sought to create their own special version of God's kingdom, from Yorkshire, England. In 1719, wealthy merchant William Trent arrived from Philadelphia to build his stylish brick mansion near the wide, fast-flowing river to escape the city's urban blight, congestion, and summer diseases. He had then laid out the town's blueprint in a triangular design based upon two lengthy, parallel main streets, King and Queen, running north-south from the commanding heights on the north and down to nearly the Delaware's waters and the low-lying river bottoms.

On the high ground to the north gained by the foremost troops of central column of Greene's Division, these two main streets of Trenton gradually narrowed to meet, along with the intersection Pennington Road, which reached the town from the northwest, and the Princeton-Trenton Road that entered this intersection from the northeast, on the commanding heights. Near the head of Trent's carefully laid out triangle, all of these roads intersected on dominant terrain overlooking Trenton. The founder's beautiful Queen Anne-style brick mansion, the Trent House, which was situated on the river's level floodplain, was now occupied by a thirty-man Hessian detachment under Ensign Heinrich Zimmerman.

As dully noted by Zimmerman and his men, one of Trenton's popular taverns was distinguished by its colorfully painted sign of a energetic beaver felling a tree above the virtuous Latin word "perseverando," which symbolized two primary sources of American national pride and amazing success as a people in the New World: hard work and industriousness. In his diary and with the keen eye of an Irish immigrant from Ulster Province, Colonel Fitzpatrick described Trenton as "a pretty village, containing about 130 houses and a Presbyterian meeting-house [and] There are apple orchards and gardens."[4]

The "greatest English political writer" of the eighteenth century, who so masterfully articulated the very essence of the revolutionary struggle's meaning with an unmatched eloquence of the common people, Thomas Paine described how "Trenton is situated on a rising ground" that gradually rose northward from the low-lying Delaware.[5]And in a letter to his wife, Colonel Knox, who early detected Trenton's serious defensive limitations because of the lack of fortifications and the blessings of geography that benefitted Washington's attackers once they gained the all-important high ground north of town, explained how "Of these [British] cantonments Trenton was the most considerable [and] Trenton is an open town, situated nearly on the banks of the Delaware, accessible on all sides."[6]

Presenting Washington with the most golden opportunity of his military career, Trenton was indeed easily "accessible" on every side, especially the strategic heights at the north end of King and Queen Streets partly because the military manual of Hessian regulations had been ignored by Rall and his British superiors, who were unable to read German. This revered German textbook specifically emphasized how whenever a German "Regiment or Battalion is posted in village, which is not far from the enemy, the Chief or Commander must immediately cause a Redoubt to be erected on a chosen spot or height, or where it is in some way advantageous" for the town's defense.[7]

After having been defeated in four major battles and then driven back around a hundred miles from New York to eastern Pennsylvania's cold woodlands at a time when seemingly everything had gone to "the Devil," in Lieutenant Colonel Samuel Blachley Webb's words, Washington's troops now had much to prove to themselves and their infant nation, hovering on the verge of a premature death. Ironically, like the General Greene whose ill-found tactical judgment paved the way for Fort Washington's loss, the New Englanders, mostly in Sullivan's First Division, were determined to demonstrate their combat prowess to the non-New Englanders, especially the Virginians, because of their long-existing, intense rivalry.[8]

Hurrying forward his two New York six-pounders at the head of Stirling's Pennsylvania, Virginia, and Delaware brigade over bumpy ground and the freshly fallen snow without falling behind in Greene's column, the rambunctious Captain Alexander Hamilton, always eager for a fight, noticed the heightened esprit de corps that now bolstered the Second Division's surging ranks, martial sinews, and combat capabilities. Therefore, the young, irrepressible New Yorker was convinced that Washington's homespun warriors of diehard faith, both revolutionary and religious, were now ready to "storm hell's battlements," if necessary, and never more so than on the morning of December 26.[9]

With newfound confidence, recently issued flints, and full cartridge-boxes and all available bayonets now fixed on muskets, Washington's young men and boys from Massachusetts, Virginia, Connecticut, Pennsylvania, Delaware, New York, Maryland, New Hampshire, and New Jersey had finally put aside all past sectional and cultural differences to come together as one and as free Americans to face their supreme crisis together. More than ever before, these soldiers were now united by a solitary purpose and goal: to reap the most desperately needed victory of the war to ensure a new republic's survival.

Most of Washington's Continentals were yeomen farmers, not unlike the mostly lower class farmers who primarily filled Rall's enlisted ranks. The ad hoc composition of Washington's main strike force, so hurriedly thrown together by fate and circumstances for this desperate attack to save the day, was actually its hidden strength and one secret of its newly forged resiliency and confidence: the series of past reversals and retreats no longer weighed so heavily to sap confidence about what they could accomplish this morning, because this newly formed contingent of freedom fighters had not previously experienced humiliating defeats together. But most of all, Washington's common soldiers, now coughing, sneezing, and snorting from having caught colds during the tortuous river crossing and the night march, felt the added weight of a heavy burden on their shoulders,, while pushing at a good pace across the white landscape under a cold, leaden sky. Surging ahead through the deluge of steadily falling snow, the fighting men from across America felt a solemn, if not sacred, responsibility because "America in 1776 could have field[ed] an army of 280,000 men, but [now] just 2,400 held the fate of a continent in their hands."[10]

But Washington's remaining soldiers, the most never-say-die Continentals in America, were determined to succeed at any cost this eventful morning. Perhaps some of these men now remembered a Pennsylvania minister's inspiring words to the troops who had been humiliated so often by the British and Hessians: "Courage, my brave American soldiers, if God be for you, who can be against you? . . . be equipt for this warfare [and] put on . . . the gospel armour."[11]

For Captain Alexander Hamilton, a most promising, self-made man who had risen far and fast and must have wished that he was still enjoying sun-splashed days of his youth in his native West Indies, this confrontation at Trenton was much more than simply a desperate, last-ditch attempt by Washington to vanquish the three well-trained regiments of a Hessian brigade, despite the seemingly impossibility of that feat. To Hamilton, this sudden clash of arms that had descended upon the little town of Trenton like a summer thunderstorm was also much about a long-term national destiny of limitless potential.

Despite being a relative newcomer to America's shores, the ambitious Hamilton was already an early nationalistic visionary imbued with a vivid sense of what would later be called Manifest Destiny. Hamilton, ever perceptive and precociously analytical, saw the real root of this conflict as having largely stemmed from "a jealousy of our dawning splendour [and] The boundless extent of the territory we possess, the wholesome temperament of our climate, the luxuriance and fertility of our soil, the variety of our products, the rapidity of our population [growth], the industry of our country men," which ordained America's grandiose national destiny and a bright future for the United States second to none.

But Hamilton, Washington, and their soldiers' utopian visions of a great republican empire and bright future could not be fulfilled unless a dramatic victory was first secured this bitterly cold morning of December. Therefore, these idealistic, God-fearing men firmly believed that Colonel Rall and his elite German brigade were all that now stood in the way of America's future rising to eventually fulfill a grand, divinely sanctioned destiny as a great nation, an inspirational shining beacon of hope for the rest of the world, and a new, brighter day for all mankind.[12]

For such pressing reasons that were as personal as they were national for Washington's men, Rall's three crack regiments had to be swiftly eliminated in one stroke and as thoroughly as possible because so much was now at stake. In Washington's own strategic view and words, the attack on Trenton was very much about "preserving a city [the capital of Philadelphia and also the larger Puritan-inspired national vision of a "City on a Hill"], whose loss must prove of the most fatal consequence to the cause of America."[13] Quite simply, the battle of Trenton was also very much about preserving what was in essence the best hope for mankind.

Consequently, on multiple levels, the motivation among Washington's troops, now moving at a smart trot over the snowy terrain and closer to their great goal of Trenton, could not have been higher this morning. Not long after 8:00 a.m., Washington ordered the foremost soldiers of the central column of Greene's Division, Stephen's vanguard brigade just behind Captain Washington's Virginians, to form in battleline along the cold, wind-swept heights about a quarter mile north from Trenton's center and at King Street's head. Moving forward into their hastily assigned, but excellent, commanding positions on the high ground at a time when knapsacks never seemed heavier and legs more weary, Greene's breathless soldiers, panting from almost unbelievable exertions that had begun more than twelve hours before, shifted swiftly into their assigned places. All the while, Washington looked on through the cascading snow, as if yet attempting to gauge the fighting spirit among his troops, and with some satisfaction.

Most importantly in overall strategic terms, Washington was in the process of gaining a tighter and more firm grip on the high ground that dominated Trenton. In record time, Stephen's Virginia troops hustled across the strategic high ground, which was the key to Trenton this morning, with the easy precision of veterans, despite the thick snow covering the ground. Like the rest of Washington's soldiers, the Virginians were worn-down from the nightmarish Delaware crossing and the harrowing march through the snowstorm and over seemingly endless miles, but they were now ready for the challenge, thanks to no small part of Washington's inspired leadership that bestowed confidence and bolstered fighting spirit. Washington's example ensured that the often-defeated soldiers now would do their best and perform at their highest levels, which was unprecedented at this point in the war.

Here Washington "ordered us to form, that the [foremost two] cannon [of Captain Forrest's artillery which had advanced at the column's head with Mercer's brigade, so that they] might play" upon the enemy, wrote Major George Johnston, Fifth Virginia Continental Regiment. Washington skillfully orchestrated the deployment of Greene's troops of the center column with precision. Washington now demonstrated an uncanny ability in knowing exactly where and how to position his units to order to get the best out of them and their commanders. Because he rode at the column's head, Washington had earlier ascertained the best terrain to exploit it to the fullest. Along with the reassuring conviction that he now held the most strategic ground that completely dominated the town and spanned southward a considerable distance to the lower ground, Washington also possessed the vital intersection of the two most important roads—King and Queen Streets—that ran downhill through the heart of Trenton and toward the river. Too many times in the past, Washington had been forced to fight on less than favorable terrain not of his choosing. Quite simply, he had been almost always out-generaled. And now this most favorable of tactical situations was the exception to the rule for the hard-luck Virginian. Indeed, Washington was now the master of Trenton's most dominant terrain and literally king of the hill.

As if performing on a drill field, the fast-moving troops of Mercer's brigade, the right column of Greene's Division, continued to move west at a brisk pace to secure the most advantageous positions as directed by Washington. Very likely wondering if he would survive this day to finally see his son, who had been born last August back at his modest Fredericksburg home and named after him, General Mercer quickly deployed his veteran Maryland, Connecticut, and Massachusetts brigade along the high ground west of King Street. Meanwhile, Stirling's brigade of Delaware, Pennsylvania, and Virginia troops, coming up fast behind Mercer, was aligned in Washington's center, and stood astride the head of King Street, but mostly to its west. Eventually, Stirling's line was extended farther east so that the brigade's left extended to a point just northeast of the head of Queen Street.

Chevalier Matthias Alexis Roche de Fermoy's Pennsylvania brigade, including the bulging ranks of the robust German Regiment, secured the left of Washington's fast-forming battleline to the east. Mercer now commanded a newly created brigade of veteran regiments and knew how to use them with skill. This fine Continental brigade had been recently clubbed together by Washington so that his tactically astute Scottish friend would have an opportunity to lead it into action in just such key combat situations, after the troops of Mercer's Flying Camp had been either captured at Fort Washington or faded away when the Maryland and New Jersey enlistments expired. But to Mercer's absolute delight at this time, one of the hard-hitting regiments that now protected his left flank was his reliable old regiment, the Third Virginia Continental Regiment, Stirling's brigade, which was now commanded by the Scotsman's own brother-in-law Colonel Weedon.

A rarity in this army, Fermoy's Continental brigade was led by an aristocratic Frenchman. In part because America was so desperately in need of professionally trained soldiers, General Fermoy was very much of a mystery man of an entirely unknown ability, which was an unsettling fact that might yet come back to haunt Washington this morning. However, Washington had been saddled with this proud, aristocratic French volunteer, who could not speak English, for political purposes. An ever-meddling Congress had recently bestowed a brigadier general's rank upon the Frenchman based upon hardly more than his dubious word. Nevertheless, it was both necessary and symbolic that a French volunteer general, despite his highly-questionable and unverified qualifications, now commanded one of Washington's brigades, including his largest regiment.

Most of all, America desperately needed France as an official ally for any hope of surviving a war of attrition. Suddenly more hesitant to assist the young republic after so many miserable defeats, especially New York City's loss, the carefully calculating French king and government now only awaited for the good news of a rebel victory from the Mount Vernon planter to continue the flow of secret military aid—such as Captain Moulder's three French four-pounders—and inch closer to the all-important official recognition. Clearly, in regard to the prospects for the young republic's bid to gain foreign recognition, everything was now at stake at Trenton. And now vanquishing an entire battle-seasoned Hessian brigade at Trenton would send a powerful and most timely message to the French king and his pro-interventionist cronies.

As throughout this winter campaign, Washington continued to think ahead in tactical terms. Indeed, just before reaching Trenton's northern outskirts immediately northwest of the head of King and Queen Streets, Washington had dispatched Fermoy's brigade, the last brigade in column behind Stirling's brigade, to "file off" from Greene's main Second Division column, march across country to the east, and bypass Trenton's upper end in an attempt to gain the Princeton-Trenton Road and extend Washington's left east toward Assunpink Creek. Washington's farsighted and timely tactical maneuver to block the Princeton-Trenton Road was also calculated: most importantly, to prevent the Rall brigade's escape and to stop the arrival of any reinforcements, General Leslie's British troops, who might be dispatched south from Princeton and down this icy road, that led northeast from Trenton to Princeton, to assist the isolated Rall, who was on his own.

With muskets on shoulders, therefore, Colonels Hand and Haussegger's troops of Fermoy's brigade had earlier trekked off east through the open, windblown fields of white on their key assignment to gain the Princeton Road beyond the upper town, northeast of Queen Street, and an elevated position blocking the escape northeast, between Queen Street to the west and Assunpink Creek to the east, out of town. Most importantly in overall strategic terms, Washington was about to shortly possess all three roads—blocked by Sullivan, Greene, and Fermoy, respectively, from west to east—that led north from Trenton, additionally sealing the Hessian brigade's fate hardly before the battle had begun. Not only the whitish haze of the dropping snow but also a belt of dark woodlands masked Fermoy's stealthy push eastward across relatively high ground from prying Hessian eyes, to the south on much lower terrain, to eventually present yet another nasty surprise for Rall and his troops when least expected this morning.[14]

Born in the Caribbean (like Captain Hamilton) island of the French island of Martinique around 1737, the ever-opportunistic Fermoy had only recently reached American soil to create a name for himself in battling for liberty. He claimed to have been a colonel—but most likely only a mere captain—of French engineers, a highly respected elite corps of educated officers. Seeking to add prestige to the ancient aristocratic Rochedefermoy family name and strike a blow against France's ancient enemy, Fermoy's hasty appointment to brigadier general came less than two months before—on November 5, 1776—from highly impressible Congressional members, who knew little about military matters. Fortunately, for America's fortunes, the showdown at Trenton was to be the only engagement in which the liberty-loving Frenchman demonstrated the military competence that he had bragged so loudly about so often.[15]

Meanwhile, the rearmost of Greene's soldiers in the lengthy Second Division column continued to be spurred onward and into their assigned positions by the sound of Sullivan's booming artillery to the southwest, indicating the rapid progress of the lower, or right, arm of Washington's pincer movement. Not long after the first artillery fire had erupted from the two three-pounders of the Eastern Company New Jersey State Artillery, under young Captain Neil, who was assigned to Sullivan's vanguard brigade under Colonel Sargent, Sullivan's other cannon of the First Division added their fury that descended so unexpectedly upon the Rall brigade. Moving up quickly behind Sargent's onrushing troops and now assigned to Glover's brigade, high-spirited New England gunners of the Massachusetts Company of Continental Artillery pushed their two six-pounders forward.

Working fast in the snow to get their field pieces into their assigned positions, which helped warm themselves up on the frozen morning, the 55 Bay State artillerymen of young Captain Winthrop Sargent soon blasted away with authority. Captain Sargent was an intellectual and enlightened scholar. Additionally, he was a graduate of Harvard College, hailing from the fishing port of Gloucester, Massachusetts.

The rolling peals of crashing musketry from the smoothbore muskets of Captain Flanhaven's New Jersey Continentals, who continued to lead the way for Sullivan's surging First Division, and the thundering First Division artillery-fire to the southwest told Washington, basking in the initial success already achieved by his double envelopment, that Sullivan was continuing to push the foremost Hessians rearward and closer to Trenton's southwestern and lower end.

As he deployed his battle-hardened Continentals north of town with alacrity under heavy gray skies that hovered low over the whitish landscape of ice and snow, Washington relished the thought of having so easily gained the strategic high ground at the head of King and Queen Streets. From this elevated point of strategic importance, Washington could easily ascertain any future Hessian intentions, movements, or tactics on the lower ground below that was mostly open and with relatively few trees, except next to houses. Most importantly, the seasoned Virginians of Stephen's brigade, whose right was situated near King Street's head just to the left-rear of Stirling's brigade, were in good position to shift farther east to fill in the gap to Fermoy's right to the east whenever Washington felt that it was tactically necessary.

All of Washington's well-conceived chess-like moves in a complex series of unit deployments on carefully chosen ground were calculated to firmly set in place his most reliable commanders and his finest veteran troops, who were most capable of handling important assignments, in the most advanced positions from where they could either inflict the most damage or make the most staunch defense in case the Hessian brigade counterattacked. Washington's uncanny ability to match up just the right assignment to best fit his subordinate commander's capabilities and his troop's overall quality resulted in the lead regiment of Stirling's brigade, Weedon's Third Virginia which was now the right-center of Stirling's brigade, having been deployed for action at the head of King Street.

Demonstrating additional sound tactical judgment, Washington also set Captain Washington's vanguard, Third Virginia boys who had been long infused with a crusading fervor by Chaplain Griffith, at the most advanced position at the top of King Street, before the nondescript ranks of Weedon's Virginia Regiment. Washington ensured that he now had his crack Virginians, both Captain Washington's vanguard and the Third Virginia Continental Regiment, in ideal positions to lead an infantry attack straight down King Street whenever he gave the word. Seemingly thinking of everything, he now allowed his more exhausted vanguard troops of Stephen's brigade some badly needed rest just to the left-rear of the Third Virginia, after having shifted his relatively better conditioned troops—the Third Virginia Continental Regiment—into the key position on the high ground at King Street's head: the perfect location to not only open the main battle, but also to play a leading role, defensive or offensive, once the fighting began in earnest.

Meanwhile, the pounding of the beating instruments of young Hessian drummer boys and the crisp blasts of a cavalry bugle blown by a sleepy-eyed redcoat musician of the Sixteenth Light Dragoons, part of the British detachment of only twenty finely uniformed light horse cavalrymen stationed at Trenton, blared loudly. While the bugle's sharp notes slanted through the cold air and across the relatively narrow east-west (compared to north-south) width of Trenton in the bugler's frantic attempt to rally the Hessian brigade, Washington barked out orders for Knox's guns to hurry forward and deploy along the commanding high ground.

Drawn by weakened horses that were as worn as the weather-beaten gunners of Captain Forrest's Pennsylvania Second Company of the Pennsylvania State Artillery, and with the usual sound of the cannon's movements yet muffled by the freshly fallen snow, these foremost field pieces and the wooden powder carts had kept up with the head of Mercer's brigade as ordered. Demonstrating a more thorough appreciation—almost an advanced, Napoleon-like understanding—of artillery's decisiveness on the battlefield, especially a wintery one, than ever before, Washington personally accompanied the first two guns at the column's head, encouraging them forward on the double. Most of all, he was determined to make sure that these Pennsylvania cannon and their well-trained gunners were deployed correctly at the best terrain and in the most advantageous position to reap the greatest dividends: the commanding high ground perch at King Street's head around 250 yards directly north of the town's center.

Utilizing the keen tactical sense and well-honed instincts of a veteran artillery commander, Washington knew that a proper deployment of these two big six-pounders and two five and a half-inch howitzers of Forrest's Pennsylvania battery along the high ground overlooking Trenton might well spell the difference between success and failure on this momentous morning upon which the winner would take all. As Knox and Washington fully realized, Forrest's long six-pounders packed the most devastating punch, especially against infantry: double the firepower of the Hessian's six bronze three-pounders, and almost equal in firepower to the hard-hitting eight-pounders. Such a decided firepower advantage on the battlefield, especially in an engagement's beginning, was a fundamental reason why the master artilleryman Napoleon had made sure that the reliable six-pounder became his army's primary field gun for his unbeatable

French armies that rampaged across Europe and toppled one opponent's army after another for years.

What has been most often overlooked by generations of historians is Washington's acute tactical sense in regard to artillery prioritization and careful placement, based specifically upon his artillery's capabilities that rose to an unprecedented height, revealing his insights as to gun size, the quality of artillery leadership, and the capabilities of his high-spirited gunners. Frederick the Great understood that a great commander possessed what was known as coup d'oeil, or the "sweep of the eye," that instantly ascertained the advantages of terrain and immediately exploited it to the fullest: exactly what Washington quickly accomplished in so early and firmly securing the high ground at the head of King and Queen Streets and the careful placement of artillery to dominate all of Trenton.

With an amazing perceptiveness and quick decisiveness in a key situation, Washington had early tailored his cannon and their capabilities to precisely meet a host of specific and key mission requirements: first and foremost, in deciding that the most lethal of Knox's artillery—the four guns of Forrest's elite Pennsylvania artillery company—should advance at the head of Greene's column, proper, with Mercer's brigade. Then, to ensure their swift deployment as early as possible on the high ground north of Trenton, Forrest's guns had advanced with Weedon's Third Virginia, which led Stirling's brigade, just behind Stephen's Virginia vanguard brigade, after the Maryland, Connecticut, and Massachusetts infantry of Mercer's brigade shifted south from the main column to advance westward.

With a most keen eye for securing the most advantageous terrain that dominated the town on the north, Washington was already familiar with Trenton's environs and its most advantageous geography that he exploited to his maximum benefit: timely, insightful knowledge originally gained from the observant Virginian's close attention to detail that he had long kept sequestered in his agile, reflective mind—not unlike Arthur Wellesley, or the Duke of Wellington, in regard to vividly recalling and then utilizing the most favorable terrain on the battlefield of Waterloo, Belgium, to decisively defeat Napoleon—and now exploited in masterful fashion.

Washington's relatively easy securing of the strategic high ground north of Trenton for his judicious placement of his artillery to command the entire town now combined nicely with his greater appreciation of his artillery arm's capabilities and decisive potential, which mirrored Knox's own forward-thinking opinions about artillery's decisiveness on the battlefield. All in all, Washington now demonstrated distinguished trademark of a great commander: virtually winning an important battle before the first shot in anger is fired.

Washington's eagerness to place his largest guns, best led, and finest trained artillerymen atop the commanding perch above Trenton as soon as possible clearly indicated that he realized exactly what the key to victory was this morning. Like Napoleon from an early date, Washington fully appreciated and acted upon the axiom that "battles are won by artillery," in the Corsican's words. At long last, the farsighted wisdom of Washington's tactical sense and keen insight in regard to artillery's decisiveness began to be fulfilled in its most tangible form when his first cannon, Captain Forrest's guns, neared the most advantageous position, as designated by Washington, on the commanding terrain that over-looked Trenton. To fulfill his ambitious tactical vision of a lengthy, neat row of Knox's finest artillery pieces set up along the high ground to dominate the town and hence the fast-forming Rall brigade, Washington ordered the Pennsylvania guns to be hurried into their key position.

Clearly, the Virginian wanted to make sure that Forrest's cannon were placed at exactly the right spot along the heights. Washington continued to benefit from his prior decisions of not only adding far more guns to his strike force than usual, but also from the novel process of integrating artillery with infantry to enhance the combat capabilities of both arms. As early envisioned by Washington, Knox's artillery pieces were about to be employed as highly effective assault weapons to maximize hard-hitting capabilities by transforming a single Continental infantry brigade into a much more formidable fighting machine. This was a wise tactical decision because the "true secret" of Napoleon's remarkable battlefield successes across Europe called for a close, mutually sup-portive, and precise coordination of infantry and artillery into "one continuous process of attack," with each arm bolstering the capabilities of the other to maximumize the hard-hitting power of a combined one-two offensive punch of artillery and infantry to destroy the enemy's will to resist as soon as possible.

Under dark, cloud-covered skies that blocked the frigid sun of late December, a mounted Washington shouted to Captain Forrest, whose Pennsylvania battery had advanced in the van of Greene's column proper, to set up his first two cannon along the heights. As Napoleon himself would accom-plish in so many key battlefield situations across Europe, Washington carefully directed the Pennsylvania gun's placement along the open high ground, which was just south of a brown-hued belt of leafless trees that ran along the road's north side, about 250 yards north of Trenton's center and perpendicular to the two parallel main streets, King and Queen. As both exhausted artillery horses and cannoneers, led by Forrest's top lieutenants, Hercules Courtney, Francis Procter, and Patrick Duffy, struggled through the snow, while the frozen breath of both exhausted animals and gunners hung momentarily in the cold air, the first two cannon of Greene's column gained their key positions—as assigned by Washington—on the most strategic high ground position at Trenton.

In record time, Forrest's two Pennsylvania cannon were then dragged into position and wheeled into line by enthusiastic young cannoneers. Knowing the importance of their key role and with adrenaline rushing through reinvigorated systems to negate some lingering effects of weariness, sleeplessness, and even the bone-numbing cold, Forrest's gunners worked faster than usual. The two guns were quickly loaded by expert artillerymen, who then took their assigned firing positions. With the seconds passing like ages to these cannoneers, including smooth-faced teenagers, in awaiting the order to fire, anxious Philadelphia gunners felt especially eager to punish the Hessians on the lower ground below them to eliminate potential threats to their own hometown, the new republic's capital, located farther down the Delaware. Meanwhile, at Washington's incessant urging, Captain Forrest's other two cannon were coming up quickly through the now-furrowed snow to add more muscle to the elevated position at King Street's head.

At this critical moment, Washington wanted all four guns—the two six-pounders and the two five and a half-inch howitzers—of Forrest's Second Company, Pennsylvania State Artillery, which was the largest and best trained battery in Knox's Regiment of Continental Artillery, to be positioned along the commanding ground at King Street's head. Some of Washington's heaviest guns, the two long-barreled six-pounders that fired solid iron cannonballs, were large enough to adequately safeguard his east-west-stretching formation of Continental troops in static defensive positions, while Forrest's two short- and wide-barreled howitzers were more effective in firing explosive shell at high angles. And both the six-pounders and five and a half-inch howitzers were especially deadly at close range when firing grapeshot or canister.

Forrest's long six-pounders and his most prized guns—the versatile howitzers—once placed at this most advantageous commanding point (ironically the exact location where a disinterested Rall had been advised by Donop's engineer to erect the artillery redoubt) allowed Washington's most lethal firepower to thoroughly dominate the open lower ground of Trenton below while yet situated comfortably beyond range of Hessian's smooth-bore muskets and artillery in the river valley below. In a masterful orchestration, Washington had carefully calculated in getting his largest caliber and best serviced guns—the iron six-pounders of Knox's artillery arm consisting mostly of small three-pounders—aligned on the most dominant terrain on the Trenton battlefield as soon as possible. Fulfilling his lofty ambition on his finest hour, the Virginian knew that the battle's course depended upon just such a timely, judicious placement of artillery.

Destined for a well-deserved lieutenant colonel's rank largely because of what he accomplished during this winter campaign, Captain Forrest was an officer of considerable talent and ability. Forrest, a future Pennsylvania Congressman, was determined to make a name for himself and his Pennsylvania artillery unit on his lofty perch overlooking the commercial town draped in a whitish pall. Most importantly, Forrest's largest guns now commanded not only Trenton but also the primary avenue, King Street, of approach into the town, if the Hessian brigade counterattacked north up the gently slope ground upon which this main thoroughfare ran in a straight line.

In overall tactical terms, Washington's cannon poised across the high ground also supported the advance of Mercer's brigade, west of King Street, Stirling's brigade mostly west of King Street, and Fermoy's brigade, consisting of a Pennsylvania regiment and the German regiment, east of these twin avenues, King and Queen Streets. To protect Knox's cannon and this vital road intersection on the high ground if Rall organized his forces and mounted a counterattack up King Street, both Stirling and Stephen's infantry brigades were now situated in a foremost position across commanding terrain to provide fire support.[16]

Incredibly, Washington had secured the strategic high ground without so much as facing a single Hessian soldier or artillery piece posted at this elevated point that completely commanded the town. In essence and in masterful fashion, Washington had already fulfilled what became one of Napoleon's fundamental maxims in the art of waging successful war: "the artillery should be advantageously placed, ground should be selected which is not commanded or liable to be turned, and, as far as possible, the guns should cover and command the surrounding country."[17] Enjoying a commanding view of Trenton at King Street's head and with Captain Forrest's two six-inch cannon deployed to command the extensive length of King Street flowing down the snow-covered slope, Washington now made a key decision on a stormy morning in which virtually every one of his command decisions went according to his well-conceived, prearranged plan. Instead of waiting for the arrival of Captain Forrest's other two guns, the five and a half-inch howitzers, and Captains Hamilton's and Baumann's artillery, to come up to the head of King Street, Washington fully understood that time was now of the essence. With the initiative, momentum, and advantage now decidedly in his favor, the commander-in-chief was not about to waste a second of time while hundreds of Hessians attempted to form for action in town on lower ground below him.

To fully exploit the element of surprise, Washington instinctively realized that he simply could not waste any precious time for the slower-moving cannon to be brought up before opening fire to reap the maximum advantage by inflicting shock, damage, and more chaos upon his opponent. Ensuring that their guns were now dry and clean so as not to diminish firepower capabilities, Forrest's Philadelphia artillerymen had kept the muzzles and touch holes, or vents, of barrels securely plugged with tompions during both the hazardous river crossing and the long, nighttime march. Even now, these expert Pennsylvania gunners yet protected touch holes and their precious loads of black powder from the moisture and snow. Knox's wooden ammunition carts were likewise waterproof, thanks to thick, sturdy lids, a peaked roof design that allowed water to roll off the sides, and oilcloth coverings that provided protection to keep black powder dry.

A mounted Colonel Knox, literally larger than life in girth, personality, and command presence on a decisive morning when dynamic leadership was most needed, barked out the exact range of the forming Hessians on King Street below the muzzles of the two six-pounders and with Trenton's center only around 250 yards distant. Forrest's well-trained gunners, representing various ethnic groups that included artillerymen like Irishman Thomas Kennedy and German Jacob Harkishimer, made careful calculations in regard to precise elevation and range adjustments of the long cannon barrels of the six-pounders.

Having endured the nightmarish march to Trenton without "Shoes and Watch Coats," as lamented the Philadelphia-born Captain Forrest, who had watched the men's suffering in anguish, the Pennsylvania artillerymen took careful aim with their big six-pounders, aligning cannon barrels to fire straight down King Street and sighting on the mass of Hessians attempting to organize below them. Well-trained to hit British warships at long range to defend their hometown of Philadelphia, these expert cannoneers aimed their six-pounders on targets now at much closer range, calculating to unleash their fire at a low angle to sweep the open street clean of Hessian soldiers.

Now beside his personal escort of the young, aristocratic dandies of the Philadelphia Light Horse, under the chivalric, Philadelphia-born Captain Morris, while the cavalrymen's distinctive yellow silk banner snapped in the stiff wind blowing across the frozen heights, a mounted Washington surveyed all before him without missing a detail, taking everything in. While the snow tumbled down in its quiet, monotonous fashion without a let up, he suddenly felt an increasing measure of impatience, desiring for his worn-out cannoneers and artillery horses to move even faster in order to get all of Knox's artillery pieces into their proper, advantageous positions along the high ground. Meanwhile, Forrest's first guns, the big six-pounders, were ready to unleash their wrath upon the most hated soldiers in all America. The mastermind behind the farsighted decision to transport all eighteen guns across the Delaware and all the way to the King Street's head nearly ten miles distant, Washington appropriately now gave the first order to open, shouting "Fire!" for all to hear.

Now waging war on his own home soil of New Jersey and before his veteran brigade aligned in protective fashion near Forrest's six-pounders, Stirling described with pride in a letter how, "we soon got two field pieces at play."Breaking the heightened tension among Washington's anxious troops aligned in a lengthy line at King Street's head, Captain Forrest's six-pounders, which were sufficiently depressed to fire down King Street, opened up, roaring angrily in unison. Ringing over Trenton, this first eruption of Knox's artillery from the high ground north of Trenton announced to a very surprised Rall brigade that the much-ridiculed Washington had not only secured the strategic high ground, but also had gained a tight grip on the area's most strategic position.

Beautiful music to American ears, the resounding crash of Forrest's Philadelphia guns warmed the spirits of Washington and his soldiers, who now realized that their most powerful arm was in action. No doubt, an enthusiastic cheer was raised by nearby infantrymen, yet shivering in the cold, who knew that their chances for success were continuing to rise. Best of all, Washington neither saw nor heard any Hessian return fire erupting from any of the Rall brigade's half dozen cannon in response. Ordered to open up by Washington himself who remained near Captain Forrest's booming guns and looked on benignly like an admiring parent on the chaos among the Hessians in Trenton with a calm certitude that denoted satisfaction, the fiery eruption of the Pennsylvanian's cannonfire so soon after the first American troops had secured the high ground at King Street's head caused considerable consterna-tion among the Germans. Manned by expert cannoneers whom fairly lusted for the opportunity to punish Rall's men who had vanquished so many Americans in the past, the Pennsylvania field pieces bucked and fumed in rapid sequence after hurling their deadly missiles down King Street.

It is not known, but perhaps Captain Forrest's Irish fifer, Daniel Dennis, now played an inspiring, lively martial air, or a number of young drummer boys, such as George Weaver, Christopher Coleman, or Daniel Syfred, beat their drums to encourage their "long-arm" comrades, who busily worked their six-pounders that belched fire down the slopes. If so, then any such American martial music echoing from the high ground north symbolically countered the frantic beating of drums by Hessian drummer boys to rally Rall's troops in the lower ground below. [18]

Meanwhile, about a quarter mile to the southwest of Forrest's commanding position and following on the heels of Captain Flahaven's onrushing vanguard of New Jersey Continentals after the stubborn German jaegers were hurled rearward from Dickinson's stately Hermitage, Colonel John Stark continued to lead Sullivan's Division straight down the River Road that now offered an open avenue into the lower, or southwestern end of Trenton. Shocked by the sight of so many of Flahaven's New Jersey and Stark's New Hampshire soldiers charging at them with fixed bayonets, Lieutenant Grothausen led his green-clad jaegers farther down the River Road in a rapid retreat, while the elated Continental's war-cries split the icy air. Before they were overrun by the New Englanders, the reeling jaegers headed toward the safety of the lower town, seeking shelter from Sullivan's raging storm.[19]

With Stark's rawboned New Hampshire boys now leading the way with their typical aggressiveness, the first of Sullivan's Continentals gained the town's southwestern outskirts. Here, on open ground, snow-covered fields and meadows, and facing the corner of the River Road and Second Street, Captain Moulder's Philadelphia gunners brought their four-pounders, imported all the way from an Atlantic port in France like Brest, to the forefront in support of Sullivan's onrushing infantrymen, who pushed steadily eastward in a deter-mined effort to gain a toehold on Second Street and toward Trenton's com-mercial district in the lower town. With silk battle flags snapping in the brisk winds that howled from the northeast, Sullivan's troops swarmed onward at a rapid pace, despite the clinging snow, surging into harm's way with unbridled enthusiasm. These veteran New Englanders were on a collision course with the elite troops of the Knyphausen Regiment, which was yet forming for action on Queen Street both above and below Second Street.[20]

While Sullivan's and Greene's columns had launched their simultaneous offensive effort from two different directions to fulfill Washington's tactical vision of a double envelopment, no such close defensive coordination existed between the British and their German allies. Panicked members of the "British light horse" immediately deserted the Rall brigade. They rushed out of their assigned quarters at the two-story Friends (Quaker) Meeting House, built in 1739, on Fourth Street, and hurriedly mounted up. Shocked that they had been surprised by Americans, these unnerved Englishmen then galloped across the Assunpink bridge, forsaking their German allies and Trenton's defense.

With Washington's cannon roaring from two directions and the cannonade's fury echoing ominously over the snowy landscape like a summer lightning storm sweeping along the humid Potomac at Washington's Mount Vernon, these panicked Englishmen, who considered themselves elite troopers, forgot all about their pride and lofty reputations. They now only thought about escaping the howling tide of onrushing rebels. But these Britons were not alone in their wild flight from Trenton. In a letter, Richard Henry Lee described with contempt how a good many "Tories that were in Town scampered off at the beginning of the engagement."[21]

Meanwhile, knowing the supreme importance of amassing as many of Knox's cannon as possible in the most advantageous terrain, Washington continued to bolster his artillery alignment across the high ground at the head of King Street. Drawn by frothing, sweat-streaked horses that could hardly pull their heavy loads any farther from the night-long exertions, Forrest's other two guns, the five and a half-inch howitzers at last reached the commanding terrain above Trenton. The two howitzers were hurriedly set up by the Philadelphia artillerymen in the freshly fallen snow just to the left of the two blazing six-pounders, which continued to hurl a hail of iron solid projectiles down King Street.

Like its sister six-pounders, Forrest's howitzers, "the best of [their] class," packed a mighty punch: exactly why Washington now desired their careful placement on strategic high ground overlooking Trenton. In fact, they were Washington's most lethal artillery pieces at long range, which was an invaluable asset on a wintery battlefield. Unlike Forrest's six-pounders that fired only a single round ball of solid iron at long range targets, Knox's five and a half-inch guns hurled hollow cannonballs—or shells—that exploded in murderous shell-bursts above densely packed enemy formations to cause a deadly hail of shrapnel to break out from a thin iron casing, spiraling downward and wreaking havoc on the heads and shoulders of massed infantry.

By adding more muscle to Forrest's fast-firing cannon from the snowy heights and knowing that massing artillery firepower was the key to vanquishing a full brigade of Hessians—a feat not yet accomplished in this war—Washington was only beginning to wage his own personal artillery war this cold morning. With all of Forrest's Pennsylvania guns now blasting away in the softly falling snow, Washington now directed a newly arrived battery of capable New York gunners into action. And in the process, he additionally verified the wisdom of having placed artillery units at the head of brigades in column in order to get as many cannon in action as soon as possible. Arriving on the commanding terrain after much strenuous effort, this fine New York artillery company of two six-pounders was led by an especially aggressive, talented young commander, Alexander Hamilton. Ironically, however, this transplanted New Yorker felt that he had much to prove to himself and a good many others in part because he was yet considered a foreigner by other Americans because of his West Indies roots.

Upon first glance at the firebrand West Indian, such outstanding officer qualities seemed almost incongruous because of Hamilton's small size (slender, not short, as generally assumed) and youthful appearance that beguiled the depth of his tenacity, fierce ambition, and the hot competitive fire that burned within him. However, Washington early recognized and appreciated Hamilton's sterling leadership qualities that were exceptional for such a young artillery commander. For this reason, Hamilton's New York State Company of Artillery had advanced at the head of Stirling's Virginia, Delaware, and Pennsylvania brigade during the trek to Trenton. In a commanding voice, Hamilton barked out a set of orders and his six-pounders were quickly set up by his New York gunners on the high ground at the head of Queen Street, just to the right, or east, of King Street, on the left of Forrest's four guns that continued to roar as if there was no tomorrow.

Here, at the head of Queen Street and beside Washington's guardian troopers of the Philadelphia Light Horse, under the recently chastised Captain Morris, whose cavalrymen's neighing horses showed nervousness when positioned so close to Knox's booming cannon, Washington also orchestrated the deployment of the two six-pounders of Hamilton's New York company on the high ground without a moment's delay. Bellowing orders, he extended the row of artillery eastward across the snow-covered heights.

Hamilton's guns were now in the best of hands, with Lieutenants Thomas Deane and Thomas Thompson providing solid leadership to inspire their artillerymen to do their best this morning. Most of all, the aristocratic Virginian had complete confidence in this gregarious New York captain from a lowly background, and his faith was rewarded. Especially on this morning of decision, Hamilton was especially "enterprising, quick in his perceptions and his judgment intuitively great," wrote the admiring commander-in-chief of his hard-fighting gamecock. Not surprisingly, Washington maintained his high esteem for the gifted West Indian to his life's end, never forgetting what Hamilton had accomplished in the struggle for liberty, especially at Trenton.

Of course, Colonel Knox also greatly assisted in the judicious placement of his artillery along the high ground perch, allowing his seemingly limitless "long-arm" expertise to rise to the fore. The swift deployment of Hamilton's New York cannon in this key high ground position was not without risk because Lieutenant Wiederhold's Knyphausen pickets in the first houses at northern end of Queen Street yet "fired at the enemy, who were forming for battle on the city's height," scribbled the lieutenant in his diary. As if to compensate for his "small [but not short], slender, and with a delicate frame," the handsome, teenage captain was known not only for his feisty fighting spirit, but also for wearing his cocked hat pulled low at a jaunty angle, even in fair weather.

At this time, Hamilton also wore a plain, but surprisingly warm, winter cape that had been crudely fashioned manner from an old, dirty blanket into a durable, makeshift winter overcoat. Looking almost like a drab Mexican poncho, this unique "military" apparel was likewise worn by Hamilton's New York cannoneers, who had smartly adjusted to wintertime conditions through clever improvisation. But Hamilton hardly needed any specific instructions about the urgency of getting his six-pounders in action as quickly as possible because he was entirely capable to choosing the best ground to maximize his gun's capabilities to the utmost. Hamilton's high-spirited gunners were now more than "ready, every devil of them," wrote the dashing captain, whose intelligence beamed like a shining star. Along with Forrest's artillery unit that represented Pennsylvania with typical regional pride, Hamilton's artillery company of sixty-eight officers and enlisted men was also not a Continental unit, but a New York state command that operated under within the overall framework of Knox's Continental Regiment of Artillery.[22]

By this time, Captain Hamilton, despite only age nineteen and hardly looking the part, was one of the army's best artillery officers. He was also a natural leader of men. And this self-confident young man already possessed a lofty reputation as a brilliant philosophical writer of influential, and rather remarkable, revolutionary pamphlets. Even more than writing with a skill seldom seen in the colonies, he loved and admired his six-pounders almost as if they were his children, and not something of cold iron cast in a foundry for the express purpose of blowing apart British and Hessian soldiers. With a ruddy-faced complexion and thick mane of sandy-colored hair that appealed to the ladies young and old, Hamilton was the highest-ranking West Indian in Washington's Army. Although Hamilton, born on the isle of Nevis, grew up in a slave-owning, dysfunctional family on the tropical island St. Croix, dominated by slavery, he shortly became an outspoken opponent of slavery, adhering to the revolution's most enlightened principles.

Lithe and overflowing with nervous energy, Hamilton was not only a bright, studious intellectual, but also every inch a fighter. At the age of twelve and despite a pious nature, Hamilton had written to a letter to a friend that he wished for a war to escape the Caribbean and to make a name for himself. He now possessed not only that long-awaited coveted opportunity, but also an irrepressible spirit and a temperament that blazed as hot as his native Caribbean sun on a July day. From a somewhat hazy, mysterious family background of a generally unsavory nature and marked by a "whole countenance that was decidedly Scottish," this young immigrant from the Caribbean hoped to gain widespread recognition, if not a measure of redemption, from battlefield accomplishments. Therefore, this complex intellectual who was fluent in French, a brilliant writer and revolutionary pamphleteer of note, and a lover of the classics, was highly motivated amid the cold hell of this morning that he would never forget. Like a Crusader of old campaigning in the Holy Land, Hamilton wanted to win his fair share of the glory, as if to erase a dark, trouble-filled family past that had left him virtually an orphan after his mother's early death.

Hamilton was the precocious, youngest son of a ne'er-do-well Scottish merchant, who abandoned his mother of French Huguenot descent. His father's sudden departure resulted in his mother's remarriage, which were considered illegal under Danish law. In consequence, Alexander had been considered illegitimate under the convoluted legal logic and inane complexities of eighteenth-century Danish law that yet confounds legal experts to this day. His mother had been overburdened by the tainted social stigma of "adultery," causing the young man much personal grief and humiliation. Hamilton's troubled, dark past in

Christiansted, St. Croix's capital, was something that he wanted to wipe out by personal achievements on the snowy field of Trenton.

A recent newcomer, Hamilton had first migrated to America in 1772 to start life anew at age seventeen, fulfilling his burning ambition of leaving the Caribbean's restrictive confines and lack of opportunities far behind. Consequently, this fiery, young captain—a rising star early (before Washington) recognized by Greene—of so much potential was yet haunted by the fact that he had been "a bastard [and] an orphaned immigrant." A hard-fighting Presbyterian warrior like so many of Knox's Irish and Scotch-Irish gunners at Trenton, Hamilton began his military career in St. Croix, where the threat of slave revolts on the sugar island were omnipresent.

Reflecting his lowly origins and free, but disciplined, spirit, he had early developed a hatred of arbitrary authority, monarchy, and the corrupt British upper class ruling elite, first in the British Caribbean and then in America. Hamilton also detested the Church of England's abuses and hypocrisy with a passion while warmly embracing John Locke's liberal Enlightenment ideals. Therefore, he became an early and leading spirit of the Sons of Liberty in New York City when not attending to his classical studies at King's College, founded by royal charter in 1754, the future Columbia University. Thanks to his writing skills, this bright, natural revolutionary, who enjoyed lengthy periods of quiet time to read and study like an ancient Greek scholar, evolved into "the darling of New York's radicals," winning for him early high-level personal and political support because of his radical pamphlets that galvanized opposition to the Crown. Most of all, Hamilton was a diehard nationalist who believed, in his own words, "in the future grandeur and glory of America."

No dreamy, inactive bookworm, Hamilton had early organized a volunteer company, known as the Hearts of Oak, of mostly King's College students. Hour after hour, he drilled these "young gentleman" soldiers, including a number of friends, in green uniforms before classes. Along with his school boy volunteers, who were nicknamed the "Corsicans" for these freedom-fighters' rebellion against Italy, he proudly wore a stylish leather cap embroidered with the revolutionary slogan, "Freedom or Death." Despite his youth (and he looked younger than his years) that guaranteed no urgent need of a razor, the ambitious Hamilton had already declined an offer to serve in the prestigious position as an aide on the personal staffs of both Lord Stirling and General Greene, just to have an opportunity at independent command so that he could distinguish himself in combat.

In March 1776, he finally garnered an artillery officer's rank from the State of New York and then set out to make a name for himself. Captain Hamilton recruited his own artillery company of English, Irish, Scottish, Scotch-Irish, and some German, including a prized first sergeant and zealous, young cannoneers of the "Provincial Company of Artillery" from New York. After studying everything about artillery that he could get his hands on, young Hamilton early gained an exceptionally high level of expertise in commanding the "sole" artillery company of New York. Because he was an immigrant and knew hard times in the Caribbean, Hamilton felt no prejudice for foreigners, including the German sergeant that he advocated his promotion to lieutenant, which was granted despite violation of hierarchical and traditional class customs. Here, along the high ground north of Trenton, Hamilton's young Teutonic gunners, including immigrants who identified with their West Indian commander, very likely now contemplated the irony of hurling death and destruction upon their fellow countrymen on the low ground below them.

Yet basking in the renown that garnered early recognition, Hamilton had been one of the first Americans of the revolution to unlimber a cannon in liberty's defense. Early rising to the fore, he covered the army's rear during the withdrawal north from New York City, after the disastrous defeat on Long Island. Hamilton's steadfast battlefield performances, including at Harlem Heights and White Plains, early attracted Washington's attention, who bestowed greater challenges upon the impetuous West Indian. Hamilton was an able drillmaster, transforming his artillery command into a well-trained and disciplined unit, which had caught first Greene's and then Washington's eye.

Before the showdown at Trenton, the young captain's finest day as a battery commander had come in protecting the rear of Washington's withdrawing army with a defiant stand on elevated terrain opposite the Raritan River crossing, where the wooden bridge had been destroyed by the retiring Americans, at New Brunswick on November 29, 1776. Here, in ensuring Howe's forces were unable to cross the fordable river, the spunky Hamilton held the pursuing British and Hessians, including killing of Captain Friedrich Karl von Weitershausen of the Knyphausen Regiment, which he now faced once again at Trenton, at bay. Deployed in good firing positions on the elevated south bank, Hamilton's cannon roared defiance across the Raritan River, buying precious time for Washington's army to retreat safely to Trenton and then to escape across the Delaware.

The boyish-looking captain, embodying an odd mix of wise philosopher and youthful daredevil, who always relished the thrill of combat as much as lively philosophical debate with the brightest and most enlightened minds, had played the Continental Army's vital role as Horatio at the bridge on the sluggish Raritan, an Algonquian name. Most importantly, by the time of the dramatic showdown at Trenton to decide America's fate, Hamilton had molded his artillery unit into a model of discipline and an elite command that Washington could depend upon in a crisis situation.

Despite his intense, scholarly ways, this young West Indian, ever an enigma, was also a carefree dandy and a dashing ladies' man. Hamilton's free-wheeling dancing for three hours with General Greene's pretty, vivacious wife Catharine (Caty), who was fourteen years younger than her husband, was eventually destined to raise a good many eyebrows and rumors at headquarters. This brazen, open flirtation certainly was no way to endear the ever-opportunistic young man (then on Washington's staff) to her sensitive, non-dancing, and former Quaker husband, who now had Hamilton and his New York artillery unit in his Second Division. Nevertheless, Hamilton's widespread appeal stemmed from a blend of audacity and courage, bordering on recklessness, both on and off the battlefield. His ardent, simultaneous pursuit of glory and pretty ladies, married or not, earned him a mixture of envy and jealousy among his many less romantically skilled peers. For a host of noteworthy personal qualities and in consideration of his youthful appearance, chestnut-colored hair, and slender build, Hamilton was widely known throughout the Continental Army by the endearing sobriquet "The Little Lion."[23]

Demonstrating wisdom beyond his years in regard to his strategic thinking and in striking contrast to most army leaders, Hamilton early advocated the wisdom of waging guerrilla warfare, which was now represented in the strike on Trenton: "The circumstances of our country put it in our power to evade a pitched battle [and] It would be better policy to harass and exhaust the soldiery by frequent skirmishes and incursions. . . ."[24] Symbolically, even in Trenton's blowing snows, Hamilton was yet inspired by ancient military heroics made famous in Plutarch's classic *Lives of Noble Grecians and Romans,* including Caesar.[25]

Washington's hardworking secretary on his headquarters staff, Lieutenant Tench Tilghman, a wealthy Philadelphia merchant and another young bachelor and ladies' man who could never keep up (like most others) with Hamilton's frantic pace of bedroom conquests and smitten admirers, sarcastically referred to the energetic, fun-loving New Yorker as "the little saint," which had nothing to do with the West Indian's Presbyterian faith that reflected his Scottish heritage. Now with his New York six-pounders deployed for action on the high ground at the head of Queen Street, "The Little Lion" was about to enjoy his finest day.[26]

In a dramatic meeting between two natural leaders on the field of strife, Colonel Rall, age fifty, was about to taste the artillery wrath of this young "Little Lion," who was an ever-aggressive, new generation warrior. Ironically, Rall was also known as "The Lion" for his sheer ferocity and courage in vanquishing American rebels with his bayonet-wielding Grenadiers, who never had been beaten. Here at Trenton, despite their age differences and in mutually battling for what they believed was right, Rall and Hamilton were very much kindred spirits in the searing heat of combat.[27]

Captain Hamilton's earlier—although seemingly premature at the time— astute analysis about the inner resolve of America's homespun revolutionaries (now the key to Washington's success) was now fully demonstrated all around him on the snowy field of Trenton: "there is a certain enthusiasm in liberty, that makes human nature rise above itself in acts of bravery and heroism."[28]

After Captain Hamilton and his thirty-six New York artillerymen quickly deployed their two six-pounders across the high ground at Queen Street's head, these Empire State guns were soon ready for immediate firing because all touch holes on cannon barrels had been well protected by the gunners and were now dry. Consequently, these New York cannon were now moisture-free only because of the use of metal plugs (tompions) which would not expand to get stuck in barrel vents, like wooden ones, during inclement weather conditions.

These protective devices had been kept tightly in place by Hamilton's New Yorkers during the treacherous crossing and the long march south toward the stormy unknown. And with ample ammunition, which had been kept dry in sturdy artillery ammunition carts, Washington was able to place six guns, commanded by two of his most promising artillery officers, Forrest and Hamilton, in excellent firing positions at the heads of both King and Queen Streets, respectively. Ignoring the steady cascade of snow flurries driven by a harsh northeast wind, New York artillerymen hurriedly rammed down charges of black powder, and then solid iron shot down cannon barrels. Working briskly, they then primed their powder charges. Eager New York gunners lit matches for firing and stood beside their cannon in pre-assigned position, waiting for the word to open up. Either Washington or Knox gave the eagerly awaited order to Hamilton to fire down into the valley below.

Situated in ideal firing positions, Forrest and Hamilton's cannon, aligned close together from right to left, or west to east, now blasted away as one. Both fast-working batteries, one from Pennsylvania and New York fired down both King and Queen Streets, respectively, from their high ground perches with authority. Each well-directed blast from Forrest's cannon, hurling iron balls down King Street, and Hamilton's artillery, sending shells down Queen Street, caused more confusion among the Hessians, still disorganized and half-stunned from the first shock of Washington's surprise attack, who were attempting to rally as best they could. Firing rapidly at targets of opportunity, the row of American cannon bucked and roared in quick succession with a rapidity that must have caused Washington and Knox to smile to themselves with a comforting satisfaction.

Most effective against infantrymen forming in Trenton's snowy streets were the exploding shells from Forrest's five and a half-inch howitzers. These projectiles dispersed a hail of iron fragments after exploding in midair. Raining death from above, these overhead shell-bursts were demoralizing to the Hessians exposed in the open. Just as Hamilton had been "one of the first Americans of the War of Independence to unlimber a cannon," so he now fired the first cannon shot to scream down Queen Street toward Trenton, heading for members of Major Dechow's Knyphausen Regiment. All the while, Forrest's and Hamilton's cannon thundered as one, then were quickly reloaded once they were rolled back into place by strong-armed artillerymen, after the guns recoiled with each fiery blast. Whistling cannonballs and iron fragments from exploding shells showered over Trenton's center and above the Hessians, issuing death from above.

In essence by early securing the strategic heights north of town, Washington had already outflanked the Hessian position at Trenton with the upper, or left, arm of his pincer movement not only because he had gained the high ground, but also, and more importantly, because so much of Knox's artillery had been so quickly unlimbered in excellent firing positions perpendicular to the two parallel arteries that led north-south through Trenton's length. And consequently, the only way that the Hessians now could possibly win today was by counterattacking north up the main thoroughfares to push the Americans off their commanding perch and capture Forrest and Hamilton's artillery, which now roared unimpeded from the head of King and Queen Streets.[29] All the while and with calm assurance as if he was back reading military books in his beloved London Book Shop in Boston, Knox continued to demonstrate America's good fortune that he from "the very first campaign [had been] entrusted with the command of the artillery, and it has turned out that it could not have been placed in better hands," penned one officer.[30]

As important as the fact that Hamilton's and Forrest's guns now blazed away as one from the head of King and Queen Streets, Washington had positioned his veteran infantry strike force—the right-center of Stirling's brigade and the right-rear of Stephen's Virginia brigade—at the key location on the high ground at King Street's head. Stirling's veteran Pennsylvania, Delaware, and Virginia troops were now in a good position not only to protect Forrest's blazing cannons, at the head of King Street, but also to charge down the sprawling length of King Street, the main artery leading through Trenton, into the town's heart and smash into the center of the Hessian position, if unleashed by Washington. To hit the Hessians on the left, or western, flank in the town's center, Washington ordered Greene's rightmost brigade, Mercer's Maryland, Connecticut, and Massachusetts troops, to undertake a wide enveloping movement. Mercer, consequently, led his thoroughly chilled troops farther south across the open fields of snow to King Street's west.

Most importantly, Washington had already made two key tactical decisions that would eventually pay high dividends: placing Stirling's hard-fighting Continental brigade astride King Street and one of his best regiments, the Third Virginia, on the brigade's right-center; and the right-rear of Stephen's Old Dominion brigade at the exact location on the snow-covered high ground at King Street's head to inflict the most damage in either defending the elevated terrain, or if Washington ordered an attack down King Street.

Despite the aristocratic title of lord that was not only a rare but also paradoxical distinction in Washington's Army, thoroughly infused with lofty republican ideology and sentiment, Lord Stirling was as combative as he was controversial in part because of his inflated claims to nobility and an earldom in Scotland. Demonstrating his high level of trust on other battlefields, Washington had previously relied upon Stirling in both independent and main army roles, including flank maneuvers. And most recently, Washington had occasionally employed Stirling and his Virginia, Delaware, and Pennsylvania veterans with complete confidence as the dependable rear-guard during the long withdrawal through New Jersey.

Although he knew that Stirling often found considerable "relief in [a good] toddy" which was understandable under the war's pressures and horrors, Washington possessed ample good reason to place his faith in this hard-fighting, transplanted aristocrat, who was a natural leader of men. Stirling first gained widespread recognition for his defiant actions at the battle of Long Island. When nearly surrounded after hundreds of Hessians and British soldiers gained his command's rear, at no tactical fault of his own, Stirling led half of the well-trained Marylanders of Colonel Smallwood's Maryland Continental battalion, consisting of "men of honour, family, and fortune," in a bold attack up the dusty Gowanus Road with fixed bayonets that sparkled in the summer sunshine.

With trademark audacity, he hurled around four hundred hardy Marylanders, wearing fringed "hunting shirts" mostly of linen, in a series of charges in a desperate attempt to break through Cornwallis's dense formations around the Vechte-Cortelyou House. More importantly, Stirling's "forlorn hope [and] suicide mission" bought precious time for thousands of Washington's trapped soldiers to escape to the safety of the high ground Brooklyn defenses. In battling against the odds, Smallwood's Maryland soldiers had "fought and fell like Romans," with more than 250 Marylanders killed on bloody August 27, 1776, and more than a hundred men wounded and captured. Stirling's unforgettable combat performance in fighting "like a wolf" against the odds garnered Washington's admiration for such "brave fellows." On December 26 at Trenton, Stirling no longer possessed these tough Maryland survivors, because Lieutenant Colonel Ware's First Maryland Continental Regiment now served in Mercer's brigade. However, he yet retained his tenacious fighting qualities which Washington so admired.[31]

Because of his own personal humiliation with his capture at Long Island, Lord Stirling felt an urgent desire to redeem his personal honor on the battlefield. He, therefore, was now determined to inflict upon the Hessians of Trenton a thorough "drubbing."[32] The handsome Stirling, at a vigorous fifty-one and almost Colonel Rall's age, now possessed only around 670 fighting men of his seasoned brigade. Stirling's command consisted of the Third Virginia Continental Infantry, under Colonel "Old Joe Gourd" Weedon, the First Pennsylvania Rifle Regiment, now led capably by Colonel Ennion Williams, First Virginia Continental Regiment, and the First Delaware Continental Regiment under Ireland-born Colonel John Haslet. Basking in this representative role, Haslet now commanded the only Delaware Continental troops, the legendary "Delaware Blues" because of the color of their uniforms, in Washington's Army. This feisty Son of Erin had led these Delaware Continentals, with consummate skill and "conspicuous gallantry" since the battle of Long Island, where they were among Washington's few uniformed troops when they fought beside Smallwood's Marylanders. Haslet then gained additional recognition for having played a key protective role in recently covering the army's rear during Washington's withdrawal to Trenton.

For the rigors of winter campaigning, Stirling's troops were now in overall bad shape, however. On December 13, Major Ennion Williams, a prosperous, handsome, and proper "gentleman" with piercing blue eyes that displayed a mixture of warmth and empathy, lamented how his "poor Distressed soldiers" of his First Pennsylvania Rifle Regiment were in need of "Shirts, Shoes, Breeches, Waistcoats, Coats & Stockings, and [of course] Blankets." But dependable and top quality regimental leadership helped to partially make up for such glaring deficiencies among Stirling's troops. But even superior leadership was not a permanent equalizer. Two of Stirling's finest regimental commanders were Haslet and twenty-two-year-old Captain John Fleming, a young and "gallant officer" of Scottish heritage from Henrico County, Virginia, whose descendants had first migrated to the Jamestown Colony. Fleming now led the First Virginia Continental Regiment. He would not survive the battle of Princeton in barely a week.[33]

Just as Stirling's brigade was aligned in a good position to protect Forrest's Pennsylvania guns on this poorly lit morning, so Stephen's Virginia brigade was also situated to safeguard Forrest's guns after having been aligned mostly to the west. With its right aligned around the head of King Street to the Third Virginia's left-rear and at Queen Street's head, Stephen's Virginia brigade was also now formed up in the best position to either lead the advance of Greene's Second Division straight down Queen Street into the town's center or to extend the Old Dominion brigade's left, now situated to the left of Queen Street, farther east to link up with Fermoy's right flank.[34]

All in all and most important for the mission of overwhelming the Rall brigade, Washington could not have possessed a better officer—his former second-in-command of his Virginia Regiment during the French and Indian War—to lead the hard-fighting Virginia brigade than General Stephen. In fact, the Trenton Campaign was Stephen's twelfth military campaign during the last twenty-two years. The Scotsman's command experience went all the way back to 1755, when he had skillfully led Virginians during Braddock's fiasco in 1755.

Coinciding with an aggressive leadership style, the strong-willed Stephen seemingly had been always defiant of authority, British or colonial, including Washington himself. He was one of the most contradictory, but best, brigade commanders in Washington's Army by this time. Single-minded and focused, Stephen often proved absolutely ruthless in the quest to obtain a goal, especially on the battlefield. Stephen waged a holy war against the Mother Country that was also a very personal one for him. When Lord North, the most anti-colonial official in London, boasted that "he has a Rod in piss for the Colony of Virginia" and Maryland, Stephen had responded with a typical Celtic flair and sense of humor: "Could I see him in America! In Spite of all the Armies of Commissioners, Custom house officers & Soldiers, I would make the meanest American I know, piss upon him." Stephen had long made his sound tactical battlefield decisions on his own, excelling at independent action. In February 1776, he was appointed the colonel of the Fourth Virginia Continental Regiment by the fourth Virginia Convention, after more than two decades of military service. Stephen was promoted to brigadier general in early September 1776, enjoying Thomas Jefferson's full support.

Last October when America's prospects were much brighter, the Fourth, Fifth, and Sixth Virginia Continental Regiments—Washington's crack vanguard brigade—had originally departed Virginia to reinforce Washington's Army. And no regiment of Washington's task force was better disciplined than Stephen's own Fourth Virginia Continental Regiment. Marching north to join Washington until the Virginian's repeated defeats around New York City altered the strategic situation, the Virginia brigade, of three regiments, was then assigned to remain in position along the Delaware River. Ironically, the Board of War ordered Stephen and his brigade to Trenton. Here, they became intimately familiar with the quaint river town and the surrounding terrain, including the high ground where they now stood near King Street's head: another reason why Washington chose these hardened veterans from his home state to lead the advance on Trenton from McConkey's Ferry.

When Stephen's soldiers had marched north to join Washington, more than three hundred sick Virginians, ill-clothed and unprepared for winter's approach, were left behind in Trenton to recuperate. Stephen's more than five hundred Virginia troops, including good fighting men armed with both small-caliber Long Rifles and larger-barrel, smoothbore muskets, had finally reached Washington Army at New Brunswick during the army's retreat toward the Delaware. Almost immediately, Washington's had effectively employed Stephen and his reliable Old Dominion veterans as rearguard troops during the retreat to Trenton, including to guard the Delaware crossing in the face of Cornwallis's advance. The seasoned Fourth Virginia was under the able command of Lieutenant Colonel Robert Lawson, who now led 229 soldiers from Sussex, Isle of Wight, Charlotte, Berkeley, Price Edward, Southhampton, Brunswick, Nansemond, Surry, Princess Anne Counties, Virginia, and the Borough of

Norfolk. Lawson's Fourth Virginia was now the largest regiment of Stephen's finely tuned brigade of experienced Continentals.[35]

A proudly self-proclaimed "lover of liberty," Stephen was eager for the chance to thrash the hated Hessians. He had fought against Indians, French, Canadians, former black slaves in British service, and the English in red uniforms, but never Germans before. In righteous indignation, he yet fumed over his fast-fading republic's sad plight that he placed in Biblical-like terms: "The Enemy like locusts Sweep the Jersies with the Besom of destruction [and] They to the disgrace of a Civilized Nation Ravish the fair Sex, from the Age of Ten to Seventy."[36]

Stephen was even more motivated to perform exceptionally well this morning for another reason as well. Only a short time before on the march to Trenton, he had just suffered the stinging rebuke from an angry Washington, who only mistakenly believed that the element of surprise had been lost because of Captain Wallis's strike—unauthorized by Washington but sanctioned by Stephen—on the advanced Hessian picket post along the Pennington Road late on Christmas evening. As Wallis's regimental commander, he now wanted to wipe away the stain of that supreme embarrassment. In an attempt to ward off the biting cold and the commander-in-chief's rebuke, Stephen might have taken a deep sip of rum or whisky, of which he was occasionally fond, from a personal flask, just before meeting the foe in the final showdown at Trenton.[37]

Meanwhile, Colonel Charles Scott, commanding the Fifth Virginia Continental Regiment of Stephen's Old Dominion State brigade, briskly passed along the foremost ranks of his threadbare soldiers, who continued to suffer severely in Arctic-like blasts of cold air sweeping over the heights that overlooked Trenton. He now gave last minute advice and encouragement to his Virginia boys, whose half-frozen fingers, without gloves or mittens, ensured that firing weapons at Hessian targets would be difficult this morning: "Take care now and fire low. Bring down your pieces [and] Fire at their legs [because] One man wounded in the leg is better than a dead one for it takes two more to carry him off and there is three gone. Leg them, damn 'em. I say, leg them!"[38]

Fortunately, by this time for America's fortunes, Washington's men had been transformed by the war and its horrors that seemed to have no end. They fully realized, like their commander-in-chief, that a more ruthless kind of war was now necessary for not only an ever-elusive victory for American arms, but also for an army and nation's survival. Therefore, given their desperate situation, Washington's soldiers instinctively understood that something entirely new was now required of them to reap the war's most surprising success. All of the old established rules and rigid guidelines of conduct from the time-honored practices of conventional eighteenth-century warfare as conducted by well-educated aristocratic gentlemen from Europe's great capitals no longer applied on this snowy morning at Trenton. Washington himself already fully realized as much, revealing how a harsher way of thinking was now abso-lutely necessary to secure victory over so many of these crack Hessian troops, because the fortunes of war had already turned so drastically against America.

Washington's means of waging war, therefore, now possessed a much rougher and harder edge out of urgent necessity, because there was literally no tomorrow if yet another defeat was suffered by what little was left of the Continental Army. As he had emphasized in his orders for the attack on Trenton to Stephen's vanguard and perhaps as he now reminded his foremost Virginia Continentals, that if the Hessians took defensive positions in Trenton's houses and then if they were "annoy'd from the houses [then] set them on fire."[39]

Clearly, Washington had been seriously thinking ahead about what would be necessary to win victory at Trenton, including what was entirely new to him, the complexities and unique challenges of urban warfare for which there was no rule book or military manual: not unlike the fact that there were no rules for launching an attack in winter. Such no nonsense orders indicated that Washington fully understood that if his troops engaged in house-to-house fighting, then too much precious time, men, and momentum would be lost. Even though Washington was about to engage in the American Army's first urban battle and its greatest challenge—urban combat—for military com-manders to this day, he had already considered the unique requirements of urban combat and issued orders accordingly. Washington's tactical achieve-ment in having caught the Rall brigade so thoroughly by surprise was the fact that the Germans were unable to utilize the town for defensive purposes. Almost always an ally of urban area defenders, even the adverse weather condi-tions, which usually sapped an attacker's morale and strength, had been utilized to Washington's overall advantage. Therefore, in the end, Washington actually now possessed a better chance of achieving success in attacking an urban area or town, which ancient Chinese warfare theorist Sun Tzu had sternly advised "do not assault it."[40]

Most of all, Washington also realized that success now lay in maintaining tactical flexibility and the initiative, retaining the ability to react quickly to exploit any new developing battlefield situation. Demonstrating more versatility and flexibility as during the perilous crossing of the Delaware, Glover's mariners now pushed forward along the River Road as infantry with Sullivan's First Division column, serving as capably as infantrymen as boatmen. Fortunately, Washington benefitted from a long list of experienced brigade and regimental commanders, such as Glover, who possessed the ability to analytically and accurately judge tactical situations for themselves once unleashed on the battlefield.[41] Even more important, Washington now possessed the coveted central axiom for success at Trenton: "Soldiers and leaders committed to urban combat . . . require inordinately high morale, steadfast will, and patience to endure the stress and grueling conditions of the urban environment."[42]

Most significantly for today's fortunes, Washington realized that he now had the Hessian brigade right where he wanted it—on lower ground and unprepared for his attack—after having maneuvered skillfully to place his forces, including a good many cannon, into ideal positions on dominant terrain higher than the enemy's position. Washington, consequently, now looked with satisfaction upon his lengthy row of artillery firing with rapidity down icebound King and Queen Streets. Meanwhile, the Hessians, wearing their tall, brass-plated miter caps, of Rall's Regiment and the von Lossberg Regiment continued to pour from "alarm houses," on King Street and private quarters, rushing into formation amid the falling snow, noise, and confusion.

Thanks to touch holes of iron and bronze cannon barrels having been kept dry by well-trained artillerymen after so much effort to ensure that tompions had remained in place throughout the night, the roar of Knox's cannon echoed louder over Trenton. Additional iron cannon balls of Forrest's six-pounders were hurled down King Street, screaming overhead and causing havoc. In a letter to his lovely wife Lucy, Colonel Knox told how: "here, succeeded a scene of war of which I had often conceived, but never saw before [as] The hurry, fright, and confusion of the enemy was (not) unlike that which will be when the last trump[et] shall sound [because the Hessians] endeavoured [sic] to form in the streets, the heads of which we had previously the possession of with cannon and howitzers."[43]

Mounted on his warhorse near Washington with other staff members, Colonel Fitzgerald, who was yet as much of an Irishman (in the country less than a decade) as a true American, felt even more confident for success after Captain "Forrest [who was the senior artillery officer among Knox's long-arm commanders had] wheeled six of his cannon [his own four guns and Hamilton's two six-pounders] into position to sweep both streets," King and Queen, and now blasted away as one.[44]

Then, with time of the essence, Washington and Knox rushed additional guns forward to gain the high ground, including Captain Baumann's three three-pounders. These newly arrived guns were manned by eighty well-trained "Yorkers" led by Lieutenants Joseph Crane, George Fleming, Jacob Reed, and Cornelius Swartwout. The last artillery unit in Greene's column, Baumann's New York guns and the artillery unit's wooden ammunition carts rolled east over the snowy heights, now covered with a thinning layer of sulphurous smoke that was pushed steadily northeastward by the blustery wind sweeping off the Delaware, from Knox's blazing guns. Positioned to anchor the artillery line's left, Baumann's three cannon extended the lengthening row of Knox's artillery to the east, while Captain Forrest's Philadelphia cannon, big six-pounder and five and a half-inch howitzers, held the right end of Washington's noisy alignment of artillery.

Washington, feeling more confident with each passing minute, now had nine artillery pieces set up in excellent firing positions, aligned across high ground, and rapidly firing down both King and Queen Streets to create more chaos and confusion among the Hessians in Trenton. The uplifting sound of the angry bark of Knox's artillery pieces settled into a fast, steady rhythm that sounded like the sweet voices of the Angels to Washington.[45]

Here, on the windswept heights amid the deluge of snow and ice, it can only be speculated what Captain Baumann, who had been born at the old Medieval town of Frankfort-on-the-Main in Hesse-Cassel, in today's west-central Germany, might have felt during that eerie moment when he first barked out orders for his New York guns to open fire on his fellow countrymen below him. After all, these fast-forming Hessian troops included soldiers who hailed from his own picturesque hometown and bustling, ancient commercial and financial center situated on the right bank of the wide Main River. Baumann might have well momentarily reflected upon how shabby a wartime, half-deserted Trenton, appearing almost rustic with its mostly small, wood-frame houses, appeared compared to the cultured city of Frankfort-on-the-Main, or how the mysterious hands of fate had brought him to this obscure place and so suddenly placed him in a key combat situation in which destroying his fellow countrymen was now his foremost priority.[46]

Meanwhile, below the right flank and southwest of Stirling's brigade, Mercer's Maryland, Connecticut, and Massachusetts troops were aligned on high ground slightly closer to Trenton. They were ordered to close the sizeable gap on Trenton's west, and as effectively as Fermoy's brigade, of only two regiments, had blocked the Princeton-Trenton Road northeast of Trenton. After advancing south down gently sloping ground on the west side of the north-south running Petty's Run and parallel to the little watercourse, Mercer's troops halted on snow-covered terrain amid the snow flurries that obscured visibility. Here, Mercer's veterans aligned in a neat formation on the windswept open ground on Trenton's west side.

On Mercer's orders, they then smartly shifted east to face toward King Street and Trenton's western outskirts: the vulnerable left flank of Colonel Rall's troops now busily aligning in King Street. Without wasting time that was now precious and with a key tactical mission to fulfill, Mercer ordered his boys forward once again. They surged over the snowy terrain that gradually dropped toward the lower-lying Trenton. With the Scotland-born Mercer leading the way, the Continentals pushed east down the gently sloping ground and headed toward the Hessian brigade's left flank without meeting opposition, advancing upon the town from the west. With flintlocks on shoulders and in high spirits, Mercer's confident troops surged through the white, open fields on the run, kicking up little tufts of snow behind them. Swarming closer to Trenton's western outskirts, the emboldened soldiers of Mercer's brigade pushed down the gentle slope.

The Twentieth Connecticut Continental Regiment, under Windham, Connecticut-born Colonel John Durkee, a French and Indian War and Bunker Hill veteran who possessed the unusual of nickname of "bold bean hiller," Lieutenant Colonel Ware's First Maryland Continental Regiment, Lieutenant Colonel Moses Rawlings's Maryland Rifle Battalion, Yale College graduate Colonel Phillip Burr Bradley's Connecticut State Troops, and Colonel Israel Hutchinson's Twenty-Seventh Continental Regiment then splashed across the rain-swollen waters of Petty's Run on the double.

Flowing straight south to enter the Delaware, this little creek located just beyond the town's western outskirts was now running over its ice-encrusted banks. After surging across Petty's Run and with silk battle flags flying in the snow flurries under a darkened sky, Mercer's troops continued to push relentlessly toward Rall's vulnerable left flank on King Street. In crossing Petty's Run as in journeying across the Delaware, these veteran Continentals got their feet, already numb with cold, wet once again. Because of such a lengthy advance across so much open ground blanketed in snow, Mercer's brigade struck later than Sullivan's to the south.[47]

Washington's surging troops, pumped with adrenaline and optimism for success, became increasingly especially eager to reap "a noble revenge," because

Trenton presented the best opportunity to do so. Having long heard throughout London that Washington's soldiers were nothing but "cowards and poltroons," one American expressed a pervasive view that now existed within the hearts and minds of Washington's often-defeated Continentals, who felt that now was the time to redeem themselves and set the record straight once and for all: "It is my earnest wish [that] the despised Americans may convince these conceited islanders [of England] that without regular standing armies, our Continent can furnish brave soldiers."[48]

Chapter V

Meeting Washington's Surprise Attack

Amid the chaotic swirl of the hectic activity now dominating the icy streets of Trenton, no one was doing more to organize the thoroughly surprised Rall Brigade than Lieutenant Jacob Piel. Age thirty-four, Piel demonstrated exactly why Colonel Rall had appointed—a wise decision—this energetic lieutenant as his brigade major as soon he had taken brigade command on September 15, 1776. Upon hearing the first crackle of gun fire by the foremost Virginia Continentals upon the band of Pennington Road pickets northwest of town, he had been the first Hessian officer who attempted to galvanize initial resistence on King Street. In this crisis situation, Rall could not have possessed a more capable officer than his own adjutant, who was an esteemed von Lossberg Regimental officer now serving as adjutant for the entire Rall brigade.

Adjutant Piel's tireless efforts began early this morning and now paid dividends. He had been up early, ignoring the piercing cold and the storm's bitter wrath. Just after 5:00 a.m., despite the darkness, Piel had first departed his cozy sleeping quarters at the Rebecca Coxe House on King Street. The Coxe House was located next to Rall's King Street headquarters in the large-frame Stacy Potts's house, just to the south. Meanwhile, other von Lossberg fusiliers of Piel's regiment were quartered in the town's northern end.

A bachelor born in flourishing port city of Bremen located on the River Weser and near the North Sea, Piel had ventured out into the snowstorm on his own initiative long before the first shot was fired in anger to the northwest. Almost as if some premonition had told him that all hell was about to break loose, he had even ordered Rall's grenadiers and Lieutenant Fischer's two Rall Regiment guns of the aborted morning patrol to the South Trenton Ferry, which Major Dechow had earlier cancelled, to go back to Dechow, the Knyphausen Regiment's commander, and ask for new instructions. By this time, Dechow, as the new officer of the day, had recently departed his regimental headquarters on

Queen Street to take up new and more comfortable King Street quarters at the guardhouse just fifty paces from Rall's King Street headquarters.

Clearly, the astute Piel had wisely hoped to now compensate for Dechow's obvious tactical error in having cancelled the usual 4:00 a.m. morning patrol. Even more, the conscientious, almost prophetic, adjutant had attempted to wake Rall before 6:00 a.m., when it was yet dark, but to no avail. Then, around 7:00 a.m. and an hour before Washington struck, Adjutant Piel made another failed effort to rouse his commander at the colonel's headquarters.[1]

Therefore, when the first shots between Wiederhold's pickets and Stephen's Virginia vanguard had exploded around the Howell cooper house along the Pennington Road at 8:00 a.m., Lieutenant Piel immediately flew into action. Trying not to slip and fall on the icy street, as he was wearing a fine pair of knee-high leather boots like other Hessian officers, Piel sprinted across King Street as best he could.

After navigating the slick street, Piel then galvanized Lieutenant Johann Heinrich Sternickel's guard detachment of thirty men of the Rall Regiment, who were stationed at the headquarters watch-house, or alarm house, on King Street near Rall's headquarters. As a cruel fate would have it, Sternickel would be soon cut down this morning and later die as a prisoner-of-war far from his Germanic homeland. Then the ten other Hessian soldiers poured from their sleeping quarters in private houses along King Street, joining the aroused guard detachment amid the steadily falling snow.

Ironically, Lieutenant Piel had initially organized this group of around forty men in the hope of advancing up King Street to reinforce Wiederhold's and Altenbockum's hard-pressed pickets on the Pennington Road to the northwest. Piel realized that the band of Hessian pickets had their hands full as revealed by the escalating volume of fire rattling ever-louder over the snow-covered heights overlooking the town, and growing closer. Then, the busy adjutant raced back across King Street to the Potts's house. Frantically "hammering" away, Piel banged on his commander's headquarter's door with an urgency that could only mean that serious trouble was brewing for the Rall brigade this Thursday morning. Finally awakened and in his bedclothes, a disheveled Rall opened a second story window of Potts's house. After having been finally awakened, Rall was informed by the shouting Piel of the shocking news that he could hardly believe: Trenton was under direct attack from multiple directions by large numbers of Americans, who had so suddenly appeared out of the snow-storm and now seemed to be swarming everywhere.[2]

After departing Rall's headquarters, located on King Street's west side nearly opposite the Anglican, or English, Church, where some von Lossberg fusiliers were quartered, Adjutant Piel then dashed back to his own quarters at the Coxe House. Here, he aroused twenty-nine-year-old Lieutenant Herman Zoll, with a dozen years of military experience and a stern stickler for details, who was now the von Lossberg Regiment's acting adjutant. A reliable, unmarried officer from Rinteln who had led fifty of his von Lossberg fusiliers in a headlong bayonet charge that had cut down a good many Americans and netted sixty-four surprised prisoners at the battle of Long Island last August, Zoll had taken Piel's place as regimental adjutant.

The combined effect of the Hessian soldiers' winter night's sleep, the river valley's depth at Trenton, the howling wind, and the snowstorm's intensity had initially combined to help to muffle all sounds, even the first burst of gunfire northwest of town, to play a part in initially delaying the garrison's arousal and overall response to its greatest threat to date. As in both Rall and Zoll's cases, many Hessian soldiers, worn down by fatigue from past alarms, had remained fast asleep mostly in evacuated homes on both sides of King Street, even after the first hot skirmishing broke out between the Hessian pickets and Stephen's Virginians along the Pennington Road. Therefore, some deep-sleeping German soldiers had to be vigorously awakened from their slumbers after having failed to emerge from their sleeping quarters, especially in cozy private homes in contrast to the "alarm houses," even after the initial eruption of gun fire to the northwest.[3]

As if the very embodiment of Frederick the Great, Colonel Rall rose to the challenge in splendid fashion after having been abruptly awakened. To his utter dismay, he had been literally caught napping by the same fighting men who he had long casually and loudly denounced as nothing but "a bunch of farmers" masquerading as real soldiers. Rall quickly recovered from the shock of Washington's surprise attack. After hastily putting on his resplendent blue uniform coat of a full Hessian colonel, he grabbed his cherished saber that had presided over so many battlefield successes.

Colonel Rall then dashed from his second story bedroom, raced downstairs in his leather boots, and burst out the wooden door of Potts's house. He then emerged into the noisy confusion of King Street, where chaos yet reigned supreme. Here, excited Hessian officers ran back and forth, attempting to assemble their troops in the slippery street as best they could. Rall immediately attempted to rally his men in the open street between the row of King Street houses, as if still battling against Islam's holy warriors on behalf of an Orthodox Christianity and Catherine the Great during that seemingly endless struggle between Muslims and Russian Slavs on Europe's troubled eastern edge.

The sheer magnitude of the chaos that greeted Rall, who could hardly believe his eyes, in King Street was staggering while the heavy shower of snow and sleet continued to pour down. With Knox's cannon roaring from the heights north of town, German officers shouted orders, half-dazed soldiers rushed into line, and frightened horses neighed loudly in a scene of perfect confusion. Around a dozen Hessian drummer boys of all three regiments furiously pounded on their drums. Meanwhile, Captain Forrest's six-pounders and five and a half-inch howitzers busily hurled cannonballs and exploding shells, respectively, down King Street. Spraying a hail of iron fragments in all directions, fiery explosions caused havoc among the fast-forming German ranks amid the din.

Meanwhile, additional Hessians continued to stumble from the dark houses on both sides of King Street, spilling out into the icy street and chaos. But Rall was not deterred by a most vexing and confusing situation that would have completely overwhelmed a less determined commander. After doing all he could accomplish to organize the troops just outside his headquarters, Rall hastened down King Street to rally additional men. Although never been caught by such surprise before, Rall rose splendidly to the challenge. Here, below his headquarters on King Street, Rall attempted to organize his grenadiers for action. While the row of Washington's angry artillery boomed like thunder to the north, additional Rall Regiment grenadiers tumbled from private houses and from such large wooden structures as the Trenton post office and the Bull Head and City Taverns, a two-story brick building, and out into the teeth of the fierce northeaster and Knox's stinging cannon fire.

According to prearranged plan, about half of the regiment's blue-uniformed grenadiers gathered dutifully at the Rall Regiment's predesignated rallying point located just south of Rall's headquarters near the town's center. However, other well-trained grenadiers, especially the younger German soldiers and exhausted men, whose morale had sunk to new lows in recent days, were panic-stricken by the sheer shock of Washington's surprise attack. Amid the tumult, these shaken Hessians now headed south down King Street, making fast for the Assunpink bridge to escape, and no one could stop them.

With the situation now so critical and time to recover from Washington's surprise attack growing shorter, Rall's steady leadership in the greatest crisis situation ever faced by his troops was now vital in rallying his grenadier regiment. Rall knew that he had to get his own grenadier regiment formed for battle as soon as possible, after suffering the ignominious fate of a career soldier: a professional and experienced officer having been completely surprised by the most contemptible of opponents, a Virginia planter who lovingly tilled the soil like the ancient Roman aristocrat and republican war hero Cincinnatus, and his homespun soldiers.

Meanwhile, Lieutenants Piel and Zoll provided more timely assistance to their recently awakened brigade commander by attempting to sort everything out in the confusion. After having been awakened by Piel and obeying Rall's shouted orders, Zoll sprinted across King Street to the Anglican Church, which was located across the icy street from Rall's headquarters. Here, he awakened the brigade's bleary-eyed artillerymen, who were mostly quartered in the wooden church and also in a private house near the King Street alarm house.

Indeed, the fact that "foreign" troops were quartered in Trenton's four churches—Anglican (English), later known as St. Michael's Episcopal Church, on King Street, the Presbyterian Church on Second Street and Queen Street, the Society of Friends (Quaker) Church on Third Street, and the Methodist Church (where the British light horse had been quartered and was now empty) located at the corner of Queen Street and Fourth Street and nearly opposite the west end of Church Alley—was another outrageous sacrilege (only one of many) by the enemy that incensed pious Americans, both military and civilian. Knowing that the Rall Regiment's two bronze artillery pieces had to be placed in action as soon as possible, Zoll helped to organize the drowsy Rall Regiment's gunners, who had been asleep in full uniforms unlike the artillerymen of Rall's other two regiments, as well as the fusilier troops of Francis, or Franziscus, Scheffer's old company of the von Lossberg Regiment, as they were likewise quartered in the so called English Church.

Meanwhile, north of Rall's grenadiers, the von Lossberg fusiliers likewise continued to pour into slippery King Street from their sleeping quarters in private homes at the town's northern end, or the "right wing of the cantonment," and mostly in the wooden and brick houses on King Street's east side, and from other nearby points scattered throughout snow-covered Trenton. Von Lossberg fusiliers of both von Loss and Scheffer Companies spilled out of the Anglican Church, leaving the safety of this once-serene, revered house of God to face Washington's seemingly enraged, screaming devils from hell, who had so suddenly descended upon them out of a raging winter storm. Companies had to be formed in line in order of their commander's seniority, a time-consuming process.

Five colorful, silk battle flags of the von Lossberg Regiment were hurriedly brought out into King Street and the falling snow by the faithful color bearers in the hope of inspiring the just-awakened troops, so that they could rally around them amid the noisy confusion. Among these von Lossberg Regimental banners were the white (Life) battle flag, which every regiment carried, and company flags, or the "Compagnie-Fahne." The Compangie-Fahne flag was proudly carried by each fusilier company. Among these brightly colored banners was also that of the Lieb (first) Company, or the Life Guard or Body Guard (Leibstandarte) company, which served as the commander's honor guard and always formed on the line's right. This silk battle flag of the elite guardian company, or "corps of guards," was known as "the Liebfahne." In addition, the Avancirfahne, or soverign's colors, was also placed at the formation's head. All the Hessian flags were distinguished by the imposing "golden lion (Lieb)" of Hesse in the center, reminding these Teutonic soldiers of their distant families and homeland for whose honor and reputation they now fought to uphold.

With a clattering of gear and a considerable amount of shouting from excited officers, who wore large mustaches that were stylish among the Germans unlike the Americans or British, those von Lossberg fusiliers quartered in the houses at the town's north end and above the Rall Regiment's grenadiers rushed into formation on ice-slick King Street. Facing their greatest challenge, these battle-hardened fusiliers were distinguished by bright red uniform coats that provided excellent targets to sharp-eyed Americans with Long Rifles.

Appearing almost like a ghostly apparition in the middle of King Street amid the swirling snow, Lieutenant Colonel Francis Scheffer had somehow mustered the strength to pull himself out of his sickbed when he heard the sounding of the first alarm. He had led the von Lossberg Regiment with skill since September 23, 1776 after the previous commander died of dysentery not long after landing on American soil. Scheffer had been first aroused from his sleep by Zoll's timely efforts. Although sick for the last five days, Scheffer had not been under qualified medical care at the brigade hospital at the Presbyterian Church on Second Street, just east of its intersection with Queen Street. Instead, like a good commander, he had dutifully remained at his King Street quarters, located just north of Rall's headquarters, and near where most of his von Lossberg fusiliers were housed.

Meanwhile, the von Lossbergers continued to form on King Street in the upper end of town. Each fusilier company assembled before its own quarters at the street's north end according to prearrangement. Exposed in the open air of King Street beside his troops, Scheffer shouted for Zoll to report immediately to Rall to obtain orders about what exactly to do next in this most disadvantageous of situations. First and foremost in facing the ultimate tactical dilemma, Lieutenant Colonel Scheffer needed to know where exactly to assign the von Lossberg fusiliers, who were yet coming together, and how best to deploy the troops.

With iron cannonballs from Forrest's Pennsylvania guns hurling through the air filled with dropping flakes of snow, Lieutenant Zoll dashed up to Rall just as the distressed colonel was mounting his skittish horse, which had been brought forth from its stable by an orderly. As if compensating for Scheffer's incapacity due to illness, Rall ordered Zoll to have the von Lossberg Regiment form at a specified point east of King Street. Most of all, he wanted to get the troops out of the middle of the snowy avenue—a nice, open field of fire for Forrest's sharp-eyed Pennsylvania gunners who were now firing with a fine precision—and then out of harm's way to escape the withering fire: a wise tactical decision because hundreds of troops remaining stationary and motionless in a neat formation on the open expanse of King Street was absolute folly, when the Hessian's legendary discipline was now transformed into a serious liability in such a disadvantageous situation.

Shouting additional orders after mounting his charger, Rall directed the von Lossberg fusiliers to align just off King Street in Church Ally—situated between, linking, and perpendicular to King and Queen Streets, and located a block north of the Anglican (or English) Church and almost directly across from Rall's headquarters. Colonel Rall, shouting at the top of his voice, pointed toward where he desired the von Lossberg Regiment to form. Here, about halfway between King and Queen Streets and just east of Rall's headquarters, the von Lossberg fusiliers sought meager, but adequate shelter, behind a row of wooden structures that stood on the north side of Church Alley, from two simultaneous storms, both the northeaster and Forrest's artillery fire streaming down King Street. Most importantly and as envisioned by the clear-thinking Rall, Scheffer's von Lossbergers now occupied a position close to King Street, just to the west, within an easy distance to support the fast-forming Rall Regiment positioned lower down on King Street just to the southwest. Toward King Street's head to the north, meanwhile, Captain

Altenbockum and his fusilier company were yet holding their advanced position, remaining absent from the regimental formation. Fighting on their own hook, the tactically astute captain and his pickets were separated from the von Lossberg Regiment after having decided not to retire down the street to rejoin their command.

Finally, the formations of two regiments of the Rall brigade gradually became more complete, after the sleeping quarters had been emptied of men, in the projectile-swept King Street sector. After Lieutenant Colonel Scheffer aligned the fusilier regiment's ranks in Church Alley to face north toward Washington's bellowing cannon, the von Lossbergers now looked straight into the teeth of not only Knox's hot artillery fire but also the driving sleet and snow: a decided disadvantage, especially if the Americans suddenly attacked down King Street from the north. Some of Washington's mounted officers, including Knox who must have worried about his wife Lucy and his family if killed in this battle, watching from the windswept heights believed incorrectly that the Lossberg Regiment, the northernmost of Rall's troops, had been swept entirely from King Street without realizing that they had merely redeployed east of King Street.

Besides bestowed with a measure of shelter from Forrest's well-directed artillery-fire, the von Lossberg Regiment also gained some added strength. Out of breath after their long dash on the double-quick north from the south side of Assunpink Creek, the von Lossberg fusiliers of the von Hanstein Company, led by Captain Friedrich Wilhelm von Benning, finally reached the regiment. This contingent hurriedly took position on the regiment's left wing, adjacent to the von Loss Company, at the west end of Church Alley near King Street. Lieutenant Colonel Scheffer's Lossbergers were proud of the lengthy, distinguished lineage of their elite fusilier regiment, which had been long headquartered in Rinteln, Hesse-Cassel, on the picturesque Weser River that flowed into the North Sea. The regiment's impressive combat record extended back to the 1600s and included the battle of Minden, northern Germany, in August 1759. These von Lossbergers were tough, reliable soldiers who knew how to kill rebels. Quite simply, they were the best fighters of the Rall brigade. Tenacious fighting men, these Lossbergers had been already hardened by prewar lives as lower class farmers and from months of arduous campaigning in a strange, new land that they called Amerika. Even more than Rall's grenadiers and contrary to the popular stereotype, Scheffer's von Lossberg fusiliers were the true elite troops of the crack Rall brigade.

To make sure that his verbal orders were not misunderstood in the noisy tumult of an escalating battle, Rall personally assisted in organizing the von Lossbergers, who were now situated just northeast of his northernmost grenadiers on King Street. Then Rall galloped a short distance down snow-packed King Street and down the slope toward the town's lower end, where four companies of Rall's grenadiers, under senior regimental commander Colonel Balthasar Brethauer, had been quartered in three large buildings designated by Rall as "alarm houses." Brethauser's battalion of four companies of the Rall Regiment had formed rapidly in the upper part of the lower town, benefitting from the fact that their designated "du jour" regiment was more fully prepared for action this early morning than its two sister regiments.

Fired from smoking guns and down the gradual slope, Knox's cannonballs that were no longer hurled at lucrative von Lossberg targets at a closer range smashed into the foremost troops of the Rall Regiment's northern battalion, while other projectiles whistled harmlessly overhead to unnerve less resolute Hessians: Washington's rude wake-up call for Rall and his grenadiers on this hellish morning. Besides a direct fire, Knox's meticulous, experienced gunners also unleashed a ricochet fire. With telling accuracy because this tactic eliminated over-shooting, they skipped six-pounder cannon shot off the snowy street—a natural bowling alley—before the Rall Regiment's dense ranks to bounce downhill and continue their destructive path into the midst of their blue-colored formation. Forrest's artillerymen watched the lethal effects with glee, after having correctly gauged the exact range for a deadly display of ricocheting rounds.

Here, just below Rall's two-story headquarters at Stacy Potts's house, Rall and Lieutenant Colonel Baltasar Bretthauser, Rall's right hand man, united the four grenadier companies in the lower town with the northernmost Rall Regiment companies positioned in formation on King Street. With both battalions now linked together, the disciplined Rall Regiment grenadiers were aligned in King Street in the northern part of the lower town just south of Rall's headquarters, to meet the anticipated attack from a yet unknown number of Americans. With his grenadiers in neat lines and braced for Washington's anticipated assault, Rall then led his own regiment a short distance up through the snow of King Street and straight through the hail of projectiles from Knox's booming guns.

Meanwhile, these battle-hardened grenadiers advanced with discipline while cannonballs and shells smashed into their ranks. To escape the incessant fire of Captain Forrest's six-pounders and five and a half-howitzers, as he had earlier done with the von Lossberg Regiment, Rall then adroitly shifted the foremost half (his northernmost battalion) of his grenadiers—east off King Street and into Pinkerton's Alley, a block below, or south, of Church Alley and the stationary von Lossberg Regiment. Once positioned in the Anglican Church's rear and behind a row of tall popular trees, thin and appearing skinny without leaves that swayed in the gusty northeaster, this new location provided some shelter from the rain of cannonballs from Forrest's Pennsylvania guns, both howitzers and long six-pounders. By having positioned so many troops east off King Street, Rall was now attempting to buy time, anticipating that the Knyphausen Regiment would advance north from Queen Street in the lower town to reinforce him and his two regiments to unite the entire brigade on King Street.

However, in the smoky confusion and noise, Colonel Rall was not yet fully aware of how much pressure Sullivan and his onrushing First Division were applying to the south. Indeed, Flahaven and Stark's aggressiveness focused most of the Knyphausen Regiment's attention on the more immediate threat from Sullivan's Division in the lower town to Rall's southwest. Nor was Rall cognizant that Major Dechow, a highly respected commander who had gained solid experience as a captain under Frederick the Great, was less supportive than anticipated. Dechow hailed from Ratzeburg, surrounded by four lakes in today's northern Germany. Rall and Dechow were at odds personally and professionally at a crucial time when complete unity was essential for the Rall Brigade's survival. But the fact that Washington had struck from two directions simultaneously most of all sabotaged any hope of close and effective cooperation of all three regiments.

Despite his careful tactical calculations, Rall was not to benefit long from his wise decision of shifting most of his troops just off King Street to minimize losses. A far more serious and closer threat for Rall suddenly emerged— yet another surprise on a morning full of surprises for the Hessians—in a new direction, when the first American musketry rattled loudly from west of King Street, when Mercer, at the head of his brigade, struck. This swiftly developing emergency situation called for yet another a new tactical deployment by Rall to meet this escalating threat. While the foremost Rall Regiment battalion faced north along Pinkerton's Alley in the rear, or south, of the Anglican Church, and east of King Street, Rall was now forced to redeploy his troops. Reacting quickly, he turned his southernmost battalion of four companies—a Hessian regiment consisted of two battalions—along King Street to face west, after ascertaining the emerging threat of the foremost attackers of Mercer's Maryland, Connecticut, and Massachusetts brigade swarming forward through the open ground of snow-covered fields and meadows west of town. Rall's swift tactical adjustment was timely since the Hessians would have been forced entirely from King Street and then from Queen Street to the east, with Rall brigade positions falling like dominos when systematically outflanked by Mercer's attackers from the west.

While the von Lossberg troops continued to look north along Church Alley, Rall Regiment's grenadiers now simultaneously faced both north, via Pinkerton's Ally (the northernmost battalion), and west, via King Street (the southernmost battalion). Pinkerton's Alley ran east-west a short distance to link King and Queen Streets and was located just below, or south of, parallel Church Alley and below the von Lossbergers. At the snowy intersection of King Street and Pinkerton's Ally, Rall's newly formed defensive right angle, with its apex in King Street, now protected the Rall Regiment on two sides to face simultaneous threats from multiple directions, north and west.

Even though facing west toward Mercer's growing threat to the west meant that the Rall Regiment's southernmost battalion's right flank on the north in King Street was exposed to Forrest's artillery fire from the high ground, it was yet located sufficiently far enough south of the von Lossberger's position, to the northeast in Church Alley, to partly negate the effectiveness of Forrest's Pennsylvania field pieces. Both of these narrow alleys were situated just above, or north, from where the River Road entered King Street from the west.

To Rall and other Hessian officers and despite the initial left flank pressure applied by Mercer, who could not bring artillery (fortunately for Rall) across rain-swollen Petty's Run because no bridge existed on the town's west side, increasing from the west, the main threat to the Rall brigade yet remained to the north, where Washington's lengthy row of artillery continued to roar. Seasoned Hessian officers, who wore Prussian-style bicorn hats unlike their men, automatically knew that so many deployed American artillery pieces—ascertained only from a angry chorus of rhythmic booming, a deadly cadence that seemed to grow steadily louder, and from fiery muzzle flashes and puffs of smoke rising on the northern horizon—had to be supported by large numbers of infantry: hence, the main threat to the Rall brigade's existence clearly loomed to the north on the heights above the town.

Indeed, if this yet unknown American force was in fact larger than anyone yet imagined, then it could pour south off the high ground and down King Street to outflank the von Lossberg Regiment on its left and the Rall Regiment's southernmost battalion on its right and divide the two regiments, if the bulk of the two regiments remained mostly in relatively sheltered positions just east of King Street. But worst of all with American fire echoing louder from three sides, Rall now entertained the shocking possibility that he was in the process of being surrounded: Sullivan's attackers firing to the southwest; Mercer's men blasting away to the west; Forrest's cannon roaring to the north at King Street's head; and to the northeast at Queen Street's head, where Hamilton's two six-pounders rapidly fired south toward the Knyphausen Regiment. Believing that he was all but trapped and realizing that Washington was employing a masterful double envelopment to his utter disbelief, Rall remained not only relatively calm, but also now decided to make a determined bid to reverse the day's fortunes. Cantering back and forth on his horse before his aligned veterans, he knew that he must attack north up King Street in a desperate attempt to break out of Washington's entrapment before it was too late.

At the west end of Pinkerton's Alley, consequently, Rall now realigned his southernmost grenadier battalion in King Street to face north, regardless of Mercer's flank fire. He then ordered his own grenadiers to advance a short distance north to extend the southern battalion's northern head to touch the von Lossberg Regiment's left flank at Church Alley. After the grenadier battalion advanced a short distance up King Street, then the other Rall grenadier battalion in Pinkerton Ally was quickly shifted west and back into King Street to form behind the Rall Regiment's lead battalion, which now became the northernmost unit. In relatively short order, both battalions of the Rall Regiment were now once again in King Street and faced north and the primary threat.

Eager to unleash his troops on the offensive in the finest Prussian tradition of linear tactics, Rall prepared to order his grenadiers, now aligned in an assault column spanning from one side of the street to the other, straight north up King Street, and literally into the eye of the storm, both man-made and natural. However, Rall's adroit tactical maneuver of having smoothly faced both battalions north in an assault column and advancing a short distance up King Street, the Rall Regiment's compact ranks now offered a better target to the opportunistic Pennsylvania gunners at the head of King Street. Consequently, wide-eyed artillerymen responded with a higher rate of fire, and casualties among the grenadiers steadily rose like the snow that covered the ground.

With cannonballs from the six-pounders and five and a half-inch shells from Forrest's howitzers "flying down the street and breaking into their ranks," additional Hessian soldiers fell into nature's white carpet, now splattered and stained with red. Handfuls of other grenadiers in dark blue uniforms immediately dropped out of formation to help their wounded comrades, including those unfortunate men hit by "shrapnel" iron fragments from the exploding howitzer shells that cracked like thunder when they burst overhead. Injured Hessians were then assisted southeastward to the increasingly busy brigade hospital, which was located at the parsonage of the Presbyterian Church at Second Street and Queen Street. As so often in the past with his aggressive instincts rising to the fore despite having been caught so completely by surprise, Rall now planned to rely upon what he knew best and something that had never failed in the past: the most successful Hessian tactic of all, the bayonet attack, as demonstrated so effectively against the hapless American soldiers at Long Island, White Plains, and Fort Washington.[4]

Besides the inherent disadvantages of having been taken by surprise and with his grenadiers suffering under fire from a greater concentration of American cannon and more deadly than they had faced on previous battlefields, the overall tactical situation now faced by Rall could not have been more disadvantageous. Able to see only a few yards distant because of the pelting snow and sleet that blew into their faces while they peered north toward Knox's blazing field pieces along the high ground, Rall and his men were yet blind in regard to Washington's exact dispositions and positions, especially in regard to Sullivan's attack to the southwest, in part because no information was forthcoming from members of the Knyphausen Regiment, which was situated before their regimental headquarters in the lower town toward Queen Street's southern end.

In contrast to Washington and Knox's gunners who looked south upon a panoramic view from their high ground perch with the winter storm raging to their backs, Colonel Rall was also at a disadvantage since he and his troops were situated at a much lower point: the bottom of a natural bowl. Rall, consequently, now had to rely on his own fighting instincts, intuition, and tactical skills to get his brigade out of an exceptionally bad fix, while the sharp sounds of escalating American fire exploded around him from three directions. Hit head-on by the scorching fire of Forrest's guns, meanwhile, more finely uniformed grenadiers continued to drop out of formation, falling either dead or wounded in snowy King Street. Unknown to him at this time, however, Colonel Rall was now losing something even more significant and precious than some of his most prized grenadiers. In Lieutenant Wiederhold's words, the Hessians had already "lost the few favorable moments we might still have had to break through the enemy in one place or another with honor and without losses." From his lofty perch overlooking the town, Washington could even view signs of the steady progress of the escalating attack of Sullivan's column eastward by way of the noise of musketry, the sight of fiery flashes from muskets, and the rising smoke that was barely seen through the thick, whitish haze of falling snow.

With the round iron balls from Forrest's six-pounders and the shells from five and a half-inch howitzers streaming down King Street and knowing that getting his half dozen artillery pieces into action as soon as possible was essential for the town's defense and to support his hard-hit grenadiers, especially after they had moved a short distance up King Street to halt beside his headquarters (Stacy Potts's house) and opposite the west end of Church Alley, Rall raced over to his regiment's two-gun section to his grenadier's rear. Here, with the ever-increasing noise of battle swirling around him, this experienced colonel of middle-class background knew that he had to counter the blistering fire of Forrest's guns from Philadelphia as soon as possible. Barking in the tumult, Rall ordered for his regiment's finely uniformed gunners, who had gathered in King Street, to hurry the two three-pounders, which had been formerly parked in the snow-shrouded cemetery behind the Anglican Church, where the Rall Regiment cannoneers had been lodged, into action.

Fortunately, the grenadier regiment's two three-pounders were soon ready for action before Rall's headquarters guardhouse on King Street, located just south of his personal headquarters, instead of now guarding the South Trenton Landing just on the Assunpink's south side. Lieutenant Johann Engelhardt's top lieutenant, Friedrich Fischer, should have commanded the early morning patrol, with the two Rall Regiment artillery pieces, until cancelled by the complacent Major Dechow.

Amid the roaring noise of battle, Engelhardt's and Fischer's experienced artillerymen quickly manhandled one three-pounder into the exact position Rall designated. By hand and rope, the German gunners then hauled the field piece a short distance north up King Street to a point nearly opposite Rall's headquarters. Here, the Rall Regiment's cannoneers set up their gun in what initially appeared to be a good position. Aiming high for proper elevation to reach the heights north of town, the Hessian artillerymen then sent a screaming shot at Forrest's intimidating row of artillery pieces that were busily blasting away down King Street. But the distance was yet too far for the Hessian gun to be effective. Nevertheless, the fact the one German cannon was finally returning fire lifted the spirits among the hard-hit grenadiers, who were emboldened to know that one of their regiment's guns had gamely answered the booming American artillery at long last.

However, Rall soon realized that these two bronze guns of the Rall Regiment had to be moved much farther up King Street if they were to be effective. Therefore, the never-say-die colonel, the son of a career soldier, ordered his German gunners to retrieve the artillery horses, stabled in a nearby barn, to quickly hitch up the two field pieces in preparation for advancing the guns north up ice-covered King Street and the lengthy slope leading to the fiery heights to get within closer range of the Pennsylvania guns. In frantic haste, cannoneers dashed to the barn around fifty yards distant from the King Street alarm house, located near Rall's headquarters, to secure the eight horses for hitching to the Rall Regiment's two guns. As part of his extensive precautions just in case of an attack, Rall had wisely ordered that the brigade's artillery horses were to remain in full harness while stabled at night so that they could be more quickly hitched to artillery pieces. However, when Major Dechow cancelled the usual morning patrol due to the storm's severity and the Yuletide Season, the artillery horses of the Rall Regiment's two guns had been unhitched and then placed back in the stables.

Meanwhile, Engelhardt and Fischer rallied eighteen able artillerymen, who prepared to advance two artillery pieces up King Street and straight into the path of Forrest's withering artillery fire. Rall planned to have his regiment's two guns hauled by his well-trained gunners up King Street in order to inflict damage—hopefully even silencing some of Forrest's cannon—to pave the way for a hard-hitting infantry breakout from what Rall correctly considered a fatal entrapment. Amid the confusion swirling through King Street and around Rall's headquarters at Stacy Potts's house, teams of horses were quickly hitched by artillerymen to the two guns. Feeling that he could yet turn the tide of battle despite having been caught by surprise, Rall then screamed, "Artillery forward!" In a desperate bid to reverse the day's fortunes before it was too late, the two three-pounders were hurried north up King Street with "no [infantry] escort whatever for the cannon," because neither the artillerymen nor guns of either the von Lossberg or Knyphausen Regiments were ready to enter the action at this time. Clearly, the spunky Colonel Rall was attempting to do his best by adhering to the old adage that the best defense was a bold offensive in an almost impossible situation.[5]

Hampered by his disadvantageous position on lower ground and with a northeast wind blowing snow unceasingly hard into his soldiers' faces, Rall faced a crisis situation that now tactically required the immediate unity of all three regiments, especially the Knyphausen Regiment in the town's southern end in the Queen Street sector near the wood-frame Quaker Meeting House, to maximize offensive capabilities. Unfortunately for Rall, because his men faced multiple threats from three directions, simply too much time had been already lost by all three regiments to assemble and unite as one: the high price for having been caught by surprise and underestimating their opponent. All the while, hundreds of Americans had hurriedly not only deployed with discipline in excellent positions for action, but also had taken the initiative to gain more advantageous ground that Rall desperately needed to retain. This was especially the case on the Rall Regiment's vulnerable left flank west of King Street, where Mercer applied increasingly more pressure from the west.

Worst of all for Hessian fortunes, Rall now possessed relatively few troops who were truly combat ready and prepared for their supreme challenge. Indeed, Rall was severely handicapped by the fact that the vast majority of his enlisted soldiers—more than three-quarters of his brigade and artillerymen—were now unfit for duty. Unable to join their regiments in the town's defense, many ailing men were either housed in makeshift infirmaries, or in private houses that now served as hospitals much to their owner's regret. Additionally reducing the overall chances for reserving the day's fortunes, Rall's officer corps had been likewise thoroughly decimated by disease and illness more than battle since their arrival in this strange land known as America. These Europeans, especially those men from well-maintained German cities, hundreds of years old, where sanitation and hygiene were excellent out of necessity because of crowded conditions, were unacclimated to America's more underdeveloped environment, especially unfamiliar germs and bacteria that infected bodies which had relatively little resistance. Therefore, many leading Rall brigade officers were now either sick or dying because they now fought on American soil.

Nevertheless, many stricken men gamely answered the call to duty during the Rall brigade's moment of supreme crisis. Lieutenant Colonel Scheffer, a fifty-four-year-old married man who commanded the von Lossberg Regiment, now encouraged his troops, who hailed principally from Hesse-Cassel towns like Rinteln, Bassum, and Ucht, into action, despite having been in a sickbed for most of the last week. Although ill-clothed in only summer uniforms, a number of sick Hessians, both officers and enlisted men, had also already hobbled into line to do their duty as best they could. Rall's overall combat-ready strength was drained by other factors as well. Overcome by panic as Washington had planned, some Rall's grenadiers had already fled down King Street to cross the Assunpink bridge, escaping what they already saw with ample justification as a no-win situation for the seemingly doomed Rall brigade.

In truth, Rall was not yet surrounded as he feared, however. By this time, the initial success in the simultaneous striking of both Greene's and Sullivan's columns was not sufficient to secure a complete victory for Washington because the pincers of his double envelopment had not yet closed shut. For one, the extreme right of Stirling's brigade, Colonel John Haslet's Delaware Regiment, had to yet link with the left of Mercer's brigade to fill the gap in Washington's line on the town's northwest to ensure that Stirling's and Mercer's brigades linked together on their respective flanks to present a solid front. In addition, what also now needed to be accomplished in overall tactical terms for Washington's plan to succeed was for the right flank of Greene's troops, Mercer's Maryland, Connecticut, and Massachusetts brigade, to link with the left flank of Sullivan's attackers to the south for the initial meeting of the First and Second Divisions to complete the entrapment of the Rall brigade on three sides, north, south, and west. While Washington's veteran troops and much of his best artillery units were poised on the commanding terrain north of town, hundreds of other Americans continued to surge upon Trenton from the west (Mercer) and southwest (Sullivan). Additional numbers of Mercer's fast-arriving attackers, including more than eight hundred soldiers of the Twentieth Connecticut Continental Regiment, the Twenty-Seventh Massachusetts Continental Regiment, the First Maryland Continental Regiment, a small unit of Connecticut State Troops, and a Maryland Rifle Battalion, continued to gain advanced positions just west of King Street.

Here, on the town's western outskirts, they took cover in buildings, behind fences, and in the snow-covered lot openings between the two-story wood-frame houses, where the biting northeast wind was funneled between wooden structures to howl louder. In an urban environment and out of necessity, some of the usual tight brigade and regimental formations broke down, with companies, small groups of men, and even individuals on their own taking the best firing positions, including cellars. Initiative, adaptability, and flexibility now rose to the fore among Mercer's veterans, paying off. A good many of Mercer's foremost soldiers found good protective cover in the rear of Potts's tannery, located near his house.

From this vantage point and despite fingers numb and stiff from the cold, Mercer's infantrymen raked the Rall Regiment's left flank in King Street at close range with a stream of bullets. Gaining good firing positions in the relatively warm houses on King Street's west side immensely benefitted these Maryland, Connecticut, and Massachusetts veterans, who secured dry shelter from the incessant deluge of falling ice and snow. This advantageous situation finally allowed Mercer's men to dry their firing mechanisms, flints, and priming pans of their flintlocks. Consequently, these veterans now maintained not only a heavy but also a sustained fire from the west. This increasing volume of fire from the veterans of Mercer's brigade presented additional proof to Rall and his hard-hit troops that an audacious encirclement by Washington's suddenly daring movements was not only underway but also nearly complete, or so it seemed.[6] Especially after having suffered so many past defeats and humiliations, Washington's men had long considered themselves "lucky" for the opportunity of "killing a Hessian grenadier," and this now applied to the famed Rall Regiment.[7]

And the Americans "delighted" in nothing more than killing an aristocratic, high-born Hessian officer in a distinctive Prussian bicorn hat, eliminating a representative of the detested European ruling class. Most significantly, while the Hessians had been trained to shoot on command to unleash a volley from a neat line, the Americans knew how to kill on their own with a deadly expertise. This key difference (so significant for the eventual outcome of this urban battle) was most important, reflecting not only the Frederick the Great and Prussian tradition, but also the difference between the cultural, historical, and environmental backgrounds of Trenton's antagonists. While the average Hessian of humble origin hailed from a background where only the wealthy and social elite possessed extensive lands and engaged in the luxury of hunting in Teutonic forests as a sport, the common people of America, especially on the frontier, had early learned to stalk game, fire from cover, and shoot in order to put food on the table to survive. This notable difference began to rise to the fore in the struggle for possession of Trenton.[8]

Understandably, in such a no-win tactical situation of facing a deadly crossfire—round shot and howitzer shells from Forrest's Pennsylvania artillery from the north and Mercer's musketry at close range from the west—signs of shakiness began to ripple through the disciplined German formations. Additionally, not all of Rall's frantic orders could be heard in the tumult, leading to more confusion in the ranks now raked by multiple fires. All in all, the combined effect of the surprise attack, Knox's booming guns, and Mercer's escalating flank fire from the west provided an even greater psychological shock, because Rall and his over-confident men had been long so "sure the rebels could not," wrote grenadier Johannes Reuber, an enthusiastic teenager of the Rall Regiment, possibly launch an offensive strike, especially in such horrendous weather conditions.

Clearly, Rall now found himself in an increasingly desperate situation, with the rapid fire of Knox's artillery sweeping south off the high ground and Mercer's flank fire steaming from the west. All the while, iron round shot from Forrest's busy six-pounders, aimed to fire at a lower angle of trajectory, continued to bounce and ricochet down the sloping ground of King Street, smashing into wood-frame houses and into the dense Hessian ranks to send unlucky men flying like rag dolls. Incredibly, displaying individual initiative, some of Mercer's boldest soldiers on his brigade's left flank at the town's northern outskirts even dashed across King Street above Rall's northernmost formation to take advantageous firing positions in the rear of William Smith's and William Tindall's houses that fronted Queen Street. From these higher ground vantage points, the most opportunistic American marksmen then turned their muskets to the southwest and blasted away at foremost grenadiers in King Street, delivering a plunging fire from a new, lethal angle to cause more damage.

And, as usual, Mercer's eagle-eyed sharpshooters especially targeted Hessian officers, who stood tall before their taut formations in resplendent uniforms as dictated by unbending rules and regulations penned long ago in Hesse-Cassel. Caught in a raging cauldron of withering fires, Rall's grenadiers on King Street were now simultaneously under escalating pressure from the west by Mercer's brigade; a far lesser, but most irritating, fire from the northeast; southwest from Sullivan's onrushing attackers in the lower town; and the cannon fire to the north from Forrest's six-pounders and five and a half-inch howitzers. Facing these multiple, simultaneous fires that seemed to be coming from everywhere at once, Rall knew that he had to quickly eliminate the heaviest firepower now punishing his exposed men with impunity, or all was lost. Rall, therefore, was forced to do something desperate in a last-ditch attempt to turn the tide, and this most of all meant silencing the long row of Knox's fire-spitting cannon as soon as possible.[9]

While the beleaguered Colonel Rall was doing his best in an emergency situation, such was not the case with some of his officers. Not only were many officers now either sick and unfit for duty but also some of Rall's junior officers had never fully recovered from the initial considerable shock of Washington's surprise attack, especially the intense artillery-fire pouring down King Street.

While Lieutenant Colonel Scheffer, with thirty-five years of solid service, had willed himself out of a sickbed to take charge of the von Lossberg Regiment along with Lieutenant Colonel Brethauser, who had been ill for nearly a week but yet now commanded the grenadier regiment while Rall led the brigade, a number of junior officers were not so conscientious or determined to stand firm this morning.

Some Hessian officers failed to do their duty, remaining in their quarters and safely out of harm's way. Other shell-shocked Hessians fled south out of town, following the fast-moving British light cavalry over the Assunpink bridge, taking the snowy road south to Bordentown, on the Delaware, to escape Washington's clever tactical trap. Like the Knyphausen Regiment on Queen Street in the lower town, a number of isolated Hessian detachments also failed to reinforce Rall on King Street at this critical moment. Ensign Henrich Zimmerman, age twenty-one and born in Cassel, remained with his thirty-man detachment in the safety of the sizeable, brick William Trent House, which had been wisely bypassed by Sullivan's foremost attackers because subduing the formidable structure, located near the river and below the Assunpink, would have been time-consuming, instead of rushing north to assist their King Street comrades, since he received no new orders to do so: a classic example of Hessian superb training and discipline backfiring in a key situation.

Other German officers, like the commander of the Rall Regiment's artillery, Lieutenant Engelhardt, were inexperienced in combat: liabilities that additionally hampered Rall's overall efforts, including his "long-arm" capabilities. In such a disadvantageous situation, such novices, both officers and enlisted men, suffered from bad cases of nerves, or the shakes, with Washington's troops seemingly descending upon them from nearly all directions. Even some veteran noncommissioned officers also proved ineffective under the debilitating stress of the demanding challenges of urban combat. Therefore, and especially as the battle lengthened this morning, Colonel Rall was now more on his own than in any previous engagement. After all, this was the first time that the Hessians had ever been caught by surprise and faced a crisis situation of such a magnitude. Most of all, they were forced to fight in a confusing urban environment, where high morale, personal initiative, and tactical flexibility meant more than conventional tactics and training along Trenton's narrow streets under adverse wintertime conditions.[10]

From his advantageous high ground perch at King Street's head, a mounted Washington watched the desperate plight of the Rall brigade, now caught in its worst fix, with unrestrained amusement if not some measure of self-satisfying fascination. By way of his own intelligent tactical decisions, he had managed to ensnare an entire Hessian brigade and to get it in an incredibly bad situation, not unlike so many of his own tactical dilemmas, thanks to superior British generalship, that had confounded him throughout the course of the New York Campaign. For the first time, this customary role that had ruined Washington's reputation had now been reversed.

With considerable satisfaction, therefore, Washington surveyed the Rall regiment's quandary in the middle of King Street: seemingly unable to either advance or retreat amid the tempest of the combined effect of falling snow and the hail of Captain Forrest's artillery projectiles. Viewing how even these disciplined Hessians were disoriented by the raging snowstorm, hit by multiple fires, and surrounded by the dark buildings of a seemingly deserted, haunted Trenton, Washington described with sheer delight how "we presently saw their main body formed, but from their motions they seemed undetermined how to act."[11]

However, despite its intensifying dilemma for which there seemed no solution, the Rall brigade was yet very dangerous if suddenly unleashed, like a wounded, cornered beast, especially since the battle had fairly only begun, and with the capable Rall firmly in command. Most of all, Rall's veteran brigade possessed the will, discipline, and capabilities to strike back exceptionally hard. All the while, the northeaster continued to blow sleet and snow into Hessian faces, bestowing Washington's troops with a decided advantage in what was shaping up to be a dramatic showdown in a little river town that had suddenly become the most important in all America. As Colonel Knox, the former Boston bookseller who had "used to amuse himself in reading military books in his shop," described the significant advantages bestowed by the blessings of geography around Trenton, Washington's tactical audacity, and even the white deluge that tumbled down incessantly from black skies: "The storm continued with great violence, but was in our backs, and consequently in the faces of our enemy."[12]

In one of the battle's great ironies for the men defending Trenton, Washington had more vigorously studied the military manual known as the "King of Prussia's Instructions to his Generals" than any other.[13] And now a faithful adherence to that same set of Prussians instructions in the art of war was now in the process of dooming the Rall brigade, because Washington had learned his lessons well. Indeed, in a classic paradox, even the Hessians' own superior discipline in maintaining a neat, tight shoulder-to-shoulder formation, as if back on a sunny drill field in Hesse-Cassel, in King Street was also now proving self-defeating. Along with Mercer's relentless pressure from the west and the scorching fire from multiple directions squeezing the two German regiments like a vise and the snowstorm yet fiercely raging over Trenton, the Hessians' overall relative tactical inflexibility and iron discipline continued to prove to be Washington's forgotten allies during this climactic showdown, while American troops, especially regimental and brigade commanders, continued to exhibit tactical flexibility and initiative. Frederick the Great had long emphasized to his Prussian troops that their actions on the battlefield should be "the work of a single man," and "no one reasons, everyone executes" among the rank and file, and Rall's troops were now obeying these axioms to the letter.

Because the Germans had not been trained to fight as individuals and as only as part of large formations in a rigid linear tactical system that maneuvered as one and only on cue from the commanding officer, junior Hessian officers, including even the capable Lieutenant Wiederhold, who had already long stood his ground while waiting in vain at Pennington Road picket outpost for a superior officer to appear to hand him new instructions, failed to demonstrate badly needed tactical flexibility in this crisis situation.

Therefore, relatively few Hessian officers (and certainly not enlisted men) acted effectively on their own initiative this Thursday morning, when personal initiative was needed most of all. An enduring legacy of the revered Prussian traditions of Frederick the Great, Hessian discipline and rigid training had long eroded individual initiative and overall tactical flexibility, including offensive-mindedness, among the German officer corps. Individual Hessian officers were either unable or unwilling to successfully meet newly emerging localized threats, especially in the confusion of fighting in an urban environment, on their own without Rall's immediate supervision and direct orders.

Without new instructions in a fast-moving, fluid situation, therefore, a number of Hessian officers, commanding isolated detachments along the town's perimeter, failed to rush forward to rejoin their respective regiments on King Street, where they were needed for a concentration of effort. And here in the midst of projectile-swept King Street as dictated by the unbending rules from strict Hessian military manuals and training, German officers and enlisted men failed to break ranks for a single moment on their own (like Americans) in an emergency situation to dispatch the foremost of Mercer's sharpshooters, inflicting serious damage, in nearby houses on King Street's west side, and especially from the rear of Potts's tannery, from where a hot fire poured.

Because of such a rigid, inflexible chain of Prussian-like command and as revealed in past alarms at Trenton which exposed an inherent problem not yet rectified, Hessian junior officers were forced to repeatedly seek out their commanding officer to request permission, if they dared contemplate taking independent action, especially the initiative, without their commander's consent. Worst of all and in another striking irony, this central weakness of excessive discipline (the antithesis of a highly tactically-flexible means of waging war—essentially guerrilla warfare—as demonstrated by the Americans) had early negated the overall combat capabilities of the Knyphausen Regiment at Queen Street's lower end southeast of Rall and his two regiments. After having spilled from the Presbyterian Church at Second Street and Queen Street, and private quarters lining both sides of Assunpink Creek, Major Dechow's troops had quickly gathered and aligned in response to Greene's and Sullivan's roaring artillery pieces.

But, with Major Dechow now reassigned to his new quarters on King Street as the "staff officer of the day," hundreds of Knyphausen Regiment troops had formed according to prearranged design in front of Dechow's Queen Street headquarters without realizing that the major was absent. Here, they dutifully awaited orders for some time, as if expecting Major Dechow to magically reappear, even after their five regimental colors had been brought forth from the major's headquarters. Therefore, the entire fusilier regiment squandered the initial advantage of forming relatively quickly and early getting into action (including possibly attacking north up Queen Street if ordered) by wasting too much precious time—at least fifteen minutes—in not immediately reinforcing Rall's two regiments on King Street to the west, before Sullivan struck the lower town and gained their attention.

In consequence, the crack troops of the Knyphausen Regiment fusiliers now remained dutifully in formation waiting for Rall's specific orders before Dechow's quiet, darkened headquarters on Queen Street in the lower part of town: a lack of overall initiative and tactical flexibility that led to a waste of precious time when time was of the essence, especially when Rall's other two regiments were yet attempting to recover from the shock of Washington's surprise and under a blistering fire from two directions, north and west. Quite simply, top Knyphausen commanders demonstrated little, if any, personal initiative or imagination that diminished this fine regiment's considerable combat capabilities. In Major Dechow's absence, the finely aligned ranks of the regiment stood in a neat formation at Queen Street's southern end between Front and Second Streets and below and southwest of the modest, plain-looking Quaker Meeting House, which had been the first church established in Trenton in 1739.

Here, on low ground located just north of the foot of Queen Street at Front Street and above the Assunpink bridge, the well-trained Knyphausen fusiliers, especially the officers, continued to be severely restricted by their own superior training and Frederick the Great-inspired discipline that required them to remain dutifully in their assigned position—even if a bad one—if the brigade commander sent no specific instructions that dictated otherwise. Besides firmly fixing the Knyphausen Regiment to a stationary position and at a severe tactical disadvantage, this same tactical inflexibility also ensured a nearly flawless Frederickian close formation of Rall's troops on King Street to guarantee that encroaching perimeter threats, especially from Mercer's brigade encroaching from the west, not only went unchecked, but also continued to escalate.

Indeed, the Hessians' superior discipline in early forming for action, thanks to Rall's precautions, in the streets worked decidedly against the Germans and their attempt to effectively counter Washington's surprise attacks from two directions. Because these Teutonic soldiers were never trained or expected to fight in either urban or winter conditions—unlike the Pennsylvania and Virginia riflemen, especially hardy frontiersmen with French and Indian War experience, who knew how to keep their powder, muskets, and priming pans dry even in inclement winter weather—they were neither ready or properly clothed for winter combat. Consequently, Rall's troops lacked winter clothing, including warm underwear and especially greatcoats, while standing stoically for an extended period in tight formation like revered Prussian troops in the middle of King Street and suffering from the storm's wrath long before coming to grips with Washington's men.

At least the Americans, although ill-clothed and in tattered garments, had at least benefitted from an earlier opportunity to prepare, if only by wrapping additional dirty rags around bare feet, for active campaigning in winter weather, before crossing the Delaware. Yet wearing summer uniforms and for an extended period, Rall's grenadiers and fusiliers stood in straight lines as designated by the rule book, while the snow, driven by the northeast wind, dropped in large flakes and lashed into their faces and eyes yet to see Washington's men to the north.

In addition, these young German soldiers wore black leather shoes long since worn-out and in bad shape from the long pursuit of Washington's forces through New Jersey. Therefore, the feet of Rall's men immediately became cold and wet, while they were standing in formation in the open streets of misery. Tall Mitre helmets, fronted with highly decorative intricate brass plates and without leather bills, failed to protect Hessian faces, ears, and eyes, while also making sight and sound more difficult amid the storm that swept down King Street.

Even worse for German fortunes, the flintlock muskets and the black powder of Rall's assembled soldiers were getting wet. No precautions had been taken into account for foul weather. After all, the Hessians were not trained or accustomed to campaigning and fighting in wintertime. All the while in the King Street sector, nevertheless, these seasoned grenadiers and fusiliers maintained their tight formations as if about to be inspected by their ruling prince, Frederick II, back on a bright spring morning in Hesse-Cassel. While their frozen breath hung in the air like a thick white smoke that hovered around faces and despite all the disadvantages that they now faced, these clean-shaven Teutonic warriors, with fixed bayonets and well-founded pride in their regiments, martial legacies, and distant Germanic homeland that they feared they would never see again, now presented Rall with an opportunity to strike back at Washington.

Unlike the Hessians before them, Washington's most experienced riflemen from the western frontier, especially Colonel Hand's marksmen of the crack First Pennsylvania Continental Regiment, of Fermoy's Brigade, and now blocking the Princeton-Trenton Road just northwest of town, Colonel Ennion Williams's First Pennsylvania Rifle Regiment, of Stirling's Brigade, and the Maryland Rifle Battalion faced no such comparable dilemma as wet black powder or lack of initiative. These Marylanders had been commanded by Colonel Moses Rawlings, who had been captured at Fort Washington in mid-November 1776.

Flexible and innovative, these veteran American soldiers had already wisely utilized what was necessary to keep a hunter in the dense forests of western Pennsylvania and Maryland alive on the frontier, ensuring protection against Indians and placing food on tables in the dead of winter: leather lock scabbards, which were called a "cow's knee" because of its peculiar shape, that protected the locks, priming pans, and firing mechanisms of their flintlock rifles in wet and snowy weather conditions. The savvy New Englanders of Rogers' Rangers had utilized such effective winterizing protection during the French and Indian War. Quite possibly, the battle of Trenton was about to be decided in no small part because of this distinctive advantage over the Hessians in regard to firearm protection in inclement weather stemming from the northern and western frontier experience that now paid high dividends to Washington's riflemen.

With the esteemed Colonel Rawlings now suffering in stoic defiance as an abused prisoner in New York City along with a good many of his fellow Maryland riflemen, who had so severely punished Rall's attackers at Fort Washington, where the colonel had suffered a serious hip wound, the surviving Maryland Rifle Battalion members now possessed plenty of old scores to settle with the Hessians. Yet known as Rawlings' rifle battalion, this seasoned command consisted of deadly Maryland and Virginian marksmen. More than 450 sharp-eyed Pennsylvania veterans of both Hand and Williams's rifle commands, representing adjoining states in rebellion, were now at Trenton at considerable risk not only to themselves, but also to their western frontier families, because Quaker-dominated Pennsylvania was not adequately defended as legislation had never been passed to form a protective state militia. Even more ironic, Washington's finest riflemen now carried the sleek, finely crafted Long Rifle, possessing a lethal weapon from the western frontier. A product of the New World and western frontier experience and requirements that merged with traditional Old World designs, a legendary American firearm, that was lighter and longer than the Swiss-German Jaegar hunting rifle, first crafted ironically by German immigrant gunsmiths of Pennsylvania to create a superior long-range weapon.[14] In the capable hands of Washington's riflemen, the Long Rifle, sleek, lightweight at around nine pounds, and graceful, was so "fatally precise" in the hands of Washington's riflemen that it became known among the British and Hessians as "the widow maker."[15]

In consequence, the most outstanding rifle regiment in Washington's strike force was Colonel Hand's First Pennsylvania Continental Regiment. First led by Irish Colonel William Thompson, now a hard-fighting Continental general, who had served as a resourceful frontier captain on the daring raid that destroyed the hostile Indian village of Kittanning back in September 1756, this exceptional Pennsylvania unit of highly motivated marksmen was also the senior rifle regiment in Washington's Army. As part of Fermoy's brigade on the far left just above the upper town and beyond the left flank of Washington's lengthy row of artillery—or east of Baumann's New York guns—and astride the Princeton-Trenton Road, Hand's Pennsylvania soldiers now stood in formation amid a white shroud of freshly fallen snow under a beautiful "deep green" battle flag that snapped in the northeaster's frigid gusts. The silk banner's emerald green color reflected the distinguished historical and revolutionary legacies of the Green Isle homeland of their never-say-die commander, whom they adored, and the many Ireland-born riflemen serving in the ranks.

Made by patriotic seamstresses in Philadelphia just in time for the showdown in the snows of Trenton, this colorful battle flag portrayed a fierce-looking tigress rushing its victim-combatant armed with a spear. Distinguished by the feisty Latin motto, "Domari Nolo," or "I Refuse to be Subjugated," this distinctive flag's design was Colonel Hand's own creation, reflecting common deep-seated Celtic-Gaelic revolutionary sentiments and legacies, especially spirited defiance against arbitrary and abusive authority. While their colorful battle flag was a real beauty and a source of regimental pride, the nondescript attire of Hand's Pennsylvania boys was definitely not comparable. The fancy green uniform coats, another influential martial legacy from the Emerald Isle which equated to the revolutionary Irish tradition of the "wearing of the green," that Hand had ordered for his elite riflemen were lost to them forever in the warehouses of Fort Lee when they were captured by Howe's forces on November 20, 1776.

By this time, Colonel Hand and his Pennsylvania troops, mostly rough-and-tumble western frontiersmen, were well seasoned, dependable, and tough. Washington, consequently, relied heavily upon their ability to effectively block the vital road leading northwest from Trenton to Princeton. Like Smallwood's Marylanders and Haslet's Delaware soldiers, Hand's expert rifle regiment had received its baptismal fire before the battle of Long Island. Hand and his crack Pennsylvania riflemen had earned the distinction of having been the first American unit to harass the much-touted Hessians, when Howe's forces initially landed on Long Island. Then, along with Smallwood's Maryland and Haslet's Delaware surviving troops, Hand's Pennsylvania riflemen had remained on Long Island, under the commander-in-chief's direct orders, after the battle as a trusty rear-guard to protect the army's rear in a vital mission, while Glover's mariners transported Washington's surviving units across the East River to Manhattan Island's safety. Because of the Pennsylvania rifle regiment's reliability and elite qualities, the commander-in-chief continued to employ Hand and his seasoned riflemen in key roles throughout the Trenton-Princeton Campaign.[16]

The time-honored, popular myth that Washington's soldiers—based on only a single account by Mott who belatedly attempted to employ a handker-chief for firearm protection—held coat sleeves over the essential musket parts to keep them dry mile after mile so that they could be fired in the attack on Trenton has made little sense. Such unorganized, ad hoc precautionary procedures by individual soldiers could not possibly have been effective, given the combined effect of the difficulty in crossing the Delaware, the storm's intensity, and a time-consuming nearly ten-mile march on Trenton.

Quite simply, even a veteran Continental soldier could not have kept his musket protected with nothing more than his coat sleeve for more than twelve hours during such a lengthy, arduous ordeal. Soldiers' garments were sufficiently soaked to offer little protection to keep firing mechanisms, especially the flintlock's priming pan, dry. A heavy, sustained volume of fire of Mercer's troops from the west was only now possible because so many soldiers had taken cover in houses, where they had wiped off their firing mechanisms to blast away. Here, they dried musket flints and priming pans, cleaning off weapons when under shelter to make them operable.

All the while, the seemingly dazed Hessians, who had been asleep only a short time before, stood in formation with discipline and typical textbook order as ordered and expected, just as when they had smilingly watched the surrender of Fort Washington's long line of humiliated prisoners under the mid-November sunshine that sparkled off the Hudson's waters. And now standing up manfully to Knox's severe artillery punishment from the north and Mercer's gun fire from the west for long minutes that seemed like hours, the Rall Regiment grenadiers remained faithfully in formation as sitting ducks in King Street's awful openness, close to the colonel's headquarters near the town's center, looming as exposed targets that could not be missed by veterans.

Swept and blinded by the wind-driven flurries of snow, Rall's soldiers, without proper winter uniforms, stood in neat ranks to ensure a gradual, but thorough, erosion of firepower capabilities. Minute after minute, more snow and sleet rained down to thoroughly soak and chill the assembled Hessians, who suffered without greatcoats or winter uniforms, to the bone. Most importantly for the battle's eventual outcome, the omnipresent deluge of snow dropped relentlessly on muskets, wetting firing mechanisms, including priming pans, which contained the small black powder to ignite charges. Therefore, the sparkling clean Prussia-made flintlocks, not manufactured or ready for winter campaigning, of hundreds of Hessians, who had taken great care to keep their weapons in perfect working order and dry in their sleeping quarters to face just such an early morning threat as now posed by Washington, became increasingly compromised hardly before the engagement began.

While the storm also diminished the firing capabilities of Washington's men in the open, except those of Mercer's troops who had taken cover in houses on King Street's west side, a number of other distinct advantages were yet presented by the inclement conditions to the homespun citizen soldiers. Fortunately for Washington and his troops, the falling snow helped to mask their tactical movements, the shifting of units, the sound from hundreds of treading feet, and the deployment of cannon. At this time, the Hessians were not yet fully aware of their own seriously degraded firing capabilities unlike Washington's men, who had earlier discovered as much on the nightmarish march to Trenton.[17]

But because they never had been trained how to fight a conventional battle in a severe snowstorm, or learned how to keep muskets dry in such adverse weather conditions, the Hessians unknowingly lost more precious firepower with each passing minute. Indeed, while Forrest, Hamilton, and Baumann's cannon crashed loudly from the windswept heights above Trenton and hurled death their way, neither Rall nor his top officers noticed this stealthy, gradual erosion of combat capabilities.

Additionally, because the Hessian troops were so rigidly trained, they were less inclined to individually take protective action to ensure that muskets could fire. Therefore, even if some of Rall's more savvy grenadiers and fusiliers were now worried about their firearm's condition, they merely continued to stand up straight and tall in line as ordered with muskets held upright by their sides as during a routine inspection. All the while, the musket barrels of Rall's men pointed skyward in neat rows, and remained wide open, with no protective covering (musket tompions) to protect black powder charges in loaded muskets from the incessant falling moisture from the winterstorm.[18]

Nevertheless, Rall's two regiments were now in good positions to take the offensive. And they were poised to strike back. In obedience with the colonel's frantic orders, the Rall Grenadier Regiment had already advanced a short distance north up King Street to a point adjacent to Rall's headquarters near the town's center. Even though an increasingly number of Hessian muskets were inoperable, this grenadier regiment, and especially the even tougher von Lossberg fusiliers aligned in Church Alley, was yet formidable. Consequently, Rall's two regiments possessed not only more than ample strength, but also its most renowned offensive capabilities with its most lethal weapon that had always reaped victory in the past: the bayonet. Indeed, nothing had proved more effective in thoroughly shattering American confidence, resolve, and fighting spirit on one past battlefield after another than a bayonet attack, especially by these same crack German troops.

Colonel Rall's professional soldiers were masters in the grim art of bayonet usage. In fact, Rall now possessed a rare opportunity to not only defeat but also to perhaps destroy Washington and his band of revolutionaries with one blow, if first Greene's Second Division and then Sullivan's First Division could be kept separated and then defeated one by one. After all, Washington was now isolated on the Delaware's east side, with his back to a swollen river, after the twin failures of Ewing and Calwalader to cross the Delaware. If the closing of Washington's two pincer arms was not soon achieved, then disaster might yet result.

Washington had long realized that he must "prevent them from forming in the streets" to negate the possibility of a determined counterattack from surging up King Street to inflict a significant setback on Greene's northern, or upper, arm of the pincer movement, before Rall could then turn south to deal with Sullivan's Division in a classic case of divide and conquer. Therefore, Washington's task of reaping a decisive success was daunting because the Hessians also possessed another weapon (besides the bayonet) that neither snow, ice, nor rain would negate the firing capabilities of: artillery. The six guns of the Rall brigade were concentrated in the King Street sector, and not assigned to each regiment as usual in battle, because the Hessians had been so surprised by Washington's onslaught: a significant disadvantage for the Knyphausen Regiment and the defense of the Queen Street sector.

Thanks to a fluke of luck with Dechow's cancellation of the morning patrol that would have taken these two guns south of the Assunpink and all the way to South Trenton Ferry sector, the Rall Regiment's cannon had been the first hurled into action on King Street, while the von Lossberg artillery, which had been separated from the von Lossberg Regiment's fusiliers who had been quartered just slightly north of Rall's headquarters, were yet positioned in the Anglican Church's rear. The Knyphausen guns, near the von Lossberg cannon, were now located closer to the Rall Regiment than either the von Lossberg Regiment, and especially their proud owners, the Knyphausen Regiment. Clearly, this was an overall convoluted situation for Rall's "long-arm" that resulted in the von Lossberg Regiment eventually gaining the Knyphausen Regiment guns. But more importantly, Rall's disadvantageous situation meant that half a dozen bronze six-pounders would never be united this Thursday to meet Washington's main threat from the north with a concentrated fire.

However, under the circumstances, the Rall Regiment's artillery had responded to the challenge with a surprising alacrity; two little bronze three-pounders would now have to accomplish what all six guns should have attempted to achieve on King Street: not only regaining the initiative but also the advantage for the first time today. Commanded by Englehardt and Fischer, the eighteen well-trained artillerymen had brought the Rall Regiment's guns up King Street upon Rall's urgent orders. But these two Hessian cannon—possessing only half the firepower of two of Forrest's big six-pounders—were yet out of range of the Pennsylvania artillery that continued to blaze away from the high ground at King Street's head.

Most importantly, Washington's guns bellowed angrily without anything slowing the rapid rate of fire maintained by hard-working and seasoned gunners, who sought to exploit their advantage to the fullest. Aligned in a lengthy row along the snowy heights that frowned menacingly upon Trenton and the Rall brigade, Knox's cannon maintained a high rate of fire completely unimpeded, because they were out of range of not only Hessian muskets but also the Rall Regiment's two bronze three-pounders on King Street. Thinking aggressively, Rall realized that his regiment's two light guns could best support his upcoming counterattack only by moving farther north within closer range in an attempt to knock Forrest's booming field pieces out of action before it was too late for Hessian fortunes.[19]

Chapter VI

Rall Counterattacks

Against all expectations, therefore, Rall continued to make last-minute preparations to unleash his own counterattack to reverse the tables and catch Washington himself by surprise. In the past, many historians have incorrectly viewed this upcoming offensive effort as sheer folly, stemming from Rall's alleged incompetence and inability to develop a sensible tactical solution. In truth, Rall had made one of the best tactical decisions that he could have possibly made under the circumstances in a no-win situation. Napoleon, the ultimate master of the art of war, long emphasized the wisdom of early attempting to turn the tables on an opponent as soon as possible in a seemingly no-win situation: "When you are occupying a position which the enemy threatens to surround, collect all your force immediately, and menace *him* with an offensive movement."[1] By this time, Rall had not only rallied but also organized his own regiment and the von Lossberg Regiment, which were now poised with a steely resolve and fixed bayonets for a counterattack. But most of all, Rall knew that the best way to disrupt the closing of the arms (Greene's Second Division and Sullivan's First Division) of Washington's pincers was by attacking one of the two divisions with everything he had so that these upper and lower arms could not close shut.

Amid the blinding flurries of sleet and snow, one Hessian suddenly grabbed the bluish-green colors of the Rall Regiment, while other determined grenadiers snatched the equally colorful company banners, or the "Camagnie-Fahne," from the front of Potts's house, Rall's King Street headquarters, to inspire the troops in the upcoming offensive effort. Rall now envisioned more than simply breaking out of what he believed was Washington's clever encirclement. He desired most of all to snatch victory from the jaws of defeat.

Amid the din, Lieutenant Colonel Brethauer barked out for all of the silk battle flags of Rall's own regiment to be placed at the head of the grenadier formation, now taut and tense, in preparation for attacking up straight up King

Street and into the teeth of the storm and Knox's row of roaring artillery. As prescribed by regulations, all five flags of the Rall Regiment were now positioned before the lengthy line of bristling bayonets before the formation's center. Instilling a greater sense of pride and confidence in Rall's veteran grenadiers so far from home, these cherished war banners now flapped in the biting northeaster blowing off the heights like a windy April day along the wide Rhine River, which was more than double Delaware's size. To protect the colors snapping in the Arctic-like gusts pouring down the broad, open stretch of King Street that sloped down gradually to the river, an elite "block" of blue uniformed fusilers, or musketeers, stood in place, without moving a muscle, on either side of the massed clump of colorful war banners, the Fahner-Peloton. Hessian officers had drawn their Prussian infantry sabers and they were more than ready to lead their troops north to the high ground.

Hoping to reverse the day's fortunes by first pushing Washington's fast-working guns off the high ground and to still achieve a glorious victory for German arms as so often in the past, a mounted Colonel Rall galloped to his grenadier's front on dramatic fashion. He then ordered his troops forward up the broad slope of King Street, while "men [were] falling on every side" of him. Emboldening the grenadiers who longed for this opportunity to return punishment upon the detested rebels, Rall's regiment lurched up the lengthy slope leading to King Street's head. Young Hessian drummer boys beat their drums until it seemed as if they would burst, sounding the charge for all to hear. In almost perfect step and flags flying in the December cold, the stoic grenadiers, perhaps with some men now saying silent prayers to themselves, marched with discipline up the gradual slope of King Street. They also surged forward with the firm conviction that nothing could resist a Hessian bayonet attack. Rall had now regained the initiative.

Inspiring his troops, shouting encouragement, and waving his saber, Rall led his grenadier regiment straight up icy King Street toward the fiery eye of Knox's artillery storm. With renewed faith in hurling Washington's troops and cannon off the commanded heights in part because they were bolstered by the two three-pounders under Lieutenant Engelhardt, the densely packed Hessian ranks marched with precision through the cascading flakes of snow with firm resolution. Undeterred by the prospect of coming to close-range grips with the row of roaring American artillery, the Rall Regiment pushed up the gradually ascending ground and toward more guns than the Hessians had ever encountered before.

Leading the way as a vanguard for the lengthy formation of grenadiers in blue uniforms, Lieutenant Johann Heinrich Sternickel and his "watch-guard" company advanced before the Rall Regiment. All the while, the fast-paced pounding from more than half a dozen German drummer boys echoed through Trenton's snowy streets, keeping time for the steadily advancing grenadiers in a scene reminiscent of the glorious assault on Fort Washington barely a month before. All the while, the Hessians maintained perfect discipline, almost as if they believed that this threatening, formidable display alone would be sufficient to once again unnerve Washington's men as so often in the past.

Above all else at this crucial moment, Rall clearly understood that the true key of defense was the unleashing of the tactical offensive. To add more muscle to the infantry counterstroke by his beloved grenadiers who had never failed to taking a tactical objective, Rall ordered all the companies of the von Lossberg Regiment, in Church Alley, which the Rall Regiment had just advanced past in pushing north up King Street, to follow his grenadiers in support of the desperate offensive effort to hurl Washington off his high ground perch only around 430 paces north of his King Street headquarters. Led by Lieutenant Colonel Scheffer who now drew upon more than three decades of solid experience, hundreds of von Lossbergers filed west and out of Church Alley's relative safety, after Rall's confident grenadiers swept past them farther north up the slope.

Then, with a mechanical-like drill field precision, Scheffer's fusiliers quickly fell into an assault column just behind the Rall Regiment rank's now surging north up the lengthy expanse of King Street. Then, appreciating the importance of artillery as much as Washington and Knox whose visions of victory this cold morning depended upon the artillery, Rall bellowed to Lieutenant Engelhardt, "My God, Lieutenant Engelhardt, the picket [Captain Altenbockum's men now retiring down King Street] is already coming in! Push your cannon ahead!"

Thinking like an experienced aggressive artillery commander partly because of the tactical development of the innovative German practice of assigning artillery to infantry regiments expressly for active service in America, Rall knew that his regiment's two cannon had to be advanced much farther up King Street to be truly effective. Therefore, he now wanted these two guns deployed relatively close to King Street's head in order to get within easy range for any chance of knocking out Washington's blazing cannon, before they could blunt his counterattack's momentum: another gamble and race with time, because the Hessian guns had to inflict sufficient damage upon the Americans before they themselves were silenced in what was to become a showdown of respective wills.

With Rall's urgent directive, Lieutenants Engelhardt and Fischer shouted orders for their two three-pounders to advance north up King Street. Artillery drivers whipped horses to pull the two cannon faster up the ice-covered street and much closer to Knox's rapidly firing artillery. On King Street, the heavily breathing artillery horses strained in hauling the artillery pieces, each gun barrel and wooden carriage weighing nine hundred pounds, up the sloping ground that ascended more sharply than it initially appeared to the eye. German drivers vigorously lashed the animals of the two four-horse teams to get the two bronze guns up the slope as quickly as possible.

Shouting orders above the tumult, Lieutenants Engelhardt and Fischer led their eighteen gunners and the two bronze three-pounders, which were lighter and more mobile than Washington's iron guns because of size and weight differences between iron and bronze, straight up King Street. Staking everything on one throw of the dice, Rall was now betting that he could get his two guns rapidly moved up the slope and situated into an advanced position relatively close enough to inflict sufficient damage upon Captain Forrest's Pennsylvania guns to give his blue-coat grenadiers a chance to turn the tide with a bayonet charge. Rall envisioned that punishment inflicted by the three-pounders might open the way for his two infantry regiments to hurl Washington's guns off the high ground: a concentrated, hard-hitting one-two infantry-artillery punch that American troops had never withstood before on any battlefield of this war.

For the first time all morning, consequently, Rall felt added confidence at the sight of four stout and fresh artillery horses, evidently shod with ice-horseshoes, pulling the two three-pounders up the ascending ground of King Street. Finally, the two three-pounders reached an advanced position just north of Petty's Run, after clattering nosily across the little wooden bridge on the double. Here, only about 260 paces north of Rall's headquarters and more than halfway to the head of King Street, Lieutenant Engelhardt screamed orders for his two three-pounders to set up only around 175-180 paces south of Washington's high ground position.

However, this advanced artillery position represented an overly ambitious placement of guns and actually much too close to Washington's concentration of well-manned artillery, but this crisis situation called for desperate action and risk-taking. Indeed, with his visibility yet reduced by the snow and ice lashing into his face and because of his own inexperience, Engelhardt had placed his guns in an overly exposed position. Revealing their excellent training and nerves of steel, German artillerymen worked smoothly together as a well-oiled team, preparing their guns to fire back at their tormentors and a vastly superior array of cannon.

Perhaps Colonel Rall, therefore, would have been wiser to have merely maintained a defensive stance in town to confront Mercer's brigade to the west, because the closer his counterattack pushed north and beyond the town's center, the more vulnerable it became to Washington's greatest strength, Knox's furious artillery fire from the heights. Rall's counterattack that emerged so suddenly out of the swirling snowstorm was early ascertained by Washington and Knox. They continued to benefit from the tempest at their backs. The dense ranks of the Hessians drew nearer. With the Rall's Regiment grenadiers advancing in front and the von Lossberg fusiliers, in blue and scarlet grenadier uniforms, close behind, from north to south respectively, standing out in the open as ideal targets outlined against the white background, Washington shouted orders for Forrest's Pennsylvania gunners to prepare to warmly receive Rall's bold counter-attack up the snowy slope.

All in all, Washington and his troops on the high ground must have been amazed at the imposing sight presented below them. What they now saw was a solid Hessian wall of so-called walking muskets, a Frederick the Great legacy, surging with typical Teutonic precision up King Street. When seemingly no hope remained to reverse the day's fortunes, Rall was now relying upon his grenadier's aggressiveness, accurate artillery-fire from his two three-pounders, and, most of all, the bayonet to yet win the day. Clearly, by both nature and instinct, but tempered by well-honed experience and sound tactical judgment, Rall was clearly an enthusiastic devotee of the tactical offensive. Capable and aggressive, this grizzled veteran of more than thirty years of service knew exactly how and where to play his high card in his own tactical gamble to win not only victory, but also to reap glory, as he had demonstrated so often in the past: a well-timed coordination of close-range artilleryfire, volley firing from musketry, and a bold frontal assault with the bayonet.

However, Rall would have been wiser to have turned all six of his cannon upon Washington's infantry—especially Mercer's brigade and Haslet's regiment, north of Mercer, now hovering on his left flank and inflicting punishment—rather than attempting to engage in a lopsided artillery duel with only two little three-pounders. Handicapped on lower ground along Petty's Run and outgunned by both the number of Knox's guns and their caliber size, Rall possessed little hope of blasting far too many American cannon off a commanding position with too little firepower. But it was not Rall's style to relinquish the initiative without a determined attempt to regain it.

Therefore, he now relied upon what he knew and did best, the seemingly invincible formula of unleashing the frontal assault with the bayonet. In overall tactical terms, the two three-pounders, bolstered by Rall's two veteran infantry regiments, now presented the first serious obstacle for any American advance down King Street to deliver a knock-out blow to the Rall brigade by not only barring the way, but also threatening to upset the all-important closing of the two pincer arms of Washington's double envelopment. By delivering his own surprise attack straight up King Street, Rall hoped to steal the momentum already gained by the Virginian's surprise attack before it could be fully exploited, while keeping Washington's two pincer arms from closing tight.

With two full Hessian infantry regiments moving relentlessly up King Street as if nothing could stop them, either Washington or Knox, or both, hurriedly shouted orders for the fast-working cannoneers to now make a key adjust of munitions in an attempt to parry the day's most serious threat. This new set of directives called for the young Pennsylvania gunners positioned at King Street's head to now employ their most lethal form of anti-personnel ammunition: canister and grape (primarily a naval round). Such deadly charges, especially when delivered at close range, were the best anti-personnel munition for breaking up a massed infantry assault, especially one that was boxed in along a narrow front and crammed between rows of houses on both sides of King Street. And as Washington had earlier envisioned with tactical clarity, the best served and most lethal American artillery unit that possessed the largest supply of canister and grape in all of Washington's Army, was now located in the perfect place at exactly the right time: around the head of King Street, Captain Forrest's two six-pounders and two five and a half-inch howitzers were now poised with an eager group of experienced and well-trained gunners ready to deliver severe punishment.

At this crucial moment with everything now hanging in the balance, including America's very life, this decided "long-arm" advantage for Washington, who had already anticipated this crucial showdown on King Street, was no mere accident. Significantly, the resolute Virginian's foresight, the hallmark of both Washington's leadership throughout this morning of destiny, had masterfully set this stage for the most dramatic of showdowns, because he had long anticipated that King Street would become "the vital center of the battle." Rall, consequently, was now directing his assault formation—massed to deliver volleys and for protection against cavalry—straight into the midst of Washington's greatest concentration of strength, especially artillery but also his best infantry, as the Virginian had anticipated with clarity. Now at his best, Washington's string of insightful, well-conceived decisions went all the way back to having first integrated artillery pieces with each infantry brigade on the march to Trenton to now bestow a decided advantage at this critical moment.

Washington's initial placement of Captain Forrest's artillery at the head of the main assault column revealed exactly why the two largest Philadelphia guns, six-pounders—double the caliber size of the Hessians' cannon—and also the five and a half-inch howitzer were deployed on the most strategic position of the Trenton battlefield at King Street's head was due to Washington's well-conceived tactical design. Trained to utilize grapeshot to hammer British warships in Philadelphia's defense, Forrest's highly skilled cannoneers and guns were not only now in an ideal position but also possessed especially lethal and distinctive firepower capabilities, beyond that of any other of Washington's artillery commands.

Indeed, Captain Forrest's Pennsylvania unit possessed the most lethal capabilities, thanks to the six-pounders and howitzers which were both especially effective in firing grape and canister, to inflict the greatest possible damage upon massed infantry. Now waging war just northeast from their native Philadelphia that these Pennsylvania state cannoneers had sworn to defend with their lives, ironically, Forrest's command had yet to be formally accepted into the Continental Army by Congress. At this key moment in America's most important battle, these six-pounders and five and a half-inch howitzer even now officially operated under the overall control of the state of Pennsylvania.

With a sweeping view of the wide, expansive panorama below him from his high ground perch at King Street's head, meanwhile, Washington continued to watch the relentless advance of Rall's counterattack rolling onward up the icy slope. In some awe at the martial sight but eager to destroy the majesty of the parade ground-like formations, Washington viewed the Rall Regiment grenadiers and von Lossberg fusiliers moving closer in disciplined step and with all their colorful battle flags flapping in the brisk, northeast wind. Steeled by this imposing sight of the relentless Hessian advance and rows of steel bayonets, Washington's most timely decision was guaranteed to wreak havoc upon Rall's most audacious gamble just in time. Amid a flurry of activity ignited by Washington's more recent order, Forrest's artillerymen of the six-pounders and the five and a half-inch howitzer went to work with zeal. In frantic haste, the Philadelphia gunners began to switch from solid, or round, shot and shell, respectively, to lethal loads of both canister and grapeshot.

Relishing this golden opportunity to severely punish hundreds of finely trained grenadiers in their fancy uniforms and to smash lofty Hessian reputations and Rall's ambitions by way of their own skill, Forrest's cannoneers now brought forth heavy loads of large iron balls—canister and grapeshot—wrapped in canvas and mounted on wooded bases that perfectly fit the cannon barrel's caliber. One of the myths of the battle of Trenton was that Washington's gunners possessed only makeshift canister—pieces of iron, nails, cut-up horseshoes—which was not the case. Some young, but veteran, Pennsylvania cannoneers, with ears yet ringing from the repeated eruption of fire from iron barrels, now might have smiled at one another, because they knew that these canister loads were their most lethal anti-personnel munition in their arsenal.

For a seasoned gunner, the relatively simple procedure of switching to grapeshot and canister now transformed Captain Forrest's well-positioned cannon essentially into giant shotguns: the deadliest of weapons that could be directed against a concentrated mass of advancing infantry, especially when caught in the open at close range. Clearly, once again thinking ahead in tactical terms as throughout this Thursday morning, Washington had saved this classic artilleryman's coup-de-grace—his ultimate artillery ace in the hole—for the last, and his decision could not have been better timed. Washington might have even held up his artillery's canister and grape fire for a tense few minutes in order to allow Rall's relentless moving mass of disciplined grenadiers and fusiliers to surge even closer and farther up King Street to within a more lethal killing range. If so, then he allowed Rall's dense formations to ease up the open, ascending slope and into what in essence was a natural shooting gallery and a canister-and-grapeshot ambush of sorts. Forrest's anxious Philadelphia gunners, maintaining discipline and resisting temptation to fire, held their long linstocks with lit matches above their cannon's touch holes, while the ceaseless pounding of seemingly countless Hessian drums grew louder in the biting cold.

When the decisive moment came at last, never before had some of Washington's best artillerymen, who must have fairly salivated at the tantalizing sight of so many disciplined grenadiers advancing in formation toward them, been presented with a more inviting target. By this time, Rall's grenadiers had relentlessly pushed north up the icebound street around 150 feet and all the way "to the first houses in the street," and just before crossing the little wooden bridge over Petty's Run, the rain-swollen watercourse that ran east-west across the town's northern outskirts, before turning to flow south on King Street's west side.

What Knox's gunners, lusting at the opportunity and delighted while simultaneously yet awed by the magnificent martial sight, now saw before them was the artilleryman's greatest dream come true: a concentrated, dense formation of blue-coated soldiers—the legendary Rall grenadiers, who had long made an easy game (little more than sport) of vanquishing untrained American farm boys, masquerading as soldiers, with impunity—coming steadily on in a slow-moving mass and up the gentle, open incline lined with a soft blacket of snow. All the while, teenage Hessian drummer boys continued their rapid tapping of instruments with a steady cadence, encouraging the grenadiers and fusiliers farther up the slope and closer to Knox's now silent row of cannon.

No longer able to wait any longer with the Hessian ranks now within easy range, Washington at last roared, "Fire!" at the top of his lungs. Aligned across the snow-covered high ground while a blustery wind blew to the gunner's backs, Forrest's four cannon, loaded with grapeshot and canister, erupted in unison. Fiery blasts exploded from the Pennsylvania cannon's mouths, both the long six-pounders and the five and a half-inch howitzers, lighting up the strategic heights at King Street's head with fire. Screaming in their flight from the high ground, this deadly hail of projectiles swept down the King Street with a vengeance. Here, just below Petty's Run, the terrible impact of the lethal iron spray stopped the foremost of Rall's finely uniformed grenadiers in their tracks. Men were cut down almost as if a giant scythe was sweeping effortlessly through tall, thin stalks of ripe spring wheat on a September afternoon.

Torrents of grapeshot and canister were funneled down the sloping ground of narrow King Street like a whirlwind, striking with tremendous force. Salvoes of small-sized projectiles knocked down clumps of soldiers, cutting swathes out of the ranks. All the while, an eerie clinking sound rose from the hail of projectiles hitting the rows of upheld Hessian bayonets and accouterments. Color bearers fell into the street and colorful flags plunged downward at the head of the Hessian formation, but these cherished banners were soon picked up and then carried onward in the tumult.

After the Pennsylvania field pieces recoiled violently from the unleashing of their lethal loads, Forrest's cannoneers and nearby American riflemen marveled at the cannon's effectiveness. They very likely cheered the exhilarating sight of grenadiers falling in bunches. No doubt feeling an equal sense of satisfaction,

Washington, who never looked more inspiring to his men than when riding along the high ground, also might have momentarily joined in such an ad hoc celebration on the windswept heights.

With close friends, perhaps going back to innocent childhood days, and comrades falling around them amid the hail of iron projectiles, which proved more terrifying than the young soldier's fear of their own stern officers, the grenadier's legendary discipline began to crumble for the first time on American soil. Rall's counterattack up the ascending slope was shaken not only by the deadly combination of grapeshot and canister from the front, but also from a fiery stream of Mercer's musketry that gnawed the vulnerable left flank. Severely punished by blistering fire from two directions, north and west, the head of Rall's formation reeled from the shock of multiple blows. To escape the leaden hail, which now mixed with the yet raging snowstorm to create a wintry nightmare for massed troops surging up King Street, some panicked grenadiers on the Rall Regiment's hard-hit left flank broke ranks to seek shelter in houses on the street's west side. But these Hessians now only met an even closer-range flank-fire, and perhaps even a flurry of musket-butts and a few bayonets, of Mercer's soldiers fighting from houses bordering King Street's west side.[2]

Also adding to Rall's vexing tactical dilemma, Washington's infantrymen on the heights now unleashed a full frontal fire that also smashed into the head of the Hessian formation. For long-range firing down the open slope and to guarantee a higher degree of accuracy, Washington had gathered a detachment of the best riflemen of both Stirling's brigade and the right of Stephen's brigade, placing them on the high ground near Forrest's blazing cannon. As throughout this campaign, Washington was once again thinking ahead. Even though at a longer range from the Hessians than Mercer's and Haslet's fast-firing Continentals now hovering on Rall's left flank, this scorching frontal fire that spat flame from the Virginian's trusty Long Rifles was especially effective, much to General Stephen's delight. Reaping a grim harvest, this merciless rifle-fire was also accurate in part because Colonel Scott, the veteran Indian fighter since his teenage years, had long implored his sharp-eyed riflemen, especially the young Virginia soldiers, to aim low. Proving especially valuable this morning, Scott's astute tactical reasoning of the western frontier was as simple as it was well thought-out because his Virginia boys, in the excitement of battle, were in the "habit of shooting too high [and] you waste your powder and lead; and I have cursed you about it a hundred times [and therefore] Now, I tell you . . . nothing must be wasted, every crack must count."[3] One of Washington's most experienced regimental commanders, Scott knew that having his men aim their Virginia Long Rifles low and not overshoot in order to hit far more targets than usual was now essential for success, because "one man Wounded in the leg is better [than] a dead one for it takes two more to carry him off" the field.[4]

Meanwhile, combined with the salvoes of canister and grapeshot smashing into the Hessians' front rank from Forrest's Philadelphia guns that belched a sheet of flame, severe damage was also inflicted upon Rall's troops by the utilization of buck and ball ammunition unleashed at closer range from the west. This blistering fire delivered in enfilade from Mercer's veteran riflemen was devastating. Crackling louder in the frigid air than the rhythmic sound of the Hessians' beating drums and officers' shouted orders, the deadly flank fire streamed eastward from the row of darkened houses on King Street's west side, and from a large number of Mercer's veteran marksmen, who had aligned behind the wooden fences that encircled Stacy Potts's tanyard. Washington's soldiers in this sector benefitted from an open field of fire on the compact mass of Hessian targets, vulnerable to an enfilade fire and exposed in the openness of King Street, which loomed within easy range and could not be missed.

Pouring out of the eerily serene and silent cascade of falling snow at close range, Mercer's musketry streaming from the tanyard area on King Street's west side was especially destructive, raking Rall's foot soldiers and artillerymen with a vicious enfilade fire from the west. All in all, this punishing flank fire, especially from the close-range buck and ball ammunition unleashed from the large-caliber, smoothbore muskets of Mercer's foremost troops, was almost as effective in thwarting Rall's desperate counterstroke up the ice-slick street as the initial explosion of canister and grapeshot from Captain Forrest's six-pounders and five and a half-inch howitzers.

Along with the hardened veterans of Haslet's Delaware regiment, of Stirling's brigade, just to the north, Mercer's soldiers fully exploited a key tactical advantage over their vulnerable opponent exposed out in King Street. Protected from the storm's icy wrath, Mercer's mostly Continental troops of four regiments, from Maryland, Connecticut, and Massachusetts, continued to benefit immensely from having taken good cover in the houses on King Street's west side, which allowed them to blast away at Rall's left flank with impunity. These enclosed first and second floor firing positions ensured that the weapons, flints, and black powder of Mercer's men, whose feet were now on dry surfaces for the first time all day, stayed dry to facilitate an even heavier rate of fire. In addition, a larger trickle of Mercer's and Haslet's soldiers had crossed

King Street to the north above Petty's Run. These men then turned to unleash a plunging musketry from the street's east side upon the foremost grenadiers at the battered head of Rall's assault column.

Mercer's Continentals, armed with mostly smoothbore muskets rather than rifles, especially benefitted from the advantage of not only good firing positions but also in blasting away upon packed Hessian ranks with "Buck and Ball" at close range. Fully appreciated by the average American soldier, this deadly charge fired at close range contained the lethal combination of one large .69 caliber ball and five buckshot. Such a ratio gave the smoothbore muskets not only a shotgun-like effect with the buckshot, but also considerable knock-down, killing power with the large caliber lead ball. These common smoothbore musket loads, called "swain shot" by easterners while westerners used the more popular term of "Buck and Ball," were a key, although forgotten, factor that explained how such a bloody harvest had been reaped among the scarlet attackers at Breed's Hill: a lethal formula which was now duplicated in the bitter struggle for Trenton's possession.

With the exposed formation of Hessians on King Street at their mercy, larger numbers of Mercer's Maryland, Connecticut, and Massachusetts soldiers, all except the 105 riflemen of Colonel Rawlings's Maryland Rifle Battalion, whose men carried trusty Long Rifles, continued to blast away into the Hessians' left flank with a destructive enfilade fire. Most of Mercer's veterans unleashed sweeping loads of a single large lead "ball and buckshot," in one soldier's words. Consequently, soldiers with large-caliber smoothbore muskets maintained a more effective fire than even the Maryland riflemen in a traditional role reversal, thanks to the combined effect of their opponent's close range, buck and ball ammunition, and snowstorm conditions that limited visibility and range. The savviest of Washington's marksmen realized that the Hessians wore tall grenadier helmets in part to magnify their height to present a more fearsome appearance in order to cause opponents to fire too high and miss their targets. For long shots, the most knowledgeable American marksmen, especially the westerners, of Mercer's brigade adjusted their aim accordingly, sighting lower to squarely hit their German victims, who fell to rise no more.

No less important at this time, the smoothbores of Mercer's soldiers were now able to be loaded much faster than rifles, ensuring a higher rate and heavier volume of fire. These same Hessian grenadiers had earlier mocked—the surest way to tempt fate—the average, homespun American riflemen because of the slow process of reloading small-caliber rifles. This time-consuming procedure had often proved fatal in the past, allowing the Germans to charge and bayonet hapless American riflemen, who could not reload in time for a second fire, since it took them "an hour to load," ridiculed one Hessian. Possessing few bayonets unlike their well-equipped opponents, most of Mercer's boys now fully utilized an ideal, close-range weapon—the large caliber smoothbore—and the best anti-personnel ammunition—buck and ball—from their well-sheltered positions, both in houses and in Potts's tanyard, to deal out punishment.

Consequently, even if their aim was off, Mercer's Continentals and Connecticut state troops could yet hit lucrative targets with blasts of buck and ball, especially at close range, from smoothbores: a distinct advantage during a snowstorm when visibility was so severely hindered and limited. Some of the hottest fire now streamed from behind Rall's quarters just west of King Street, pouring from Mercer's riflemen, especially Rawlings's lethal sharpshooters of the First Regiment of Maryland Continentals, now under the able command of Lieutenant Colonel Francis Ware. These sharp-eyed Marylanders continued to demonstrate exactly why they recently had been the Hessians' nemesis at Fort Washington.

While hurriedly reloading their muskets in small, sulphurous smoke-filled rooms of darkened houses bordering King Street's west side, perhaps some of Mercer's soldiers now took a moment to marvel at the sight of the Hessians' splendid discipline and fancy uniforms. Contrary to myth, not every Hessian soldier wore the standard Prussian blue uniforms, only troops of the Rall and Knyphausen Regiments. The von Lossbergers of all six companies wore scarlet coats, like their British allies. Meanwhile, Rall's grenadiers were donned in the short blue coat patterned after the Prussian uniforms that had long distin-guished the troops under Frederick the Great, who early understood that his soldiers fought more effectively if unhindered by the traditional long waist coats worn by other European soldiers.

Rall's battle-hardened grenadiers also looked more formidable because they wore tall "mitre" hats, with large decorative brass front-plates but yet light, instead of the broad tricorne infantry hat, which had been traditionally deemed impractical for grenade throwing (the source of the word grenadier). However, at the head of their respective grenadier and fusilier companies, Rall's officers wore stylish bicorn hats as in the days of Frederick the Great, revealing their rank to Washington's marksmen. Men in such brightly colored Hessian uniforms made ideal targets for veteran American soldiers, now wearing dirty, nondescript homespun, especially when displayed against a white background. For Mercer's Maryland veterans, the systematic killing of exposed Hessian soldiers, especially officers, was almost like shooting down grazing turkeys and white-tailed deer in the Catoctin, Sugar Loaf, and South Mountains of Frederick County in western Maryland.

Swept by multiple blistering fires, Rall's counterattack floundered and front lines buckled, after having advanced more than fifty yards and about halfway up King Street, that had become a killing field, to nearly reach Petty's Run. The Rall Regiment's Christmas night and morning "watch-guard," of around thirty men, under Lieutenant Johann Heinrich Sternickel, leading the assault column forward into the eye of the storm was literally cut to pieces. Exposed in the lonely open expanse of King Street, that had become little more than a shooting gallery, just below Petty's Run, Sternickel's vanguard was almost entirely swept away by Mercer's blistering flank fire and Forrest's canister and grapeshot simultaneously striking them from the front. Along with a good many of his ill-fated men, Sternickel fell with a mortal wound. What little remained of the elite "watch-guard" survivors escaped from the nightmarish carnage of King Street, heading east toward Queen Street to seek shelter from the artillery storm. The respected lieutenant's fall into the snow and his vanguard's systematic decimation was an unnerving sight, but the grim-faced grenadiers continued to stoically push onward up the body-strewn slope with fixed bayonets and grim determination to take the high ground.

To the west, meanwhile, Mercer's rapidly firing men no doubt took some grim satisfaction in seeing the amount of devastation that they inflicted among such a feared adversary, who had beaten them so often in the past. After all, these marksmen benefitted from hitting German targets not only at close range, but also from the advantage of the higher terrain west of King Street that gradually ascended to a high point at King Street's head. The snow-covered ground on King Street's west side, which sloped gently eastward, was higher than at street level, providing Mercer's marksmen with an elevated firing position from which to deliver a plunging fire that unmercifully raked the Hessians' left flank.

After having just witnessed the disturbing sight of the thorough decimation of Lieutenant Sternickel's vanguard, a mounted Lieutenant Colonel Balthasar Brethauer halted his hard-hit grenadier ranks to restore order. Shouting directives amid the screaming hail of projectiles, he straightened the grenadier's shredded ranks as best he could. Brethauer wisely realized that continuing to advance any farther up the slope and the open street beyond Petty's Run in the face of Forrest's artillery fire was simply suicidal. Then, in a desperate effort to slow the blistering fire pouring off the high ground at King Street's head and with Sternickel's vanguard troops no longer in his front, Brethauer ordered Rall's grenadiers to realign ranks and then unleash their first volley of the day. This first eruption of musketry exploded from the grenadier's ranks, roaring through the falling snow and up King Street.

However, this initial volley from Rall's formation proved entirely ineffective for a number of reasons. First, despite the fact that the grenadiers were now deployed on open ground just south of Petty's Run, the distance and range was too great to do any damage to Washington's infantrymen and cannoneers on higher ground. And visibility was obscured with the wind, snow, and ice whipping into Hessian faces, ensuring an inaccurate fire by the Germans. The grenadier's first volley was also inconsequential because so many Hessian muskets were wet and black powder changes compromised by this time. Many Germans, therefore, were surprised that upon pulling triggers, the striking of flint on steel produced no flash in the firing pan as priming powder failed to ignite, resulting in no chain reaction of black powder charges necessary to fire muskets.

Therefore, because of these combined factors, not a single American soldier on the high ground fell dead or wounded from the first concentrated Hessian volley of the day. However, exposed in the open at the top of the heights near King Street's head, a mounted Washington experienced a close call. With raised sword and in the open, the commander-in-chief, wearing a tricorn hat and sitting tall in the saddle, which made him an excellent target, was shouting orders to his men when a Hessian bullet passed between the fingers of his raised hand. Washington, remaining calm as usual and even somewhat invigorated by the excitement of combat as since his youth when he had first discovered that "there was something charming" in the "whistle" of bullets, merely sardonically responded to a nearby staff officers with the reassuring words, "That has passed by." He then continued to inspire his soldiers to fire faster, as if nothing had happened.

Meanwhile, in contrast to the Hessians' impotent fire, the Americans, who relished the German's transition from a moving mass to a more inviting stationary target, continued to hit exposed Hessians with an accurate fire, while the crackle of gunfire echoed higher over Trenton. Then, Lieutenant Colonel Brethauer went down before the ranks of his grenadiers not long after issuing the order to fire when his horse was hit with grapeshot from the Pennsylvania field pieces. He fell hard, tumbling in the snow and ice lining King Street just below Petty's Run. Combined with the number of Hessian muskets that failed to fire, the alarming sight of Brethauer falling at the formation's head was yet another factor that shook the grenadier's confidence and morale. Nevertheless, the proud grenadiers of Rall's Regiment defiantly stood their ground amid the swirls of smoke and bloodstained snow just below little Petty's Run, continuing to put up a good fight. Then, all of a sudden, Brethauer, unlike the stricken Lieutenant Sternickel who lay in the snow, seemingly rose up from the dead. Demonstrating considerable composure amid the hail of lead, meanwhile, those grenadiers with yet operable weapons quickly reloaded them like they had practiced on a hundred drill fields, while other Hessians sought frantically to dry flints and priming pans and remove wet paper cartridges loads from flintlocks with bullet exacters that had been attached to ramrod tips. Despite his throbbing wound, hard fall from his horse, and illness of the past several days, Brehauer was suddenly back on his feet and once again in command. Gamely ignoring the pain and shaking off his lingering sickness, Brethauer roared for his grenadiers to unleash a second volley.

Another explosion of gunfire rippled down the Hessian ranks like a bolt of lightning, with a sheet of flame erupting down the line. After the grenadiers fired their second volley, Brethauer somehow managed to remain standing amid the falling snow, inspiring his troops to even greater exertions. After losing more blood and growing faint, he was soon assisted rearward by a strong-armed grenadier to seek a physician and a fresh mount to continue the fight. With a wife back in Germany, Major Johann Jost Matthaus, age fifty-eight and born in Schwarzenberg, Saxony, now took charge of what remained of the battered Rall Regiment after Brethauser's departure down body-strewn King Street. In a seamless transference of regimental command, the experienced major rose to the challenge amid the storm of projectiles that had transformed King Street into a hell on earth for the hard-hit Rall and von Lossberg Regiments. Hoping to rush the two three-pounders into action as soon as possible especially now that the infantrymen were faltering, Major Matthaus and Rall continued to implore Lieutenant Engelhardt to get the guns up in a hurry to provide support.

All the while, Haslet's Delaware soldiers, now situated in houses north of Mercer's troops, raked the head of Rall's formation, while Mercer's Maryland, Connecticut, and Massachusetts soldiers, just to the south of the Delaware Continentals, riddled the Hessians' left flank from the west. Nothing diminished the volume of galling musketry streaming from Washington's veterans because the Hessians' return fire was directed north instead of west. Like the first volley, the second volley unleashed by Rall's grenadiers, aligned just below Petty's Run, proved nothing more than a waste of ammunition.

Not one of Washington's men were hit by either volley that either sailed too high overhead, or slammed into the snow before them. But most likely, the Hessian volley struck too low, with German soldiers not aiming smooth-bore muskets well above their high ground targets in failing to adjust their aim to compensate for higher elevation firing. With snow and sleet blowing into their faces, the Hessian soldiers could barely see Washington's elevated position, except for the muffled muzzle-flashes from too many American rifles and cannon to count. However, local "tradition" has it that Washington's chestnut sorrel horse, which was not frightened under him despite the roar of cannon- and gunfire, was hit by a musket ball. If so, then it was most likely from the grenadier's fire at this point. Sitting tall in the saddle with his imposing height of more than a "full six feet, erect and well proportioned," Washington was vulnerable because he was determined to remain at the forefront beside his men along the blazing firing line.

Rall's hard-hit formations began to recoil under the relentless pounding, with more blasts of canister and grape loosed by the row of Knox's field pieces. Hundreds of grenadiers and fusiliers, exposed in King Street's deadly expansiveness, could no longer endure this brutal punishment, while delivering no damage in return during an inequitable duel from a vulnerable lower position. Rall's troops, therefore, continued to suffer under the torments of several distinct manifestations of concentrated firepower: large caliber smoothbore muskets hurling loads of buck and ball ammunition; Long Rifles unleashing a hail of small caliber balls; and explosions of canister and grapeshot from Forrest's artillery salvoes.

Ensign Carl Wilhelm Kleinschmidt, the Rall Regiment's adjutant, was stunned by the havoc wrought from the fire erupting from the roaring six-pounders and five and a half-inch howitzers, worked rapidly by expert Philadelphia gunners, who seemingly made every shot count as if they held a sadistic grudge or special desire for revenge. With the hard-hit Hessians disoriented by the combined effect of multiple fires and the snow and sleet hurled into faces, the counterattack of Rall's grenadier regiment finally broke up near Petty's Run and less than halfway from its intended target at the head of King Street.

Additional shaken grenadiers, with the screams of wounded comrades ringing in their ears, headed south down King Street with a hail of cannonballs, canister, and grapeshot escorting them rearward. Some unnerved Hessians made haste for the stone bridge across Assunpink Creek to the south. Other stunned grenadiers sought cover behind houses on the east side of King Street or down the dark, narrows alleys and backyards of houses toward Queen Street, just to the east, to escape the incessant fires. After retiring back down King Street, the vast majority of grenadiers headed to the relative safety of Pinkerton's Alley, where they had earlier formed, however. Likewise, the appropriately named Church Alley, which led to Queen Street and the Methodist Church that stood opposite the alley's west end, offered refuge a block north of Pinkerton's Alley for the northernmost grenadiers, who had not continued to retire a block south to Pinkerton's Alley.

Obeying officers' orders, the largest number of Rall's grenadiers finally began to rally where they had originally formed before the attack—along Pinkerton's Alley between King and Queen Street and just below Petty's Run. Other grenadiers continued to withdraw even farther south down King Street, passing through the supporting fusilier ranks of the von Lossberg Regiment's left wing. This flight south of some Rall's grenadiers disrupted the von Lossberger's straight line of their once-tight left wing formation on King Street.

Not deterred by the sharp setback on King Street, the feisty Rall was only beginning to fight this morning, however. Rall now ordered the well-trained fusiliers of the von Lossberg Regiment—the finest fighting men of the brigade—onward and straight up projectile-swept King Street, after Lieutenant Colonel Scheffer had restored cohesion and quickly realigned his regiment's left wing into a solid formation once more. Rall's desperate bayonet attack up King Street was continued by the crack von Lossberg fusiliers, almost as if the Rall Regiment's repulse had been a unbelievable aberration from some surreal Hessian nightmare too horrible to bear.

Just below Petty's Run and the small wooden bridge, the red-uniformed fusiliers of the von Lossberg Regiment likewise took a severe pounding during their relentless advance farther up King Street. Fusilier ranks were flailed by sheets of flame leaping from small arms and Knox's field pieces. Like the repulsed Rall's Grenadier Regiment, this punishment delivered upon the von Lossbergers came from the deadly crossfire of musketry, streaming from the west and north, and blasts of artillery-fire from the north. Indeed, Mercer and Haslet's riflemen and Forrest's gunners had redirected and concentrated their aim on the steadily advancing von Lossberg Regiment, after Rall's grenadiers were stopped in their tracks. Now it was the turn of the Lieb (first) Company— the elite Body Guards, who protected the regimental commander with their lives and was a specifically designated company of each regiment—to receive its fair share of punishment. Located on the regiment's right wing, Captain Johann von Riess commanded this elite company that now suffered severely under the pounding. Not intimidated by barking American Long Rifles in the past or present, Captain Riess had distinguished himself at the battle of White Plains in leading his cheering troops up Chatterton Hill to reap victory.

On and on up King Street came the brave fusiliers until they advanced beyond the northernmost point reached by Rall's hard-hit grenadiers. With the snow now strewn with debris, discarded equipment, and red-splattered German bodies, King Street had been transformed into a grim killing field by Knox's artillerymen, whose salvoes swept the open avenue with a ruthless, deadly efficiency. Like its earlier Rall Regiment victims, this murderous fire caught the crack fusiliers of the Lieb Company in the open. Consequently, these fusiliers now found themselves in an awfully bad fix. Blasting away at targets that they could not miss after having verified the exact range and precise trajectory in earlier smashing the neat grenadier formations to pieces, Forrest's Pennsylvania cannoneers continued to inflict damage on the hapless von Lossberg fusiliers amid the awful openness of King Street.

Additionally trusty German officers went down, perhaps including Captain Riess at this point. Under the pounding, the hard-hit right wing of the von Lossberg Regiment fell back, reeling in shock and pain like a wounded beast. As only recently seen, this same destructive formula was repeated, with the left wing of the von Lossberg Regiment wavering from the incessant flank fire, after the battered right wing had been hurled back. Led by Captain Friedrich Wilhelm von Benning, the von Hanstein Company now occupied the von Lossberg Regiment's left wing, after having belatedly just reached their fusilier regiment because it had been quartered in houses on the Assunpink's south side.

Hoping to live to fight another day, some shell-shocked von Lossbergers sought cover to escape the leaden storm while additional comrades were cut down in the body-strewn snow of King Street. Clearly, no matter how well trained or disciplined, any frontal attack with the bayonet by either grenadiers or fusiliers straight up the ascending ground along King Street was suicidal. Rall had learned the hard way that King Street was nothing more than a death trap, and the brutal lesson that not the slightest chance of scoring a breakthrough to disrupt Washington's closing vise had ever existed in the first place.

After having only recently lost so much of his own artillery arm thanks partly to the heroics of these same Hessian soldiers during the New York Campaign, Knox never forgot the invigorating sight of the systematic breaking up of the once-magnificent counterattack of both Rall and Lossberg Regiments. Young Captain Wilkinson believed that Rall's counterattack would have achieved significant gains except for the devastating salvoes of the "six-un battery opened by Captain Forrest under the immediate orders of General Washington." To escape this punishing artillery fire from the north and musketry from the west, Lieutenant Colonel Scheffer ordered his mauled fusiliers to withdraw south.

Yet maintaining discipline, the von Lossbergers headed down embattled King Street until the lieutenant colonel then wheeled his limping regiment to the right, or east, into the relative shelter of Church Alley, north of Pinkerton's Alley, from where it had originally emerged with so much confidence that was no more. Here, the von Lossberg regiment, consisting of tougher fiber, rallied with less effort than the harder-hit Rall Regiment. During the grenadier's confused withdrawal, for instance, the von Lossbergers gained possession of the Rall Regiment's colors after they had been dropped on the ground when the color guard was unmercifully shot down in the street: a loss that revealed that they had advanced farther north than the Rall Regiment. Like a number of grenadiers before them, some surviving von Lossberg fusiliers continued farther south down King Street to escape the open killing ground, amid the steadily dropping snow that gently dusted the ever-growing number of prostrate bodies of wounded and dying friends and comrades.

Encouraged by Rall's bloody repulse, Mercer's and Haslet's Delaware veterans now turned their wrath upon the gunners of the isolated two artillery pieces of Rall's Regiment. Here, on King Street just north of the little Petty's Run bridge, the two three-pounders yet stood on their own without infantry support after the von Lossbergers were hurled back. Now a high price had to be paid by the German artillerymen for "their bravery" and the audacity in holding open ground so close to Washington's cannon. Clearly, a fundamental miscalculation and tactical mistake had been made in regard to the two gun's placement. Indeed, in gambling to reverse the tide and not imagining that the assault of his two prized regiments, especially his own formerly invincible grenadiers, could possibly be repulsed by these amateur citizen soldiers, mere farmers, who proved unreliable in the past, Rall had ordered the two guns, now positioned around 260 paces north of Rall's headquarters, set up far too close to Washington's high ground position located only around 175-180 paces south of Forrest's five and a half-inch howitzers and six-pounders.

After having been drawn by a team of four horses, the two German guns had been deployed just north of Petty's Run in King Street. However, the field pieces of the Rall Regiment should have been initially placed south of the narrow watercourse for added protection and off the open street to evade the main field of fire of Forrest's artillery. But the more advanced position had been most seductive to German ambitions to reverse the tide, because the two field pieces would have been in a more advantageous position just north of Petty's Run had Rall's counterattack not been repulsed in bloody fashion just south of Petty's Run and had continued farther north as Rall had planned.

But most of all, the deployment of these two three-pounders just north of Petty's Run revealed the full extent of Rall and Engelhardt's overconfidence. Rall had never imagined or considered the possibility that his elite grenadier and fusilier regiments could possibly be repulsed to leave the two guns vulnerable and ripe for the taking, if Washington suddenly ordered a counterattack. In truth, Rall had needed all six cannon of his brigade in action at this advanced point for any chance of blasting Washington off the high ground and to have made a successful counterattack possible.

Here, just north of Petty's Run and with their infantry support having faltered, German cannoneers started to fall hardly before the two guns could return fire. Nevertheless, eighteen Teutonic gunners now waged their own private war against the might of Forrest's six-pounders in a no-win situation. Whinnying in fear and exposed in the open, additional frightened artillery horses fell in the hail of projectiles. Other panicked horses became uncontrollable, bucking and rearing, as if sensing the original sin of the Hessians' tactical error: Engelhardt's two three-pounders had simply advanced too far and were now completely vulnerable in the street, especially after infantry support had faded away. Despite the artillery duel's inequity, Engelhardt returned a lively fire upon the Pennsylvania artillerymen while bullets, grape, and canister zipped by. But like the two earlier infantry volleys unleashed by Rall's grenadiers, Engelhardt's artillery fire inflicted no damage upon the exultant Americans on the high ground. With limited visibility in the falling snow and in the noisy confusion, excited German cannoneers aimed either too high or wide or both.

To assist his hard-pressed artillerymen in their desperate situation, Lieutenant Engelhardt personally manned one bronze three-pounder while

Bombardier Westerburg and his gun crew worked the other field piece as rapidly as possible. Completely exposed in the open ground beside ice-covered Petty's Run, the busy gunners put up a good and spirited fight. But this now-isolated position along the open slope just north of Petty's Run was a death trap. Engelhardt knew that he was caught in a bad situation, especially after Rall's badly punished infantry had melted away. Suffering from flank and frontal fires, the German cannoneers did not stand a chance. Nevertheless, Lieutenant Engelhardt and his courageous band of gunners now gamely waged a lonely, solitary, and doomed battle against the odds.

Therefore, even before the first half dozen shots from the German cannon were fired, eight Hessian gunners were swiftly cut down. They lay either limp in death or writhing in pain in the trampled-down snow across the slope just on the north side of Petty's Run. Soon only four artillerymen were left standing around one bronze three-pounder, while half a dozen surviving German gunners rapidly operated the other cannon. Already too few Hessian cannoneers and horses remained standing to even safely remove the two three-pounders back down King Street, if ordered to do so, despite a handful of infantrymen from both the Rall and von Lossberg Regiments now assisting Engelhardt's outgunned artillerymen.

Therefore, with the situation growing more precarious by the minute, Lieutenant Engelhardt dispatched a messenger back to Rall with an urgent request for "protection," or infantry support, before it was too late. While Forrest's Pennsylvania cannon roared above them on the snow-lined heights, the finely uniformed Engelhardt then shouted to Major Matthaus, who was yet attempting to regroup the Rall Regiment's battered left on King Street just to the south and near Pinkerton's Alley about a block away, that the two guns would be soon lost if infantry support was not hurriedly advanced to the endangered artillery position. But by this time, Rall had his hands full east of King Street in realigning his hard-hit grenadiers in the relative shelter of Pinkerton's Alley.

Meanwhile, most ominous for Engelhardt's ever-dwindling band of cannoneers by this time, the high split-rail fences around Potts's tanyard were lit up by a sheet of crackling gunfire, which struck the left-rear of the surviving band of exposed Hessian artillerymen, situated just north of Petty's Run. Seemingly Engelhardt and every remaining cannoneer were about to be slaughtered in the open expanse of the icy street where the ambitious Hessian dreams succumbed to an early death. Additional artillery horses of the two German guns were cut down while entangled in leather harness by well-placed bullets. Screaming horses panicked, rearing in their traces and attempting to break free. Veteran German gunners, including well-trained artillerists Rieman, Poland, and Heutzemann, lay dead and wounded in the blood-splashed snow.

Meanwhile, surviving artillerymen, down and wounded, called pitifully to their comrades for help, but the stalwart gunners continued to dutifully work their field pieces as ordered, numbing their consciences out of necessity and a higher sense of duty. Even more than the bitter punishment delivered by Forrest's Pennsylvania artillery, the flank fire from Mercer and Haslet's marksmen, especially those soldiers who unleashed loads of buck and ball, continued to wreck havoc among the unfortunate German cannoneers, who were sitting ducks in the open street. While the rattling peal of musketry rose higher in the pale morning sky, Engelhardt and his artillerymen ignored the danger, maintaining a spirited return fire.

To the south below the two bronze three-pounders and on King Street's east side, one of Washington's soldiers was positioned so close to the Rall Regiment's left flank at the intersection of King Street and Pinkerton's Alley that he watched in amazement at Colonel Rall's vigorous efforts to rally his men. He saw Rall riding back and forth to reorganize his grenadiers, hearing him frantically "shouting in Dutch [German]." Beginning to lose his nerve in his first battle because of the lack of infantry support, Engelhardt knew that he and his guns were doomed.

Unable to take any more punishment, the first shaken German artillerymen finally took off, fleeing the death trap. However, most of the ever-diminishing number of Hessian gunners remained faithfully at their assigned stations in faithfully working their artillery pieces, performing their duties as if oblivious to their inevitable fates. Against the odds, Lieutenant Engelhardt and his gunners now made one of the day's most courageous last stands on the field of Trenton, hurling back defiance from their little three-pounders as best they could under the most disadvantageous circumstances.[5]

At this key moment just after Rall's and the von Lossberg Regiments had been so severely stung by not only blasts of grapeshot and canister from the north and the hot flank fire from the west by Haslet's and Mercer's troops to thwart the determined counterattack around forty to fifty yards up slippery King Street, Washington was yet saving one of his best tactical decisions for this key moment: exploiting the tactical opportunity presented by Rall's repulse and the two three-pounder's vulnerability by launching an infantry charge straight down King Street. Washington now demonstrated a high degree of tactical savvy and flexibility and an astute tactical sense of perfect timing in waiting for exactly the right time to unleash his own counterstroke. And now that golden opportunity was now presented to the tactically astute Virginian after the repulse of Rall's two infantry regiments and the increasingly dire situation of the Rall Regiment's artillery.

Washington's uncanny ability to overcome obstacles, ignore initial setbacks, and then to yet maintain tactical flexibility and a heightened opportunistic sense to exploit any newly developed tactical opportunity suddenly presented on the battlefield were all hallmarks of Napoleon's dynamic generalship. And by deliberate design, Washington now possessed some of his best fighting men, battle-hardened Virginia soldiers, in exactly the right place at the right time to lead the attack off the high ground and down King Street. Washington had been only waiting for the best opportunity to unleash a shock force of his finest infantry—lethal Virginia riflemen—to exploit the newly developed tactical situation to the fullest.

Despite being only in its initial stages, the battle of Trenton yet hung very much in the balance at this time. Both the Rall and von Lossberg Regiments had already demonstrated the rather remarkable ability to quickly rally and counterattack with considerable fighting spirit, which revealed a high level of discipline and inspired leadership: proven combat qualities which guaranteed that these veteran grenadiers and fusiliers could quickly rally and attack once again, despite the recent bloody setback on King Street. Indeed, by this time, Rall and other seasoned officers had once again organized their troops in the sheltering alleys, Church and Pinkerton's, from north to south. Clearly, the Rall and von Lossberg Regiments, both now situated just east of King Street, could yet renew the attack with Colonel Rall at their head, unless a preemptive strike was almost immediately launched by Washington south down King Street.

Meanwhile, invaluably assisting their brigade commander, some of Rall's leading subordinate officers performed exceptionally well under adversity. Despite the bloody repulse on King Street, Lieutenant Colonel Scheffer continued to demonstrate outstanding leadership ability. With his fighting spirit rising to the fore, he was determined to regain the initiative at any cost. Scheffer, consequently, ordered the crack von Lossberg fusiliers of the Scheffer Company, part of the Lieb Body Guard Company and half of the von Hanstein Company, all under thirty-nine-year-old Captain Adam Christop Steding, a confirmed bachelor born in Fischbeck, to advance a short distance to the northwest to drive out the most advanced of Stirling's riflemen, who continued to inflict damage. Exploiting their advantage, these enterprising American riflemen delivered a scorching fire from the northeast—from backyards and behind fences—along the west side of Queen Street, after having crossed King Street north of Petty's Run.

Most importantly by this time, Washington understood that the two fast-firing German guns now served as a potential rallying point for the ever-resilient, well-led Rall brigade, and they had to be eliminated as soon as possible. And the Rall and von Lossberg Regiments were yet in good positions, just east of King Street, to launch yet another counterattack north up King Street in a determined bid to take the high ground and Washington's guns. As if anticipating as much, Engelhardt had already requested urgent infantry support from not only Rall but also from Major Matthaus, or the two three-pounders and their advanced position would have to shortly be abandoned. Despite seriously outgunned, nevertheless, Rall's two field pieces now effectively barred the main route leading into the heart of Trenton. Packing a solid counterpunch, Englehardt's two bronze three-pounders were larger in bore size than the standard British three-pounder and even the French four-pounder that seemed to remind the Americans that a victory had to be won to gain vital French recognition, support, and military assistance. As Washington fully realized, this last remaining Hessian obstacle to an attack down King Street must be eliminated as soon as possible, if the Rall brigade was to be defeated on this bloody morning that was so crucial to America's survival.

Unleashing Captain Washington's Virginians On Rall's Cannon

With his tactical astuteness, aggressive natural instincts, and own eternal vigilance in having kept an eye open for a long-awaited opportunity from the commanding ground at King Street's head never so keen, Washington made one of his boldest and best tactical decisions. Besides concerned that the two Hessian guns held an advanced position and sensing a good tactical opportunity with the sight of additional Hessian artillerymen falling to the blistering fires pouring from multiple directions, Washington realized that now was exactly right time to deliver a decisive counterpunch before Rall could either bring additional artillery into action or launch another counterstroke up King Street with his seasoned grenadiers and fusiliers.

Washington, consequently, had already planned for one of his own Virginia Regiments of battle-hardened Continental troops to spearhead the infantry attack down King Street. With an acute sense of timing, Washington was going for broke, after correctly ascertaining and judging just the right psychological moment to deliver his master counterstroke. Clearly, Washington's perceptions and eye were never keener, his tactical sense sharper, and instincts more heightened than at this time.

Like Napoleon, Washington had stacked the odds in his favor by relying primarily upon a heavy concentration of artillery firepower at the forefront to smash the enemy's morale, inflict casualties, and reduce resistance capabilities while simultaneously bolstering his own troop's spirits and confidence, to now set the stage and create the key opportunity that could now be exploited to the fullest by his best infantrymen at exactly the right moment. As he had so masterfully orchestrated his artillery arm this morning, Washington was demonstrating careful coordination and perfect timing in deciding that it was now time to order an infantry charge down King Street.

First and foremost, therefore, it was no coincidence that explained why the veteran Third Virginia Continental Regiment, on the right-center of Stirling's brigade, was now the lead regiment poised at the head of King Street to lead the attack south. Indeed, Washington had carefully placed the Third Virginia Continental Regiment in an ideal position to spearhead his counterstroke down King Street to smash Rall's loftiest ambitions, whenever the tactical opportunity presented itself. And as demonstrated throughout the past, Washington could trust these seasoned Old Dominion soldiers and their experienced commanders to the utmost. On another memorable day that he yet recalled fondly, the commander-in-chief had skillfully employed these same tough Virginia riflemen to strike into the redcoats' rear at the battle of Harlem Heights to teach the Britons a rare lesson for having openly mocked the American's withdrawal with the fox-hunt bugle call of "Gone to Earth" that had brought shame upon the proud Washington.

As in having earlier placed some of his largest and best guns, with ample supplies of canister and grapeshot to repel any counterattack, at the head of King Street for the maximum defensive advantage, so Washington now possessed an ace in the hole for his upcoming offensive thrust to regain the initiative in the battlefield's most decisive sector: dependable Virginia veterans, armed with deadly Long Rifles and with well-honed combat capabilities who were known for their tactical skill, flexibility, and aggressiveness.

During the dramatic showdown at Trenton, Washington's timely and wise decision to now adhere to the tactical offensive was yet another example of the

Virginian's more thorough utilization of a masterful adaptability and tactical flexibility—an unique and balanced mixture of both offensive and defensive—than he had ever demonstrated on any previous battlefield. Enjoying his finest hour as a battlefield commander now revealed that Washington had significantly matured as a tactician, exactly when and where needed the most. At this key moment when the battle had only begun and yet hung in the balance, Washington was about to utilize his most reliable, finest, and seasoned soldiers, including his own trusty cousin, Captain William Washington, of considerable tactical ability and aggressiveness, for unleashing a hard-hitting attack off the high ground exactly when the Hessians were least prepared to meet it.

Therefore, after having been directed to do so by Washington, Knox rode up to Colonel "Old Joe Gourd" Weedon, who stood like a benevolent guardian in supervising his fast-firing Third Virginia veterans, who blazed away at lucrative targets on King Street with their deadly Long Rifles. Washington knew Weedon quite well. Weedon had long shared invigorating hot-buttered rums with Washington at his own Rising Sun Tavern in Fredericksburg on just such cold winter days. Resting heavy in the leather saddle on his war horse while heavy snowflakes tumbled down from black skies, Knox urgently asked "Old Gourd" almost rhetorically, "Can some of your men take those guns?"

Standing beside his line of seasoned Virginia Continentals under the wintry deluge, Weedon had no need to make a formal reply to Knox, because both leaders already knew the answer. Mere eye contract or a slight nod by Weedon was now fully sufficient for a suitable response. Known by his own good-natured nickname of "the Ox" because of his forceful commanding presence and hulking size but yet amiable manner, Knox expected no verbal reply from personable "Old Joe Gourd." All that Washington and Knox now expected was Weedon's immediate compliance because the tactical opportunity that now lay before them needed to be exploited immediately. Instead of discussing the plan or tactics with Knox or asking about specific details in regard to launching the charge, Weedon simply walked over to his most advanced Continentals under Captain William Washington.[6]

Fortunately, with the winter storm yet to their backs, these high-spirited Third Virginia soldiers were now ready for their supreme challenge. They hurriedly made last-minute preparations for the hard fighting that lay ahead. As placed by Washington just below where King and Queen Streets intersected to form the apex of a V-shaped formation that widened as the two streets—with King Street to the right, or west, and Queen Street to the left, or east—descended south and down the lengthy slope that ran through Trenton's center and nearly to the Delaware, these crack Virginia boys already had been carefully aligned by Washington on their windswept commanding position for this express purpose. As previously planned by Washington with tactical clarity and insight, these battle-hardened Virginians were now in a perfect position, aligned astride the narrow angle, or wedge, where the heads of Trenton's two main streets came together, to launch a counterattack straight down King Street.

However, and as long noted by the Hessians, these free-wheeling, jaunty Virginia riflemen upon which now so much depended for America's fortunes hardly looked like elite troops capable of fulfilling such an important mission. At this time, Weedon's Old Dominion soldiers, in filthy uniforms covered with body lice and wrapped in nondescript civilian clothing, were "ragged, gaunt— some barefoot—many nearly naked, most in mud and tatters." Quite simply, these young men and boys of the Third Virginia Continental Regiment were seemingly the least likely looking soldiers who could fulfill Washington's vital assignment of overrunning and capturing Lieutenant Engelhardt's two bronze cannon with so much now at stake. Fortunately for Washington, appearances were deceiving, however, because these Virginia soldiers were in fact "the flower" of Washington's Army.[7]

After receiving Weedon's orders, Captain Washington made last-minute preparations to lead the infantry attack down the broad stretch of sloping ground and straight toward Colonel Rall's headquarters and the town's center. Playing yet another one of his psychological high cards, General Washington then cantered over to this seasoned rifle command from the Old Dominion. Having a pronounced calming effect on his rawboned troops, he then shouted encouragement to lift the morale of his Virginia boys, including hardy western frontiersmen from the Piedmont of Culpeper County at the picturesque Blue Ridge foothills. Washington harbored no reservations about having presented the morning's most crucial assignment of spearheading the charge down King Street to this band of fifty Old Dominion soldiers under twenty-four-year-old Captain Washington. After having performed an earlier important mission in serving as Greene's most advanced vanguard during the nighttime march upon Trenton, these Virginia veterans were now about to perform an identical key role in leading the upcoming attack down King Street.

Almost as physically imposing as the bulky Knox, Captain Washington was such a capable, dependable officer that this vital task had been presented to him by the commander-in-chief without any reservations, despite the fact that the young man had not yet fully recovered from a nasty Long Island wound. In turn, Captain Washington himself could rely upon the leadership abilities of his able top lieutenant, James Monroe, who was General Stirling's special favorite and a future United States president. Making a hard-hitting, dynamic leadership team, Washington and Monroe now prepared to lead the infantry charge off the high ground in a desperate bid to capture the two Hessian three-pounders, which were poised in the open just north of Petty's Run.

Fortunately, the odds were now in his favor because Washington now possessed his finest combat regiment of Continentals, the Third Virginia, at the most strategic location on the field just behind Captain Washington's vanguard, and exactly where its contribution would be disproportionate in determining the battle's ultimate course. This hard-fighting Old Dominion regiment had been formerly commanded by Scottish General Mercer, who had endlessly drilled and fine-tuned these zealous Virginia Continentals to create a highly disciplined soldiery. One of the most dependable and battle-tested regiments in Washington's Army, the Third Virginia consisted of veterans from Fairfax, Stafford, Loudoun, King George, Culpeper, Prince William, and Fauquier Counties, Virginia.

Under the circumstances, the choice of Captain Washington was not only most appropriate but also most symbolic because the strapping, young officer was the commander-in-chief's second cousin. Before his tense formation of Virginia men and on foot like other lower grade officers, Captain Washington suddenly drew his saber. He now prepared to lead the vanguard of Stirling's attack, spearheaded by the Third Virginia, which was positioned on the right-center of Stirling's brigade, down King Street.

Because the ranks of Stirling's brigade were overextended west beyond King Street and because the Third Virginia's front before King Street was so narrow, Stirling's regiment on the far right, Haslet's Delaware Continental Regiment, after having advanced in a southeast direction to gain the town's upper northwest corner to fill the gap between the right of Stirling's brigade and the left of Mercer's brigade, would provide good covering fire from the northwest to support Captain Washington's charge down King Street. Therefore, along with Mercer's Maryland, Massachusetts, and Connecticut troops along King Street's west side, these dependable Delaware Continentals, just to Mercer's north, continued to occupy one of the most advantageous position to inflict damage on Engelhardt's isolated artillerymen, after having already played their part in thwarting the Rall and von Lossberg Regiment's counterattack up King Street.

Most importantly, the chances for Captain Washington's headlong charge to succeed depended in no small part upon the amount of pressure applied from the northwest. Indeed, Captain Washington possessed timely close fire support from the veterans of Haslet's Delaware regiment. These soldiers were positioned in the dark houses and snowy, open yards on the west side of King Street, just north of Mercer's brigade and perhaps as far north as nearly adjacent to Petty's Run. North of Mercer's brigade, Haslet's northernmost troops, consequently, now remained in excellent firing positions, nearly adjacent to Petty's Run and Rall's artillery situated just north of the little, frozen-over waterway.

From this vantage point, the Delaware Continentals continued to sweep the Hessian guns and what was left of the surviving cannoneers with a heavy fire from the northwest. Proud to hail from "Little Delaware" and to struggle for her honor and reputation, Haslet's veterans were the very "flower of the army" by this time. Once having worn some of the finest uniforms, blue coats trimmed in red and with white waistcoats, in Washington's Army, these elite Delaware soldiers now wore ragged clothing obtained from civilians. Looking like scarecrows, they were wrapped in dirty blankets, with bare feet bound with rags and pieces of cloth. Even now the distinctive blue uniforms and peaked mitre-shaped headgear, if any remained intact, of some of Haslet's Continentals made them look not unlike Rall's grenadiers at first glance. Not surprisingly, therefore, these crack Delaware soldiers had been mistaken for Hessians on past battlefield by the British.

Perhaps yet wearing their trademark sprigs of green from evergreens— pines or cedars—in their hats, these highly disciplined troops from the new nation's smallest state, after Rhode Island, were the sole remaining ninety-two survivors out of the 750 members rank and file, who had first marched off to war only last August. Most importantly, these Continentals were some of the best disciplined and drilled troops in Washington's Army, thanks to Haslet's tireless efforts and efficiency. One of Washington's finest regimental commanders, the Irish Haslet was a hard-fighting holy warrior who knew the Bible by heart. He had been long inspired pious congregations as a fiery Presbyterian minister on both sides of the Atlantic. A Renaissance man who waged war for God and liberty, Haslet was a respected Dover, Kent County, Delaware, physician, before the war. He was also a devoted father and husband of an attractive woman named Jemima, the same name as Lord Cornwallis's beloved wife. An overachieving scholar-soldier who had made his American dream come true, Haslet was a distinguished graduate of the prestigious

University of Glasgow, Scotland. Although a gifted politician, Haslet found his greatest personal fulfillment in cultivating the soil and operating his thriving plantation, Longfield, situated along the Mispillion River.

This tough and burley Irishman of seemingly limitless ability yet deserved brigade command. However, tiny Delaware lacked the necessary political clout in Congress to ensure Haslet's long-overdue and much-deserved advancement. Washington's trust in Haslet was partly based upon his splendid offensive performance beside Smallwood's Marylanders during the battle of Long Island, and in protecting the army's rear—the coveted "post of honor"—during the withdrawal not only from Manhattan Island, but also more recently through New Jersey. Then, barely two months before the Trenton showdown, he and his tough Delaware Continentals had even caught America's former hero Robert Rogers, now commanding the Loyalist Queen's Rangers, and his Americans by surprise, attacking with the cry, "Surrender, you Tory dogs!" and nearly missing an opportunity to annihilate the detested turncoats.

Inspiring his crack "Delawares," the "tall, erect and athletic" Haslet now fired both of his flintlock pistols, whose flints he had kept dry, at the exposed left flank of Rall's repulsed men, the von Lossberg fusiliers in Church Alley just east of King Street, and Engelhardt's gunners now caught out in the open located immediately north of the wooden bridge across Petty's Run. Given the advantageous tactical situation, Haslet shouted with glee, "We have them!" Proud of their lofty reputation that they had earned on the battlefield, these Delaware Continentals blasted away with the "most beautiful English muskets" and hit targets with careful aim. On August 27 at Long Island, when Rall Regiment grenadiers and von Lossberg fusiliers had struck the rear of Stirling's troops on the right, Haslet and his soldiers, along with Smallwood's Marylanders, had counterattacked to break the onslaught's momentum and buy time to save many survivors. Therefore, these Delaware boys now had plenty of old scores to settle with Rall and his Hessians.

In addition, many Sons of Erin of the Delaware Continental's ranks also now battled the Germans for the memory and honor of Ireland. Like so many other soldiers in Washington's Army, Haslet was a son of the "old sod." He had migrated to America from Straw, Ulster Province, northern Ireland, around 1757. Haslet was the revered "father" of his elite First Delaware Continental Regiment, which he had organized in January 1776. His hard-hitting Delaware regiment, from Kent, New Castle, and Sussex Counties, was known as the "Blue Hens' Chickens" in honor of the combative roosters of one regimental captain. Cock-fighting was popular in colonial America, especially Virginia. This popular sobriquet was warmly embraced by the Delaware boys and it later became Delaware's state motto, the Blue Hen State, which has endured to this day.

During the French and Indian War, Haslet had commanded a Pennsylvania battalion during the British expedition that captured Fort Duquesne in conjunction with a high-ranking British officer, who ironically now commanded Howe's defensive line of winter cantonments in New Jersey, General James Grant. Symbolically, Hastlet had clashed with Grant's troops at Long Island on August 27, 1776, fueling a rivalry that yet existed on this snowy morning in New Jersey. When they had been younger officers, both Haslet and Washington had protected the western Pennsylvania frontier during the French and Indian War. Drawing upon the historic analogies of English oppression of his Irish homeland, Haslet saw this present struggle as a righteous war against an immoral invader. Most of all, this former Presbyterian minister fought so that he and his people, included so many transplanted Irish, would never become the debased "vassals" of Great Britain, in his own words.

The handsome Haslet, therefore, encouraged his Delaware boys to keep blasting away to the southeast with their fine English muskets, sending more bullets toward Lieutenant Engelhardt's gunners, who continued to frantically work their two three-pounders as rapidly as possible. For those Delaware soldiers whose wet muskets could not be fired, they were at least comforted by the fact that they were among Washington's relatively few soldiers who possessed bayonets in case they met their opponent at close quarters.[8]

In many ways, this struggle raging along King Street was very much of a personal fight for Haslet and his men. After all, these same Delaware boys had been pushed off Chatterton Hill by the gleaming bayonets of Rall's grenadiers when they, along with the Knyphausen Regiment's fusiliers, turned Washington's right wing on October 28. And now Haslet's Continentals reaped a measure of revenge by punishing the Hessians to redeem their previous losses and past defeats. Not unlike the relatively few New Jersey Continentals who now served in Washington's ranks after the New Jersey militia's failure to reinforce the army, the Delaware soldiers and their hard-driving Emerald Isle colonel were highly motivated for another reason as well. In their own beloved home state, the revolutionary tide had turned in the opposite direction, thanks to so many sharp reversals. Delaware's government had all but rejoined the Crown by this time, with Tory and anti-independence moderates now dominating the state legislature. The resurgent Loyalists even threw Declaration of Independence signers, like Haslet's close friend and the brother of Captain Thomas Rodney, Caesar Rodney, out of office. Now that Haslet and his veteran Delaware soldiers had seemingly lost the political war on the home front, they were even more determined to reap a sparkling success at Trenton, because an unexpected victory on New Jersey soil would provide a most timely antidote to defeatism and a political victory of immense proportions.[9]

Meanwhile, from the high ground, Captain Forrest's cannon continued to roar during an unequal artillery duel with Rall's isolated two three-pounders, yet situated just north of Petty's Run, thanks to so many artillery horses shot down. Despite additional Hessian gunners falling dead and wounded into the blanket of snow, this intensifying artillery duel remained as spirited as it was heated. Gently falling white flakes steadily drifted down, pelting the frantically moving gunners, both American and German, working their field pieces with abandon.

Ironically, the only damage inflicted among Washington's busy artillery pieces came not from Hessian fire, but from the accumulative effect of the dual crossings of the Delaware and Jacob's Creek and the lengthy march to Trenton, however. A combination of factors caused too much wear and tear to damage at least one especially fast-firing cannon of Forrest's Second Company of the Pennsylvania State Artillery. Locally made and hence less durable, the gun's axletree grew weaker with every shot and violent recoil, while returning fire on Rall's noisy but ineffective three-pounders. While Massachusetts, Pennsylvania, and Rhode Island gunners assigned to the cannon looked on in dismay, feisty Joseph White, who had been born in Weymouth, Massachusetts and now served as the orderly sergeant in Forrest's command, described how: "The 3d shot we fired broke the axletree of the piece." This final shot hurled toward the Hessians splintered the wooden axletree, revealing a design flaw and vulnerability, before the advent of sturdy iron axletrees of the Napoleonic Era.[10]

A dedicated noncommissioned officer without a single "care about a commission," Sergeant White was a natural leader. With the broken axletree, the members of Sergeant White's artillery crew, consisting of around half a dozen New England and Pennsylvania gunners, were now without their beloved gun that they had nursed with such motherly care since the risky Delaware crossing. Therefore, Sergeant White's downcast veteran gunners felt the cannon's loss deeply. They even experienced a slight, but palpable, sense of pain, almost as if having lost a prized horse, or even a lover.

While Washington's other seventeen artillery pieces remained briskly in action in two different sectors and firing at a rapid rate, White's detachment of saddened, young artillerymen merely watched the "long-arm" duel in the King Street sector, and felt frustration over losing their prized artillery piece. As Sergeant White explained, "we stood there some time idle, they firing upon us" all the while. Then, all of a sudden, Colonel Knox, with some wry humor that reflected his gregarious nature, Scotch Irish roots, and his lively personality that could light up a room or tired soldiers on a long march, rode up to Sergeant White and his band of dejected cannoneers. With a distinct Bostonian accent and hoping to reinvigorate their sagging spirits, Knox then shouted above the thunder of his busy artillery, "My brave lads, go up and take those two field pieces sword in hand. There is a party going, you must go & join them."[11]

Knox, of course, was referring to the foremost Third Virginia soldiers under Captain Washington's and Lieutenant Monroe's command. As independent, ultra-democratically minded New Englanders and equally egalitarian Philadelphians, however, these seasoned cannoneers thought for themselves after Knox cantered off through the falling snow and drifting palls of cannon smoke. Veterans who knew strict army regulations by this time, the common soldiers felt that they must first obtain orders directly from their own immediate, even though lower-ranking, commanding officer, who they knew better than the high-ranking Knox. Therefore, Captain John Allen, having long dealt with these homespun egalitarian types who yet acted as they thought best, walked up to Sergeant White, an outspoken, intelligent former assistant adjutant, who had often defied autocratic officers, especially if wrong-headed, and emphasized, "Sergeant W[hite] you heard what the Col. Said—you must take the whole of those that belonged to that [damaged artillery] piece, and join them. This party was commanded by Capt. Washington and Lieut. Monroe [the future] President of the U. States," who were about to lead the attack down King Street. Demonstrating a can-do attitude and tactical versatility like Glover's Marbleheaders with Sullivan's First Division now advancing as infantry to the southwest, these New England and Pennsylvania cannoneers now grabbed muskets and strapped on leather cartridge-boxes, preparing to serve as infantry on the offensive.

Having left their artillery implements behind and with smoothbore flintlocks in hand, these veteran gunners then joined Captain Washington's foremost band of Virginians. Possessing a keen sense of humor, young Orderly

Sergeant White was one of the few common soldiers, who had even succeeded in not only making the austere General Washington smile, but also his wife Martha. Back at Cambridge, Massachusetts, and with a Tidewater Virginia planter's slow drawl, Washington had remarked to the teenage New England sergeant, who had yet to shave and looked like a mere boy, that he was "very young" for the responsibilities of an officer and assistant adjutant of an artillery unit "to do that duty." With some spunk mixed with a wry sense of humor, White had quickly answered the commander-in-chief diplomatically in his New England accent that he was indeed a very young man for the job, but then expressly made the point of emphasizing, with common sense wit, how he was growing older each day. About to laugh out loud and lose his legendary cool composure and strict aristocratic bearing before this outspoken, spunky boy-soldier, Washington quickly turned "his face to his wife, and both smiled" at White's witty response.[12]

Like Washington, Knox was also thinking far ahead in tactical terms this morning. He now wanted to accomplish much more than merely add extra strength to Captain Washington's Virginia vanguard by the addition of Sergeant White and his New England and Pennsylvania gun crew. Instead, the farsighted Bostonian was already contemplating about how Engelhardt's two exposed guns, if captured, could then be immediately utilized against Rall's own troops to maximize his long-arm strength in the struggle for Trenton. Therefore, Knox realized early that extra artillerymen would be needed to handle the Hessian three-pounders, if taken. Clearly, by planning to increase their artillery fire-power on a raging battlefield in this unorthodox manner, both Washington and his top artillery lieutenant continued to demonstrate that their tactical foresight and visions shined exceptionally bright on this dark, snowy morning.[13]

As understood by no one more than Washington, almost everything now depended upon the success of the upcoming attack of Captain Washington and Monroe's vanguard in spearheading the aggressive bid to capture the Hessian cannon that had to be silenced at all costs. Quite simply, unless the two Hessian guns were quickly neutralized, then the Rall brigade yet held much potential to not only inflict serious damage upon Washington's forces, but also to reverse the battle's course and the day's fortunes. In fact, time was now actually on the Hessians' side, because their superior training and discipline would certainly rise to the fore if the Americans suddenly suffered a sharp tactical setback or if they lost momentum, the initiative, or their confidence as so often in the past. After all, Washington's troops were yet in overall poor shape for a sustained battle of attrition in blizzard-like conditions: half-frozen, without sleep, weary from having marched for nearly ten miles all night, with a good many wet weapons and ammunition, and relatively few bayonets among the thinned ranks of die-hard warriors. Therefore, as soon as possible, Washington knew that he needed to deliver an offensive blow to degrade as much of the Rall brigade's yet ample combat capabilities, especially the artillery arm, as possible. Quite simply and in overall tactical terms, it was now or never for Washington and his homespun revolutionaries on this day of destiny, and they seemed intuitively knew as much without a word spoken.[14]

Meanwhile, Washington's soldiers, especially Mercer's troops but also Haslet's Delaware marksmen, just to their north, continued to inflict damage upon Rall's exposed left flank on King Street's east side, raking the von Lossberg fusiliers in Church Alley and the Rall Regiment in Pinkerton's Alley, from north to south. And the northernmost of Haslet's Delaware soldiers continued to blast away at Lieutenant Engelhardt's band of gunners from the northwest. With the battle's outcome hanging delicately, if not precariously, in the balance, Washington knew that it was now paramount to silence the Rall Regiment's two cannon before the German brigade's other four three-pounders could be rapidly brought into action by their four-horse teams to unite for the eventual unleashing of a concentrated artillery fire of six guns to at least match, if not overcome, Washington's artillery firepower at King Street's head. Ironically, the struggle for King Street's possession was about to be determined by a relatively few number of participants, a small vanguard of Virginia riflemen and a lone two-gun section of Hessian artillery yet offering spirited defiance.

Although not yet fully recovered from a nasty Long Island wound, Captain Washington was determined to do his best this morning of decision, as if not to let his second cousin, the commander-in-chief, down and to bring honor to Virginia and the Washington family name. The esteemed captain had come a long way since commanding the adventurous, young men of the Stafford County, Virginia Minutemen, who had been integrated into the Third Virginia Continental Regiment. Here, on the commanding ground where King and Queen Streets came together to form a narrow wedge, Captain Washington stood before his band of Old Dominion veterans, including former Minutemen from his own Stafford County, in the Potomac River country north, where he had been born on the second to last day of February 1752. He knew these young men and boys and their rolling, heavily forested region located just west of the Potomac River and north of Fredericksburg quite well.

Under General Washington's eyes—a motivating factor in itself—and with hundreds of Stirling's front-line troops, including his own Third Virginia, aligned across the high ground just to his rear, the young Virginia captain, with drawn saber, stood before his eager men. While the snow dropped thickly over the windy heights above Trenton and Forrest's Pennsylvania cannons roared to the rear, Captain Washington then shouted the order for his Virginia vanguard to charge down the slope that led straight into Trenton. Now unleashed like a tight, pent-up coil, the vanguard Virginians sprang forward with an enthusiastic shout. To do or die, they dashed forward, spearheading the infantry attack down King Street in an audacious bid to eliminate the "main barrier to the American advance," Lieutenant Engelhardt's booming two guns positioned on open ground just above Petty's Run.

Developing a clever solution to a vexing tactical dilemma, Captain Washington had ordered his Virginia boys to stay close to the row of wooden and brick houses in surging down both sides of King Street instead of foolishly charging down the middle of the street to present ideal targets for the German gunners. In addition, the snow was less deep close to the houses than in the street, promising an easier, faster sprint down the slope. To the young captain, the systematic breaking up of Rall's counterattack in King Street had already verified the folly of any headlong advance up or down this snowy avenue. Therefore, he was not about to repeat that same tactical mistake. Fortunately, Captain Washington and his Virginia veterans proved to be quick learners, demonstrating not only tactical flexibility and innovativeness but also a good deal of common sense. Meanwhile, to Captain Washington's rear, some of the finest riflemen of Stirling and Stephen's Virginians blasted away from the high ground at Engelhardt's exposed artillerymen, proving support fire for the vanguard's attack.

Rushing down the gradual slope at the forefront beside Captain Washington, teenage Lieutenant Monroe also led the vanguard of Virginia riflemen on the double. Ironically, Monroe should not have been now leading the desperate attack down King Street. He had only recently volunteered to join Washington's vanguard upon learning that the Virginia captain would command the vanguard. The scholarly, devout Monroe had been studying for the ministry and the Holy Bible only a short time before. Even in his own estimation, Monroe was now only "a mere youth." But he was now performing like a much older, veteran officer by providing inspiration and encouraging the Third Virginia Continentals down the sloping ground along both sides of King Street.

Tall and gangly, Monroe was a studious, cerebral intellectual with a penchant for devouring the ancient classics. From the fertile farmlands of Virginia's Northern Neck, the shy, modest young man with an amiable disposition had enrolled at William and Mary College, Williamsburg, Virginia, as a sixteen-year-old youth during the summer of 1774 in what now seemed like a lifetime ago to these Virginia Continentals. In January 1776, Monroe departed William and Mary College to fight for liberty, enlisting at the first opportunity. Of Welsh and Scottish ancestry, he had then served as a promising cadet in the Third Virginia Continental Regiment under the grizzled French and Indian War veteran Hugh Mercer, who was his Fredericksburg neighbor.

Young Monroe was born along brackish Monroe's Creek, a small tidal tributary stream of the Potomac River, that flowed east through the Northern Neck countryside of Westmoreland County, before entering the Potomac's wide waters. Here, he had swum and hunted as a younger man, which had helped to transform him into a robust officer at a time, when epidemics of disease had unmercifully decimated Washington's officer corps. Monroe was the promising son of an industrious carpenter, who knew Washington as a friend. Therefore, General Washington was long familiar with the young, unassuming officer, of so much potential, and his Northern Neck family.

Meanwhile, Monroe shouted encouragement at the head of his howling Old Dominion soldiers who continued to rush south along the sides of King Street, surging closer toward Engelhardt's two artillery pieces. Both he and Captain Washington led the charge down the sloping ground and toward Rall's headquarters, located below Petty's Run, on the run. When Captain Washington's vanguard first suddenly surged downhill, the German cannoneers were yet attempting in vain to knock out Captain Forrest's guns. Demonstrating spirited resistance, Engelhardt's gunners continued to duel with the Pennsylvania artillery on their own without either infantry or artillery support. Unfortunately for the hard-fighting lieutenant, the two three-pounders of the von Lossberg Regiment, which had not yet been deployed on King Street, were not firing toward the heights in direct support of Engelhardt's exposed position.

Soon to be manned by the Knyphausen Regiment artillerymen, these two bronze guns were located in the churchyard of Anglican Church, nestled between King and Queen Streets and nearly opposite Rall's headquarters. During the confusion caused by Washington's surprise attack, these cannon were not advanced north to join the Rall Regiment's guns for an early, all-important concentration of firepower so desperately needed by Rall from the beginning. Destined to remain at the vortex of the struggle for Trenton's possession, this small Anglican Church, established in 1703, was located on the east side of King Street in the block between Church and Pinkerton's Alleys. In a strange way, the civil war between the Germans in America that was now being played out in Trenton's snow-blown streets mirrored the congregation's own deep divisions between Loyalist and patriot, resulting in the church's closure in July 1776.

During the wild dash south, meanwhile, Captain Washington and Lieutenant Monroe continued to lead the onrushing vanguard of yelling Virginians down the slope while keeping next to the houses. In single-file, they rushed straight toward the two fast-working German cannon positioned just above the little wooden bridge spanning Petty's Run. In essence, this contest had evolved into a desperate race by the Virginia vanguard to reach the two Hessian guns before Engelhardt's cannoneers could switch to canister, and the open fire at close range to wreck havoc. Because the raging snowstorm reduced visibility and helped to early screen the charge down the slope, Captain Washington's soldiers initially possessed the advantage in surging out of the swirling snow undetected. This advantage paid off because the Virginian's race was also about attempting to reach the Hessian guns before any reinforcing German troops, as repeatedly requested by the desperate Lieutenant Engelhardt, arrived to bolster the two three-pounders. And because the Old Dominion attackers realized as much, this knowledge fueled the swift pace of their headlong surge down the slope at a faster pace.

By this time and most importantly, Captain Washington's vanguard Virginians were not advancing alone. Behind them advanced the most for-ward elements of the Third Virginia, while the rest of right-center of Stirling's brigade remained poised around King Street's head in support of Forrest's Pennsylvania battery, and most of Stephen's Virginia brigade was aligned in protective positions to the east in support Hamilton's and Baumann's roaring New York cannon, from right to left. In addition, a select group of Stephen's Virginia riflemen and Stirling's riflemen continued to fire south down King Street, providing a timely covering fire for Captain Washington's steamrolling attack. These tried riflemen, who knew how to handle their Long Rifles with skill at long range, now provided excellent fire support, raking the Hessian artil-lerymen at long distance with well-aimed shots.

Moving down both sides of King Street, the Virginians dashed through the snow down the sloping ground, surging closer to their objective. Realizing that Lieutenant Engelhardt's two three-pounders had to be captured before the veteran gunners switched their loads to lethal canister, Captain Washington ordered his veteran marksmen, with dry powder and muskets, to halt. This timely respite also allowed the Virginians an opportunity to catch their breath, which now came fast and hung heavy in the cold air in little, hazy clouds. Once his Virginia boys were aligned and ready, the Stafford County captain then yelled to open fire on Engelhardt's gunners, and especially at the finely uniformed officers, in resplendent uniforms and bicorns, and artillery horses, to prevent their removal. With these Old Dominion sharpshooters taking careful aim and then slowly squeezing triggers with cold-numbed fighters, a scorching fire erupted from the foremost Virginians. A hail of bullets swept the hapless Hessian gunners and their exposed position along Petty's Run, knocking down frightened horses, whinnying in pain and bucking, and dropping additional gunners into the snow.

In addition, the foremost of Mercer's Maryland, Connecticut, and Massachusetts troops and Haslet's Delaware soldiers, from south to north respectively, continued to blast away with rifles and smoothbores, loaded with "ball and buckshot," from the good cover of houses, fences, and yards on King Street's west side and northwest sides, respectively. The hottest fire continued to pour from the southwest from Mercer's men around the tanyard and behind the sturdy, wooden fences around it. Like shooting fish in a barrel as when these same veteran American marksmen had cut down so many of Rall's attackers in the bloody charge up Mount Washington during Fort Washington's defense, Rawlings's Maryland riflemen, of Mercer's brigade, blasted away with small caliber Long Rifles, whose sharp reports of their hunting pieces made the air sing. Therefore, raked by the combined fire of Long Rifles and smoothbores muskets, additional Hessian artillerymen fell to stain the snow with grotesque splashes of red while even more artillery horses went down in their tangled leather traces amid the torrent of zipping projectiles.

By this time, half of Engelhardt's cannoneers, nearly a dozen Rall Regiment gunners, were cut down either killed or wounded, along with dead and wounded artillery horses lying beside the guns in clumps. Captain Washington's charge also now benefitted from an earlier ill-timed command decision. Lieutenant Engelhardt had ordered one three-pounder, under veteran cannoneer Westerburg, to hurriedly shift to the left, or southwest, and open fire on Mercer's fast-firing riflemen grouped together at the tanyard and behind the wooden fences around the small structure covered in snow. In the vain hope of suppressing this blistering fire, Engelhardt had directed Westerburg's cannon to be loaded with canister. Therefore, the gun's thirteenth and last shot was directed in the wrong direction: not toward Captain Washington's Virginians, but toward Stacy Potts's tanyard, which had helped to make him a wealthy man, from where Rawlings's Marylanders inflicted damage with their blazing Long Rifles.

All the while, sleet and snow tumbled down from black, churning skies without a break to meet the rising pall of sulphurous smoke that hovered over embattled King Street before lazily drifting away by the northeast wind, providing a hazy partial screen for the Virginia attackers. Even worse for the dwindling band of German cannoneers caught out in the open, the whitish downpour continued to blow into their faces to not only obscure visibility but also to hamper, along with cold hands and half-numb fingers, loading and firing. Converging on their "long-arm" target during this race of death, the Virginia farm boys, hunters, and woodsmen proved swifter than the isolated band of Hessian artillerymen on their own.

For good reason, Engelhardt's gunners became more unnerved from multiple fires and the sight of the seemingly crazed Virginians, tall and formidable-looking men from the western frontier who were shouting like a pack of Indians and acting half-crazed in so brazenly defying death, charging toward them with wild abandon. Captain Washington's onrushing men now benefitted from the fact that Westerburg's cannon, which had been just turned southwest to fire on the tanyard, was yet in the process of being shifted back to face north and fire upon them, consuming more time to save Virginia lives. Meanwhile, the savvy Virginians continued to perform like urban warfare experts, smartly sticking close to the row of brick and wood-frame houses to avoid the blasts of cannonfire. To escape the howling Virginians, a handful of Hessian cannoneers threw down handspikes, rammers, and sponge-staffs, deserting their artillery pieces and running away. Unable to get both of his bronze three-pounders once again simultaneously firing north in unison and in time, Lieutenant Engelhardt shortly realized that he and his men were doomed.

But a handful of Hessian gunners defiantly refused to run, standing their ground beside their prized cannon just north of Petty's Run. After much effort with handspikes and rope to maneuver the cumbersome field piece that weighed nearly a thousand pounds, Westerburg and his remaining gunners finally turned the other cannon around in the proper direction, facing north toward Captain Washington's vanguard. But not enough time remained to load the field piece with canister with the cheering Virginians practically atop them.

Therefore, the last group of German cannoneers finally abandoned the gun. Meanwhile, Engelhardt's artillerymen of the other cannon courageously attempted to get off one final shot. After switching from round shot to canister and despite caught out in the open, the last remaining German gunners continued to faithfully perform their solemn duty like good soldiers to the very end. Captain Washington's riflemen now raced down the slope with renewed speed, sensing the kill and hoping to reach the cannon before it could be fired. With howling Americans getting close, Engelhardt ordered his gunners to retreat before it was too late. Partly thanks to hot frontal and flank fires that decimated the cannoneers, none of Captain Washington's Virginians were hit.[15]

Watching the drama playing out along King Street from the windswept heights, General Stephen had never seen such expert shooting from his own Virginia riflemen on his brigade's right flank and Third Virginia soldiers, on Stirling's right-center, to the west. In timely fashion, these experienced Virginians had effectively supported Captain Washington and Lieutenant Monroe's charge down King Street with an accurate fire from their Long Rifles that hit targets at long range before the attackers swarmed close to Engelhardt's cannon. Positioned on higher ground than Captain Washington's Virginia men surging down the broad slope before them, expert riflemen from Stephen and Stirling's commands had fired straight down middle of the street, while the vanguard attackers hugged the sides of King Street, staying close to the houses to provide an open field of fire down the street. Meanwhile, the sharp barking of the Long Rifles echoed from the snowy heights, and the Virginians of Stephen's brigade took pride in having administrated severe punishment upon lower-lying Hessian targets around the two artillery pieces situated just north of Petty's Run. In a letter, an amazed Stephen described how, "You never Saw so many good Shot[s] made in your life time—We drove the Enemy from their Cannon in our Shooting."[16]

Meanwhile, the rawboned Virginians closed in on the two German field pieces, and nothing could now stop them. In his diary, Colonel Fitzgerald described the dramatic moment when, "The Hessians were just ready to open fire [with canister] with two of their cannon when Captain Washington and Lieutenant Monroe with their men rushed forward and captured them."[17] With a drawn artillery saber and leading his onrushing fellow New England and Pennsylvania artillerymen, in their first and last infantry charge of the war, young Orderly Sergeant White was at the forefront of the rapid descent down the slope upon the two vulnerableguns of the Rall Regiment. The young former assistant adjutant, who was proud of being "a good speller," was now on the field of Trenton only after barely surviving a near fatal "dangerous sickness" a short time before.

White, who hailed from the fishing and commercial port of Weymouth, Massachusetts, which was named after an English coastal community in Dorset, England, described the desperate life-and-death race to reach the Rall Regiment's three-pounders, just before the last German artillerymen unleashed a hail of canister upon Captain Washington's vanguard: "I hallowed as loud as I could scream, to the men to run for their lives right up to the pieces [and] I was the first that reach[ed] them. They had all left it, expect one man tending vent—run you dog, cried I, holding my sword over his head, he looked up and saw it, then run" for his life.[18]

Watching the stirring scene on King Street from the high ground, General Stephen penned in a letter how this single "brave" Hessian cannoneer, who remained at his gun "was loading her by him self after the Rest had left him—a Virginian as brave as he, would not let him [and] but run up knockd [sic] him down w[i]t[h] the butt of his Gun & took him prisoner."[19] And in a letter from his father, Marylander Tench Tilghman described Captain Washington's bold charge down King Street, writing how: "our people advanced up [to] the Mouths of their Field pieces, shot down their Horses [to ensure that they could not bring] off the Cannon."[20]

But what also made Captain Washington's daring charge succeed in the end was the accurate musketry that streamed from both front (north) and flank (west). Upon ascertaining the vanguard's initial progress, General Washington had ordered more Virginia Continentals into the fray and straight down King Street, exploiting the tactical opportunity to capitalize on the hard-won tactical gains. Advancing behind Captain Washington's vanguard, consequently, the sharpshooters of the Third Virginia Continental Regiment had provided excellent fire support, while they surged down the snowy slope, firing on the move in true frontier fashion. In addition, some of the finest marksmen of Major George Johnston's Fifth Virginia Continental Regiment, situated on the far right of Stephen's brigade, also had early provided fire support with long-range rifle fire from the high ground. Organized in May 1776, the Fifth Virginia Continental Regiment consisted of veterans from Henrico, Westmoreland, Lancaster, Bedford, Loudoun, Northumberland, Richmond, Hanover, Chesterfield, and Spotsylvania Counties, Virginia.[21]

Most importantly, the capture of the two three-pounders to remove the last and principal barrier that had stubbornly loomed in his way before General

Washington could unleash a general advance down King Street also now opened up new tactical opportunities. Emboldened by his success in overrunning the Hessian cannon, Captain Washington instinctively felt the pressing urgency to keep moving and driving a retreating opponent ever-farther down King Street. In a chain reaction, Captain Washington's tactical success in capturing the two three-pounders fueled "Old Joe Gourd" Weedon's general assault of the Third Virginia farther down King Street. Meanwhile and equally significant, the Third Virginia's push south coincided with the advance of troops on the left of Stirling's brigade, with its right flank now secure and protected by Captain Washington's successful charge down King Street just to the west, which began to inch down icy Queen Street.

At this time, a good opportunity now existed on King Street below Petty's Run for additional tactical gains to be reaped by the attackers also because the Lieb Company of Rall's Regiment, on the left flank, continued to be raked by the gunfire from Mercer's men from the west. Resulting in a chain reaction, the grenadier's dilemma then spilled over to other westernmost companies on the Rall Regiment's left in Pinkerton's Alley, and also on the von Lossberg Regiment's left flank, in Church Alley, which was located just below Petty's Run, causing some confusion.

After overrunning the two three-pounders and after Englehardt's gunners had "suffered for their bravery," Captain Washington's elated victors raised a resounding "Huzza" that rang through Trenton's darkened streets now brightened by the attacker's high spirits. This Old Dominion victory cheer echoed above the sharp crackle of escalating gunfire, cutting through the thick battle-smoke that left a hazy, sulphurous atmosphere, already dimmed by the winter's weak light and dense cloud cover, hanging over Trenton like a dark cloud.

With their fighting blood up, Captain Washington and Lieutenant Monroe, despite being out of breath from their daring sprint down King Street in leading the charge, now resisted the temptation of resting, catching their breath, or celebrating their success to waste precious time. These two young leaders wisely avoided this all-too-common tactical mistake too often made by even the most experienced commanders during the excitement of victory. Once again proving the wisdom of their commander-in-chief's confidence in them, the two enterprising Virginia officers knew better than to unnecessarily risk sacrificing the hard-won momentum and the initiative by wasting precious time.

With Captain Washington and Lieutenant Monroe continuing to lead the way, the Virginia riflemen once again swarmed south across the little, wooden bridge spanning Petty's Run, resuming their bold rush into Trenton. Captain Washington's Virginia boys surged farther down King Street, almost as if the snowy sloping ground and slippery street surface alone now carried them toward the town's center, without losing momentum or the initiative. Intoxicated by their heady success in capturing the two Hessian guns and envisioning greater tactical gains in pushing farther south, some elated attackers shouted the unforgettable words of Paine's *The American Crisis*. Just hearing Tom Paine's inspiring sentiments repeated on the battlefield spread greater enthusiasm among the common soldiers now spearheading the Second Division's offensive effort. Clearly, Washington's wise decision to have the words of Paine's pamphlet read out loud to the troops just before crossing the Delaware continued to pay dividends.[22]

All the while, Captain Washington's Virginians surged farther down King Street in the hope of breaking up additional Hessian resistance situated below Petty's Run before Rall's troops had an opportunity to rally and again launch a counterattack. Attempting to defend themselves against the Virginian's attack steamrolling down King Street, some westernmost German troops, of both the Rall and von Lossberg Regiments on the left flank, in King Street retired farther south for better protection. But most grenadiers and fusiliers remained in relatively sheltered positions in Church and Pinkerton's Alleys east of King Street to escape the worst of Forrest's artillery fire. However, with Captain Washington's elated men, tasting victory and desired additional success, surging down the sloping ground, either a group of Hessian skirmishers or a reinforcing party belatedly sent north by Rall in an attempt to save Engelhardt's guns, was forced to take position in houses at the upper end of King Street just below Petty's Run on the street's east side.

In Church Alley on King Street's east side to the south, meanwhile, Lieutenant Colonel Scheffer shifted the pressured left of his von Lossberg Regiment to protect his now suddenly more vulnerable left flank. Then, the von Lossberg fusiliers defended their vulnerable flank as best they could from the dual threats of Captain Washington's surge south and Mercer's withering fire just to King Street's west. And from advantageous positions in the private houses (sleeping quarters) at King's Street's northern end just below Petty's Run, German soldiers, who never retired south, held firm, refusing to budge.

Blasting away from good cover, these ensconced Hessians opened up at close range from houses situated along the east side of King Street upon the left flank of Captain Washington's vanguard, which continued to lead "Old Gourd"

Third Virginia Weedon's advance. However, the fact that some von Lossbergers, from the regiment's left flank, who had been pushed down King Street opened fire from the south resulted in a vicious crossfire—up the street to the south and from the houses to the west—that raked the surging Virginia vanguard. To prevent their capture, meanwhile, the two three-pounders of the Knyphausen Regiment were prudently hauled east toward Queen Street and united with the von Lossberg Regiment for safekeeping during the chaos of battle.

Leading the way farther down King Street, the sheer commanding size of General Washington's esteemed second cousin at the forefront made him an ideal target. He had a close call when a large-caliber lead musket ball passed between his fingers of the right hand gripping his saber. Captain Washington, age twenty-four, was now completely exposed in the eye of the storm with Hessians firing upon him from nearby houses on King Street's east side at close range and also up the open street from the south. Towering above his fellow Virginians and with whistling bullets by his ears and tempting fate once too often, Captain Washington was hit. This aggressive, resourceful commander, a well-educated member of the planter class, suffered painful wounds to both hands. Then gangly Lieutenant Monroe, a fresh-faced youth of only eighteen, took charge of the Virginia vanguard survivors, who were yet determined to exploit their success to the fullest.

With the savvy instincts of a veteran officer wise beyond his years, young Monroe wasted not a moment in taking command, despite the vicious cross fire and his men's exhaustion. "At the head of the corps," Monroe hurriedly prepared his band of Virginia Continentals to continue their attack farther down King Street. Monroe's decision to continue to exploit the hard-won advantage was wise. The lieutenant's Virginia boys, breathless but more than ready to continue the attack, were yet invigorated by their sparkling success in capturing two cannon. Knowing the importance of maintaining the initiative by continuing to push even farther down King Street to break up as much Hessian resistance and as quickly as possible, the young scholar-officer shouted, "Charge!" With drawn saber, the mature teenager, demonstrating that he was a tactically astute officer, then led his cheering Old Dominion riflemen deeper toward the smoke-laden center of the town, blanketed in a fresh sheet of snow, which had transformed into a raging battlefield.

Gaining more momentum in the wild charge south along the slick, icy sloping ground that gradually descended toward the river, the Virginia vanguard's assault continued down King Street and ever-closer to Rall's headquarters. In the forefront and like Captain Washington who had fallen wounded in consequence, Monroe was especially vulnerable. While surging onward through the falling snow and the hail of bullets that whizzed by from nearby houses that spat a blistering sheet of flame at close range, Monroe was soon hit by a lead ball in the tempest. As fate would have it, the future president of the United States now suffered the most serious wound of any American soldier on December 26. He had volunteered for this key mission, and now paid the price.

With the lead ball passing through Monroe's breast and shoulder, the gapping wound appeared mortal. At a makeshift field hospital, two American medical men later saved the life of the good-natured young lieutenant of so much promise when one physician hurriedly tied the severed artery in Monroe's shoulder just in time. Monroe not only gained a captain's rank for his heroism at Trenton, but also established a lofty reputation that helped to pave the way for him to eventually become the republic's fifth president in 1817.

As fate would have it, Monroe carried this large-caliber lead ball in his shoulder all the way to the White House and to another American battlefield at Bladensburg, Maryland. Here, just northeast of Washington, DC, where the rout of American forces resulted in the British task force's entry and the capital's burning in September 1814, as President James Madison's secretary of state Monroe made tactical deployments with untrained Maryland militia in the vain hope of repelling a new generation of British invaders of America's sacred soil.[23]

Finally, on embattled King Street, the Virginia vanguard's slashing attack ran out of steam, losing momentum with the fall of its two inspirational leaders and stymied by exhaustion, especially when combined with an escalating of Hessian fire from the south in front, and a flank fire from the east. But most importantly and as envisioned by the commander-in-chief, a great deal had been already achieved by the spirited onslaught of Captain Washington's Virginians. At the cost of Monroe and Washington's wounding, what these two promising, young Virginia officers had accomplished in a relatively short time was the removal of the main obstacle, Engelhardt's two three-pounders, to Washington's general advance down King Street. By regaining of the initiative and momentum at a key moment so soon after the repulse of Rall's two regiments attacking up King Street, these hard-charging Virginia Continentals paved the way for Washington's soldiers to continue surging farther down King Street and toward the heart of Trenton while not allowing the Hessians to gain time to solidify resistance or to launch another counterattack northward.

Most importantly, Captain Washington's timely tactical achievement stemmed not only from inspired leadership but also from something instinctual and almost primeval that brought out the aggressiveness of the common Virginia soldiers in the ranks, almost as if they were yet hunting and chasing down wounded prey for sport or to put food on the dinner table. In a letter to his Maryland Tory father, Lieutenant Tilghman described the dramatic moment how the elated Virginia Continentals had "pushed on with so much rapidity that the Enemy had scarce time to form, our people advanced up to the Mouths of their Field pieces" and then beyond these significant gains and farther down King Street.[24]

All in all, Captain Washington's tactical success was in fact a key turning point of the battle, helping to pave the way for the overall fulfillment of General Washington's tactical design of a double envelopment, drawing one arm of pincer much closer to the other. Revealing no regional prejudices, Colonel Haslet bestowed proper recognition where it was due, although he was from Delaware, by writing in a letter to his good friend Caesar Rodney, a Declaration of Independence signer and Delaware delegate in the Continental Congress, how "a party of Virginians formed the vanguard and did most of the fighting" this morning.[25]

The dashing Irish colonel's words were no exaggeration in regard to the tenacious struggle for King Street's possession. Quite simply, Washington's and Monroe's timely "capture of the two Hessian cannon was, in fact, a turning point of the Battle of Trenton [because] The clearing of the upper end of King Street permitted George Washington to [eventually] complete a maneuver that led to the entrapment and surrender of hundreds of the defenders [in the end] And no act of individual bravery had more bearing on the outcome of the battle than the wild charge against the Hessian cannon on King Street. . . ."[26]

Indeed, the Virginian's sparkling success in capturing the two three-pounders resulted in a double psychological blow that deflated the morale of Rall's soldiers, who had never known defeat at the Americans' inexperienced hands. First, the sheer shock of Washington's surprise attack—the one-two punch of the artillery bombardment and then the infantry attack down King Street—was enough to shake even the best trained troops, especially during a snowstorm. But the most devastating psychological blow suffered by the Hessians this morning was in losing their two artillery pieces, which was second only to losing a cherished battle flag painted with "the golden lion of Hesse."

Rall's only real hope for successfully defending Trenton, especially against Washington's seventeen artillery pieces that seemed never to cease roaring with authority, and resisting Washington's infantry attacks had been only possible, if all of his brigade's artillery, six guns, were earlier concentrated this morning. Combined with many Hessian muskets now unable to fire because of wetness, the loss of such a large percentage, or one-third, of Rall's most dependable all-weather weapons, the Rall Regiment's two three-pounders, took away even more of the German's already limited capabilities to defend not only the town but also themselves, especially from two simultaneous assaults from different directions. Consequently, the Rall brigade was now less likely to foil any single arm of Washington's double envelopment while the two arms of his pincer movement closed tighter.[27]

Most importantly, Washington's leadership ability and tactical skill continued to rise to the fore in splendid fashion. So far on this most inclement of mornings, Rall and his veteran brigade were simply unable to match Washington's superior tactical flexibility and insight, mobility, firepower, fluidity, imaginative counter maneuvers, concentration of force, and quickness to exploit tactical opportunities and advantages. Washington's formula for success that relied upon a combination of surprise, speed, stealth, and shock that simply could not be successfully countered by even the best efforts of the crack Rall brigade.

In striking contrast to the ineffectiveness of the Rall brigade's cannon with only one-third, now lost to American arms, having been brought into action, Knox's artillery—now reduced to seventeen guns—was having its finest day this morning. From two directions, Knox's artillery from both Greene and Sullivan's columns continued to unleash a heavy volume of firepower that could not be either matched or withstood by the hard-hit Hessians in any sector. No one more than Lieutenant Colonel Scheffer, commanding the von Lossberg Regiment of fusiliers, who had already faced that awful storm of round shot and grapeshot pouring down King Street, fully realized as much.

Washington's astute wisdom in placing his best artillery units, especially Forrest's Philadelphia company with its big six-pounders and five and a half-inch howitzers, close together across the high ground at King Street's head to unleash an early concentrated fire had all but negated any possibility of an effective defense of Trenton in the King Street sector. Scheffer described the worsening dilemma faced by the reeling Hessians, who had so suddenly found themselves in a no-win situation in large part because of the vast superiority of Washington's artillery firepower: "It rained Cannonballs and grapeshot here, and snow, rain, and sleet came constantly into our faces," while more Hessians fell and their wet muskets could no longer fire.[28]

Ironically, among the projectiles now unleashed upon Rall's troops were those of their own captured artillery. Fulfilling their predesignated role thanks to spare artillery equipment brought along for this express purpose as directed by Knox, the foremost artillerymen assigned to manning captured guns now took over one of the captured three-pounders on King Street. Orderly Sergeant White and his New Englanders and Pennsylvanians, meanwhile, serviced the other captured field piece. Here, just north of Petty's Run, he described how: "We put in a cannister of shot, (they had put in the [black powder] cartridge before they left it,) and fired" at the reeling Hessians, adding insult to injury.[29]

With the tide having turned decidedly against Rall and his battered troops on King Street and knowing that the battle's course had gradually shifted eastward, thanks to the gains achieved by Captain Washington's successful attack down King Street, Mercer's relentless application of pressure on the Hessians from the west and Sullivan from the southwest, Washington now felt sufficiently confident to make yet another well thought-out tactical move. Thinking ahead as if knowing that the battle would eventually shift eastward, he dispatched the trusty General Stephen and his three regiments, the Fourth, Fifth, and Sixth Virginia Continental Regiments, farther eastward to plug a gap between Stirling's left, now extended farther east to cover the head of Queen Street with Stephen's departure from this sector, and Fermoy's right, adding more strength in blocking the Princeton-Trenton Road to more solidly eliminate a northwest escape route for the hard-hit Rall brigade.[30]

Vicious Fighting Rages on Queen Street

After the von Lossberg Regiment's repulse and despite the capture of the Rall Regiment's two three-pounders, Lieutenant Colonel Scheffer's fusilier regiment, thanks in no small part to his inspired leadership, was yet in relatively good shape with around two hundred men in the ranks, and even in better condition at this time than the Rall Regiment in part because—besides out of the line of fire from Forrest's Pennsylvania cannon—it had been positioned behind the grenadier regiment, or farther south, during Rall's counterattack up King

Street. In addition, the von Lossberg Regiment had been initially shifted out of harm's way by way of Church Alley, and eventually a short distance farther south down King Street and behind the Anglican Church between King and Queen Streets, preserving more of its strength and cohesion while also suffering less from Mercer's flank fire.

Even more, the von Lossberg Regiment of fusiliers was now in overall better shape than its sister grenadier regiment because it consisted of more veterans than the Rall Regiment. For all of these reasons, the von Lossberg Regiment performed better and with more cohesion throughout this morning than any Rall brigade regiment; a fact later acknowledged in an official investigation and even appearing in British reports. Indeed, the von Lossberg fusiliers now possessed the silk colors of the Rall Regiment because the grenadier's faithful color guard had been cut down during the ill-fated counterattack up bullet-swept King Street. After the bloody King Street setback, consequently, the von Lossberg Regiment was now more intact than the grenadier regiment, retaining more of its considerable combat capabilities and lofty esprit de corps. However, the von Lossberg Regiment had already met with two significant failures by this time: the failure of Lieutenant Colonel Scheffer's initiative in having hurled a detachment of light troops northeast to eliminate the harassing fire from the east side of the northern end of Queen Street; and the failure to halt Captain Washington's counterattack from pushing farther south down King Street, gaining more ground, and inflicting more damage.[31]

In overall tactical terms, Captain Washington and his vanguard of Virginia riflemen had been fortunate to have proceeded so far south down King Street. After having escaped Captain Washington's charge, a shaken Lieutenant Engelhardt reported to Colonel Rall, who had shifted the Rall Regiment farther east, near the corner of Church Alley and Queen Street. Here, Engelhardt appealed to Rall, who rode back and forth with drawn saber to realign his troops: "Colonel Rall, there is yet time to save the cannon." But disoriented by the blinding snowstorm and the confused street fighting instead of the usual set-piece battle of neatly aligned formations facing each other on a broad, open field as in Europe, and while the rolls of musketry from Sullivan's attackers crashed louder to the southwest, Rall gave no immediate answer. Caught in the most perplexing tactical dilemma of his career—facing what was evolving into "a grand melee" and gripped with indecision, this veteran commander, however, knew that the overall situation was now far more complex and grave than he had originally imagined, after having lost two cannon and with so much of King Street that was now in Washington's hands by this time.

Two comparable urgent pleas, including from Lieutenant Gregorious Salzmann, a brave German Jewish officer of the Rall Regiment, who repeated Engelhardt's initial request for assistance, were posed in no uncertain terms to the colonel. Both requests solicited no reaction from Rall, however. Nevertheless, the hard-fighting colonel from Hesse-Cassel was determined to regain all that he had already lost to the detested rebels and of all generals, Washington. The sharp sting of this unthinkable humiliation only fortified Rall's resolve to somehow reverse the day's fortunes. Despite hemmed in by houses and swirling battle-smoke in what had become a nightmarish urban "battle royal" in the icy streets amid the steadily falling snow that almost seemed to mock man's folly of waging war on his fellow man, Rall solemnly promised his troops "we will soon have them [the two lost cannon] back." Yet smarting from the blistering flank fire of Mercer's infantrymen and the salvoes of Forrest's canister and grape, only a relatively few of Rall's grenadiers took heart at the thought of mounting yet another headlong offensive effort to retake the two lost three-pounders at this time, however.

Once the alignment of his formations was complete, Rall attempted to implore his troops westward once again, toward hundreds of American soldiers, and into the vortex of the raging storm that had been manufactured so cunningly by Washington. But too many good Hessian officers already had been cut down and picked off by experienced American sharpshooters with deadly, small-caliber rifles. Many grenadiers were shell-shocked by the swirl and chaos of urban combat, Knox's cannonade, the blinding storm, and Mercer's withering enfilade fire. Some fainthearted Rall Regiment grenadiers, mostly conscripted peasants, fled the raging battle, heading south down Queen Street to escape the escalating combat.[32]

While the Rall Regiment's two three-pounders, now in the capable hands of Orderly Sergeant White and his New Englanders and Pennsylvanians and one of Knox's extra gun crews, had been silenced on King Street, the von Lossberg Regiment's two cannon had been moved southeast to unite with the Knyphausen Regiment. Here, at Queen Street's lower end, these two von Lossberg guns were now manned by Knyphausen Regiment cannoneers, after having been hauled from the back yard of the Anglican Church and then southeast to the lower Queen Street sector to escape Captain Washington's and Lieutenant Monroe's steamrolling attack down King Street just to the west. Consequently, the von

Lossberg Regiment's three-pounders now roared defiance in opposing Sullivan's advance, hoping to stem the onrushing American tide.

But before the onslaught of Sullivan's First Division, these von Lossberg cannon on the south proved as ineffective as the Rall Regiment's guns on the north before Greene's Second Division. Commanded by an artillery lieutenant who evidently was not aware how fast and far Sullivan's foremost soldiers had already penetrated east toward the outer edge of the lower town, these guns fired too high. To the amusement of Sullivan's First Division troops, the first Hessian cannon shots in the Knyphausen Regiment's southern sector missed the onrushing tide of mostly New Englanders, who suddenly appeared like ghostly apparitions charging out of the snowstorm. Creating more noise than casualties, Hessian cannonballs in the southern sector arched west toward the River Road, where most of Sullivan's troops continued to surge onward through the falling snow. With the German cannoneers' aim also impeded by the rows of two-story houses that resulted in an over-elevation of cannon barrels, cannon shots continued to roar well over the heads of Sullivan's foremost troops, under Stark, Sargent, and Glover, respectively. Instead of smashing into Sullivan's leading attackers and inflicting damage, these cannonballs simply sailed high overhead to hit near the rear of St. Clair's column, the reserve brigade of New Hampshire and Massachusetts troops, moving east down the River Road.

By this time, Colonel John Paterson's Fifteenth Massachusetts Continental Regiment was the rearmost unit of St. Clair's reserve brigade, consisting of four seasoned Continental regiments, now moving rapidly eastward down the River Road near the end of Sullivan's column and descending toward Trenton's southwestern edge. This veteran Massachusetts regiment, consisting of Continental troops from Middlesex, York, Worcester, Suffolk, Hampshire, and Berkshire Counties and Litchfield County, Connecticut, was the only Bay State unit in a fine brigade of three New Hampshire Continental regiments, including Stark's regiment (the hard-hitting First New Hampshire), which now led the brigade's advance. A relatively recent arrival from the disastrous Canadian Campaign, including duty in captured Montreal, and part of Gates's northern army reinforcements, the Fifteenth Massachusetts, also known as "the 15th Foot," had been assigned to St. Clair's brigade in late November.

Encountering a rude awakening upon nearing the town's southwestern edge, Johnny Greenwood, the high-spirited fifer of the Fifteenth Massachusetts, described how amid the lengthy column, now enveloped in a haze of snow flurries and human breath from the panting New Englanders, "as we were marching near the town, the first intimation I received of our going to fight was the firing of a 6-pound [three-pound] cannon at us, the ball from which struck the fore horse that was dragging our only pieces of artillery, a three-pounder [of Captain Hugg's Western Company, New Jersey State Artillery]. The animal which was near me [and] was struck in its belly and knocked over on its back [and] While it lay there kicking the cannon was stopped . . . ."[33]

In striking contrast to the fire from the von Lossberg two bronze three-pounders from the defensive position of the Knyphausen Regiment in the lower town, Sullivan's artillery proved more effective, especially Captain's Neil's New Jersey two iron three-pounders, which blasted away in the forefront with Sargent's advancing Massachusetts, New York, and Connecticut brigade. Additionally, the Knyphausen Regiment at Queen Street's lower end also simultaneously took long-range punishment from primarily Captain Hamilton's New York artillery-fire, the far-reaching long six-pounders that now barked loudly from not only the high ground at Queen Street's head, but also from Sullivan's foremost cannon to the southwest. Much like Colonel Rall in having earlier ordered both the von Lossberg and Rall Regiments to shift out of the middle of King Street to escape Forrest's artillery fire by realigning in Church and Pinkerton Alleys, respectively, just east just off King Street, so Major Dechow ordered the Knyhausen Regiment to move out of the deadly line of fire of Captain Hamilton's and Baumann's New York artillery, that were likewise aligned across dominating terrain, firing down Queen Street, which ran down the wide, descending slope to the low-lying river like King Street just to the west.

A veteran commander who was widely respected, Dechow led the bulk of his fusilier regiment farther south and then a short distance east of Queen Street toward the open ground around the suitably plain Quaker Meeting House. In addition, this new position offered the majority of Knyphausen troops protection from the fire of Mercer's soldiers, who were now mostly located about two blocks to the west. Therefore, Dechow's formation was now safely beyond the field of fire from two directions, including from the west, thanks in part to the intense snowstorm and the intervening two-story wooden houses that obstructed views.

However, additional numbers of Stirling and Mercer's soldiers continued to inch forward on their own hook, pushing east and crossing King Street in the town's upper end. Larger numbers of these veterans were fighting by companies and squads, and even individuals, relying on their own flexibility, initiative, and fighting skill to drive the Hessians back. On the north, however, Lieutenant Wiederhold and his hard-fighting pickets, who fired with spirit from the first houses at Queen Street's upper end, helped to deter the advance of the left of Stirling's brigade, to the north, down Queen Street, before he eventually linked with his own Knyphausen Regiment to the south.[34]

After having been swept off King Street, Lieutenant Engelhardt and his withdrawing artillerymen, without their two three-pounders, finally reached the Knyphausen regiment in the lower town, after having fled down the snow-filled alleys east of King Street, before turning right, or south, on Queen Street. Here, near the Quaker Meeting House, where the British light horse detachment had been quartered before riding out of town in a great hurry, Engelhardt informed Major Dechow of the shocking loss of his two guns and Rall's repulse on King Street. This disturbing news revealed that the deteriorating tactical situation was far more serious than Dechow realized.

Stained with black powder, Engelhardt's breathless report caused an alarmed Major Dechow, with nerves already severely strained amid the heat of combat, to snap, "For God's sake, I understand!" Major Dechow now ordered troops west down east-west running Second Street, in the town's low-lying commercial district near the river and perpendicular to Queen Street which it intersected, to confront Sullivan's attackers head-on. After reporting his grim tidings, Engelhardt and his shell-shocked gunners continued their flight, heading south down Queen Street and making fast for the stone bridge across the Assunpink to escape what had become a surreal Hessian nightmare of epic proportions.

Meanwhile, toward King Street's lower end, the southernmost von Lossberg fusiliers were likewise surprised about this time after having escaped Captain Washington's attack from the north by retiring farther south down the embattled street. After they had played a role in thwarting Captain Washington's Virginians from pushing farther south down King Street, these experienced fusiliers then retired east from King Street's lower end toward Queen Street. Both fusilier sections, the one east of King Street in Church Alley that had been outflanked by Captain Washington's attack and the one at King Street's southern end, of Scheffer's von Lossberg Regiment was now united east of King Street. All of a sudden, Lieutenant Colonel Scheffer was shocked to receive a smart fire in his left-rear, to the southwest, from the most advanced of Sullivan's swarming attackers, Captain Flahaven and his New Jersey Continentals, who were followed by the foremost of Stark's onrushing New Hampshire troops, who were eager to meet the much-touted Hessians.

Like Major Dechow in saving the lives of his Knyphausen troops and Scheffer in doing the same for the von Lossberg Regiment by having moved to less exposed positions to the east, meanwhile, Rall had once again wisely withdrew his grenadiers farther away from multiple encroaching fires that seemed to have no end. Consequently, like the von Lossberg fusiliers, the hard-hit grenadiers had initially shifted away in two directions from the wrath of Forrest's artillery-fire: heading farther down King Street and then east by way of the sheltering alleys, especially Pinkerton's Alley, perpendicular to King Street.

Despite the noisy confusion and under skies that were as menacingly ominous as the fire of Washington's sharpshooting riflemen, Rall rallied additional troops (no small accomplishment) from King Street, while most Rall Regiment grenadiers remained in a defensive position in the open ground to the rear of the Anglican Church, between King and Queen Streets and Church and in Pinkerton's Alley just south of the church. All the while, Rall continued to display inspired leadership, refusing to concede the day. Riding back and forth in frantic haste and shouting encouragement, he instilled a measure of resolve and confidence in his grenadiers.

Despite having been first caught by surprise and then repulsed in attacking up King Street, these Hessians proved to be highly durable and resilient troops, refusing to accept defeat at the hands of the detested Americans, who seemingly never won a battle. In terms of numbers and resolve, they had rallied sufficiently to yet retain the considerable offensive capabilities for yet another determined counterstroke if ordered, because these veterans were willing to follow Rall from hell and back, if he only led the way as so often in the past.

With the tumult swirling around him, forty-six-year-old Major Ludwig August von Hanstein, a married man born in Obernhof with twenty-eight years of experience, of the von Lossberg Regiment, took action. At this time, the von Lossberg Regiment remained in position around a block north of the Rall Regiment—as the two regiments had been previously situated on King Street—after gaining Queen Street, north of the Knyphausen Regiment, by way of west-east running Church Alley. Hanstein emphatically appealed to the colonel, who was yet attempting to sort everything out of the swirling chaos and fog of war. The tactically astute major implored Rall to order an immediate frontal attack north up Queen Street. All in all, a determined Hessian counterattack up Queen Street made good tactical sense to the receptive Rall, promising to outflank from the east the Virginian's deep, southward penetration down King Street. Therefore, an advance up Queen Street now offered Rall a viable tactical solution, or so it seemed.

After all, by this time, even more of King Street's extensive length was firmly in American hands, with gains extending a good distance below Petty's Run. Indeed, Stirling's foremost troops—while other soldiers remained at King Street's head to protect the high ground perch—on the brigade's right-center and center had also advanced down the King Street's northern end, swinging east to push past the deserted, dark houses and through the icy alleys between King and Queen Streets to close in on Queen Street's west side, after crossing to the south side Petty's Run.

Meanwhile, to the southwest, Sullivan's foremost First Division attackers, Flahaven's New Jersey men, swarmed deeper into the town's southwestern outskirts with cheers and muskets blazing, as they had already unleashed a hot fire into an exposed portion of the von Lossberg Regiment's left-rear after Scheffer's fusiliers had fallen back south with their repulse on King Street, and before they slipped eastward toward Queen Street to find better protection. By this time, the overall tactical situation was desperate for the Rall brigade, with blistering fires from the north (Stirling), west (Mercer), and southwest (Sullivan) raking the Hessians now caught amid the horror of urban combat during a raging snowstorm that impaired visibility and fueled confusion. In helping to convince Rall of the tactical wisdom of attacking north up Queen Street, meanwhile, Major Hanstein continued to argue in no uncertain terms how:"If you will not let us press forward up this street [Queen], then we must retreat to the bridge [across the Assunpink]; otherwise the whole affair will end disastrously."[35]

With his own aggressive instincts rising to the fore, therefore, Rall began to shift his fusilier companies of Scheffer's regiment farther east along Church Alley, between King and Queen Streets, to form up the von Lossberg Regiment roughly at a midpoint in snowy Queen Street in preparation to once again launch another counterattack north. Armed with fusils, rather than standard smoothbore muskets, and with bayonets fixed, the von Lossberg fusiliers made ready to surge up Queen Street in yet another offensive effort. Clearly, Rall was determined to regain the initiative at all costs. Once again Rall's favorite grenadiers, who were of only average height rather than much taller which was usually the case for these crack troops, prepared to attack up the slope with the bayonet.

Most importantly, Rall's next offensive effort was now bolstered by the two Knyphausen Regiment guns. The two Knyphausen Regiment three-pounders were now with the von Lossberg Regiment, restoring confidence among the grenadiers after the bloody King Street repulse. After King Street just to the west had been lost, Rall was determined to tighten his grip on Queen Street, after Major Dechow had left a void in having earlier ordered his Knyphausen Regiment south to near the Quaker Meeting House to escape the cannon-fire from Hamilton's and Baumann's guns streaming down Queen Street and the increasing flank fire from the west by the foremost of Mercer's onrushing soldiers, especially the sharp-shooting riflemen of the Maryland Rifle Battalion, and those foremost attackers of Mercer's and Stirling's brigades, who had crossed to King Street's east side on the north.

Despite all of the recent setbacks and spiraling casualties, Colonel Rall was confident for success because the von Lossberg guns now bolstered the Knyphausen Regiment, adding much-needed strength, enhancing combat capabilities, and raising morale of the men in the ranks. Ironically, all four three-pounders of the Rall brigade were now with the wrong regiments at this time, which indicated the amount of confusion wrought by the fury of Washington's surprise attack. With a flurry of hectic movement, brightly colored Hessian regimental flags were quickly passed to the front to take their usual places in the front-center of each regimental formation. Finely uniformed officers with their long hair tied in stylish queues, dressed the lengthy ranks, while German musicians, including those same young drummer boys who had scampered up the cliffs during the attack on Fort Washington while American bullets whistled by, struck up a martial air to inspire regimental members as on so many past battlefields where impressive victories had been won.

With renewed determination to yet redeem the day in part because of some slackening of American gunfire due to wet powder and muskets, a reinvigorated Rall screamed out orders for Lieutenant Colonel Francis Scheffer and his crack Lossberg fusilier "to clear" Queen Street of the foremost groups of Stirling's and Mercer's troops to the north. Displaying the same kind of aggressiveness that had so gallantly carried the high ground at Fort Washington in one bold rush, Rall screamed, "Forward March!" The lengthy line of von Lossberg fusiliers surged ahead up the snow-covered slope with confidence in a much-feared bayonet attack up Queen Street.

Moving relentlessly forward with a momentum all its own, this determined assault was led by Scheffer, who commanded the six veteran companies of the von Lossberg Regiment. Flapping in the wintry gales sweeping off the heights, the large Hesse eagle and motto of "Pro Principe et Patrica," embroidered in gold silk, adorned across the von Lossberg battle flags inspired the advancing fusiliers, who now embarked upon their second offensive thrust of the morning and straight north toward Knox's awaiting cannon. But this time and unlike when Rall's grenadiers had spearheaded the first counterattack up King Street now strewn with Hessian bodies, the von Lossbergers launched their own assault, heading north up Queen Street with confidence and closer to the killing zone of Captain Hamilton's and Baumann's New York guns. Meanwhile, just to the west, Rall simultaneously encouraged his disciplined grenadiers west along Pinkerton's Alley and toward King Street in the hope of regaining his two lost cannon: a humiliating setback that nagged at his soldier's conscience and pride.

Seasoned Von Lossbergers moved steadily north up the gentle slope with firm step and fixed bayonets. Scheffer led the way, urging everyone forward into the face of the snow flurries. Born in the town of Hermsdorf which was nestled amid the virgin evergreen forests of east Prussia in 1722, Scheffer was an inspirational commander with thirty-five years of solid experience that now rose to the fore in splendid fashion. But not long after having turned north to advance up Queen Street from the relative shelter of Church Alley, the von Lossberg regiment's vanguard was raked with round shot fired from Hamilton's two New York six-pounders and Baumann's three-pounders that hurled a hail of projectiles straight down Queen Street, which became a shooting gallery as deadly as nearby King Street.

However, Rall's grenadiers possessed even less chance for achieving gains in surging toward King Street because the Virginians, both Captain Washington's vanguard and the Third Virginia, had already advanced so far south down King Street and Mercer's troops had surged farther eastward. Therefore, Rall's grenadiers were almost immediately rudely greeted by an explosion of musket and rifle fire that erupted from the rifles and smoothbore muskets of Mercer and Stirling's troops east of King Street. Additionally, Sergeant White and his New England and Pennsylvania gunners and Knox's extra gun crew also blasted away at Rall's grenadiers with the two captured Hessian guns at close range, after turning around the three-pounders to face east in anticipating Rall's spirited resurgence. Therefore, the grenadier's tentative surge toward King Street was stopped hardly before it had begun along Pinkerton's Alley that had become a death trap for Rall's most prized soldiers: an ill-fated, almost hesitant advance that got nowhere under a furious storm of lead and with elated Americans seemingly swarming everywhere through the town, now shrouded with a thick pall of battle-smoke, which had been transformed into a raging battlefield.

Through the storm of projectiles and nature's wrath, the hard-hit Rall Regiment fell back under the punishment, retiring east to regroup and lick its wounds. For the second time, the much-touted grenadiers, who had never known defeat, had been repulsed to Rall's utter disbelief. To escape the swirling urban combat, the Rall Regiment troops limped back east through Pinkerton's Alley toward Queen Street. Understandably, the troops of Mercer's brigade, seasoned Maryland, Connecticut, and Massachusetts boys, were emboldened by the rather remarkable sight of these fabled grenadiers, battered and bruised, retreating east, leaving their dead behind them.

Raising a resounding victory cheer, the elated Americans pursued their reeling opponent to exploit their success and the tactical opportunity, charging eastward through the blizzard of snow and drifting palls of battle-smoke. After repulsing the finely uniformed grenadiers and advancing east through the dark alleys and between the snow-covered houses to take up new firing positions vacant wooden structures along the west side of Queen Street, behind fences, and in backyards around smokehouses, outhouses, and wells, Mercer's marksmen now spied new and most lucrative targets to the east: the suddenly exposed left flank of the von Lossberg Regiment advancing relentlessly up Queen Street, surging north with flags flying, bayonets flashing, and drums beating. Now unleashing a vicious fire on the vulnerable left flank of the Scheffer's fusiliers, Mercer's opportunistic infantrymen, including men advancing closer and fighting on their own hook, had fully exploited the tactical advantages bestowed by Rall Regiment's repulse just west of Queen Street.

Caught in a deadly quandary, the von Lossberg regiment was especially devastated by the fire of Hamilton's six-pounders at Queen Street's head. From their elevated terrain, the fairly salivating New York gunners unleashed blasts of canister down the long slope that tore remorselessly through the fusilier's ranks. At even closer range, scorching enfilade fires from the west poured forth from Stirling, Haslet, and Mercer's riflemen, from north to south respectively, who had surged forward in pursuit of Rall's hard-hit grenadiers, when they limped eastward and all the way to Queen Street. Because the grenadiers had been thwarted more quickly in attacking west of Queen Street than the von Lossberger's northward surge up Queen Street, Scheffer's counterattack was thoroughly outflanked and hence doomed to failure.

Consequently, the von Lossbergers took severe punishment from both north and west, causing an ever-increasing number of fusilier bodies to litter Queen Street. The fallen Hessians stained the snow-covered artery in bright red, leaving Prussian-style weapons and the debris of accouterments scattered across the road. After having just rejoined his fusilier regiment with his powder-streaked pickets from the northern part of Queen Street in the upper town, Captain Altenbockum's band of warriors was caught in an exposed position. A volley exploded from attackers on the left of Stirling's Pennsylvania, Virginia, and Delaware brigade and tore down Queen Street, striking Altenbockum and killing two of his men, Heinrich Spier and Heinrich Baude of Wieden, Bavaria, in today's southeast Germany.

Suffering a grazing head wound when a bullet broke the skin and splattered him with blood, the highly respected captain was knocked unconscious, dropping to the snowy ground. Altenbockum, however, was soon revived by his men. He then managed to get back to his feet with assistance. While his head was hastily bandaged, the resilient captain was determined to stay in action as long as possible to share the fate of his tough fusilier comrades whatever that may be. Gamely shaking off the pain, the half-dazed Altenbockum continued to encourage his hard-fighting men, who busily loaded and fired at their swarming tormentors.

Only age seventeen but with four years of solid service, Ensign Franz Friedrich Grabe, who had been born in Rinteln, Hesse-Cassel, took over the hard-hit company, leading the battered left of the von Lossberg Regiment. But in the same volley that dropped Altenbockum, other von Lossberg fusiliers went down to rise no more, such as Sergeant Christian Eyssel, who hailed from the rolling, neatly cultivated hills of the Rinteln area. Both Eyssel and Baude were members of Captain Altenbockum's company that had picketed the Pennington Road until they had been swept aside by the onrushing Virginians. As earlier on body-covered King Street, the von Lossbergers lost more good men for no tactical gain or glory in suffering another bloody setback, but this time on Queen Street.

Indeed, in record time, the smartly uniformed Lossbergers suffered the identical dismal fate (hit by fires from multiple directions) earlier suffered by the Rall Regiment just to the west: punished by artillery—Hamilton's two barking six-pounders at the head of Queen Street and Baumann's nearby three three-pounders—from the front and by a hail of musket and riflefire of Mercer's and Stirling's troops from the west, or flank, and front, respectively. Even the

Knyphausen Regiment's cannon had proved ineffective in adequately sup- porting Rall's bold offensive effort straight up the broad stretch of Queen Street.

As Washington had long known with certainty, no troops, no matter how experienced or disciplined, could long withstand such concentrated and severe artillery punishment, especially from a dominant, high ground position. Consequently, and as ordered by Rall, the badly chastised von Lossberg Regiment, now situated just north of the Rall Regiment, began to fall back toward the town's east side to escape the leaden storm sweeping down Queen Street. The grim harvest reaped by Hamilton's and Baumann's death-dealing row of New York field pieces, State and Continental, respec- tively, created a good many new widows and orphans across the land that would become Germany one day.

Then, to exploit the sudden withdrawal of the von Lossbergers, Stirling's soldiers, mostly the brigade's left, renewed their push down the northern part of Queen Street, now lined with debris of battle, broken German dreams, and bodies. Wrapped in their odd assortment of ragged civilian winter apparel and parts of well-worn uniforms, these veterans now surged south with banners, most likely Liberty flags since the Stars and Stripes was not yet adopted by the fledgling nation, waving through the steady deluge of snowflakes, while a chorus of American cheers rose higher in the sulphurous haze laying low over Trenton. However, the overall lack of close coordination and the time lapse (inevitable during a snowstorm and swirling urban combat) between Captain Washington's and Lieutenant Monroe's earlier attack down King Street before the advance of the left of Stirling's brigade south and down on the parallel street (Queen) had bought Rall some precious time and a badly needed respite.[36]

Indeed, as ordered by Colonel Rall to duplicate the eastward withdrawal of his own grenadier regiment, the battered von Lossbergers retired slightly northeastward and farther off bloody Queen Street and toward the head of the small, snow-covered avenue known to locals as Dark Lane, that ran northeast from Queen Street and parallel to the Princeton-Trenton Road to the north, and the lower ground and relatively slight natural cover along Petty's Run to escape the brutal punishment. Yet mounted and exposed, Rall accompanied the mauled von Lossberg fusiliers slightly northeast through the choking battle- smoke, while a handful of reliable grenadiers of his own regiment guarded the fusilier's rear in protective fashion to keep the surging Americans at bay.

Meanwhile, just to the south, Ensign Carl Wilhelm Kleinschmidt, adju- tant of the Rall Regiment, likewise led the Rall Regiment on a parallel course northeastward toward the open ground east of town. Clearly, escaping the deadly fires and confused street fighting of Trenton—a raging urban environment that had become almost a mini-Stalingrad-like struggle to the greatest disadvantage to such conventionally trained troops as the Hessians—was now the top priority of Rall and his hard-hit men.

Meanwhile, during the march to slip away from the escalating urban tempest that resembled a scene from Dante's inferno, Rall sent an urgent order to Major Dechow and his Knyphausen Regiment, now positioned southeast of Rall's headquarters and around the wood-frame Quaker Church, to link with his two roughed up regiments by moving north to gain the upper part of town, if Sullivan's attackers could not be successfully resisted on the south. Most of all, Rall smartly realized that he had to offer solid resistance on both fronts—northern and southern—as long as possible to keep Washington's pincer movement from closing in a Cannae-like double envelopment.[37]

With Hessian initiative having lost steam in all sectors, thirty-eight-year-old Lieutenant Friedrich Fischer rose to the challenge on Queen Street upon Rall's orders to protect the rear of the withdrawing von Lossberg and Rall Regiments, from north to south, respectively, and to prevent an advance of Stirling's troops farther down Queen Street to protect his open left flank, after he crossed to the street's east side. As the experienced senior artillery officer in this sector and Engelhardt's top lieutenant, Fischer was now in command of the only available artillery which had accompanied the von Lossbergers after Lieutenant Engelhardt and his Rall Regiment gunners had fled across the Assunpink. Fortunately, a contingent of rearmost von Lossberg fusiliers was nearby to provide some initial, timely support to these defiant German gunners, but not for long. Shouting out instructions above the tumult, Lieutenant Colonel Scheffer ordered a number of red-uniformed von Lossbergers to assist Fischer, who was short on cannoneers but not on nerve.

With the assistance of veteran bombardier Conrad Volprecht, Fischer took command of an ad hoc gathering of fifteen artillerymen and infantrymen-turned-gunners, amid the confused fog of war that had consumed all of Trenton and the hard-hit Rall brigade. While the battle roared to new furies and the deluge of snow and ice continued to descend from blackened skies unabated, they then pushed forward the Knyphausen Regiment's two three-pounders farther north up Queen Street. Sweating despite the cold from their exertions, this united band of determined German infantrymen and artillerymen hauled the two guns north up the slope on this Thursday morning in hell.

Once deployed by Fischer in an advanced position and a good distance north of the austere Quaker Church, but not as far north as the Rall Regiment's guns had been set up just north of Petty's Creek on King Street immediately to the west, these two cannon were now in a position to not only protect the rear of the withdrawing Rall and the von Lossberg regiments, while moving slightly northeast, but also to keep open one of the two main arteries that led through Trenton and to the stone bridge across the Assunpink and by which reinforcements from Bordentown could come, if dispatched in time. However, setting up the two cannon so far up, or north, slippery Queen Street without the protection of advancing infantry was a risky decision, especially with an unknown number of Stirling's troops before them to the north and with the foremost of Haslet's and Mercer's surging men, to the west, having advanced east to reach Queen Street's west side. One of Fischer's three-pounders was placed squarely in Queen Street and the other artillery piece was situated on open ground just to the street's left.

As earlier when the Rall Regiment's ill-fated two gun section had been positioned just north of Petty's Run on King Street, Lieutenant Fischer's two three-pounders now stood alone amid the omnipresent snowfall without sufficient infantry support because the Knyphausen Regiment was positioned too far south and farther down Queen Street in the lower town. With well-oiled efficiency fueled by a heightened sense of desperation, Fischer's gunners went to work to respond to the barking New York cannon. Eight shots were quickly fired toward the high ground from the two three-pounders, even though they were no longer manned entirely by highly trained gunners of Engelhardt's detachment, but by some versatile infantrymen, perhaps former gunners, detailed from the von Lossberg Regiment.

Most importantly in tactical terms, Fischer's timely advanced placement of the two Knyphausen cannon presented a formidable obstacle to the continuation of Stirling's advance down Queen Street. Therefore, Fischer's feisty band of Teutonic gunners and their two three-pounders had to be eliminated as soon as possible. From the high ground at Queen Street's head, Captain Hamilton and his New Yorkers sighted his six-pounders on the two lone Hessian field pieces, now exposed in the open. Hamilton's New York cannon bellowed angrily, raking the lower ground along Queen Street with an accurate fire. One well-placed iron cannonball ripped through and mangled three unlucky artillery horses, all but ensuring the impossibility of removing the gun in time with so many Americans converging from multiple directions.

Hamilton's keen-eyed New Yorkers had zeroed in on the exact range in record time. One Hessian gunner was cut down while other cannoneers experienced close calls amid the torrent of screaming projectiles. Then a three-pounder was disabled in Queen Street by an excellent shot from the New York artillerymen and the gun could no longer be fired. Simultaneously, the hail of American musketry from multiple directions increased in lethality to additionally reduce Fischer's band, who were now the northernmost, and hence most exposed, Rall brigade members on blood-stained Queen Street. More Hessian gunners and artillery horses fell around the two isolated field pieces aligned in the snow. Lieutenant Fischer's dwindling band of gunners was now in the process of being surrounded by the relentless advance of seemingly countless Americans.

In grim desperation, therefore, Fischer ordered the sole remaining functional cannon to be loaded with canister in a last-ditch effort to keep Stirling's encroaching troops, inching south down Queen Street and eager to capture Hessian artillery by killing all the gunners, at bay. However, only a single blast of canister was unleashed upon the swarming executioners, especially sharp-eyed riflemen, of Hessian artillerymen, just before Fischer's horse was shot from under him. With some of his men already streaming south down Queen Street to either escape or rejoin their fusilier regiment under Scheffer, Lieutenant Fischer screamed orders to hitch up the surviving gun of the Knyphausen Regiment before it was too late.

The able artillery lieutenant, filling Engelhardt's shoes in excellent fashion, planned to escape east to link up with the von Lossberg and Rall Regiments. Providing solid leadership in a crisis situation, bombardier Volprecht, and a handful of Fischer's surviving artillerymen of the Knyphausen guns, hoped to escape to join the cannoneers of the two three-pounders, the von Lossberg guns, now with the Knyphausen Regiment, while bullets hummed around them like angry bees among spring flowers on a sunny April morning back along the Rhine. Lieutenant Fischer, born in Niedernhausen and with two decades of military experience, had performed admirably during this showdown on embattled Queen Street in which his two guns had been silenced in less than ten minutes by the much-maligned Americans who were now fighting with a spirit not previously seen.[38]

WASHINGTON CROSSING THE DELAWARE.

Washington Crossing the Delaware, originally published in *Life of George Washington* by Washington Irving, 1859. Author's collection. Depicts Washington orchestrating the crossing of the Delaware with several members of his esteemed "family" of capable officers.

Realistic sketch of the crossing, originally published in 1926 by New York Interstate News Service. Author's collection.

GESCHIEDENIS DER VERENIGDE STATEN
1. Washington steekt de Delaware over (1776).
LIEBIG BOUILLON BLOKJE: soepen, sausen, groenten, deegwaren
Nadruk verboden   Verklaring op keerzijde

German print of the crossing. Author's collection.

Stamp of the crossing from the Republic of Liberia. Author's collection.

Headquarters of Colonel Rall located at the two story Stacy Potts's House on King Street in the heart of Trenton. Author's collection.

The Alexander Calhoun House, the Hessian picket outpost attacked by Washington's advanced guard of Virginians during the first skirmish of the battle of Trenton. Originally published in *The Battles of Trenton and Princeton* by William S. Stryker in 1989. Author's collection.

A depiction of Colonel Henry Knox's artillery firing from Trenton's northern edge, where Washington's second division under General Nathanael Greene also attacked. Originally published in *Life of George Washington* by Washington Irving, 1859. Author's collection.

The house of General Philemon Dickinson of the New Jersey Militia, named "The Hermitage" and positioned near the Delaware River, where General John Sullivan's first division advanced. Originally published in *The Battles of Trenton and Princeton* by William S. Stryker in 1989. Author's collection.

A postcard depicting the Old Barracks, which was defended by a small Hessian detachment during the battle of Trenton. Author's collection.

A sketch of Washington's attack on Trenton by American artist F. O. C. Darley. Author's collection.

A portrait of Lieutenant Tench Tilghman, originally published in *Memoir of Lieut. Col. Tench Tilghman* by Samuel A. Harrison, 1876. Author's collection.

Original sketch of the mortally wounded Colonel Rall's formal surrender of his garrison to Washington by American artist Frederic E. Ray. Author's collection.

The Victory at Trenton by Charles Kendrick, 1896. Author's collection.

Surrender of Col. Rall at the Battle of Trenton by Alonzo Chappel, 1866. Author's collection.

Surrender of Col. Johann Rall by E. Percy Moran, approximately 1909. Author's collection.

Portrait of Captain Thomas Forrest by Charles Willson Peale. © Independence National Historical Park, Philadelphia, Pennsylvania.

Portrait of General William Alexander, known as Lord Stirling, by Bass Otis. © Independence National Historical Park, Philadelphia, Pennsylvania.

Portrait of Colonel William Washington by Charles Willson Peale. © Independence National Historical Park, Philadelphia, Pennsylvania.

One of the hardy mariners of Colonel John Glover's crack unit, the 14th Massachusetts Continental Regiment. These versatile fighting men not only manned the flotilla of Durham boats during Washington's crossing of the Delaware, but also played a key role in capturing the lower town on the morning of December 26, 1776. Original Sketch by American artist Gary S. Zaboly.

Portrait of Captain Alexander Hamilton, originally published in *The Battles of Trenton and Princeton* by William S. Stryker in 1989.

Chapter VII

Bitter Struggle for the Lower Town

General Sullivan, a thirty-six-year-old Scotch-Irish warrior and the son of immigrants from Ulster Province, northern Ireland, kept his First Division troops on the move, closing the southern arm of Washington's pincer movement tighter around its reeling Teutonic victim. One observer wrote with some amazement how it would "astonish our European military men, to learn that General Sullivan was only a lawyer in 1775," and now leading his unleashed First Division with consummate skill.[1] Like Washington, the New Hampshire-born Sullivan was now having his finest day at Trenton, fighting like a man possessed.

In overall tactical terms and as Washington fully realized, the key to keeping the Rall, Knyphausen, and von Lossberg Regiments from uniting and performing effectively as one—the only real hope for Rall to break through Washington's tightening vise of a Cannae-like double envelopment—lay in striking from two directions and maintaining heavy pressure: the first phase of Washington's encirclement and then annihilation of Rall's brigade. Therefore, adhering to the sound tactical principle of divide and conquer, Washington's elated troops of Greene's and Sullivan's Divisions were now "pressing in on every side" in a determined bid to seal the Hessians' fate. Knowing that exact timing of Washington's well-planned double envelopment was vital for achieving decisive victory, Lieutenant Elisha Bostwick described Washington's masterful tactical formula that all but ensured victory, because the two divisions of "our army . . . with a quick Step [were] pushing on upon both roads at the Same time entering the town" from two different directions and then orchestrating a pincer movement in an urban environment by hard fighting.[2]

While Washington had initially halted Greene's Division in a stationary position on the high ground north of town to await favorable tactical developments before launching his infantry attack down King Street, the assault of Sullivan's Division was slowed because the advance covered a greater distance and initially entered a confusing tangle of snowbound streets in the lower town's outskirts below and just southeast of the River Road. Mirroring the hard-hitting performance of the left of Stirling's Brigade in sweeping aside resistance at Queen Street's northern end and the Virginia Continentals on King Street, Sullivan's New Englanders continued to surge into Trenton's southwestern edge, battling through the darkened streets in the hope of reaping a dramatic victory "for the salvation of America."[3]

Fortunately, to achieve this lofty goal, Sullivan possessed a secret weapon in his sweeping charge into lower Trenton; Colonel Stark, a fellow Scotch-Irish warrior well-known for this aggressive style and tactical skill. Colonel Stark. Commanding the veterans of the First New Hampshire Continental Regiment, the irrepressible Stark, with his fighting blood up, continued to lead the surge of Sullivan's division—with Sargent's brigade in the lead, followed by Glover's and then St. Clair's brigades—through the snowy streets. On the double and backed by the booming cannon-fire of Captain Neil's New Jersey two three-pounders, Stark and his New Hampshire troops, the first regiment in Sullivan's column, surged ahead just behind Captain Flahaven's band of New Jersey solders.

The fighting spirits among Sullivan's attackers was high after overcoming all initial resistance. These onrushing New Hampshire and New Jersey soldiers had already tasted victory in having chased the green-uniformed jaegers out of Dickinson's Hermitage and in driving back the foremost, or westernmost, Knyphausen Regiment's fusiliers eastward. Meanwhile, Major Dechow had led his regiment from the Quaker Church area and to Queen Street's west side in a belated attempt to meet Sullivan's onslaught. As the southern arm of Washington's pincer movement, Sullivan's First Division troops charging into the darkened edge of the lower town were eager to prove themselves.

After all, these same men of Sullivan's First Division, mostly New Englanders, had been often mocked by British leaders as nothing but "a dirty pack of New England long-faces," while upper class Virginians, especially the planter's sons, felt a comparable contempt. Therefore, on this cold morning when so much was at stake for America, Sullivan's New Englanders, ignoring tired legs, the biting cold, and mind-numbing fatigue, were determined to prove to the Virginians, the haughty British, and especially the equally arro-gant Hessians that they were completely wrong about the prowess of the north-eastern fighting man.[4]

And fortunately for Washington, no New Englander was more determined to prove himself this bitterly cold morning than Stark himself. Now never so far from his heavily forested mountains of his New Hampshire Grants, Stark was a natural brawler blessed with considerable tactical ability. The straightforward, opinionated Stark had only recently strongly objected to Washington's face (something no one ever did to America's highest ranking commander who was called "His Excellency") about having been ordered by him to erect defenses along the Delaware's west bank because he believed that his New Hampshire boys could be more wisely utilized in attacking the enemy. In fact, an impatient Stark had even "boldly demanded to know [exactly] when Washington would order an attack" to redeem America's honor. This bold, tactically gifted commander from New England's frontier was now unleashed in the key role that he most relished and best suited him, leading the steamrolling attack of an entire division in America's most important battle to date.[5]

Overwhelming the Barracks

Just a block below Stark's New Hampshire attackers, who faced the foremost, or westernmost, Knyphausen Regiment soldiers, defending positions on, above, and below Second Street and after having earlier turned south off the River Road, meanwhile, Sullivan's troops closed in on targets south of the River Road and Second Street, after departing the east-running River Road by way of a snowbound road leading south toward the Delaware. In his usual hard-hitting style, Sullivan led Sargent's and Glover's brigades south to gain the head, or the western end of Front Street, while Stark and Flahaven continued to surge eastward to apply pressure on the westernmost Knyphausen Regiment fusiliers in the Second Street sector. Here, at this intersection where the road descended to the right, or south, from the River Road met the west end of Front Street, the old barracks, the largest structure in all Trenton, stood to the road's right about a block west of King Street.

Located in the snow-covered river bottom just east of Petty's Run before it entered the overflowing waters of the Delaware and just below where the River Road entered King Street, this imposing stone bastion could not be allowed to remain in Sullivan's rear with the foremost troops, under Stark and Flahaven, now advancing east down the western end of Front Street. Therefore, after Sullivan's First Division had earlier overrun the Dickinson House picket position on the River Road, the U-shaped barracks on the southwest corner of the town's outskirts loomed as the most formidable objective of Washington's right wing in Trenton's lower part. To fulfill this key mission, Sullivan had already dispatched troops south below Second Street for the express purpose of neutralizing the barracks: a costly tactical diversion in terms of time and effort.

Here, opposite the western end of Front Street, Grothausen's breathless "greencoats" from the River Road had earlier reached the two-story barracks to link up with additional Hessian troops housed in these sturdy quarters. All in all, this barracks was an excellent place to make a defensive stand to slow up Sullivan's steamrolling attackers because by this time "the Americans were thick in their front," recalled one stunned Hessian. Therefore, Lieutenant Grothausen hurriedly organized an ad hoc defense before the barracks, which had been built by the Colony of New Jersey in 1758.

In a highly questionable decision, Grothausen decided not to utilize the imposing barracks to make a last stand, however. Instead the green-coated jaegers and barracks troops formed a defensive line just before the barracks, evidently in the open parade ground on the barracks' open side that faced east toward the town's southern end and toward the road by which Sullivan's Continentals poured down in the conventional manner, as prescribed by military textbook. Here, in attempting to defend yet another exposed position, the Hessians prepared to receive Sullivan's attackers swarming southward with cheers. In a strange paradox, these jaegers, trained for dense woodlands fighting, were attempting to defend an urban position on open ground. This isolated band of Hessians had no idea that this formidable barracks had been originally constructed as part of a lengthy defensive line, that included New Brunswick, Elizabethtown, and other New Jersey communities for both British regulars and American militia, whose mission was to safeguard British Empire possessions during the French and Indian War as part of a global struggle between England and France for supremacy.[6]

Situated on the low ground of the river bottoms not far from the ice-filled Delaware, the barracks, fronted by a full-length wooden balcony, was located just two blocks south of the River Road and only a block west of King Street. With sufficient space to house around three hundred soldiers in more than twenty rooms, the stout barracks served not only as quarters for the jaegers but also for relocated Tory refugee families from Burlington and Monmouth Counties and New Jersey and Hessian wives and their children. For the most part, these German women, or camp followers, were a tough, feisty lot, enduring months of active campaigning with their soldier husbands and lovers. They were known for their special hatred of American rebels, having been "abusive" toward Fort Washington prisoners back in mid-November. Presenting a formidable obstacle, the well-constructed barracks was Trenton's largest structure, consisting of native undressed stone erected with skill by master craftsmen. Clearly, the barracks should have served as an ideal defensive bastion that would have been impregnable to delay Sullivan's attack. The well-trained Lieutenant Grothausen, who had been long schooled to fight in conventional ways, thought otherwise, however.

As Sullivan had realized upon first sight, the imposing stone barracks had to be overwhelmed as soon as possible. The barracks, looming like a menacing beacon against a snowy landscape within sight of the dark-colored Delaware, posed a threat that promised not only to slow up but also to sap the overall momentum of Sullivan's attack. To fulfill Washington's ambitious tactical vision of a double envelopment, Sullivan's onslaught had to be continued east unabated down Second and Front Streets, from north to south, to maintain pressure on the Knyphausen Regiment, which was positioned on, above, and below Second Street, and threaten the rear of the Rall and von Lossberg Regiments, facing north in confronting Greene's Second Division.

Therefore, this sharp clash for the barrack's possession was no simple or inconsequential tactical confrontation—although often overlooked or minimized by historians—when Sullivan's onrushing soldiers descended upon a thin, green line of jaegers and other barracks troops deployed. Reacting quickly, the Hessians unleashed a concentrated volley when the foremost Americans, half obscured by a white veil of falling snow, surged forward. But nothing could stop Sullivan's New Englanders by this time. Little, if any, damage was inflicted on the swarming attackers, who continued onward without even halting to return fire.

Lieutenant Grothausen, without sufficient time for his troops to reload for a second volley, had no choice but to order everyone rearward. On the double, the green-coated jaegers and barracks soldiers now made haste for the Assunpink Bridge to escape Sullivan's screaming attackers before it was too late. However, the slight detour of Sullivan's troops—Sargent and Glover—farther south and below the Knyphausen Regiment's westernmost fusiliers around Second Street to the north in descending upon the barracks position and capturing the structure took precious time and slowed the closing of Washington's pincer movement on the south.[7]

After sweeping through the barracks sector, the troops of Sargent and Glover's brigades continued their seemingly unstoppable advance east down Front Street, a block south of Second Street. Meanwhile, on this frozen morning in the snowy lowlands along the Delaware, Stark demonstrated in the Second Street sector in the lower town that he was Washington's best man to spearhead the lower arm of the double envelopment from the south. An ideal choice and a hardened veteran of winter warfare, he possessed hard-hitting qualities well suited for the many stern challenges of the urban warfare and close-quarter fighting now raging through the narrow streets. After pouring deeper into the town's southwest outskirts, Stark and his New Hampshire boys continued to steadily push back the foremost, or westernmost, Knyphausen fusiliers in and around Second Street in the dark streets and narrow, snow-filled alleys of southwest Trenton while surging steadily east toward where the frozen sun had risen.

As if yet battling against the hated French, Indians, and Canadians in wintertime during the last war, the grizzled, former Rogers' Ranger captain caught the foremost Hessians unready to muster an adequate defense against his surging attack that continued to gather momentum. Quickly ascertaining the tactical situation despite the confusion of fighting in the slick streets cloaked in limited visibility, Stark hurled a reliable officer, Captain Ebenezer Frye, and a lengthy line of New Hampshire skirmishers forward through the falling snow.

Now unleashed, these veteran New Englanders dashed ahead on Stark's flanking mission, racing forward with flintlocks at the ready. With his sizeable girth made even larger by a bundle of winter garments, Frye presented a most unsoldierly-like appearance. But Frye was a dependable French and Indian War veteran with good tactical sense and sound judgment. Stark trusted these hard-hitting New Hampshire soldiers, including men from his own hometown, who fought well in Trenton's snowy streets as if they were yet battling Abenaki warriors in the New England's thick, virgin woodlands of summer. Stark's faith was immediately rewarded.

Therefore, immediately upon spying a good tactical opportunity to out-flank Knyphausen troops, Stark dispatched Captain Frye and seventeen veterans from Derryfield (today's Manchester), New Hampshire, and the Merrimack River country forward on the double for a new mission. Maneuvering rapidly to suddenly swoop down upon a party of around sixty Hessians from the flank, this "little ragged squad" of resourceful New Hampshire Continentals quickly captured every fusilier of the advanced detail.

Thanks in part to Captain Frye's outflanking tactics, Stark's New Hampshire soldiers now advanced at a more brick pace over the snowy land-scape to easily overrun the foremost, or westernmost, Knyphausen Regiment troops. Fortunately for Stark, Frye, and Sullivan, the isolated fusilier regiment had wasted too much time in having initially formed in front of Dechow's own headquarters and then around the lower end of Queen Street, near Second Street, just below the plain Quaker Meeting House and around two blocks southeast of Rall's King Street headquarters. The indecision, confusion, and delinquency of the Knyphausen Regiment's leadership allowed for Sullivan's First Division's troops to gain an early toehold on Trenton's southwestern edge: a solid grip that would not be relinquished this morning. Playing a key role, the northernmost of Stark's hard-hitting advance had also threatened the Rall and Von Lossberg's Regiments from the rear to help disrupt Rall's second counterattack while Stirling struck from the north, Haslet advanced from the northwest, and Mercer pushed forward from the west: the well-timed, hard-hitting combination of heavy pressure that had forced both the Rall and von Lossberg Regiments, and then the westernmost elements of the Knyphausen Regiment, to retire eastward to escape the closing jaws of Washington's pincers.

Besides the effective support fire streaming from Captains Neil's New Jersey, Moulder's Pennsylvania, and Sargent's Massachusetts blazing artillery pieces, Stark's infantry attack was also bolstered by cannonfire from Ewing's Pennsylvania militia brigade positioned on the Delaware's west bank. Guns of seven batteries had earlier played a role in forcing the foremost Knyphausen soldiers rearward and away from the riverfront area. Then these Pennsylvania militia gunners turned their fire farther north, hurling projectiles across the river and causing consternation among the foremost Knyphausen Regiment members in the lower town. Caught in a low-ground position with limited visibility that was heightened by the falling snow, Major Dechow's troops were astounded to hear a semicircle of unseen American artillery fire rumbling like thunder seemingly from an angry Hessian-hating god of war from three directions.

None of Washington's colonels possessed a more lengthy record of punishing America's enemies—from Indian, French, Canadians, and British to the equally despised Hessians—than Colonel Stark, the consummate Scotch-Irish frontier warrior. With Stark himself leading the way, the crack First New Hampshire Continental Regiment attacked not only as the vanguard of Sullivan's First Division but also the advance of Sargent's Massachusetts, New York, and Connecticut brigade, which was the first brigade, followed by Glover's and St. Clair's brigades, in Sullivan's assault column.

With well-honed tactical skill, Scottish General St. Clair had been educated at the University of Edinburgh. Like Stark and as if avenging the subjugation of his own Celtic homeland by the British regulars who were experts at crushing rebellion, he battled the enemy with a burning William Wallace-like intensity. Consisting of 110 soldiers of mostly Hillsborough and Rockingham Counties, Stark's First New Hampshire Continental Regiment (now on paper officially the Fifth New Hampshire, but soon to be renamed the First New Hampshire on January 1, 1777) had been relieved from duty in Stark's brigade, of the Northern Department, to join Washington's Army on November 26, 1776.[8] Like Stark, General Sullivan possessed a fine top lieutenant in St. Clair. This hard-fighting Celtic brigade commander was described by one highly impressed officer as having been "born in Scotland, where he has a family and property; he is esteemed a good officer, and . . . will certainly act a principal part in the army."[9]

As in past savage, often no-quarter, skirmishes and battles against the French, Canadians, and Indians during the French and Indian War in the north country's snowy wilderness lying above the most remote New England frontier settlements of mostly Scotch-Irish pioneers, Stark led his New Hampshire boys with the same abandon as when he had won legendary renown as one of the top leaders of Rogers' Rangers who attacked his opponent with audacity and a distinctive "the Indian hollow."[10]

Proud of his Celtic heritage, Colonel Stark was a tenacious Scotch-Irish holy warrior from the unmapped evergreen wilderness of the New Hampshire Grants, seemingly a righteous redeemer, with sword in hand, right out of the Old Testament. Battling with that same intensity across Trenton's smoke-shrouded lower town, Stark now demonstrated that he was one of Washington's hardest fighting regimental commanders. He possessed perhaps more frontier combat experience than any Continental officer in Washington's Army. At the head of his rampaging New Hampshire troops, Stark's mere physical presence inspired his Continentals to rise to their greatest challenge.

With typically prominent Scotch-Irish features, including a sharp nose and high cheek bones, some people believed that the swarthy Stack possessed Indian ancestry. Instead, Stark was an unprivileged son of lowly Irish immigrants from Ulster Province, northern Ireland. Stark's fame as one of America's authentic French and Indian War heroes, second only to Major Rogers, had preceded him. He had earned widespread renown as Robert Rogers' top lieutenant during some of the ranger's most famous wilderness battles and skirmishes against enemies who long devastated the New England frontier. In the present war against the Mother country, he first served as a volunteer beside other rough-and-tumble frontiersmen of the Bennington Rifles. Like some ancient Scottish clan chieftain from the Highlands, Stark led a good many Scotch-Irish soldiers—the primary composition of Rogers' Rangers and tough fighting men who had been members of his First New Hampshire when first organized in May 1775—against the foremost Knyphausen fusiliers in the lower town. In a name that evolved from his vanquishing and domination of so many German soldiers at Trenton, he later christened his war horse "Hessian."[11]

Upon spying a good tactical opportunity, Stark descended upon the Knyphausen Regiment's defensive line aligned in a neat formation before the Henry Drake's Bull Head Tavern, the largest building on the block and where rum had often flowed late into the night, on Second Street near Queen Street. Like the snowstorm propelled by the howling northeast winds, seemingly nothing could now stop Stark from pushing deeper into the dark recesses of the lower town by way of Second Street, despite the fact that this was exactly where the Knyphausen Regiment resistance was most concentrated. Above all, Stark knew that whenever he had an enemy on the run, then his reeling opponent had to be pressed as hard as possible.

Therefore, and despite being subordinate in rank to Sullivan, Glover, and St. Clair, Stark was not only leading the way, but also making his own tactical decisions in the frontier tradition, striking his own selected targets, and fighting very much on his own hook. Supported by the fire of Moulder's Philadelphia, Sargent's Massachusetts and Neil's New Jersey field pieces that were leap-frogged eastward to get within close range of the Knyphausen Regiment soldiers, Stark's advance steadily gained more ground. Demonstrating a blend of typical Scotch-Irish combativeness and independent-mindedness, this New Hampshire frontiersman wasted no precious time waiting for specific orders when on the move in the heat of combat. Doing what he did best based upon his own instincts and tactical decision-making literally on the run, Stark continued to exploit the tactical advantage gained by his own aggressiveness and initiative, leading his Continental troops deeper through the icy streets of lower Trenton. With his hard-fighting First New Hampshire regiment, he charged anything and everything that he saw before him, gaining more vital ground for the First Division in the process, while spearheading the pincer movement of Washington's southern arm.

At this time, Major Dechow's responsibility was to protect not only Rall's rear, but also the approaches to the Assunpink Bridge. Rall's first order only recently reached the major who was in the lower town's depths, directing Dechow to keep the approaches to the stone bridge over the creek wide open. Therefore, Dechow was forced to align troops facing north as well as west. While Stark's First New Hampshire troops advanced east down Second Street and Sargent and Glover's brigades, respectively, surged forward in the same direction down Front Street one block to the south, the vast majority of Dechow's troops west of Queen Street faced mostly west to meet the First Division's escalating threat southwest of town. Commissioned as a captain in the Second Continental Infantry, Major James Wilkinson never forgot how Colonel Stark, Washington's most unorthodox, maverick Continental regimental commander, led his First New Hampshire soldiers in a "thundering charge" with the bayonet and wild cheers from the dense forests of the northwestern frontier.[12]

Fairly lusting after a most inviting tactical opportunity, Stark now took dead aim on the left, or southernmost, flank of the Knyphausen Regiment positioned west of Queen Street. If anyone could defeat the elite Knyphausen fusiliers, then the roughhewn Stark, age forty-eight, was that dynamic leader. Besides love of country and the struggle for liberty, this natural warrior, known for his audacity, was now in essence battling fiercely in defense of his New Hampshire farm on the Merrimack River near Amoskeag Falls. All the while, the magnetic power of Stark's leadership inspired his 110 onrushing soldiers of the First New Hampshire Continental Regiment to charge deeper into the labyrinth of ice-crusted alleys and streets of darkened lower Trenton, and closer to the Knyphausen Regiment's left flank. With their muskets and ammunition wet from melting sleet and snow of the incessant deluge, Stark had already implored his men to get as close as possible to the Hessians and then to rely upon the bayonet.

Most of all, Stark was now rising to the challenge in the narrow streets of the smoke-filled lower town, as so often during the French and Indian War. Even Major Rogers's widely circulated journals, published in London in 1765 and immensely popular on both sides of the Atlantic, had applauded Stark's leadership ability and skill as a natural guerrilla fighter. Gaining experience in conventional warfare, he had played a key role in leading his New Hampshire regiment, consisting of large numbers of Scotch-Irish, in saving the day at the battle of Bunker Hill. Here, on his own tactical initiative, Stark had wisely decided to extend the vulnerable defensive line northeast all the way to the Mystic River to protect the amateur revolutionaries' exposed left flank of Breed's Hill. When the rustic New England defender's limited support of ammunition dwindled during the third British assault that overwhelmed the high ground defensive position, he had then formed an effective rear-guard against the charging British regular, buying invaluable time to protect the mob of New Englanders streaming out of the earthen fort atop Breed's Hill to escape. Then in an equally skillful repeat performance, Stark also protected the army's rear during the American withdrawal from ill-fated Canada, proving invaluable service and helping to save the day.

But overcoming the odds and doing the impossible, regardless of the opponent, was nothing new to Stark. He had even survived capture by the much-feared Abenaki, doing what few others have ever accomplished. In the beginning, Stark even gained the Indians' rare respect for a white man by striking back at the largest, fiercest-looking warrior and threatening "to kiss all their women" when running the deadly gauntlet at the village of Saint Francois. Revealing depth of character and empathy for Native Americans, Stark had refused to participate in the devastating, early October 1759 raid of Rogers' Rangers on his befriended former captors at Saint Francis.

When not battling America's enemies and as could be expected, the ever-combative Stark often clashed with his fellow Americans. Stark had long demonstrated a typically Scotch-Irish hatred of arbitrary political and governmental authority. He had long openly denounced corrupt, abusive politicians on both sides of the Atlantic. Stark proclaimed that he didn't "care a damn" for established legislative institutions, British or American, if not properly serving the people. Refusing to play the backdoor game of self-serving politics for personal advancement, Stark instead allowed his sparkling battlefield successes to speak for themselves. And now this irrepressible son of the New Hampshire Grants was fiercely battling Dechow's Knyphausen fusiliers in the sulphurous smoke and snow blowing across the low ground of Second Street with a righteous intensity that was reflected in his personal motto of "Live Free or Die."

In addition, Stark possessed a good many personal scores to settle this morning. Two of Stark's nephews had already sacrificed their lives in America's struggle for liberty, which only fueled his motivation. All the while, therefore, Stark continued to keep his First New Hampshire Continentals together and on the move while surging in the same direction in the blinding snowfall. Shouting orders in his booming voice that no one challenged, Stark's words betrayed a recognizable Scotch-Irish brogue that reflected the rich Celtic cultural heritage of Ulster Province and the transplanted Scotch-Irish community of Londonderry, New Hampshire, which had been named after northern Ireland's largest city.[13]

As so often in the past, Stark proved unstoppable in the bullet-swept streets of lower Trenton, brushing aside all initial Knyphausen Regiment resistance before the fusilier regiment's increasingly vulnerable left flank. Most of all, he now sought to deliver a sledgehammer-like blow against Dechow's veteran regiment "to prevent my country from being Ravaged and Enslaved by our cruel and unnatural Enemies" from England and Germany.[14] Determined to capture the lower town to fulfill Washington's lofty tactical vision of a double envelopment, Stark was also fueled by an undying contempt for his Hessian opponents because they were nothing more than mercenaries who had been "bought for seven pounds and tenpence a man."[15]

Stark, consequently, was very much waging his own personal war, striking everything in sight. All the while, he continued to encourage his yelling New Hampshire boys, no longer feeling the late December cold in their adrenaline-infused excitement and thrill of success, onward through Second Street, pushing aside more fusiliers and surging past the little vacant shops and stores, now darkened and silent, of the once-thriving commercial district in a determined effort to strike and then roll up the Knyphausen Regiment's left flank. As if avenging Gaelic-Celtic family members who had been fiery rebels on both sides of the Atlantic, Stark applied ever-increasing relentless pressure on Dechow's vulnerable left. In awe, Major Wilkinson never forgot how "the dauntless Stark dealt death wherever he found resistance, and broke down all opposition before him."[16]

Meanwhile, while Stark's New Hampshire Continentals charged east through Second Street, low-lying on the river's floodplain, and hurled back additional fusiliers toward the Knyphausen Regiment's left flank, the remainder of Sullivan's First Division maneuvered just below Stark to pour down Front Street, where the popular Black Horse Tavern had long satisfied thirsty patrons, only one block south and deeper into the smoke-laden maze of southwestern Trenton.

As planned, Sullivan's onrushing troops now exploited Stark's success in sweeping aside all initial resistance. Colonels Sargent and Glover's brigades, bolstered by the rapid fire of Neil's New Jersey, Moulder's Pennsylvania, and Sargent's Massachusetts batteries, respectively, surged slightly northeast toward the Knyphausen Regiment's left from the south just below Stark. Seemingly like a man possessed, Sullivan was now determined to smash through all Knyphausen resistance to gain Queen Street, the strategic artery just to the east and whose possession promised victory now that the Continentals had secured

King Street, to cut off the Rall brigade's escape south out of town by gaining the foot of Queen Street in the lower town and the Assunpink bridge—the only means of escaping across the rain-swollen creek.[17]

With a comparable strategic objective in mind and just north of Sargent's and Glover's eastward-surging brigades, respectively, Stark remained keenly focused on rolling up the Knyphausen's left flank, which now defended the vicinity of Queen and Second Streets, while St. Clair's New Hampshire and Massachusetts regiments surged ahead to Stark's rear. Running a gauntlet of fire from nearby houses, Stark and his New Hampshire troops smashed into Dechow's left with a vengeance, inflicting damage and knocking additional crack fusiliers out of action. More importantly in tactical terms, Stark was driving the westernmost troops of the Knyphausen Regiment gradually east toward Queen Street, driving closer to his primary tactical objective.

Young Major Wilkinson was part of Stark's attack that steamrolled through the lower town to give the Knyphausen Regiment more than it could handle, describing how "the enemy made a momentary shew of resistance by a wild and undirected fire from the windows of their quarters [private homes] which they abandoned as we advanced, and made an attempt to form in the main street [Second], which might have succeeded." With the fusilier regiment's left now heavily pressured from the howling tide of Sullivan's attackers, from both north (Stark on Second Street and with the rest of St. Clair's brigade following) and south (Sargent and Glover, respectively, on Front Street), Dechow ordered his hard-hit troops to fall back before they were completely overwhelmed. Therefore, the northernmost fusiliers on the Kynphausen Regiment's right began to withdraw east and then north up Queen Street with the objective of marching east out of the swirling urban combat into a broad, open field just east of the Quaker Meeting House, which was located about a block east of Queen Street.[18]

Feeling that victory was ordained by God, Stark continued to push aside every fusilier whom he found opposing him in the streets, alleys, and houses along Second Street and its dank environs. Destroying the enemy was simply a case of "doing my God and Country the Greatest service" to this Scotch-Irish holy warrior. Colonel Stark's sustained pressure was strategically important and timely, ensuring that the Knyphausen Regiment was not initially going to link up with the Rall and von Lossberg Regiments, which had now continued to retire northeast to Queen Street's east side, for an united offensive effort of the entire brigade to escape Washington's entangling web: another key tactical requirement for the eventual fulfillment of Washington's grand tactical design of a double envelopment. Therefore, all three regiments of the previously undefeated Rall brigade would never unite as one for either an offensive or defensive effort this morning.[19]

Most importantly by this time, Washington's fast-moving infantry units of his unleashed First and Second Divisions on every sector of the field refused to relinquish either the initiative or momentum as if holding tightly onto something precious precisely because it had been so rarely grasped. Meanwhile, after having been thwarted in its determined counterattacks and even in regard to the permanent placement of its artillery in advanced positions on both main parallel arteries leading into Trenton's center, the Rall Regiment and von Lossberg Regiments remained just east of Queen Street at this time while the Knyphausen Regiment fought on its own to the south against Sullivan's Division, which continued to achieve significant gains in the embattled lower town.

While the Rall Regiment of grenadiers remained in the area just east of Church Alley on Queen Street's east side, the von Lossberg Regiment's left flank likewise remained on Queen Street, with most of this crack fusilier command aligned in the more open ground to the east. Here, the Hessians maintained stationary positions after having learned the wisdom of keeping formations out of the middle streets dominated by Knox's artillery. Rall and other top officers restored order, despite consecutive offensive setbacks and spiraling losses. Begrimed in black powder and exhausted, these experienced grenadiers and fusiliers yet remained seemingly half-stunned from the recent punishment delivered by the salvoes of artillery and sheets of musketry, however. Never before had these crack fighting men seen so many American soldiers displaying so such aggressiveness, skill, and initiative, shattering long-existing stereotypes that had been long accepted without question.

Most shocking of all, Rall's most determined offensive efforts had been twice thwarted: something that had never happened before to Hessian troops on American soil. Rall listened nervously to the escalating crash of musketry to the southwest with Sullivan's troops pouring through the lower town with ever-increasing momentum. Now the exploding musketry from Washington's onrushing troops echoed like a summer thunderstorm over Trenton from the north, south, and west. Even though the Hessians could see relatively little of what was exactly happening around them in the snowstorm and drifting clouds of sulphurous smoke, they knew from the cacophony of rattling musketry and crashing cannonfire that Washington's encirclement was continuing to succeed as planned.

Since remaining stationary and idle in Trenton was a no-win situation, Rall's faithful adjutant and conscientious bachelor, Lieutenant Jakob Piel, approached Rall, who continued his attempts to stabilize his hard-hit command. Knowing that the opportunistic Americans were making a determined offensive effort to gain Queen Street in the lower town below their position to cut off their main avenue of escape south from Trenton, now engulfed by Washington's closing arms of a pincer movement, the lieutenant attempted to convince Rall that now was the time to withdraw south and escape across the Assunpink Bridge— by which many Germans, Engelhart's gunners, the British light horse, and a number of fusiliers and grenadiers had already slipped out of harm's way—at the foot of Queen Street. Even Grothausen's elite "greencoats" had already fled across the bridge never to return, bursting the persistent myth that a single "jager is worth more than ten rebels." Clearly, as Washington had planned with such care, his surprise attack had caused a paralytic sense of disorientation, bewilderment, and indecision among the Rall brigade's veterans. Combined with the realization that his once-magnificent brigade had been victimized by the smooth orchestration of Washington's double envelopment that caught everyone by suprise, discretion was now the better part of valor for a good many Hessian soldiers.

And now Rall finally began to understand as much, accepting the bitter truth that was now no longer possible to ignore. Out of tactical solutions and options, Rall reluctantly agreed with Piel's advice that seemed like a sound tactical solution by this time. But was the Assunpink bridge even open with the troops of Sullivan's First Division, especially with relentless Stark leading the way, advancing so rapidly to the south and pushing aside all resistance, as indicated by the ever-eastward rolling cascade of musketry?

Prudently, Rall had earlier sent word to Dechow to do whatever was necessary to keep the bridge open, but Sullivan's First Division had gained much more ground in the lower town since that time. Rall, consequently, dispatched this experienced lieutenant (Piel), with fourteen years of service, south to the foot of Queen Street to ascertain if this vital stone bridge across the wide, rain-swollen, tidal stream, was yet free of Washington's attackers, who now seemed to be swarming everywhere and as omnipresent as the flurries of snow descending upon Trenton nonstop.[20]

However, a host of pressing factors caused even this resourceful, never-say-die German brigade commander, who had reaped victory on every 1776 battlefield, to now contemplate escape as the only solution. First and foremost, the most distinctive feature of this hard-fought battle that it was a savage, close-range urban struggle that continued to frustrate Rall's best efforts. Rall and his men possessed no prior experience with the almost unfathomable challenges of the savage, close-range nature of urban combat. Nor had they faced so much well-serviced American artillery, which was having its finest day, placed in such advantageous positions.

To additionally confound the Hessians, Washington's soldiers fought largely on their own hook and as individuals in true frontier fashion, advancing and fighting on their own without the usual conventional rules restricting their movements, initiative, and natural aggressiveness. Proving expert street fighters and natural brawlers in which they utilized their own good tactical sense, they battled Rall's befuddled troops in an eerie, almost surreal setting of a night-marish urban environment, during an intense snowstorm's "unnatural darkess-by-day" atmosphere, made gloomier by the thick palls of battle-smoke hovering over Trenton like a cloud.

From the beginning in fighting by regiments, companies, squads, and individuals, Washington's soldiers fully utilized this individualistic brand of warfare at which they now proved themselves masters. More like Indian raiders unleashed rather than conventional soldiers, the fast-moving Continentals advanced through the streets, alleys, and backyards before taking good cover to blast away at targets from behind fences, houses, and trees. Throughout this freezing morning, these young yeomen farmer-soldiers relied upon their own initiative, experience, and intelligence to repeatedly outmaneuver and tactically outthink their opponents, pushing aside Rall's formations and overwhelming stubborn pockets of Hessian resistance.

In contrast, Rall's Germans depended upon maneuvering, firing, and attacking in close coordination and as one in neat, tight formations for massed volley firing in the Prussian tradition of Frederick the Great: the anthesis of the individualist American soldier's way of fighting. And in this regard, Rall and his officers were the key to keeping everything moving and flowing in a precise, disciplined, and correct manner. Knowing as much, consequently, Washington's men naturally sought to eliminate these key linchpins of the smooth functioning of this businesslike Prussian system, focusing on shooting down German officers as soon as possible. The fact that lower- and middle-class

American riflemen relished the opportunity to kill upper-class members in the name of God and country was yet another incentive to cut down Hessian officers without mercy.

Knowing how to keep their weapons dry, soldiers frantically chipped their newly issued musket flints to ensure sparks, recently issued upon Washington's orders—another example of their commander's foresight—to guarantee that most of their rifles and muskets would fire even during a raging snowstorm. Washington's astute, versatile attackers also hurriedly loaded and fired while on the move, carefully picking out and cutting down targets, especially Hessian officers exposed in their resplendent uniforms. In the heat of battle, no officer had to tell Washington's savvy veterans, especially frontiersmen from the wilds of western Maryland, Virginia, or Pennsylvania, how to keep flintlocks firing at a rapid pace, or which target to pick out and knock down with a well-placed shot.[21]

With the swirling combat reaching a crescendo in an urban environment that was alien for Rall and his troops untrained in the novel art of urban warfare that was not in the eighteenth-century European military manual, the American's distinctive frontier style of fighting rose to the fore in Trenton's streets. Most of all, the individual common soldiers and officers from New England to Virginia now relied upon their own well-honed instincts and skills in fighting as individuals who could think and act for themselves. In this way and most importantly for a successful double envelopment as envisioned by Washington, the elated common soldiers—from beardless teenagers to grizzled veterans with long gray hair—maintained the initiative and momentum throughout this morning of decision.

Meanwhile, the surging Americans gained additional ground by advancing on their hook and firing from cover. During this combat raging through Trenton, the natural inclinations, including killer instincts, took control of a good many individual Continental soldiers, who now battled in a Darwinian survival of the fittest showdown in Trenton's narrow streets against the elite Rall brigade, as if yet confronting Indians in their own manner of warfare. Clearly, Washington's fighting men benefitted immensely from the fact that the close-range combat swirling through Trenton's avenues and alleys provided an ideal setting for the individualistic, free-thinking soldiers of a desperate American army that now needed to win a victory for its very survival.

Consequently, many Hessian officers and enlisted men were befuddled in attempting in vain to cope with this frontier style of fighting in a hellish urban environment. Few Hessians believed that these often-defeated Americans would have dared to attack a full grenadier-fusilier brigade, especially in the midst of a blinding winter storm. For Rall's men, therefore, this vicious urban-winter combat raging through Trenton's streets seemed like an ugly, surreal nightmare—much too close-range and personal—from which they seemingly could not awake. In the midst of a bitter winter storm (waging winter combat, especially siege warfare, was considered "impossible" in conventional and traditional European minds) at a time when European soldiers were normally sitting beside their warm fires in comfortable winter quarters, the elated Americans, yelling like Indians from the darkest recesses of a primeval wilderness, seemed to be everywhere and firing from behind every house and rail fence.

Taking careful aim and slowly squeezing Long Rifles and smoothbores with "ball and buckshot," Washington's soldiers blasted away from good cover to rake the exposed Hessians, who hardly knew where to turn amid the confusing din. To the Hessians' endless lament, the Americans' close-quarter style of combat was the very anthesis of traditional European warfare. Therefore, the Hessians were perplexed by this novel way of fighting, a blend of western frontier, guerrilla warfare, and urban combat mixed into one. All the while and as deemed by regulations, proud Hessian officers stood out before their formations in their fancy uniforms, wearing shiny regimental silver, copper, or brass gorgets which hung from necks and covered upper chests, and large bicornered hats, which only drew an accurate fire of sharp-eyed western frontier sharpshooters with trusty Long Rifles.

All of the old conventional rules for waging war, as ordained by the most respected European and German textbooks and military colleges, had said nothing about defending positions in a congested urban area during the most appalling winter conditions. Emerging suddenly out the snowstorm, the shocking sight of Washington's cheering soldiers, loading and firing on the run, swarming off the high ground to the north and off the low ground to the south in overwhelming numbers was an almost mind-numbing, if not unbelievable, spectacle to disciplined Teutonic soldiers long trained and conditioned to confront conventional opponents in neat, straight linear formations on Europe's open fields.

Almost as if hoping to demonstrate that the Old World's traditional ways of waging war were really not yet obsolete at Trenton, young Hessian musicians played martial music in the midst of the raging battle. Even while under a heavy fire, the Hessian musicians played their most inspiring tunes almost certainly to the amusement, if not disbelief, of unsophisticated, illiterate American farm boys, who continued to shoot down additional German soldiers, especially finely educated and priviledged officers, with the ease of hunting white-tailed deer or turkeys in the dense, hardwood forests of western Maryland, Pennsylvania, and Virginia. Under such circumstances, these German musicians, drummer boys and flutists, should have been ordered by officers to grab muskets and to assist in fighting off Washington's swarming attackers from multiple directions, because every man was now needed in the hard-hit ranks if the Rall brigade was to survive its greatest challenge this morning in hell.[22]

While the talented German musicians of the fine brass band played their martial tunes that rippled eerily over a war-ravished Trenton, the thundering symphony of Sullivan's cannon grew louder in the town's southern end. In a strange way, the angry growl of Knox's guns appropriately matched the fury of the wintry tempest in sheer intensity, while hundreds of Washington's veterans continued to advance at a brisk pace through the icy streets, snow flurries, and suffocating clouds of battle-smoke. All the while and sensing victory as never before, the Americans moved relentlessly onward as if nothing could stop them.

Even though Washington possessed no comparable brass bandsmen to counter the playing of spirited Teutonic music that echoed through Trenton's streets, the onrushing Americans were fueled by their own source of inspiration—more philosophical, intellectual, and spiritual—that fortified an even greater resolve. Shutting the door on the Rall brigade's escape from the south, hundreds of Sullivan's First Division troops surged ever-eastward toward the lower end of Queen Street, while shouting an invigorating war cry straight from the hallowed pages of Paine's *The American Crisis*: "These are times that try men's souls." Amid the heat of battle, the shouting of Paine's words by the common soldiers was a most symbolic development because the ever-contrarian Englishman, when General Greene's volunteer aide, had shed tears upon the sickening sight of the fall of Fort Washington. After all, here, Colonel Rall and his elite brigade had reached the zenith of their success and lofty reputations for invincibility in reaping their most impressive battlefield success on American soil. At long last, the war was now coming full circle at a little New Jersey town nestled on the Delaware, and the haunting, searing memories of all those past defeats and humiliations now motivated Washington's breathless troops as never before, inspiring them to keep charging through the snowy streets of Trenton, shouting, loading, and firing on the run.[23]

Glover Maneuvers Skillfully, As If At Sea

While Colonel Stark continued to lead the way east along Second Street with his onrushing New Hampshire regiment, batter the Knyphausen Regiment's crumbling left, and fight his way closer to the strategic Queen Street sector, the charging soldiers of Colonel Sargent's New York, Connecticut, and Massachusetts brigade also maintained equally heavy pressure on the Knyhausen Regiment in pushing east along Front Street only a block to the south. Meanwhile, the largest brigade of Sullivan's Division, Glover's New England brigade, advanced behind Sargent's surging brigade. Meanwhile, just to the northwest, Sullivan's rearmost regiments, or reserves, yet pushed down the River Road, where the snow had been trodden down by this time to leave a sheet of ice that made footing treacherous. Moving at the double quick behind Glover's Bay State and Connecticut soldiers, the most rearmost of St. Clair's troops, New Hampshire and Massachusetts Continentals, poured down the River Road toward Trenton's southwestern edge and the intensifying battle.

As a well-deserved reward for having saved such a large percentage of Washington's Army by evacuating them safely off Long Island and out of Howe's clutches in late August, Glover now commanded a full brigade of 865 veterans in one Connecticut and four Massachusetts Continental regiments. His veteran Massachusetts contingent included his fellow 177 Marbleheaders of the Fourteenth Massachusetts Continental Regiment, which was Glover's favorite (his old command), if not somewhat pampered, regiment. Unleashing high-pitched, piercing war cries straight from the depths of New Hampshire's pine and spruce backwoods, Stark and Sargent's troops, from north to south respectively, continued to surge through the town's southern end, loading and firing on the run.

While Sullivan's foremost soldiers, under Stark and Flahaven's New Jersey vanguard, had first entered the frozen lower town by having followed the southeast-running River Road that terminated at King Street in the northern sector of the lower town before plunging farther south and deeper into the southern, or lower, end of Trenton to apply pressure on the Knyphausen Regiment's left, Sullivan's rearmost troops, St. Clair's New Hampshire and Massachusetts brigade, had continued to advance down the River Road, bringing up the column's

rear. At the River Road intersection of the first north-south-running, or perpendicular, street that was King Street, St. Clair's brigade had then divided:
with the first arriving regiments of Sargent and Glover's brigades having shifted
south first to Second Street and then to Front Street one block to the south,
while the last of St. Clair's regiments, the Fifteenth Massachusetts Continental
Regiment, pushed steadily east toward King Street north of Colonel Stark, who
advanced east on Second Street along with the "right" of St. Clair's brigade
consisting of two regiments, and Sargent and Glover's troops, respectively, likewise poured east a block south along Front Street below Stark's surging New
Hampshire Regiment.

While colorful Massachusetts battle flags snapped in the stiff breeze blowing
from the northeast, Glover's elated New England soldiers continued to swarm
east into snowy Front Street, a parallel artery just below the River Road, where
both King and Queen Streets terminated in Trenton's southern end and the
street closest to the river. This southernmost and lowest-lying area of town was
the commercial district of shops and private businesses that had long intercepted, and then sold, the heavy flow of all variety of goods transported down
the Delaware on the short journey to Philadelphia.

With the hard-fighting Colonel Paul Dudley Sargent leading the way, below
Stark's regiment, the mostly New Englanders of this fine Continental brigade
surged east toward Queen Street with cheers echoing through the frigid air and
unnerving even some veteran Knyphausen fusiliers, who must have thought
that demons were descending upon them. Unlike most soldiers of Sullivan
and Greene's columns, Glover's mariners charged through the streets behind
Sargent's troops with the distinct advantage of fixed bayonets. Therefore, during
close quarter fighting that swirled through the deserted lower town when visibility was low and quite unlike Mercer's troops, especially the frontier westerners armed with deadly Long Rifles, who possessed relatively few bayonets, to
the north, Glover's feisty soldiers met Knyphausen fusiliers on their own terms
with steel bayonets in the swirl of confused fighting along the snow-covered side
streets, backyards, and alleys of the darkened lower town.[24]

But most significantly, some of Glover's men, almost certainly the old
mariners, carried the longtime weapon of choice of men at sea, the blunderbuss. The large-caliber, short-range musket, actually more of a shotgun because
it fired clusters of shot, was the best possible weapon for not only fighting
at close quarters, but also during a raging snowstorm when relatively little
could be seen. In fact, no weapon was more ideally suited for the conditions

of urban warfare, and Glover's former seamen proved themselves especially formidable with this short shotgun-like musket with the flared barrel at the end. A non-issued weapon long beloved by pirates, the blunderbuss was early brought into Glover's ranks from home by individuals, who appreciated the lethality of this unique firearm that was carried by no other troops on either side at Trenton.[25]

By this time, Glover's multi-dimensional and versatile men, who now demonstrated that they could perform as well on land as hard-hitting infantrymen as mariners on water, felt supremely confident, especially after their sterling performance during the river crossing. After all, these hardy "fishermen from Marblehead had sure shown [all] those landlubbers from New York and Pennsylvania how to handle a boat—even in a damn flat-bottomed river boat surrounded by ice cakes!"[26]

Now the Marblehead mariners were determined to prove to the haughty Virginia cavaliers of Greene's Second Division how well they could perform as infantrymen on land. However, in truth, Glover and his Bay State Continentals had nothing to prove in this healthy, but often intense, rivalry, especially after all that they had already accomplished on New York soil on an unforgettable October 18, 1776, barely two months ago. At that time, Glover and his well-trained Massachusetts brigade, including his own Fourteenth Massachusetts Continental Regiment, had fought magnificently along the coast to save Washington's Army while it withdrew north for the safety of White Plains at the battle of Pell's Point, or Pelham Bay. After Howe's Army had surprised Washington by a successful amphibious landing on Westchester County, New York, soil north of New York City, Glover's Massachusetts brigade rushed to the rescue to meet the threat. Fighting tenaciously, they bought precious time by frustrating Howe's ambitions, keeping a powerful invading British-Hessian army from advancing rapidly inland in one of the war's most brilliant delaying actions. Without Glover's skillfully orchestrated defensive stands behind a series of lengthy stonewalls that spanned Westchester County's fields and meadows against the odds, Howe would have smashed into Washington's slow-moving retreat to White Plains or gained the Continental Army's rear.[27]

While battling his way through the snow-filled streets, the swirl of sulphurous haze, and the most southernmost elements of the Knyphausen Regiment, Glover now especially relied upon the formidable combat capabilities of two veteran regiments that had played such a vital role in saving the day at Pell's Point: Colonel William Shepard's Third Massachusetts Continental

Regiment, of 217 men, and Colonel Loammi Baldwin's 113 soldiers of the Twenty-Sixth Massachusetts Continental Regiment.[28]

Colonel Baldwin was just the kind of aggressive regimental commander who made Glover's brigade such an excellent command. At age thirty-two, Baldwin was a Renaissance man of ability and promise, but he never lost the common touch. A dotting father of "our little son," he was a highly educated civil engineer from Woburn, Massachusetts. This well-laid out agricultural community, located just north of Boston and at the principal source of the Mystic River, had been founded by the colonel's own enterprising father. Baldwin was a scholar-soldier, who was blessed with an inquisitive mind made sharper at Harvard College. The son was also good with his hands as a master cabinetmaker. Later Baldwin's love of nature and the soil literally bore fruit, when he later became the widely acclaimed father of the "Baldwin" apple, which he developed on his own manicured farm. Even more, he eventually gained renown as the distinguished father of American engineering. As seemingly in everything that he embarked upon in life, Baldwin excelled as an inspiring regimental commander, leading his Bay State soldiers onward on the double through the lower town's snowy streets. He was so highly motivated at Trenton because, as he recently penned in a December 19, 1776 letter to his pretty Salem wife, Mary Fowle, whom he had married in July 1772, he was "determined to exert my self to the last" to win a new nation's independence.[29]

While the falling snow continued to hamper visibility during the close-quarter, urban combat raging through the smoke-wreathed lower town, Glover's Marbleheaders once again demonstrated the same kind of feisty fighting spirit seen on that October 18 day at Pell's Point. Pouring east along Front Street with New England battle flags waving in the stiff northeast breeze, Sargent and Glover's charging soldiers, respectively and with the southernmost of St. Clair's onrushing New Hampshire and Massachusetts troops on their heels, ran a gauntlet of fusilier bullets. Proving as handy with a flintlock and blunderbuss as a lengthy wooden oar, Glover's men blasted away at fusilier targets of opportunity. Massachusetts men armed with conventional weapons then rammed bullets down large-caliber smoothbore musket barrels with wooden ramrods for the next shot at Dechow's finely uniformed men in bright red coats. With the snow and sleet pelting down that bestowed a certain surreal quality to the combat in the streets, the foremost New Hampshire, Massachusetts, and Connecticut soldiers hurriedly took an advanced position behind a sturdy wooden fence, painted bright red by its image-conscious owner, of too much pride and vanity for a Quaker, to deliver greater punishment upon the southern flank of Dechow's Knyphausen Regiment. Wrapped in threadbare garments and anything that they could lay their hands on before crossing the Delaware, veteran New England officers had also halted their panting men at this point so that they could gain their breath.

Along the wooden fence standing alone in the snow, Sargent and Glover's Continentals, along with veterans on the right of Stark's New Hampshire Regiment just to the north on their left, rested their flintlocks on sturdy wooden rails. Here, they steadied their aim to unleash an accurate fire upon on the southernmost of Dechow's fusiliers. Blasting away with volleys and then firing at will at Hessians too close to miss, Stark's New Hampshire men and three regiments of St. Clair's brigade, all except the Fifteenth Massachusetts Continental Regiment that remained on King Street, following behind them, hammered the most lucrative Second Street fusilier targets with a hot fire while Sargent and Glover's Continentals on Front Street forced the reeling Hessians, caught in a cross fire, to retire farther east and north. Most of all, Dechow's fusiliers now hoped to escape the nightmare of battling Sullivan's converging units in a confusing urban environment. Raising a cheer that rang through the embattled lower town, the ecstatic New Englanders then continued onward with renewed confidence and fixed bayonets through the low-hanging palls of battle-smoke, charging east toward Queen Street.

Gathering momentum, Stark, on the north, and Sargent and Glover, respectively and to the south, continued to hurl the Knyphausen troops northeastward, applying more pressure upon the stubborn fusiliers who had met their match in Trenton's streets. The Marblehead soldiers, especially in blasting away with their giant shotguns the blunderbusses, now relished reaping a measure of sweet revenge upon their old opponent from the battle of Pell's Point, the Kynphausen Regiment.

But Glover's soldiers now felt greater satisfaction in thoroughly punishing Dechow's fusiliers because the British government had deprived them and their lower- and middle-class families of their traditional economic livelihoods by keeping Marblehead sailing ships from fishing the Grand Banks. Therefore, Glover's Massachusetts and Connecticut troops were especially elated by the sight of troops on the Knyphausen Regiment's mauled left on the south falling back under the relentless pressure, and additional fusiliers starting to head northeast toward Queen Street and the Quaker Meeting House while other Hessians broke ranks to either seek cover in vacant houses without angry patriot owners or raced south to reach Assunpink bridge and the road, which led south to Bordentown and safety.[30]

For the first time, Glover now basked in the sight of so many Germans on the run. Meanwhile, he attempted to do all that he could to fulfill Washington's lofty tactical requirements of achieving an elusive double envelopment. With undisguised contempt, the former Marblehead sea captain viewed Dechow's fusiliers as detested "poltroons." Glover knew that this hard-fought struggle raging fiercely through Trenton's streets would determine if Americans were to be "either freemen or slaves." In his own words, this hard-nosed Marblehead colonel now led his seafaring "boys" farther into the smoky depths of the lower town so that the people of America and future generations would never become debased "slaves, which is [a fate] worse than death [and] We can but die in conquering them, which will be dying gloriously."[31]

With more than two thousand fighting men so imbued with such idealistic sentiments and eager to exploit their already significant tactical gains, Washington and his Continental and state troops were not to be denied this morning. In fact, Glover was only beginning to fight in the urban combat swirling through the lower town. Because Ewing's Pennsylvania militia troops had been unable to cross over the Delaware and advance into Trenton's lower end to capture the Assunpink bridge, the most strategic lower town objective, and then join the First and Second Divisions as ordered by Washington, the stone structure was not yet secured to eliminate Rall's escape route south. Squinting his eyes, Glover peered southeastward through the falling snow toward the Assunpink bridge, expecting to catch sight of Ewing's Pennsylvania militia troops occupying advanced positions in the lower town. But this full brigade of Pennsylvanians was now mysteriously absent from Trenton's streets. A perplexed Glover was not yet aware of Ewing's failed crossing attempt, but he almost certainly surmised as much.

On his own, consequently, Glover remained undaunted. He now began to realize that he and his Massachusetts boys would have to accomplish what Ewing's Pennsylvania brigade had been assigned to do: capturing the strategic Assunpink bridge to bar the escape of the Rall brigade or reinforcements dispatched north from Bordentown. Washington later lamented how a large percentage of Rall's garrison escaped over the bridge because "Ewing was to have crossed before day at [the South] Trenton Ferry, and taken possession of the Bridge leading out of Town, but the Quantity of Ice was so great" to allow a crossing of the Delaware. For ample good reason, consequently, the ever-vigilant

Glover now feared that the Knyphausen Regiment could yet escape Washington's closing entrapment by making a dash south and down Queen Street to gain the key bridge over Assunpink Creek. At this time, the stone bridge at Queen Street's lower end yet remained in Hessian hands, offering an open avenue for the Rall brigade's escape. Glover, therefore, knew that something had to be done to slam this open door shut and as soon as possible if the Rall brigade was to be entrapped as Washington envisioned with the complete closing of the arms of his pincer movement.

Making his own independent tactical decision on the spot, Glover hurriedly made preparations to capture the Assunpink bridge, which had suddenly become the most strategic point on the battlefield, on his own. As so often in the past, the former sea captain and his disciplined Massachusetts Continentals would have to fulfill this vital tactical mission that less capable troops—untrained and undisciplined militia—had already failed to accomplish.

With no time to seek orders from Sullivan or Washington, Glover now acted on his own, as if yet commanding his own ship once again on a lengthy voyage to the Grand Banks. As usual, he once more relied on his own initiative, aggressiveness, and tactical instincts in a key battlefield situation. Knowing instinctively that no time could be wasted, Glover led his Massachusetts troops onward in a bid to secure the bridge, spanning dark, flooded waters, to cut off Rall's southern escape route. With muskets and blunderbusses on shoulders, Glover's soldier-sailors sprinted southeast through the whitish downpour in an effort calculated to drive yet another nail in the Rall brigade's coffin. On the double, Colonel Glover led his Bay Staters southeast below Sullivan's main body of advancing troops, including Sargent and St. Clair's brigade, respectively, to tighten the fatal noose around Rall's three regiments by capturing the bridge.[32]

Guarded by only a forlorn eighteen-man Hessian detail under the command of Sergeant Johannes Mueller, who had been given an impossible task, the stone bridge with three graceful arches over the Assunpink was now ripe for the taking. Glover was now taking full advantage of the overall lack of initiative demonstrated by the Kuynapshusen Regiment throughout the cold morning. Clearly, Dechow's regiment was guilty of having made its initial fatal delay by remaining stationary in the vicinity of Queen and Second Streets for too long Indeed, when first formed in front of Major Dechow's Queen Street headquarters and later just below the Quaker Meeting House, the Knyphausen Regiment troops had stood in position far too long, thanks to its officers failing to act on their own initiative, even while escalating cannonfire from Knox's guns boomed to the northwest and Sullivan's musketry crackled to the southwest.

However, in truth, some of this lengthy delay that allowed Sullivan's First Division to penetrate into Trenton's southwest outskirts was entirely excusable. Because the Knyphausen Regiment's fusiliers had been quartered on both sides of Assunpink Creek—perhaps as far west as the Barracks located on the river bottoms and as far south as the wooden houses situated along the road on the creek's south side—and over a wider area than either of its two sister regiments, Major Dechow's troops had initially taken longer to come together and form for action to meet the threat than either the Rall or von Lossberg Regiments.

But even after the regiment aligned and when initiative was most required to parry Washington's multiple threats from two directions, leading Knyphausen officers had initially wasted too much precious time—at least fifteen minutes but certainly even more—in awaiting Rall's orders about what to do next while Washington, Greene, and Sullivan rapidly maneuvered in attempting to close the trap around the entire Rall brigade with a double envelopment. Most of all, Rall had needed his top lieutenant, Major Dechow, to have quickly advanced north to support either one, or both, of his counterattacks, but the major had been in the King Street sector when Washington unleashed his assault. And, of course, Sullivan's aggressiveness had also ensured that the Knyphausen Regiment remained in the lower town and fought on its own hook, keeping the command firmly in place. But at least half of Dechow's fusilier regiment could have joined Rall with the other half conducting a holding action in the lower town to protect the Rall and von Lossberg Regiment's rear during Rall's counterattack northward and to keep Sullivan and Greene's Divisions from closing their pincer movement.

However, Major Dechow might have deliberately withheld his support from Rall in part because they were bitter enemies. Dechow had recently dispatched a letter of complaint against Rall to General von Heister at his New York City headquarters. Dechow's report arrived at headquarters on Christmas Day: an insubordinate act that violated the proper chain of command to reveal the depth of the dissension and dysfunction within the Rall brigade's highest leadership ranks. Additionally, both Rall and Dechow yet thought in conventional terms on the most unconventional of battlegrounds, viewing the Knyphausen Regiment as a strategic reserve: an unaffordable luxury.

Therefore, when Lieutenant Wiederhold, one of the Knyphausen Regiment's best officers and a skilled cartographer, rejoined Dechow's fusilier regiment after he and his band of pickets were driven south and after having delayed the initial advance of the left of Stirling's brigade down Queen Street, he was astounded by the lack of activity and initiative that he saw around him. As early ascertained by Wiederhold, the lethargic Knyphausen Regiment demonstrated far too little initiative when bold action was most needed.

In dismay while the firing of American muskets and cannons reached a new crescendo to reveal to him that Washington's troops were undertaking a sweeping encircling movement, a disbelieving Lieutenant Wiederhold screamed at regimental commander Dechow, "In God's name! Why have we not occupied the bridge?" Wiederhold was also venting his mounting anger at his older and more aristocratic superior. After all, Dechow had cancelled the usual morning patrol that might have early detected Ewing's attempt to cross at the South Trenton Ferry and alerted the garrison before Washington struck. Dechow had then only implored his eighteen fusiliers at the Assunpink bridge "to hold out as long as possible," instead of sending reinforcements. But Dechow could have been excused for his unfortunate lack of initiative when Rall counterattacked northward, because he was now unfit for active duty. Attempting to do his best under the most difficult circumstances, Major Dechow had yet to recover from multiple wounds received during the headlong assaults up the bullet-swept slopes of Chatterton's Hill and at Fort Washington.[33]

America's First Flying Artillery

Meanwhile, in support of the onrushing infantrymen who were rising to the challenge, Washington's artillery of both divisions continued to rule the streets, dominating the swirling combat. To fully capitalize on Captain Washington's success of capturing the Rall Regiment's two three-pounders, the general infantry advance down King Street, and the repulse of Rall's two counterattacks, Washington continued to exploit his tactical advantage to the fullest. As demonstrated throughout this morning, he instinctively understood what would become one of Napoleon's central axioms in the art of war: first break an enemy's "equilibrium" or "balance," and then "the rest is nothing," and no single factor verified the wisdom of this key battlefield tenet more thoroughly than the aggressive employment of artillery.[34]

Therefore, Washington understood the tactical wisdom of not allowing all of the artillery assigned Greene's Second Division to remain poised idle on the high ground at the head of King and Queen Streets, after Rall's dual repulses up both avenues. To exploit the long-arm tactical opportunity, Washington ordered artillery pieces forward, or south, to add more firepower pressure upon the reeling Hessians. Washington and Knox had already proved that they were innovative tacticians not only in the art of maneuvering artillery pieces at the heads of columns for quick deployment at a battle's beginning and then concentrating their artillery en mass, but also in maximizing artillery mobility in the midst of battle to exploit newly developed tactical opportunities.

With an increasing number of American muskets unable to fire because of wet powder, Washington and Knox continued to utilize the artillery's wet-weather, or uneroded, capabilities and maximize their gunner's soaring morale, now sky high after winning the duel against the Rall Regiment's artillery on the King Street and the Knyphausen Regiment cannon on Queen Street. Washington now possessed the ideal ingredients, including an overabundance of artillery, for aggressively employing his guns in the most forward positions. Washington, consequently, ordered some of Forrest's gunners to take their cannon down King Street and to follow in the wake of the advance of Captain Washington's vanguard and the Third Virginia to exploit the tactical advantage to the fullest.

Such forward-thinking modern tactical concepts of aggressively utilizing the artillery arm as a highly mobile and flexible form of firepower became a fundamental key to the battlefield successes of Napoleon, who began his military career as a none-too-promising artillery officer. The superior mobility and tactical flexibility of Napoleon's horse, or flying, artillery ensured that his guns were almost always brought rapidly to the front and close to enemy formations, Austrian, Prussia, or Russian, to systematically smash them to pieces with superior firepower: in essence, Washington's and Knox's same artillery tactics utilized so effectively at Trenton, whose streets, despite the ice and snow, offered relatively easy mobility for both gunners and artillery horses compared to a traditional, non-urban or wooded battlefield, especially in rainy weather conditions.[35]

Rising to yet another challenge with a combination of imagination and initiative, the dynamic Washington-Knox team now employed their novel tactical concept—fundamentally Napoleonic—of flying artillery, before it was developed in Europe, including France which experimented with the concept in the late 1770s. This aggressive tactic was now even more appropriate and timely because the cannon were essentially "waterproof" compared to soldiers' muskets on this stormy morning. Washington's timely exploitation of the artillery arm's capability and mobility as a front-line weapon explained in part why Major Wilkinson, the ambitious Marylander of merit, marveled how the tactical flexibility of Forrest's artillery "annoyed the enemy in various directions," especially after Washington ordered a detachment of Forrest's Pennsylvania guns to advance down King Street and the sloping ground in the manner of flying artillery.

Forrest's capable Irish lieutenant, Patrick Duffy, led his Pennsylvania gunners down King Street with a six-pounder, following Captain Washington's and the Virginian's successful attack south down the sloping ground. In the Irishman's words from a December 28 letter: "I had the Honour of being detach'd up the Main [King] Street in front of the [Hessian] Savages, without any other piece," and unlimbered in the middle of frigid King Street.[36] But in fact in his eagerness, "Pat" Duffy, who had migrated from the Emerald Isle and still spoke with a thick Irish brogue, had deployed his lone six-pounder too far down the street. In this sector above Sullivan's assault in the lower town, lingering Hessians, either the southernmost von Lossbergers, or Rall grenadiers, or the northernmost element of the Knyphausen Regiment fusiliers, unleashed a sharp fire from nearby houses lining King Street's east side within easy range of Lieutenant Duffy and his strong-armed cannoneers. Nevertheless, these Pennsylvania state artillerymen remained out in the open on the snowy street, busily loading and firing at targets of opportunity. The bold Irish lieutenant wrote how he and his Philadelphia boys "sustained the fire of Several gunns [sic] from the Houses on each side without the least loss [and therefore I] must attribute my protection to the hand of Providence."[37]

While a hail of Hessian bullets whistled by, Lieutenant Duffy and his adrenaline-ridden gunners maintained discipline and their nerve under the hot fire, working their six-pounder with businesslike efficiency, firing first to the south down King Street and then east after the Germans were hurled off the body-covered street and driven east. With some understatement, therefore, Duffy later wrote how, "[I] can assure you the Artillery got applause" for what it accomplished this morning.[38]

In addition just to the northeast of Duffy's busy cannon, Hamilton's New York guns were also employed by Washington as effective flying artillery, thanks to Stirling's advancing infantrymen on the brigade's left opening up the way south down Queen Street. Naturally, the aggressive Hamilton was in his element amid the swirling combat along Queen Street. On the snowy landscape north of Petty's Run, the handsome New York captain led his guns a short distance down the sloping street with his usual combination of dash and skill. Once unleashed from Hamilton's stationary defensive role on the high ground at Queen Street's head, his battery of two six-pounders inched south to ease within better range of their opponent. Therefore, Washington's northern arm of his pincer movement in gradually closing southward was considerably strengthened by the advance of flying artillery on both King and Queen Streets.

In addition, Washington's artillery firepower became more formidable on King Street by the added muscle of the two captured Rall Regiment guns. Loaded with canister by its former owners, one captured Hessian three-pounder was now manned by Sergeant White's hard-luck artillery crew from the disabled field piece at King Street's head. Meanwhile, the other Rall Regiment cannon was utilized by Knox's predesignated gun crew, which had been equipped with rammers and primers to turn captured artillery upon the Hessians. In a hurry, young Orderly Sergeant White and his New England and Pennsylvania gunners opened up with canister on the Hessians, first south and then east of King Street. These roaring cannon, Hamilton's New York and Duffy's Pennsylvania's guns—all six-pounders—and the two captured Hessian three-pounders, benefitted from dry, black powder ammunition, belching fire to inflict additional body blows upon Rall's hard-hit brigade from multiple directions in the snowfall-diffused sunlight.[39]

Yet mounted in defiance of canister fired from Captain Hamilton's six-pounders, which were now closer to him than Baumann's three three-pounders, and a stream of rebel bullets as he had braved at Long Island, White Plains, and Fort Washington, an anxious Rall awaited Lieutenant Piel's return from his reconnaissance, as ordered by him, to ascertain if the stone Assunpink bridge was open to provide an escape route. Meanwhile, just east of Queen Street and yet fuming over his lost cannon, Rall tightened up his formations under the leaden storm. All the while, the disabled Knyphausen three-pounder, knocked out by Hamilton's cannon fire, remained abandoned on Queen Street, standing useless and silent in the snow while low-lying clouds of dense smoke hung heavy in the frozen air.

Engaged in urban combat for the first time, the young Philadelphia gunners, mostly hardworking men from the seedy rough waterfront, of Captain Moulder's city battery, with its three French four-pounders aligned near Second Street and Neil's two New Jersey three-pounders continued to unleash fire from the west on the Knyphausen Regiment. The scorching fire of Moulder's guns of the Second Company of Philadelphia Associators from the east and the flying artillery, Hamilton's two six-pounders, from the northwest was increasingly unbearable for Dechow's fusiliers. In addition, the onrushing troops of Stark, Glover, and St. Clair brought greater pressure on the Knyphausen Regiment while surging closer to Queen Street to ensure that any chance for the Rall brigade to escape south grew slimmer with each passing minute. Meanwhile, additional hard-hit Hessians broke ranks, heading east and toward the only end of Trenton yet open and free from Washington's tightening noose that was slowly squeezing the life out of the reeling Rall brigade.[40]

The Knyphausen Regiment's Dilemma

Knowing that the stone bridge across the Assunpink had to be secured at all costs, Glover's fast-moving Massachusetts and Connecticut troops continued to surge farther southeastward, heading rapidly toward the swollen Assunpink Creek to cut off the Hessians' line of retreat. Glover was once again exhibiting a remarkable display of individual initiative, unlike what had been demonstrated by the Knyphausen Regiment's leaders. Throughout the smoke-choked lower town, Sargent and St. Clair's soldiers advanced relentlessly to gain more ground. Like a giant broom sweeping down Front and Second Streets from the west, Sullivan's mostly New England attackers hurled the last remaining southern-most Knyphausen Regiment fusiliers eastward while expanding their already tight grip on the lower town. Colonel Paul Dudley Sargent, born in the fishing port of Salem, Massachusetts in 1745, and hailing from Hillsborough County, Massachusetts, was another hard-hitting brigade commander, like Glover, who now rose to the fore. Sargent led his more than eight hundred onrushing New York, Massachusetts, and Connecticut troops through the wind- and bullet-swept streets of the south side of Trenton that had to be captured as soon as possible.[41]

Out in front as usual and keeping up the momentum, meanwhile, Stark led the surging right wing of St. Clair's brigade—three regiments—with his charging New Hampshire Continentals, who were sucking in air in the cold, pushing east to gain possession of almost all of Second Street that ran parallel to Assumpink Creek. Applying increasing pressure as when one of the most daring officer of Rogers' Rangers so long ago, Stark succeeded in turning the left flank of the Knyphausen Regiment, which yielded more ground under the New Englander's relentless pressure.

The last of the finely uniformed soldiers in scarlet on the Knyphausen Regiment's buckling left standing firm were finally uprooted from their lower Queen Street position. These stubborn fusiliers were then pushed across to the street's east side with a flurry of bayonets, musket-butts, and bullets in ugly, close-range fighting around darkened houses. Farther north on the Knyphausen Regiment's right, larger numbers of fusiliers withdrew northeast toward the vicinity of the little Quaker Meeting House to escape the wrath of Sullivan's onrushing troops pouring through the cold streets with victory cheers that split the air. All the while, Dechow continued to hurriedly reposition additional fusiliers just south of the Quaker Meeting House and closer to the von Lossberg and Rall Regiments, from north to south, just east of Queen Street, to the north.[42]

Like the rampaging soldiers of Stark's New Hampshire Continental Regiment, other New Hampshire regiments of St. Clair's brigade also continued to exploit their tactical gains as if determined to wipe out their opponent's old Kip's Bay stereotype that "without New-England rum" northeastern soldiers lacked the courage to face Hessian soldiers on the battlefield. Of English ancestry, Lieutenant Colonel Israel Gilman, who hailed from one of New Hampshire's most respected families, now led around 135 Second New Hampshire Continental Regiment soldiers forward to redeem New England's honor.

Consisting primarily of Continentals from Rockingham and Strafford Counties, New Hampshire, the attacking troops of the Second New Hampshire Continental Regiment were inspired by the beautiful sight of their waving blue silk flag, which was embroidered with the motto "The Glory Not the Prey." Fluttering in the icy wind sweeping across the regiment's head, this colorful battle flag was distinguished by a circular design of interlocking chain links, which represented each new state and the nationalistic concept of strength through unity, in the center. Like their veteran commander from the small fishing town of New Market, Rockingham County, in New Hampshire's southeast corner on the Lamprey River and located on an expansive inland bay near the Atlantic, Gilman's New Hampshire boys were hard-nosed fighters. They had methodically cut down a good many attacking redcoat regulars on the long, grassy slope of Breed's Hill when New Englander soldiery saw their finest day on June 17, 1775. A former respected member of the General Assembly and community leader, Lieutenant Colonel Gilman might have now wondered if he would ever again see his wife, Hannah Smith, while charging through the snow-covered streets—now dominated by a mixture of confusion, fear, courage, and death—and trying to catch his breath on a frigid morning in hell that he would never forget.[43]

Capturing the Stone Bridge Across the Assunpink

Moving fast through the flurries of snow as if they had not already rowed the Durham boats across the Delaware and marched all night to Trenton, Glover's hard-charging soldiers, wheezing for air, neared their next objective after having played its part in hurling the Knyphausen Regiment aside. Glover was determined to secure the stone bridge across the Assunpink. To ensure that no Hessians were bypassed on the south that would make his right flank vulnerable, Glover extended right farther south across the snowy river bottoms and all the way to the Delaware.

Ignoring their weariness and the strength-sapping cold, the Massachusetts soldiers on Glover's right advanced across the level, open ground of the river's windswept flood plain, meeting no natural or man-made obstacles. Demonstrating firm discipline by keeping their fast-moving line relatively straight despite slippery footing on the ice and snow, Glover's Massachusetts and Connecticut troops swarmed onward on the double-quick "with their right to the Delaware, and with their left to the town, straight away to the bridge."[44]

Descending like locusts upon the stone bridge over the Assunpink's high waters, Glover's Massachusetts troops, with two battle flags waving in front and cheering wildly, pushed aside Sergeant Muller and his eighteen-man detachment of Knyphausen Regiment fusiliers, smashing through their thin line guarding the stone bridge. To the very end, the battle-hardened sergeant obeyed Major Dechow's orders, recently barked out by their mounted commander, to "hold out as long as possible." Facing far too many swarming New Englanders, Sergeant Muller and his guardian detachment never knew what hit them. In fact, Glover overwhelmed the bridge so easily that the Hessians believed that they had been attacked by "three battalions [or regiments] of the enemy." Now with the strategic Assunpink bridge firmly in Glover's capable hands, no additional troops of Rall's diminishing garrison could escape south over the bridge while also eliminating the possibility of arriving Hessian reinforcements from Bordentown. But the fainthearted British cavalrymen of the Sixteenth Light Dragoons, Captain Grothausen's jaegers, Captain Engelhardt and his shell-shocked cannoneers, and Sergeant Muller's bridge guardians, respectively, had already slipped across the Assunpink before Glover's elated Massachusetts soldiers, forgetting their fatigue but not their hard-won reputations, captured the bridge.

Meanwhile, to continue to cut off Rall's line of retreat and to play his leading role in closing the southern arm of Washington's encirclement movement in the lower town, Glover encouraged his mariners onward across the Assunpink Creek Bridge. With bayonet-attached muskets, the breathless New Englanders filed across the stone bridge, trotting through the steadily dropping snow in high spirits, as if on a light rain shower on a soft April morning along the rocky coast of eastern Massachusetts, and basking in another sparkling tactical success.

Moving swiftly, these tough New England veterans, with muskets and blunderbusses on shoulders, were careful about their footing on the stone surface covered with ice. As a precaution and thinking ahead as usual, Glover barked out orders for two Marblehead companies to serve as guardians at each end of the bridge. Glover knew that the Assunpink bridge had to be now kept in American hands at all costs. After skillful tactical maneuvering that was as swift as it was efficient, Glover now held the key position to effectively block any future Hessian effort to force passage over the easiest crossing point along this rain-swollen tidal creek.

However, Glover typically refused to rest on his laurels or bask in his most recent success while an intensifying battle was yet raging fiercely under dark, leaden skies. The opportunistic Marblehead commander instinctively knew that he had to keep his troops moving on the double to exploit the tactical advantage and achieve greater gains. Keeping up the momentum, Glover, consequently, continued to demonstrate even more resourcefulness and initiative that separated winner from loser on this bitter Thursday morning.

After crossing the Assunpink, therefore, he immediately shifted his troops to the left, or east. Glover's men then pushed up a lengthy east-west ridge, nestled between the overflowing creek and the equally high Delaware, which commanded the wide creek bottom to the north. Here, immediately below, or south, of the stone bridge, the narrow road to Bordentown turned east to ascend the ridge that closely paralleled the creek before following this snow-covered strip of high ground in an easterly direction. Fortunately, this little road, Glover's new avenue to reaping additional tactical gains, provided easy access for his brigade's artillery to be hauled up the snowy slope by teams of hard-working New England gunners' tired horses lashed by drivers. Across the commanding terrain, Captain Winthrop Sargent then hurriedly deployed his two Massachusetts six-pounders to protect the bridge and support the two companies of Glover's infantrymen, who now gained their breath after having won the race to gain the vital bridge. Most importantly, Knox's artillerymen now held the most dominant high ground on both the north and south of Trenton, sandwiching the battered Hessian brigade between an encroaching ring of cannonfire, whose deep, harsher voices thundered above the crisp and sharper chorus of crackling musketry.

Now saddled with the key mission of safeguarding the Assunpink bridge, Captain Winthrop Sargent, a young artillery officer from Boston, was Colonel Sargent's intellectual nephew, who had graduated from Harvard. The young man had been born in the fishing port of Gloucester, Massachusetts, as the prodigal son of a wealthy Massachusetts militia colonel. Therefore, brigade commander Sargent felt pride upon viewing the sight of nephew Winthrop's fast-working six-pounders firing on the Knyphausen Regiment, including fusiliers like twenty-one-year-old Ensign Heinrich Zimmermann, from the high ground just below the Assunpink bridge. Such timely action continued a distinguished Sargent family tradition of invaluable military service in their homeland's defense. Despite his youth and scholarly ways, Captain Sargent was a resourceful long-arm commander. He also possessed longtime common maritime experiences like Glover, having served as a seafaring captain on one of his father's sailing ships.[45] As fully expected by Washington, meanwhile, Colonel Glover and his swarthy fishermen and rawboned sailors continued to surpass themselves as hard-hitting infantrymen, demonstrating how these versatile Marbleheaders, as they had so boldly warned earlier in 1776, "would not tamely part with their rights and Liberties," especially to foreign soldiers from Germany.[46]

Just north of the Assunpink's dark, high waters, meanwhile, Colonel Stark overcame all resistance to finally reach his tactical objective of Queen Street. Stark typically remained at the forefront near where Second Street met Queen Street, with his New Hampshire boys blasting away at the remaining Knyphausen soldiers. Like an ancient Celtic warrior from his family's picturesque ancestral homeland of Ulster Province, Stark continued to perform like an unleashed force of nature. Exceeding expectations was nothing new for Stark. He had encouraged his Continentals to aim lower and fire faster on that bloody June day at Breed's Hill. But Stark was now essentially accomplishing what he had always done best when he had led his green-coated mostly Scotch-Irish frontiersmen of Rogers' Rangers as the legendary major's dependable right-hand man for four years. As an impetuous young man from the unruly Merrimack Valley frontier he had hunted the White Hills with Rogers himself, so these harsh winter conditions were nothing new to him. In fact, Stark seemed almost invigorated by the snowstorm's rigors, leading his New Hampshire Continentals with a demonic fury that even astounded the reeling Hessians. Most of all, he was motivated by the burning desire to crush every single Hessian who stood before him, as when he, in authentic Indian dress, had led Rogers' Rangers against the hated "French dogs" in the north country wilderness.[47]

Lieutenant Piel, dispatched by Rall on the crucial mission to ascertain if the Assunpink bridge was open, finally reached the bridge's vicinity. Here, he was shocked to see that the entire area, including the snow-covered high ground located just south of the creek, was swarming with Americans. In astonishment, the yet unmarried lieutenant, in his mid-thirties, also saw that Glover had already set up a secure roadblock on the bridge's other side, holding a good defensive position bolstered by Captain Sargent's two Massachusetts six-pounders. Clearly, the escape route south across the bridge to safety was now closed shut not only to the Knyphausen Regiment but also the von Lossberg and Rall Regiments.

An out-of-breath, glum Lieutenant Piel finally returned north up Queen Street to his beleaguered command and brought the disturbing news to Rall. With Piel's stunning report tumbling from his mouth and the angry growl of Captain Sargent's Massachusetts cannon to the south echoing like thunder in his ears to mock his best efforts, Colonel Rall, an overachieving sergeant's son from Hesse-Cassel, now realized that he had missed his last chance to escape south. Ironically, the strategic Assunpink bridge had remained firmly in Hessian hands for nearly an hour this morning after the battle opened: a missed opportunity for the Rall brigade to slip away from Washington's entrapment and fight another day. While Washington's masterful double envelopment closed tighter like a noose to slowly choke more of the fast-fading life out of the Hessian brigade, Rall's never-say-die attitude, determination to prevail in the end, and sense of professional pride had ensured that this elite brigade had not attempted to escape south.

After digesting the gloomy tidings that the Assunpink bridge was firmly in Glover's hands, Rall realized that his tactical dilemma was even greater than anticipated. Indeed, by this time, hundreds of shouting, elated Americans continued to advance and fire on the run toward the hemmed-up Hessians on three sides, while an ever-increasing volume announced the glowing success of Washington's almost complete encirclement of the Rall brigade, which was now all but vanquished, or so it seemed to the most optimistic Americans.[48]

Indeed, while Washington's troops of both divisions advanced from three directions, Rall's brigade was not yet united. Hessian offensive and defensive efforts had been disjointed and piecemeal all morning, assisting in the fulfillment of Washington's divide-and-conquer formulate for success. A host of self-inflicted wounds by the Hessians themselves had significantly reduced the Rall brigade's overall combat capabilities and, hence, chances for survival by this time.

On this day of destiny when every soldier in the ranks was needed to prevail, Washington was not hampered by hesitation, self-doubt, or indecision unlike his vexed opponent, who had been victimized by the most brilliant tactical plan of the war. Seemingly, every Continental soldier on the field was now actively engaged in doing all their power to vanquish the Hessian brigade when so much was at stake. And now with the Assunpink bridge secured by Glover, the Rall's brigade's best escape route south out of the nightmarish urban cauldron was now closed forever, ensuring that the Hessians would have to do or die on this bloody morning. All the while, Washington's brilliant tactical trap was closing tighter around the finest Hessian brigade in America, and sealing its fate as never before.

Desperate Attempt to Gain the Trenton-Princeton Road

No eighteenth-century soldiers could stand up to such severe punishment, both artillery and musketry, which was now delivered upon the Hessians, just east of Queen Street, from three sides. To additionally diminish the Rall brigade's combat capabilities, two field pieces had been captured, leaving only three three-pounders operable after the disabling of one Knyphausen field piece on Queen Street by the accurate fire of Hamilton's New York gunners. This rapidly deteriorating situation and the systematic silencing of half of the Rall's brigade's artillery now meant that the von Lossberg, Rall, and Knyphausen Regiments, from north to south and just east of Queen Street, were now outgunned by more than five-to-one by Knox's guns: a disastrous ratio for Hessian fortunes.

While the dwindling number of Hessians were steadily punished by cannonfire and musketry in the front from the north, they also continued to be raked on the left flank by Mercer and Stirling's troops from the west and northwest, and Sullivan's soldiers fired into them from the south and south-west as well. After additional muskets were cleaned off and flints were dried or chipped and larger numbers of Washington's men found better firing positions, the volume of gun fire increased from the troops of Mercer's brigade from the west, Haslet's Delaware men from the northwest, and Stirling's other soldiers of his Delaware, Virginia, and Pennsylvania brigade from the north. With blazing rifles and smoothbore muskets, these well-positioned soldiers from Maryland, Connecticut, and Massachusetts of Mercer's brigade blasted away from the windows of second-story wooden structures and from open spaces between houses. What was becoming increasingly obvious was that for Rall's three regiments to simply remain stationary was now a certain guarantee of not only a thorough decimation of ranks, but also of the brigade's complete encirclement and destruction.

However, caught amid a confusing urban battle and surrounded on three sides by elated American soldiers surging forward and firing on the move, Rall possessed very few tactical options or solutions at this time. Many Hessian troops had been already cut down or escaped across the Assunpink bridge, before secured permanently by Glover. And an unknown number of Rall's soldiers, unnerved by the savagery of urban combat, stayed under cover or hid in darkened houses to escape Washington's wrath rather than attempting to fight out in the open against the harsh elements and the even harsher American tide that was unstoppable.

By this time, Ensign Carl Wilhelm Kleinschmidt, the Rall Regiment's acting adjutant, who had killed a fellow officer in a duel aboard their ship during the long journey to America and who became an American soldier in 1781, had regained the regimental banners from the von Lossberg fusiliers of the von Hanstein Company. While lamenting how so "many men of the regiment had already been wounded," he then restored these sacred flags to the Rall Regiment's color company to lift the grenadier's morale and fighting spirit.

With his formations realigned just east of Queen Street north of the Knyphausen Regiment, Rall then wisely ordered his troops to march farther out of town, which had become the swirling eye of the storm. Rall knew that he had to escape the confused fighting and horror of urban warfare that continued to rage fiercely through the streets and along even narrower alleys and houses against a resourceful, highly motivated opponent, who already sensed victory. Rall, therefore, then led his troops farther east beyond Queen Street with intact discipline and the determination to get "out of town" before it was too late.

Most of all, Rall fully realized that he had to move both regiments farther away from the clusters of wooden-frame houses spitting a stream of gunfire and out of what had become a roaring hornet's nest. Rall made his decision. With his one remaining field piece in tow, consequently, Rall's troops headed toward the relative safety of open ground on the town's eastern outskirts, the apple orchard. The generally level terrain of the apple orchard, located to the east and just south of Petty's Run, offered a relatively safe haven for the two regiments to reorganize and gain a breather from Washington's fierce onslaught.

Here, in the relative security of the little apple orchard, Rall would also gain time to confer with his top lieutenants and contemplate his next tactical move in an increasingly no-win situation. However, the Rall and von Lossberg Regiments had to first cross over marshy, low-lying ground just south of Petty's Run, known as "the Swamp" to locals, who wisely knew better than to enter this morass, even in winter.[49] Relieved to finally escape the blinding swirl of urban combat and the palls of battle-smoke that lay like a cloud over Trenton, Lieutenant Wiederhold described in his diary how Rall, after displaying some hesitation about the proper course of action, then "moved out his regiment to the right [east] of the city, under the apple trees," and away from Trenton that had become hell on earth for the hard-pressed Germans.[50] In a letter to "my dear Lucy," Knox basked in the glow of what had been accomplished in hurling the Hessians out of the war-torn town: "It must give a sensible pleasure to every friend of the rights of man to think with how much intrepidity our people pushed the enemy" out of Trenton.[51]

The unbelievable sight of so many Hessians retiring east and moving like clockwork in a close-order formation out of Trenton provided an instinctive signal, unleashing Washington's troops to take off in pursuit of their quarry. In the words of one Virginian who described how "Our cannon [especially Captain Hamilton's guns in firing down Queen Street by also from cannon firing from the west] dispersed them and the fight became a chase" through the smoke-filled streets amid the falling snow and sleet.[52] By marching his well-organized troops east to reach the open ground "under the apple trees," Rall hoped to gain better visibility away from Trenton's fiery cauldron and develop new tactical options. Most of all, Rall also sought to minimize his losses and maintain command cohesion in the hope of somehow regaining the initiative to strike back and yet turn the tide. Escaping Trenton's deadly streets, slick with a mixture of ice, snow and blood, and reaching the open ground of the apple orchard east of town offered a sanctuary of sorts for the Hessians, but only in relative terms.

Once he aligned his disciplined grenadiers and fusiliers in the apple orchard beyond the dark row of Trenton's outlying fringe of easternmost houses, the shrieks of the dying, and the sulphurous canopy, Rall carefully surveyed the tactical situation. He now quickly developed a new plan that was as bold as it was audacious. Most of all, Rall was proving that he was a tactically flexible commander, who had long smoothly adjusted to fast-paced tactical developments on conventional battlefields and excelled in consequence.

However, everything was now entirely different. Rall faced the unprecedented and imposing challenge of confronting a victorious, confident opponent advancing on two fronts, which guaranteed no ready answers or easy tactical solutions. As in earlier having taken the offensive in an attempt to capture the commanding terrain at King Street's head, Rall once again realized that he had to launch another desperate offensive effort, or his cherished brigade was doomed to certain annihilation.

Consequently, Rall flew into action, making hasty preparations to lash out once again at his swarming tormentors. He now planned hit and turn Washington's exposed left flank (the left of Stirling's brigade), which was yet hanging in midair, just northeast of the head of Queen Street. But in no small part because the unrelenting storm was yet to his back, Washington's high ground perch allowed the commander-in-chief, who was like a vigilant hawk this morning, to survey the roaring battlefield, unlike Rall who could see relatively little from lower-lying ground, where a rising pall of sulphurous smoke and the falling snow obscured vision on a morning when the sun was obscured by black clouds, at the apple orchard along Petty's Run. Therefore, Rall's preparations for his next move in what was turning out to be a chess game for the possession of Trenton and his adroit tactical adjustments out of urgent necessity were early ascertained by Washington.[53]

Even though Rall had escaped Trenton's suffocating confines and gained more ability to maneuver after reaching the open ground of the apple orchard, Washington's vise was still rapidly closing in on the Hessian colonel and his beleaguered survivors, who were now positioned just south of Petty's Run. In fact, the Rall and von Lossberg Regiments were now more exposed on the open ground, blanketed in a thick layer of snow, east of town, if the Americans continued to advance east and converge upon them in overwhelming numbers. Perhaps Rall might have been wiser to have made a defensive stand inside the row of wooden houses on Trenton's eastern outskirts, where his Rall and von Lossbergtroops could have at least dried off weapons and had a better chance to defend themselves while awaiting reinforcements—first from the Knyphausen Regiment just to the south and then garrison troops from either Princeton or Bordentown, or both—rather than aligning out in an exposed position amid open orchard east of Queen Street.

Under the bare apple trees which offered scant protection from neither the harsh elements nor projectiles, Rall at least gained not only a respite but also some much-needed room for tactical maneuver, however. Now the Rall and von Lossberg Regiments with their feisty fighting spirit yet intact despite the losses and setbacks suffered on this nightmarish morning, were finally united as one and in a good position for a renewal of an offensive thrust. Therefore, thanks to this timely unity of force in a more advantageous position east of town, Rall now planned to march north in an attempt to gain the strategic Princeton-Trenton Road to not only escape Washington's trap, but also to hit the American's left flank (Stirling's left just beyond—or northeast—the head of Queen Street) to the right of Fermoy's Continental brigade.

Because of the density of the falling snow, Rall was unable to see the position of Fermoy's brigade. Dressed in his resplendent uniform and with his men poised to strike in a new direction, a mounted Rall shouted orders for his two veteran regiments to take the offensive, "Forward! Advance! Advance!" With perfect discipline and executing Rall's orders with alacrity, the neat ranks of two regiments, the von Lossberg Regiment on the north and the Rall Regiment on the south, marched north toward the Trenton-Princeton Road in the vicinity of the Fox Chase Tavern, operated by Mrs. Joseph Bond, northeast of Queen Street's head. With the Rall Regiment on the left and the von Lossbergers on the right, the lengthy line advanced toward the high ground just northeast of town. Courageous color-bearers led the way for the Rall and von Lossberg Regiments, while Washington's artillery continued to roar unceasingly, thanks to Knox's farsighted decision to bring a sufficient supply of black powder (that had caused Glover's men greater exertions) across the river for a lengthy battle of attrition, even during blizzard-like conditions. A long row of bayonets, dull and not reflecting light from the hidden, weak sun shrouded by the thick cloud cover, were held by veteran grenadiers and fusiliers now emboldened with the determination to drive the Americans off the high ground to reverse the day's fortunes. Rall's bluecoat grenadiers felt an electric surge of new confidence, especially after having only recently regained their precious battle flags, now tattered by bullets and buckshot from hunters and marksmen from across America.

Thanks to Washington's eternal vigilance on a morning on which he was never more perceptive and tactically astute, he was already fully prepared for Rall's next countermove during this intricate chess game now being played out at Trenton for such high stakes. As if having already anticipated Rall's ambitious design to make a desperate attempt to steal the tactical advantage by striking Washington's vulnerable left flank and gain the Princeton-Trenton Road, Fermoy's brigade already had been placed by the forward-thinking commander-in-chief in an ideal place, on the far left wing, to close the door to the north by blocking the Princeton-Trenton Road. This new threat from the resurgent Hessians was serious because the apple orchard had provided an ideal staging area for Rall's push north across Petty's Run, which was much narrower at this point upstream and more easily fordable compared to where it crossed King Street, around 250-300 yards to the west after curving southwestward toward the Delaware, to gain the Princeton-Trenton Road.

In the front ranks unlike so many other eighteenth-century commanders in order to closely monitor the tactical situation, Washington early ascertained exactly what was now developing below him in the apple orchard to the southeast: Rall was now advancing in a new direction that presented an immediate threat to Washington's exposed left flank, or the right of Fermoy's brigade. Clearly, this new threat would steadily escalate unless decisive and quick action was taken to immediately checkmate Rall's next maneuver. After literally reading Rall's opportunistic mind and predicting his tactical intentions, Washington barked out new orders to parry the escalating threat just in time. Meanwhile, Rall's two regiments had just begun to push north across Petty's Run and up the snow-covered slope toward the strategic Princeton-Trenton Road and Stirling's left flank and Fermoy's right flank. Hundreds of finely disciplined Hessians surged forward in lengthy lines with businesslike efficiency. Like an experienced battlefield commander with well-honed instincts and an astute tactical sense, Rall was not wasting any time to exploit the existing tactical advantage.

To parry the most serious threat yet posed to his weak left flank (Stirling's left) because he had concentrated so much infantry strength and artillery fire-power in the King and Queen Street sectors and for the earlier offensive thrusts down both avenues, Washington dispatched a mounted courier with a new set of orders to the inexperienced brigade commander Fermoy. Washington directed for Fermoy and his experienced Pennsylvania brigade "to throw themselves before" Rall's latest bid to regain the initiative and even possibly yet reap the most improbable of successes before it was too late. To counter this new threat, Fermoy's two Pennsylvania regiments faced toward the low ground of Petty's Run and the apple orchard from where Rall's two advancing regiments had so suddenly emerged with disciplined step.

After extending ranks to cover more ground to the west, Hand and Hausseggers' regiments, consisting mostly of Pennsylvanians, then pushed south on the double to counter Rall's determined attempt to gain Washington's exposed left flank. Fermoy's brigade, in double rows that blocked the vital road leading northeast toward Princeton, pushed rapidly toward the advancing Rall's grenadiers and the von Lossberg fusiliers. Washington's German Regiment's disciplined Pennsylvania and Maryland Continentals surged toward the dense formation of Hessians, who now pushed up the snow-covered, barren slope in a lengthy line. But Fermoy's onrushing troops possessed the advantages of higher ground, a clear field of fire, and more operable flintlocks and rifles than the wet smoothbore muskets and powder of Rall's troops: a mismatch in this showdown northeast of Trenton.

In one of the battle's classic ironies, nearly four hundred soldiers of Washington's largest regiment—the officially designated German Regiment—pushed down the slope beside Colonel Hand Continental riflemen of the elite First Pennsylvania. Colonel Haussegger's German and German American Continentals, whose numbers exceeded those of Hand's rifle regiment by more than one hundred men, were now playing the leading role in countering Rall's desperate bid to reach the Princeton-Trenton Road and turn Washington's left flank just northeast of the head of Queen Street. Most of all, from his high ground perch near Queen Street's head, Washington was awed by the impressive sight of the alacrity in which Hand and Haussegger's soldiers hurled themselves before the advancing Hessian ranks with an unsurpassed "Spirit and Rapidity" that he never forgot, especially with so much at stake.

Indeed, Washington's maneuver to stem this latest crisis was tactically well-conceived and most timely, having been calculated to effectively checkmate Rall's latest gamble to turn the tide. As Washington described the pressing tactical situation: "they attempted to file off by a road on their right leading to Princeton, but perceiving their Intention, I threw a Body of Troops [638 men of two regiments] in their Way . . . ." In masterful fashion, Washington had correctly ascertained not only the extent of the most serious threat to his left flank situated on elevated terrain, but also that Rall was attempting to gain an advantageous high ground position by which to launch a breakout to gain the Princeton-Trenton Road.[54]

Meanwhile, Colonel Haussegger, who had served capably beside Washington in the Virginia Regiment during the French and Indian War, led hundreds of his German Continentals, both American- and Germany-born from Pennsylvania and Maryland, onward down the open ground that descended toward Petty's Run and the bare trees of the apple orchard just south of the little watercourse. If this experienced German colonel, born in the old country, from Pennsylvania now had any qualms about vanquishing his fellow Germans, he revealed no outward indications or overt signs to his men.

Meanwhile, the German Regiment's young musicians, including fifers Adam Bush and drummers Frederick Mulz and Paul Schley, who was fated to die in this war, of Pennsylvania, and Marylanders John Heffner and George Hyatt, who had served in the Baltimore Town Militia Battalion, provided lively martial music to encourage hundreds of patriotic Germans toward their fellow countrymen, who had no idea that they were about to face fellow Germans in battle.[55]

Lieutenant Colonel George Stricker, second in command of the German Regiment, led his troops southward, surging though the fallow fields, covered in white, just north of Petty's Run. All the while, the lieutenant colonel's son, seventeen-year-old Cadet John Stricker, who had been born on the western frontier community of Frederick, Maryland, in February 1759, marched by his side. This devoted father-son team had first fought together as members of Colonel William Smallwood's First Maryland Battalion, in which the father had served as a captain since March 1776 before his promotion to the German Regiment's lieutenant colonel in mid-July 1776. Mature beyond his years, the western Maryland teenager garnered a well-deserved sergeant's rank in January 1777, thanks in part to heroism demonstrated at Trenton. John Stricker, Jr., eventually earned a general's rank in commanding Maryland militia during the next war with Great Britain, or the Second War for American Independence. During the War of 1812, Stricker played a leading role in helping to stop the British invasion on Maryland soil just outside Baltimore, after the British's invasion by water had been thwarted at the masonry bastion known as Fort McHenry.[56]

Pushing south down sloping ground and through the open fields and meadows toward icy Petty's Run, Washington's onrushing German Regiment faced no natural obstacles to impede its steamrolling advance that continued to gain momentum with each passing minute, despite the thick layer of snow covering the slope. With regimental banners flying, these Pennsylvania and Maryland Continentals surged relentlessly toward the apple orchard and straight at the advancing von Lossberg and Rall Regiments while also continuing to extend Washington's left flank by veering slightly southeastward to better protect the road. Ensuring that the Teutonic soldiers of Haussegger's German Regiment maintained their line's integrity, tried officers, like Colonel Rall's own cousin, made sure that their men maintained firm discipline. Captain George Keeports, who had served in Captain Samuel Smith's Baltimore Company of Independent Maryland Militia, which then became an elite core unit of Smallwood's Maryland Battalion that had fought so splendidly at Long Island during the August showdown between Washington and Howe, was yet another excellent officer who now led his troops downhill before the German Regiment's surging ranks in the aggressive bid to parry Rall's counterstroke.[57]

Washington's adroit, timely tactical maneuver in a last-minute attempt to counter Rall's latest offensive threat paid off handsomely. Watching from the high ground near the head of Queen Street, Washington never forgot the exhilarating sight of Fermoy's onrushing Pennsylvania and Maryland troops fulfilling his urgent order "to throw themselves before them [which] immediately checked them" with their own timely counter stroke. Most of all, Washington's extreme left flank (Stirling's left) was saved by his timely reliance upon what was always the best defense: the tactical offensive.[58]

Throughout this climactic Trenton showdown that was becoming ever more desperate, Washington yet remained at his tactical best, always staying one tactical step ahead of Colonel Rall. Rall continued to be out-thought, out-gunned, and out-fought by Washington during this increasingly bitter struggle for Trenton's possession. But on this snowy morning on which America's destiny yet hung in the balance, Rall was far from finished from unleashing his increasingly desperate attempts to outwit and outfight the commander, who he had long disparaged as nothing more than a backward Virginia farmer of little ability or intelligence. Rall was learning a bitter lesson in regard to the folly of underestimating an opponent, especially one who was desperate and defending home soil.

Chapter VIII

Rall Lashes Back With Renewed Fury

From the open ground just above the apple orchard, whose northern edge lay along the south bank of Petty's Run, Rall now realized that his ambitious plan of pushing north to catch Washington by surprise by gaining the high terrain, turning the American's left flank, and reaching the vital Princeton-Trenton Road was no longer a possibility upon seeing the dense double lines of Fermoy brigade surging south across the snow-covered slopes that descended all the way to the orchard. Likewise, Stephen's brigade of three Virginia regiments, now positioned on the left of Stirling's brigade, had shifted farther east to also bolster Washington's left by this time to face Rall's last offensive effort to fire into or strike the Hessians' left flank if they successfully broke through, advancing south just to the right-rear of Fermoy's brigade.

Thanks to Washington's quick reading of the opposing commander's mind to decipher his ambitious tactical design and his equally swift countermove to thwart this resilient opponent, Rall was now thoroughly checkmated on the north. The timely, almost simultaneous combination of Hand and Haussegger's precision maneuvering and swift advance across the snowy landscape to so quickly parry Rall's latest threat on the north and Sullivan's tactical successes, especially Glover in capturing the Assunpink bridge, to the south in the lower town continued to swiftly seal the Rall brigade's fate.

As if these significant tactical setbacks were not sufficient to additionally sink the Rall brigade's fortunes, a breathless Hessian officer, gasping for air, suddenly brought more bad news to Rall: the two captured three-pounders of Rall's own regiment were now in action against their former owners to deliver insult as well as injury. Therefore, with tactical alternatives diminishing until seemingly no realistic options remained, Rall was completely frustrated by the most vexing tactical dilemma and no-win situation that he had ever faced after he returned with his troops to the apple orchard. Rall's tactical quandary seemingly could not be overcome, despite all the Hessian courage, discipline, training, sacrifice, and shiny bayonets. Quite simply, Rall was fundamentally without a tactical solution by this time after having been repeatedly checkmated on every front. Then, all of a sudden, a never-say-die junior officer snapped Rall out of his seemingly multiple setback-induced daze by offering the most radical of all tactical decisions: to now turn his two regiments entirely around, march out of the apple orchard, and mount a headlong attack straight west and back into the heart of Trenton!

The most audacious of tactical ideas that appealed to his aggressive instincts well-honed by decades of wartime experience, Rall warmly embraced the audacious concept this last remaining—and almost unthinkable—tactical option now left open to him: relying on the bayonet in one last gamble to attempt to snatch a victory from the jaws of defeat. As Rall now realized, launching a frontal assault back into Trenton's center made good sense for a variety of reasons. First, simply engaging Fermoy's brigade, which had deployed in a lengthy line for action north of the apple orchard, in an indecisive slugfest of exchanging volleys across the open ground would accomplish nothing but inflicting additional casualties that Rall's already two decimated regiments could ill afford.

In addition to Rall's reasoning based upon years of experience, after crossing the Delaware, marching at night, and fighting all morning, the Americans had to be so physically exhausted as now to be vulnerable. And even more weapons of Washington's troops were inoperable from wetness and fouled by this time, and American ammunition was beginning to run low, as revealed by a gradual diminishing rate of fire that was discernable to Rall's trained ear. And, best of all, reinforcements were nearby. Hurled by the onrush of Sullivan's attackers out of the lower town, the Knyphausen Regiment now retired slightly northeast of Queen Street and the Quaker Meeting House. With Dechow's fusiliers getting closer to his position, Rall ordered the Knyphausen Regiment farther north to unite with his other two regiments in preparation for the maximum offensive effort calculated to yet win the day. Even now and despite its mauling in the lower town, the Knyphausen Regiment was in overall better shape than its two sister regiments. For the first time all day and at long last, Rall was seemingly about to have his entire brigade united and together to strike back with a concentrated offensive blow.

Ironically, Sullivan's hard-hitting team of top lieutenants, Stark, Sargent, Glover, and St. Clair had finally driven all of the Knyphausen Regiment out of the lower town to make the vital linkage—more by accident than deliberate tactical design—possible with Rall's other two regiments to the north at exactly the right time. Most of all, the resilient Rall brigade was yet proving that it possessed plenty of fight remaining. At long last, fortune seemed now to be smiling and swinging in Rall's favor.

As an ironic fate would have it, Washington's checkmate of Rall's determined effort to gain the Princeton-Trenton on the north combined with Sullivan's success to the south created the possibility for the uniting of all of Rall's three regiments and the launching of his most powerful Hessian counterattack this morning. And because Washington's forces were divided into two divisions and widely extended in advancing over a lengthy front to nearly encircle Trenton, Rall actually enjoyed a numerical advantage whenever and wherever he confronted Washington's troops at a single point. He, therefore, would now possess an even greater numerical advantage with the impending arrival of the Knyphausen Regiment for one final, united offensive effort to reverse the day's fortunes by turning around and pushing the Americans out of Trenton once and for all.

Most importantly, Rall also knew that he needed to bolster his attack with all the artillery that he could get his hands on if he was to succeed in his most daring offensive thrust. Rall, therefore, had already ordered Lieutenant Wiederhold to hurriedly bring up the two three-pounders with his Knyphausen regiment from the south. These were the von Lossberg Regiment's artillery pieces that had become separated from Scheffer's fusilier regiment during the confusion caused by Washington's initial attack down King Street. Lieutenant Fischer, of the Rall Regiment's artillery, had been assigned to command the Knyphausen guns in time for their ill-fated solo advance up Queen Street. However, by this time, both Knyphausen Regiment's cannon had become disabled after "their touch-pans had burned out," in one Hessian's estimation, but in fact one gun had been hit by the artillery-fire of Hamilton's New York boys. Four of the Rall brigade's six cannon, consequently, were now of no active service to Colonel Rall by this crucial moment when he desperately needed as much massed artillery firepower as possible to assault the town from the east and to prevail in the end. Therefore, Rall was now severely handicapped without the availability of two-thirds of his artillery, while Washington possessed seventeen guns in action, enjoying an eight-to-one advantage.

Not deterred by multiple setbacks and soaring casualties, Colonel Rall was determined to reverse the day's fortunes that had turned so suddenly and decidedly against him. As in just having attempted to gain the Princeton-Trenton Road and turn Washington's left flank around Queen Street, he now hoped to return the tactical favor of doing what seemed all but impossible by this time: launching a final, all-out offensive effort—a headlong charge—back into the narrow streets of Trenton to catch Washington and his now overconfident soldiers completely by surprise. Indeed, Rall's most determined counterattack of the day was about to be unleashed in full fury, when a good many American soldiers believed that they already had a resounding victory well in hand, especially after occupying all of Trenton. However, perhaps one other possible tactical option remained open to Rall. Instead of attacking back into the midst of another vicious round of nightmarish urban combat at close range, Rall might have decided to turn his troops southeast in an attempt to ford the creek northeast of the bridge, where the Assunpink, a tidal stream, narrowed. If more prudent and less bold, he then could have attempted to escape to save what remained of his hard-hit command rather than now risking everything, including his entire brigade, on one throw of the dice.

However, this never-say-die colonel, too proud and capable to consider even the thought of surrender, was yet emboldened by vivid memories of so many past glorious victories, including sparkling successes against yatagan sword-wielding Turks in the Crimea, and especially recent victories reaped by Hessian bayonet charges that had so easily overwhelmed America's hapless citizen soldiers. Most of all, Rall wanted to redeem his brigade's badly bruised honor and to regain his two lost artillery pieces, now manned by Orderly Sergeant White's New Englanders and Pennsylvanians and Knox's extra artillery crew specially assigned by Knox for the taking over captured guns, of his own regiment. A devastating psychological blow, the loss of one-third of the Hessian brigade's guns was the ultimate humiliation to Rall and the men of his famed brigade.

Worst of all, Rall had been surprised and committed the unthinkable by withdrawing completely out of Trenton, before this often-defeated former Virginia militia colonel, who long had been a laughingstock of multitudes of people on both sides of the Atlantic. Rall, therefore, was upset and angry. In consequence, Rall's upcoming attack was driven in part by a potent mixture of rage, contempt for the American fighting man, and an excessive Teutonic pride, even while the booming of the near-circle of Knox's cannon grew louder in the late December air.

Rall was now determined to win it all, and at any cost. He once again gamely prepared to lead the Rall and the von Lossberg regiments, back into the smoky center of American-held Trenton, or Dante's, inferno. Rall believed that if he regained possession of the town, then Washington's unprecedented string of tactical successes in the debris-strewn streets of Trenton would be quickly negated in one bold stroke. After all, if the even most fanatical Islamic warriors had been beaten with Rall's bayonet attacks when in Russian service, then he could certainly yet turn the tables on these upstart American rebels, who had exceeded their capabilities and good fortune this morning.

Ignoring the earlier wise council from Lieutenant Wiederhold for Rall not to make the classic mistake of underestimating either the size and determination of so many emboldened Americans now swarming all over Trenton, which was filled with drifting clouds of burst-powder smoke that looked eerie under the dim winter sunlight and snow flurries, because they were so "very strong," the veteran colonel from Hesse-Cassel was undeterred. He now prepared his grenadiers and fusiliers for their most desperate undertaking of the day.

In a booming voice, Rall ordered his troops, who benefitted at this critical moment from the instilled Prussian-style discipline thanks in part to the tough-minded martinet Adjutant Kleinschmidt's tireless efforts, to about face and turn around away from Fermoy's Continental brigade to the north in preparation for the formidable challenge of attempting to overwhelm Trenton to the west. With his fighting blood up, Rall directed Lieutenant Colonel Schneff to form up the two regiments in battle lines facing west and directly toward the town, from where plumes of sulphurous smoke rose higher into the thin winter air until pushed away by the winter wind. Once again with another display of firm discipline and excellent training, the surviving troops of the von Lossberg Regiment aligned on the right, or north, and the Rall Regiment on the left, or south, in mechanical fashion.

Against the odds, the Hessians were about to launch a frontal assault on the town now swarming with triumphant American troops, whose confidence and spirits were sky-high. Incredibly, Rall had only begun to fight this morning when death hung so heavy in the air, refusing to admit defeat regardless of the tactical situation. As in the past, he was now once again relying upon what Hessian bayonets could accomplish against mostly American farm boys. Quite simply, Rall simply refused to consider doing what almost any other commander, Hessian, British, or American, would have done in a comparable no-win situation: surrender. Yet feeling that this drawn-out battle had only begun—like Napoleon who believed that all was lost and hovered near disaster at Marengo until the battle's course was reversed near the day's end—despite seemingly everything having turned against him and lingering on the verge of the most humiliating defeat of his career, Colonel Rall rode rapidly up and down the front of his two veteran regiments.

As on so many previous battlefields where victory was reaped, Rall's dynamic leadership style fortified his grenadiers and fusiliers with greater resolve for embarking upon one final effort to win the day. In addition, the colonel ordered his brass band to play a spirited martial tune to inspire his troops for one last counterattack to reverse the day's fortunes. Once again and ever so briefly, the romance and glory of war returned to reinvigorate Rall, who basked in that old sense of invincibility that had existed before Washington's surprise attack.

In a strange way, this tenacious struggle for the possession of Trenton had been now transformed for Rall into a high-stakes contest very much about personal, regimental, and brigade honor, an unblemished reputation, and a good deal of professional pride of a career soldier. After all and something that he could never forget, Rall was the non-noble son of Captain Joachim Rall of Stralsund, situated on a picturesque, blue-colored sound on the Baltic Sea, and former cadet who had fought with distinction in Russia, Bavaria, the Rhineland, the Netherlands, and even in Scotland. And, most of all, Rall was not about to let his men, especially his cherished grenadier regiment named in his honor, down by allowing the dark stain of defeat to blemish the most distinguished military record and reputation in America.

Besides having lost the two Rall Regiment cannon on King Street, the two guns of the von Knyphausen Regiment were disabled. One Knyphausen gun had been left behind in Queen Street and the other field piece was yet in the von Lossberg Regiment's possession, while the remaining two von Lossberg Regiment three-pounders were with the Knyphausen Regiment to the south. If Rall could get these two three-pounders up to bolster his upcoming offensive effort and if the two lost cannon on King Street could be recaptured from Orderly Sergeant White and his New England and Pennsylvania cannoneers and then turned on the Americans, then Rall believed that a good chance remained to achieve a remarkable success. Nevertheless, Rall's upcoming counterattack with the bayonet was in fact little more than a desperate last-ditch effort, but it was the best possible remaining tactical alternative in part because so many Hessian muskets had become inoperable from the steady deluge from blackened skies. As Rall hopefully calculated, the Knyhausen Regiment's arrival from the south to reinforce his two regiments might well be sufficient for him to yet turn the tide.

However, two unexpected and sudden tactical developments—one on the Hessian side and the other stemming from Washington's own tactical decision—suddenly occurred that significantly affected the battle's final outcome. Ironically, Rall's hopes and his men's spirits additionally brightened when hundreds of Dechow's fusiliers suddenly appeared from out of the white haze of the falling snow, after having marched up Queen Street from the south. However, just when all three of Rall's regiments finally came together and were united as one, about to take the offensive together for the first time all day, a strange twist of fate suddenly intervened.

A Knyphausen Regiment officer, either a top lieutenant or perhaps even an aide to Major Dechow, who was yet hobbled from illness and an aggravated former wound not yet completely healed, reported to Rall. He then asked Colonel Rall if his newly arrived fusilier regiment "should march about left." At the front of his grenadiers and the von Lossberg fusiliers, Rall answered with a single word, "Yes." At this time, Rall desired for the Knyphausen Regiment to "about face" to the left, which meant shifting from facing north to facing west toward Trenton.

Such a relatively simple tactical maneuver should have placed the Knyphausen Regiment neatly aligned and in formation, as Rall envisioned, alongside his other two regiments, which were poised to attack back into Trenton. However, amid the tumult of crashing musketry, the pandemonium and intimidating growl of Greene and Sullivan's cannon from multiple directions, and the steady snow flurries that limited visibility which all attributed to the general confusion, Major Dechow either misunderstood the transmitted directive from Rall or the communication was jumbled. Dechow, therefore, issued orders that suddenly caused his Knyphausen Regiment to about face. Moving in a neat formation, Dechow's fusiliers now turned not west toward Trenton as Rall desired, but south toward the Quaker Meeting House and the lower town from where the fusilier regiment had just marched.

Immediately north of Dechow's Knyphausen Regiment and with the intoxicating pageantry of war having seemingly briefly returned once more to Trenton, meanwhile, a mounted Rall inspired his lengthy line of two regiments by his example. He was determined to recapture not only his lost cannon but also cherished battle flags. Yet believing that the Knyphausen Regiment was in alignment to the south, Rall turned to face his grenadiers and fusiliers, who loved him like a father and would follow him to hell and back if necessary. He then screamed, "Forward march! And attack them with the bayonet." To the blue-uniformed men of his own well-trained regiment, he then shouted for all to hear: "All my grenadiers, forward!"[1]

Clearly, Rall's determination to take the initiative and launch a frontal attack was the best tactical decision under the circumstances. After all, Napoleon explained how a military commander "of ordinary talent occupying a bad position, and surprised by a superior force, seeks his safety in retreat; but a great captain supplies all deficiencies by his courage and marches boldly to meet the attack. By this means he disconcerts his adversary, and if this last shows any irresolution in his movements, a skillful leader profiting by his indecision may even hope for victory . . . ." Rall was now fulfilling this timeless maxim in the art of war.[2]

But Washington's acute tactical sense, never more on target than on this frozen morning, had once again risen to the fore. Even before an emboldened Rall shouted to this grenadiers, "alle was meine Grenatir seyn, vor werds," Washington had already maneuvered to protect his hard-earned prize that had been secured thanks to a hazardous river crossing, a lengthy nighttime march, and much hard fighting—the battle-scared, smoking town of Trenton. As tenacious as a bulldog this morning, especially when his fighting blood was up, the resilient commander from Mount Vernon was not about to relinquish Trenton to a resurgent Rall brigade without a tough fight.

Therefore, watching hundreds of German soldiers marching closer and spying an opportunity upon sighting the exposed right flank of the von Lossberg Regiment that extended north toward Petty's Run, Washington "ordered Lord Stirling to advance [the left of] his brigade [south and farther down and parallel to Queen Street] upon their other [right] flank" that was unprotected. Also on Washington or Knox's order, Captain Hamilton hurriedly shifted his two six-pounders guns a short distance south and down Queen Street, moving his New York cannon into a better position to inflict more damage at closer range. Stirling's opportunistic troops, consequently, on the Virginia, Pennsylvania, and Delaware brigade's left also inched farther down the gently sloping ground to provide support for Hamilton, while those New York cannoneers on Stirling's center descended mostly in a southeast direction to defend the town from the northwest. Meanwhile, Stirling's Virginians on the brigade's right remained at King Street's head to protect Forrest's Philadelphia artillery.[3]

Against rows of American smoothbore muskets and rifles bristling from advantageous firing positions all along the town's eastern edge over a wide area from north to south, the lengthy Hessian formation surged west with drill ground precision. With Rall riding at their head and cantering forward on his war horse while snowflakes tumbled down from black skies, the finely uniformed grenadiers and fusiliers advanced in amazingly "good order." Each German soldier seemed to be in perfect step. From all appearances, the relentless advance of Rall's troops, in a tight, neat formation, looked like a solid wall of invincible Teutonic might. The two veteran regiments moved together as if of one soul and purpose, which was to push every last rebel out of the town and to recapture Trenton at any cost.

To the ragamuffin American citizen soldiers who could not yet maneuver or march with the same crisp precision as their opponent, Rall's disciplined advance across the snowy landscape toward Trenton was a magnificent, if not slightly unnerving, sight to behold by even Washington's veterans. After all, in defending the town, the Hessians "gave smart resistance," wrote Clement Biddle in a letter, and Washington's men still felt the sting of that spirited resistance. In the von Lossberg Regiment's fusilier ranks surging relentlessly onward through the snow to the right, or north, of the Rall Regiment and despite the recent loss of so many comrades, Lieutenant Ernst Christian Schwabe, age thirty, felt a growing sense of admiration as the two determined Hessian regiments "advanced on the town with drums beating" and flags flying in the stiff winter breeze.[4]

Nineteen-year-old Lieutenant Carl Andreas Kinen and his brother Ensign Ludwig Kinen, age eighteen, both Dillenburg-born members of the Rall Regiment, were not advancing toward Trenton together. Carl, who had been wounded in the assault on Fort Washington and was unable to fight this morning, was captured earlier by Glover's men in attempting to cross over the Assunpink bridge. Therefore, teenage Ludwig Kinen now advanced on Trenton in formation without his older brother by his side.[5]

Attempting to do the unexpected in a seemingly no-win situation and as if having recently learned a tactical lesson, Rall was determined to wrestle not only the initiative away from Washington, but also the same tactical weapon that had bestowed Washington with so much unprecedented success this Thursday morning: the element of surprise. To Washington's amazement, Rall had unleashed a classic eighteenth-century bayonet attack right out of the pages of Frederick the Great's *Instructions*, as if once again charging up the high ground at Fort Washington, the commander's own namesake. Worn, black powder-smeared American soldiers, who had thought the battle for Trenton's possession had already been won, looked on in wonder as the Rall brigade's brass band of fully uniformed musicians advanced in front of lengthy formations as if on parade, playing a lively Germanic martial air to inspire the survivors of these two elite regiments in their all-out effort to reverse the day's fortunes.

Despite the fact that the Germans realized that they were about to enter the vortex of the storm in a nightmarish urban environment, Rall's order for his grenadiers and the von Lossbergers to push straight west and toward the town's smoke-filled center lifted the fighting spirit of these tough, professional soldiers who believed that they could yet turn the tide. Like Colonel Rall, these proud Teutonic fighting men were eager to redeem German honor and the Rall brigade's lofty reputation by regaining not only Trenton but also their cannon. After all, never before had a Hessian field piece been lost in action to Washington's homespun revolutionaries.

And their deep-seated disdain (although now lessened after this morning's dramatic turn of events) for American citizen soldiers itself was even now propelling Rall and his finest troops back into the midst of a hornet's nest with a burning desire to avenge all the bad that had happened to them this morning. Therefore, with colorful battle flags waving in the stiff winter breeze and young drummer boys furiously pounding their instruments, decorated with ornate, brightly painted sides, in a rhythmical cadence that inspired the men in the ranks, these well-trained Hessians advanced steadily west across the gently sloping ground below Petty's Run.

Like a well-oiled machine, grenadiers and fusiliers surged onward through the snow flurries, moving parallel to that ice-covered watercourse. Proud veterans of the von Lossberg Regiment and Rall Regiment, from north to south, pushed forward with fixed bayonets "to recapture the cannons" of the Rall Regiment, in the words of Private Johannes Ruber, the seventeen-year-old grenadier. All the while, the spirited beating of the Hessian drums rose higher and split the morning air, alerting Washington's troops of the full-scale assault and allowing them time for appropriate preparations. However, Rall's final opportunity to reap a dramatic tactical success had been already largely negated by one single misunderstood order, thanks to the confusing fog of war that helped to doom what should have been the mightiest, and very likely overwhelming, Hessian offensive effort—from all three regiments—of the day.

Unfortunately for Rall, meanwhile, the Knyphausen Regiment, including much-needed fighting men like eighteen-year-old Ensign Wilhelm von Drach, born in Ellrichshausen, continued to push relentlessly onward in another direction entirely different from his two other regiments. Hundreds of Dechow's experienced fusiliers now marched not side by side with their sister regiments advancing on a western course, but due south and all alone.

In misinterpreting Rall's verbal directive communicated by a Knyphausen officer, Dechow evidently believed—and this made some sound tactical sense for perhaps yet thwarting Washington's double envelopment—that Rall would push Greene's Second Division troops out of Trenton's northern end, while he would accomplish the same tactical feat against Sullivan's First Division troops in the lower town in a dual offensive effort: a last-ditch attempt to reverse the extensive gains of the Americans and to pry open the closing arms of Washington's pincer movement meant to encircle the Rall brigade and destroy it. In addition, the left flank of Rall's two counterattacking regiments on the south needed protection against Sullivan's surging troops, especially its highly mobile guns that moved forward through the streets as flying artillery. And Major Dechow, who had served in the Prussian Army under Frederick the Great, knew that this pressing tactical objective of protecting the vulnerable flank of Rall's assault on Trenton could only be accomplished by the Knyphausen Regiment moving south instead of west to give a chance for Rall's counterattack to succeed.

Indeed, if all three regiments had advanced together west into the north-western edge of Trenton as Rall wished, then their collective left flank would be completely exposed to a flank fire from Sullivan's Division to the south. Consequently, the tactical concept that the Knyphausen Regiment should pro-tect the southern end, or left flank, of Rall's frontal assault back into the mael-strom of Trenton made such good tactical sense that Lieutenant Wiederhold, and no doubt other experienced officers as well, now believed that his fusilier regiment "had been ordered to cover the [left or southern] flank:" an exposed flank that would shortly be hit by Sullivan's troops attacking north up King Street at the most critical moment.

Consequently, Rall's jumbled order that the Knyphausen Regiment "should march about left," had resulted in the fact that the Rall brigade was once again separated in a key battlefield situation as throughout this morning of decision: the old classic case of divide-and-conquer. Amid the thick layers of battle-smoke hovering over the frozen field and the cascading snow showers that refused to let up, Rall had failed to see this startling tactical development that had so sud-denly taken place just beyond the Rall Regiment's left, or southern, flank: the von Knyhausen Regiment was in fact moving off at a good pace in the wrong direction—south—while he led the Rall and von Lossberg Regiments west.

Most of all, Colonel Rall needed all three regiments together because he now hoped to reverse the day's fortunes by negating the dramatic gains achieved by Washington's left wing, Greene's Second Division, by prying open one-half of the lethal pincer movement to upset the double envelopment by regaining control of King Street, especially the high ground at the street's head. Because the apple orchard was located just below Petty's Run and only slightly northeast of his old King Street headquarters at Stacy Potts's house near the town's center, Rall led his two regiments in a slightly southwest direction. Before reaching the first small wooden houses on the town's northeast outskirts, the lengthy Hessian formation of two regiments pushed across open country west of the apple orchard and north of Perry Street, a block above Fourth Street, running parallel to Petty's Run to the north. Perry Street was the northernmost street to enter Queen Street, before eventually entering King Street, one block to the west.

Imploring everyone onward while the sharp rattling of Hessian drums echoed louder through the streets to warn Washington's men, Rall led his grenadiers and fusiliers toward the old battleground of King Street, where bodies of dead, wounded, and dying comrades lay in the snow, as if certain of reaping yet another victory over the rustic Americans as so often in the past. Rall directed his two regiments, moving with disciplined ease, toward the relative shelter offered by the northern row of wood-frame houses on Perry Street to avoid the blistering fire of Washington's cannons on the high ground above, especially Hamilton's two New York six-pounders that had eased down Queen Street to an advanced position just below Queen Street's head.

Meanwhile, Haslet and Mercer's infantrymen were already ready and waiting in good firing positions with loaded flintlocks in and around the midsection of the town's eastern outskirts, after having sprinted across Queen Street to take good firing positions from the vantage point of second-story houses that overlooked the snowy approaches and open ground to the east. Here, from the protective cover and especially from the lofty perch of wide-open second story windows that allowed gusts of freezing air inside, these veteran marksmen prepared to deliver more punishment upon the fast-approaching Rall and von Lossberg Regiments. All the while, Rall's two embattled regiments surged relentlessly onward and roughly parallel to the Princeton-Trenton Road, nearing the town's eastern edge.

As if nothing could stop it, Rall's lengthy formation rolled over the open fields of white just east of the town's eastern outskirts, until rudely greeted by a fiery explosion of gunfire that erupted from doorways and windows, including two-story vantage points, and from behind wells, wooden fences, smokehouses, cellarways, and outhouses on the town's east side. To the Hessians who continued onward through the leaden storm, it now seemed that "Americans [were] firing from every window" of every house in Trenton.

Additionally, Forrest's "flying" artillery, under Irish Lieutenant Duffy, in King Street had been pushed east by the hardworking Pennsylvania artillerymen toward Queen Street and now opened fire. The two captured Rall Regiment cannon, brought south down debris-strewn King Street from where they had been taken just north of Petty's Creek, were also in action, blazing away. Sergeant White and his New Englanders and Pennsylvania gunners blasted away with one three-pounder while the other gun was fired by Knox's preassigned gun crew. These veteran artillerymen relished using the German's own ammunition to cause havoc among the advancing Hessians.

But the most punishment delivered upon Rall's counterattackers stemmed from a blistering fire unleashed by Mercer's Maryland, Connecticut, and Massachusetts men, with dried muskets, firing pans, flints, and plenty of equally dry black powder. Taking careful aim, these savvy veterans blasted away from the west at Rall's foremost ranks, while Haslet's Delaware Continentals, above Mercer, and some of Stirling's men from the brigade's right fired from the northwest and Stark's New Hampshire soldiers fired northeastward from the south and into Rall's exposed left flank. Not committing the folly of marching through the open fields and meadows, just south of Petty's Run, to the north, the von Lossberg fusiliers gained the vicinity of Perry Street, where houses on the street's north side offered some protection, while the grenadiers just to the south surged west in the Fourth Street sector. By this time, Rall's two resurgent regiments again neared embattled Queen Street, with Schneffer's von Lossbergers continuing to advance above, or north, of Rall's grenadiers, who pushed toward Rall's King Street headquarters near the town's center. Then, just below the head of Queen Street on the open slope, Hamilton's New York guns unleashed fire from the north, raking the von Lossberg Regiment's right flank once exposed in the street. Blasts of canister swept down Queen Street and into the von Lossberger's exposed right flank, dropping more young fusiliers in the snow. But most of the Lossbergers, like Lieutenant Ludwig Wilhelm Keller who died of disease in October 1777, survived the hail of lead and continued onward, following their colorful battle flags in the tempest. Caught in the open and without any cover, Rall's troops, especially on the north, were so hard-hit by the maelstrom of projectiles, including from Baumann's guns to the left-rear of Hamilton's artillery, that some confusion resulted. Nevertheless, Rall's two regiments somehow continued to push onward and across Queen Street under fire, while the Germans continued to ignore not only their losses but also their greatly reduced capabilities to return fire with wet muskets and ammunition.

In the meantime, Rall and other experienced officers restored order in the shaky ranks on the hard-hit right. Running the deadly gauntlet, the grenadiers and fusiliers continued to push west through the storm, both leaden and from Mother Nature. Finally, after passing across the killing ground of bullet- and cannonball-swept Queen Street, the steadily advancing Hessians then entered the more sheltered area between King and Queen Streets, especially protective Church Alley. Mounted before his surging troops and with snow-laden houses spitting fire and seemingly overflowing with sharp-eyed American marksmen, a mounted Rall suffered a "slight wound." But the colonel ignored the pain, remaining in front of his troops to set the inspirational example, waving his saber and shouting orders.

Colonel Rall then continued to lead his grenadiers toward King Street in a determined bid to regain possession of his old headquarters and his two lost cannon that had been brought farther south by the victors from where they had been captured just north of Petty's Run. While a hail of bullets zipped by, Rall implored his troops farther west by way of the relative shelter of Church Alley, which led straight to his headquarters near King Street's midpoint. Amid the excitement of battle and only concerned about salvaging a no-win situation, Rall was evidently not aware of steadily growing weaker from the loss of blood from his wound.

Farther south in the smoke-laced lower town, meanwhile, Sullivan's veterans continued to perform exceptionally well. Leading his hard-charging brigade of New Hampshire and Massachusetts Continentals, General St. Clair's experience as a respected British officer under General James Wolfe, who was a Culloden veteran like Mercer but on the winning side, in the decisive English victory at Quebec in 1759, continued to pay dividends. "Genl Saint Clear," in one New England soldier's words, was popular among his Continentals, who fought as much for him as for heady Age of Enlightenment ideology. The tactically astute Scotsman's leadership experience now translated into a long line of his veterans blasting away at the Rall Regiment's exposed left flank and inflicting damage.[6]

As Haslet and Mercer's riflemen punished the dark-colored ranks of Rall's disciplined grenadiers surging west through the whipping wind and snow flurries, additional troops on the right-center of Stirling's brigade continued to ease southeast down the sloping ground at the town's north end while firing to bring heavier pressure on Rall's vulnerable right flank. More importantly to the south, a New England regiment of St. Clair's brigade, the reserve unit of Sullivan's First Division column and in the rear, was ordered farther north up King Street not only to fulfill Washington's tactical ambitions of uniting with Greene's Second Division, but also to intercept head-on Rall's desperate attempt to regain King Street at any cost. With battle flags flying and an eagerness to meet the Hessians, Colonel John Paterson's Fifteenth Massachusetts Continentals pushed north to parry Rall's counterattack, heading toward the Rall Regiment's exposed left flank as it neared its tactical objective of King Street.

While the foremost three New Hampshire regiments of four-regiment St. Clair's New England brigade had surged east in pursuit of the Knyphausen Regiment, after crossing King Street to eventually gain the vicinity of Queen Street just below Mercer's men, the last regiment—St. Clair's rearmost unit, Colonel John Paterson's Fifteenth Massachusetts Continental Regiment—had turned north and now advanced up King Street. In pushing north with smooth-bore flintlocks on shoulders, Paterson, a Yale graduate, and his Massachusetts troops were in an advantageous position to confront the fast-emerging threat of Rall's counterattack, steamrolling toward King Street, to the northeast. But Paterson's veteran Bay State regiment was not alone in advancing north to intercept Rall's counterattack. The Sixteenth Massachusetts Continental Infantry, Sargent's brigade, was also hurled north up King Street, by either Sargent or Sullivan, to support the northward advance of Paterson's Fifteenth Massachusetts up King Street in the bid to head off Hessian westward counter-attack now targeting Rall's headquarters.

With Mercer in front to the west, Haslet to the northwest, Stirling to the north, and St. Clair south of Rall's two advancing regiments and while two Massachusetts Continental Regiments rushed north up King Street to inter-cept Rall's desperate bid calculated to regain King Street, Washington's First and Second Divisions continued to gradually move nearer to each other to close the noose around the two advancing Hessian regiments, which were now unknowingly entering a deadly trap. Consequently, and unknown to Rall, the jaws of Washington's pincers were finally about to slam shut on King Street and on the final Hessian ambitions on December 26. Evidently, Haslet and Mercer's riflemen immediately before Rall's advance retired back from the fore-most houses on the town's eastern outskirts to lure—although out of necessity rather than by deliberate design or plan—Rall's two regiments deeper into the heart of town.

Worst of all for Rall although he did not realize it at the time, some enterprising Americans, mostly likely Pennsylvania, Virginia, or Maryland riflemen, remained inside houses to allow the Hessian formations to pass by. These opportunistic soldiers then pushed forward to ease around the flanks of Rall's two regiments, getting into advantageous positions behind the advancing Hessian formations to threaten a complete encirclement. Meanwhile, isolated bands of Washington's troops continued to gain ground in other sectors, rushing ahead to find better firing positions to inflict more damage upon the German interlopers. Meanwhile, with each passing minute in surging farther west and deeper into Trenton, Rall's two regiments found themselves even more isolated, becoming separated farther from the Knyphausen Regiment to the south. Indeed, Major Dechow and his fusiliers had not only withdrawn farther south down Queen Street but also were forced by Sullivan's northernmost attackers farther southwest of Rall's counterattack, to where they could offer no assistance when most needed by Rall to the north.

All the while, the clatter of musketry erupting from Washington's men picked up in volume and intensity, with lucrative targets, especially Hessian officers in resplendent uniforms, closer and easier for sharpshooting veterans to hit, especially with clean head shots, during Rall's thrust back into Trenton. Rall's two regiments marched west along narrow, darkened avenues lined with flashes of American gun fire. Leaping flames of musket-fire licked at and raked the Rall and von Lossberg Regiments from three sides, and especially at the exposed flanks: along with officers leading the way through the storm of crackling musketry, these were the coveted targets of opportunity for Washington's marksmen armed with Long Rifles. During his determined push west to regain King Street in his headquarters area, Rall led his fusilier and grenadier regiments into a three-quarters circle of blazing gunfire, amid a sulphurous cauldron of intensifying close-range combat, which made the Hessians even more vulnerable.

After running the gauntlet and somehow reaching a "place obliquely opposite Rall's quarters," in the words of thirty-year-old Lieutenant Ernst Christian Schwabe, who indicated how far the von Lossbergers, led by the stalwarts of the "body company" of which he was a proud member, had now advanced west to a point just northeast of Stacy Potts's house, the Hessians now found themselves in the very vortex of Trenton's fiery storm. With wet muskets and firing pans, a large percentage of Rall's men could no longer return fire, however. In easing closer to Rall's tactical objective of reaching King Street, the battle-hardened grenadiers and von Lossberg fusiliers were consumed by a surreal nightmare of bitter, close-range combat in a confused urban setting, which was dominated by thick layers of battle-smoke, too many swarming American soldiers to count, and an ugly death that could come at any moment.[7]

In the embattled northern sector located just above Church Alley, where the blaze of musketry directed upon the von Lossberg fusiliers on the north became even heavier when "obliquely opposite Rall's quarters" at the two-story Potts's house, Lieutenant Schwabe wondered if he would ever see his native Rinteln again. He never forgot the vicious swirl of a full-blown urban conflict that raged like an uncontrollable wildfire around him. Here, in this hellish sector, the von Lossbergers "fired on the enemy who were hidden in the houses, cellars and behind fences . . . and through a continual snowfall and heavy rain and the men's guns would not in some instances fire off any longer."[8]

In desperation, Captain Adam Christoph Steding, age thirty-nine, yelled for his frustrated von Lossberg fusiliers to chip their musket flints in the hope that fresh sparks from newly cut—or dry—flints (something that the Americans had already done) might ignite powder charges in smoothbore muskets. Clearly, this hard-fighting bachelor from the little town of Fischbeck near Rinteln who possessed more than two decades of solid military experience, knew exactly what to do in this emergency situation. Steding's fast-thinking initiative might have succeeded except that the black powder in most German's muskets, and evidently leather cartridge-boxes as well, was wet by this time, negating the impact of larger sparks from steel hammers striking re-cut musket flints to ignite powder charges in musket barrels.[9]

By this time when the grenadiers and fusiliers had penetrated so deeply into the town's darkened depths amid the suffocating palls of sulphurous smoke that hovered over King Street like an ominous cloud for German fortunes, some emboldened patriotic citizens of Trenton joined in the escalating fray to assist their hard-pressed countrymen in arms. Making the most of the opportunity, these townsfolk now blasted away with muskets from the shelter of their own homes.

But the greatest punishment inflicted upon the exposed fusiliers was unleashed from the right of Stirling's men, especially Virginia Continentals— who Washington had smartly held in place as a strategic reserve on King Street sector—armed with deadly Long Rifles, on the north. Here, on the north, the exposed right flank of Scheffer's von Lossberg Regiment was cut to pieces, and the hard-hit ranks began to waver under the severe pounding, falling into some initial disarray. In record time, fourteen von Lossberg fusiliers were killed and wounded, dropping like autumn leaves on a windy October day in the Rhineland so far away. It was the unfortunate fate of the von Lossberg fusiliers to have earlier passed not only closest to Hamilton's two six-pounders, now positioned just below Queen Street's head, but also Forrest's Pennsylvania guns, as they approached King Street. Unable to return fire, cursing, shrieking, and shouting fusiliers reached new levels of desperation in attempting to fight back as best they could in the noisy confusion.

Ironically, after many Americans had only recently believed that the contest had been won by Washington's surprise attack, the struggle for Trenton's possession was only now beginning to reach its zenith on the grim, urban killing ground between King and Queen Streets. With choking battle-smoke continuing to reduce visibility along with low, dark clouds blotting out the sun, this surreal, close-quarter fighting amid such an overall darkened atmosphere under a poorly lit sky was the ultimate nightmare for highly disciplined professional soldiers. After all, the Hessians were neither trained nor familiar with the horrors of urban combat, the nastiest kind of warfare. While Continentals fired from standing, kneeling, and prone positions and with individualistic fighting men from across America darting about fleetingly like ghosts between houses and along alleys, expert American marksmen seemed to Rall's soldiers to be blasting away from every point. While the snow continued to tumble down over fallen bodies, flashes of flame erupted from marksmen who blasted away from behind trees, outhouses, and fences and even out of cellars to cut down more Germans.

As the relentlessly moving Hessian ranks pushed closer to King Street with flags waving, music blaring, and drums pounding in a regular cadence, as if waging war on a conventional European battlefield on the continent's central plains, in the mistaken hope of intimidating Washington's citizen soldiers, at least one Trenton woman picked up a trusty flintlock with deadly intent. She took careful aim at the most noticeable target that she could ascertain amid the drifting clouds of burnt-powder smoke and chaos that swirled below her. Then, this lady rebel pulled (most likely jerked rather than squeezed) the trigger, firing at one of the foremost foreign occupiers of her own hometown. Wearing bicorn hats, these finely uniformed Hessians, especially upper class, aristocratic officers, presented ideal targets against the white background of snow on the street below.

Most of all, this daring American woman, of unknown age and background, could not resist the temptation to do her patriotic duty. Venting her anger at great risk to herself and perhaps Trenton family, this New Jersey patriot now reloaded her musket and again fired at Rall's troops also because if married, then her husband might have been even now serving in Washington's Army. As if facing the scorching fires of Washington's men was not enough, Rall's soldiers were shocked by the sight of this American woman firing at them from a window—something not seen by these German veterans during many years of military service on both sides of the Atlantic. For the more philosophical Hessians who witnessed firsthand her pent-up fury, these mostly Lutheran fighting men must have now realized that such spirited homespun resistance revealed that they were encountering a new kind of people—fanatical, diehard republicans—who were now waging a holy war against hated invaders.

With Rall's encroaching soldiers at close range to her own home, one of the woman's shots mortally wounded a conspicuous Hessian "captain," either thirty-one-year-old Johann Fredrich, or Kasper, von Riess or Friedrich Wilhelm von Benning, serving in the regiment since 1766, who were leading their troops bravely onward into the maelstrom. Described as a "brave and gallant officer," Captain Riess, born on Frankfort-on-the-Main in 1745 and hailing from an upper-class Stallburg family, which owned the salt mines at Allendorf, on the Lumda River, amid towering, evergreen-covered mountains, was instantly killed. He fell near Captain Benning, who likewise was killed in the vicious cross fire raking the two exposed regiments without mercy.

The name of this accurate-firing patriotic Trenton woman, who almost certainly deliberately targeted one of these Hessian officers, thanks to his fancy uniform, and as if instinctively knowing the urgent need to eliminate the most inspiring Hessian leaders in their final bid to reap victory by regaining King Street, has never been ascertained. A trustworthy officer, Benning commanded the Sixth Company, von Lossberg Regiment, when cut down in the body-littered street. He had served capably as a fusilier officer for at least a decade, and had been appointed Staff Captain of the von Lossberg Regiment in 1773. When Benning was killed, he was standing near the mounted Rall while the colonel continued to encourage his troops west toward King Street and a hail of bullets zipped by. In doing his duty, Rall ignored the sight of his fallen friend and his own slight wound. This sharp-shooting female patriot might well have been of German heritage, adding another unique dimension of the surreal civil war among Germans in America during this bloody showdown at Trenton.[10]

Meanwhile, not long after the fall of Captains Riess and Benning while leading their troops onward into the face of the roaring musketry that seemingly was erupting from all sides, Lieutenant Ernst Christian Schwabe, who had served with distinction in the Lieb Body Guard Company, von Lossberg Regiment, since age fourteen, was hit in the thigh and went down on the snow-covered ground. While the bleeding Schwabe was carried to the shelter behind a nearby house not held by revenge-seeking Americans, nineteen-year-old Ensign Friedrich von Zengen, born in Bonenburg and recently promoted to an officer's rank from the enlisted ranks, took command of the crack Lieb Body Guard Company, which continued to put up a good fight against Washington's sharp-shooting executioners who seemed all around the dwindling number of boxed-in von Lossberg fusiliers.[11]

While the von Lossberg Regiment's advance stalled among the houses immediately north of Rall's grenadiers between Queen and Kings Streets just above Church Alley, where the distance between these two north-south main thoroughfares was narrower than farther south as the parallel roads gradually widened in descending south toward the foot of both arteries, the Rall Regiment grenadiers kept moving relentlessly west along Church Alley on the von Lossberger's left just to the south. Boring a narrow hole through the cauldron of increasingly determined American resistance, these well-trained grenadiers forced Mercer's foremost soldiers to withdraw west, finally opening the way up to King Street.

Through the hail of lead projectiles, Rall's grenadiers struggled onward with determination to finally reach their objective of King Street by way of Church Alley after running a deadly gauntlet of fire. Even though the Hessians could yet hardly see anything in the thick, swirling smoke and with wet muskets and powder which ensured that the American ring of fire could not be responded to in kind, the foremost Rall's grenadiers at last managed to gain their coveted goal of King Street, wielding bayonets like pikes and expending more lives of German men and boys as if they no longer mattered to their concerned families back in Germany.

Against the odds, the foremost surviving Rall Regiment grenadiers spilled into King Street near the town's center and Rall's headquarters, driving away supporting infantrymen and a handful of American gunners, who operated the two captured three-pounders, which had been brought by the victors farther south from their original location just north of Petty's Run. No doubt a Hessian victory cheer rang down body-strewn King Street when the two Rall Regiment guns were finally taken back into the grenadier fold after even more lives were lost: a remarkable tactical accomplishment under the circumstances, especially considering the fact that Trenton was held by a larger number (around a thousand more) of Americans.

Teenage Grenadier Johannes Reuber, of the Rall Regiment, described with pride in only a few words of the turning point in the tenacious struggle for possession of King Street, when the unstoppable grenadiers descended upon the defenders and captured their two field pieces that they thought they would never see again: "We got them back." Colonel Rall was elated by his most improbable tactical success that he had achieved on King Street near his own headquarters at Potts's house. After all, he had accomplished much more than the recapture of two lost cannon. At long last and at least for the moment, Rall had wrestled away and regained the initiative, stealing the momentum from a seemingly already victorious Washington, while also wiping clean the dark stain upon his grenadier regiment's spotless record and reputation in this war.

Additionally, after more hard fighting in the embattled heart of Trenton, the colonel reclaimed the badly bruised honor of his entire brigade, the pride of Hesse-Cassel and other Germanic regions of the ancient Teutonic homeland, by regaining the two little three-pounders. After having stirred up a hornet's nest deep within Trenton's bowels, Rall's sparkling tactical success of reaching King Street and recapturing his two cannon was short lived, however.[12]

At this time, an increasing amount of pressure continued to be applied by Sullivan's First Division troops south of Rall's successful counterattack all the way back into King Street: Glover possessed the Assunpink brigade and Sargent's New England and New York brigade continued to confront the feisty Knyphausen Regiment at Queen Street's lower end. Meanwhile, Colonel Paterson's Fifteenth Massachusetts Continental Regiment, St. Clair's reserve brigade, led the way north and straight up King Street and through the drifting smoke. A direct order had been issued to Paterson to intercept and parry Rall's westward-lunging counterattack by either Sullivan, division commander, or St. Clair, brigade commander.

Not long after Rall gained his precious toehold on King Street and the hard-fighting grenadiers reached their deepest penetration point west to gain an advanced point near Rall's headquarters, these yet unbloodied New England troops, with full cartridge-boxes and plenty of fighting spirit, swarmed north up

King Street at the most opportune moment; one regiment from St. Clair's brigade, the Fifteenth Massachusetts Continental Regiment, and the other from Sargent's brigade, the Sixteenth Massachusetts Continental Regiment, from north to south, respectively.

Moving forward in the Sixteenth Massachusetts's surging ranks, African American Private Jacob Francis described how, after first having pushed down the River Road, his regiment had then entered "into the town to the corner where it crossed the street running up towards [or north] the Scotch Road and [the regiment] turned up [King] street," to advance behind Paterson's Bay State regiment. And in the forefront of this timely counter stroke pouring north up King Street toward Rall's headquarters, Sullivan now possessed a most capable commander and a battle-tested regiment for leading the counterattack from the south that now threatened Rall's southern, or left, flank that had gained a toehold on King Street: Colonel Paterson and his Fifteenth Massachusetts. When needed the most to stem the crisis, this seasoned Continental regiment was about to make its presence felt far beyond its numbers and in a disproportionate manner, even though this Massachusetts regiment had been recently cruelly decimated by smallpox, until only the colonel and half a dozen soldiers had remained fit for duty as late as June 1776.

Most importantly for meeting Rall's counterstroke in King Street, Paterson's Fifteenth Massachusetts Continental Regiment had early gained a lofty reputation as "the flower" of New England's Continentals. Paterson was a Yale College graduate (Class of 1762) and a sharp lawyer of Scottish ancestry. He looked back with pride to a rebellion-minded and British-hating grandfather, who had fled the native Celtic and Protestant homeland for political reasons. This capable Massachusetts colonel was versatile and tough-minded, having gained timely support, including "patriot" Indian volunteers, from the Stockbridge Tribe in the spring of 1775.

Leaving his son a distinguished martial legacy, Paterson's father had died of yellow fever in the same year that his promising son graduated from Yale, while serving in Havana, Cuba, not long after the Spanish port's capture. Modest by nature, Paterson was a community and early revolutionary political leader from Lenox, Massachusetts. He was also the loving husband of Elizabeth Warren Lee after having married the love of his life in 1766. However, he missed their ten-year wedding anniversary because of his patriotism and this war's stern demands, which somewhat soothed Elizabeth's anger. At the risk of making them orphans so that he could lead his men to victory at Trenton, Paterson was also the father of three daughters—Hannah, Polly, and Ruth, respectively—and one son, Josiah.

Most importantly in overall tactical terms, Colonel Paterson and his Massachusetts Continentals were now exactly in the right place at the right time: fresh troops, with full cartridge-boxes, now advancing north up King Street, just below Rall's deepest westward penetration and most successful counterattack of the day, surging ahead on a direct collusion course with the Rall Regiment that had secured a tight grip on King Street from where more extensive gains could be reaped if exploited. At this critical moment, Greenwood described the charge of Colonel Paterson and 170 mostly "Berkshire [County, Massachusetts] men" of his seasoned Fifteenth Massachusetts Continental Regiment—St. Clair's brigade's largest regiment—which included hard-fighting Scotch-Irish officers, like Lieutenants John and Thomas McKinstry, north up King Street and the gently sloping ground from the south: "As we advanced, it being dark and stormy so that we could not see very far ahead, we got within 200 yards of about 300 or 400 Hessians who were paraded, two deep, in a straight line with Colonel Roll (Rall or Rahl), their commander, on horseback, to the right of them."[13]

Not long after they regained King Street and recaptured their two three-pounders, this most advanced concentration of Rall's foremost grenadiers who had reached a point near their commander's headquarters on King Street was yet formidable, despite having suffered heavy losses. Meanwhile, just northeast of Rall's Regiment and Church Alley and immediately east of King Street, the von Lossberg Regiment was now in more serious trouble than its sister regiment situated just to the southwest. Here, immediately above Church Alley, "the bravest men" of the von Lossberg Regiment made a defensive stand, after a good many fusiliers were already cut down by the flank fire sweeping down from the north from the right of Stirling's troops that had remained in position—upon Washington's orders—on commanding ground at the head of King Street. This von Lossberg defensive stand was primarily orchestrated by Captain Steding, age thirty-nine, who was yet full of fight despite repeated setbacks. He stubbornly refused to be denied on this hellish morning, mirroring the tenacity of his strong-willed brigade commander, who was now battling just to the southwest on bullet-swept King Street. Both Hessian leaders were determined not to relinquish any ground after it had been so hard won at the cost of some of the brigade's best soldiers.

Exhibiting the natural phenomena of hard-hit soldiers in an awfully bad fix under a scorching fire, some of Rall's men began what was known as "bunching" out of instinct. Nevertheless, despite soaring losses, the Hessians continued "fighting as hard as they could" in the blood-soaked King Street sector. A hardened veteran and equally committed bachelor whose hard-earned cynicism mocked marriage and romantic notions, Captain Steding, and his top lieutenants, including twenty-two-year-old Ensign Christian August von Hobe, born in Mecklenburg in northern Germany in 1754 and the Sixth Company's commander, and Lieutenant Wilhelm Christian Muller, born in Ziegenheim in the Rhineland in 1749 and who had served in the Fourth Company since age sixteen, steadied the reeling Lossbergers, who suffered from a vicious flank fire from the north and a frontal fire from the west.

Amid the din, veteran Hessian officers shouted barely audible orders, and the fusiliers attempted to return fire the best they could, blasting away at both concealed and stealthily-moving Americans darting in and out of the smoke and firing from houses and from behind fences. All the while, these well-trained soldiers stood vulnerable in formation in the open to be methodically shot down with relative ease. Leading the Sixth Company, Ensign von Hobe, age twenty-two and born in Mecklenburg like Ensign von Hobe, steadied his punished fusiliers amid the scorching fires, shouting encouragement in the tumult. Despite caught amid a confusing nightmare of urban combat that was utterly baffling, Lieutenant Colonel Scheffer's feisty von Lossbergers yet possessed plenty of fighting spirit and gamely battled on against the odds.[14]

Peering through the drifting layers of sulphurous smoke and hazy veil of snowflakes descending over King Street and its combatants locked in a mortal struggle, Rall suddenly spied the northernmost elements of the unexpected advance of St. Clair's lone Massachusetts regiment surging up the street from the south just in the nick of time. He, therefore, barked out orders and hurriedly shifted his southernmost grenadiers on his left flank, after having been surprised once again on King Street. As if already facing a hot fire from two directions, north and west, was not enough, Rall was now forced to form his troops to face south in an entirely new direction in a last-minute attempt to parry the newest emerging threat. Out of urgent necessity and while Forrest's cannon fired down King Street and toward their vulnerable rear, Rall's grenadiers on the south now looked down King Street while bracing for the upcoming clash with the rapidly advancing Bay Staters.

With sword in hand, the colonel from Hesse-Cassel then ordered his neatly aligned grenadiers to open up on Paterson's menacing mass of highly motivated New Englanders, who was yet half-obscured by the density of the falling snow. Positioned in a east-west formation across King Street, these southernmost Hessians unleashed a volley, which caught St. Clair's northern-most Continentals, who could see relatively little with the northeast wind and snow blowing in their faces, by surprise. However, the grenadier's volley sailed high in firing downhill at Paterson's Massachusetts troops, ascending ground along King Street, negating the Hessians' advantage of finally benefitting from the storm to their backs and blasting away from a higher elevation. Although not able to see a great deal in the snowstorm, Greenwood described how "They made a full fire at us, but I did not see that they killed any one."[15]

Indeed, the grenadier's blast of musketry erupting out of the snowy haze proved harmless to St. Clair's Massachusetts troops on their lower position down the icy slope on King Street, thanks also to the fact that so many Hessian muskets were unable to function properly in the driving storm. In contrast, a blistering fire of riflemen from the right of Stirling's brigade and Mercer's men, who had pulled back, north and west of Scheffer's fusilier troops, respectively, continued to wreak havoc on the gallant last stand of the von Lossberg Regiment, now positioned just northeast of Rall's heavily pressured grenadiers on King Street.

The deep penetration of the von Lossbergers so close to King Street and so far within Trenton's smoke-wreathed depths only made them more vulnerable to the hail of lead from multiple fires. All the while, additional veteran fusiliers of Scheffer's regiment went down, tumbling into the snow to rise no more. Because the von Lossbergers had not quite pushed far enough west to reach the open expanse of King Street, like Rall's grenadiers just to the southwest thanks to Rall's inspired leadership and their own determination, they were relatively safe from the fire of Captain Forrest's six-pounders and five and a half-inch howitzers that yet dominated the high ground at King Street's head just to the northwest. Nevertheless, Scheffer's fusiliers continued to pay a frightfully high price for their audacity and courage in nearly reaching King Street and in waging an intense, close-range urban battle while confined and surrounded by rows of houses filled with American marksmen, who took no mercy on their opponent exposed in the open streets. Trenton had become a certain death trap.

But this high, if not heroic, sacrifice of von Lossbergers, both officers and enlisted men, was not in vain. Here, just north of Church Alley, this determined defensive stand of the defiant von Lossbergers, whose blood of its most unfortu-nate members was now splattered on their fine scarlet uniforms, just northeast of Rall's headquarters, bought some precious time "to delay and, if possible, to prevent a retreat" that very likely would have ensured either the annihilation or capture of one or even both German regiments. And as equally important just below the position of the von Lossberg Regiment, the disciplined volleys of Rall's well-trained grenadiers also bought additional time to solidify both hard-hit regiments. After Rall's first "full volley" had suddenly poured south and down King Street too close for comfort when it sailed just high over Bay State heads, Major Henry Shelburne, a seasoned commander from Newport on Aquidneck Island in southeast Rhode Island, and now leading the northernmost portion of Colonel Paterson's Fifteenth Massachusetts Continental Regiment, shouted out a set of new orders to his boys.

He now directed his Bay State troops, who were much too close to Rall's southernmost formation of grenadiers thanks to the lack of visibility amid the snow flurries, to fall back and ease south out of deadly range. Also a withdrawal was now absolutely necessary because the Massachusetts regiment's combat capabilities were greatly eroded with many soldiers unable to fire their weapons because of wet muskets and damp black powder. Here, on lower ground farther down King Street south of Pinkerton's Alley after retiring south down the gentle slope that led to the lower town, this popular Massachusetts major then shouted for his Continentals to take off their packs and knapsacks, full of three days' rations and extra gear, in preparation for again soon meeting the Hessians, but only when they were better prepared for tangling with the tough grenadiers in close combat.

Only in his mid-thirties and a gifted graduate (Class of 1759) of the College of New Jersey at nearby Princeton, Shelburne now employed a masterful psychological ploy to inspire these troops in this key situation on the southern flank of Rall's counterattack. These Massachusetts soldiers were convinced that "a braver man never was made" than the tough-as-nails major, and they loved him like a father, despite his strict martinet ways that had created a very good regiment and even better fighting men. At this key moment, Shelburne shouted carefully chosen words to fortify his Massachusetts soldiers' resolve for the next attack north up King Street with the bayonet to meet the Rall Regiment grenadiers once again, but at much closer range: "Now, my boys, pass the word through the ranks that he who is afraid to follow me, let him stay behind and take care of the packs!"[16]

As planned, the major's cleverly calculated taunt made his Fifteenth Massachusetts Continental Regiment boys, including Fifer Greenwood who already possessed a year and a half of experience despite only age sixteen, only more determined to demonstrate their worth to their esteemed commander.

Consequently, the Massachusetts soldiers could hardly wait to be unleashed and led forward by their beloved Major Shelburne in another attack north up the gentle slope and upon the southernmost Rall's grenadiers aligned across King Street near Stacy Potts's house, Rall's headquarters, despite wet powder and muskets that could no longer be fired.

Meanwhile, Washington prepared to hurl larger numbers of Stirling's infantry on the brigade's right down King Street to sandwich Rall's finely uniformed grenadiers between them and the foremost, or northernmost, of Sullivan's troops lower down on King Street, especially after more damage was inflicted upon Rall's grenadiers by withering musketry and Knox's artillery. Indeed, Rall's northern most grenadiers in King Street were fully exposed to the bitter wrath of Washington's most lethal artillery unit, Captain Forrest's big six-pounders and five and a half-inch howitzers. After having watched the Rall Regiment grenadiers overrun their two lost three-pounders in King Street with a shout of triumph that raised their ire, the well-trained Philadelphia gunners blasted away at Rall's northernmost grenadiers deployed and exposed in the open street from the north, while the von Lossberg Regiment made its last stand in a less vulnerable position situated just north of Church Alley and just east of King Street.

Therefore, severely punished by the terrible salvoes of canister and grape from the roaring Pennsylvania cannon, Rall's northernmost grenadiers were finally forced south and a short distance down King Street, grudgingly giving up hard-earned ground now littered with equipment, headgear, and fallen soldiers from across their Teutonic homeland so far away. Thoroughly punished but not defeated, the grenadiers headed south down King Street—the avenue of broken Hessian dreams on this bloody morning—and closer to the foremost, or northernmost, of soldiers of Sullivan's First Division, the Fifteenth Massachusetts Continental Regiment, to escape the leaden storm. Then, rejuvenated by the sight of grenadiers giving ground, Stirling's troops on the Virginia brigade's right renewed the offensive effort down King Street in the hope of driving Rall out of Trenton's principal westernmost thoroughfare for the second time this morning and once and for all.

One lucky survivor of Rall's Regiment, young Private Reuber described the resurgence of Stirling's attackers, thanks to Washington's timely orders, in surging downhill from the north in a determined effort to push the hardfighting Hessians out of King Street. With more Continentals charging out of the howling snowstorm and off the dominant high ground, Colonel Rall quickly shouted orders to shift his regiment to face north to meet the new threat. In his diary, Grenadier Reuber, only age seventeen, wrote of the intensity of this second bitter struggle for King Street's possession, which remained the primary bone of contention, when Washington's soldiers "attacked us furiously [and] Near Rall's quarters there was a barricade of boards and in front of that stood our two company [regimental] cannon [that the grenadier's had captured]. As the Americans were attempting to reach the cannon [to capture them for the second time] we of Rall's Grenadier regiment encountered them, directly in front of Rall's headquarters [and] The fight was furious [and then] The rebels dismantled the barricade and now we lost the greater part of our artillery [once again] and the rebels were about to use them," during some of the morning's most bitter fighting.

At the same time that Rall's grenadiers were raked by musketry from the north by the westernmost of Stirling's Second Division troops, they were simultaneously pressured from the south by the northernmost of the First Division's soldiers, Colonel Paterson's Fifteenth Massachusetts Regiment, of Sullivan's First Division. Like the southernmost of Rall's grenadiers before them, ironically, the foremost (northernmost) soldiers of St. Clair's brigade were about to rely upon sheer force of momentum and weight of impact of their offensive effort, with weapons unable to fire and possessing so few bayonets. Despite these setbacks, Major Shelburne ordered his Fifteenth Massachusetts troops to attack north up King Street. As Private Greenwood wrote: "When we were all ready we advanced, and, although there was not more than one bayonet to five men, orders were given to 'Charge bayonets and rush on!' and rush on we did. Within pistol shot they again fired point-blank at us; we dodged and they did not hit a man, while before they had time to reload we were within three feet of them, when they broke in an instant and ran like so many frightened devils [and] we [went] after them pell-mell."[17]

Once again, the grenadiers on the Rall Regiment's southern, or left, flank on King Street broke eastward just before the Massachusetts Continentals, elated by the sight of running Hessians, reached them. Just northeast of Rall's northernmost grenadiers above Church Ally, meanwhile, von Lossberg Regimental cohesion and resistance were also rapidly breaking down, with spiraling losses and incessant fires raking them from multiple directions. Even some able-bodied common soldiers began to drop out of ranks, dashing east to escape the awful crossfires. In the von Lossberg Regiment alone, four company captains were cut down. And some of the best junior officers of the Rall brigade's finest regiment were hit as well.

After Lieutenant Ernst Christian Schwabe had been struck by a bullet in the thigh while leading the elite Lieb Company, he had been carried out of the hail of bullets to the relative shelter of a nearby tree by teenage Ensign Zengen. Despite his only four years of experience and age of nineteen, Zengen had then rushed back into formation to encourage the Lieb Company's survivors, helping to solidify the last stand just north of Church Ally and northeast of Rall's headquarters. Incredibly, the von Lossberg Regiment maintained not only its discipline but also its cohesion longer than the Rall grenadiers, even while taking severe punishment in the murderous snowbound streets ringed by gun fire and swarming Americans sensing the kill.

In fact, greater adversity and spiraling losses only seemed somehow, in some inexplicable way, to bond and draw the surviving von Lossberg fusiliers closer together, as if by way of a collective survival instinct. Consequently, they continued to stand tall and firm under the merciless pounding: the epitome of a crack regiment's toughness and character rising to the supreme challenge of a crisis situation. Here, the defiant fusiliers gamely faced up to their attackers in the most embattled sector that had been transformed into a pitiless killing ground where more good Lutherans from Germany met their Maker far from home.

However, this once-fine fusilier regiment had no realistic hope of holding its advanced position with so many good men and officers, who were the heart and soul of the von Lossberg Regiment, cut down. Ensign Christian August von Hobe, born in 1743, had taken a bullet through the leg. Leaving a trail of blood splashes in the snow, von Hobe limped eastward through the whistling bullets and falling snow, hoping to escape a nightmare. He eventually made it all the way to Queen Street to gain the safety of the Methodist Church at the corner of Queen and Fourth Streets. Standing before his surviving fusiliers to inspire them to greater exertions, Lieutenant George Hermann Zoll, the Lossberg Regiment's adjutant, fell with an ugly wound in the back.

All in all, nearly seventy von Lossbergers were already cut down amid the scorching cross fires seemingly coming from all directions. Demonstrating a mixture of iron discipline and a fighting spirit that could not be broken, the most diehard fusiliers formed up in protective fashion with fixed bayonets to guard the bullet-shredded colors, clumps of fallen comrades yet alive, and the battered rear of what relatively little was left of Scheffer's proud von Lossberg Regiment. Pressure was now increasing with Lord Stirling's troops, on the brigade's right, blasting away and attacking south down King Street to punish Rall's right flank from the north, while St. Clair's Fifteenth Massachusetts and

Sargent's Sixteenth Massachusetts, from north to south, respectively, advanced north and farther up the slope toward Rall's left flank on the south. With more resistance collapsing and additional dazed soldiers of both Hessian regiments beginning to head east to escape a dying town that had transformed into a tragic graveyard for the Rall brigade's ambitions and its brave followers, these hard-hit Germans, half stumbling in their weariness, horror, and agony, sought to escape the urban combat hell and certain destruction.

But what line of retreat now offered the best avenue of escape amid the closing pincer arms of Washington's double envelopment? By a process of elimination, only one answer remained for the reeling Rall brigade because the Assunpink Creek bridge had been captured by Glover and his Massachusetts and Connecticut troops as reported to Rall by Adjutant Piel. The thirty-four-year-old Piel had been almost killed in having reconnoitered too close to the bridge when he had mistakenly believed that Glover's darkly clad soldiers guarding the Assunpink bridge were Knyphausen troops in the blinding snowfall. Ironically, the stone bridge, which had already served as the escape avenue for so many garrison members this morning, had remained open for only a relatively short time until permanently secured by Glover's swift maneuvering and timely initiative. Therefore, by this time, von Lossberg and Rall Regiment survivors knew that they could not withdraw to the north, south, or west after they had stopped in their tracks during their deepest penetration to the west.

Indeed, south of the struggle raging to new furies along King Street, meanwhile, the heavily pressured Knyphausen's regiment was pushed by Sullivan's First Division troops southeast toward Assunpink Creek. Major Dechow's fusiliers headed for the bridge in an attempt to escape the punishing fire, especially the canister pouring east from the iron barrels of Captain Neil's New Jersey three-pounders. Likewise, Captain Moulder's French four-pounders were also served skillfully by veteran gun crews commanded by the capable captain and his top lieutenants, William Linnard and Anthony Cuthbert, from Philadelphia, and they blasted away at close range. Anticipating the approach of Dechow's command, Glover had positioned some of his most reliable Massachusetts troops, now ready and waiting for the Knyphausen Regiment's inevitable arrival, in good defensive positions around the bridge, effectively sealing off this escape route across the Assunpink. Clearly, Washington's double envelopment and entrapment was becoming more complete, while the bitter end was drawing nearer for the most celebrated German brigade in America.[18]

While Colonel Paterson's Fifteenth Massachusetts troops, St. Clair's brigade, pursued the southernmost of Rall grenadiers first north and then east through the streets with victory cheers that split the frigid morning air, the Sixteenth Massachusetts soldiers, Sargent's brigade, continued to surge farther north up King Street to drive more of the last remaining southernmost grenadiers off the street, which had been named after the English sovereign for which even more Hessians were now dying. Cheering African American soldiers now advanced side by side with Anglo-Saxon and Anglo-Celtic attackers as members of the only Continental regiment of Sargent's brigade, which now pushed up King Street behind Paterson's Bay State men.

Here, in the chaos of close-range urban combat made more surreal by the icy force of the northeaster and eerie half light of a dim December morning, the fiery forge of battle combined with comradeship bonds to now unite black and white soldiers of America more firmly together as one, transcending racial, societal, and class differences, with the hated Hessians having become the sole object of their pent-up fury. Advancing beside his Caucasian brothers-in-arms, Private Jacob Francis charged in the Sixteenth Massachusetts Continental Regiment's ranks, surging through the whizzing bullets and hail of ice pellets that swept body-littered King Street that now looked as if a tornado had raged through it. Like other African American Continentals battling in Washington's ranks, Private Francis felt that he had much to prove this morning to himself, his comrades, and, most of all, the detested Hessians.

This seasoned Continental regiment—the Sixteenth Massachusetts—now consisted of 152 Massachusetts men of Colonel Sargent's old regiment that he had molded into an excellent command. Private Francis, a fortunate survivor of the disastrous battle of Long Island, was only one of Washington's African American soldiers who fought with distinction in Trenton's maelstrom this morning. A proud free black man, twenty-one-year-old Jacob Francis had already served for more than a year in the struggle for liberty. At the first opportunity, he had enlisted in Sargent's regiment at the fishing port of Salem from where so many privateers sailed to wage war against English vessels. Here, in picturesque Salem, once consumed by the mass hysteria of witch trials, Colonel Sargent's Massachusetts regiment had been organized in the fall of 1775. Ironically, Private Francis knew Hunterdon County, New Jersey, quite well, having been born and raised not far from Trenton.

He was the son of a black slave mother and a white father, who was very likely her owner, in the little town of Amwell, around fifteen miles north of Trenton, which had been founded by idealistic German Baptists. After having served five different masters of varying dispositions—some good, some bad—who he had carefully gauged for survival under slavery, Francis had only recently gained his long-coveted freedom. Consequently, the young black Continental soldier from Hunterdon County, where Trenton served as the county seat, now charged up King Street with flintlock in hand amid the fast-moving ranks of Sargent's old Massachusetts regiment to preserve not only his infant nation's independence, but also his own precious freedom. Private Francis was determined that no whites—British, Hessian, or American—would ever dare attempt to take his freedom away again.[19]

Colonel Rall Cut Down

Amid the choking smoke and deafening noise engulfing King Street, Rall was haunted not only by the loss of his two prized three-pounders for the second time on the same ill-fated avenue of death, but also by Lieutenant Piel's earlier searing words that the Assunpink bridge was now held by far too many American soldiers and artillery to push aside. What Washington and his troops were now demonstrating most convincingly was that the Hessians' glory days, as witnessed for one and all to see at Long Island, White Plains and Fort Washington, were no more. Consequently, Rall might well have known that it was all but over by this time, especially after the left, or southern end, of his own grenadier regiment crumpled from the combined pressure of close-range volleys, the spirited charge up King Street by Paterson's Massachusetts Regiment, and especially after having seen so many grenadiers, the best and brightest, cut down in the roaring tempest.

And worst of all for Rall, his surviving men were now even less able to return fire because of their wet muskets and powder, leaving them all but defenseless except for steel bayonets. Meanwhile, after the collapse of grenadier resistance in King Street's southern sector, the tactical situation worsened even more for the northern end of Rall's regiment on King Street, with increasing numbers of soldiers breaking rearward, or east, on their own. Quite simply, these punished grenadiers were no longer able to face the terrible fires of musketry streaming from the open windows of houses, whose second stories, filled with lethal marksmen, overlooked Hessian positions in the snow-covered King Street below.

Nevertheless, the mounted Colonel Rall continued to defy the ever-fickle hands of fate, tough luck, and death all morning. Rall already had been hit by an American bullet, which "annoyed him very much" and "weakened him" with each passing minute. But the bloodstained colonel ignored the pain and blood loss to keep encouraging his grenadiers to fight on against the American tide, while battling against the odds in the bullet- and canister-swept northern sector of King Street. Finally, with so many von Lossberg troops having retired to leave his northern flank on King Street more vulnerable to a blistering enfilade fire and with large numbers of his own southernmost grenadiers likewise retiring east from King Street that left what relatively little remained of the grenadier regiment which was sandwiched by ever-increasing pressure—a deadly closing vise—from north and south, Rall had no choice but to reluctantly give the anguished order for the northernmost grenadier survivors to move east off King Street by way of sheltering Church Alley.

What had been truly amazing was the fact that Rall had come so close to snatching a sparkling victory away from Washington almost at the last minute. Accepting his fate because no hope remained, Rall now sought to retire safely eastward along Fourth Street, one block south of Perry Street, leading to the town's opposite end. With bullets whizzing around him amid the falling snow, Rall planned to escape Trenton and regain his former relatively secure position on the open ground of the little apple orchard. Here, away from gunfire-spitting houses full of American sharpshooters and the nightmarish swirl of urban combat, he believed that he could once again organize and realign his battered units for either a defensive stand or perhaps another counterattack.[20]

Not long after the southern portion of his own grenadier regiment broke from the rippling volley fire and determined charge of Colonel Paterson's Massachusetts troops roared up King Street and north along the lengthy slope, Rall ordered everyone, including just under two hundred remaining fusiliers of the von Lossberg regiment just to the northeast immediately above Church Alley to escape the urban cauldron that had become a hellish deathtrap. While growing weaker from blood loss, Colonel Rall was now largely on his own by this time, after additional experienced officers had been cut down, and with some unnerved subordinate officers having failed to do their duty. But this leadership failure among an increasing number of Hessian officers was understandable given the soaring casualties, especially since the German officer corps which had been cut to pieces by sharpshooters and salvoes of canister and grape. Clearly, both the Rall and von Lossberg Regiments had paid a high price for briefly recapturing the two lost Rall Regiment cannon and regaining their honor. Without the Knyphausen Regiment's much-needed assistance, Rall's final attack all the way to King Street had only resulted in getting a good many excellent soldiers and officers shot down with impunity by expert Pennsylvania, Maryland, and Virginia riflemen.

By gaining a precious toehold on body-strewn King Street in the day's most determined counterattack and briefly recapturing his regiment's artillery, Rall had battled against far too many handicaps to possibly overcome, including too few troops, the Knyphausen Regiment's absence, and the lack of the timely support of his brigade's remaining artillery—the von Lossberg Regiment's two cannon now with Dechow's regiment. Rall's determined bid to not only reclaim the two lost three-pounders and cherished battle flags but also his regiment's reputation, as well as that of his hard-fighting grenadiers, had nearly succeeded. But Rall had not been adequately supported or assisted in his desperate counterstroke to reverse the day's fortunes. In a letter, Richard Henry Lee, Virginia Congressman from Westmoreland County, merely concluded how the "Hessian officers in general behaved infamously in this battle," letting Colonel Rall down at Trenton.[21]

Despite his best efforts, Colonel Rall simply could not keep the tightening arms of Washington's pincers from closing just in time to thwart his most determined offensive effort of the day. In addition, Rall's no-win situation stemmed from the inherent complexities of a bloody battle of attrition amid the chaotic nature of urban warfare for which the Hessians were not trained. Lieutenant Wiederhold, whose Knyphausen Regiment had been mercifully spared, quite by accident, from participating in Rall's desperate counterattack all the way of King Street, fully realized as much. Although guilty in exaggerating Washington's numbers by more than double and in exhibiting personal prejudice against Rall, the hard-fighting lieutenant wrote in his diary how in regard to Rall's final all-out offensive effort to King Street: "What nonsense this was! To try to retake, with 600 to 700 men, a city which was of no value and which had been left ten or fifteen minutes previously, which was now filled with 3,000 to 4,000 enemy, in houses, and behind the walls and fences."[22]

But the high price for Rall's audacious decision to attack straight back into Trenton's fiery center in a desperate bid to reverse the battle's course was not yet paid in full. Not long after Rall gave the painful final order for his surviving grenadiers to retire east, Washington's marksmen increasingly focused their special attention upon the finely uniformed, mounted figure—obviously a high-ranking officer and the most active Hessian leader—before his surviving men just across from his headquarters at Stacy Potts's house. At this time and despite his own pain and blood loss from an earlier wound, Rall offered solace to yet another fallen officer cut down by the incessant bursts of musketry that exploded around him. A sharp-eyed sharpshooter, very likely a western Virginia or Maryland frontiersman of Lieutenant Colonel Moses Rawlings's Maryland Rifle Battalion, Mercer's brigade, took careful aim with a Kentucky, or Pennsylvania, Long Rifle, at the thoroughly exposed Colonel Rall on horseback.

Ironically, in a strange twist of fate, Rall had already earlier defied a good many bullets of these same lethal Maryland marksmen, including western frontier sharpshooters, in leading the sweeping attack up Mount Washington at Fort Washington. In a striking paradox that now came back to haunt him, the veteran colonel had long held American riflemen in contempt. When he had led his grenadiers to victory at Fort Washington, Rall had seemingly possessed with a death wish, which had caused Lieutenant Wiederhold to wonder how he possibly "came off [the field] without being killed or wounded" on that mid-November day along the Hudson. And now, Colonel Rall, riding before his troops, was even more in the open and completely exposed to Washington's sharpshooters, while the jaws of Washington's ever-tightening pincers closed tighter around him. He, consequently, became the top priority of keen-eyed American marksmen, who had long made shooting down Hessian officers their favorite pastime. By his actions, shouted orders that were obeyed instantly, and resplendent uniform, it was clear that the officer mounted on a white horse was indeed the dynamic leader of the Rall brigade.

Somehow yet defying the odds and the hail of projectiles as if wearing an ancient Teutonic charm or amulet to ward off the stream of bullets, Rall yet remained in the open expanse of King Street with the northern section of his hard-hit grenadier regiment. Especially while mounted, the colonel now presented an ideal target, especially from veteran marksmen ensconced in nearby houses, where they had kept their weapons, flints, and powder dry, on both sides of King Street. Peering through the dense flurries of snow and with cold-numbed fingers, an unknown American rifleman slowly squeezed the trigger of his Long Rifle carefully aimed at his prominent mounted target at close range. Sparks from the rifle flint flew just before the marksman's face when it struck the frizzen pan, igniting the powder in a delayed flash. A small burst of flame then flashed through the tiny hole in the breech of the barrel to ignite the powder charge, resulting in a smooth firing of the bullet, which was accompanied by the musket's sharp kick that was cushioned by the sharpshooter's shoulder. Fortunately, the marksman's powder stayed dry.

A round, lead ball from a small-caliber hunting rifle, very likely one fashioned by an enterprising German immigrant gunsmith from Pennsylvania, whistled into Rall's side from close range. With the direct hit, Rall immediately buckled in the saddle in the body's natural response, which indicated to Washington's experienced hunter-marksmen that a serious wound had been inflicted in the colonel's midsection. But Rall did not go down. In excruiating pain, he reeled in the saddle, with his well-trained horse neither plunging nor rearing in fright to throw its rider on the icy ground. Somehow Rall maintained his balance while losing more blood, which mixed with the flow of his earlier wound. Only the colonel's ornate saber dropped on the snowy ground: a symbolic fall of the sword from Rall's hand that seemed to foretell how both the elite Rall brigade and its revered commander were now doomed. Rall cried out to nearby grenadiers that he was been hit. After his many years of experience, Rall, age fifty, most likely knew that his wound was fatal.[23]

As usual, Rall was yet gamely inspiring his grenadiers to the very end. In Major Wilkinson's words, the colonel was struck while "exerting himself to form the dismayed and disordered corps."[24] In a letter, Knox merely penned how, "A Colonel Rawle commanded, who was wounded" in the lead storm.[25] While yet mounted, Rall continued to present a fine target while riding before his grenadiers and dripping blood. Not surprisingly, he was shortly hit by another bullet in the same side. The mortally wounded Rall, who possessed the yet unread note from the German farmer warning of Washington's impending attack in his uniform coat pocket from the previous night, now slumped lower in the saddle. Nearby grenadiers reached up to keep the reeling colonel from tumbling off his horse. Rall was caught in mid-fall before he hit the ground. He was then gently assisted off his steed, which was grabbed by Captain Altenbockhum, who continued to serve with bandaged and bloody head. The captain shortly mounted the colonel's horse to eventually reach his withdrawing von Lossberg comrades.

After lying in pain on the ground for a few minutes, Rall was then assisted up by two grenadiers. Rall was then carried east by his grieving men, who knew a mortal wound when they saw one, toward the haven of the Methodist Church on Queen and Fourth Streets. In passing a fallen, blood-splattered Lieutenant Zoll who possessed a dozen years of faithful service, Rall's compassion rose to the fore when he asked if the handsome lieutenant was badly injured. When Zoll, age twenty-nine, replied that the wound appeared mortal, Rall said, "I pity you."

Here, in the wood-frame church, the suffering colonel was gently laid on a wooden bench, where devout worshipers had only recently prayed for peace on earth. Rall might have felt a certain sense of comfort by the fact that he was now safely in a peaceful house of God, where the cold silence and the relative calm seemed to mock the folly of the battle roaring just outside and the brutal reality that additional Hessians were dying for no gain. King Street had been transformed into a bloody avenue of broken dreams and ambitions for the mortally wounded Colonel Rall and his brigade, which had never before known defeat.[26]

After having suffered heavy losses, faced by multiple blistering fires, especially from the nearby houses on both sides of King Street, and with their inspirational commander cut down, the remaining grenadiers marched for the relatively safety of the apple orchard outside of Trenton.

But the surviving Hessians had to first run yet another gauntlet to escape this urban hell. Rall's westward penetration was so deep into town and so time-consuming that Washington's men to the east had been busy attempting to make sure that Rall's two regiments never escaped the town. In a letter to his wife, Colonel Knox described how "During the contest in the streets measures were taken for putting an entire stop to their retreat by posting troops and cannon in such passes and roads as it was possible for them to get away by."[27]

However, Rall's surviving troops now possessed one remaining open avenue east down Fourth Street (about half way between Front Street and the head of Queen Street), which led out of town and to a country lane (Quaker Lane), parallel to and east of Queen Street and below Dark Lane, that led a short distance north to the orchard. As could be expected, Rall's fall from his horse before his troops eroded morale, signaling the end of all efforts in attempting to hold onto any embattled sector near ill-fated King Street. Grenadier Reuber lamented that the bitter struggle for King Street's possession had to be forsaken. He attributed this final bloody repulse to Rall's mortal wounding and the failure of many junior officers to rise to the challenge of the swirling urban combat: "If he had not been severely wounded they would not have been able to take us prisoners . . . his three regiments of brave men would have disputed every foot of the land. But when he was shot there was not an officer who had the courage to take up the half-lost battle" this morning.[28]

As a respected aide to General St. Clair and not far from Paterson's Massachusetts Regiment on King Street, teenage Major Wilkinson described Rall's mortal wounding that finally broke the back of the last grenadier and von Lossberg fusilier resistance in the King Street sector, when the colonel was "shot from his horse, the main body retired" out of the smoking town that had become a hell on earth.[29]

But in truth the repulse of the final Hessian offensive effort was due much more to a host of factors rather than to the loss of a single man. Most of all, combined with the fact that the hard-fighting grenadiers and fusiliers were unable to return fire because of wet powder and muskets, both regiments had taken a more severe beating, suffering higher losses than in any previous battle. One von Lossberg soldier lamented with anguish how his crack fusilier command suffered more casualties than any Rall brigade regiment, and "lost in this affair 70 men killed and wounded [during] Our whole disaster" at Trenton.[30]

Meanwhile, the fusilier and grenadier's sullen retreat east toward the apple orchard was hampered by the loss of leadership, escalating casualties, and a growing sense of defeatism. However, the vast majority of these withdrawing troops yet maintained a surprising degree of discipline, despite their inability to fire muskets and the severe beating that they had suffered at Washington's hands. However, rather than run the gauntlet of fire in tight formations, some Hessians obeyed the higher calling of natural survival instincts. Therefore, these individuals, dazed by the surreal urban combat, broke out of ranks to seek shelter inside houses, basements, and churches to finally escape the wrath of so many deadly American marksmen.

Most of all, the true reason for Rall's repulse at King Street was the fulfillment of Washington's bold tactical vision of a double envelopment, the closing of the two arms of the pincer movement. Among the onrushing soldiers of the Fifteenth Massachusetts Continental Regiment, of St. Clair's brigade, Fifer Greenwood never forgot how the elated troops charged "after them pell-mell," after the last remaining Rall Regiment grenadiers broke eastward. In pouring north up King Street in a sweeping charge led by Major Shelburne and then eastward in pursuit of the defeated Germans, Greenwood described how: "Some Hessians took refuge in [the Anglican] church at the door of which we stationed a guard to keep them in, and taking no farther care of them for the present, advanced to find more, for many had run down into cellars of the houses. I passed two of their cannon, brass [three-] pounders [of the Rall Regiment that had been momentarily recaptured during the counterattack], by the side of which lay seven dead Hessians and a brass drum [and] I stopped to look at it, but it was quickly taken possession [one of a dozen drums captured this day] by one of our drummers, who threw away his own instrument. At the same time I obtained a sword from one of the bodies, and we then ran

on to join the regiment, which was marching down the main [King] street .
. . . General Washington, on horseback and alone, came up to our major and
said, 'March on, my brave fellows, after me!' and rode off." Finally and most
importantly, Greene's troops (the right of Stirling's brigade) from the north and
Sullivan's troops (Paterson's Fifteenth Massachusetts, St. Clair's New Hampshire
and Massachusetts brigade, and the Sixteenth Massachusetts, Sargent's brigade)
from the south met on King Street, gaining permanent possession of Trenton's
main street now littered with the carnage of hardest fought battle in recent
memory.

Most importantly and in dramatic fashion, the two arms of Washington's
envisioned pincer movement now tightly closed shut on King Street, with the
double envelopment finally becoming a long-awaited reality in this crucial
sector at the most critical moment to hurl back Rall's most determined counterattack of the day.[31] At long last in a most significant merger of the First
and Second Divisions, the two Massachusetts regiments surging north up King
Street now met face-to-face the Stirling's Virginia soldiers pushing south down
King Street from the north.

Private Jacob Francis, the resilient African American soldier of the Sixteenth
Massachusetts Continental Regiment, which advanced north up King Street
just behind Paterson's regiment, described this timely uniting that ensured the
winning of the battle of Trenton and the final verification of the tactical wisdom
of Washington's risky double envelopment, when the surging troops of Greene's
Second and Sullivan's First Divisions finally came together in King Street in
what was perhaps the most dramatic meeting of the American Revolution:
"General Washington [who] was at the head of that street [King] coming down
towards us and some of the Hessian between us and them [and] We had the
fight," before driving the last Rall's grenadiers out of King Street.[32]

Even those Hessians who had secured relatively good defensive positions
were pushed out of their King Street hiding places by fast-moving units like
Paterson's Fifteenth Massachusetts from the south and Stirling's Virginians from
the north. As Knox penned in a letter, "The backs of the houses were resorted to
for shelter [but] These proved ineffectual: the musketry soon dislodged them."[33]

Running the flaming gauntlet, the battered Rall and von Lossberg Regiments
continued to limp east through Trenton, maintaining good order under the circumstances, as if instinctively understanding that safety in numbers—as learned
during ceaseless training—meant staying close together, especially when seemingly surrounded by a howling tide of Washington's encroaching attackers. As

throughout the day, Lieutenant Colonel Scheffer, who had taken command as the brigade's senior commander after Rall's fall, now led not only what was left of his own von Lossbergers, but also the Rall Regiment's bloodied remains during the withdrawal east toward the little apple orchard. Sensing the kill, the emboldened Americans pursued the battered grenadier and fusilier regiments east through the smoke-filled streets, firing and loading on the run. Keeping up heavy pressure, Washington's cheering troops chased Rall's survivors as close as only fifty feet away, leaving a trail of Hessian bodies in the snow along Fourth Street and its environs as a bloody testimonial to their superior marksmanship and aggressiveness.

After reaping success on King Street and leading the way, Paterson's elated Massachusetts soldiers pursued the hard-hit Rall's grenadiers relentlessly through the palls of drifting smoke. Wisely, with the Hessians on the run, the hard-charging Continentals possessed the good sense—or simply obeyed Washington's astute orders—not to stop to engage in the time-consuming job of rooting out individual or small groups of exhausted Germans who had taken shelter in houses, basements, and cellars. Instead, Washington's surging troops simply bypassed these defensive positions, continuing onward in fast pursuit with cheers.

Wrapped in civilian clothes and dirty blankets, the pursing veterans of Bunker Hill, Long Island, and Harlem Heights instinctively knew that they had to keep the pressure up to secure a complete victory this morning. Through the dropping snowflakes, consequently, the animated Americans closely pursued Rall's legendary professional soldiers in fancy blue and red uniforms in a life-and-death race in which the winner would take all.[34] As in no previous battle, Washington now had the Hessians beaten and on the run. But the commander-in-chief's challenges were far from over. Most of all, Washington understood what yet had to be achieved in full: Napoleon's key to achieving decisive success in the art of war, which was the psychological destruction of an opponent's will to resist to force complete submission and capitulation.[35]

On this day of destiny 180 miles northeast of his stately Mount Vernon on the Potomac, to fulfill the requirements of his first battlefield success of the American Revolution, one of Washington's best tactical decisions had been to order the German Regiment and Hand's First Pennsylvania Continental Regiment, of Fermoy's brigade, to "about face" and advance upon Trenton's northeastern outskirts to thwart Rall's earlier bid to gain the Trenton-Princeton Road. Therefore, situated to the left of Stephen's Virginia Brigade, these two fine infantry units, mostly a Pennsylvania attacking force, of Fermoy's brigade were yet in a perfect position to intercept the retiring Hessians struggling east toward the apple orchard. In another case of good timing, Fermoy's troops, with the little-known, aristocratic French general at its head, surged off elevated ground from the northeast in a bid to intercept the withdrawing Hessian troops moving east to escape Trenton's surreal tempest.[36]

No one could have been better chosen for this vital mission of closing the trap on the reeling von Lossberg and Rall Regiments from the north than the tactically astute Colonel Hand. With Fermoy's liabilities in never having led a brigade in combat before, Hand was an experienced commander of outstanding ability. He now fully compensated for what the newly appointed French general, his rookie brigade commander, lacked at this crucial moment. Therefore, Major Wilkinson was not guilty of exaggeration in lavishly praising the key role played by "the brave Colonel Hand" and "his distinguished rifle corps" of expert marksmen, who primarily hailed from the wilds of Pennsylvania's western frontier.[37]

In timely fashion, Hand played a pivotal tactical role in closing the door not only to the escape route to the Princeton-Trenton Road, but also in tightening the noose around the Hessians retiring toward the leafless trees of the apple orchard. In his typical hard-hitting style, Hand led his Pennsylvanians down the snow-covered slope on the double, toward Petty's Run, and straight toward the Hessians streaming out of Trenton and out into the expanse of open ground east of town: exactly where Washington most desired this combative, dependable commander and his veteran Pennsylvania riflemen to be situated at this time.[38]

Meanwhile, as during the arduous night crossing of the Delaware and on yet another one of his finest days as a hard-hitting brigade commander of outstanding tactical ability, Colonel Glover continued to excel southeast of where Rall's final counterattack was repulsed on King Street. After having led his four Massachusetts regiments and one Connecticut unit southeast and parallel to the river in surging through the lower town, he continued to firmly hold onto the little stone bridge across the Assumpink: a tight grip that would not be relinquished today. Not satisfied simply with the bridge's capture to effectively block Rall's southern escape route, Glover had early foreseen what an essential next tactical step was in order to secure a complete victory at Trenton.

Pushed rearward as if with a giant broom by Sullivan's swarming attackers, with Stark and his New Hampshire Continentals yet leading the way, after the Knyphausen Regiment had marched by mistake back down Queen Street and into the lower Trenton, Major Dechow led several hundred Knyphausen Regiment fusiliers and its two three-pounders south in a final attempt to reach the stone bridge to escape Washington's closing trap and Sullivan's wrath. But thanks to Glover's timely initiative of securing the Assunpink bridge, the Knyphausen fusiliers received their second nasty surprise of the day when thwarted by the presence of a good many of Glover's Continental veterans, backed up by Captain Sargent's Massachusetts artillery, ready to greet them at the bridge.

Here, the tactically astute colonel from Marblehead had placed an ample number of veterans in good defensive positions before the bridge and across the elevated terrain along the Assunpink's south bank. Consequently, the thwarted Knyphausen soldiers were forced to turn away from the stone bridge and Glover's sturdy roadblock bolstered by artillery. Major Dechow's fusiliers then pushed straight east, following the Assunpink's north side in an attempt to find a way across the overflowing waterway, hoping to escape by a ford higher up the creek. All the while, the desperate Knyphausen soldiers were raked by scorching fires from two directions: from the west by Washington's relentless pursuers and from the south by Sargent and Glover's mostly New Englanders across, or on the south side of, the tidal creek.

To head off the withdrawing Knyphausen Regiment and acting without orders, Glover hurried the largest part of his Massachusetts and Connecticut brigade eastward on the double quick and parallel to the broad, dark-colored creek. Glover's troops followed the Assunpink's frozen, brush-covered south bank of the rain-swollen watercourse. With keen foresight, Colonel Glover also ordered twenty-three-year-old Captain Sargent, the gifted Harvard graduate (Class of 1771), to hurry two six-pounders east with his onrushing infantry to provide "long-arm" support. Most importantly, Glover was yet in the process of filling a crucial tactical gap for the realization of Washington's double envelopment, accomplishing what Ewing's Pennsylvania militia had failed to tactically achieve by not crossing the Delaware at Trenton Ferry. With his usual skill, Glover extended the southern arm of Washington's pincer movement eastward to broaden the grip of the ever-tightening noose around the Rall brigade.

By this time around five hundred yards below, or south of, the apple orchard just below Petty's Run northeast of town and east of Queen Street, Sullivan ordered his foremost troops, St. Clair's three regiments with Stark still leading the way, to continue advancing east toward the Knyphausen Regiment's rear guard, which now protected Dechow's retreat eastward. Firing and inflicting punishment from the west, these rejuvenated soldiers drove the Knyphausen Regiment's survivors farther toward where the dim winter sun tried in vain to poke through the dark bank of snow clouds. Keeping up heavy, relentless pressure, these onrushing attackers literally herded Major Dechow's troops into a low swampy and underbrush-choked area, now covered in ice and snow but also muddy after having been churned up by soldiers' feet, along the creek's north side east of the stone bridge: a natural trap for these weary, half-beaten fusiliers, who had seen everything turn against them.[39]

All the while, the elated Continentals continued to converge on their outgunned Knyphausen victim, applying steady pressure and inflicting additional damage, both physical and psychological, to steadily erode Hessian combat capabilities and, most importantly, the will to resist, while Washington's net drew tighter. Rall's dying hope of revering the day's fortunes faded even further away, along with the white haze of battle-smoke blowing off and eventually slipping away into nothingness like the loftiest Hessian ambitions for reaping victory and winning glory at the small river town of Trenton.

Running the Deadly Gauntlet

Meanwhile, the battered troops of the Rall and von Lossberg Regiments continued to stumble east through the driving snow between King and Queen Streets. They yet suffered from multiple fires unleashed by Washington's soldiers, including troops advancing on a parallel course through adjoining streets and alleys, and a few emboldened Trenton civilians, ensconced in houses, who continued to blast away at finely uniformed officers. Running the blazing gauntlet of fire, the surviving Hessians eventually gained Queen Street, whose icy openness became the next shooting gallery, proving as lethal as King Street. From the higher ground along the northern part of Queen Street, Hamilton's New York six-pounders belched a blistering fire on the Hessians' left flank, while Captain Moulder's barking four-pounders that had been imported all the way from France fired northward from the corner of Queen and Second Streets into the German's right flank on the south.

Combined with bursts of musketry erupting from Stirling's left from the north and Sullivan's troops from the south and southwest, this sweeping artillery cross fire sandwiched the German grenadier and fusilier regiments in yet another bad fix when they attempted to pass across Queen Street's open expanse. Grenadier Reuber described the horror of attempting to get across Queen Street: "The Americans had seven artillery pieces in position there [but] We had to get through. It was very hard for us, very costly" in attempting to reach the relative safety of the apple orchard.[40] In a jubilant letter to his wife, Knox described the success, writing how, "Finally they were driven through the town and into the open plain beyond."[41] Displaying a sense of empathy for the crack fighting men whom Americans had only recently feared as no other troops on the North American continent, Knox even felt a bit sorry for the plight of the "poor fellows" of the Rall brigade.[42]

Indeed, after streaming east out of Trenton primarily by way of Fourth Street, but also through dark, bullet-swept alley ways, especially Church Alley, which ran perpendicular to Queen Street, the Rall and von Lossberg Regiments followed their three remaining field officers east, after crossing projectile-swept Queen Street and heading toward the final north-south road on Trenton's eastern outskirts, Quaker Lane that intersected Dark Lane above Petty's Run. With the mortally wounded Rall left behind in his agony, the highest ranking surviving Hessian officers yet hoped to move their hard-hit troops back to where Rall's ill-fated counterattack had begun with so much promise among the bare trees of the apple orchard. All the while, Rall's surviving Germans ran a perfect gauntlet of fire pouring forth from Knox's blazing cannon, positioned on high ground just north of Petty's Run, which had been pushed farther south to close Washington's trap. The fact that these two hard-hit Hessian regiments yet retained even a small measure of discipline and cohesion, not to mention fighting spirit, was a high testament to the fusilier and grenadier's high level of experience, resolve, and discipline.

At last, the battered Hessian force of two regiments finally gained a much-needed, but brief, respite upon once again reaching the apple orchard where "they formed in an instant," penned an impressed Knox, after having pushed north a short distance up Quaker Lane. Here, just south of Petty's Run, Rall's survivors soon realized that they were almost as vulnerable as if they had remained in the smoke-filled town. Therefore, with their esteemed brigade commander and so many capable company leaders already having been cut down, the highest ranking surviving trio of the two regiment's field officers met in a hasty conference under the brown branches of a leafless apple tree that offered scant protection from American bullets. By this time, however, the overall situation could not have been worse for the Rall and von Lossberg Regiments: repeatedly repulsed in town, brigade commander Rall now dying a slow, agonizing death, and Washington's advancing soldiers closing in and now descending upon the outnumbered Rall and von Lossberg Regiments in a sweeping, giant "half-moon" that promised to soon engulf, if not destroy, them. Clearly, Washington's double envelopment and the fatal vise of the two pincer arms could be neither slowed nor stopped by this time.

After a hasty conference, therefore, Lieutenant Colonel Scheffner and Major Ludwig von Hanstein of the von Lossberg Regiment, and Major Johann Jost Matthaeus of the Rall Regiment, who was taller than his fellow senior officers and known for his exceptionally "long legs," decided to attempt a break out to escape Washington's tightening noose. They now prepared "to make a hole" through the advancing American formations by pushing northeast and then farther up the Assunpink in a desperate attempt to gain an upper ford and eventually gain the Princeton-Trenton Road by which they could reach the British garrison at Princeton. At this time, Major Matthaeus, nearly age sixty and a professional soldier since a teenager, was yet haunted by the fact that he had in vain urged Rall of the urgent tactical necessity of patrolling Johnson's Ferry to prevent a surprise crossing of the Delaware and attack upon Trenton.

Hoping for the best after having gained the apple orchard, meanwhile, Lieutenant Colonel Scheffer walked down the diminishing fusilier ranks, getting ready to lead the von Lossbergers northeast in a final bid to escape Washington's tightening tactical trap. However, the von Lossberg fusiliers were now out of both time and luck, as an unkind fate was fast catching up with the surviving Hessians. Swarms of Washington's advancing infantrymen and cannon seemed to be everywhere, unleashing additional musketry and doses of death to young men and boys from across Germany.

Even before they could undertake their last bid for freedom, the fusiliers and grenadiers were blocked by the relentless advance of Stirling and Stephen's troops and especially Fermoy's brigade, Hand's Pennsylvania riflemen and the sizeable German Regiment, from the northeast, from right to left, respectively. Most importantly, this powerful array of onrushing veteran infantrymen was backed up by the considerable firepower of Captains Forrest's Pennsylvania, and Hamilton's and Baumann's New York artillery on the north. These well-manned field pieces, mostly three-pounders and six-pounders, were shifted to point a menacing row of iron and bronze barrels toward the southeast, targeting the floundering Hessians in the open space of the apple orchard. Now in advanced positions to complete the process of entrapping the Rall brigade, these experienced American units had extended not only farther south, but also east and closer to the Assunpink's west bank, which turned north from the town's southern end, to ensure that there would be no escape for the two Hessian regiments this morning.

Once again, Forrest and his Philadelphia guns, the six-pounders and five and a half-inch howitzers, were in the right place at the right time, and they opened fire with authority and a renewed fury. Additionally, Captain Moulder's French four-pounders from Philadelphia and other field pieces of Sullivan's Division had been moved to east to Queen Street and beyond. But inflicting the most damage were the artillery pieces that blased away at close range and from higher ground just north of Petty's Run. These well-placed cannon fired on Scheffer's von Lossberg troops fusiliers situated on lower terrain just below the ice-covered watercourse. Unleashed in unison, this combined cannonfire from two directions, north and west, whizzed around the surviving grenadiers and fusiliers, who were exposed on the open ground of the apple orchard "like a swarm of bees."[43]

Consequently, Scheffer's final attempt to escape to the northeast was thwarted hardly before it had begun, with the concentrated fire of Washington's artillery throwing the two boxed-in regiments into some confusion. Artillery explosions erupting around the Hessian ranks caused the two battered regiments to become "mixed together," ensuring the lack of concerted action. Having played their last hand in yet another thwarted tactical gamble, the bloodied fusiliers and grenadiers were now trapped in the apple orchard, just below the frigid waters of Petty's Run that afforded little cover. Once again the Hessians attempted to regroup as best they could in the apple orchard. Here, trapped on relatively low ground and in an exposed position upon which it "rained cannon balls and grapeshot here, and the snow, rain and sleet came constantly into our faces," in Scheffer's words, the severely punished remnants of the Rall and von Lossberg Regiments awaited their grim fate that was now inevitable.[44]

North of Petty's Run, meanwhile, Colonel Hand played the leading role in the final entrapment of the Rall brigade's two best regiments. The young, dashing Marylander Major Wilkinson felt confident because the Hessians had sought in vain to move "up the Assunpink, with the apparent inclination to escape to Princeton [but] General Washington threw the brave Colonel Hand and his distinguished rifle corps [and the German Regiment] in their way," sealing their doom.[45] Hand had been born in a little thatched roof cottage in the small farming village of Clyduff, Ireland, just west of Dublin, on Christmas Eve 1744. The twisting course of Hand's life and even his coincidental birth date (age thirty-two) seemed to have ordained that this hard-fighting Irishman would play a prominent role in reaping decisive victory this Thursday morning.

Even more ironically, Hand's combat prowess and leadership skills had been partly the product of more than half a decade of British Army service. He had served in the Eighteenth Regiment of Foot, or the Royal Irish. Besides the honor and memory of old Ireland, Hand also now battled the Hessians for the defense of his transplanted Lancaster, Pennsylvania, homeland, and wife Katharine, called Kitty. Hand had married "My Dearest Kitty," a young, pretty Scotch-Irish girl, in March 1775, less than three years before. She was the mother of his beloved "Little Sally," who had been born on December 8, 1775. Hand's personal odyssey began when he retired from the Royal Irish, who fought at Lexington and Concord, in June 1774, before taking command of his elite rifle regiment of Pennsylvania frontiersmen. The Irishman's audacious battlefield feats early became the talk of the Continental Army. As written in a recent prophetic letter, Hand fully realized that Philadelphia's "fate must soon be determin'd," and this destiny for America's capital was now being played out the field of Trenton. As revealed in a letter with words that now applied to the climactic showdown at Trenton, Hand had been confident for ultimate success, because "If confidence can be put in a good Cause, and Numbers of as Good Soldiers as I ever saw, we need not doubt success."[46]

Appropriately and to Hand's liking, no American fighting force now delivered more severe punishment upon the boxed-in Hessians with cascading volleys of close-range musketry during their relentless surge south toward the apple orchard than Colonel Hand and his Pennsylvania boys—Washington's best rifle regiment—from the counties of Northampton, Cumberland, Lancaster, Berks, Northumberland, Bedford, and York. These veteran Pennsylvania frontiersmen, consumed by the sheer excitement of the fight that overcame fatigue, fired with a high degree of accuracy. Beside these Pennsylvanians, meanwhile, the Continentals of Washington's German Regiment likewise advanced in high spirits. These Teutonic warriors now blasted away at their fellow countrymen with clear consciences in what had become a bitter civil war among Germans that possessed a host of surreal aspects.

In a sweeping charge from the northeast, from exactly where Scheffer had earlier hoped to escape Washington's rapidly closing trap, to seal the doom of the von Lossbergers and the Rall grenadiers in the apple orchard, Hand's expert riflemen of the First Pennsylvania Continental Regiment could not be stopped. Hand's Pennsylvanians fired small-caliber Long Rifles, while the onrushing soldiers of Haussegger's German Regiment split the air with crashing musketry from their large-caliber smoothbores. Both Continental regiments unleashed a blistering fire along a lengthy front of blazing musketry, exploding in a sheet of flame across the snow-covered slope.

With his well-honed Pennsylvania frontier, where he had been stationed for seven years as a redcoat officer before the revolution, instincts rising to the fore, Colonel Hand knew to keep the pressure on the hard-hit Hessians, who were now completely exposed amid the low ground of the apple orchard. In a futile attempt to defend themselves, the desperate Hessians hurriedly formed up in an U-shaped alignment, with the two regiments poised and facing three sides with bristling rows of bayonets to confront simultaneous threats. Above all else, Hand was determined to continue to advance south to maintain an even heavier and closer fire upon the Rall and von Lossberg regimental soldiers to allow them no respite.

Leading the way as usual, therefore, Hand encouraged his Pennsylvania riflemen farther down the snow-covered slope and toward Petty's Run to deliver punishment at closer range. With only Petty's Run now separating rivals, Hand's veteran marksmen, who could not miss at such a close range despite the blinding haze of falling snow, fired into the defenseless Hessian formation at a distance of only fifty paces. While the acid stench of drifting battle-smoke stinging lungs and mouths, the Americans were able to get so close to their opponents, wrote one German, because "no fire was opened upon the enemy in front of them," due to wet muskets and ammunition.

To the rear of Washington's fast-advancing lines, meanwhile, Knox's cannon of Greene's Second Division continued to be inched south by hardworking gunners to occupy even more advantageous, high ground above Petty's Run and closer to their blue- and red-uniformed quarry exposed in neat ranks on the open ground. By this time, the surviving band of pinned up Hessians in the apple orchard were practically surrounded "by a semicircle of field guns," and hundreds of onrushing, elated Americans, who could now taste a decisive battlefield success as never before. Indeed, Hamilton's two six-pounders had moved south down Queen Street by the New Yorkers and were then turned east to face the two Hessian regiments at close range from the west, while Forrest's four Pennsylvania artillery pieces were aligned on the north and Baumann's three three-pounders to the east.

With the double-lines of Fermoy's and Stephen's Continental brigades, from left to right, rolling south and ever-closer to the hemmed-in Hesssians and with Washington's lengthy formations now dominating the northern horizon above the grenadiers and fusiliers, the battle was beginning to turn into a slaughter. Raked by a torrent of multiple close-range fires, the U-shaped formation of weary German defenders began to crumble, falling to pieces. Once-neat Hessian ranks were transformed into a bloody "disorganized force" that was now doomed. With their quarry hopelessly cornered on the orchard's lower ground just below Petty's Run and with even more Hessian soldiers dropping to a hot, close-range fire that could not be returned because of wet powder, something quite remarkable now happened among the converging line of American soldiers, who were on the verge of their most remarkable victory to date.

Some of the foremost Continentals of Washington's German Regiment, including Colonel Haussegger, whose empathy for his fellow countrymen ran especially deep, suddenly began to have a change of heart. Instead of systematically destroying the almost helpless Hessians or "poor fellows," in Knox's words, standing before them, some Americans began to wonder if perhaps these unfortunate, all-but-vanquished soldiers from mostly Hesse-Cassel, who were about to be wiped out, could be saved from needless slaughter. Even in the heat of battle, some of Washington's German Continentals not only felt sympathy for their seemingly about to be exterminated opponents, but also a sudden sense of compassion.

Meanwhile, other members of the German Regiment, both those men born in Germany and in Pennsylvania and Maryland, were sickened at the sight of the cruel decimation of the two proud Hessian regiments right before their eyes. At close range, the German Regiment's Pennsylvania and Maryland soldiers now witnessed this destruction of helpless grenadiers and fusiliers on the battlefield for the first time with a growing sense of revulsion.

Without orders to do so, therefore, additional numbers of Haussegger's common soldiers now hesitated to slaughter their defenseless fellow countrymen, who were firmly ensnared in Washington's spider web and with no escape. Instead of killing the surviving Hessians without mercy, these compassionate Continentals, who had already seen enough of killing for one day, now either cradled muskets in arms or dropped stocks of their weapons to the snowy ground. With flintlocks soaked and fouled, the Hessians were unable to fire back. They, consequently, were now entirely defenseless, only waiting to die. As Lieutenant Colonel Scheffer explained the cruel fate and dilemma, "None of our muskets could fire any longer." Worse of all for Hessian fortunes, additional guns of Knox's artillery (Forrest on the north, Hamilton to the west, and Baumann to the east), loaded with grapeshot (Forrest) and canister, were steadily pushed closer to the two hapless Hessian regiments trapped in the apple orchard.

Clearly, Washington's wise decision to significantly empower his around 2,400 attackers with eighteen (now seventeen) field pieces, while even Napoleon later operated by the firm principle that "it is necessary to have four guns to every thousand men," (a ratio nearly doubled by Washington) continued to pay more high dividends and just at the right time. Disturbed by the sight of defenseless grenadiers and fusiliers falling to a scorching fire at only fifty feet unleashed by Hand's fast-firing marksmen, who systematically cut down Rall's soldiers with the well-honed ease of shooting turkeys off their elevated roosts on an early spring Pennsylvania evening, an unknown German-speaking member of Washington's German Regiment himself suddenly took action on his own. He shouted out unexpected words in flawless German, calling for his fellow countrymen to surrender to avoid certain annihilation.[47]

Then, in a spontaneous act of mercy amid the gently falling snow, other Maryland and Pennsylvania Germans, who refused to kill any more of Rall's helpless men, likewise picked up the merciful cry in the hope of preventing more slaughter, imploring the Hessians to surrender before it was too late. Then, a chorus of shouts, almost frantic pleas, in both German and English rang out echoed down Washington's ranks and over the windswept apple orchard, calling for the Hessians "to stack their arms and surrender" to prevent a massacre. Perhaps Washington's German Regimental members implored their fellow countrymen to give up in part because of the fear that they would receive no mercy from Washington's much less sympathetic Anglo-Saxon, Scottish, and Irish Continentals, who looked upon these Hessians with far less benevolent sentiments.[48]

Clearly, what was now happening among the rows of bullet-scarred apple trees just below Petty's Run was actually something rather remarkable, rising partly out of the tragedy of a civil war between Germans on American soil. Most significantly, this spontaneous compassionate effort to halt the mindless killing came not from high-ranking officers, but from the humble privates and common soldiers who thought for themselves, especially about doing what was morally right based upon the Bible's moral lessons and not flowery directives or dry, textbook regulations from army headquarters.

Some American historians have recently attributed this unauthorized effort to bestow last-minute mercy on the Trenton battlefield as resulting from entirely unique sets of American cultural values and a more humanitarian New World morality, stemming partly from humanistic revolutionary ideology. But in truth, this relatively rare display of mercy—generally not shown by the most enthusiastic Age of Enlightenment idealists toward Indians—amid the heat of combat in the little apple orchard, located just outside Trenton, was instead sparked primarily by the Hessians' own Teutonic countrymen of Washington's German Regiment and among the Pennsylvania Germans of Hand's regiment: a more valid and less American-centric Old World explanation as opposed to an alleged wholly New World phenomenon of the bestowing of mercy and Christian compassion that was missing in savage wars against Native Americans.

Revealing the complexities of comparable emotional, cultural, and psychological factors, the same empathy among the Maryland and Pennsylvania soldiers of Haussegger's German Regiment, and to a lesser degree among the Pennsylvania Continentals of Hand's rifle regiment, on December 26 also can be seen in the representative analogous words written in a letter by a German American, who returned to the Old World as a dough boy in 1918 to fight against his fellow countrymen on the western front in France during the First World War: "I never know when I might be shooting at one of my own cousins or uncles."[49]

So that the virtually defenseless Hessians would not suffer the tragic fate of so many of his fellow Celtic-Gaelic countrymen, who had been vanquished for generations in their own wars of liberation against Ireland's conquer from England, Colonel Hand, a hard-fighting Emerald Islander of Christian (Presbyterian) faith and compassion, confessed in a letter to his wife back in Pennsylvania how "nothing on earth could Give me Greater pleasure than to embrace my Wife & Child," also played a key role in eventually halting the scorching fire of his Pennsylvania marksmen to stop the slaughter of additional Hessians in the apple orchard.[50]

Chapter IX

Final Drama Played Out in a
Snowy Apple Orchard

However, some cynical Hessian officers yet worried about the prospect of surrendering to these same Americans—they had no idea that they were facing an entire German Regiment which was Washington's largest such unit of more than 370 men—who they had previously treated harshly, especially at the battle of Long Island.[1] After all, Washington's veterans had heard all of the grim stories about the liberal bloody use of bayonets, rough treatment of prisoners, and the rape of New Jersey girls by the evil Hessians. Therefore, Rall's von Lossberg fusiliers and grenadiers, who were all but surrounded in the apple orchard, possessed ample good reason to be apprehensive, even after hearing the first calls to surrender, because some of Washington's soldiers now wanted to exact revenge on the most hated soldiers in America.[2]

But by this time, the outgunned Hessians in the orchard just below Petty's Run really had no choice or alternatives remaining with Washington's formations closing in from seemingly every direction and additional cannon of Knox's Regiment pushed forward within even closer range. In a letter that caught the representative mood among Washington's men, William Hull described with pride how the "Resolution and Bravery of our Men, their Order and Regularity, gave me the highest Sensation of Pleasure."[3]

A former British captain, Twenty-Seventh Regiment of Foot, who had seen duty in occupied Ireland, Major Apollos Morris, a Philadelphia Quaker who now served as a volunteer aide to Washington, realized that the bitter end was fast approaching for these two proud German regiments. Hailing from an old distinguished Irish family which had owned the Fifteenth Century Salem Castle in County Cork, Ireland, ever since the crushing of the 1641 Irish revolt and a patriarchal, freedom-loving Son of Erin, who had resigned from British service to fight for America's liberty, Morris described how by this time: "The only resource left [for the Hessians] was to force their way [and therefore] They did not relish" the prospect of fighting their way through Washington's dense formations of confident soldiers, who possessed plenty of dry powder, securely in cartridge-boxes and powder horns, and whose muskets and rifles were yet operable for the most part.[4]

To Americans long conditioned by so many past defeats that the novel concept of victory seemed almost incomprehensible at this time, it now seemed as if the battle was far from over. If nothing else, the ever-combative Rall brigade was most of all a resilient, never-say-die unit, as only recently had been so convincingly demonstrated by the colonel's final counterattack that penetrated all the way to King Street to momentarily recapture two cannon of the Rall Regiment. In a letter written by Philadelphian Colonel Clement Biddle, a member of the privileged upper class, he described the fate of the Rall and von Lossberg Regiments after "their parties in town gave smart resistance for a while [but then] they passed up the Creek [Petty's Run] bank [northeast] of the [Quaker] Meeting House where they formed and thought we should have had a smart engagement but they were by that time nearly surrounded . . . ."[5]

Perhaps relishing more combat in keeping with his fiery nature, Lord Stirling also expected additional hard fighting to erupt in a final last stand at the apple orchard. As he described in a letter written not long after the battle: "They retreated towards a field behind a piece of wood up the creek [Petty's Run], from Trenton, and formed in two bodies [the Rall and von Lossberg Regiments], which I expected would have brought on a smart engagement from the troops, who had formed very near them, from the back of the wood, with his Excellency General Washington . . . ."[6]

Fortunately, for the surviving Hessians who were most vulnerable in the apple orchard, Haussegger's German Regiment remained in the forefront to the north, and additional sympathetic soldiers in Washington's only Teutonic regiment continued to call out to their fellow countrymen, who were yet being cut down by a murderous fire streaming from Hand's Pennsylvania marksmen, especially the non-Germans, to lay down their weapons. Clearly, this fortunate happenstance of the largest body of Washington's Germans meeting the largest body of Rall's Germans at the exact same time and location at the decisive moment might well have been a key forgotten factor that explained the lack of greater resistance at a time, when the troops of the Rall and von Lossberg Regiments still possessed the bayonet and could use it with a bloody expertise.

Indeed, with the surrender summons in German repeatedly echoing across the snow-lined landscape from officers and enlisted men of Haussegger's regiment, the Hessians felt more assured that these wild-looking men from across America would not inflict a brutal no-quarter policy upon them for past sins, both real and imagined, if they capitulated in the apple orchard.

Therefore, Lieutenant Colonel Scheffer, who had led the von Lossberg Regiment with distinction in capturing strategic Chatterton Hill at White Plains and on other hard-fought fields, suddenly stepped forward from his boxed-in fusilier ranks. He then shouted out in German to Haussengger's troops to verify that the surrender summons was indeed legitimate, attempting to make sure that it had been sanctioned at higher levels and not by mere American privates without authority. Responding to the ringing chorus of calls for submission, Scheffer then formally requested that quarter be shown to his men if they formally surrendered.

Knowing that time was now of the essence, Washington relayed liberal capitulation terms, fearing that Hessian and British reinforcements might now be marching rapidly toward Trenton to reinforce the Rall brigade. Not long thereafter, consequently, a young American officer, riding like the wind, "came galloping up" to Scheffer and his von Lossberg troops, whose aristocratic officers held bicorn hats aloft on sword tips as symbols of at least a temporary submission. Such timely gestures, especially from Hessian officers, had early convinced more adrenaline-flushed and excited young Americans, with loaded muskets and rifles and an eagerness to kill more Germans, to cease firing, saving a good many lives.

Dispatched by Washington, this dashing, young officer who galloped rapidly through the snow as only a planter class and fox-hunting Virginian could ride on a momentous December morning was Lieutenant Colonel George Baylor. The twenty-four-year-old officer was destined to be commended for valor for his sterling Trenton performance. Baylor was one of Washington's most trusted aide-de-camps, who had "to possess the soul of the general," in Washington's words, to be truly effective. In regard to Baylor, Washington had only one complaint. Back in November 1775, Washington wrote how "contrary to my expectation [Baylor] is not in the slightest degree a penman, though spirited and willing." Clearly, Colonel Baylor, or "Mr. Baylor" in Washington's words, was more of a man of action.

Another privileged member of the Virginia aristocracy, like his revered commander-in-chief who personally knew this ambitious young man and his respected, upper-class planter family, including his brother Walker Baylor who commanded Washington's Life Guards in 1777, Baylor was a most promising officer. He hailed from the agricultural community of New Market in western Virginia, nestled in the picturesque Shenandoah Valley, which was safe from the enemy's incursions.

Most importantly for communicating precise details of surrender with Hessian officers, Baylor spoke German because his picturesque valley homeland was populated by many German settlers. Serving as adjutant general on Washington's staff, the debonair Virginian conferred with Scheffer, senior brigade officer after Rall's fall, and Major Johann Matthaeus, who had taken command of the mauled Rall Regiment. Amazingly, no anxious soldier on either side opened fire in this fluid, tense situation, yet half-obscured by the sulphurous smoke drifting through the bullet-pocked apple trees just below Petty's Run. This bright Virginian of high expectations was fated to be badly wounded by a British bayonet through one lung in late September 1778, which eventually proved fatal. The popular Baylor died five years later in the West Indies, where he hoped in vain to recover from the wound's effects.

Loaded with grape and canister upon Washington's specific orders, Forrest and Hamilton's six guns were ready to fire from the north and three New York three-pounders commanded by German-born Captain Baumann were poised to fire on the east. And lengthy formations of veteran Continentals circled around the two Hessian regiments on the north, west, southwest, and east. In this nerve-racking situation, an ad hoc conference took place at the body-strewn apple orchard, while the snow continued to fall softly upon the silent ranks of anxious Americans and Hessians. Tension and anxiety could not have been higher. Speaking both English and German, Baylor offered liberal surrender terms as expressly emphasized by Washington, including fair treatment to all prisoners and good medical treatment for the wounded.

To verify the promise of decent treatment for so many wounded Hessians, Baylor offered to immediately take the confirmed bachelor Captain Altenbockum, of the von Lossberg Regiment, back with him to town to receive medical care from two capable American physicians, including forty-six-year-old Surgeon John Cochran, who was much admired by Washington. From New Brunswick, New Jersey, now occupied by the British, and married for more than sixteen years to the widow of Peter Schuyler, Cochran was a Pennsylvania-born Scotch-Irish immigrant from Ulster Province. He possessed excellent medical experience gained from service as a "surgeon's mate" in the British Army during the French and Indian War.

The widely respected Cochran was also the principal founder and former president of the New Jersey Medical Society. As an able assistant to Cochran, the other American physician at the makeshift Trenton field hospital was the equally competent Dr. Rikker, a private New Jersey physician of German ancestry, who had joined Washington's Army only the night before. By this time, both of these skilled physicians had already saved Lieutenant Monroe's life. Captain Altenbockum, age forty, had suffered a nasty head wound during the doomed counterattack up bullet-swept Queen Street. But Altenbockum had remained in the ranks to lead his fusilier company to the bitter end, continuing to perform exceptionally well.

After additional discussion, while the snow fell through the apple trees and a cold, blustery wind from the northeast cut like a knife, between Lieutenant Colonel Scheffer and Major von Hanstein, born in Obernhof nestled in western Germany's Rhineland and the seasoned commander of the Fourth Company, von Lossberg Regiment, these highest ranking German officers finally agreed to Washington's liberal capitulation terms. Mounting his fleet horse, Baylor dashed off toward Trenton with Altenbockum, now with a bloodstained bandage wrapped around his head and yet mounted on Rall's war horse, to present Washington with the exhilarating, if not unbelievable, news: Scheffer agreed to surrender terms, and two-thirds of the Rall brigade had been systematically eliminated by some of the hardest fighting of the war. Meanwhile, the dedicated captain from Courland was treated by either Cockran or Rikker, or both. Altenbockum eventually recovered from his wound to serve with distinction in the Napoleonic Wars.

Proud officers like Hanstein, with thirty-five years of experience and who had fought so tenaciously to stave off defeat this morning, never before felt a greater sense of humiliation than now at the snow-covered apple orchard just east of Queen Street and about halfway between Fourth Street, to the south, and the Trenton-Princeton Road to the north. Doing what these legendary fighting men had never imagined was even remotely possible, the formerly invincible grenadiers of the Rall grenadiers and von Lossberg fusiliers began to ground arms.

Then, in the most painful act and ultimate display of capitulation for the vanquished Hessians, color-bearers lowered their cherished regimental and company battle flags of silk, now tattered from the torrent of bullets and buckshot. These brightly painted banners, distinguished by the standing "golden lion" of Hesse, would no longer fly proudly at the head of Rall's fierce bayonet charges as so often in the past. The Rall Regiment's beautiful, bluish-green colors dropped to the snowy ground in the final act of submission, while exhausted grenadiers felt a searing anguish not previously experienced. Some of Rall's men shed tears at the painful sight. Proud Hessian officers, who yet grieved at having lost their brigade commander in the bitter fighting on King Street, surrendered under the apple trees, which were now scarred with bullets, canister, and grapeshot that had been meant to kill them only a short time before.[7]

Despite his well-served artillery having played such a key role making this surrender of two crack regiments possible, Colonel Knox could hardly believe the sight, writing in a letter how that after the Hessians "were formed on the plain [of the apple orchard] found themselves completely surrounded [and they] were obliged to surrender upon the spot . . . ."[8] In a letter written only days after the battle, Connecticut-born Captain William Hull described the scenario that resulted in the sweetest of victories for Washington, when the "fire begun on every Side at the same instant, their Main body had just Time to form when there ensued a heavy Cannonade from our Field Pieces and a fine brisk and lively fire from our Infantry [and] This continued but a Short Time before the Enemy finding themselves flanked on every Side laid down their Arms."[9]

With a heavy shower of snow dropping gently over the surrender scene amid the apple orchard just south of Petty's Run to present an eerie, if not slightly surreal, setting, the von Lossberg and Rall Regiment soldiers methodically laid down well-cared for weapons and equipment, which were far superior to those of Washington's men. Overcome by the unbelievable sight of the surrender of two full regiments of the most feared fighting men in America, William Hull admitted in a letter how, "tis impossible to describe the snowy scene to you as it appeared." Indeed, a strange graveyard-like silence dominated the submission scene in the apple orchard, with the Americans looking on seemingly in absolute disbelief, while catching their breath, and yet too tired to celebrate their most sparkling success.

Appearing more like ragged scarecrows than the vanquishers of an elite German brigade, the threadbare victors marveled at the sight of such fine Hessian weapons and fancy accouterments of these legendary fighting men from across the sea. All surrendered German weapons, accouterments, and equipment conformed to the strict regulations of the autocratic Frederick II, who ruled Hesse-Cassel with a tight fist. The principal Hessian weapon, now tossed into the snow, which had unexpectedly played a role in Washington's amazing victory by proving useless in a snowstorm was the smoothbore musket. Other weapons now surrendered included lengthy partizans—essentially a pike weapon—engraved officer's swords, and the long officer's spontoons (that designated rank), which could effectively dispatch American soldiers in close combat.

Sturdy flintlocks, now either thrown down in anger or laid in piles by the grenadiers and fusiliers, were primarily Prussian model 1740 muskets manufactured in Potsdam, Germany. Short, light Jaegar rifles (from which America's Long Rifle later evolved) of large caliber and other pattern muskets, which were made at large arms factories at Suhl on the edge of the mostly evergreen Thuringian Forest, at Herzberg in lower Saxony, and at Schmalkalden, on the Schmalkalde River, were also surrendered. The most fearsome of all these weapons were the Hessian bayonets, including sharp, six-sided implements, which had taken a good many American soldiers' lives in the past. After their hardest-fought battle to date, Washington's weary men must have breathed a great collective sign of relief upon the sight of hundreds of Hessian bayonets, mostly of the "Potsdam" pattern, being tossed in a pile on the snowy ground to ensure that they would kill no more American boys in the future.[10]

While light, drifting layers of battle-smoke yet partly shrouded the final drama, including Baylor and Scheffer's hasty negotiation, played out in the snow-covered apple orchard, Washington was not yet aware of the two regiment's capitulation. Instead, the Virginian's fighting blood was up when he was never closer to his most important victory of his lackluster career as the revolutionary leader of America's Army. He, therefore, was not taking any unnecessary chances this unforgettable morning. Washington feared that the Hessians had only employed a clever ruse in a lengthy discussion of terms to buy time for either the Knyphausen Regiment or reinforcements from Princeton or Bordentown to come to the aid of the Rall and von Lossberg Regiments.

As when an ambitious youth during the French and Indian War, Washington was still caught up in the excitement of battle. After all, Washington had never seen so many enemy soldiers, especially Hessians, on the run before, and the sight was exhilarating for a hard-luck leader, who was seemingly cursed with an excessively long losing streak. Therefore, throughout this morning in directing unit placements and maneuvering his troops, Washington had lingered too near the firing line for a prudent commander-in-chief. Making sure that the artillery was ready and loaded with grape (Forrest's battery) and canister for a possible final showdown from two suddenly resurgent Hessian regiments if they suddenly resumed the offensive, he was now mounted near Captain Forrest and his smoking Pennsylvania guns.

His trusty Irish Catholic aide, Colonel Fitzgerald, who no doubt now wore a crucifix, was by Washington's side, sharing the same dangers with him on this morning of decision as on past battlefields. Eighteen-year-old Major Wilkinson was also mounted with other staff members near Washington, who had presented a perfect target on horseback throughout this morning because of his towering height, sheer recklessness, and bravery. The young Alexandrian described how earlier the commander-in-chief's "position was an exposed one, and he was frequently entreated to fall back, of which he took no notice [and then] He had turned the guns on the retreating enemy," hoping to inflict the maximum damage and force a surrender.[11]

Washington, as if unable to comprehend that he was on the verge of reaping a remarkable success over a much-touted Hessian brigade and his first real battlefield victory of the war, was yet preparing to continue the fight, until Captain Forrest, whose confident Philadelphia gunners stood poised like statues in the snow beside their six-pounders and five and a half-inch howitzers loaded with grape, had ascertained the capitulation through the clouds of sulphurous smoke covering the field. The jubilant Pennsylvanian then shouted to Washington in excitement: "Sir, they have struck" their colors. Hardly believing that such a surrender was even possible, Washington merely responded with a single word in question form that betrayed his disbelief: "Struck?" No doubt with a smile on his face, the dashing Captain Forrest answered in regard to what had been truly unbelievable only a short time before: "Yes, their colors are down."[12]

At long last and after so many bitter setbacks, fortune had finally smiled upon Washington as a battlefield commander in this war of broken dreams and cruelly shattered illusions. A relieved Washington galloped down the snow-covered slope to formally receive the surrender of both regiments. Evidently he met fellow Virginian Adjutant General Baylor on his return. After some of the most intense combat waged almost entirely in a nightmarish urban environment, and as if both sides were too exhausted to continue the bitter contest any longer, the struggle for the possession of Trenton in this sector had finally sputtered to an end just east of town.[13] One highly respected modern historian, Christopher Ward, emphasized the dominance of the urban combat of the battle, which "in detail . . . is indescribable [because the contest] was a grand melee, a great, informal 'battle royal'."[14]

Ironically, perhaps even more shocking to Washington than the sudden surrender of two-thirds of the Rall brigade was the fact that with great "Pleasure observed, that he had been in Many Actions before, but always perceived some Misbehaviour [sic] in some individuals, but [at Trenton] he saw none."[15] Boston-born, Lieutenant Samuel Shaw, a twenty-two-year of Knox's Artillery Regiment, scribbled in his journal without exaggeration, "I think it impossible for any troops to behave better than ours did."[16]

As Washington had first envisioned at his headquarters west of the Delaware both the von Lossberg and Rall Regiments had lost the ability to resist and the will to fight after encroaching American lines had coiled tightly around them like a giant anaconda to squeeze the life out of the will to resist: the tactical fulfillment of Washington's masterful double envelopment. Knowing the extreme importance that the artillery arm had played in determining the battle's final outcome, Lieutenant Elisha Bostwick described the key equation that only highlighted the fact that Washington's artillery had just enjoyed its finest day to date, in sharp contrast to the Rall brigade's artillery that had experienced its worst day: "[T]heir artillery taken [by our troops] they resign'd with little opposition."[17]

Indeed and most significantly, two crack Hessian regiments had been forced to submit largely because of what Washington's artillery had already accomplished in repulsing multiple attacks and overpowering resistance at every point. Survivors of the von Lossberg and the Rall Regiments surrendered only because they were ringed by seventeen artillery pieces, loaded with canister and grape, poised at close range and mostly on higher ground. And hundreds of American smoothbores, loaded with buck and ball, and rifles could have eliminated the survivors of both regiments in short order. Armed with Long Rifles, Colonel Hand's veteran riflemen, including western soldiers with white buck tails angled in jaunty fashion in hats, stood within only fifty paces of their opponents: a most convincing argument to surrender.[18]

Perhaps Colonel Knox, who felt some sympathy for his enemy's plight, best described the totality of the Hessians' no-win situation: "The poor fellows [were] completely surrounded [after] The Hessians lost part of their cannon in the town," and were doomed by Washington's encroaching formations and the rows of cannon surrounding them.[19]

From the Mispillion River country of southern Delaware, Ireland-born Colonel Haslet, although slightly exaggerating the total number of disconsolate prisoners by around one hundred, wrote in a letter how Stirling's troops forced "1000 Hessians" to surrender.[20] Indeed, the hard-fighting Scotsman, who was initially the senior ranking officer at the apple orchard surrender site before Washington's arrival, received the saber of the highest ranking Hessian officer, Lieutenant Colonel Scheffer, who commanded the von Lossberg Regiment before taking overall brigade command after Rall was fatally shot down.[21]

In a December 28 letter, the understandably proud Stirling emphasized his key role without a trace of modesty. As Stirling penned to Governor William

Livingston, his own brother-in-law, how during: "our little expedition to Trenton . . . we made a complete surprise of them [and] I had the honour to make two regiments of them surrender prisoners of war" to his Pennsylvania, Virginia, and Delaware soldiers, who gained a measure of vengeance for losing so many comrades on Long Island.[22]

In waging his own holy war to free his occupied home state, Stirling was New Jersey's premier officer by this time. At the battle of Long Island, one Hessian officer was convinced that this self-styled "lord" with "sword in hand, had forced his people to fight against the King." Stirling was only too familiar with the twisting, ever-unpredictable fortunes of war. He had been captured after having orchestrated one of the war's most audacious charges upon the stone house, held by Cornwallis's legions, on the Gowanus Road during the battle of Long Island on August 27. This aristocratic gentleman who fought Hessians as hard as he drank, Stirling now felt absolute jubilation about the remarkable scene presented to the beaming victors in the apple orchard. After all, Washington's most one-sided victory to date had occurred on Stirling's own home soil of New Jersey.[23]

Since Stirling commanded two Virginia units, the First and Third Virginia Continental Regiments, of his four-regiment brigade, and especially because of the success of Captain Washington's vanguard attack which had captured the Rall Regiment's two cannon on King Street, many Americans, especially Southerners consumed with sectional pride, believed that "the Virginians won Trenton." For what he accomplished at Trenton, Stirling earned a well-deserved promotion to major general in February 1777.[24] Additional regional rivalry was evident in the words of New Englander William Hull, who penned in a letter how "Pennsylvania itself is obliged to acknowledge the Bravery of New Eng'd Troops" at Trenton.[25]

Besides the Virginians, Stirling's other two regiments, one from Pennsylvania and the other from Delaware, reaped more than their fair share of laurels. Colonel Haslet and his First Delaware Continental Regiment had performed magnificently on December 26. A former Presbyterian minister from Ulster Province, Ireland, Haslet emphasized how the entire brigade, and not just the Virginians, had been instrumental in winning the most glorious of victories. In a January 1, 1777, letter to Caesar Rodney, which was one of his last letters before the combative Irishman's January 3, 1777 death at Princeton, Haslet described how Stirling's brigade "had the honor of fighting 1000 Hessians to a surrender."[26]

Although he would "not pass for a Lord in England," as one amused Hessian officer lampooned, Stirling was especially elated by what his tough Continentals had accomplished under his capable leadership. In a strange twist of fate after "the proud Scotsman" had been captured in a hot Long Island cornfield in late August, while waving a flintlock pistol in each hand in attempting to rally his outnumbered troops, Stirling had sought out the highest ranking Hessian officer to surrender his sword to rather than a hated British officer. Stirling had then handed his saber over to General Leopold Philip von Heister, overall commander of Hessian troops in America, when surrounded by a throng of British soldiers. Stirling had surrendered his sword to the German general, suffering the greatest humiliation of his life. Then, he had been roughed up and "treated . . . so badly" by some strong-armed Hessian enlisted men that he sought protection from a high-ranking commander. Stirling, consequently, gained a great measure of personal satisfaction—although he demonstrated no bitterness or vengeance this cold morning—in accepting the surrender of so many downcast Hessians and in receiving Scheffer's ornate saber.[27]

All in all under black, stormy skies, the Rall and von Lossberg Regiment's sullen surrender in the apple orchard was well-deserved payback for the Long Island fiasco, where the Hessians had captured more than five hundred Americans and eleven battle flags, including revolutionary banners embroidered with "Liberty." However, an unexpected, eerie silence yet prevailed over the apple orchard with the unbelievable sight of so many Hessians surrendering, which was almost beyond comprehension to the ragtag Americans.

Then, all of a sudden, the strange spell suddenly broke. Across the open ground surrounding the windswept apple orchard and amid the falling snow, Washington's victorious soldiers unleashed a spontaneous chorus of wild cheering. Sounding and acting almost like crazy men in a spontaneous explosion of pent-up emotions, American soldiers were more than jubilant. Some men even became a bit unmanageable for the first time since embarking upon their greatest challenge more than a dozen hours before, throwing hats into the air and shouting their lungs out. The freezing cold no longer felt so severe as these ragged young men and boys, so often defeated in battle against these same crack grenadiers and fusiliers, shouted themselves hoarse. Back-slapping, hugging, and hearty handshakes rippled down the now-broken ranks, while discipline vanished into thin air. Announcing America's most unexpected and surprising victory of the war, a resounding "Huzza" echoed across the apple orchard and farmer's fields covered in a shroud of freshly fallen snow.

Almost as if yet back in the busy streets of Dublin, at a popular County Cork festival, or along the picturesque coast in Galway, Ireland, perhaps some of Washington's Celtic-Gaelic soldiers, who had been long held in such contempt by the British, briefly danced Irish jigs from their ancient Celtic-Gaelic home-land so far away to celebrate. Half-frozen feet, empty stomachs, and the loss of so many comrades and the humiliating disasters of Long Island, Kip's Bay, and Fort Washington were momentarily forgotten in the joyous celebration. Meanwhile, more pious soldiers, especially New Englanders of strict Puritan backgrounds, said silent prayers to themselves as if back home at the family's pew, giving thanks where it was due for survival. No doubt like Washington, they also offered praise to God for the most improbable of victories to breathe new life into what had been a failed resistance effort before they crossed the Delaware. At long last, young soldiers, including beardless teenagers, nearly barefoot men, and drummer boys, from Massachusetts, Virginia, Pennsylvania, Connecticut, and other states felt a new lease on life for themselves and their infant nation conceived in liberty.

Meanwhile hundreds of benumbed Hessians were practically in a state of shock in experiencing their first defeat at the hands of their most contempt-ible opponent. In consequence, these soldiers who had never tasted defeat were silent and angry in the gathering gloom of the apple orchard, while the Americans celebrated. A deep sense of humiliation overwhelmed these van-quished fusiliers and grenadiers on this most nightmarish of mornings in a strange land far from home. Forced to swallow their pride and relinquish the thought that the American rebellion, unlike in Ireland and Scotland, was all but over, a good many von Lossberg fusiliers and Rall grenadiers became especially bitter, experiencing a shame that cut more severely than the piercing cold. One upset Hessian corporal swore how in no uncertain terms "had not Colonel Rahl been severely wounded, we would never have been taken alive!"[28]

However, Washington himself said it best, because if the Rall and von Lossberg Regiments had not surrendered at this time, then "they must inevi-tably be cut to pieces" by the lengthy rows of muskets and cannon manned by determined veterans, who had refused to believe or admit that they were in fact a vanquished people, after so many 1776 reversals.[29] For the crestfallen Rall Regiment grenadiers and von Lossberg Regiment fusiliers, they now must have wondered about the strange destiny that had brought them to this little, but prosperous, commercial town along the Delaware River, where they had finally met their match in a rawboned, gentleman farmer from Mount Vernon and his band of ragamuffin citizen soldiers, who had indeed followed him to hell and back on December 26.

Chapter X

The Knyphausen Regiment's Submission

About a quarter of a mile directly south of the final capitulation drama played out in the apple orchard where the von Lossberg and Rall Regiments surrendered, around three hundred fusiliers of the Knyphausen Regiment were stunned by the sound of the sudden explosion of wild cheering—the high-pitched kind never heard from Hessian throats on the battlefield—to the north. Because of the blinding snow flurries unleashed by the "northeaster," Major Dechow's fusiliers could not see that far north. But they knew only too well the awful truth of what had happened to their grenadier and fusilier comrades to the north from the sheer length of the loud cheering. Like its two ill-fated sister regiments, the Knyphausen Regiment was also caught in its own particular dilemma, attempting to cross the wide, swollen Assunpink. Making this feat exceptionally difficult for Dechow's regiment was that fact that its members were overcome by exhaustion and its movements were belabored by a mob of camp followers, including the wives and lovers of the men in the ranks.

In addition, now in the Knyphausen Regiment's possession, the Rall brigade's sole remaining two three-pounders, the von Lossberg cannon, became mired in the water and mud of the Assunpink's flooded bottom along the north bank just east of the stone bridge, which was yet held securely by Glover's tough New Englanders. Struggling to free the bronze guns from the swampy ground took much too much time, additionally hampering the attempt of Major Dechow's soldiers to escape Washington's entrapment. Fighting against the odds to avoid a most humiliating end, the Knyphausen Regiment's final gasp for life by escaping south was thwarted not only by the morass, but also because the creek widened into an impassible mill pond just east of the bridge

Therefore, Dechow's regiment was now caught in the natural trap of the muddy swamp beside the swollen Assunpink, sandwiched between an ever-tightening vise of attackers from Greene's First and Sullivan's Second Divisions on three sides: Stirling and Mercer's brigades on the north and northwest, respectively, while St. Clair's New Hampshire and Massachusetts troops followed the Knyphausen Regiment east along the creek's north side from the west. Glover's veterans, who held the Assunpink bridge and the area immediately east, and Sargent's New England and New York brigade were aligned across the high ground below the creek to the south. Therefore, multiple fires raked the slow-moving Knyphausen Regiment from three sides, inflicting additional damage. Facing a dilemma for the first magnitude, Dechow's harried Knyphausen Regiment had no chance to escape south across the Assunpink with the creek's waters so high, especially the wide, deep waters of the mill pond; Glover and Sargent's brigades positioned in lengthy lines below the creek; and the two Massachusetts six-pounders, under Harvard College's young Captain Sargent, which peppered Dechow's command from the south with a vigorous fire.[1]

Meanwhile, Glover, the former ship captain, who consistently performed as well on land as on water, continued to dictate the tactical situation after early surmising that Dechow's fusilier regiment would attempt to push farther east to gain a small ford higher just beyond the mill pond. Not content to having merely cut off the best escape route by blocking the Assunpink bridge on both sides, Glover maintained the tactical initiative. He ordered some of his best men double-quick east along the ridge that ran parallel to the creek's southern bank to gain an upper ford, just beyond the eastern head of the Mill Pond, where the creek narrowed. With flintlocks on shoulders, these hand-picked New England Continentals raced eastward in Glover's initial effort to outflank Dechow's desperate bid to move up the creek and gain a point ahead, or east, of the Knyphausen Regiment on the Assunpink's other side.

After dashing east for about a quarter mile, some of Glover and Sargent's boldest men, including Marbleheaders who possessed no trepidation whatso-ever about entering the Assunpink's dark, frigid waters because of their former hazardous lives at sea, waded out in the raging creek at the mill pond's head. Private John Dewey was one such enterprising soldier, who forded the swollen creek with musket held high. He described how this advanced party of winded New Englanders plunged into the icy waters and then waded "about mid-thigh to cross the creek in order to cut off the enemy's retreat." With their strenuous efforts, these Massachusetts Continentals helped to close the door shut on the Knyphausen Regiment's determined effort to escape east, after gaining the creek's north side to out flank and inflict damage with a hail of fire that raked the fusilier's advance from the east.[2]

Clearly, Dechow's situation on low-lying and underbrush-clogged ground along the creek was becoming increasingly hopeless. The devastating effect of too many good Knyphausen officers cut down and having wasted too much precious time in attempting to free the two von Lossberg guns from the flooded creek bottom, when combined with the fires pouring from front, rear, and both flanks, now left Major Dechow's regiment with even fewer tactical options and less hope for escape. About a quarter mile east of the bridge on the north bank, the Knyphausen Regiment was now practically surrounded by Stirling and Mercer's troops advancing from the northwest; St. Clair's brigade to the west; Sargent and Glover's brigade, with Captain Sargent's Massachusetts six-pounders, firing from commanding terrain, to the south across the creek; and now Glover's advanced detachment of Massachusetts mariners on the east.

By this time and in true flying artillery style, most of Sullivan's guns had already advanced through the icy streets of the lower town and across Queen Street to descend upon the Kynphausen Regiment from the west. Clearly, Major Dechow had no choice now but to entertain the only existing alternative to annihilation: surrender. Additionally, he already realized that the Rall and von Lossberg Regiments had submitted to Washington's swarming soldiers just to the north, losing "their well-earned reputation" in the process. Dechow was now on his own without a prayer, and he knew it.

Indeed, by this time, Captain Moulder's three Philadelphia guns, French four-pounders with loads of canister, had steadily leap frogged east with St. Clair's New England troops through the icy streets of the lower town to gain an advantageous position to hit Dechow's fusiliers from the west with a close fire. Here, just east of Queen Street, veteran New Jersey artillerymen under Captain Neil and his top lieutenants, John Doughty, Thomas Clark, Aaron Clark, and John Vandyke, fired projectiles from their two three-pounders at the beleaguered fusilier regiment. With Sullivan's artillery and rows of muskets and rifles of infantrymen blasting away at such close range, casualties mounted among the hapless Knyhausen fusiliers.

Just north and near the head of the overflowing mill pond, Major Dechow took a mortal wound in the left hip. However, he remained faithfully with his fusiliers. Dechow was determined to share their fate, whatever might come this nightmarish morning. Far from his home and family, Dechow's illustrious military career was nearing its inglorious end amid the clinging mud, futility, and shattered Teutonic hopes along the muddy Assunpink southeast of Trenton and under black, menacing New Jersey skies. With the Knyphausen Regiment under pressure from every side and with the fusilers finding themselves in the same no-win situation that had forced its two sister regiments to submit, no tactical alternatives remained but capitulation by this time.

However, some of Major Dechow's most determined officers, especially Captain Georg Wilhelm Biesenrodt, yet remained defiant. A hulking, distinguished-looking captain, who resembled General Washington in size and with the same inspiring command presence, with more than two decades of service, Biesenrodt was every inch a fighter. As the regiment's senior company commander, the forty-year-old Biesenrodt was determined to continue fighting regardless of the odds.

Consequently, an angry Biesenrodt, with drawn saber and yet full of fight, shouted to Dechow that "we cannot give ourselves up like this." But the mortally stricken major, who also had been badly wounded less than six weeks before in the assault on Fort Washington, understood the folly of attempting to stop the raging tide of so many advancing Americans, bolstered with a disproportionate amount of artillery, on every side. Clearly, the bitter end was drawing near for both this distinguished officer and his proud fusilier regiment along the high-flowing Assunpink. Reeling in pain and after relinquishing command to the regiment's surviving senior captain, the badly bleeding Dechow declared in response to his adamant younger officers, who agreed with Biesenrodt and were determined to continue fighting against fate regardless of the cost, "My dear sirs, do as you like, I am wounded." At least, Dechow, who had served with distinction in the Prussian Army under Frederick the Great and had never surrendered to any opponent before, felt a measure of personal relief. He had spared himself the pain of ordering the surrender of what he loved the most and like an adorning parent: the Knyphausen Regiment. Although suffering from a mortal wound, Dechow now possessed a clear conscience while limping away in pain from his boxed-in command after leaving Captain Biesenrodt in command.

With twenty-six years of solid military experience, Captain Jacob Baum, age forty-four, was not the kind of officer who was easily discouraged, even though "we were the only ones left to fight" by this time. An imaginative, flexible commander of the elite Lieb Company, Baum had long garnered respect and popularity among the enlisted ranks. While Captain Biesenrodt now believed that it was his duty to obey Major Dechow's final wish as senior commander, Captain Baum felt no such binding obligation. Continuing to display initiative in this desperate situation, and hoping to avoid any fate but surrender, Captain Baum was determined to survive and fight another day. Fifty other fusiliers felt the same way, following the irrepressible Baum farther up the Assunpink on their own.

Dashing ahead before their fusilier regiment mired and floundering in the freezing creek bottoms, these desperate men, mostly of the Lieb Company, headed farther up the creek, struggling through flooded low spots, tangles of brownish-hued underbrush, and clinging mud along the north bank. After pushing farther east up the creek and then northeastward as the Assunpink turned and narrowed in that direction—roughly parallel to the Princeton-Trenton Road—and with Baum in front leading the way, this band of determined fusiliers finally reached the upper fording point. Here, the fusiliers prepared to enter the icy waters just beyond the reach of Sargent's Massachusetts, New York, and Connecticut troops to the southwest and Glover's most advanced parties to the south. Those fusiliers who knew how to swim immediately stripped off cartridge-boxes and other cumbersome equipment. They then plunged into the cold waters without knowing its depths or strength of its currents. But the majority of Baum's fusiliers were forced to turn back to the west bank because the swirling tidal water was too deep and they could not swim.

Captain Baum, who knew how to swim, entered the freezing waters and escaped Washington's tightening snare, reaching the steep bank on the creek's other, or east, side. Lieutenant Heinrich Reinhard Hille, twenty-two and from Rinteln, also managed to reach the opposite bank, slipping away in the pale morning light to fight rebels another day. After looking back to the southwest to catch a glimpse of the heart-wrenching sight of ever-increasing numbers of Washington's troops and cannon descending upon the doomed Knyphausen Regiment now trapped on the low ground along the creek, Baum and Hille then dashed across the snowy fields east of the Assunpink with other escapees. Basking in his good fortune, Baum retained his fine officer's saber, honor, and sense of pride, accomplishing what his senior commanders had deemed impossible

After having hurried his confident troops and artillery pieces south and southeast from the apple orchard (the surrender site) and down the snow-covered slope descending toward the low-lying creek bottoms just northeast of the intersection of the Delaware River and Assunpink Creek, Stirling prepared to deal a death blow to the Knyphausen Regiment with his veteran brigade. By this time, Stirling's Virginia, Delaware, and Pennsylvania troops were now aligned for action north of and only forty paces away from the Knyphausen Regiment trapped on the low ground of the Assunpink's bottom. Here, Stirling shouted orders for the hurried deployment of Stephen's Virginia and Fermoy's Pennsylvania and Maryland troops in "two columns with two cannon directly in front," presenting a most formidable front on the north and serious threat to the fusilier regiment's fast-fading existence.

Meanwhile, the never-say-die Biesenrodt was about to embark upon one last gamble. In a final bid to break out of Washington's closing double envelopment, a frantic Captain Biesenrodt led the fusilier regiment farther east parallel to the Assunpink in the hope of fording the creek at a narrow point, the upper ford about a half mile slightly northeast of the bridge, where Baum and his men had escaped Washington's converging tide and tightening grip. However, the ever-vigilant Glover spied Bisenrodt's final bid for freedom in pushing farther east, which was yet unblocked except for a relatively handful of Glover's men, to cross the creek.

Therefore, in a checkmate maneuver, Glover ordered the bulk of his Massachusetts and Connecticut brigade even farther east to follow on the heels of his most advanced detachment on the east, which he had earlier dispatched across the Assunpink at the mill pond's head "in order to cut off the enemys retreat." Because the narrow ridge that paralleled the creek below the Assunpunk was open and the road extended east along the ridge-top, Glover's troops moved faster eastward along more firm ground than the Knyphausen Regiment floundering through the mud, tangled thickets, and flooded low terrain on the Assunpink's north side. After another long sprint, Glover's troops finally poured across another narrow point of the Assunpink about an eighth of a mile east of the mill pond's head, spilling across in large numbers and gaining the north bank. They then maneuvered to the north and turned to face west, effectively blocking the Knyphausen Regiment's escape route, while the hopeful fusiliers yet followed their last fading chance to slip away from Washington's clutches without fully realizing that this opportunity had already passed.

Amid the low-lying creek bottoms filled with ice and snow, the Knyphausen Regiment's head suddenly came face to face with the solid front of Glover's Massachusetts and Connecticut brigade, which had spilled across this narrow point of the Assunpink about one-third of a mile to the bridge's east. The closing tactical trap of the last surviving regiment of the Rall brigade was nearly complete. After advancing farther east, Captain Sargent's experienced Massachusetts gunners, led byLieutenants Isaac Packard, David Preston, and

Joseph Blake, had taken good firing positions on high ground along the creek's south bank, turning their aim northwest to inflict additional punishment upon the front of the hard-luck fusiliers.

In his diary, Lieutenant Wiederhold, who would defiantly refuse to sign a parole paper, described the final entrapment of the fusiliers: "We sought to wade through the water but it was not practical at this point and as two enemy battalions, with four cannons, marched up close in front of us and seized the right flank, which was our only escape, the only possible means of rescue." Indeed, the Knyphausen Regiment was effectively checkmated on the east, thanks to Glover's tactical foresight and timely initiative. Biesenrodt, therefore, ordered his troops to march north away from the raging Assunpink and move inland over the frozen ground. But he soon ran straight into the long lines of Mercer's and Stirling's troops descending upon them from the northwest and north, respectively. Clearly, by having shifted so much infantry, with accompanying well-served artillery, first east and then to the creek's north side, Glover had already eliminated any chance for the Kynphausen's escape. Consequently, the tactical entrapment of the last remaining regiment was now complete.

Sensing an impending meaningless slaughter if additional unnecessary fighting continued, young Major Wilkinson, on St. Clair's staff, boldly walked toward Dechow's fusiliers, emerging on his own from the Continental ranks of St. Clair's New Hampshire and Massachusetts brigade to the west. The ambitious Maryland officer attempted to open negotiations with Captain Biesenrodt. However, Biesenrodt's sense of pride and honor, and that of his legendary fusilier regiment, were now at stake. Not trusting heretical rebels who fought unfairly from behind any cover that they could find and from the safety of private houses, he also suspected an American ruse.

By way of acting interpreter Lieutenant Weiderhold, consequently, Bisenrodt bluntly informed the promising teenager from the gently rolling tobacco country from southern Maryland not to advance any farther, or he would order his fusiliers to open fire. However, the battle-hardened Hessian captain soon softened his hardline stance, coming to his senses while literally looking down the barrels of a good many American cannon. Therefore, Biesenrodt dispatched well-educated Lieutenant Wiederhold, who spoke excellent English unlike himself, to meet Wilkinson to ascertain his exact purpose. No Hessian lieutenant had been more at the forefront of so many key developments in the fast-paced battle of Trenton from beginning to end than Wiederhold. He shortly returned to his hemmed-in fusilier regiment, informing Captain Biesenrodt of the Scotland-born St. Clair's demand to surrender.

While the hobbled regimental commander, Major Dechow, was helped west toward the lower town by two sergeants with a dirty white handkerchief tied to an uplifted musket's end to signify submission, Captain Biesenrodt yet refused to comply. In fact, Biesenrodt earlier informed Captain Baum that he would fight his way out of Washington's snare. A disbelieving Wilkinson then hurriedly reported back to St. Clair, who stood at the head of his mostly New Hampshire brigade west of the nearly surrounded fusiliers, with the resplendently uniformed Lieutenant Wiederhold in tow.

St. Clair, a highly respected Continental brigade commander and a French and Indian War veteran, now learned to his dismay that the Knyphausen Regiment had refused to surrender. Not to be tampered with unnecessarily given his deeply nurtured Celtic hatred of the British imperialism and mercenaries, St. Clair became incensed with the incredible news. The tough Scotsman was stunned by the Hessian defiance when further resistance was futile. Resorting to reason and suspecting that Biesenrodt was only trying to buy time in the hope that reinforcements might arrive, St. Clair informed Wiederhold that all the roads leading out of Trenton were blocked, the fords and bridge across the creek occupied, and, most importantly, that the Knyphausen Regiment was now completely surrounded. Indeed, Stephen and Fermoy's brigades held the ground on the north; Mercer on the northwest; St. Clair on the west; Sargent to the south; and Glover to the east: the ultimate fulfillment of Washington's double envelopment and the thorough closing shut of the two pincer arms from opposite directions.

But St. Clair saved his most forceful argument for last. With the muskets of his New Hampshire and Massachusetts Continentals cocked and his seasoned artillerymen, with nerves taunt and their ears yet ringing from booming guns, about to fire loads of grapeshot and canister at point-blank range from the west, St. Clair presented his most convincing ultimatum that left no more room for negotiation, doubt, or debate in an increasingly touchy situation: "Tell your commanding officer that if you do not surrender immediately, I will blow you to pieces."[3]

No idle bluff, this ominous threat from the fiery St. Clair, who held no outdated romantic notions of a gentleman's war, was immediately backed up in a more convincing manner, when he suddenly ordered his nearby New Hampshire and Massachusetts soldiers to unleash a high, close-range volley from the west. This explosion of gunfire echoed just over the heads of the dumbfounded, if not terrified, Knyphausen Regiment soldiers, who now saw that they were totally at the mercy of hundreds of Americans who seemed about to unleash a good deal of pent-up fury if an immediate capitulation was not soon forthcoming.[4]

Therefore, Captain Biesenrodt finally relented. He sullenly gave up all ideas of attempting to fight his way out of Washington's trap after the arms of Washington's pincer movement had closed shut around the ill-fated Knyphausen Regiment on the low ground north of the eastern end of the mill pond about a quarter mile east of Queen Street. Biesenrodt agreed to discuss surrender terms with St. Clair and Stirling, while Wiederhold served as translator. Desiring to preserve a measure of honor and dignity, the feisty fusilier captain requested that his officers be allowed to keep their swords and his men their personal baggage stored in Trenton.

Scotland-born St. Clair agreed to the request, sealing the ad hoc deal with a firm handshake. Without any hope remaining, the Knyphausen fusiliers, who wore their long hair in queues, threw down their weapons in a huge pile. The tall, pointed miter-shaped caps, with decorative brass front plates, distinguished by the majestic standing Hessian lion, which was the coat of arms of the princely house of Hesse-Cassel, soon became the homespun victor's favorite souvenir. These treasured reminders of Washington's one-sided success on a freezing New Jersey morning were kept as heirlooms in American families for generations.[5]

Lieutenant Wiederhold described the fusilier regiment's final humiliation just southeast of Trenton and located almost directly below the smoke-laced apple orchard in his diary: "We had to follow the other two regiments and surrender as prisoners of war. In so doing, we were able to arrange a sort of capitulation whereby we retained our swords and baggage and the troops their knapsacks [and] General Stirling promised this on his word of honor."[6]

The enthusiastic, free black soldier of Sargent's brigade, Private Jacob Francis, had never seen so many white men humiliated and humbled before in his life, a shock in itself. No doubt, this incredible sight was a hidden delight for Private Francis in a host of complex, almost subconscious ways that transcended a simple sense of righteous patriotism: symbolically an unforgettable scene played out at a Delaware River town near where he had been born and, which had been founded by abolitionist Quakers, who helped to inspire Thomas Paine to likewise devote his energies toward destroying America's "peculiar" institution. And now, this young African American Continental private, wearing little more than rags for a uniform, stood watching the Hessians' supreme moment of humiliation as a jubilant victor of Washington's republican army, which had battled all morning in blizzard-like conditions in the name of something that held very special meaning to Francis: equality. In disbelief, Private Francis described how several hundred "Hessians grounded their arms and left them there" in the downtrodden snow, ending the impressive winning streak of the elite Knyphausen Regiment, which had never previously known defeat.[7]

Meanwhile, Washington continued to ride south over a landscape draped in a layer of freshly fallen snow, galloping past the downcast, mortally wounded Dechow, who limped painfully rearward with a mangled left hip. He continued to be assisted by two faithful fusilier sergeants, who supported and kept him upright. As a sad fate would have it, the major would never see his beloved Ratzeburg again. Dechow was destined to die far from his Teutonic homeland on December 27. At such a momentous time, Washington had no time to stop to exchange words with Major Dechow. Mounted on his favorite war horse, the commander-in-chief hurried forth to ascertain the most recent tactical developments and the exact situation of Rall's last remaining regiment in the low-lying area to the south, where he had heard the final, sharp crackle of musketry from St. Clair's New Hampshire and Masschusetts troops near Assunpink Creek

With the Knyphausen Regiment's final submission, Major Wilkinson, St. Clair's young adjutant, was ordered by the elated Celtic general to carry the astounding news of the last surrender to Washington. Wilkinson mounted his horse and galloped north to inform Washington that the Knyphausen Regiment had finally submitted on the low ground located just above the Assunpink. Washington, now riding south, met Wilkinson near Queen Street's lower end. Here, the aristocratic Marylander from the gently rolling, forested hills and tobacco country of Calvert County informed Washington of the equally unbelievable news of the Knyphausen Regiment's capitulation to close some of the most intense fighting of the war.

Incredibly, a complete victory had been won by Washington for the first time in his military career. To Washington's way of thinking, it was appropriate that a dashing Southern officer reported the incredible news of the winning of the first thorough victory achieved by a much-maligned Southern commander-in-chief, who especially loved his Virginia boys. A beaming Washington shook the hand of the personable young man, who would one day betray the United States. Basking in his proudest moment as a military commander in this war, an ecstatic Washington then shouted to the ambitious Marylander that "this is a glorious day for our country."[8]

Exceeding Washington's fondest expectations, all three regiments of the Rall brigade had surrendered at two different points across an eerie, snow-covered landscape that had now become cherished ground for America: one capitulation on the north and the other one on the south and separated by about a quarter mile, but at nearly the same distance east of Trenton. The Fifteenth Massachusetts Continental Regiment was one of the last commands to belatedly dash into the apple orchard, after having pushed east all the way from King Street. These winded Bay State soldiers, sweating and sucking in the cold air, had not yet learned of the surrender of the Rall and von Lossberg Regiments.

Despite some of Paterson's Massachusetts soldiers "without a collar to their half-shirt [and] no shoes," and with most men possessing few bayonets, wet powder, and soaked muskets, these highly motivated veterans were yet ready for additional combat. Fifer Greenwood recorded how, "After passing a number of dead and wounded Hessians we reached the other [east] side of the town and on our right beheld about 500 or 600 of the enemy paraded, two deep, in a field. At the time we were marching in grand divisions which filled up the street, but as we got opposite the enemy we halted and, filing off two deep, marched right by them, –yes, and as regular as a Prussian troop. When we had reached the end of their line we were ordered to wheel to the right, which brought us face to face six feet apart, at which time, though not before, I discovered they had no guns. They had been taken prisoners by another party and we had marched between them and their guns, which they had laid down."[9]

Amid the handshaking, merrymaking, and back-slapping among the celebrating victors on the snowy ground below the apple orchard with the proud Knyphausen Regiment's demise, none of Washington's men noticed or even cared that Captain Baum and fifty fellow Knyphausen fusiliers, including two officers, had waded across the Assunpink to escape. From the creek's other (east) side and before making for Princeton on the double, these fortunate Hessians watched the humiliating surrender of their proud fusilier regiment just north of the Assunpink. They naturally felt the sting of a "painful mortification" at the sounds of the American's wild celebration, which rang as loudly as clanging church bells over the battle-scarred town of Trenton, while racing across the snowy fields to escape to safety. These fusilier survivors headed for Princeton with the sickening realization that the proud, once-invincible Rall brigade had been thoroughly vanquished by ill-trained citizen soldiers in the most improbable of successes.[10]

Against all expectations of the most respected military leaders on both sides of the Atlantic and in one of the great ironies of fate, the day had been won by a former Virginia militia colonel and a resilient band of desperate, ill-clothed rebels, who had simply refused to accept the fact that they were already vanquished and that their revolution had been all but crushed. Quite simply, "it may be doubted whether so small a number of men ever employed so short a space of time with greater or more lasting results upon the history of the world."[11]

The scope of Washington's most dramatic victory was breathtaking. During the surrender, Lieutenant Elisha Bostwick and his Connecticut comrades of Glover's brigade could hardly believe their eyes because "about nine hundred all Hessians with 4 brass field pieces [were taken while] the remainder crossing the bridge at the lower end of the town escaped [and T]heir Commander Col Rhale [sic] was Mortally Wounded & perhaps 15 or 20 kill'd[, while] our loss [was] only two men kill'd & 2 officers & a few Soldiers Wounded."[12]

Another member of Sullivan's Division, David How, who hailed from the little farming community of Methuen, Massachusetts, located in Merrimack Valley of Essex County and situated on the Merrimack River, of Sargent's New York, Connecticut, and Massachusetts brigade, described in a letter how "we Toock 1000 of them besides [we] killed Some."[13] In a rare letter that revealed a mixture of glee and humor, General Stephen described how "We had a Christmas frolick at Trenton [and] We have killd [sic] & wounded the most of three Regimts [sic] of Hessians" on a day that he would never forget.[14] More specifically, William Hull penned in a letter how in regard to the numbers of Hessian killed and wounded: "1 Col. [Rall] wounded since dead, 2 Lieut. Cols taken, 3 Majors, 4 Capts, 8 Lieuts, 12 Ens'ns, 92 Serg'ts, 9 Musicians, 12 Drums, 25 Servants, 842 Privates, 2 Capt's killed, 2 Lieut's killed, 50 privates, Six Brass Field Pieces, One Mortar and about 1500 Stand of Arms. A large Number of Horses and a vast Quantity of Plunder of every kind."[15]

The hard-fought field of Trenton, especially the town itself, now presented a scene of carnage, destruction, and death. Sickened by the sight, young Orderly Sergeant White, far from his New England home and family, described "my blood chill'd to see such horror and distress, blood mingling together—the dying groans, and 'garments rolling in blood' [and] The sight was too much to hear; I left it soon" to escape the battlefield's surreal horrors.

Clearly, Washington's cannon, rifles, and smoothbore muskets had reaped a grim harvest from the Rall brigade's ranks on this New Jersey morning.

In total, the Rall brigade lost at least twenty-two men killed and another eighty-three seriously wounded, while a good many Hessian soldiers suffered lesser wounds. Three Hessian officers lay dead on the field beside their fallen enlisted men. And along with Colonel Rall, two other officers, Major Dechow and the brave captain shot down in Rall's final counterattack through the town's center by the anonymous lady rebel of Trenton, were mortally wounded. Sixteen Hessian enlisted men and one noncommissioned officer likewise lay dead in the streets, alleys, and fields covered in a soft, white blanket of snow and the scattered debris of a once-invincible brigade and lost opportunities.[16]

Perhaps no soldiers in the ranks were more elated by Washington's one-sided success than the disproportionate number of Irish and Scotch-Irish soldiers, who had been part of the Irish diaspora. A respected member of Washington's staff, Ireland-born Colonel Fitzgerald was one such elated Son of Erin. He eventually took pride in being the cousin of future Irish revolutionary Edward Fitzgerald, an Ireland-born member of a leading aristocratic family, who now served in a British regiment: a painful remainder that, like the Germans, the Irish were also engaged in battling against their fellow countrymen in what was a forgotten Celtic-Gaelic civil war on American soil.[17]

And in regard to both planning at Washington's headquarters and fighting on the field, Scotland-born General Mercer, the former Jacobite rebel, had played a leading role in vanquishing a full German brigade of elite troops. He had already witnessed a Celtic people's revolt crushed at Culloden by superior British discipline, firepower, and generalship. With Irish ancestors on his mother's side, Lieutenant Tilghman, Washington's faithful personal secretary and staff member, wrote in an understated December 27, 1776 letter to his Loyalist father, who he yet addressed as "Honored Sir," how: "About 600 [of the Hessians] run off upon the Bordentown Road the moment the Attack began, the remainder finding themselves surrounded laid down their Arms. We have taken 30 Officers and 886 privates among the former Col. Rahls the Commandant who is wounded."[18]

As an esteemed member of Washington's headquarters "family," Lieutenant Tilghman's tabulation was quite accurate. Indeed, some 653 of the 1,586 total under Rall's command just narrowly escaped Washington's masterful double envelopment. Therefore, more than 40 percent of the Trenton garrison slipped away to fight another day. This wild flight south included entire detachments: the British light horse, the Assunpink bridge guardians, the green-uniformed jaegers commanded by Lieutenant Grothausen, who was destined to receive his death stroke in only a few days, Lieutenant Engelhardt and his surviving Rall Regiment cannoneers, the Trent House detachment under Lieutenant Zimmerman, and a good many German soldiers who had been quartered south of the Assunpink. A number of Hessian musicians—unlike the nine captured musicians who soon formed Philadelphia's first brass band that played patriotic music on the first anniversary of the Declaration of Independence's signing—also escaped the battle along with the Rall brigade's chaplains, who now acquired more reason to give thanks, and medical corps. This flight south had also included a heavy flow of noncombatants: the town's citizens, Hessian wives and children, camp followers, no doubt including ubiquitous prostitutes, and refugee Tory families, who escaped Washington's clever tactical trap to tell their tales of woe to the British upon reaching safety.[19]

Witnessing the incredible sight of Great Britain's most formidable allies humbled at Trenton was an exhilarating, unforgettable experience for Washington's victors. The only regret, if any, for the many Emerald Islanders in Washington's ranks was that these conquered foes were not British soldiers. After the surrender and despite their exhaustion and sore shoulders from the kick of muskets in having fired so many rounds, Washington's men now received their first close-up views of these legendary German professionals, who had spread so much fear across America.

Especially after a hard-fought battle, something strange, but not entirely unexpected, now happened on the field of Trenton. Victorious soldiers suddenly turned into gaping spectators, curious about their vanquished opponent. Groups of Washington's men, with faces smeared in black powder, especially right cheeks, ambled forward in a friendly manner to get a close look at these finely uniformed Hessians, whose reputations for ferocity had proceeded them. In a surprising development, all past bitterness that had been considerably built up within the hearts of these young American soldiers, especially after so many bitter 1776 defeats, faded away like the rising smoke of battle that was gradually diffused northeastward by the winter breeze, leaving no sense of vengeance.

Instead, an unexpected friendliness developed among the Americans toward the vanquished Hessians. An easy flow of conversation even opened up between the prisoners and the German-speaking men of Haussegger's German

Regiment. The zealous Irish volunteer with a good many years of British Army experience, Major Apollos Morris, never forgot how the American soldiers "after satisfying their curiosity a little, they began to converse familiarly in broken English and German."[20]

Curious about these tough Teutonic fighting men, New Englander Lieutenant Elisha Bostwick never forgot his first close-up view of these legendary soldiers from so far away: "They are of a Moderate Stature rather broad Shoulders [and] their limbs not of equal proportion[,] light complexion with a b[l]ueish tinge[d] [and long] hair cued [behind their heads] as tight to the head as possible [and] Sticking straight back like the handle of an iron Skillet. Their uniform blue with black facings [,] brass drums which made a timbling sound [, and] their flag or Standard of the richest black silk & the devices upon it & the lettering in gold leaf."[21]

Likewise, the Hessians were similarly surprised by the sight of the ever-aggressive commander of the New York cannon that had roared so much fury at them this morning, because "at their head was a boy, and I wondered at his youth," wrote one observer about Captain Alexander Hamilton.[22] But certainly most shocking to Rall's defeated men was the sight of so many ill-clad Americans, including soldiers in their thigh-length hunting shirts, the traditional "rustic uniform" of the Continental Army. [23]

Here, about a quarter mile to the south of the apple orchard near the Assunpink where the Knyphausen Regiment had surrendered in an open, snow-covered field, Washington's men were surprised to see that these German soldiers were quite ordinary-looking individuals, and not as they had imagined. They were also shocked to learn that many Hessians were in fact lowly and humble tillers of the soil, carpenters, blacksmiths, and cobblers like themselves. Even the famed blue-uniformed grenadiers of Rall's Regiment were not the much-feared giants as long portrayed by legend and lore to enhance their fearsome reputations. Instead, they were quite ordinary men of only average, and even below average, height, especially when compared to the generally taller Americans. And Rall's grenadiers possessed no lengthy, waxed mustaches of the grenadier tradition. Ironically, the men of the Rall Regiment were clean-shaven like Washington's Continentals, although now with stubbled faces from having had no time for their early morning shaves, thanks to the success of the surprise attack.[24]

Perhaps no one was more delighted in viewing so many captured Hessians than Colonel Glover and his barely 175 Marblehead seafarers. After all, these mariners had earler played a leading role in making Washington's remarkable success at Trenton possible by performing as magnificently on water as on land. Of course, these versatile Massachusetts fishermen, who knew the Grand Banks as well, if not better, than their own home port of Marblehead, had no idea that these captured Germans had seen their prime fishing grounds more recently than themselves during the Hessians' summer 1776 journey across the Atlantic. Not surprisingly, Glover was proud of what he and his Marblehead boys had accomplished against the odds within the past twenty-four hours, especially in regard to the perilous crossing of Washington's entire strike force across the rampaging Delaware. This stocky, pious, and short former ship captain and righteous holy warrior especially detested these Teutonic "mercenary tools of Britain" and the coercive imperialistic powers that they now represented by serving in the British Army.[25]

Unfortunately, surviving Hessians left few first-person accounts of their views of the surprisingly humble, even respectful, American victors at Trenton. However, Rall's men very likely were equally astounded by their first close-up look at these unorthodox Americans, now streaked with black powder stains, thin from malnourishment, and haggard from loss of sleep. However, the sight presented of Washington's men to the Rall brigade's survivors might well have been comparable to the opinions of Hessians who surrendered at Saratoga.

Describing the October 17, 1777 surrender in a letter, one Hessian closely analyzed these hard-fighting New World men from the forests, small towns, and urban centers across America, who risked their lives in the name of liberty, God, and country: "Not a man of them was regularly equipped [and] Each one had on the clothes which he was accustomed to wear in the field, the tavern, the church, and in everyday life. No fault, however, could be found with their military appearance, for they stood in an erect and a soldierly attitude . . . all the men who stood in array before us were so slender, fine-looking, and sinewy, that it was a pleasure to look at them."[26]

But on this freezing morning under the dark, menacing skies, Washington's victors now looked far more like the vanquished than the winners. America's finest soldiers were exhausted, diseased, sickly, and covered with grease, lice, and dirt. Private Greenwood, the spunky, teenage soldier-musician from Boston, "had the itch then so bad . . . and there were hundreds of vermin upon me . . . ."[27]

In part because they were so well-treated and in a gentlemanly manner, especially by Stirling, the cowed Hessians demonstrated relatively little arrogance or excessive pride so common with British soldiers, especially officers, who naturally despised rebels. Not long after the surrender, Greenwood never forgot how the Hessians "seeing some of our men were much pleased with the brass caps which they had taken from the dead Hessians, our prisoners . . . pulled off those that they were wearing, and, giving them away, put on the hats which they carried tied behind their packs. With these brass caps on it was laughable to see how our soldiers would strut" in their new trophies.[28]

Expecting unbearable arrogance and harshness from their captors, the captive Hessians were amazed by the good treatment that they received. As revealed in his diary, Adjutant Piel described how "the rebel Colonel [George] Weedon [who led the Third Virginia Continental Regiment]. To say a little about this man—His lowly origins spoke to his advantage, and thus he won all of our hearts through his friendly treatment toward us [and] General Lord Stirling [also] conducted himself in a very friendly manner toward us [and even] General Washington . . . received us very politely [on December 28] . . . ."[29]

During this dinner held by at his personal headquarters only two days after the battle and attended by the captured Hessian officers, Washington also paid a nice compliment to Lieutenant Wiederhold, a sensitive lover of nature who marveled at the majesty of God's creations and bemoaned the sad plight of African Americans in bondage, in regard to his tenacious delaying action with his band of advanced pickets on the Pennington Road at the battle's beginning. As he recorded in his diary: "With the seventeen men I had with me [on the morning of December 26], I did all that was possible and all that an honorable man could be responsible for doing. Even the enemy, and especially Lord Stirling, who commanded the advance guard, and as a result was engaged with me, added his praise an acknowledgment, which is of special worth [and] When I dined with General Washington he made the pleasant compliment, and expressly asked to meet me in order, as he said, to get to known such an excellent officer in person. He had asked about my name and character and noted such . . . ."[30]

Almost as if entertaining upper-class guests back in his sprawling dining room at Mount Vernon, Washington's sense of Southern chivalry and magnanimity toward the vanquished was manifested in other ways. In his diary, Lieutenant Wiederhold recorded how Washington ordered the captured swords of Hessian officer returned to their rightful owners after they had been eagerly snatched by souvenir seekers in violation of the surrender pact's stipulations.

A thoroughly pleased Wiederhold explained in his diary how General Sullivan "had taken one of our swords and gave his in exchange."[31]

With an uncanny ability to circumvent the military regulations and proper protocol to his officer's consternation, Orderly Sergeant White, the feisty teenage New Englander, was not about to relinquish his most coveted prize from Trenton: "I saw a field officer laying dead on the ground and his sword by him, I took it up [and] It was an elegant sword, and I wore it all the time I staid in the army . . . ."[32]

Astounded by the widespread displays of American generosity and overall decency, Adjutant Piel wrote in his diary how General Stirling "conducted himself in a very manner toward us [and at Washington's formal dinner on December 28] he received us with the words, 'Your General von Heister treated me like a brother when I was a prisoner [when captured at the battle of Long Island], and so, Gentlemen, you shall be treated by me in the same manner'."[33]

What has been overlooked about the story of Trenton was the fact that Washington's amazing success was also a victory of sorts for Ireland and Scotland in the eyes of leading Continental commanders from Ireland and Scotland: Scotland-born Mercer, the survivor of Culloden's slaughter on a grassy Moor; Ireland-born Stark, the resourceful frontier fighter of countless wilderness fights against the French, Canadians, and Indians as the top lieutenant of Major Rogers of Rogers' Rangers fame; Ireland-born Haslet, the former Presbyterian minister, who commanded the elite Delaware Continental troops and one of the few American heroes of the battle of Long Island; the urbane, popular Colonel Hand, likewise born on the Emerald Isle and who had held the advance of Howe's Army at bay at Throg's Neck with only a mere handful of his Pennsylvania frontier marksmen; and the hard-fighting, New Hampshire-born General Sullivan, the son of lowly Irish indentured servants and who had been captured by Hessians at the battle of Long Island.[34]

Most of all, the world, especially England but also Germany, was shocked by the news of Washington's surprising victory and conquest of a full Hessian brigade of legendary warriors. A stunned editor of the *Annual Register*, London, England, was incredulous, reflecting the common prevalent view across Europe and around the world. No one could believe that "three old established regiments, of a people who make war their profession, had laid down their arms after inflicting only twelve [actually less than half that number] casualties on the hitherto contemptible Americans."[35]

With his plans for his long-awaited return to England and his sickly wife now dashed by the success of Washington's brilliant surprise attack at Trenton, Cornwallis was thunderstruck with the news of the Trenton disaster. The aristocratic lord of outstanding military ability wrote with sadness and regret, "I did not think that all the Rebels in America would have taken that brigade prisoners."[36] Even the ever-ambitious Bostonite and president of the Continental Congress, John Hancock, was equally incredulous. Of Irish ancestry, he marveled how Washington's "extraordinary" success at Trenton had been achieved by a motley band of ragged revolutionaries, even though they were "broken by fatigue and ill-fortune."[37]

Ironically, Washington's tactical brilliance that reaped such a remarkable victory has been minimized because of the standard explanation that the Hessian garrison was drunk and hungover from a wild Yuletide celebration: one of the oldest stereotypes and most persistent myths of the American Revolution. Young fifer Greenwood revealed the truth: "It was likewise asserted at the same time that the enemy were all drunk [but] I am willing to go upon oath that I did not see even a solitary drunken soldier belonging to the enemy."[38]

Instead of drunkenness, one often overlooked factor that explained the relatively low American casualties was the shortage of dry ammunition among the Hessians. In fact, the muskets of von Lossberg Regiment members were able to fire by the time of the surrender, according to the frustrated regimental commander, Scheffer. In contrast, Washington's troops were blessed with an "overwhelming numerical superiority of artillery and muskets," especially Knox's eighteen "water-proof" cannon. Indeed, the splendid performance of Washington's artillery "had a tremendous amount to do" not only with the victory, but also with the low American casualties from the battle's beginning to end.[39] In conclusion, Lieutenant Piel lamented how: "Our muskets could not fire any more on account of the rain and snow" unlike the weapons of most Americans. Consequently, there was "Nothing therefore was left to us but to surrender as prisoners of war," wrote an embittered Piel, who hailed from Bremen, in northwest Germany, on the Weser River and not far from the North Sea.[40]

In one of the most forgotten and ironic stories of the battle of Trenton, Rall's own cousin, a Maryland Continental officer and a former cobbler of Washington's German Regiment, Fermoy's brigade, accepted the informal surrender of the mortally wounded Rall, perhaps even acquiring the colonel's sword to keep it in the family. Rall felt some comfort from words spoken in German by his Teutonic relative, who wore the ragged uniform of a Continental, concerned about his personal welfare. Almost all members of the crack Hessian brigade "understood not a word of English." Before he died of his wounds, Rall might have been stunned to hear officers and enlisted men of Washington's German Regiment and other commands, especially those from Pennsylvania, speaking in perfect German as if they were back in the fertile Rhineland, along the picturesque Neckar and Leine Rivers, or in Hesse-Cassel.[41]

Ironically, the feelings and emotions of some German soldiers in Washington's Army were mixed because they had killed their own countrymen at Trenton. Colonel Haussegger deserted Washington's German Regiment, joining the Hessians at Princeton on January 1, 1777, after the town's evacuation. But this veteran German-born colonel acted alone, while hundreds of Germans and German American Continentals continued to faithfully serve in the German Regiment's ranks year after year. Unfortunately, however, the colonel's actions, which resulted in the confiscation of Haussegger's home, business—a hatter's shop—and property in Lebanon, Pennsylvania, by angry patriots, placed a dark stain on the reputation of the hard-fighting German Regiment, which played such a key role in reaping victory at Trenton. Captain Alexander Graydon theorized in regard to Colonel Haussegger: "Thinking that our cause was going down rapidly, he saw no reason" to continue to struggle for America's liberty.[42]

A forgotten factor that diminished overall morale by the time of the battle, Rall's troops at Trenton found themselves in a surreal situation in which Germans had fought and killed fellow Germans in what was essentially a civil war. Beginning at the battle of Long Island in late August, Rall's grenadiers were astounded that among their many American prisoners was a combat unit "mostly composed of Germans recruited in Pennsylvania."[43] Therefore, Hessian soldiers had gradually began to view themselves as engaged in something far more complex and contradictory than simply the usual nasty business of crushing yet another rebellion of rural peasants as in Ireland or Scotland. To their shock, the Hessians discovered that they had been thrown into the midst of a nightmarish civil war against their own people, who had previously migrated to America, including from the very same regions and communities of Germany where they themselves hailed. Consequently, captured Hessians were early astounded by the presence of so many German-speaking American soldiers, who were "men of our own blood," including former comrades who they had served beside in European Wars, wrote one perplexed German in a letter.[44]

Enlightened German intellectuals and liberals criticized the exploitation of their own citizens who were dying in faraway America as mercenaries. Likewise, the inspirational example of the common people of America battling for their liberty bestowed new insights to many German soldiers, who were never exposed to Age of Enlightenment ideology, especially in rural areas, like Americans. Back home, larger numbers of progressive Germans began to condemn a "oriental tyranny" of the despotic ruling princes of the German states.

And the greatest autocratic abuse committed by the petty princes, especially the Landgrave of Hesse-Cassel, was the hiring out their mostly lower subjects from impoverished peasant families to England to wage war against largely middle-class Americans of primarily humble origins for sheer profit that was then reinvested, including in the lucrative Dutch stock market, to reap greater gains. Very little of the profits trickled down to lower-class soldiers' families struggling to survive: a classic case of a rich man's war and a poor man's fight. Consequently, Rall's men began to realize that they had been sent to suppress a free people at a time when Germans possessed little of the same liberty that these Teutonic warriors now sought to deny Americans. Ironically, had the Landgrave not been a cousin of King George, Colonel Rall and troops would never have found themselves at Trenton on the frigid morning of December 26.[45]

Contrary to the stereotype of unthinking pawns, the Hessians in America were not immune to the rise in either liberal thought or egalitarian longings by the time of the climactic showdown at Trenton. Liberty's ample blessings were readily seen by the Hessian soldiers in the New World's seemingly endless prosperity that contrasted with their impoverished homelands, especially Hesse-Cassel. Another little-known factor that also partly undermined Hessian morale at Trenton was a rumor that emphasized the wisdom of personal preservation, rather than fighting to the bitter end on December 26, because the German homeland shortly needed to be defended by these troops: circulating news of the pending "recal [sic] [of] the Hessian troops, for the dominions of the prince of Hesse were invaded by the French king."[46]

By the time of the battle of Trenton, consequently, increasing numbers of Hessians began to realize that they were in fact fighting on the wrong side by opposing basic human progress, freedom, and equality for the common man. And Rall's men had already read or heard about the August 14, 1776 proclamation from the Continental Congress, which sought to "seduce" the Hessians who served on American soil: the "states will receive all foreigners who shall leave the armies of his Britannic majesty in America and shall chuse

[sic] to become members of any of these states; that they shall be protected in the free exercise of their respective religions, and be invested with the rights, privileges and immunities of natives . . . And, moreover, that this Congress will provide, for every person, 50 acres of unappropriated lands in some of these states . . . ."[47]

This powerful appeal that offered the tantalizing possibility of a lower-class German of few prospects rather suddenly becoming a prosperous United States citizen and starting a new life in a bountiful land with a pretty young American girl certainly was an almost irresistible lure to lonely, Hessian farm boys far from home. Such factors, even if only on an unconscious level, played a forgotten role in undermining Hessian morale even before the final confrontation at Trenton.[48]

Chapter XI

A Most Remarkable Victory

At age forty-five, Washington's most surprising and amazing success of his military career to date in achieving his "lucky stroke," in his own understated words, was primarily due to another factor, however. Washington's remarkable victory lay primarily with his brilliant battle plan that would not have been possible without the strength of the commander-in-chief's own moral and spiritual leadership and his fierce determination to reap victory at any cost. He was the only leader in America who could have inspired his troops to do the impossible on December 25.

From deep within himself during the supreme moment of crisis, Washington drew upon his own moral will and religious faith in taking the great risk of deciding to attack a formidable brigade of elite soldiers who had never known defeat. Washington's blitzkrieg assault, a hard-hitting pincer movement or double envelopment, succeeded because it was so masterfully calculated to catch the enemy by surprise and destroy the opponent's will to resist by delivering an overpowering moral, physical, and psychological blow that could not be resisted: the essence of what later became Napoleonic warfare.

But, of course, Washington's tactical plan could not have succeeded without the heightened resolve and determination of his common soldiers, who saw their finest day on this freezing morning at Trenton and rose to their greatest challenge like their commander-in-chief. Never before had American soldiers served with more discipline or with greater determination to succeed than on this single New Jersey morning: qualities attributed directly to Washington's superior leadership qualities, which reached new heights during the arduous Delaware crossing, the long, nighttime march on Trenton, and throughout the furious urban battle that presented a host of daunting challenges. From the beginning, Washington made sure that the battlefield's most strategic points were held by his finest infantry and artillery commands and leaders, matching crucial assignments with the most formidable combat capabilities of his best units.

Like Napoleon, Washington demonstrated an uncanny ability to get his often-defeated troops to perform at a lofty operational and personal level not seen before. In his report to John Hancock, the president of the Continental Congress, on December 27, a thankful Washington summarized without exaggeration: "In justice to the Officers and Men, I must add, that their Behaviour upon this Occasion, reflects the highest honor upon them [and] when it came to the Charge, each seemed to vie with the other in pressing forward, and were I to give a preference to any particular Corps, I should do great injustice to the others . . . ."[1]

Born of sheer desperation at the most desperate of times when another setback could no longer be afforded by America, this stealthy transformation from losers to winners was almost miraculous. Barely three months before at the Kip's Bay fiasco when hundreds of American soldiers fled for their lives without offering even token resistance, including against Hessian troops, and ignoring the Virginian's desperate appeals to rally, a disgusted Washington had thrown his hat to the ground and exclaimed in anguish, "Are these the men with which I am to defend America!"[2]

Most importantly, Washington effectively orchestrated and skillfully utilized his Continentals, state troops, and militia in a masterful balanced manner throughout this vital campaign that simply could not be lost because America's survival was at stake. Even the much-ridiculed militia, especially from New Jersey, rose to meet this seemingly insurmountable late December challenge. And one high-ranking officer of Washington's Army wrote how: "Great credit is due to the Philadelphia Militia; their behaviour [sic] at Trenton . . . was brave, firm and manly."[3]

Yet another forgotten factor that played a part in Washington's amazing victory: the bitter rivalry existing between the British and their German allies. Hessian successes, especially at Fort Washington, had only fueled greater British resentment and jealousy. As revealed in a letter published in a London newspaper: "The defeat of the Hessians at Trenton was primarily owing to a dispute which subsisted between the English and the German troops. Col. Rhall [sic] apprehending he should be attacked by superior numbers, required of lord Cornwallis a reinforcement. Two regiments, under col. Grant [in his cozy quarters at New Brunswick] were detached for the purpose. The English troops showed a reluctance to assist the Hessians [and] They halted for a few hours, during which interval col. Rhall was defeated."[4]

Thanks in part to this ongoing and quite heated rivalry, the redcoat cavaliers of the Sixteenth Light Horse at Trenton took no part in the battle. They early deserted their German allies as soon as they sprang out the wooden doors of the nondescript, two-story Quaker Meeting House, where they were quartered, and "made off on our first appearance," wrote one of Washington's amused officers. The British horsemen then dashed out of Trenton to eventually reach the road leading to Princeton. In fact, these twenty British light horsemen had earlier refused to patrol the area, including the key Delaware River crossings (especially without adequate Hessian infantry support), for fear of ambush. As Rall's only cavalry, consequently, these Britons indirectly played a part in allowing Washington to cross the Delaware undetected and unmolested.[5]

Minimizing Washington's generalship, another popular stereotype developed that sought to explain the systematic surrender of so many crack Hessian troops. Two investigating British captains, not without prejudice, reported to London how the Hessians "behaved indifferently, having an eye to the preservation of their plunder [taken from citizens] more than to fighting."[6] No admirer of his brigade commander, Lieutenant Wiederhold later accused Rall of having launched the final counterattack into the heart of Trenton from the desire to regain the brigade's lost baggage. However, this denunciation—or character assassination in this case—was just another effort to blame Trenton's loss on Rall, who had been determined to recapture his lost guns, flags, and the brigade's reputation, and win the day by launching his final counterattack to King Street. Therefore, like the popular tale of German drunkenness at Trenton, the myth was born that the Hessians had failed at Trenton because of Rall's incompetence, "hot-headedness," and "great rashness" stemming from an excessive concern for their baggage, or plunder.[7]

In truth, Washington's attack was successful because he fully exploited not only the element of surprise but also the physical, mental, and psychological exhaustion of worn, stressed-out German soldiers, who only thought about winning the battle instead of the safety of their baggage. Just before the attack, one Hessian officer at Trenton felt that his troops "can endure no longer" the constant duty and stern demands. In psychological terms, Rall brigade members had expected in vain to spend the winter in a captured Philadelphia rather than in a half-deserted, bleak Trenton, causing Hessian morale to plummet to an all-time low by December 26. In overall terms, Hessian spirits had been partly crushed when they received orders to winter at Trenton instead of at New Brunswick, which was "famous in peacetime for its beautiful women and good Madiera wines." But instead of enjoying good times in a quiet sector and with young ladies, either virgins or experienced, unfaithful wives whose husbands off to war regardless on which side they fought, Rall and his troops soon discovered at Trenton that they were surrounded by an escalating insurgency of a good many angry New Jersey patriots, who possessed plenty of scores to settle with a foreign invader. For the average Hessian soldier, this profound shock resulted from suddenly facing a new kind of war, a full-blown insurgency, and one that they were not adequately prepared to fight.[8]

Additionally deep class divisions resulted in the overall poor performance by the German officer corps at Trenton. After the battle, both upper-class and middle-class officers of the Rall brigade, representing the nobility and their prince, banded together to transform Rall, the man and friend of the common soldiers, into the scapegoat for Trenton's loss. Class fissures had long existed in the upper class officer ranks which partly explained why the Rall brigade failed to function at its best on December 26. Just before the battle along the Delaware, upper-class representatives Dechow and Scheffner, commanding the Knyphausen and von Lossberg Regiments, respectively, had sent a long list of complaints against Rall, a middle-class product, to German headquarters in New York City.

Equally crippling was the fact that the entire Hessian command structure had been severely decimated by disease, death, and wounds. By December 26, top Hessian commanders of the German expeditionary force were either dead, wounded, sick in the hospital, or retired from the most arduous service. Even those experienced commanders who led their units at Trenton were in bad shape: Lieutenant Colonel Scheffer, commanding the von Lossberg Regiment, was so ill that he was lying in a sickbed at the attack's beginning, and Major Dechow, leading the Knyphausen Regiment, had yet to fully recover from previous wounds. Therefore, two of Rall's three regimental commanders should have been in the hospital instead of leading their troops in action during the confused combat that swirled through Trenton's streets.

Other factors explained why Rall was not adequately supported by his subordinate officers at Trenton. Because of sedentary years of garrison duty in Germany, many Hessian officers were in overall poor condition for the challenges of vigorous campaigning in America. Quite simply, the Rall brigade was led by an aging officer corps. In the von Lossberg Regiment, many officers and noncommissioned officers were in their forties and fifties, sickly and even frail, limiting stamina and overall leadership abilities to engage in a lengthy battle under winter conditions. Nevertheless, the officer corps of the von Lossberg

Regiment—more than its sister regiments—rose splendidly to the Trenton challenge, and more so than in any other Rall brigade regiment.

By December 26, this aging Hessian officer corps and their units had been decimated by the ravages of disease during the long summer and fall 1776 campaign. Barely a week before the attack on Trenton, only one hundred men per regiment in the Rall brigade of around 1,400 men were fit for duty. A bitter Grenadier Johannes Reuber charged that no Rall Regimental officer possessed sufficient "courage to take up the half-lost battle" at the decisive moment, after Rall's mortal wounding on King Street. But in fact, this was only primarily the case only after Rall fell mortally wounded, because the overall valor of the German officer corps was fully verified by the long list of officer casualties and well-documented heroics.[9]

However, not only had some officers let Rall down, but also a good many common soldiers failed to live up to their lofty reputations, including the much-touted grenadiers. After all, more than 40 percent of the Trenton garrison, including officers, fled the battle hardly before it began. Instead of the stereotypical hardened professionals of European Wars, the vast majority of the young men and boys of Rall's brigade were actually quite different, contradicting stereotypes that emphasized ferocity and savagery. Upon closer investigation, even the Rall Regiment's grenadiers were much less ruthless Teutonic warriors than has been commonly portrayed by American historians, however.

More of a localized militia unit, with relatively low standards in European terms, than a truly elite (a well-deserved renown earned on America's battlefields) and professional combat command before reaching America's shores, the Rall Regiment consisted of a good many "callow farm lads," who had been conscripted. And contrary to the stereotype, the typical Rall Regiment grenadier lacked imposing height and brawny physicality. In fact, these grenadiers were even smaller in height and size then other soldiers of their own German division in America. Seventeen-year-old grenadier Johannes Reuber was barely five foot tall: the anthesis of the stereotypical fearsome image of the towering professional grenadier. However, Reuber was an average-sized Rall Regiment grenadier, who were even smaller and "much inferior" to other Hessian troops in size.[10]

And, of course, another key ingredient in the equation of the Hessian brigade's defeat along the Delaware was the thorough erosion of combat capabilities during the winter storm. On this bitterly cold morning, Rall's men had been suddenly roused from their deep winter sleep without time to eat breakfast, warm up with coffee or tea, or even put on extra clothing over summer uniforms, which were entirely unsuited for winter conditions. The Hessians' warm winter greatcoats were stored in New York City warehouses with other regimental baggage not yet forwarded to remote Trenton. By this time, even the Hessians' collarless summer uniform coats were worn thin by the usual wear and tear of arduous summer and fall campaign.

Consequently, the Rall brigade troops had attempted to defend themselves and wage a winter urban battle amid Trenton's windswept, snow-covered streets in thin, worn-out uniforms. At the exact time that Washington struck with a vengeance, the German quartermasters were undertaking a belated mission to New York City to secure the brigade's winter clothing. When the Rall brigade first formed up in the icy streets to meet Washington's attack, therefore, the common soldiers of all three German regiments were "destitute of small clothes," in Lieutenant Wiederhold's words from his diary, and lacking in adequate "pants, shoes, [and] shirt[s]."[11]

Every single narrative of the battle of Trenton has failed to take into account that the Hessians, except for officers, were in fact even more ill-clothed for winter combat than Washington's troops in most cases. Ironically, because of so many past successes that had propelled Rall's Hessians all the way to the Delaware, logistical challenges, and with the pesky New Jersey insurgency in full swing, an invaluable stockpile of winter clothing was never forthcoming to the isolated Rall brigade at Trenton from a lengthy train of quartermaster wagons. Washington's soldiers had least made some necessary make-shift preparations and received some belated supplies, including shoes and blankets, from nearby Philadelphia before crossing the Delaware.[12] In the end, what was most remarkable about the spirited performance of the Rall brigade was that it had in fact fought so well and for so long, even though these grenadiers and fusiliers were unable to adequately resist Washington's onslaught with wet weapons and black powder and without winter uniforms.

Washington's Most Decisive Arm, the Artillery

In a letter written to his wife Lucy not long after the battle of Trenton, Colonel Knox described how "His Excellency the General has done me the unmerited great honour [sic] of thanking me in public orders in terms strong and polite. This I would blush to mention to any other than to you my dear Lucy; and I am fearful that even my Lucy may think her Harry possesses a species of little vanity in doing [it] at all."[13] Neither Washington or Knox were guilty of exaggeration, because artillery was crucial to winning the battle.

Thanks to Washington's premeditated decisions, never have so relatively few artillery pieces played such a more important, disproportionate, or decisive role in winning a more crucial battle for American fortunes than at Trenton. Washington demonstrated the wisdom of massed artillery, concentrating all his guns of both divisions at the front, where they played a leading role in securing decisive victory. Quite simply, Washington's "field guns were never better employed" in any battle of the American Revolution. In contrast to the dismal performance of the Rall brigade's six cannon, Knox's seventeen (originally eighteen) guns played a decisive role in forcing the surrender of all three German regiments. All in all, Washington would not have won the battle of Trenton without having brought so much artillery—his own farsighted decision—across the Delaware, or without his aggressive and masterful utilization of his artillery arm in the manner of Napoleon.[14]

Quite correctly, Napoleon famously emphasized how: "It is the artillery that takes places; the infantry can only aid it."[15] This Napoleonic axiom well applied to Washington's brilliant utilization of his artillery arm at Trenton. Perhaps Major George Johnston, second in command of the Fifth Virginia Continental Regiment, Stephen's vanguard brigade, said it best in describing the battle's primary turning point in a letter, when the Virginians attacked down King Street and "pursued to the very middle of the Town, where the whole Body of the Enemy, drawn up in a solid column, kept up a heavy fire with Cannon and Muskets, till our Cannon threw them into confusion."[16]

Another one of the central myths of the battle of Trenton was that the vast majority of the American's rifles and smoothbores were wet and inoperable, and that the conflict that swirled through Trenton's narrow streets and darkened alleys was waged in relative "silence" for a hard-fought contest. However, bayonets were in short supply in Washington's Army, unlike in Rall's brigade. Therefore, the bayonet had not decided the day in the tradition of eighteenth-century warfare. In truth, Washington's soldiers, firing small-caliber balls from rifled bores and buck and ball ammunition from smoothbores, proved far more formidable than the bayonet during combat in a close-range, urban environment, especially after weapons, flints, and firing mechanisms were dried in houses.

But most of all, the American artillery arm largely decided the day, thanks to the dynamic, highly effective leadership team of Washington and Knox and a host of young, capable artillery officers, who performed at their best on the morning of December 26. Washington's aggressive, imaginative, and flexible tactics of early employing flying artillery were an often-overlooked key to his Trenton victory that astounded the world. Far from his native Irish homeland, feisty "Pat" Duffy, Forrest's top lieutenant, and his Philadelphia cannoneers first advanced south down King Street and then east through the snowy streets as flying artillery to inflict greater damage. Likewise, all of Washington's artillery units advanced over wide stretches of ground to play leading roles in applying heavy pressure and eventually forcing all three Hessian regiments to surrender. In a December 28, 1776 letter, Duffy marveled about the decisive role played by Washington's artillery arm. He concluded with a sense of accomplishment how, "We made prisoner of about nine hundred together with the number killed which I cannot exactly ascertain, but we took six brass [bronze] field pieces and a small number of small arms which have been safely carried off."[17]

Irishman Lieutenant Duffy justifiably gloated about the American's capture of the six three-pounders, which represented the largest capture of artillery on the battlefield by Washington's citizen soldiers to date. The tactically gifted Knox, Washington's irrepressible chief artillery commander, who saw his finest day at Trenton and soon garnered a well-deserved promotion to a general's rank, was proven correct in his prophetic December 18, 1776 evaluation of the artillery's supreme importance on the battlefield, which echoed the core elements of Napoleon's tactical thinking, "Great battles are won by artillery," including flying artillery: "In the modern mode of carrying on a war, there is nothing which contributes more to make an Army victorious than a well regulated & well disciplined Artillery, provided with a sufficiency of Cannon & Stores."[18]

From beginning to end, the Hessians were simply unable to withstand the wrath of Knox's cannon during an artillery hell, which "rained Cannonballs and grapeshot," in the words of one of Rall's survivors, smashing morale, young German bodies, and the will to resist to the bitter end. As Napoleon well understood, and as masterfully demonstrated by Washington at Trenton, abundant and aggressive artillery support played a leading role in fortifying soldier morale and fueling fighting spirit, allowing even ill-trained citizen soldiers to exceed expectations.

The Hessians' own superior discipline and training resulted in close order ranks of a tight, linear formation, as so long demanded by officers according to the textbook and regulations in the Prussian tradition, proved to be their undoing in the end. Because of this well-honed proficiency, the Hessians continuously presented the most inviting of targets to Knox's veteran artillerymen, especially when the guns were advanced closer as flying artillery, in all sectors throughout the morning. Thanks to Washington's aggressive utilization of a disproportionate amount of artillery manned by highly motivated veteran gunners, he transformed the Hessians' most celebrated asset into their greatest liability.[19]

Paving the way to victory before the first shot was fired in anger at Trenton, Washington's farsighted increase of his artillery ratio to infantry and his integration of his cannon at the head of brigades and columns to greatly enhance each individual brigade's firepower and overall combat capabilities was all-important in achieving the final victory. The smooth-working and hard-hitting team of Washington-Knox proved highly effective in employing their cannon at the forefront as lethal assault weapons and maneuvering the artillery with unprecedented skill, aggressiveness, and precision. And like Washington, Knox inspired his "brave lads" to victory by personal example by remaining at the forefront, which provided a vital element to success. No wonder that Washington had earlier recommended Knox for a brigadier general's rank to Congress. Like so many others, Dr. Benjamin Rush, now serving as a Continental Army surgeon, was greatly impressed by what he saw in the aggressive leadership style of this gifted, innovative Scotch-Irish commander, who possessed a distinguished Celtic-Gaelic lineage that extended back to Scotland's ancient nobility. As he wrote to Virginia Congressman Richard Henry Lee: "I saw [Knox's] behavior in the Battle of Trenton; he was cool, cheerful and was present everywhere" on the frozen field of strife, animating his young artillerymen to victory by example and displaying inspired leadership qualities.[20]

As planned by employing so much of Knox's artillery—three times more than possessed by the Rall brigade—especially along the high ground at the head of King and Queen Streets, Washington had early largely checkmated not only the Rall brigade's artillery, but also the Hessians' most potent weapon, the bayonet, and their most successful tactic, the bayonet charge. Devastating blasts from the lengthy row of Knox's artillery pieces that Washington, who masterfully grasped the novel concept of massed "long-arm" firepower, had carefully aligned across the high ground ensured that the Hessians could never get close enough to King Street's head to utilize their most effective weapon and inflict maximum damage of their own. In the end, the real key to victory at Trenton was Washington's farsighted and tactically astute Napoleon-like decision to transport all of his artillery—eighteen guns—across the Delaware and then to divide his field pieces equally between each arm (or division) of the pincers of his masterful double envelopment.

These wise, farsighted decisions, including having no artillery reserve that would have kept guns idle and useless at the battle's beginning, allowed him the opportunity to early deploy all of his artillery into action, to mass his most effective guns on the most commanding terrain, to concentrate his artillery firepower to maximize his own strength, and to minimize his opponent's strengths, both defensive or offensive, while also negating the firepower of the Rall brigade's six artillery pieces. Throughout the morning with Washington's troops striking from two directions, therefore, Rall was unable to concentrate all of his infantry and artillery at the most advantageous points for maximum benefit unlike Washington.

Indeed, Washington's artillery had been early and effectively placed in action in the best strategic positions along the high ground to maximize not only the element of surprise, but also to unleash a concentrated firepower to prevent a successful counterattack that might have swept the American guns off their commanding perch to reverse the battle's entire course. Then, like the master artilleryman Napoleon and predating some of the finest artillery tactical lessons of the Napoleonic Wars that allowed the artillery arm to so thoroughly dominate the early nineteenth-century battlefield, the dual concepts of concentrated artillery and then flying artillery allowed Washington to not only strike early, but also to maintain heavy pressure with a forward, close-range fire in a modern way not previously seen on a Revolutionary War battlefield.

To reap one of the war's most unexpected victories in relatively short order, Washington had not only embraced classic tactics of insurgency and partisan warfare, but also some of the most successful Napoleonic concepts of aggressive artillery utilization on the battlefield, especially the novel concept of flying artillery: a masterful blend of both past and future ways of waging war, which played a decisive role in Washington's remarkable success at Trenton.[21]

With the irrepressible Knox by his side and playing a leading role not only in orchestrating the Delaware crossing but also in securing victory at Trenton, Washington could not have possibly benefitted more from the contributions of his able top artillery lieutenant. As he had prophetically written to his wife, the enchanting, Boston-born Lucy, after so many humiliating defeats around New York City, a philosophical Knox had been correct not only about the important role that his artillery shortly played at Trenton, but also about the fact that: "One or two drubbings will be of service to us; and one defeat to the enemy, ruin."[22] On the field of Trenton, the "entire course of the war had been changed [and]Knox and his gunners had contributed mightily, not only to two small victories, but also to the making of an army and a nation."[23] Most of all in tactical terms, Washington's "victory demonstrated how effective the use of mobile field guns could be in leading an assault [as in] a modern war with guns ahead of columns [and] this strategy was the same one that Napoleon" depended upon for success across the breath of Europe.[24]

And as part of his daring plan to attack Trenton, Washington had increased his artillery arm by one-fourth with the addition of the six captured cannon, thanks to victory at Trenton. These "double fortified Brass [bronze] three pounders" made a timely addition to Knox's existing eighteen cannon, and in fact were the "most prized" new addition to considerably strengthen the army's capabilities.[25] Elated over what his Pennsylvania field pieces had accomplished this morning on New Jersey soil, Captain Forrest wrote with much pride in a letter of "defeating the Brass Caps and Crous coups" at Trenton.[26]

Despite his success, Colonel Knox was not basking in his finest day to date. Instead, he was yet haunted by the savagery and horror of the urban combat that he had witnessed. In a letter to his wife, the sensitive "Harry" Knox described his innermost feelings that ran deep: "The attack of Trenton was a most horrid scene to the poor inhabitants. War, my Lucy, is not a humane trade, and the man who follows [it] as such will meet with his proper demerits in another world."[27]

Washington's Improbable Victory

Perhaps one of Washington's staff officers best summarized Washington's masterstroke at Trenton in only a few backwoods words as spoken by the common folk: "He pounced upon the Hessians like an eagle upon a hen" in a farmyard.[28] But Washington's broad strategic vision won the battle of Trenton long before the first shot had been fired in anger on New Jersey soil and long before crossing the Delaware: the combination of the utilization of so much artillery and the ordering of Griffin's highly effective diversion to Mount Holly to ensure that Rall would not be reinforced. Such well-conceived ingredients for success set the stage for unleashing a surprise attack just after dawn, and reaping the most unexpected and improbable of victories.

In addition, the Rall brigade was also doomed by its faithful adherence to its own much celebrated skill in conventional tactics, especially the bayonet attack, that were made obsolete by the unprecedented challenges of urban combat and Washington's foresight and tactical innovations and sound judgment. Most of all, Washington reaped his most dramatic victory by delivering a one-two punch: expertly planned and manned Knox's artillery played first the long-range role (and then later a closer-range role) in stopping the counterattacking Hessian formations in the main streets of Trenton, while American muskets and rifles, especially weapons dried off in houses, won the close-range contest in Trenton's alleys, backyards, and houses.

Indeed, from beginning to end, the Rall brigade of three veteran regiments had been completely outgunned at Trenton not only by superior artillery firepower but also by veteran soldiers, especially western frontiersmen, whose superior marksmanship with both rifles and muskets dominated the fast-paced contest in the snowy streets and fields. Much of the engagement was ultimately decided by the showdown between the sharply contrasting inherent characteristics of two distinct bodies of soldiers, from vastly different cultural backgrounds, value systems, and military heritages who met face-to-face in a bitter urban conflict that determined which popular myth—the sharpshooting American soldier or the disciplined Hessian soldier with the bayonet—would prevail in the end. Therefore, what resulted at Trenton was the systematic destruction of the corresponding myths of the decisiveness of the Hessian bayonet attack, superiority, and invincibility. Most of all, the tenacious struggle for Trenton's possession revealed that the real "secret of being formidable in battle [in this war or any other] depends not on looking ferocious, but on aiming correctly."[29]

In his diary, Lieutenant Wiederhold recorded how General Stirling told him that Washington secured his victory because of an ample number of Continental infantry regiments and "fourteen cannon and two howitzers [two guns short of the actual total and] This was enough to surround 1,000 men as they were not in the best disposition . . . Our fame and honor, earned at White Plains and Fort Knyphausen [Fort Washington] suffered a severe blow here" at Trenton.[30]

Not long after the surrender when the rows of Knox's artillery stood silent with smoking barrels yet hot from firing so long and fast, the victorious Americans discovered new things about not only their vanquished opponents, but also about themselves. After all, this was the first experience of Washington's soldiers in winning a complete battlefield victory of such wideranging political, strategic, and psychological consequences in the American Revolution. Like so many other young soldiers in Washington's tattered ranks,

Cadet Joseph Stricker, Jr., the high-spirited teenager who served faithfully and with distinction in the German Regiment, and his lieutenant-colonel father, George, from the forested hills of Frederick County, Maryland, never forgot the intoxicating thrill of victory.

Like no other single event since the Declaration of Independence's signing on July 4, 1776, the Rall brigade's demise at Trenton was widely celebrated across America. Rall's defeat was viewed by the war-weary American people as a miraculous victory sanctioned by a just God's favor that verified the moral righteousness of America's struggle for liberty. The popular myth of Hessian drunkenness (the stereotypical Old World decadence and depravity) as paving the way to their own defeat at Trenton was embellished by generations of American historians to explain Washington's sparkling, one-sided success in order to vindicate American righteousness and moral superiority. But the truth of the dramatic story of the battle of Trenton was very different.

As penned by a Hessian officer, Captain Johann von Ewald, who had been born in Kiel, on the Baltic Sea, summarized the overall German experience in America with a measure of well-deserved pride untainted by hyperbole and with refreshing insight so often ignored by American historians: "Few people know the brilliant part played by our Hessian corps in America, and history has failed to do them justice. The outcome of that war [and the battle of Trenton] was the result of the bad management of the British government, and not the fault of British soldiers, or their allies, the Germans."[31]

When the unbelievable news of Rall's defeat first reached the main Hessian headquarters in New York City, it was widely reported, as revealed in a letter from one of Washington's delighted officers, that "the Hessian general Scratched out one half of his hair, on hearing the news at Trenton."[32] This anguished Teutonic commander was none other than the overall commander-in-chief of Hessian forces in America, General Leopold Philip von Heister. He was an aristocratic blueblood who had recently won glory at Long Island. He had even accepted General Stirling's sword in surrender and treated him with extreme kindness as a captive. On November 19, 1777 and after having been replaced by Baron von Knyphausen, Heister's anguish and shame finally ended forever. According to the Baroness von Riedesel, he died in his beloved Hesse-Cassel "of grief and disappointment" because of the shameful Trenton debacle.[33] At last finding a measure of peace in death not found on American soil, perhaps General Heister can be properly considered as the last Hessian officer fatality of the battle of Trenton. In this sense, the name of Heister might well be added to a deceased officers' list that included Colonel Rall, Major Dechow, Captains von Benning and Riess, and Lieutenants George Christoph Kimm and Kuehne.

But even capture by Washington's ragamuffins at Trenton was no guarantee of survival for the Rall brigade's officers. An unkind fate awaited some of the highest ranking and best officers of the von Lossberg Regiment, including men who had played inspired leadership roles during the showdown at Trenton: born in Fischbeck near Rinteln in 1737 and with twenty-three years of experience by the time of the battle of Trenton, Captain Adam Christop Steding, a bachelor who had first joined the von Lossberg Regiment at age sixteen; Ensign Heinrich Carl von Zengen and Lieutenant Wilhelm Christian Muller, born in Ziegenhain in the Rhineland, in 1749 and a soldier since age sixteen; and Major Ludwig August von Hanstein. Having escaped the salvoes of Washington's cannon, sharpshooting riflemen, and captivity after taken at Trenton, all of these von Lossberg Regiment officers were lost at sea on the same ship, the *Adamant*, during an October 1778 hurricane off the east coast.[34]

This ignominious ending in the Atlantic's cold waters was an especially ironic and tragic fate for these fine German officers, who had been key players in Trenton's defense. After all, they had rallied and then skillfully led the von Lossberg fusiliers, who performed with more distinction than any other Rall brigade troops at Trenton. Consequently, the von Lossberg Regiment suffered the lion's share of the Rall brigade's losses, with twenty-two killed and eighty-four wounded, a total of 106 casualties. Of this total, seven Lossbergers were killed, while another fifty-nine fusiliers fell wounded. In compiling a distinguished record on the morning of December 26, the von Lossberg Regiment suffered more than 60 percent of the Rall brigade's total casualties at Trenton.[35] In his December 27 report to John Hancock and the Continental Congress, Washington merely concluded in regard to Hessian losses: "I dont exactly know how many they had killed, but I fancy not above twenty or thirty . . . ."[36]

Washington's victory at Trenton was not only one of the most one-sided and unexpected of the American Revolution, but also the first real American battlefield success—and Washington's first after a year and a half in the field—after the battle of Bunker Hill on June 17, 1775. Incredibly, only six Americans fell wounded on the morning of December 26. And even more remarkably, none of Washington's casualties were fatalities, despite the popular Trenton myth of two soldiers—who have conveniently never been identified by either name or regiment—who allegedly froze to death on the march to Trenton.[37]

In a letter, an incredulous William Hull wrote accurately how Washington had suffered "only the Loss of six [the correct number] or seven on our side, this is no Exaggeration but simple fact . . . . "[38]

Washington himself was a forgotten casualty of not the battle, but of the march upon Trenton. By December 28, the night march's ordeal had left him with a "lame hand" that disabled Washington from writing his usual prolific amount of correspondence. Therefore, General Stirling penned Washington's battle report to Governor Livingston, while praying that "I hope it [Washington's hand] will soon be well enough to give them another drubbing soon."[39]

In a letter evidently written by an aide or Stirling, Washington described his minuscule losses from his two divisions at Trenton as "very trifling indeed." He informed the Continental Congress that two officers and "one or two privates [were] wounded" and none killed. But Washington in fact had six officers, who were leading the way, wounded during the battle. Captain Washington and Lieutenant Monroe were the best known casualties. Captain Charles Mynn Thruston was another officer who was wounded on December 26. This gentry-class Virginian from the Shenandoah Valley was a soldier-scholar of promise, having attended College of William and Mary in Williamsburg, Virginia.

Thurston had studied theology on the distant Albion nation that he now waged war against with righteous zeal at Trenton. He was a popular Episcopal minister, who also served as an inspirational militia officer in the 1750s. Doing his dual Godly and patriotic duties, Thruston raised a volunteer company in the America Revolution's beginning during the exciting spring of 1775, including men from his own liberty-loving congregation. At Trenton, this hard-fighting "warrior parson" led his Virginians forward until "badly wounded." Thruston recovered from his Trenton wound, gaining a colonel's rank before the revolution's conclusion.[40]

Young Ensign James Buxton, Fourth Virginia Continental Regiment, was also wounded while playing his part in securing the most improbable of victories at Trenton with his Virginia comrades of General Stephen's vanguard.[41] Wounded in the defense of Breed's Hill, Lieutenant Colonel Samuel Blatchey Webb, who had served capably as Washington's aide-de-camp since June 21, 1776, took his second wound of the war at Trenton.[42]

In addition, Lieutenant Richard Clough Anderson, born in Virginia in 1750, was another one of Washington's officers who fell wounded at Trenton. Anderson led a company of Colonel Scott's Fifth Virginia Continental Regiment of Stephen's vanguard. Anderson was second in command of

Captain Wallis's company that struck the Hessian pickets on the Pennington Road, before the arrival of Greene's Second Division column. He was also the father of Richard Anderson, a Mexican War veteran and future commander of Fort Sumter, South Carolina, when Confederate artillery opened fire on the masonry fort in Charleston harbor on the morning of April 12, 1861 to spark the Civil War's fratricidal horrors. Both father and son later laid their muskets and sabers aside to settle on fine country estates of the same name, Soldier's Retreat.[43] In total, consequently, Washington's loss at Trenton was only six officers wounded and not a single enlisted man killed or wounded can be explained by the Hessians' reduced firepower because of wet powder and weapons. Most importantly, this relatively small sacrifice among Washington's attackers soon paid off when hundreds of American prisoners in New York City were soon exchanged for Rall's captured soldiers.[44]

Ironically, in a forgotten tragedy of the story of Trenton, far more of Washington's veterans of the battle of Trenton died in the weeks, months, and sometimes even years after America's most fortunate day (December 26, 1776), falling victim to disease, exhaustion, and more from the combined effect of the arduous river crossing, the long night march, and the intense urban combat than from all the Hessian bullets, cannonfire, and bayonets combined.[45] After his dual strikes—Trenton and then Princeton in early January 1777—east of the Delaware, Washington's Army withdrew to the small town of Four Lanes End (now Langhorne, Pennsylvania across the Delaware from Trenton), where more than 150 men died of disease, battle wounds, and winter's ravages at four houses-turned-hospitals.[46]

While no injured American soldiers immediately succumbed to their Trenton wounds, the severely suffering Colonel Rall died in his own headquarters, Stacy Potts's house on King Street's west side, on the night of December 27, the same day that Major Dechow perished. Dying with Rall was his considerable own personal anguish for having lost Trenton and his entire brigade to Washington's ragtag rebels, who almost never won a battle. After having been cut down, Rall had been carried west through the debris-strewn Church alley from the Methodist Church in a wooden pew and then placed back at his headquarters at Potts's house by his mourning grenadiers. At age fifty, far from home, and lamenting the recent course of events, Rall's final thoughts, while suffering from the pain of two agonizing stomach wounds, might well have been upon fond memories of his distant

Hesse-Cassel homeland and the soft voice and loving ways of his affectionate mother, Catharina Elisabeth Dreyeich-Rall.

But before the colonel died, Rall felt some solace in the proud memory of how his prized grenadiers had recovered magnificently from Washington's greatest surprise and then fought courageously against a cruel fate and too many disadvantages to possibly overcome at Trenton. Such final fond memories might have well blotted out some of the pain of losing his fine combat brigade and horror of the screams and moans of his dying men, who had fallen in vain far from home. During Rall's "last agony, he yet thought of his grenadiers and entreated General Washington that nothing might be taken from them but their arms."[47]

The much-acclaimed victor of every battle in which he fought on American soil until Washington and the Gods of War had seemingly turned against him and united as one to vanquish his crack brigade was laid unceremoniously in a lonely grave at Trenton. Today, the exact location of Colonel Rall's grave is known only to God. Rall shared the same fate—a general obscurity—with his dead officers and enlisted men, who met their untimely deaths at Trenton.[48]

In his diary, the Knyphausen Regiment's Lieutenant Wiederhold, of humble origins and a reflective nature, merely recorded how Rall "was twice fatally wounded because of making the ill-considered attack [into Trenton], died the same evening, and lies buried at the Presbyterian Church in this place which he made so famous. Sleep well, dear commander! The Americans reportedly erected a marker on his grave later, and wrote the following words, 'Here lies Colonel Rall. His life is over.'"[49]

An introspective, senstive Lieutenant Piel presented a more human portrait of his hard-fighting commander, who died for the honor of his beloved grenadier regiment and his Germanic state and people. Piel described how Rall was "a generous, magnanimous, hospitable, and polite to everyone; never groveling before his superiors, but indulgent to his subordinates. To his servants [perhaps black as well as white], he was more friend than master. He was an exceptional friend of music and a pleasant companion."[50]

For whatever reason, Washington's victors had not ordered the Hessian prisoners to dig the graves for their comrades. Instead American soldiers themselves dug a mass grave, in ground not yet frozen solid, near the Presbyterian Church. Then, they unceremoniously deposited the bodies of bloodstained grenadiers and fusiliers, who only recently had been the most feared troops from Europe on American soil. Perhaps an American chaplain—ironically the first chaplain to die "in the service of America" was later buried at this same Presbyterian Church cemetery—or even a sympathetic common soldier, perhaps a former minister, offered a final prayer for these young men and boys, at least twenty Hessians, who died so far from their Teutonic homeland. Filling the shallow burial pit were the bodies of three excellent officers of the von Lossberg Regiment: Lieutenant Georg Christoph, or Christian, Kimm, born in 1743; Captain Johann Friedrich, or Kasper, von Riess; and Captain Friedrich Wilhelm von Benning. Thirty-three-year-old Kimm had been appointed to lieutenant of the von Lossberg Regiment in 1773 at only age twenty because of his demonstrated leadership abilities. Like Colonel Rall's grave, the exact location of this Hessian burial pit has remained unknown to this day. However, it has been generally assumed by historians and students of the battle of Trenton that the Hessian bodies lay in the cemetery of the First Presbyterian Church.[51]

Like a Teutonic phoenix rising, Rall's body resurfaced quite by accident in 1839. At that time, the new 1805 church, which had been built over the site of the old 1726 Presbyterian Church, was torn down. And "in the middle of the sanctuary floor a tomb was discovered that contained the body of a soldier buried with flag." According to a knowledgeable Pastor John R. Allen, "What better place to bury the colonel [Rall] than under the floor of the church [so] that it could not be desecrated."[52]

Then Colonel Rall's earthly remains were either reburied at some unknown location—perhaps deliberately unmarked—to avoid discovery, or perhaps even returned to Germany by family members. However, other evidence has been found that the worst indignity eventually befell the remains of the Hessian dead, including Colonel Rall. In 1916 and two years after the "guns of August" initiated the horrors of the First World War, the rising tide of anti-Germany feeling, fueled by vigorous program of American and Allied propaganda, reached new heights across America, including at Trenton.

In a misguided and rather perverse demonstration of American "patriotism," the marked Hessian graves, thanks to past efforts of relatives and Germans in America, were dug up by indignant New Jersey citizens. Then, the bones of the Teutonic warriors, and most likely including Colonel Rall, were unceremoniously tossed into the slow-moving drift of the Delaware flowing south since time immemorial. Symbolically and in a strange twist of fate, therefore, Rall evidently found his final resting place in America's December 1776 river of destiny, so far from his Hesse-Cassel homeland, which had played such a central role in his own ultimate downfall. This especially ugly incident by outraged Trenton citizens explained why the location of Hessians' final remains, including Rall who might have well become King George and the British Army's greatest military hero for having all but crushed the revolution, if he had beaten Washington at Trenton perhaps if only his troops had possessed dry muskets and powder, cannot be located today.[53]

But the most bizarre fate of any Hessian soldier captured at Trenton occurred at Newton, Pennsylvania, only around a dozen miles from the battlefield. The unfortunate German died of disease while held a prisoner at Newton. A Continental surgeon, Pennsylvanian James Tate, exhumed the German corpse in order to learn more about anatomy by way of dissection. He then buried what was left of one of Rall's proud fighting men in the basement of his stone house.[54]

As shabbily as this individual Hessian and Colonel Rall's last remains were treated by angry Americans, circumstances, and the unpredictable hands of fate, Rall's reputation suffered even greater abuse and indignity. The popular image (post-Trenton rather than pre-Trenton) of Rall's alleged military incompetence rose to truly monumental heights from the prolific pens of generations of American historians—based upon the military kangaroo court findings of a self-serving court of inquiry that "investigated" the Trenton fiasco—including the twentieth century and beyond. The creation of this most popular myth of Trenton historiography was all but inevitable, because Rall was the loser of the battle of Trenton and lost his life, paying the ultimate price.

When Colonel Rall died and as could be expected in such a monumental fiasco that stunned the British Army, he immediately became the most convenient scapegoat for the British command structure. After all, Howe, Cornwallis, and Grant were largely responsible for the Trenton debacle, and Hessian commanders, Heister and Donop, who also had bungled badly, had been responsible for setting the stage for the Rall brigade's demise at Trenton. However, all responsibility for the disaster was conveniently assigned to Rall, who obviously could not defend himself from the charges in what was a classic case of "piling on." But in truth, this highly respected Hessian colonel had been a center stage player of more tactical successes in America in 1776 than any other German or British brigade commander. Nevertheless, he has become widely demonized as a drunkard, an incompetent buffoon, and an outright fool, who lost Trenton all by himself.

In the end, consequently, Rall became the perfect fall guy for the lengthy list of glaring strategic and tactical failures of a fumbling British leadership at the highest levels. For generations of Americans, from schoolchildren to leading, respected historians, Rall has always served as the ideal foil that contrasted perfectly with the romantic image of a saintly, divinely inspired Washington: a most symbolic example of Old World decadence vanquished by New World virtue in what transformed into a moral showdown at Trenton. In truth, Rall was defeated for the most part because of the lack of support, reinforcements, and assistance from his superiors, both British and German. Consequently, Rall and his crack grenadier and fusilier brigade were largely doomed even before the first shot of the battle of Trenton had been fired. Rarely in the annals of military history have the reputations, popular images, and fortunes of two opposing commanders—Washington and Rall—been so more dramatically reversed during one of the war's shortest battles, around forty-five minutes, that was distinguished by a hectic, fast-paced swirl of urban combat.

Colonel Rall became the most convenient scapegoat for the loss of his three well-trained regiments and Trenton on both sides of the Atlantic not only at the time, but also well into the twenty-first century. During an official army court of inquiry that only ended half a decade after the battle of Trenton, surviving Hessian officers of the Trenton fiasco neatly shifted all blame from themselves to preserve their lofty reputations and future career prospects. In a gross injustice, they placed the disaster entirely upon the shoulders of a former colonel of so much merit, while he lay in his remote New Jersey grave far from home. By making Rall solely responsible for the Trenton disaster, the Rall brigade's officers were acquitted of wrongdoing. The German officer corps exonerated, because they (except for Rall) "all done their duty," as required and expected.

Elitist, aristocratic British and German officer class (of a social class higher than Rall) possessed more than a vested interest in smearing the stainless reputation of a capable and fearless commoner, who died for their collective military sins. By heaping all blame on Rall, who was unable to defend himself, the names and reputations of three German regiments and the fabled Hessian officer corps escaped all tarnish. In the end, ironically, Rall's spotless record and lofty reputation were unfairly stained by his own men, his British and German superiors, and generations of Americans and historians as the sole author of the "fatal affair" at Trenton. Significantly, when left on his own in the Virginia theater in 1781, Lord Cornwallis, the man most responsible for advocating the garrisoning the advanced, isolated, and exposed position of Trenton, would have no one else to blame for a far greater disaster but himself for his own considerable strategic errors and miscalculations that led to his entrapment and surrender at Yorktown in October.[55]

While his superiors were left blameless for the Trenton defeat, Rall immediately became the fashionable whipping boy. By April 1777, the son of the langrave of Hesse-Cassel regretted how the "death of Colonel Rall has taken him away from my wrath which he so well deserved in allowing himself in so inexcusable a way to be surprised."[56] In contrast, a descendant of Colonel Rall correctly emphasized how it is now time—more than two centuries after the battle of Trenton—for the "dispelling myths [in regard to Colonel Rall because he] was a good soldier from a very young age . . . and quite a respected one among his troops [and] The portrayal of the 'drunken boob' at Trenton" is a myth.[57]

Born in Westmoreland County, Virginia, Richard Henry Lee, Declaration of Independence signer and a leading member of Congress, came closer to the truth of what really happened at the battle of Trenton and exactly why, refusing to lay solitary blame for the unprecedented fiasco on Rall. In a most revealing letter, he strongly condemned the "infamously" bad conduct of Rall's subordinate officers—ironically the same ones who later condemned him—during the course of the battle. Indeed, a number of Hessian officers were early unnerved by Washington's surprise attack from two directions, and escaped the Virginian's brilliant double envelopment by early deserting their troops and forsaking their brigade commander in a crisis situation and in his hour of greatest need.[58]

However, Lee's well-deserved denunciation of the Hessian officer corps overlooked the demoralizing effect of urban combat on conventional troops, especially officers who faced their first urban combat challenge. In truth, the majority of German officers faithfully remained beside their men throughout the battle and until the final surrender. However, once a number of leading officers were cut down, some surviving Hessian officers provided less than inspired leadership, leaving Rall largely on his own. Many of these officers were privileged members of aristocratic Hesse-Cassel families, bearing minor noble titles, thanks to close family and political ties with the prince. Consequently, some top Rall brigade's leaders, although Rall was a notable exception, were privileged upper-class elitists, who often viewed fighting and dying as something left primarily to the lowest ranks, or the common soldiers or peasants: guaranteed cannon fodder because of lower class status and rank.[59]

For generations, Rall's many past successes have been conveniently forgotten by his legion of fault-finders. Therefore, he became the epitome of the father of folly in the annals of American history. Rall was widely condemned for allegedly having doomed his brigade entirely on his own because he had been "too proud to retreat a step before such an enemy as the Americans," in the prejudiced words of the von Lossberg Regiment's quartermaster.[60]

Of course, in the end, Colonel Rall's only fault for losing Trenton was the fact that he was a victim of Washington's brilliant tactical plan. Thanks partly to the humbling experience derived from the disastrous New York Campaign, one of Virginia's richest planters finally became successful in fully disengaging from a popular, but fatal, strategic thinking known as Bunkerhillism just in time to boldly embrace a most innovative, novel, and masterful battle plan. Most importantly, Washington possessed the wisdom to switch from a disastrous reliance on losing conventional tactics to those of asymmetrical—partisan or insurgency—warfare out of necessity in an emergency situation.

On December 26 and at long last, Washington relied upon a new tactical solution by forsaking the traditional European ways of waging war of his counterparts—England's elite officer class—and embracing the more practical tactics of America's common people of the western frontier, where innovative battle plans had been long formulated out of desperation and necessity for simple survival: catching an unwary, overconfident opponent by surprise by attacking at dawn and unleashing a pincer movement, while employing stealth and speed to minimize casualties (as in Indian warfare) in order to inflict as much damage as possible upon the enemy in a total war that knew no conventional rules or eighteenth-century niceties.

By relying upon such a new, distinctive American way of fighting—more brutal and ruthless than England and Europe's more gentlemanly ways of conducting war—that was largely a feature of Indian and frontier warfare based upon the simple premise of survival of the fittest that had emerged out of bitter struggle for possession of America's primeval wilderness, Washington finally utilized the ideal winning tactical formula in a delicate balancing act between the proven tactics of conventional and irregular warfare by combining the most suitable qualities of each in order to develop the best tactics to achieve success at Trenton: the double envelopment and the Indian-like raid that was essentially a lightning strike based on the element of surprise. By never giving up hope for an eventual success and audaciously reclaiming the initiative and the tactical offensive on December 26 when least expected by his opponent, Washington achieved a significant battlefield success at very small cost in true guerrilla fashion to reap the most important American victory of the war to date, and one that was far out of proportion to the numbers involved on both sides.

When most needed by the dying American nation and an often-defeated citizen soldier army literally on its last legs, Washington's remarkable achievement was only possible because he persisted in believing that success was yet possible by relying upon a central concept of insurgency warfare: the lightning quick raid to catch the opponent by surprise to reap a decisive success, which was the winning formula for overwhelming a conventional adversary who was far superior in training, equipment, and discipline. During the French and Indian War, Captain James Smith, of the Pennsylvania militia, lamented how the American people and militia had inexplicably not "made greater proficiency of the Indian art of war [and theorized that this noticeable lack of tactical evolution among the colonial fighting man, both officers and men, was due because] we are too proud" to accept even a winning tactical formula for success.[61]

Fortunately for the young republic struggling for its very existence in its darkest hour, the austere Washington was not too proud or vain to shed his aristocratic, conventional notions of war waging. Therefore, he evolved just in the nick of time for America, placing his faith in the most ungentlemanly, unorthodox of tactical battle plans, rooted primarily in the frontier experience of the lowly common people of the American wilderness. For the Trenton showdown, he adapted and changed to become a more imaginative, flexible, and mature commander-in-chief, who thought more like a partisan, relying upon speed, stealth, mobility, tactical flexibility, and the element of surprise, to shock his overconfident opponent and destroy his will to resist to reap the most unexpected victory to date.

Drawing from multiple sources, Washington also relied upon a novel mix of some of the best lessons of both ancient and conventional European warfare, especially the pincer movement, or the double envelopment, a rapid concentration of force, and the massing of superior artillery firepower to overwhelm his adversary. Therefore, as demonstrated at Trenton and improvised out of urgent necessity and the most bleak of situations, this new way of waging war—a truly American way—utilized by Washington in masterful fashion was a balanced blend of the most appropriate tactics and lessons derived from both the American and European military experiences on both sides of the Atlantic that were best suited for the tactical situation presented at Trenton, combining both conventional and irregular concepts of war in a masterful fusion and a most timely synthesis of tactical lessons to reap his most dramatic victory of the war.[62]

Trenton's Heroes Fall at Princeton

Worried that British and Hessian reinforcements were converging upon Trenton, Washington prepared to again cross the Delaware to reach Pennsylvania's safety. The failure of Ewing and Cadwalader to cross the Delaware as planned made it impossible for Washington to continue his offensive operations and fulfill his larger objective to also launch strikes on Princeton and then New Brunswick. But he unexpectedly encountered a new problem not long after the final shot was fired in anger at Trenton. A good many American soldiers became roaring drunk to celebrate their rare victory, after breaking into casks of rum. Fortunately, Washington's strategy of focusing Donop's attention on Mount Holly, south of the Hessians' headquarters at Bordentown, continued to prove effective. Had Donop attacked Trenton with Washington's back to the swollen river and with so many Continental soldiers drunk, America's people's revolution against monarchy might have yet ended in the most embarrassing and tragic of fashions along the ice-choked Delaware. Emboldened by his Trenton success, nevertheless, Washington was yet determined to maintain the initiative and "pursue the enemy in their retreat," as he wrote to Congress on December 29, continuing to think more like a daring partisan leader than a conventional eighteenth-century commander.[63]

Therefore, knowing that it was now time to strike once again in the hope of achieving another Trenton-like success by catching his opponent by surprise, Washington set his sights on another cantonment along Howe's sprawling defensive line that had been earlier targeted: Princeton. But Washington yet possessed even greater ambitions. In his own words, "My original plan when I set out from Trenton was to have pushed to [New] Brunswick."[64]

Washington divided his command, with Mercer's brigade, of less than four hundred men, detached from the main column. Anticipating Washington's plan to snatch another isolated and vulnerable winter outpost, Howe reacted quickly to Trenton's loss by dispatching Cornwallis and eight thousand reinforcements. The thirty-eight-year-old Cornwallis now sought revenge for the Trenton humiliation, after having been forced to return from his much-anticipated trip to visit his sickly wife in England, which had been abruptly cancelled with Washington's victory at Trenton.

Realizing that he would be crushed if he remained in position along the Assunpink with his back to the Delaware, after having re-crossed the river—and then hurling back Cornwallis's attack from defensive positions on the creek's south bank, during the so-called Second battle of Trenton (or the Battle of Assunpink Creek) on January 2—Washington made his bold move to exploit the favorable tactical opportunity. Washington slipped around Cornwallis's left in another night march and advanced upon Princeton in stealthy fashion. However, Mercer's troops, hoping to strike Cornwallis's rear, were caught out in the open at William Clark's orchard, when they ran head-on into veteran British regulars marching along the road to reinforce Cornwallis at Trenton on January 3, 1777. A brisk fire was exchanged in this accidental battle, and then the British regulars suddenly charged with fixed bayonets. Hardly had Mercer, on horseback, formed his troops before the attacking Britons were upon the startled Americans. Nothing could now stop the fierce onslaught of Lieutenant Colonel Charles Mawhood's brigade of veteran redcoats, not even fiery blasts from Captain Neil's New Jersey artillery. Continentals fled the unstoppable attack, with the British bayoneting their way through the shocked Americans in the orchard. Refusing to run and continuing to fire his three-pounder beside his fellow New Jersey cannoneers, Captain Neil defended his two guns to the last. Without infantry support, the young New Jersey officer stood firm against the surging red tide. Refusing to run, Neil received no quarter, and expected none, receiving his death stroke.

Attempting to rally his shattered ranks, Mercer went down when his gray-colored horse was shot and he suffered a shattered leg. After struggling to his feet, Mercer again tried to rally his men, while elated redcoats descended upon the Scottish general like locusts. Much like the ill-fated Captain Neil, Mercer also refused to run. Mercer was in no mood to become a captive of the hated English. Even though Captain Neil's New Jersey cannon were captured and the Americans' flight became a rout, Mercer continued to fight back with spirit. He ignored British cries of "Surrender, you damn rebel." Mercer, who had made out his final will at Fredericksburg on March 20, 1776, was determined to fight against a cruel fate and too many redcoats to count.

All the while, General Mercer slashed with his saber at the surging tide of red encircling him. He was repeatedly bayoneted and then clubbed to the ground with musket-butts, while cursed as a damned "rebel general." The cruel bayoneting only stopped when Mercer feigned death. On his death bed, Mercer explained: "My death is owing to myself [as when] I brought to the ground by a blow from a musket . . . I felt that I deserved not so approbrious an epithet and determined to die as I had lived, an honored soldier in a just and righteous cause, and with out begging my life or making a reply. I lunged with my sword at the nearest man. They then bayoneted me and left me" on the ground. Attempting to rally Mercer's shattered ranks after his own troops had been forced rearward by the fierce bayonet attack, Colonel Haslet dashed forward and was shot in the head, dying instantly. Haslet's death before his troops caused more panic among the reeling Americans, who continued to flee across the snowy landscape, before Washington and reinforcements arrived just in the nick of time to reverse the tide with a determined counterattack that steamrolled all the way into Princeton to reap another surprising victory.[65]

Unlike at Trenton, the Princeton victory was most costly, especially among Washington's officer corps. In the words of one of Washington's men from a January 5, 1777 letter: "Colonels Haslet, and [Ireland-born James] Potter [who commanded the Northumberland County, Pennsylvania, militia, and a veteran of the 1756 Kittanning Expedition was initially reported killed, but was only wounded and captured], capt. [Daniel] Neal [Neil who commanded the Eastern Company, New Jersey State Artillery at Trenton], of the artillery, capt [John] Fleming, who commanded the first Virginia regiment [and led them at the battle of Trenton], and four or five other valuable officers [also] were slain on the field."[66]

After they had just demonstrated kind treatment to the captured and wounded Hessians at Trenton, most of these gifted officers were shown no quarter by the redcoats. Thanks to the surprising Trenton success of these resurgent Americans, the British fully realized that such dynamic military leaders, regimental, battery, and brigade commanders, were Washington's best and brightest who had to be eliminated, ensuring a brutal no-quarter policy. Washington received a stunning blow in the loss of General Mercer and Colonel Haslet, who were his two most capable Celtic warriors, with one born in Scotland and the other in Ireland, respectively.

Combined with the sparkling Trenton success, the news of Washington's dramatic victory at Princeton also lifted spirits across America. Proving a rare, almost unbelievable, sight to the American people, the Hessians captured at Trenton were marched through Philadelphia to dispel the myth of invincibility by providing proof that Germans could be vanquished by American fighting men: a possibility not previously entertained. However, many Philadelphians were disappointed to discover that the dejected Germans looked not like fierce warriors and devils incarnate but just like ordinary men.

Not long thereafter, the citizens of America's capital were greeted with a painful reminder of the high cost of freedom, however. Colonel Haslet's body was the first to arrive in Philadelphia for burial. As revealed in a leading Philadelphia newspaper on February 4, 1777: "In the action at Princeton . . . the brave col. John Haslet was mortally wounded and his remains were brought to this city . . . with the honours [sic] of war . . . Since his arrival in this country [from northern Ireland] he remained a fair and unblemished character [and possessed an] inextinguishable love of his country and unconquerable zeal for the invaded rights of America . . . undismayed at the danger of war, he nobly sacrificed his invaluable life at the shrine of American liberty."[67]

The Ireland-born Haslet left behind an attractive wife named Jemima, a brood of children, a bountiful plantation along the Millpillion River that flowed gently into Delaware Bay, and a nice house, where he should have been reposing at the time of the battle of Trenton. Ironically, he was killed at Princeton with Washington's orders in his pocket to proceed to Delaware to recruit a new battalion. But Haslet had been determined to lead his men into battle one more time, ignoring Washington's directive in his eagerness. Symbolically, Haslet had been killed while coming to the assistance of his fallen Celtic friend, General Mercer. The martyred Irishman's uniformed body was placed at Philadelphia's State House yard for an official public viewing and a solemn memorial observance, which was shortly repeated for Mercer.

Colonel Haslet was buried at the First Presbyterian Church's cemetery in a casket draped with a large American flag. Symbolically, a good many Irish soldiers from Haslet's native Ulster homeland, including the finely uniformed cavalrymen of Captain Morris's First Troop of Philadelphia Light Horse which fought at Trenton, served as the silent honor guard during the funeral. Only two weeks later, another forgotten casualty of the Trenton-Princeton Campaign was Haslet's wife Jemima. She died of grief and heartache back in Delaware, never rising from her bed after receiving the tragic news of her husband's death at Princeton.[68]

Then yet another shock soon struck the American people like a lightning bolt: General Mercer's death. With head injuries and multiple bayonet wounds to his stomach, Mercer lingered in agony at the Thomas Clark house on the Princeton battlefield for nine days before dying. When Washington's good friend and fellow Virginian died, the recognition of Mercer's important contributions in the formulation of the most brilliant tactical plan of the American Revolution died with him.

The sad news of Mercer's death was printed in the *Maryland Gazette* on January 23, 1777: "Last Sunday evening died near Princeton, of the wounds he received in the engagement at that place on the 3d instant, HUGH MERCER, Esq; brigadier general in the Continental Army. On Wednesday his body was brought to his city [Philadelphia], and yesterday buried in Christ Church yard with [full] military honours . . . The uniform character and exalted abilities and virtues of this illustrouss [sic] officer, will render his name equally dear to America with the liberty for which he" died to preserve.[69] Mercer's many admirers, and no one more than Washington, never forgot the Scotsman's fiery words that proved most prophetic in the end: "For my part, I have but one object in view, and that is, the success of the cause; and God can witness how cheerfully I would lay down my life to secure it."[70]

The high sacrifice of so many of Washington's leading officers at Princeton was unprecedented. Besides Mercer and Haslet, some of Washington's most promising leaders were fatally cut down: Captain Daniel Neil, who commanded the East Company, New Jersey State Artillery with distinction at the battle of Trenton; twenty-two-year-old "heroic" Captain John Fleming, the promising Henrico County, Virginia, commander of the First Virginia Continental Regiment and descendant of Jamestown settlers, who fell "at the head of his company in defence [sic] of American freedom" in leading the counterattack; Lieutenant Bartholomew Yeates and Ensign Anthony Morris, Jr., who were both killed on the field; and Lieutenant John Read, Fourth Virginia Continental Regiment, who was mortally wounded, dying on January 25, 1777. Along with so many other promising officers, Major John Armstrong, Jr., Mercer's faithful aide-de-camp at Trenton, also fell wounded in Princeton's close-range combat. Ironically, not only the son of the Kittanning Expedition's daring commander but also one of the experienced Pennsylvania officers of that audacious September 1756 raid over the Allegheny Mountains, Ireland-born Colonel James Potter, was also cut down in the bloodletting at Princeton.[71]

After having refused to run unlike so many other soldiers and getting off a final shot from his three-pounder before the onrushing redcoats descended upon him with bayonets, Captain Neil's final resting place has remained at an unknown location on the Princeton battlefield. Tradition has it that Neil's body was brought back to his wife Eliza and his two children in the enemy-occupied Passaic River country, but such was not the case. In regard to the tragic death of one of Trenton's heroes and one of his best artillery officers of Sullivan's First

Division in the December 26 victory that gave new life to the infant nation, General Greene lamented how: "The enemy [had] refused him quarter after he was wounded [and] He has left behind a grieving widow overwhelmed with grief . . . ."[72]

Washington's improbable dual successes at Trenton and Princeton accomplished the impossible, turning the tide of the revolution and saving the young republic from an early death. While General Mercer died ingloriously at the Thomas Clark house at Princeton, where young Major Armstrong had carried him in tears, the leading capitals across Europe were abuzz with the unbelievable news of Washington's twin New Jersey successes when least expected by one and all. Europe's rulers and leaders were dazzled by the audacity of Washington's crossing of the Delaware and unexpected attack in wintertime, when no one else waged war. Frederick the Great, whose own veterans, like Major Dechow who led the Knyphausen Regiment at Trenton and paid for the success of Washington's daring battle plan with his life, had served in Rall's brigade, wrote how the remarkable "achievements of Washington and his little band of compatriots . . . were the most brilliant of any recorded in the history of military achievements."[73]

While Washington was acknowledged around the world as a gifted commander when in the most severe crisis situation, Mercer's body lay in his final resting place in Philadelphia far from his Fredericksburg home and his five children—Anna, John, William, George, and Hugh, Jr. Fortunately, Mercer's orphans were later cared for by Mercer's brother-in-law, Colonel George Weedon, who led the Third Virginia Continental Regiment with distinction at Trenton. However, the aristocratic kings, princes, and upper-class generals of Europe could hardly have imaged that an immigrant, transplanted Scotsman, and former Jacobite rebel, who had been only an obscure Fredericksburg physician at the revolution's beginning, was in fact a primary tactical architect of the battle plan that resulted in the war's most surprising victory.[74]

In total and in an unprecedented feat, Washington's homespun revolutionaries captured fifteen Hessian flags at Trenton, five from each of the three regiments of the now non-existent brigade. Symbolically, at least two of Trenton's revered trophies was proudly hung in the main meeting hall of the Continental Congress which was located not far from the fifty-two-year-old Scotsman's final resting place, where General Mercer's remains were honored: the bluish green silk flag of Rall's elite grenadier regiment and the beautiful white silk banner, with its majestic House of Hesse eagle emblem, of the von Lossberg Regiment.

These bullet-shredded trophies had been carried to Congress by Washington's Virginia friend and aide Lieutenant Colonel Baylor on a fast horse.[75]

As penned by a Continental Army surgeon, Dr. Jonathan Potts, with obvious pride in what Washington had accomplished against the odds to surprise the world and infuse new life into a dying resistance effort across America, the Hessians "were drubbed and out-generaled in every respect" at the little town of Trenton.[76] All in all, Washington's victory at Trenton upset a host of traditional beliefs and assumptions, sending shock waves reverberating around the world. When America's armed citizen soldiers dared to first take up arms in a popular uprising to confront a monarchy's almost limitless might and Europe's best professional leaders and soldiers, they boldly challenged the preeminent military establishment and the traditional order of the eighteenth-century world.

Before December 26, the humiliating defeats suffered by Washington's Army in disastrous 1776 had seemingly verified to the world that a common people's revolt—as long demonstrated with tragic results for fiery Celtic rebels during the course of hundreds of years in Ireland and Scotland—against this Old World power structure and professional army was an absolute impossibility. To everyone's surprise, a resilient Washington had demonstrated that success could be achieved against the odds and an established military system by innovative tactical thinking, audacity, and bold action. Even more, Washington's dramatic victory at Trenton proved that the old, entrenched military system was unable to demonstrate the necessary flexibility or adjust sufficiently to cope with new challenges of an asymmetrical nature to decisively defeat highly motivated soldiers of a revolutionary army, when it utilized a new American way of waging war.

By overpowering an entire Hessian brigade of crack warriors on December 26, Washington first demonstrated this new realization by way of a masterful blending of the best tactical lessons of traditional European warfare—especially amassing artillery and the ever-elusive double envelopment—with the more innovative and successful New World tactical lessons—especially the guerrilla-like raid and surprise attack at first light learned from battling Native Americans. Washington's surprising victory at Trenton was the first demonstration of the symbiotic and synergetic fusion of the most successful unconventional military lessons—a surprise attack near dawn combined with massive artillery firepower and a reliance upon tactical flexibility, mobility, speed, stealth, and hard-hitting shock in the Napoleonic tradition of the next century—from both sides of the Atlantic, serving as a harbinger of a new day to come in modern warfare.

In overall strategic terms, Washington's remarkable success at Trenton provided the first concrete example that Great Britain, in fighting a limited war of attrition far from home with its small professional army, would be unable to develop a workable military solution to thwart a popular uprising among a politically motivated and religiously inspired people, who were well armed, waging more of a total war than their opponents, and inhabiting an expansive land: insurmountable moral and physical barriers to conquest. Indeed, Washington had convincingly demonstrated that a sprawling country and a people's rebellion could not be quickly, easily, or completely overwhelmed, even after large cities, such as New York, were lost to the conquerors.

The most insightful British officers and leaders now began to understand what had been once unthinkable just before Washington's shocking victory at Trenton: that this strange, new kind of war in faraway America—so unlike the traditional conflicts in Europe and even in regard to people's rebellions in Ireland and Scotland—simply could not be won against a highly politicized and mobilized people, mere lowly peasants in European eyes, who had been galvanized and radicalized by Age of Enlightenment ideology and a popular uprising. With Washington's most improbable of successes at Trenton, even King George's mercenary policy had been now exposed as folly by the defeat of an entire Hessian brigade that had been considered invincible by one and all.[77]

Revealing the emergence of this new equation for waging war in America in a letter, Richard Henry Lee, a respected member of the Virginia planter class who was educated in England, was correct in his prophetic estimation how even if Philadelphia was eventually captured, then "the loss of ten such cities would not ruin the American cause [because] at the beginning of this quarrel we told our enemies that we knew they could take our cities and our sea coast, but that still enough would be left to secure American freedom."[78]

As never before, the stiff challenges and trials, especially crossing the turbulent Delaware, united Washington's soldiers, cementing divergent parts and molding them into a more cohesive fighting force that emerged into something that was more national than sectional by the morning of December 26 and just in time for America's fortunes. More than lofty Age of Enlightenment rhetoric, the Declaration of Independence, or even Tom Paine's *Common Sense* or *The American Crisis*, the bonds of comradeship of Washington's soldiers were solidly forged by the sufferings, fires, and sacrifices by the Trenton challenge, uniting divergent soldiers from across America and creating a nationalistic bond that rose to the fore during the overwhelming of a Hessian brigade.

Indeed, the bidding ties of nationhood and brotherhood were permanently forged among America's soldiers and larger numbers of people across the land with Washington's twin wintertime victories in New Jersey. The wide regional, class, and cultural differences between soldiers from east and west, and especially those men from north and south, finally began to be erased by the formidable Trenton challenge when complete unity was necessary for victory: a forgotten, but vital, ingredient for the development of a true American national identity, character, and army with Washington at its head, that led to the real—rather than theoretical because independence could only be won on the battlefield and not by Founding Fathers simply issuing a lofty declaration—creation of an authentic American nation and people.

The rough-and-tumble, Scotch-Irish fighter from the backwoods of New Hampshire, John Sullivan, understood the nature of this silent evolution in hearts and minds and the more thorough Americanization process among the ranks, after having seen so many young men and boys from both the North and South, or the "Yankee" and the "Buck-Skin," respectively, fighting side-by-side and celebrating their sparkling success at Trenton together as one. Overcoming their own considerable personal and regional prejudices and gaping sectional differences, soldiers from across America gained a new healthy respect for each other during the recent trials, forging a greater sense of unity and a tighter bond that was truly nationalistic.

As General Sullivan in a letter described this most timely Trenton synthesis in which New Englanders and Virginians fought united as one and as a highly effective team to reap the most dramatic of victories: "I have been much pleased to See a Day approaching to try the Difference between yankee Cowardice & Southern valor [and] The Day has or Rather the Days have arrived and all The General officers allowed & do allow that the yankee Cowardice assumes the shape of True valor in the field & The Southern valor appears to be a Composition of Boasting & Conceit."[79]

At the same time that these regional and sectional differences diminished with shared hardship, suffering, and the sweet taste of success at Trenton, another synthesis had occurred when Washington relied upon a masterful blend of the most successful Native American, frontier, and European tactics, mixing conventional with asymmetrical ways of waging war. This timely tactical synthesis had brought much more than victory at Trenton, having a profound, far-reaching impact, because now "the British saw their comfortable plan for winning the war utterly shattered."[80]

At long last and most importantly, Washington had broken the long winning streak of a seemingly invincible opponent while also infusing the young Continental Army and infant nation with a new vibrant energy and sense of determination to keep the once-dying embers of revolution alive, which had seemed about to be extinguished for all time. After the twin winter setbacks in western New Jersey, Howe's lengthy defensive line, that pointed straight at Philadelphia like a dagger, was rolled all the way back to New Brunswick: a most symbolic retreat and admission that attested to the fact that America could not be conquered by conventional and traditional means as long as Washington's army remained a mobile, unpredictable fighting force in the field.

In overall strategic terms and boding well for America's prospects in a lengthy war of attrition, what was most convincingly demonstrated by Washington's victory at Trenton was that the British and Hessians were simply far too few numbers to successfully combat the irregular, or guerrilla, tactics of insurgency warfare over a wide expanse of North America with conventional tactics. Indeed, the land's vastness—a thousand miles in length and several hundred miles in width—and the multitudes of Americans, including patriot pioneers west of the mountains, could not be subjugated by a relatively small standing army (without England relying on conscription despite global commitments), especially a "foreign" one, far from home and with a government divided in sentiment.

These true realizations—first verified with Washington's victory at Trenton—in regard to the true strategic situation in America only belatedly enlightened British political and military leaders of an undeniable new and harsh reality.[81] When Lord George Germain, the powerful Secretary of State for the Colonies since November 1775, first learned of Washington's success at Trenton in February 1777, he lamented how: "All our hopes were blasted by the unhappy affair at Trenton."[82] And in a December 31, 1776 letter to Lord Germain, a stunned William Tryon, New York's royal governor, was equally disconsolate: "The Rebels carrying off the Hessian Brigade under Coll. Rall at Trenton, has given me more real chagrin than any other circumstance [of] this war."[83]

In Trenton's wake, the British press, military, and political leaders condemned the formerly invincible Hessians, who became scapegoats like Rall for the Germans. The Hessians were now widely denounced as "the worst troops," receiving the entire blame for the Trenton debacle instead of top

British leadership. Therefore, Howe, Cornwallis, and Grant, who was most of all responsible for the Trenton fiasco, were not blamed or widely condemned. Clearly, Sir Howe had been knighted by the king as a prestigious Companion of the Bath far too soon before the crushing of Washington's Army had been completed, thanks to London's assumption that he had all but ended the war by late December 1776, and until that fateful late December morning when everything changed forever with Washington's surprise attack that so suddenly emerged out of a blinding snowstorm from two directions.[84]

In contrast to the pervasive lament of golden opportunities lost with the wreckage of Howe's carefully laid strategy that crushed the British government's hopes for ending the war, Americans across the land now sensed a decisive turning of the tide. While morale soared and prospects brightened across the breath of America, British and Hessian spirits sank to new lows: a dramatic reversal of fortune and public opinion, thanks to what Washington had accomplished during a mere forty-five minutes of intense combat at Trenton. In the words of one rejuvenated colonist, who expressed this new electrifying faith in the revolution's ultimate success that had spread like wildfire with the unbelievable news of Washington's winter successes: "by the late providential turn of affairs, the God Almighty was visibly on our side."[85]

Likewise, Colonel Knox, giving thanks to God, emphasized in a letter how "Providence seemed to have smiled on every part of this enterprise."[86] Meanwhile, from an uneasy White Hall shrouded by the darkening gloom of the stunning Trenton reversal, Lord George Germain, the leading voice on Lord North's cabinet, provided a cautionary warning for the future: "It is to be hoped that the dangerous practice of underestimating the enemy may make a lasting impression on the rest of the army."[87]

Thanks to Washington's brilliant stroke, German arms had been tarnished as never before. A stunned Donop admitted to Grant on December 29, 1776: "the shame . . . for our nation to have lost six cannon, with fifteen banners and three regiments at one attack and this in a section of the country greatly demoralized [while] Colonel Rall was to have been buried with his Lieutenant Colonel [Dechow] yesterday."[88]

Epilogue

Trenton's Long Shadow

In late November 1776 during the struggle for liberty's darkest period, a letter written by an American from France revealed how the series of sharp American reverses, especially New York City's loss, had all but ended any possibility of French intervention, which was absolutely necessary for a successful experiment in rebellion: "The success of the King's forces against the revolted provinces has been so rapid, and the panic which this success has struck through the rebels . . . that the court of Versailles . . . must now abandon so weak a system of policy [because] the present winter, will most probably terminate the rebellion before the next spring . . . ."[1]

Howe's relatively easy capture of New York City, the victorious push all the way to the Delaware, and the ambitious plan to capture Philadelphia, America's capital, were deliberately calculated to discourage England's ancient foe, France, from entering the conflict on the American revolutionaries' side. France had long anxiously awaited convincing tangible evidence—a solitary victory of importance by Washington—that this common people's rebellion against a major European power was not just another ill-fated revolt of starry-eyed, fumbling rebel leaders, as in Ireland or Scotland, that was easily crushed by superior British military might.

A string of British victories in 1776 seemed to have eliminated any possibility of a successful American resistance effort. France, therefore, began to lose all hope of avenging New France's 1759 loss by depriving England of her thirteen colonies. France also hoped to tie the British down in a lengthy conflict of attrition—a "ruinous war against herself"—to steadily drain the British Empire's manpower, morale, prestige, and resources. But before France could officially intervene, the American revolutionaries must first demonstrate that they were worthy of official support—a formal French alliance—by proving that they could actually win a significant battlefield victory. To prevent the possibility of a French alliance (England's worst nightmare in overall global terms),

England had gambled on winning the war with one single, knockout blow during a single campaign season of 1776. But Washington ruined that possibility by safely retiring across the Delaware in early December and denying Howe the means to cross the river and capture Philadelphia.[2]

Ironically, Washington's victories at Trenton and Princeton—essentially hard-hitting raids in force—were viewed as insignificant by those British military commanders and civilian leaders who were not yet aware of the nuisances, implications, and complexities of insurgency warfare. In consequence, Washington's dual winter successes were generally considered "only skirmishes" by the least enlightened British leadership, but he had in fact inflicted significant losses of more than two thousand men while losing only one-tenth of that number during the Trenton-Princeton Campaign: a new way of waging war.

As one complacent correspondent, who attempted to put Trenton's loss in perspective, penned to William Eden in London, "The British cause in American certainly does not depend on the conduct of a Hessian Colonel [named Rall because] The back of the snake [rebellion] is [yet] broken."[3] But traditional English political leaders failed to understand the complex psychological, symbolic, and moral dimensions of Washington's most unexpected success in reinvigorating the pulse of America's common people, restoring their faith and resolve.

Thousands of colonists across America now sensed that something meaningful—a great spiritual and moral vindication and rejuvenation of the revolutionary faith—lay in the surprising Trenton victory, and to a lesser degree at Princeton, and not unlike the Court of Versailles in faraway Paris. Consequently, Washington's unprecedented Trenton success altered the overall balance of the strategic situation by once again opening the door to significant French invention, including vital Gallic naval support and ground troops on a widespread scale, which was necessary for decisive victory. After the Continental Congress had fled Philadelphia for Baltimore to additionally lessen the possibility of French intervention in a significant political setback, Washington and his senior officers had fully understood by Christmas Day that a victory at Trenton was necessary to send a powerful message to the wavering French King Louis XVI and the Court of Versailles, which was now under the sway of the anti-interventionists, after New York City's capture and Washington's dismal retreat across New Jersey.

Consequently, like a sudden thunderbolt from the sky, no single event of the American Revolution more thoroughly shocked foreign leaders and capitals across Europe, from Madrid, Spain, to Moscow, Russia, and turned the political tide in America's favor than the unbelievable news of the almost incomprehensible capture of an entire Hessian brigade at Trenton. Washington's victory was widely proclaimed as a "masterpiece of military skill." Wise heads realized that Washington's remarkable success at Trenton now placed France in an advantageous position to eventually bestow full recognition and open the door to large-scale intervention (with the 1777 Saratoga victory concluding what Trenton had begun) that was necessary for winning the revolution.

But none of this remarkable reversal of fortune would have been possible without the December 26 victory at Trenton. Quite simply, Washington's success at Trenton was the beginning of the end of British imperial ambitions for the conquest of America. Thanks to Washington's Trenton victory, for the upcoming spring campaign of 1777 until the final October 1781 showdown at Yorktown, where a combined American-French Army reaped the final decisive victory on the James River, Washington's Continental Army was supplied with tons of the best French arms, especially the model 1766 French musket, munitions, and supplies.

In a chain reason, Washington's Trenton success (won without French weapons except for a handful of cannon) set the stage for massive French aid that paved the way for victory at Saratoga, where Horatio Gates's Army scored a victory in no small part because 90 percent of its weaponry and munitions were obtained from France. Washington's Trenton and Princeton winter victories so upset the strategic situation in 1777 that Howe remained too far south of Albany, New York, at a most decisive moment. Instead, he was too intently focused on Washington's unpredictable army that might again suddenly lash out as at Trenton, taking his strategic focus away from a crucial linkage with General John Burgoyne's march south from Canada and down the Hudson toward Albany to split the colonies in half to reap decisive victory in the northern theater. Therefore, in the end, Trenton's legacy played a key role in sealing the fate of "Gentleman Johnny" at Saratoga and British fortunes in America.[4]

Quite simply, without Washington's dramatic victory at Trenton which was the "necessary precursor," neither the Saratoga victory or the all-important French Alliance were possible. In his diary, Reverend Erza Stiles, the esteemed president of Yale University in 1778, made the connection between "the Action at Trenton [and] a Gent[leman who] arrived [from England where he had] heard Gen.[Ireland-born Eyre] Massey declare on Change that a french War was [now] inevitable & that the Rebels would hold America."[5]

Thanks to the timely French Alliance of February 1778 that bestowed official recognition on the new people's republic, a proud Great Britain suffered its "only clear defeat" in what was its lengthy global struggle against France and an expansive conflict of attrition that stretched from the Revolution of 1688 to Napoleon's defeat in the Belgium fields and meadows of Waterloo in mid-June 1815.[6]

In analyzing the supreme importance of Washington's improbable victories at Trenton and Princeton in the shaping of not American but also world history, British historian George Trevelyan summarized without hyperbole how: "It may be doubted whether so small a number of men ever employed so short a space of time with greater or more lasting effects upon the history of the world."[7] Quite simply, the tide had been turned by Washington during the Trenton-Princeton Campaign. In a letter to Thomas Jefferson who eventually preceded him as Virginia's wartime governor, Yorktown-born Thomas Nelson, Jr., penned in a letter: "Our affairs have had a black appearance for the two last months, but [now] We have at last turned the Tables upon these scoundrels by surprize."[8]

And a prophetic Robert Morris, who had defiantly remained in Philadelphia while the rest of Congress fled to Baltimore, praised Washington in a December 28 letter: "we rejoice in your [recent] success at Trenton as we conceive it will have the most important publick consequences . . . ."[9] Indeed, "no other victory has meant more to American history, and very few battles in all history have had the lasting significance of Trenton." Washington's Trenton-Princeton Campaign "changed the history of the world" and in the most dramatic way possible.[10]

In the words of one modern historian, "Had Washington lost this battle [of Trenton], the defeat almost certainly would have spelled the end of the revolutionary army and therefore the revolution itself, leaving Britain in control of the North American colonies for an indeterminate period in the future . . . ."[11] In a strange irony, perhaps the only patriot in America who was not thoroughly impressed by Washington's amazing success at Trenton was his own mother. When she first heard of her son's remarkable victories at Trenton and Princeton, Mary Ball Washington merely dismissed the exciting news and lavish praise heaped upon her commander-in-chief son as, "Here is too much flattery."[12]

A lampooning Benjamin Franklin, who gained a great deal more credibility as the American ambassador in Paris to secure the decisive French Alliance with the Trenton victory, waxed satirically in February 1777 in regard to the large payment due from the British government to the German princes for each Hessian soldier lost at Trenton by presenting a biting satire about the prince of Hesse-Cassel's imagined cynical, sarcastic response to the Trenton disaster: "I have learned with unspeakable pleasure [of] the courage our troops exhibited at Trenton, and you cannot image my joy on being told that of the 1,950 Hessians engaged in the fight but 345 escaped . . . Do you remember that of the 300 Lacedaemonians [Spartans] who defended the defile of Thermopylae, not one returned? How happy should I be could I say the same of my brave Hessians! It is true that their king, Leonidas, perished with them: but things have changed, and it is no longer the custom of princes of the empire to go and fight in America for a cause with which they have no concern . . . I am not at all content with [the] saving [of] the 345 men who escaped the massacre at Trenton."[13]

Most importantly, Washington's one-sided success at Trenton gave new life not only to the resistance effort, but also to the very existence of the Continental Army that had been headed for certain extinction. For the first time, Washington proved that the most feared professional soldiers in the British Army could be vanquished by mostly ex-farmers, poorly trained and ill-clothed, imbued with a burning love of liberty. Washington's amazing victory at Trenton, therefore, guaranteed that a good many new recruits rallied to Washington's Army by the start of the 1777 Campaign, regenerating and fueling the resistance effort from its pre-Trenton nadir.[14]

While America celebrated Washington's one-sided success at Trenton, other patriots felt a good deal less joyous. The young wife of Captain Daniel Neil, Eliza, suffered her most devastating personal loss that overshadowed news of the Trenton and Princeton victories. Neill, who was "personally very brave and greatly beloved by his men," had just won a well-deserved promotion to major for his splendid performance at Trenton, but never saw it officially confirmed, falling to rise no more at Princeton. Eliza Neil was not even comforted by the return of her husband's body to their Acquackanonk farm along the Passaic River because the promising New Jersey artillery captain was buried at an unknown location just north of Clark's farm at Princeton. With her husband dead and once-splendid New Jersey farm ransacked by the British and Hessians, a grieving Eliza, with two young children to support on her own, found herself without a provider. Therefore, during the same harsh winter that her young husband was killed, she and her children became entirely "destitute."

On February 19, 1777, Eliza penned a desperate, pathetic appeal directly to Washington: "The unhappy situation in which I am left by the late Catastrophe of my Husband, major Daniel Neil of the Artillery who was slain at the Battle in Princeton January 3, 1777–induces me to apply to your Excellency [because] the Farm on Wich [sic] wee [sic] lived is rendered useless by the Enemy–so that I am left with two small Children destitute of Support, unless the honorable the Continental Congress will allow me the Benefit of a Resolution I am informed was made relative to the support of the Widows & orphans, who will be rendered thereby comfortable during the Calamities of War."[15]

Nevertheless, an impoverished Eliza and her two infants continued to suffer during one of the worst winters in recent memory. Deeply moved by the family tragedy, Washington sent Eliza's plea for relief to Congress with his own February 28 letter of support: "Inclosed you have a Letter from the Widow of a brave Officer who was killed at princeton [and] I can venture to recommend her as a proper Object, to made some Reparation for her great Loss."[16] Unfortunately, for Eliza and other grieving, destitute widows of deceased Continental soldiers across America, Congress had not yet created a relief program for women who had lost their soldier-husbands in battle. Therefore, near the end of April 1777, a somewhat embarrassed Washington informed Eliza Neil how "that Honble body have, I presume, thought it too early to adopt a measure of this kind . . . as I sincerely feel for your distress, I beg your acceptance of the Inclosed [$50.00], as a small testament of my Inclination to serve you upon any future occasion."[17] Bestowing a timely charity long unrecognized by historians and forgotten, the compassionate Washington assisted Captain Neil's widow with funds out of his own pocket.

New York-born Governor William Livingston later appealed to the state legislature in mid-September 1777 for relief to the "distressed Widow and orphans of that brave Officer," Daniel Neil. But even this appeal from the state's highest ranking official, New Jersey's first revolutionary governor, fell on deaf ears. New Jersey, now that the revolution's tide had turned thanks partly to Captain Neil's courageous efforts at Trenton, had seemingly turned its back on Mrs. Neil in "her present Situation [that] is truly deplorable . . . . "[18]

In a letter, Rhode Island-born General Greene, who led the Second Division with distinction at Trenton, lamented Eliza's tragic situation, which "melts the hearts of all."[19] Not until June 1781—only a few months before the final victory at Yorktown, and more than four and a half years after Captain Neil's battle-field death—and thanks to the unsung humanitarian efforts of Washington and Knox, who mutually lamented how the handsome, young artillery captain had been killed "at the head of his [artillery] Company while nobly supporting the Liberties of his Country," was Eliza and her children finally awarded some financial relief, although yet insufficient, from the state.[20]

Although long overlooked and forgotten by America, Washington's capable infantry and artillery commanders, like Captain Neil, played stirring roles in securing victory at Trenton. A secret of his remarkable success on December 26, Washington benefitted immensely from commanding a determined, highly motivated soldiery, especially so many talented leaders of his unsung officer corps: ironically, generally young men who could never have obtained officer's commissions in the British Army. But this secret formula for success was no accident. Early recognizing talent and leadership ability, Washington had personally groomed and promoted militarily inexperienced men from civilian life, especially Knox and Greene, who evolved into his capable top lieutenants, who rose to the fore at Trenton. All in all, Washington could not have achieved victory at Trenton without the boundless ability, skill, and resourcefulness of some of the finest natural regimental, brigade, and division commanders ever to serve together on a single battlefield from 1775-1783.

Captain Neil was only one such dynamic young leader who rose splen-didly to Trenton's formidable challenge. Fortunately, the forty-five-year-old Washington had possessed an excellent supporting cast of capable, hard-fighting top lieutenants, general officers, and colonels for the dramatic showdown at Trenton: John Glover, John Stark, Hugh Mercer, Henry Knox, Alexander Hamilton, John Haslet, John Sullivan, Nathaniel Greene, Edward Hand, Lord Stirling, and fine lower-grade officers and unit commanders like Captains William Washington, Joseph Moulder, Thomas Forrest, Winthrop Sargent, John Fleming, and Lieutenant James Monroe and other fine leaders, who were no less determined to achieve victory on December 26. These were self-made men whose natural talents and gifts would not have risen to the fore in the old class-based European system based on proper aristocratic bloodlines, especially Hamilton and even Washington, and hence they would have been doomed to relative obscurity. These resourceful, enterprising leaders of outstanding natural ability were literally America's best and brightest, and they demonstrated as much at Trenton in splendid fashion. Such shining stars in the constellation of Washington's officer corps represented the rise of a new generation of young, dynamic leaders. Without the many contributions of this extraordinary group of exceptional leaders, who rewarded Washington's trust and faith on December 26, the final outcome at Trenton might have been altogether different.[21] These men of promise rose magnificently to the challenge and put their lives on the line at Trenton because, as explained by the eloquent words of John Adams, "I must study . . . war, that my sons may have liberty to study mathematics and philosophy" and other higher pursuits in life.[22]

All of these enterprising junior officers except Washington's senior commanders, such as Mercer and Stirling who were in their early fifties, were younger than most of Rall's officers, who were in their forties and fifties. At the time of the battle of Trenton, Greene was thirty-four, Knox twenty-six, Hamilton nineteen, and Captain John Fleming, another rising star, twenty-one. Fleming commanded the First Virginia Continental Regiment at Trenton until killed at Princeton.

This highly motivated, energetic officer corps represented the development of something special: an elite officer corps, which had subtly occurred without anyone quite fully realizing it, and just in time for the Trenton challenge. Without a standing army or professional military tradition as in Prussia and England, a good many gifted, talented American civilians, including men with little or no prior military experience or training and from all walks of life, had come together in a people's revolution to lead mostly untrained, ill-equipped troops to prevail over veteran professional soldiers under European military-educated leaders. Most importantly, they demonstrated that older, more experienced Hessian leaders, who fought by the rule book in a traditional manner, could no longer so easily dominate this new generation of America's revolutionary leaders, who had relied upon flexibility, innovativeness, and suppleness, rather than revered European military educations and convention, to overcome their opponents at Trenton: the rise of the American way of war.

Washington, five years younger than Colonel Rall, had persevered amid the greatest adversity and series of defeats which had allowed him the opportunity to evolve, adapt, and mature until he emerged as a flexible, masterful orchestrator of brilliant innovative tactics at Trenton literally at the last minute. Washington had been thoroughly tempered by the almost unbearable weight of military and political uncertainties, lack of support on every level, and embarrassing defeats (a harsh tactical and leadership school of hard knocks that forced the commander-in-chief to more thoroughly appreciate the wisdom of the distinct, inherent tactical advantages of the unconventional tactics of partisan, or insurgency, warfare) to set the stage for the timely creation of his tactical masterpiece at Trenton.

By relying upon a masterful blend of mobility, stealth, and surprise to strike an overpowering blow to break an opponent's will to resist, Washington in essence emulated Napoleon's most successful tactics and a dynamic leadership style that inspired his troops to achieve the impossible during the most adverse situation and conditions. America's nearly fatal, illusionary, and badly misplaced faiths—too much reliance placed upon militia instead of a professional army and the folly of defending fortified positions (the "war of posts") against a vastly superior and better-trained opponent, an overeagerness to replace Washington as the Continental Army's commander, and the myth of Hessian invincibility—vanished forever, when hundreds of stunned Rall brigade grenadiers and fusiliers raised their hands to surrender at Trenton: an unbelievable sight never imagined or seen before.

Like Washington himself, so the young men and boys in Washington ranks were likewise transformed and rejuvenated into something entirely new (winners, not losers) by the multiple challenges of crossing the ice-clogged Delaware, the grueling nighttime march through a blinding snowstorm, and engaging in the close-range, urban combat that raged through Trenton's snowy streets. Because of this searing process that was in essence a character-building forge, they evolved into real professional soldiers who were suddenly were made more formidable by a heightened level of discipline, morale, and determination, thanks to Washington's leadership skill in honing a keener edge in his men's abilities, skills, and attitudes that rose to the fore during the Trenton challenge: a most timely development that was necessary to reap the war's most surprising victory at Trenton. A yet amazed Washington, therefore, warmly praised his men in his official report "for their gallant and spirited behavior [as] he did not see a single instance of bad behavior in either officers or privates."[23]

America and the revolutionary struggle's darkest hour and lowest ebb had finally passed after Washington's sparkling victory at Trenton, vanishing like Howe and Great Britain's loftiest imperial ambitions in the snows of Trenton. Nevertheless, the battle of Trenton had been a very close thing, and much more so than generally recognized by historians. The impetuous, infant American republic came precariously close to succumbing to an early, agonizing death, until Washington gambled everything on one throw of the dice by unleashing the carefully calculated and most audacious surprise attack in American history.

Less than a quarter century after the battle of Trenton and long after more than three thousand Hessians, including those Germans captured at Trenton and George Armstrong Custer's ancestor—a Hessian sergeant captured at Saratoga—either settled in America or returned to Germany, Washington departed his stately Mount Vernon mansion on horseback in softly falling snow. This gentle snowfall might well have reminded him of that unforgettable December 26 morning along the Delaware in western New Jersey so long ago. As was his custom, Washington rode out into the biting cold to survey the sprawling lands, covered in bare trees and brown fields, of his Mount Vernon estate on December 12, 1799, which was possibly on the anniversary of the very day some twenty-three years before when he had decided to assault Trenton.

Preoccupied with the upkeep of his extensive properties, Washington remained out longer in the cold, windy weather than was prudent. All the while, the snow and sleet steadily fell across the farming lands that bordered the wide Potomac, covering the landscape in a blanket of white. But Washington simply ignored the incessant deluge just like during the nightmarish, December 25-26, 1776 march upon Trenton through a swirling snowstorm that seemed to have no end. Washington was about to catch a nasty cold and a "very sore" throat from a severe bacterial infection, while snowflakes dropped softly around him like on that cold, unforgettable December morning so long ago, when it had seemed that America's republican experiment in nationhood was doomed to certain annihilation.

Instead of returning to a warm fireplace at his Mount Vernon mansion to change his wet clothing, Washington, age sixty-seven, continued to gallop over the winter-hued land that he loved. Amid the gently falling snow that descended over the Virginia Tidewater, perhaps he once again felt a certain sense of exhilaration with the fond memory of his most brilliant tactical achievement of the war when he had been in his prime. After all, Washington's remarkable success at Trenton was in part due to the fierce snowstorm that had served as an effective screen for his attackers, demonstrating that such inclement conditions favored a guerrilla-like offensive strike even in winter, while good weather conditions always favored regular troops and conventional warfare.

Therefore, if such comforting thoughts of past glory were in mind, Washington might well have even savored nature's wintertime beauty and the serene, calm silence of the cascading snow, which shortly piled up to several inches. But any such invigorating thoughts about that all-important late December morning in 1776, when he won his most audacious gamble of the war to revive the faith of a fast-fading people's revolution, had dimmed considerably by the time that Washington lay dying in his bed. Ironically, partly because of a physician's excessive ill-advised bleeding that resulted in a much greater loss of Washington's blood than he had shed on that cold Thursday morning at Trenton, Washington's last day of life, when he was bled four times and lost five pints of blood that devastated his massive body and left him near hemorrhagic shock, came on December 14: the anniversary of when he had been planning his surprise attack on Trenton nearly a quarter century before.

Ironically, Washington's end came as swiftly and as unexpectedly as when he had delivered his tactical masterstroke and surprise attack that doomed an entire Hessian brigade to inglorious defeat at Trenton. Perhaps, in his final hour with his life slowly fading away thanks in no small part to so-called remedies and medicines of his physicians, Washington yet heard the cold, winter wind howl outside Mount Vernon's windows as when it had raged so fiercely in sweeping through his thin column of ragged soldiers, while they toiled relentlessly through the snow toward Trenton and a rendezvous with destiny. Therefore, Washington now might well have thought back upon or dreamed one final time about that unforgettable December 26 morning and his remarkable success, when he was never prouder of the splendid performance of his long-suffering, stoic men, who rose so magnificently to their greatest challenge.[24]

While Mount Vernon lay under a white shroud of snow like the little Delaware River town of Trenton so long ago when he was a much younger man, Washington also might have found a measure of solace in perhaps recalling his best leadership decision of that memorable campaign that had made his surprise of the Trenton garrison possible, when he issued his December 1, 1776 order for his men to secure "particularly . . . the Durham Boats which are very proper" for crossing the Delaware to make possible the most audacious and unexpected success of the American Revolution.[25]

Ironically, and most symbolically, Washington had also ordered the assembly of "all vessels to ferry the armies [American and French in August 1781] across the Delaware" on the march to Yorktown and the final decisive victory against his old antagonist, Cornwallis, who had chased him across the Delaware in early December 1776, just before he reversed the tide at Trenton.[26]

Clearly, in his final hours, Washington possessed ample good reason to have reflected with fondness on what he had accomplished against the odds at Trenton, and how he had confounded all of the leading military experts. The revolution's course could not have been reversed at Trenton without the

Virginian having first employed the most appropriate tactical lessons from both sides of the Atlantic which combined—a most timely fusion and fortuitous synergy—at a time, when Washington had desperately needed to do something radically different in tactical terms to rescue America's struggle from the jaws of defeat. Indeed, the insightful words of Sun Tzu, written around 500 BC, which emphasized the importance of a military commander having the uncanny ability to evolve and change his outdated thinking and obsolete, failing tactics, adopting to more fluid, innovative, and flexible tactics to achieve victory, demonstrate the true secret to Washington's remarkable success at Trenton. The philosophic Chinese war theorist wrote how "Military tactics are like unto water, for water in its natural course runs away from high places and hastens downwards. So in war, the way to avoid what is strong is to strike what is weak . . . He who can modify his tactics in relation to his opponent and thereby succeed in winning, may be called a heaven-born captain."[27]

At Trenton, Washington mastered these fundamental ancient truths, timeless lessons, and secrets of Sun Tzu's *The Art of War* to reap his first real battlefield success in dramatic fashion. As revealed in an editorial in the January 21, 1777 issue of the *Pennsylvania Evening Post* and that hinted of Sun Tzu's ancient axioms of war: "Gen. Washington, perceiving this favourable [sic] opportunity, on a sudden resolves to take advantage of it. In one of those dark and dismal nights, which the greatest masters in the art of war recommend for an enterprise of this kind, he passes over the Delaware with only twenty-four hundred men and quick as lightening falls on the astonished and surprised enemy [and] He wins an almost bloodless victory . . . ."[28]

"Nowhere in the annals of warfare can be found a counterpart of the winter campaign of Washington and his army," wrote historian William S. Stryker. America was fortunate to have had exactly the right man, at the right place, and at the right time to reverse a new nation's destiny in late December 1776. Victory at Trenton was simply not possible without Washington's "incredible ability to persist in the face of uncertainties, agonizing betrayals, frustrations and prolonged desperate physical demands that would have stopped almost any other man."[29] In fact, never in the history of nations was a people's revolution closer to the brink of certain extinction and dark oblivion than immediately before Washington struck with an unexpected blow at Trenton to reverse the course and fortunes of war.

However, in the unforgettable story of Trenton, other leading players and architects of this most dramatic of Washington's victories have been doomed to obscurity. Even the irrepressible, can-do brigade commander who had made it possible for Washington to cross the Delaware, John Glover, was not only soon forgotten, but also wreaked emotionally, physically, and financially by the war's demands and horrors. Glover's large family, without a main provider while the patriarch served for years under Washington and at a time when Marblehead's economy was wrecked by the British blockage of the Grand Banks, suffered most severely. While battling for a new nation's liberty, Glover lost much of what was most precious to him, including his eldest son, who had marched beside him during the stormy descent upon Trenton, and his wife Hannah, who died of disease at Marblehead in 1778. As Glover penned to Washington of his sad personal situation in 1778 less than two years after the battle of Trenton: "When I entered the service in 1775 I had as good a constitution as any man of my age, but it's now broken and shattered to pieces," thanks in no small part to his leading role in orchestrating the Delaware crossing, leading his New England Continentals into the raging battle at Trenton, and achieving significant tactical gains in the lower town.[30]

At the war's conclusion and after having obtained a general's rank, Glover returned "home a Beggar" to his motherless family, failed business, and modest wooden Georgian gambrel, two-story house that faced the sea, which had once provided his family with prosperity. Tragically, Glover described how years of faithful service to his country under Washington came at "the expense of my Little fortune, earned by hard labor and industry; to the sacrifice . . . and total ruin of a family of [eight] young children. . . ."[31]

Like the irrepressible Glover, Washington's common soldiers also paid a high price in order to reap their unforgettable victory at Trenton. While no Americans had been killed and only six wounded at Trenton, the final tally of the sacrifice was actually much higher among these tried veterans in the months and even years after the battle. Exactly how many of Washington's soldiers eventually died of exhaustion, disease, and exposure from the winter campaign's harsh rigors will never be known, but this number was almost certainly higher than the total Hessian casualties of more than one hundred. One of Washington's typical Trenton veterans who paid a high price for this all-important victory on that late December morning was Ireland-born soldier Private William McCarty, of Lieutenant Colonel Francis Ware's First Maryland Continental Regiment, which was part of Mercer's brigade.

Crippled by the arduous 1776 winter campaign and plagued with worthless Continental money from spiraling inflation while his Maryland family suffered from his lengthy absence, this forgotten hero of the battle of Trenton finally deserted out of an urgent need to at long last go home, but only after the revolution's fortunes had been successfully reversed. In a February 1777 *Maryland Gazette* newspaper ad, placed by his captain, Alexander Murray, that offered a four dollar reward for his capture, William McCarty was described as "an Irishman, about forty years old, [and he] had on when he deserted, a blanket over-coat, round hat, and his shoes tied with strings, his feet have been frostbitten. He says he was an old soldier in the British service, he has something of the [Irish] brogue in his language."[32]

Although Private McCarty's sacrifice was never listed in his official army service records, McCarty's tragic case revealed the high hidden and tragic costs that continued to be paid in full by Trenton veterans long after the battle. These were Washington's forgotten, untabulated casualties of the perilous river crossing, the nightmarish march to Trenton, harsh winter conditions, and the bitter street fighting: true losses that were in striking contrast to the mythical, much-embellished, and endlessly repeated story of the two never-identified American soldiers who supposedly froze to death during the snowy trek to Trenton.[33]

Even General Stirling, who had been relatively well-clothed for winter's harshest offerings compared to the threadbare enlisted men, became "very ill . . . owing to what I suffered on our Expedition to Trenton," as penned in a January 8, 1777 letter.[34] All that Washington's common soldiers received for their supreme efforts and high sacrifices, except for considerable personal satisfaction, was sincere thanks from Congress: although these young men and boys from across America had been "broken by Fatigue & ill-Fortune" on December 26, they nevertheless were "inspired, and animated by a just Confidence in their Leader," and greatly "exceed[ed] E[x]pection [and] the Limits of Probability."[35]

Paradoxically, even a good many Hessians captured at Trenton were more fortunate than Washington's victors, like Private McCarty, even as prisoners. German soldiers, both before and after their capture, fell in love with America, which they viewed as an "earthly paradise" and "the land of promise—the land where milk and honey flows," as one Hessian captain wrote in a letter.[36] Another Hessian officer marveled about America's seemingly endless promise: "Here a man, even of the meanest [lowest] station, provided he will only do something, can live as well as the richest." Therefore, a large percentage of the captured Hessians, including Lieutenant Wiederhold, eventually became good, faithful American citizens after their parole and release. In this new land of endless bounty and promise so unlike impoverished Hesse-Cassel, many of Rall's veterans gained liberal land grants and found loving American wives, raising families and blending in with the young nation's melting pot population after the war's end. In a strange twist of fate, a large percentage of surviving grenadiers and fusiliers eventually became part of what they once had fought so hard against on that late December morning in Trenton's snowy streets.[37]

Equally ironic in the years ahead, America eventually developed a closer identification with Germany—in no large part because of a shared Protestantism—instead of its wartime ally, Catholic France, which was sufficiently inspired by the American Revolution to embark upon its own people's revolution against monarchy in 1789, despite the vital strategic alliance between the two nations that Washington helped to secure with his victory at Trenton.[38]

Despite a remarkable victory of mostly Protestants over fellow Protestants in a non-religious war, Washington's success at Trenton was most of all a great moral victory for a beleaguered nation, providing America with a timely reconfirmation that God was indeed on the revolutionaries' side. Washington's seemingly divinely bestowed Trenton success verified the validity of the American people's strong Old Testament faith, now infused with Age of Enlightenment ideology, and reinvigorated the conceptual and spiritual idea that America was a sacred, moral, and holy place under the sun. Viewed as a symbolic moral showdown, Washington's remarkable success at Trenton reconfirmed in people's minds that America was indeed a specially blessed place in God's grand scheme of things, far removed from Old World corruption and decadence. In this sense, Washington, like an ancient Old Testament prophet, had indeed led his people to the promised land by crossing the Delaware and capturing Trenton. Consequently, Washington's December 26 victory rekindled the righteous faith that America was destined to fulfill its sacred mission as a blessed land of liberty and holy place, based upon cherished Old Testament moral principles and values.

More than any other single episode of the American Revolution's tortured course, Washington's impossible success—seemingly an actual miracle to people on both sides of the Atlantic—at Trenton revived the almost-extinguished spiritual and seemingly mystical faith that America offered a righteous new beginning not only to Americans, but also to people around the world, fulfilling John Winthrop's original utopian vision "that wee shall be a Citty upon a Hill . . . ."[39]

At the last moment when seemingly the idealstic dream of America had died, Washington's outstanding success at Trenton breathed new life into the new republican faith in which the common people ruled themselves and determined their own destiny in "a new Jerusalem" according to God's wishes without the arbitrary dictates of autocratic kings, class, privilege, and wealth. In the end, Washington's Trenton victory ensured that America's popular uprising would not be crushed like so many other people's rebellions as in Ireland and Scotland. Americans once again began to believe that moral good could indeed conquer evil, and that even the mighty English Empire, and its Hessian allies, could be defeated because God was indeed on the American revolutionaries' side. Most of all, Washington's sparkling victory at Trenton not only set the stage for the eventual winning of the struggle for liberty, but also provided an indispensable stepping stone along the evolutionary path of overall human progress with the widespread recognition that a people's republic, and its golden promise of a fresh, new beginning for mankind, was the best form of government for Americans and people around the world.[40]

More than eighty years after the battle of Trenton and on another bitterly cold winter day like that which had been endured by Washington and his half-frozen, hopeful soldiers during their grueling march through the winter storm to a rendezvous with destiny at Trenton, newly elected President Abraham Lincoln traveled east from the windswept Illinois prairies of the vastness of America's heartland with his own sense of destiny. He journeyed toward the nation's capital (no longer Philadelphia as in 1776), now named in honor of the revered Virginian, by train in February 1861. Lincoln was on his way to take the highest office of the self-destructing American republic with the American experiment in democracy unraveling at its very seams after seven Southern states had already seceded from the Union during the turbulent winter of 1860-1861. This was now the darkest hour for America's fortunes since just before Washington launched his high stakes attack on Trenton.

Drawing upon the meaningful historical lessons of the last time that the American republic had confronted a greater national crisis and life-threatening peril, Lincoln realized that he now faced a task "greater than that which rested upon Washington" in late December 1776, and that he could only succeed with "the assistance of the Divine Being." For the first time in his life, Lincoln stopped at Trenton in a symbolic pilgrimage, after just having visited Philadelphia, the "Cradle of Liberty," on George Washington's birthday. But eerily, it was almost as if the president-elect had been to Trenton before, because Lincoln had so often read about the stirring story of Washington's Delaware crossing and the famous battle of Trenton since the lazy days of his youth.

Therefore, the deep moral inspiration of Washington's Trenton victory that saved a dying infant nation and a revolutionary struggle yet burned vividly in the mind, heart, and memory of the spare, fifty-one-year-old Illinoisan (near Colonel Rall's age when he died at Trenton) who had traveled from deep inside America's sprawling heartland of endless bounty. Here, at Trenton, Lincoln felt the ghostly, inspirational presence and moral weight of when Washington had been at his best to literally save the day for America at the last minute. Consequently, Lincoln now saw Washington as "the mightiest name of earth," in no small part because of what he had accomplished at this very place located along the Delaware River.

Inspired by the American Revolution's enduring moral and spiritual legacies and Washington's timeless example, Lincoln feared that the American nation was about to lose forever what Washington and his ill-clad soldiers of courage and faith had reaped at Trenton and what the revolutionary generation—truly America's greatest—had created with so much blood, toil, and sacrifice. Therefore, for Lincoln, Washington and his improbable Trenton success provided the best inspirational example about what it would take to rejuvenate an even more progressive revolution in America, while restoring the American revolution's original idealistic promise—yet unfulfilled—of equality for all men. Here, during the third week of February 1861 and basking in the symbolic and historic significance of standing on the most sacred ground of America's fabled saga in the nation's creation story, Lincoln spoke slowly, but eloquently, with growing emotion to the New Jersey legislature on the very spot where Washington had reaped his incredible victory. Lincoln immediately drew a direct parallel between the American nation's two greatest national trials and fiery upheavals: 1776 and 1861.

With the late February weather betraying the first slight hint of an early New Jersey spring and a symbolic, although unrealized at the time, new beginning for America, the president-elect reflected with awed, solemn reverence upon Washington's inspirational example in leading his tattered band of followers across the Delaware on the darkest of nights during a fierce northeaster to achieve the most improbable and surprising of victories at the very spot where he now stood. In a most thoughtful Gettysburg Address-like speech to the New Jersey Senate at Trenton, Lincoln explained the essence of his own personal sense of moral mission and sacred duty as the American nation's newly chosen leader to preserve the Union, on the verge of the ultimate nightmare of civil war, while sounding eerily much like an equally determined General

Washington, whose motivation had been "Victory or Death," back when the young nation's greatest crisis situation seemed without any solution whatsoever and America's fortunes had never been lower than on that frozen December morning in western New Jersey: "away back in my childhood, the earliest days of my being able to read, I got hold of a small book, such a one as few of the younger members have ever seen, 'Weem's *Life of Washington.*' I remember all the accounts there given of the battle-fields and struggles for the liberties of the country, and none fixed themselves upon my imagination so deeply as the struggle here at Trenton, New Jersey. The crossing of the river; the contest with the Hessians; the great hardships endured at that time, all fixed themselves on my memory, more than any single revolutionary event; and you all know, for you have all been boys, how these early impressions last longer than any others, I recollect thinking then, boy even though I was, that there must have been something more than common that these men struggled for. I am exceedingly anxious that thing which they struggled for; that something even more than National Independence; that something that held out a great promise to all the people of the world in all time to come. I am exceedingly anxious that this Union, the Constitution and the liberties of the people shall be perpetuated in accordance with the original Ideas for which that struggle was made, and I shall be most happy indeed if I shall be an humble instrument in the hands of the Almighty, and of this, his almost chosen people, as the chosen instrument, also in the hands of the Almighty, for perpetuating the object of that great struggle."[41]

Indeed, near the one hundred, twenty-ninth anniversary of Washington's birthday, barely a week after his own birthday some fifty-two years before in the rolling hills of north central Kentucky, Lincoln fully understood exactly what had most of all inspired Washington's young men and boys, both northerners and southerners to unite together as one, to risk all in the war's most desperate gamble to win an impossible victory that so few people—perhaps only themselves—had believed even remotely possible. Reflecting upon the very core of America's true meaning and revered symbolic place as a shining beacon of liberty for people around the world, Lincoln reached deep down within his own soul to articulate the most concise answer to the mystery as to why Washington and his hungry, cold, and ill-shod men had fought with so such spirit, courage, and determination to achieve a remarkable victory at Trenton.

With an insightful brilliance that revealed his unshaken conviction in the meaning of the "self-evident" truths expressed in the Declaration of

Independence as his ever-reliable moral compass, Lincoln emphasized the inherent essence of America's true meaning while also explaining his own determination to make the correct decisions in the future that were necessary to preserve the Union. Inspired by Washington's dynamic leadership example at this very special place on another cold winter day so long ago, Lincoln was emboldened, feeling more confident in facing the great trials of 1861-1865 that lay ahead, because he understood above all that "There must have been something more than common that those men struggled for [and] something that held out a great promise to all the people of the world for all time to come."[42]

Even more than Age of Enlightenment rhetoric or the Declaration of Independence, what Washington and his tattered, ill-equipped citizen soldiers had kept alive with their long-shot victory at Trenton was the golden dream, idealistic hope, and "the original idea" of America, which bestowed the great "promise that in due time the weights should be lifted from the shoulders of all men, and that *all* should have an equal chance" in life.[43]

Lincoln also echoed the utopian words and egalitarian vision of Thomas Paine, who had inspired hundreds of Continental troops, thanks largely to Washington's well-conceived, timely directive to have Paine's *The American Crisis* read by officers to his anxious, young soldiers just before they embarked on the perilous crossing of the Delaware on that bitterly cold Christmas evening, heightening their resolve and determination to succeed in successfully meeting their greatest challenge. As Paine had proclaimed with his masterful blend of passion, common man's logic, and historical insight: "The cause of America is in a great measure the cause of all mankind."[44]

Indeed, the "great promise" that America held out to the world was the optimistic vision and egalitarian dream of a free people pursuing their own "happiness" while ruling themselves by way of consent in a representative government and republic based upon individual liberty: the day's most enlightened and idealistic philosophical concept that proclaimed an unprecedented birth of freedom in the New World and the emergence of a new kind of truly egalitarian society that was more individualistic, free, and democratic than any other on earth: all of which Washington kept alive and preserved with his sparkling victory at Trenton.[45]

As Lincoln revealed in his moving words at Trenton in February 1861 on the Civil War's eve, the inspirational legacy of Washington's amazing success at Trenton continued to linger deeply in the hearts and minds of future generations of patriotic Americans across the United States. When General Robert

Edward Lee's Army of Northern Virginia invaded Pennsylvania in June 1863 and headed toward the crossroads town of Gettysburg, citizen soldiers of a threatened Philadelphia rallied around an old, silk battle flag carried by Pennsylvania soldiers in the battle of Trenton. Meanwhile, Lee's ragged invaders—looking more like Washington's men than the Yankees—identified with the suffering of Washington's soldiers at Trenton, embracing the appropriate revolutionary analogies and comparing their personal sacrifices to the ragged victors of December 26, 1776. Something legendary and almost mystical, this enduring example of the dedication and faith of Washington's ill-clothed Continental and state troops at Trenton has continued to inspire American fighting men around the world to this day.

Therefore, it was especially ironic that young American troops, perhaps including descendants of Washington's soldiers who fought at Trenton or even Colonel Rall's Hessians who had remained in America after the American Revolution, captured Cassel, Germany, in April 1945. This picturesque ancient city, once known as Hesse-Cassel, consisted of a population that yet included many old families who had once sent their sons and fathers to fight and die in faraway Trenton as proud members of the Rall's Grenadier Regiment so long ago.

Equally ironic, British Royal Air Force bombers dropped tons of heavy ordnance upon the German town of Bremen—another home community of Rall brigade soldiers—on September 5, 1942. Some bombs struck the Bremen Art Museum, destroying the first artistic rendition of the famous painting by Emanuel Leutze, the idealistic German liberal from Wurttemberg, who had created an iconic American work of art in part to remind the German people of the evils of monarchical abuses, including the hiring out of young men and boys as mercenaries to die in faraway lands, *Washington Crossing the Delaware*. With the cycles of history coming full circle, the United States and Great Britain became allies in a world war in which a new opponent, Germany, was viewed as evil as American colonists had once seen King George III and his invading legions from England and Germany.[46]

More than 160 years before the end of the Second World War and as written in the first sentence of his December 27, 1776 report to John Hancock, Continental Congress, a typically modest Washington gave no hint of the importance of what he and his mostly Continentals had accomplished against all odds on snowy December 26. However, this had been in fact the most "decisive day for the creation of the United States": a near miraculous feat of endurance and arms accomplished by only a relatively few resolute Continental and state soldiers, from America, Ireland, Germany, Scotland, and other faraway nations, because they had stubbornly refused to accept defeat and persevered at a time when no hope for success seemed possible. Never before and afterward would America owe so much to so few fighting men, and especially their never-say-die commander, who overcame almost unimaginable obstacles and the highest odds to ensure that a new republican nation conceived in liberty, rising like a phoenix from near extinction.

Revealing his sense of humility, Washington began his official Trenton battle report to John Hancock and the Continental Congress by merely presenting plain, matter-of-fact words that little seemed to be an adequate description of the war's most important victory to date, and a major turning point in American history, in which he and his band of citizen soldiers rose so magnificently to successfully meet their supreme challenge in what was their finest hour: "I have the pleasure of congratulating you upon the Success of an Enterprise, which I had formed against a Detachment of the Enemy lying in Trenton, and which was executed yesterday Morning."[47]

Washington's hastily written words might well have represented the greatest understatement in American history. In fact, never before had so few fighting men in the annals of military history accomplished so much to achieve a more improbable or important success with a more significant long-term impact for the American nation and the world than Washington and his soldiers of liberty. And no single person was more responsible for this dramatic, unexpected reversal of America's fortunes that saved the revolution and newborn republic from collapse than Washington.

During the nation's darkest hour, he inspired his often-beaten mostly yeomen farmers to believe in themselves—despite everything that said and emphasized the contrary—and to overcome the almost inconceivable challenge of crossing the raging Delaware during a perilous nighttime passage, and then a grueling march of nearly ten miles at night through an unfamiliar countryside amid a snowstorm to descend upon a full Hessian brigade with a vengeance, as if they were refreshed, never defeated, and properly clothed for winter warfare. With dazzling skill, Washington's brilliantly conceived orchestration of flexible, innovative tactics, both infantry and artillery, overcame the stale, formal, and overly complex tradition of linear tactics of Frederickan warfare and a bygone era. Europe's greatest conqueror of his generation and Napoleon's idol, Frederick the Great, was correct in his final summarization of Washington's

Trenton-Princeton Campaign: "The achievements of Washington and his little band of compatriots [in] a space of 10 days, were the most brilliant of any recorded in the annals of military achievements."[48]

Clearly, in the end, only one man in all America could have been so often defeated, criticized, and widely denounced by so many people on both sides, felt a greater measure of personal anguish, and experienced greater depths of frustration, but yet somehow not only persevered against seemingly endless difficulties but prevailed at a time when a revolution's end seemed inevitable and when the odds for success were seemingly impossible. Emerging stronger instead of having been overwhelmed by all manner of adversity, thanks in part to channeling his "gigantic and troubling" passions toward the goal of vanquishing a full Hessian brigade (something that had not been accomplished before) at Trenton, Washington possessed the uncanny ability to rise up during America's and his own darkest hour to face his infant nation's greatest challenge like the proverbial phoenix and to inspire his young, ill-trained troops and convince them that they could indeed accomplish anything against the odds, if they only believed in themselves.

Emboldened by strength of character, an unshakable faith in God and America's idealistic, egalitarian promise, and the most brilliant battle plan of the American Revolution, Washington magnificently led his often-defeated revolutionaries to achieve their greatest moral, psychological, and political victory of the American Revolution at Trenton to save an unprecedented republican dream and egalitarian experiment, which Lincoln described as the zenith of mankind's "political and moral freedom," from an early tragic death so that America could survive as a shining beacon of hope for the world. Praising the hidden, miraculous work of a divine helping hand (Washington's often-emphasized "Providence") which president-elect Lincoln also emphasized in his stirring speech at Trenton on the Civil War's eve, Colonel Knox wrote in a letter to "my dear [wife] Lucy" on December 28, 1776, how the victory at Trenton was due to "Providence [which] smiled" on America two winter days before.[49]

And in another most revealing letter about the Trenton and Princeton victories, the incomparable Knox concluded that he and America should "thank the great Governor of the Universe for producing this turn in our affairs."[50] In regard to his one-sided success at Trenton that led to America's rebirth, Washington praised God without ever using the word, writing with undisguised awe how "Providence has heretofore saved us in a remarkable manner."[51]

Indeed, most of all, Washington's victory at Trenton represented a great moral redemption and vindication for "the sacred cause . . . of Liberty," in Washington's words, where the determined Virginian and his equally resolute citizen soldiers had backed up Tom Paine's inspiring words by winning the war's most dramatic victory to reconfirm to people across America that the real "King of America" in fact "reigns above and doth not make havock [sic] of mankind like the Brute of Britain."[52]

Washington's remarkable success at Trenton most conclusively delivered a death stroke to the lofty, mystical aura of monarchy's sacredness and righteous authority by proving that its best professional soldiers in America could be decisively overcome by ordinary men of unshakeable faith against what was widely viewed as an invincible divinely sanctioned and omnipotent power. Perhaps New Englander Captain William Hull said it best in a letter in summarizing the miracle of Trenton: "What can't Men do when engaged in so noble a Cause."[53]

Won by mostly young, middle-class soldiers, primarily yeoman farmers, who fought and died for "the rights of man," in Colonel Knox's words as penned in a late December 1776 letter to his wife who was ahead of her time, Washington's Trenton victory that surprised the world convincingly demonstrated that anything was possible, including a prosperous life for the infant United States of America, which was no longer fated to die in its cradle, much to almost everyone's astonishment. After barely surviving its supreme moment of crisis by the narrowest of margins, a new day had dawned for America and the sacred "cause of freedom," in General Greene's words, with the most improbable of victories at Trenton, where a dying cause was reborn in the most miraculous fashion when time was running out. Because they never lost faith in America's golden promise and unprecedented meaning, Washington and his resilient band of homespun soldiers saved a fledgling republic that seemed destined for certain extinction.[54]

In the day's most brilliant political improvisation that resulted in America's Declaration of Independence, so another creative effort and masterful improvisation only a few months later led to the development of the most brilliant battle plan and the most surprising, unexpected victory in the annals of American history at Trenton. While no political event in American history was more pivotal than the Declaration of Independence, so no battle was more pivotal in the American saga than Trenton.

Not only saving the Continental Army and a newborn people's republic— the first created ever "intentionally by thought and moral choice" in mankind's history and the blueprint for the successful modern nation-state—by his most improbable of all victories, Washington most of all saved the "great idea" of America as the world's enduring symbol, its limitless promise, and the bright vision of a new beginning for the common man. The idealistic, utopian dream of America and the infant republic, "founded on the intrinsic sacredness of all men and women," would have perished if Washington, who was at his best when the situation was darkest, had lost his greatest gamble when everything was at stake at a little western New Jersey town during the most important battle in American history.[55]

In a most revealing letter, Captain William Hull, Nineteenth Connecticut Continental Regiment, Glover's brigade, perhaps said it best. He described exactly why and how Washington and his citizen soldiers, who had been united as a determined band of brothers by the forge of adversity for the greater good as never before, had overcome the odds to prevail, when "the fate of America," in Washington's words, hung in the balance on the bleak, frigid morning of December 26, 1776, when he undertook his greatest, but well-calculated, gamble with the life of America at stake in going for broke, because he most of all sincerely believed in what his men could accomplish because they were "engaged in so noble a Cause."[56]

After the American-French victory at Yorktown in October 1781, Washington stopped at Annapolis, Maryland, and received a heartfelt "City Address" (printed in the *Maryland Gazette* on November 29, 1781) from the people of the state capital that emphasized without exaggeration or hyperbole the supreme importance of Washington's winter 1776 campaign that saved America, "We derive peculiar pleasure from the contemplation, that the successes at Trenton and Princeton laid the corner stone of our freedom and independence:" the true birth and real beginning of the United States of America.[57]

Notes

Introduction

1. *Maryland Gazette*, Annapolis, November 29, 1781.
2. John Ferling, *The Ascent of George Washington, The Hidden Political Genius of an American Icon*, (New York: Bloomsbury Press, 2009), pp. 89-123; Rodney Atwood, *The Hessians, Mercenaries From Hessen-Kassel in the American Revolution*, (Cambridge: Cambridge University Press, 2002), pp. 95-96, 100; William Heath, *Memoirs of Major-General William Heath by Himself*, (New York: William Abbatt, 1901), p. 95; William S. Stryker, *The Battles of Trenton and Princeton*, (Trenton: Old Barracks Association, 2001), pp. 176, 187, 194; Rod Gragg, *By the Hand of Providence, How Faith Shaped the American Revolution*, (New York: Simon and Schuster, Inc., 2011), pp. 87, 89-91; David Hackett Fischer, *Washington's Crossing*, (New York: Oxford University Press, 2004), p. ix; Alan Dershowitx, *America Declares Independence*, (New York: John Wiley & Sons, Inc., 2003), p. 1; Robert Harvey, "A Few Bloody Noses," *The Realities and Mythologies of the American Revolution*, (New York: The Overlook Press, 2003), pp. 214-215; Suetonius Transquillus, *Suetonius, The Twelve Caesars*, (New York: Penguin Books, 2007), pp. 29-30.
3. Joseph J. Ellis, *American Creation, Triumphs and Tragedies at the Founding of the Republic*, (New York: Alfred A. Knopf, 2007), p. 6; Fischer, *Washington's Crossing*, pp. 206-244.
4. Ray Raphael, *Founding Myths, Stories That Hide Our Patriotic Past*, (New York: MJF Books, 2004), pp. 1-266.
5. Edward G. Lengel, *Inventing George Washington*, (New York: HarperCollins Publishers, 2011), pp. 1-5, 132-135.
6. Ibid., pp. 1-5, 8-214; Robert K. Wright, *The Continental Army*, (Washington, D.C.: The Center of Military History, United States Army, 1983), p. 320; David Bonk, *Trenton and Princeton 1776-77*, (Oxford: Osprey Publishing, 2009), pp. 19-20; John B. B. Trussell, *ThePennsylvania Line, Regimental Organization and Operations, 1775-1783*, (Harrisburg: Pennsylvania Historical and Museum Commission, 1993), pp. 225-226; Victor Von Hagen, *TheGermanic People in America*, (Norman: University of Oklahoma Press, 1976), pp. 159-162.
7. Scott G. Rall, Waldorf, Maryland, to author, July 22, 2010; Henry J. Retzer, *The German Regiment of Maryland and Pennsylvania in the Continental Army 1776-1781*,

(Bowie: Heritage Books, 2006), pp. 5, 51, 79, 131; Weiser Family Information, Conrad Weiser Homestead Archives, State Historic Site, Womelsdorf, Pennsylvania.

8. Atwood, *The Hessians*, pp. 12, 41, 99, note 82; Bonk, *Trenton and Princeton 1776-1777*, p. 49; Fischer, *Washington's Crossing*, pp. 201, 239-240, 256; Joseph M. Malit, Hessian historian, Maplewood, New Jersey, to author, July 9, 2010; Lengel, *Inventing George Washington*, p. 200.

9. W. E. Woodward, *George Washington*, (Greenwich, Conn: Fawcett Publications, 1956), p. 206.

10. Ibid., pp. 10, 35; Ron Chernow, *Washington, A Life*, (New York: Penguin Press, 2010), pp. 15-268; Fischer, *Washington's Crossing*, pp. 203, 264-265; Ray Raphael, *Founders, The People Who Brought You A Nation*, (New York: MJF Books, 2009), p. 267; Ferling, *The Ascent of George Washington*, p. 92; Fischer, *Washington's Crossing*, pp. 202-203

11. Ferling, *The Ascent of George Washington*, pp. 89-122; Lengel, *Inventing George Washington*, pp. 77-92, 132-135, 201; Willard M. Wallace, *Appealto Arms, A Military History of the American Revolution*, (New York: Harpers and Brothers, 1951), p. 127; Fischer, *Washington's Crossing*, pp. 260-261, 423; Stryker, *The Battles of Trenton and Princeton*, p. 402.

12. Lawrence E. Babits, *A Devil of a Whipping, The Battle of Cowpens*, (Chapel Hill: University of North Carolina Press, 1998), pp. Xiii-10, 61-160; Harry M. Ward, *Major General Adam Stephen and the Cause of American Liberty*, (Charlottesville: University Press of Virginia, 1989), p. 100; John T. Goolrick, *The Life of General Hugh Mercer*, (New York: The Neal Publishing Company, 1906), pp. 13-74; Frederick English, *General Hugh Mercer, Forgotten Hero of the American Revolution*, (Lawrenceville: Princeton Academic Press, 1975), pp. xii, 25-28, 58-59, 81; B. H. Liddell Hart, *Strategy*, (New York: Frederick A. Praeger Publishers, 1961), pp. 48-49.

13. Gragg, *In the Hands of Providence*, pp. 89-96; Thomas Fleming, *Liberty! The American Revolution*, (New York: Viking, 1997), pp. 217-218, 245, 253-262, 324-226.

14. Alan Valentine, *Lord Stirling, Colonial Gentleman and General in Washington's Army* (New York: Oxford University Press, 1969).

Chapter I

1. Ellis, *American Creation*, p. 43.

2. William Dwyer, *"The Day is Ours!," An Inside View of the Battles of Trenton and Princeton, November 1776-January 1777*, (New Brunswick, N. J.: Rutger's University Press, 1983), p. 108.

3. Worthington C. Ford, "British and American Prisoners of War, 1778," *The Pennsylvania Magazine of History and Biography*, no. 2, vol. 17, (1893), pp. 159; Dwyer, *The Day is Ours!*, p. 165.

4. Fischer, *Washington's Crossing*, pp. 216-216, 392-393; Bonk, *Trenton and Princeton 1776-77*, p. 35; Stryker, *The Battle of Trenton and Princeton*, pp. 129, 130, note 1, 360;

Alan Valentine, *Lord Stirling, Colonial Gentleman and General in Washington's Army*, (New York: Oxford University Press, 1969), p. 196; George Athan Billias, *General John Glover and his Marblehead Mariners*, (New York: Henry Holt and Company, 1960), pp. 6-7; Mark V. Kwasny, *Washington's Partisan War, 1775-1783*, (Kent: Kent State University Press, 1998), p. 98; Richard M. Ketchum, *The Winter Soldiers*, (New York: Henry Holt and Company, 1973), pp. 247-248; "The History of Johnson's Ferry," Information Guide, Washington's Crossing, New Jersey State Historic Site, New Jersey; *A Young Patriot in the American Revolution*, p. 80; Samuel Steele Smith, *The Battle of Trenton*, (Monmouth Beach: Philip Freneau Press, 1965), p. 18; Richard Hanser, *The Glorious Hour of Lt. Monroe*, (Brattleboro: The Book Press, 1975), p. 126; "Historic Resources of Washington's Crossing the Delaware," Paper, National Register of Historic Places, National Park Service, United States Department of Interior, Washington, D.C.; Ron Chernow, *Washington, A Life*, (New York: Penguin Press, 1910), p. 270; Chastullex, Marquis d., *Travels in North-America in the Years 1780-1781*, (New York: 1882), p. 122; David G. Chandler, *The Campaigns of Napoleon, The Mind and Methods of History's Greatest Soldier*, (New York: Scribner 1966), p. 145; Raphael, *Founders*, p. 286.

5. Stryker, *The Battles of Trenton and Princeton*, p. 360; Martin I. J. Griffin, *Catholics and the American Revolution*, (2 vols., Ridley Park: Martin I. J. Griffin, 1907), vol. 2, p. 382; Billias, *General John Glover and his Marblehead Mariners*, pp. 6-7; John Buchanan, *The Road to Valley Forge, How Washington Built the Army That Won the Revolution*, (Hoboken: John Wiley and Sons, Inc., 2004), p. 156.

6. Andro Linklater, *An Artist in Treason, The Extraordinary Double Life of General James Wilkinson*, (New York: Walker and Company, 2009), pp. 27-28; Chernow, *Washington*, p. 273; Fischer, *Washington's Crossing*, p. 210; Francis Rufus Bellamy, *The Private Life of George Washington*, (New York: Thomas Y. Crowell Company, 1951), pp. 53-54, 315, 347.

7. Gregory T. Edgar, *Campaign of 1776, The Road to Trenton*, (Bowie: Heritage Books, 2008), p 330; Chernow, *Washington*, pp. 269, 272-273; Gerald Mulvey and Elliot Abrams, "A Forensic Meteorological Perspective on the American Revolutionary War, Battles of Trenton and Princeton, AccuWeather, September 17, 2009, Power Point Presentation, internet.

8. Ronald N. Tagney, *A County in Revolution, Essex County at the Dawning of Independence*, (Manchester: The Crickett Press, Inc., 1976), p. 297-298; Ketchum, *The Winter Soldiers*, pp. 246, 248-249; Smith, *The Battle of Trenton*, p. 18.

9. Chastellux, *Travels in North-America*, pp. 69-70.

10. Billias, *General John Glover and his Marblehead Mariners*, pp. xi-xii, 1-34, 59-131; Tagney, *A County in Revolution, Essex County at the Dawning of Independence*), pp. 10-11, 161, 207; Samuel Roads, Jr., *The History and Traditions of Marblehead*, (Marblehead: Press of N. Allen Lindsey & Company, 1897), pp. 1-7, 46-48, 131; Priscilla Sawyer Lord and Virginia Clegg Gamage, *Marblehead, The Spirit of '76 Lives Here*, (New York: Chilton Book Company, 1972), pp. 16-17, 19-35, 61, 63, 69, 84, 91; Ronald N. Tagney, *The World Turned Upside Down, Essex County During*

America's Turbulent Years, 1763-1790, (West Newbury: Hamilton Printing Company, 1989), pp. 18, 21-23, 32; Wright, *The Continental Army*, p. 218; Mark Kurlansky, *Cod, A Biography of the Fish that Changed the World*, (New York: Penguin Books, 1998), pp. 59-114; William Upham, *A Memoir of General John Glover, of Marblehead*, (Charlottesville: University of Virginia Press, 1999), pp. 2, 4; Priscilla Sawyer Lord and Virginia Clegg Gamage, *The Lure of Marblehead, A New Guidebook to its colonial houses–crooked streets–and historic sites*, (Marblehead: Marblehead Publications, 1973), pp. 2, 5, 45; Fischer, *Washington's Crossing*, pp. 21-22, 219; Egar, *The Campaign of 1776*, pp. 157-159; Stryker, *The Battles of Trenton and Princeton*, p. 356

11. Roads, *The History and Traditions of Marblehead*, pp. 48, 67-68, 70, 78, 97; Gamage, *Marblehead*, pp. 30-35, 92; Gamage and Lord, *The Lure of Marblehead*, pp. 7, 13, 23-24, 27, 32, 34-35, 43, 45, 47; William L. Stone, *Letters of Brunswick and Hessian Officers During the American Revolution*, (Cranbury: Scholar's Bookshelf, 2005), p. 192; Bruce E. Burgoyne, *Defeat, Disaster, and Dedication, The Diaries of the Hessian Officers Jakob Piel and Andreas Wiederhold*, (Bowie: Heritage Books, 2009), pp. 10-11; Chernow, *Washington*, p. 271; Don Troiani, *Military Buttons of the American Revolution*, (Gettysburg: Thomas Publications, 2001), p. 93.

12. Stryker, *The Battles of Trenton and Princeton*, p. 361.

13. Griffin, *Catholics and the American Revolution*, vol. 2, pp. 252-253, 256, 267, 270-271, 305; *The American Daily Advertiser*, Philadelphia, Pennsylvania, April 16, 1811; Mark Mayo Boatner, III, *Encyclopedia of the American Revolution*, (New York: David McKay, Inc., 1966), pp. 751-752; Marquis de Chastellux, *Travels in North-America in the Years 1780-1781*, (New York 1882), pp. 62, 74.

14. Billias, *General John Glover and his Marblehead Mariners*, pp. xi-xii, 1-34, 59-131; Tagney, *The World Turned Upside Down*, p. 284; Kurlansky, *Cod*, pp. 112-113; Stryker, *TheBattles of Trenton and Princeton*, p. 130; Henry Wiencek, *An Imperfect God, George Washington, His Slaves, and the Creation of America*, (New York: Farrar, Straus and Giroux, 2003), pp. 216-217; Buchanan, *The Road to Valley Forge*, p. 161; Barnet Schecter, *The BattleFor New York*, (New York: Walker and Company, 2002), pp. 161-167; Benton Rain Patterson, *Washingtonand Cornwallis, The Battle for America, 1775-1783*, (New York: Taylor Trade Publications, 2004), pp. 73, 83; Fischer, *Washington's Crossing*, pp. 203, 217, 399-401; Smith, *TheBattle of Trenton*, p. 18; Hanser, *The Glorious Hour of Lt. Monroe*, p. 136; Chernow, *Washington*, p. 272; Mulvey and Abrams, A Forensic Meteorological Perspective on the American Revolutionary War, Battles of Trenton and Princeton, AccuWeather, September 17, 2009, Power Point Presentation, internet.

15. Billias, *General John Glover and his Marblehead Mariners*, p. 71; Fischer, *Washington'sCrossing*, p. 22; Stryker, *Battles of Trenton and Princeton*, pp. 263-264; Smith, *The Battle of Trenton*, 22.

16. Wiencek, *An Imperfect God*, pp. 215-216; Fischer, *Washington's Crossing*, pp. 22, 25.

17. Alice M. Hinkle, *Prince Estabrook slave and soldier*, (Lexington: Pleasant Mountain Press, 2001), pp. 19, 61-62; Bonk, *Trenton and Princeton 1776-77*, p. 19; Caroline Cox, *A Proper Sense of Honor, Service and Sacrifice in George Washington's Army*, (Chapel

Hill: University of North Carolina Press, 2004), p. 8; John F. Ross, *War on the Run, The Epic Story of Robert Rogers and the Conquest of America's First Frontier*, (New York: Bantam Books, 2011) pp. 149, 262; Richard S. Walling, "Prince Whipple: Symbol of African Americans at the battle of Trenton," December 2001, internet..

18. Bonk, *Trenton and Princeton 1776-77*, p. 9; Don Troiani and James L. Kochan, *Don Troiani's Soldiers of the American Revolution*, (Mechanicsburg, Pa.: Stackpole Books, 2007), p. 93.

19. Wiencek, *An Imperfect God*, pp. 216-217; Billias, *General John Glover and his Marblehead Mariners,* pp. 68-69; Tagney, *A County in Revolution*, pp. 196-197; Roads, *TheHistory and Traditions of Marblehead*, pp. 78, 87, 281-289, 558-561; Gamage, *Marblehead*, pp. 77-78; Tagney, *The World Turned Upside Down*, pp. 19, 115; W. Jeffrey Bolster, *Black Jacks, African American Seamen in the Age of Sail*, (Cambridge: Harvard University Press, 1997), pp. 1-232; Moses Brown Orderly Book, Beverly Historical Society, Beverly, Massachusetts; Upham, *A Memoir of General John Glover*, pp. 2, 4; Brookhiser, *George Washington* on *Leadership*, pp. 97-98; Lord and Gamage, *The Lure of Marblehead*, pp. 35, 47; Fischer, *Washington's Crossing*, pp. 21-22; Edgar, *Campaign of 1776*, p. 328; John U. Rees, "'They were good soldiers'," African Americans in the Continental Army, and General Glover's Soldier-Servants," *Military Collector & Historian*, vol. 62, no. 2, (Summer 2010), p. 141; Ellis, *American Creation*, pp. 34-35.

20. Tagney, *A County in Revolution*, p. 136; Ellis, *American Creation*, pp. 34-35.

21. Roads, *The History and Traditions of Marblehead*, p. 136; Tagney, *The World Turned Upside Down*, pp. 116, 119, 168; Lord and Gamage, *Marblehead*, p. 123; Kurlansky, *Cod*, p. 98; Edgar, *Campaign of 1776*, p. 327.

22. Bostwick Memoir, YUL.

23. Lengel, *General George Washington*, p. 182; Smith, *The Battle of Trenton*, p. 18.

24 .Charles Royster, *Light-Horse Harry Lee and the Legacy of the American Revolution*, (Cambridge: Cambridge University Press, 1981), p. 201.

25. Ferling, *Almost A Miracle*, pp. 175-176; Wood, *Battles of the Revolutionary War*, p. 62; Chadwick, *George Washington's War*, p. 14; Smith, *The Battle of Trenton*, p. 18.

26. Samuel J. Newland, *The Pennsylvania Militia, The Early Years*, (Philadelphia: Commonwealth of Pennsylvania, Department of Military and Veterans Affairs, 1997), p. 144; Lord and Gamage, *Marblehead*, pp. 121-122, 125; Tagney, *The World Turned Upside Down*, 240, 283-284, 492; Billias, *General John Glover and his Marblehead Mariners*, pp. 9, 66; Stryker, *The Battles of Trenton and Princeton*, pp. 129-130, 137, 141, 233; Roads, *The History and Traditions of Marblehead*, pp. 120-121, 493, 527; Peter Sarlie, "Tucker's Wharf," *Marblehead Magazine*, internet; Buchanan, *The Road to Valley Forge*, pp. 156, 162; Farling, *Almost A Miracle*, p. 176; Barbara J. Mitnick, ed., *New Jersey and the American Revolution*, (New Brunswick: Rivergate Books, 2005), p. 97; Bruce Chadwick, *George Washington's War, The Forging of a Revolutionary Leader and the American Presidency*, (Napierville: Sourcebooks, 2005), pp. 14-15; Fischer, *Washington's Crossing*, pp. 27, 209, 216-217, 219; Mark Puls, *Henry Knox, Visionary General of the American Revolution*, (New York: Palgrace Macmillian, 2008) p. 74; Smith, *The Battle of Trenton*, pp. 18-19; Hanser, *The*

Glorious Hour of Lt. Monroe, pp. 131-132, 136-137; Herbert C. Bell, *The History of Durham Township*, (Durham: Durham Historical Society, 1993), pp. 1-32; Brochure, "The Durham Boat," Washington Crossing Historic Park, Pennsylvania Historical and Museum Commission; LCVP, Wikipedia, internet; Robert G. Ferris, editor, *Signers of the Declaration*, (Washington, D.C.: National Park Service, 1975), pp. 137-138; Chernow, *Washington*, pp. 270, 272-273, 279; Edwin M. Stone, *The Life and Recollections of John Howland*, (Providence: George H. Whitney, 1857), pp. 71-82; John Rhodes Russell Biography, Geni, internet; D. B. Robinson's Genealogy Data Base, Rootsweb internet; Lineage Book, National Society of the Daughters of the American Revolution, vol. 8, (1895), (Harrisburg: Harrisburg Publishing Company, 1899), p. 229; *Marblehead Marriages, Vital Records of Marblehead, Massachusetts, to the End of the Year 1849, Marriages and Deaths*, vol. 2, (Public Essex Institute, 1904), p. 18; Joseph Widger, "These are My People," April 9, 2011, internet; Frank A. Garcher, *Glover's Marblehead Regiment in the War of the Revolution*, (Salem: The Salem Press, n. D.), p. 18; David Waldstreicher, *Slavery's Constitution, From Revolution to Ratification*, (New York: Hill and Wang, 2009), p. 26; Ward, *The War of the Revolution*, pp. 293-294.

27. Caesar A. Rodney, *Diary of Captain Thomas Rodney, Diary of Captain Thomas Rodney 1776-1777*, (Wilmington: The Historical Society of Delaware, 1888), pp. 12, 22-23; Smith, *The Battle of Trenton*, p. 19; Troiani, *Military Buttons of the American Revolution*, p. 137.

28. Stryker, *The Battles of Trenton and Princeton*, p. 233; Wood, *Battles of the Revolutionary War*, p. 62; Fischer, *Washington's Crossing*, p. 222.

29. Mulvey and Abrams, A Forensic Meteorological Perspective on the American Revolutionary War, Battles of Trenton and Princeton, AccuWeather, September 17, 2009, Power Point Presentation, internet; Fischer, *Washington's Crossing*, pp. 217-218, 397; Lengel, *General George Washington*, p. 182; *New York Times*, New York, January 24, 1932; Smith, *The Battle of Trenton*, pp. 18-19; Boatner, *Encyclopedia of the American Revolution*, p. 1205.

30. Stryker, *The Battles of Trenton and Princeton*, p. 371; Boatner, Encyclopedia of the American Revolution, pp. 587-588; Puls, *Henry Knox*, pp. 34-42, 73-75; Smith, The Battle of Trenton, p. 19; Hanser, The Glorious Hour of Lt. Monroe, p. 137; Chernow, Washington, p. 273.

31. Stryker, *The Battles of Trenton and Princeton*, pp. 134, 136 note 1, 358; Fischer, *Washington's Crossing*, p. 217; Bill, *The Campaign of Princeton*, p. 45; Newland, *ThePennsylvania Militia*, pp. 129-131; John W. Jordan, editor, *Colonial and Revolutionary Families of Pennsylvania*, vol. 2, (2 vols: Baltimore: Genealogical Publishing Company, Inc., 1978), p. 467.

32. Lengel, *General George Washington*, p. 182.

33. Charles R. Smith, *Marines in the Revolution, A History of the Continental Marines in the American Revolution, 1775-1783*, (Washington, D.C., History and Museums Divisions 1975), p. 95; Lengel, *General George Washington*, p. 177; "Washington Crossing Visitor Center Museum," Information Brochure, New Jersey State Historic

Site, New Jersey; Hanser, *The Glorious Hour of Lt. Monroe*, p. 18; Caroline Alexander, *The War That Killed Achilles*, (New York: Viking Penguin, 2009), pp. 25, 236, note 5; Ian C. Johnston, *The Ironies of War, An Introduction to Homer's Illiad*, (New York: University Press of America, 1988), pp. 1-145; Puls, *Henry Knox*, pp. 74-75; Hanser, *The Glorious Hour of Lt. Monroe*, p. 132; Chernow, *Washington*, p. 273; Marble, *James Monroe*, p. 42.

34. *New York Times*, December 28, 1876; Kurlansky, *Cod*, pp. 114-115; Ketchum, *The Winter Soldiers*, pp. 250-251; Smith, *The Battle of Trenton*, p. 19.

35. Roads, *The History and Traditions of Marblehead*, pp. 67, 549-550, 553, 557, 559; Thomas Grant, Sr. And Thomas Grant, Jr., American Silversmiths, Ancestry.com, rootsweb, internet..

36. Roads, *The History and Traditions of Marblehead*, pp. 240-242.

37. *The Washington Post*, Washington, D.C., February 11, 1883; Lengel, *General George Washington*, p. 182; *New York Times*, December 26, 1876; Fischer, *Washington's Crossing*, pp. 219, 390-391; *A Young Patriot in the American Revolution*, p. 80; Edgar, *Campaign of 1776*, p. 329; Chernow, *Washington*, p. 273.

38. Billias, *General John Glover and His Marblehead Mariners*, p. 68-69; Fischer, *Washington's Crossing*, p. 1; Oliver Cromwell Biographical Sketch, Oliver Cromwell, Black History Society, Inc., Burlington, New Jersey; Mitnick, ed., *New Jersey in the American Revolution*, p. 129; Wiencek, *An Imperfect God*, p. 217; Boatner, *Encyclopedia of the American Revolution*, pp. 1198-1199; Paul Johnson, *Heroes, From Alexander the Great to Julius Caesar to Churchill to De Gaulle*, (New York: HarperCollins Publishers, 2007), p. 115.

39. *New York Times*, December 26, 1876; Jacob Needleman, *The American Soul, Rediscovering the Wisdom of the Founders,* (New York: Jeremy P. Tarcher/Putnam, 2003), pp. 86-87; Buchanan, *The Road to Valley Forge*, p. 161; Robert Middlekauff, *The Glorious Cause, The American Revolution, 1763-1789,* (New York: Oxford University Press, 2005), p. 366; Fischer, *Washington's Crossing*, p. 222; Wright, *TheContinental Army*, p. 255; "The History of Johnson's Ferry," NJSHA; English, *General Hugh Mercer*, p. 84; Smith, *The Battle of Trenton*, p. 18; Hanser, *The Glorious Hour of Lt. Monroe*, pp. 137-138; Stryker, *The Battles of Trenton and Princeton*, p. 137; Edgar, *Campaign of 1776*, p. 159; Lengel, *Inventing George Washington*, pp. 122-123; Chernow, *Washington*, p. 273; Joseph G. Bilby and Katherine Bilby Jenkins, "The Woodwards Rise Up: Revolution as Civil War in Monmouth County, New Jersey, 1776-1777," *Patriots of the American Revolution*, vol. 4, issue 3, (May/June 2011), p. 46; Harriett Clement Marble, *James Monroe, Patriot and President*, (New York: G. P. Putnam's Sons, 1970), p. 42.

40. Needleman, *The American Soul*, pp. 86-87; Chernow, *Washington*, pp. 271-272; William Tudor, Wikipedia, internet; Cox, *A Proper Sense of Honor*, pp. 16, 44.

41. William Tudor letter to Delia Jarvis, December 24, 1776, Tudor Family Papers, 1773-1822, Massachusetts Historical Society, Boston, Massachusetts; Needleman, *The American Soul*, pp. 86-87; Chernow, *Washington*, p. 273.

42. "The History of Johnson's Ferry," NJSHS; Johnson Ferry House, Information Guide, New Jersey State Historical Site; Smith, *The Battle of Trenton*, pp. 26, 30-31; Needleman, *TheAmerican Soul*, pp. 86-87.

43. "The History of Johnson's Ferry," NJSHS; Hanser, *The Glorious Hour of Lt. Monroe*, p. 128; Smith, *The Battle of Trenton*, pp. 26, 30-31.

44. *Maryland Gazette*, January 23, 1777; Billias, *General John Glover and his Marblehead Mariners*, p. 7; Ferling, *Almost A Miracle*, p. 165; Boatner, *Encyclopedia of the American Revolution*, pp. 993-995.

45. Elisha Bostwick Memoir, Yale University Library, New Haven, Connecticut; Roads, *The History and Traditions of Marblehead*, pp. 47-48, 67-68; Lord and Gamage, *Marblehead*, pp. 121-122; Stryker, *The Battles of Trenton and Princeton*, pp. 134, 136, 358; Billias, *General John Glover and his Marblehead Mariners*, pp. 7-8; Buchanan, *The Road to Valley Force*, p. 161; Ketchum, *The Winter Soldiers*, p. 249; Fischer, *Washington's Crossing*, pp. 216, 220-222, 391; "The History of Johnson's Ferry," NJSHS; Smith, *The Battle of Trenton*, pp. 11, 19; Chernow, *Washington*, p. 273; Marble, *James Monroe*, p. 42.

46. Thomas McCarthy Diary, William Croghan Papers, Lyman Copeland Draper Collection, State Historical Society of Wisconsin, Madison, Wisconsin. Buchanan, *The Road to Valley Forge*, p. 162.

47. Linklater, *An Artist in Treason*, p. 28.

48. Fischer, *Washington's Crossing*, p. 217; Don Troiani and James L. Kochan, *Don Troiani's Soldiers of the American Revolution*, (Mechanicsburg: Stackpole Books, 2007), p. 116; Bill, *The Campaign of Princeton*, p. 29.

49. *A Young Patriot in the American Revolution*, (Westvaco Corporation, 1981), pp. 78, 80; Smith, *The Battle of Trenton*, p. 19; Edgar, *Campaign of 1776*, p. 330.

50. Ketchum, *The Winter Soldiers*, pp. 210-211; Chernow, *Washington*, p. 270.

51. Fischer, *Washington's Crossing*, pp. 209, 216, 221-222; Bonk, *Trenton and Princeton 1776-77*, pp. 20, 55; Wallace, *Appeal to Arms*, pp. 123, 130; Billias, *General John Glover and his Marblehead Mariners*, p. 8; Stryker, *The Battles of Trenton and Princeton*, pp. 46, 371; Buchanan, *The Road to Valley Force*, p. 161; Farling, *Almost A Miracle*, p. 176; Bill, *The Campaign of Princeton*, p. 107; John Laffin, *Jackboot, A History of the German Soldier, 1713-1945*, (New York: Barnes and Noble, 1995), p. 13; Owen Connelly, *Blundering to Glory, Napoleon's Military Campaigns*, (Wilmington: Scholarly Resources Inc., 1999), p. 3; Marble, *JamesMonroe*, p. 42; Dwyer, *"The Day Is Ours!,"* p. 254; Smith, *The Battle of Trenton*, pp. 17, 19-20; Puls, *Henry Knox*, pp. 40-42, 67, 73-74; Hanser, *The Glorious Hour of Lt. Monroe*, pp. 118, 137; Edgar, *Campaign of 1776*, p. 328; Chernow, *Washington*, p. 273; Bellamy, *The Private Life of George Washington*, pp. 143-144; Mark Neaves, "Henry Knox, A Brief Biography," *Patriots of the American Revolution*, vol. 3, issue 4 (July/August 2010), pp. 14-15; Chandler, *The Campaigns of Napoleon*, p. 340; Jac Weller, "Guns of Destiny, Field Artillery in the Trenton-Princeton Campaign, 25 December 1776 to 3 January 1777" *Military Affairs*, vol. 20, no. 1 (Spring 1956), pp. 4, 8, 13; Marble, *James Monroe*, p. 42.

52. Griffin, *Catholics and the American Revolution*, vol. 2, p. 368; Michael Stephenson, *Patriot Battles, How the War of Independence was Fought*, (New York: Harper Collins Publishers, 2007), pp. 252, 257; Lengel, *General George Washington*, p. 182; Michael Rose, *Washington's War, The American War of Independence to the Iraqi Insurgency*, (New York: Pegasus Books, 2008), p. 81; Billias, *General John Glover and his Marblehead Mariners*, p. 17; Willard Sterne Randall, *George Washington, A Life*, (New York: Henry Holt Publishers, 1998), p. 323; W. J. Wood, *Battles of the Revolutionary War*, (New York: Da Capo Press, 2003), pp. 58, 62; Chadwick, *George Washington's War*, p. 13; Fleming, *1776*, 425; Connelly, *Blundering to Glory*, p. 3; Troiani, *Military Buttons of the American Revolution*, p. 103; Chris McNab, *Armies of the Napoleonic Wars*, (Oxford: Osprey Publishing, 2009), p. 245; Fischer, *Washington'sCrossing*, pp. 216, 225; "The History of Johnson's Ferry," NJSHS; Puhls, *Henry Knox*, pp. 73-75; Smith, *The Battle of Trenton*, pp. 18-19; Linklater, *An Artist in Treason*, p. 28; Edgar, *Campaignof 1776*, pp. 328-329; Chernow, *Washington*, p. 273; Chastellux, *Travels in North-America*, pp. 28, 70; Weller, "Guns of Destiny," *MA*, pp. 6-7.

53. Chandler, *The Campaigns of Napoleon*, p. 360.

54. Howard H. Peckham, *The War of Independence*, (Chicago: The University of Chicago Press, 1958), pp. 52-53; Buchanan, *The Road to Valley Forge*, pp. 152, 158; Chadwick, *George Washington's War*, pp. 13-15; "The History of Johnson's Ferry," NJSHS; Puls, *Henry Knox*, pp. 73-75; Theodore P. Savas and J. David Dameron, *The New American Revolution Handbook*, (El Dorado Hills: Savas Beatie, 2010), p. 5; Chernow, *Washington*, p. 273; Fischer, *Washington's Crossing*, p. 397.

55. Fischer, *Washington's Crossing*, pp. 225, 397; Lord and Gamage, *Marblehead*, p. 122; Stryker, *The Battles of Trenton and Princeton*, pp. 136,138 note 2, 358, 371, 394; Bonk, *Trentonand Princeton 1776-77*, pp. 19-20; Tagney, *The World Turned Upside Down*, pp. 283-284; Farling, *Almost A Miracle*, p. 176; Chadwick, *George Washington's War*, p. 15; Ketchum, *TheWinter Soldiers*, p. 252; "The History of Johnson's Ferry," NJSHS; "Washington Crossing Visitor Center Museum," Information Guide, NJSHS; Smith, *The Battle of Trenton*, p. 20; Chernow, *Washington*, p. 273; Chastellux, *Travels in North-America*, p. 28.

56. Rodney, *Diary of Captain Thomas Rodney*, p. 51; Fischer, *Washington's Crossing*, p. 391.

57. Stryker, *The Battles of Trenton and Princeton*, p. 371.

58. Ibid., pp. 134, 371;Upham, *A Memoir of General John Glover*, p. 21; Boatner, *The Encyclopedia of the American Revolution*, p.657; Chadwick, *George Washington's War*, p. 15; Hanser, *The Glorious Hour of Lt. Monroe*, p. 122.

59. Smith, *Marines in the Revolution*, pp. 94-96; Stephenson, *Patriot Battles*, p. 256; Lengel, *General George Washington*, p. 182; Billias, *General John Glover and his Marblehead Mariners*, pp. 3, 6; Chadwick, *George Washington's War*, p. 15; Fischer, *Washington's Crossing*, pp. 25-28, 209, 213; Stryker, *The Battles of Trenton and Princeton*, pp. 136, 358, 423; Chernow, *Washington*, p. 274.

60. Lengel, *General George Washington*, p. 182.

61. Lengel, *This Glorious Struggle*, p. 87.

62. Clark, All Cloudless Glory, p. 304.

63. Fischer, *Washington's Crossing*, pp. 216-217, 219; Buchanan, *The Road to Valley Forge*, pp. 152, 158; Lengel, *General George Washington*, p. 182; Bonk, *Trenton and Princeton 1776-77*, p. 20; Farling, *Almost A Miracle*, p. 176; Wood, *Battles of the Revolutionary War*, p. 62; Ketchum, *The Winter Soldiers*, p. 202; "The History of Johnson's Ferry," NJSHS; Smith, *TheBattle of Trenton*, p. 19; Hanser, *The Glorious Hour of Lt. Monroe*, pp. 136-138; Edgar, *Campaign of 1776*, p. 328.

64. Wood, *Battles of the Revolutionary War*, p. 62; Buchanan, *The Road to Valley Forge*, p. 158; Chadwick, *George Washington's War*, p. 16; Fischer, *Washington's Crossing*, pp. 374, 391; Hanser, *The Glorious Hour of Lt. Monroe*, p. 138; Chandler, *The Campaigns of Napoleon*, pp. 708, 734; Weller, "Guns of Destiny," *MA*, p. 9; Smith, *The Battle of Trenton*, p. 20

65. *A Young Patriot in the American Revolution*, p. 80; Fischer, *Washington's Crossing*, p. 391; Trenton, *The Battle of Trenton*, p. 20.

66. *New York Times*, January 18, 1862; Chadwick, *George Washington's War*, p. 15; Edgar, *Campaign of 1776*, p. 328; Chernow, *Washington*, pp. 270-273.

67. Bill, *The Campaign of Princeton*, pp. 13, 17; *New York Times*, December 26, 1876; Hanser, *The Glorious Hour of Lt. Monroe*, p. 111.

68. *A Young Patriot in the American Revolution*, p. 80; Hanser, *The Glorious Hour of Lt. Monroe*, pp. 83, 137.

69. Bellamy, *The Private Life of George Washington*, p. 194.

70. Stryker, *The Battles of Trenton and Princeton*, p. 139; Rose, *Washington's War*, p. 81; Hanser, *The Glorious Hour of Lt. Monroe*, pp. 110-111, 137.

Chapter II

1. Bellamy, *The Private Life of George Washington*, p. 183.

2. Lengel, *This Glorious Struggle*, p. 87; Chernow, *Washington*, p. 274; Fischer, *Washington'sCrossing*, p. 209; Clark, *All Cloudless Glory*, p. 304..

3. Royster, *Light-Horse Harry Lee*, p. 201.

4. Bellamy, *The Private Life of George Washington*, p. 204.

5. Ward, *The War of the Revolution*, p. 295.

6. Elisha Bostwick Memoir, YUL.

7. Chernow, *Washington*, p. 274; Ward, *The War of the Revolution*, p. 295; Ferling, *The Ascent of George Washington*, pp. 99, 120; Bellamy, *The Private Life of George Washington*, p. 148; Gragg, *By the Hand of Providence*, pp. 5-91.

8. Gragg, *By the Hand of Providence*, p. 91.

9. Johnson, *Heroes*, p. 119.

10. Fischer, *Washington's Crossing*, p. 207.

11. Ferling, *The Ascent of George Washington*, p. 102.

12. Bellemy, *The Private Life of George Washington*, p. 199.

13. Ferling, *The Ascent of George Washington*, p. 99; Lengel, *This Glorious Struggle*, p. 87; *Maryland Gazette*, January 2, 1777; Lengel, *GeneralGeorge Washington*, pp. 87,181-182;

New York Times, December 26, 1876; Billias, *General John Glover and his Marblehead Mariners*, pp. 10-11, 70; Fischer, *Washington's Crossing*, pp. 55-56, 209, 219, 225, 391; Smith, *The Battle of Trenton*, p. 14; English, *General Hugh Mercer*, p. 85; Hanser, *The Glorious Hour of Lt. Monroe*, pp. 138-139; Chernow, *Washington*, p. 274; Bellamy, *The Private Life of George Washington*, p. 61; Weller, "Guns of Destiny," *MA*, p. 9; Johnson, *Heroes*, pp. 115-116.

14. Buchanan, *The Road to Valley Forge*, p. 163; William Hull Biography, Virtual American Biographies, internet; "The History of the Johnson's Ferry," NJSHS; Washington Crossing State Park Literature, Washington Crossing State Park, New Jersey; Edgar, *Campaign of 1776*, p. 205; Chernow, *Washington*, p. 274; Derby, Connecticut, Wikipedia, internet.

15. Fischer, *Washington's Crossing*, pp. 221-222, 230-231; Marble, *James Monroe*, p. 42; *Records of the American Catholic Historical Society of Philadelphia*, (Philadelphia: American Catholic Historical Society, 1904), vol. 15, pp. 415-417; St. Mary's Catholic Church, Philadelphia, internet; Ford, "British and American Prisoners of War, 1778," *The Magazine of Pennsylvania History and Biography*, pp. 159-174; Smith, *The Battle of Trenton*, p. 20.

16. Smith, *The Battle of Trenton*, p. 20; Gamage and Lord, *The Lure of Marblehead*, p. 9; Bill, *The Campaign of Princeton*, p. 45; Smith, *The Battle of Trenton*, p. 20; Fischer, *Washington'sCrossing*, p. 391; Stryker, *The Battles of Trenton and Princeton*, pp. 136, 358; Weller, "Guns of Destiny," *MA*, pp. 4,8, 13

17. *Maryland Gazette*, January 2, 1777,

18. Stryker, *The Battles of Trenton and Princeton*, p. 140; Dwyer, *"The Day Is Ours!,"* p. 246; Fischer, *Washington's Crossing*, p. 222; Buchanan, *The Road to Valley Forge*, p. 156.

19. *A Young Patriot in the American Revolution*, p. 81.

20. Elisha Bostwick Memoir, YUL; Lengel, *General George Washington*, pp. 182-183; Farling, *Almost A Miracle*, p. 176; Dwyer, *"The Day Is Ours!,"* pp. 247-248; Wright, *The Continental Army*, p. 239; Smith, *The Battle of Trenton*, p. 19.

21. Elisha Bostwick Memoir, YUL; Buchanan, *The Road to Valley Forge*, p. 169; Fischer, *Washington's Crossing*, p. 225.

22. Bill, *The Campaign of Princeton*, pp. 50; Weller, "Guns of Destiny," *MA*, p. 8.

23. Ketchum, *The Winter Soldiers*, p. 266; Styker, *The Battles of Trenton and Princeton*, p. 479; Weller, "Guns of Destiny," *MA*, p. 9; Smith, *The Battle of Trenton*, p. 22.

24. Fischer, *Washington's Crossing*, pp. 210, 225-226; Smith, *The Battle of Trenton*, p. 20; Stryker, *The Battles of Trenton and Princeton*, pp. 62, 139.

25. Fischer, *Washington's Crossing*, pp. 210, 234; Bill, *The Campaign of Princeton*, p. 46; Ketchum, *The Winter Soldiers*, p. 246; *A Young Patriot in the American Revolution*, p. 80; Weller, "Guns of Destiny," *MA*, pp. 9, 15.

26. Fischer, *Washington's Crossing*, pp. 207, 234; Stryker, *The Battles of Trenton and Princeton*, p. 371; Gary Zaboly, *American Colonial Rangers, The Northern Colonies 1724-64*, (Oxford: Osphrey Publishing Limited, 2004), pp. 4, Plate H; Tim J. Todish and Terry S. Todish, *AlamoSourcebook 1836: A Comprehensive Guide to the Alamo and the Texas Revolution*, (Austin: Eakin Press, 1998), p. 160; Bill Mauldin, *Mud &*

Guts, A Look at the common soldier of the American Revolution, (Washington, D.C.: National Park Service, 1978), p. 31; Hanser, *The Glorious Career of Lt. Monroe*, pp. 99, 111, 136-137; Smith, *The Battle of Trenton*, pp. 16, 20; Stryker, *The Battles of Trenton and Princeton*, p. 86; Bellamy, *The Private Life of George Washington*, p. 236; Edgar, *Campaign of 1776*, p. 304; Chernow, *Washington*, p. 269, 273-274; Ross, *War on the Run*, p. 98; Chastellux, *Travels in North-America*, p. 100..

27. Hanser, *The Glorious Hour of Lt. Monroe*, p. 141; Fleming, *1776*, p. 458; Stryker, *TheBattles of Trenton and Princeton*, p. 140.

28. Hanser, *The Glorious Hour of Lt. Monroe*, p. 141; Lengel, *This Glorious Struggle*, p. 99.

29. Loammi Baldwin December 19, 1776 letter, Loammi Baldwin Papers, 1768-1872, Houghton Library, Harvard University, Cambridge, Massachusetts.

30. Joseph J. Ellis, *His Excellency, George Washington*, (New York: Vintage Books, 2004), p. 23; Phillip Thomas Tucker, *The Important Role of the Irish in the American Revolution*, (Bowie: Heritage Books, 2009), pp. 12-31; Papers of George Washington, Aldeman Library, University of Virginia, Charlottesville, Virginia; Ward, *The War of the Revolution*, p. 292.

31. Bellamy, *The Private Life of George Washington*, pp. 19-20.

32. Hanser, *The Glorious Hour of Lt. Monroe*, p. 113.

33. Harrison Clark, *All Cloudless Glory, The Life of George Washington, From Youth to Yorktown*, (Washington, D.C.: Regnery Publishing, Inc., 1995), p. 223.

34. Ben Z. Rose, *John Stark, Maverick General*, (Waverly: Treeline Press, 2007), pp. 23-40; Ross, *War on the Run*, pp. 137, 129, 137-138.

35. Stryker, *The Battles of Trenton and Princeton*, p. 360

36. Bellamy, *The Private Life of George Washington*, p. 180.

37. Clark, *All Cloudless Glory*, p. 265.

38. Fischer, *Washington's Crossing*, p. 25; Bonk, *Trenton and Princeton 1776-77*, p. 20; Stryker, *The Battles of Trenton and Princeton*, pp. 142, 284; Buchanan, *The Road to Valley Forge*, p. 158; Alfred Hoyt Bill, *The Campaign of Princeton 1776-1777*, (Princeton: Princeton University Press, 1975), p. 45; Weller, "Guns of Destiny,"*MA*, p. 8.

39. Fischer, *Washington's Crossing*, pp. 208, 226; Smith, *The Battle of Trenton*, p. 20.

40. Clark, *All Cloudless Glory*, p. 209.

41. *A Young Patriot in the American Revolution*, p. 81; Smith, *The Battle of Trenton*, p. 20.

42. Stryker, *The Battles of Trenton and Princeton*, p. 140; Bonk, *Trenton and Princeton 1776-77*, pp. 52, 55; Diccon Hyatt, "History Buffs have a stake in bridge battle," HopewellSpace, internet; Fischer, *Washington's Crossing*, pp. 225, 227; Chernow, *Washington*, p. 274; Smith, *The Battle of Trenton*, p. 20.

43. Clark, *All Cloudless Glory*, p. 284.

44. Elisha Bostwick Memoir, YUL; Bill, *The Campaign of Princeton*, p. 46; Fischer, *Washington's Crossing*, p. 227; Bonk, *Trenton and Princeton 1776-77*, 52, 55; Stryker, *TheBattles of Trenton and Princeton*, p. 141; Chernow, *Washington*, p. 274; Cox, *A Proper Sense of Honor*, pp. 11-12.

45. Elisha Bostwick Memoir, YU; Fischer, *Washington's Crossing*, p. 227; Chernow, *Washington*, p. 274; Johnson, *Heroes*, pp. 115, 123.

46. Chastellux, *Travels in North-America*, p. 60.

47. Elisha Bostwick Memoir, YUL; Israel Angell, *Diary of Colonel Israel Angell, Commanding the Second Rhode Island Continental Regiment During the American Revolution*, (Providence: Preston and Rounds Company, 1899), p. 43, note.

48. Bellamy, *The Private Life of George Washington*, p. 317.

49. Bellamy, *The Private Life of George Washington*, p. 184.

50. Billias, *General John Glover and his Marblehead Mariners*, pp. 15, 203, note 20; Stryker, *The Battles of Trenton and Princeton*, p. 194; Fleming, *1776*, p. 463; Fischer, *Washington's Crossing*, pp. 225, 227.

51. Wright, *The Continental Army*, pp. 102-103, 339; Trussell, *The Pennsylvania Line*, pp. 7,189-193; Thomas Forrest biography, Wikipedia, internet; Newland, *The Pennsylvania Militia*, pp. 113-114, 130-131,137-139; Stryker, *The Battles of Trenton and Princeton*, p. 370; Griffin, *Catholics and the American Revolution*, vol. 2, pp. 201-202; Buchanan, *The Road to Valley Forge*, p. 158; Fischer, *Washington's Crossing*, p. 227; Benjamin M. Nead, "A Sketch of General Thomas Procter, With Some Account of the First Pennsylvania Artillery in the Revolution," *Pennsylvania Magazine of History and Biography*, vol. 4, no. 4, (1880), pp. 454-470; Weller, "Guns of Destiny," *MA*, p. 8; Smith, *The Battle of Trenton*, pp. 20, 22.

52. Trussell, *The Pennsylvania Line*, pp. 7, 192, 194, 200, 203; Nead, "A Sketch of General Thomas Proctor," *PMHB*, pp. 454-470; Chernow, *Washington*, p. 274; Weller, "Guns of Destiny," *MA*, p. 8; Smith, *The Battle of Trenton*, pp. 20, 22; Cox, *A Proper Sense of Honor*, pp. 58-59.

53. Bellamy, *The Private Life of George Washington*, p. 288.

54. Randall, *George Washington*, p. 318; Newland, *The Pennsylvania Militia*, pp. 135, 139, 141-142-143; Nead, "A Sketch of General Thomas Proctor," *PMHB*, pp. 454-470.

55. Elisha Bostwick Memoir, YUL.

56. Ibid; Fischer, *Washington's Crossing*, pp. 225, 227; Bonk, *Trenton and Princeton 1776-77*, pp. 52, 55; Weller, "Guns of Destiny," *MA*, p. 5; Smith, *The Battle of Trenton*, p. 22.

57. Thomas Fleming, *Washington's Secret War, The Hidden History of Valley Forge*, (New York: HarperCollins Publishers, 2005), p. 87.

58. Buchanan, *The Road to Valley Forge*, pp. 152, 158; Ketchum, *The Winter Soldiers*, p. 246; Weller, "Guns of Destiny," *MA*, p. 8; Smith, *The Battle of Trenton*, pp. 20, 22; Fischer, *Washington's Crossing*, p. 210.

59. *A Young Soldier in the American Revolution*, p-. 1-4, 82; Gragg, *By the Hand of Providence*, pp. 84-85; Edgar, *Campaign of 1776*, p. 326; Bill, *The Campaign of Princeton*, pp. 20-21.

60. Gragg, *By the Hand of Providence*, p. 84.

61. Robert C. Baron, editor, *Soul of America, Documenting Our Past, 1492-1974*, (Golden: Fulcrum Inc., 1989), p. 50.

62. Bellamy, *The Private Life of George Washington*, p. 200.

63. Clark, *All Cloudless Glory*, pp. 246-247.

64. Wright, *The Continental Army*, p. 203; Chastellux, *Travels in North-America*, pp. 35-36; Burrows, *Forgotten Patriots*, p. 64.

65. *Maryland Gazette*, March 20, 1777; Dwyer, *"The Day is Ours!,"* pp. 85-86; Henry B. Dawson, *Westchester-County, New York, during the American Revolution*, (Morrisania, N. Y.: 1886), p. 263; Fischer, *Washington's Crossing*, pp. 28-29, 222, 225, 228; Jon Kukla, *Mr. Jefferson's Women*, (New York: Vintage Books, 2008), p. 89; Cox, *A Proper Sense of Honor*, pp. 54-59.

66. Clark, *All Cloudless Glory*, p. 304.

67. Fischer, *Washington's Crossing*, p. 227-228; Topographical Map, Hunterdon County, New Jersey; Smith, *The Battle of Trenton*, p. 20; Chernow, *Washington*, p. 273.

68. Elisha Bostwick Memoir, YUL; Smith, *The Battle of Trenton*, p. 20; Chernow, *Washington*, p. 274; Bill, *The Campaign for Princeton*, p. 46.

69. Bellamy, *The Private Life of George Washington*, p. 213.

70. Elisha Bostwick Memoir, YUL; Bellamy, *The Private Life of George Washington*, p. 200.

71. Golway, *Washington's General*, pp. 110-112; Lengel, *General George Washington*, p. 183; Billias, *General John Glover and his Marblehead Mariners*, pp. 10-11; Buchanan, *The Road to Valley Forge*, p. 158; Farling, *Almost A Miracle*, p. 177; Bill, *The Campaign of Princeton*, pp. 45-46; Ketchem, *The Winter Soldiers*, pp. 26-27, 253, 266; Fischer, *Washington's Crossing*, p. 209, 228, 230; Hanser, *The Glorious Hour of Lt. Monroe*, pp. 124, 140-141, 143; Chernow, *Washington*, pp. 274-275; Smith, *The Battle of Trenton*, p. 20; Charles Rappleye, *Sons of Providence, The Brown Brothers, the Slave Trade, and the American Revolution*, (New York: Simon and Schuster, 2007), p. 175; Valentine, *Lord Stirling*, p. 193.

72. Norman Gelb, *Less Than Glory, A Revisionist View of the American Revolution*, (New York: G. P. Putnam's Sons, 1984), p. 141.

73. Weller, "Guns of Destiny," *MA*, pp. 8-9, 15; Fischer, *Washington's Crossing*, pp. 223-224, 244-245, 392; Ketchum, *The Winter Soldiers*, p. 246; Stryker, *The Battles of Trenton and Princeton*, pp. 6, 136, 358; Wright, *The Continental Army*, p. 62; Bonk, *Trenton and Princeton 1776-77*, pp. 20, 55, 57; Bill, *The Campaign of Princeton*, p. 45; Buchanan, *The Road to Valley Forge*, p. 158; Billias, *General John Glover and his Marblehead Mariners*, pp. 10-11; Stone, *Letters of Brunswick and Hessian Officers During the American Revolution*, p. 123; Chandler, *The Campaigns of Napoleon*, pp. 504-505, 708, 734.

74. Bill, *The Campaign of Trenton*, pp. 45-46; Ketchum, *The Winter Soldiers*, pp. 246, 253, Fischer, *Washington's Crossing*, pp. 192, 222, 225; Stryker, *The Battles of Trenton and Princeton* pp. 140-142; Bonk, *Trenton and Princeton 1776-77*, p. 19; Dwyer, *"The Day Is Ours!,"* pp. 246, 430; Chernow, *Washington*, pp. 274-275; Bellamy, *The Private Life of George Washington*, p. 144.

75. Marble, *James Monroe*, p. 42.

76. Fischer, *Washington's Crossing*, pp. 230-231; *A Young Patriot in the American Revolution*, p. 81; Marble, *James Monroe*, p. 42.

77. *A Young Patriot in the American Revolution*, p. 81; Fischer, *Washington's Crossing*, p. 208.

78. Stryker, *The Battles of Trenton and Princeton*, pp. 140-141, 154; Fischer, *Washington'sCrossing*, pp. 222, 230; Ketchum, *The Winter Soldiers*, p. 246; Bonk, *Trenton and Princeton 1776-77*, p. 19; Ward, *Major General Adam Stephen and the*

Cause of American Liberty, pp. 145, 149; Clark, *All Cloudless Glory*, p. 205; Smith, *The Battle of Trenton*, p. 20; Chernow, *Washington*, p. 274.

79. Baron, ed., *Soul of America*, p. 51.

80. Harry M. Ward, *Major General Adam Stephen and the Cause of American Liberty*, (Charlottesville: University Press of Virginia, 1988), pp. ix-245; Chastellux, *Travels in North-America*, p. 41, note.

81. Harry M. Ward, *Charles Scott and the "Spirit of '76,"* (Charlottesville: University Press of Virginia, 1988), pp. ix-197; Wright, *The Continental Army*, p. 286; Smith, *The Battle of Trenton*, p. 20.

82. Ward, *Charles Scott and the "Spirit of '76,"* pp. 14, 41.

83. William Armstrong Crozier, William Dickinson Buckner, and Howard Randolph Bayne, *The Buckners of Virginia and the allied families of Strother and Ashby*, (New York: The Genealogical Association, 1907), pp. 157-159; Wright, *The Continental Army*, p. 287; Smith, *The Battle of Trenton*, p. 20.

84. Donald N. Moran, Caleb Gibbs, Commander of the Commander-in-Chief Guards, Sons of Liberty Chapter, Sons of the American Revolution, internet archives; Smith, *The Battle of Trenton*, pp. 5, 20; Bonk, *Trenton and Princeton 1776-77*, p. 19; James Haltigan, *The Irish in the American Revolution and their Early Influence in the Colonies*, (Washington, D.C.: Patrick J. Haltigan, 1908), pp. 400-401; Fischer, *Washington's Crossing*, pp. 228, 230, 390, 393; Stryker, *The Battles of Trenton and Princeton*, pp. 142, 362; Dwyer, *"The Day Is Ours!,"* p. 246; Griffin, *Catholics and the American Revolution*, vol. 2, p. 217; Smith, *The Battle of Trenton*, p. 20; Boatner, *Encyclopedia of the American Revolution*, p. 601; Robert Lawson, Wikapedia Encyclopedia, internet; David Hackett Fischer, *Liberty and Freedom, A Visual History of America's Founding Ideas* (New York: Oxford University Press, 2004), pp. 135-136, 158; Chastellux, *Travels in North-America*, p. 62; Chernow, *Washington*, pp. 274-275

85. Tench Tilghman, *Memoir of Lieutenant Colonel Tench Tilghman, Secretary and Aid to Washington*, (Albany: J. Munsell, 1876), pp. 5-173; Fleming, *Washington's Secret War*, pp. 107-108; Stryker, *The Battles of Trenton and Princeton*, pp. 84, 366; Tench Tilghman Biographical Sketch, Valley Forge National Historical Park, Pennsylvania; Tench Tilghman Biographical Sketch, Wikipedia; Boatner, *Encyclopedia of the American Revolution*, pp. 1108-1109; Douglas Cubbison, "Forgotten Hero of the Continental Army, Tench Tilghman carried the news of Yorktown," September 27, 2011, Stone Fort Consulting, internet.

86. Stryker, *The Battles of Trenton and Princeton*, p. 371.

87. Baron, ed., *Soul of America*, p. 50.

88. James McCarty, editor and compiler, *Ireland, From the Flight of the Earls to Grattan's Parliament*, (Dublin: C. J. Fallon Limited, 1957), pp. 64-66; Tucker, *The Important Role of the Irish in the American Revolution*, pp. 12-31, 65-87; Cox, *A Proper Sense of Honor*, p. 238; Fleming, *Washington's Secret War*, pp. 140-142, 285; Owen B. Hunt, *The Irish and the American Revolution, Three Essays*, (Philadelphia: Owen B. Hunt, 1976), pp. 24-26; David Noel Doyle, *Ireland, Irishmen and Revolutionary America, 1760-1820*, (Cork: The Mercier Press, 1981), 109-151; James Webb, *Born Fighting,*

How the Scots-Irish Shaped America, (New York: Broadway Books, 2004), pp. 9-165; Smith, *The Battle of Trenton*, p. 20.

89. Fleming, *Washington's Secret War*, p. 140-142, 285; Doyle, *Ireland, Irishmen and Revolutionary America*, pp. 118, 149-150; Hunt, *The Irish and the American Revolution*, pp. 24-26; Goolrick, *The Life of General Hugh Mercer*, pp. 28-29, 31, 37.

90. Theodore Roosevelt, *New York*, (Delray Beach: Levenger Press, 2004), p. 107, note 4.

91. Cox, *A Proper Sense of Honor*, p. 238.

92. Michael Fry, *How the Scots Made America*, (New York: St. Martin's Press, 2003), pp. 1-67; Arthur Herman, *How the Scots Invented the Modern World, The Story of How Western Europe's Poorest Nation Created Our World and Everything in It*, (New York: Broadway Books, 2002), pp. 108-160; Valentine, *Lord Stirling*, pp. 3-56; Stryker, *The Battles of Trenton and Princeton*, pp. 116, 367; James Mackay, *William Wallace, Brave Heart*, (Edinburgh: Mainstream Publishing, 1995), pp. 9-268; Clark, *AllCloudless Glory*, p. 307; Fischer, *Washington's Crossing*, pp. 183-184; Cathleen Crown and Carol Rogers, *Images of America, Trenton*, (Chicago: Arcadia Publishing, 2000), p. 10; Chastellux, *Travels in North-America*, p. 41, note; A. F. Murison, *Scottish Histories, Sir William Wallace*, (New Lanark: Geddes and Grosset, 2008), pp. 43-125; Literature, "Meet William Trent," William Trent House Museum, Trenton, New Jersey; Lord Stirling Biographical Information, William Alexander Collection, 1778-1813, Princeton University Library Manuscript Division, Princeton University Library, Princeton, New Jersey.

93. Chastellux, *Travels in North-America*, p. 64.

94. Dwyer, *"The Day is Ours!,"* pp. 37, 119; Smith, *The Battle of Trenton*, p. 5; Boatner, *Encyclopedia of the American Revolution*, p. 1179; Bonk, *Trenton and Princeton 1776-77*, p. 19; Michael Cecere, *They Behaved Like Soldiers, Captain John Chilton and the Third Virginia Regiment 1775-1778*, (Bowie: Heritage Books, 2004), pp. 13-29; Wright, *The Continental Army*, p, 285; Dorothy Twohig, ed., *George Washington's Diaries, An Abridgement* (Charlottesville, Va.: University of Virginia Press, 1999), pp. 124-125, 145, 177, 106; Ward, *Major General Adam Stephen and the Cause of American Liberty*, p. 197; Hanser, *The Glorious Hour of Lt. Monroe*, pp. 57-59; Goolrick, *The Life of General Hugh Mercer*, pp. 79, 83, 196; English, *General Hugh Mercer*, p. 51.

95. Harry Ammon, *James Monroe, The Quest for National Identity*, (Charlottesville: University of Virginia Press, 1990), pp. 7-8; Boatner, *Encyclopedia of the American Revolution*, pp. 618-619; Cecere, *They Behaved Like Soldiers*, pp. 3-29; Hanser, *The Glorious Hour of Lt. Monroe*, pp. 42, 53-55, 60, 73-76, 97.

96. Cecere, *They Behaved Like Soldiers*, pp. 13-15, 19, 21.

97. Ketchum, *The Winter Soldiers*, p. 146.

98. Ibid., pp. 4, 25-26, 67, 145-146; Bonk, *Trenton and Princeton 1776-77*, pp. 19-20; Cecere, *They Behaved Like Soldiers*, pp. 84, 91; Cox, *A Proper Sense of Honor*, p. 194; Bellamy, *The Private Life of George Washington*, p. 189.

99. Carolly Erickson, *Bonnie Prince Charlie, A Biography*, (New York: William Morrow and Company, Inc., 1989), pp. 1-201.

100. Bellamy, *The Private Life of George Washington*, p. 57; Fischer, *Washington's Crossing*, p. 209.

101. Bellamy, The Private Life of George Washington, p. 60.

102. Billias, *General John Glover and His Marblehead Mariners*, pp. 11, 30-31, 35, 37, 67; Upham, *A Memoir of General John Glover*, p. 11; Lord and Gamage, *The Lure of Marblehead*, p. 42; Carin Gordon, "The Ornes," *Marblehead Magazine*, Marblehead, Massachusetts, internet; Stryker, *The Battles of Trenton and Princeton*, p. 140; Smith, *The Battle of Trenton*, p. 20.

103. *A Young Soldier in the American Revolution*, p. 82; Smith, *The Battle of Trenton*, p. 20.

104. Douglas R. Egerton, *Death or Liberty, African Americans and Revolutionary America*, *(New York: Oxford University Press, 2009)*, p. 74.

105. Ibid., p. 76.

106. Billias, *General John Glover and His Marblehead Mariners*, pp. 11, 22, 66-67, 70, 75, 84, 149; Lord and Gamage, *Marblehead*, p. 121; Kurlansky, *Cod*, p. 98; Roads, *The History and Traditions of Marblehead*, pp. 136, 223; Upham, *A Memoir of General John Glover*, pp. 11, 59; Fischer, *Washington's Crossing*, pp. 219, 270; Stryker, *The Battles of Trenton and Princeton*, pp. 140, 362; *A Young Patriot in the American Revolution*, p. 80; Smith, *The Battle of Trenton*, p. 21; Boatner, *Encyclopedia of the American Revolution*, p. 1178; Charles C. Coffin, *The Boys of 76*, (Gainesville: Maranatha Publications, Inc., 1998), p. 8; Chernow, *Washington*, p. 275

107. Roads, *The History and Traditions of Marblehead*, p. 176; Billias, *General John Glover and his Marblehead Mariners*, pp. 11, 70.

108. Hanser, *The Glorious Hour of Lieutenant Monroe*, p. 141; Troiani and Kochan, *Don Troiani's Soldiers of the American Revolution*, p. 107; Fleming, *1776*, p. 458; Fischer, *Washington's Crossing*, p. 192; Bellamy, *The Private Life of George Washington*, p. 57.

108. *A Young Patriot in the American Revolution*, p. 83; Chandler, *The Campaigns of Napoleon*, p. 136.

109. Ketchum, *The Winter Soldiers*, p. 197.

110. Bellamy, *The Private Life of George Washington*, p. 106.

111. *Pennsylvania Gazette*, Philadelphia, Pennsylvania, September 30, 1756.

112. Ellis, *American Creation*, pp. 35-36

113. Stryker, *The Battles of Trenton and Princeton*, pp. 143-144; Fischer, *Washington'sCrossing*, pp. 228, 230; Chernow, *Washington*, p. 275; Marble, *James Monroe*, p. 42.

115. *A Young Patriot in the American Revolution*, pp. 31-80.

116. Linklater, *An Artist in Treason*, pp. 5-28; Willard Sterne Randall, *Benedict Arnold, Patriot and Traitor*, (New York: William Morrow, 1990), pp. 84-317; Bellamy, *The Private Life of George Washington*, p. 189.

117. Lengel, *This Glorious Struggle*, p. 84; Stryker, *The Battles of Trenton and Princeton*, pp. 141; Gragg, *By the Hand of Providence*, p. 27; Boatner, *Encyclopedia of the American Revolution*, p. 925; Chernow, *Washington*, pp. 274-275.

118. Bellamy, *The Private Life of George Washington*, p. 109.

119. Ibid., p. 149; Stryker, *The Battles of Trenton and Princeton*, pp. 139-140, 143; Elisha Bostwick Memoir, YUL; Hanser, *The Glorious Hour of Lt. Monroe*, pp. 127, 134, 139;

Edward G. Lengel, *This Glorious Struggle, George Washington's Revolutionary Letters,* *(New York: Harper Collins Publishers, 1993)*, pp. 79, 85; Elisha Bostwick, YUL; David S. Reynolds, *John Brown, Abolitionist, The Man Who Killed Slavery, Sparked the Civil War, and Seeded Civil Rights*, (New York: Alfred A. Knopf, 2005), pp. 16-20; Zondervan, *NIV Study Bible*, (Grand Rapids, Mi.: Zondervan Publishing, 2008), pp. 378-402; Edgar, *Campaign of 1776*, pp. 157-159, 171, 243, 310; Boatner, *Encyclopedia of the American Revolution,* p. 953; Chernow, *Washington*, pp. 274-275; *Daughters of the American Revolution Magazine*, vol. XLIV, no. 1, (January 1914), p. 7; Gragg, *By the Hand of Providence*, pp. 3-87.

120. Stryker, *The Battles of Trenton and Princeton*, p. 375; Clark, *All Cloudless Glory*, p. 223; Elisha Bostwick Memoir, YUL.

121. Lengel, *This Glorious Struggle*, p. 89.

Chapter III

1. *Pennsylvania Evening Post*, July 26, 1777; Troyer Steele Anderson, *The Command of the Howe Brothers During the American Revolution*, (Cranbury: Scholar's Bookshelf, 2005), pp. 204-206, 212; Burgoyne, *Defeat, Disaster, and Dedication*, p. 27; Stryker, *The Battles of Trenton and Princeton*, p. 38.

2. *Pennsylvania Evening Post*, July 26, 1777; Charles Nieder, editor, *George Washington, A Biography by Washington Irving*, (New York: Da Capo, 1994), pp. 326-328, 337-338; *New York Times*, December 27, 1880; Fischer, *Washington's Crossing*, pp. 59, 364; Burgoyne, *Defeat, Disaster, and Dedication*, pp. i-ii, v-vii.

3. *Pennsylvania Evening Post*, July 26, 1777; Von Hagen, *The Germanic People in America*, p. 161; Douglas Edward Leach, *Roots of Conflict, British Armed Forces and Colonial Americans, 1677-1763*, (Chapel Hill: University of North Carolina Press, 1986), pp. 130-131; Neider, ed., *George Washington*, p. 326; Dwyer, *"The Day Is Ours!,"* p. 12; Linklater, *An Artist in Treason*, pp. 31, 60; Burgoyne, *Defeat, Disaster, and Dedication*, p. 18.

4. Dwyer, *"The Day is Ours!,"* p. 13.

5. Chadwick, *George Washington's War*, p. 4; Edgar, *Campaign of 1776*, p. 118; Boatner, *Encyclopedia of the American Revolution*, p. 997.

6. *New York Times*, July 3, 1932.

7. *Pennsylvania Evening Post*, July 26, 1777; Dwyer, *"The Day is Ours!,"* p. 11; *New York Times*, December 27, 1880; Burgoyne, *Defeat, Disaster, and Dedication*, p. 20.

8. *New York Times*, December 27, 1880.

9. Slagle, "The Von Lossberg Regiment," AU, pp. 7-9; *Pennsylvania Evening Post*, July 26, 1777; Atwood, The Hessians, pp. 7-37; Fischer, *Washington's Crossing*, pp. 51-65, 364; Smith, *TheBattle of Trenton*, p. 31; Burgoyne, *Defeat, Disaster, and Dedication*, p. v; Helen Roeder, editor and translator, *The Ordeal of Captain Roeder*, (London: Methuen and Company, Ltd., 1960), p. 42; Reid, *Culloden Moor 1746*, p. 48; Clark, *All Cloudless Glory*, p. 222.

10. Von Hagen, *The Germanic People in America*, p. 162; Boatner, *Encyclopedia of the American Revolution*, p. 911; Charles Bracelen Flood, *Rise, And Fight Again, Perilous Times Along the Road to Independence*, (New York: Dodd, Mead and Company, 1976), p. 98; Donald N. Moran, "Colonel Johann Gottlieb Rall, Guilty of Tactical Negligence or Guiltless Circumstances?," *The Liberty Tree Newsletter*, November/December 2007.

11. Atwood, *The Hessians*, p. 70.

12. Robert Oakley Slagle, "The Von Lossberg Regiment: A Chronicle of Hessian Participation in the American Revolution," PhD Disseration, 1965, American University, Washington, D.C.: pp. 49-50; 83-84; *Pennsylvania Evening Post*, July 26, 1777; Neider, ed., *George Washington*, pp. 326-328, 338; Boatner, *Encyclopedia of the American Revolution*, p. 911; John G. Miller, *Alexander Hamilton, Portrait in Paradox*, (New York: Barnes and Noble, n. D.), p. 21; Flood, *Rise, And Fight Again*, pp. 98, 127-132; *New York Times*, December 27, 1880; Atwood, *The Hessians*, pp. 43, 64, 73-75, 77-79; Fischer, *Washington's Crossing*, pp. 55-57; Dominic Lieven, *Russia Against Napoleon, The True Story of the Campaigns of War and Peace*, (New York: Viking, 2010), pp. 23-24, 195; Moran, "Colonel Johann Gottlieb Rall," *LTN*; Smith, *New York 1776*, p. 78; Smith, *The Battle of Trenton*, pp. 27-28; Burgoyne, *Defeat, Disaster, and Dedication*, pp. i-iii, v, 2,18-19, 66, 71-72; Edgar, *Campaign of 1776*, p. 320.

13. Slagle, "The Von Lossberg Regiment," AU, p. 215; *Pennsylvania Evening Post*, July 26, 1777; Wheeler, *Voices of 1776*, p. 195; Stryker, *The Battles of Trenton and Princeton*, p. 392.

14. Von Hagen, *The Germanic People in America*, p. 162; Billias, *General John Glover and his Marblehead Mariners*, pp. 17-18.

15. Neider, ed., *George Washington*, p. 326; Boatner, *Encyclopedia of the American Revolution*, p. 911; Flood, *Rise, And Fight Again*, p. 98; Smith, *The Battle of Trenton*, p. 8.

16. Neider, ed., *George Washington*, p. 327; Michael A. Davis, *The Trial of Lt. Colonel Abraham Hunt, September 22, 1777, Trenton, New Jersey*, (Bloomington: Xlibris Corporation, n. D.) p. 170; Fischer, *Washington's Crossing*, p. 170; Smith, *The Battle of Trenton*, p. 13; Burgoyne, *Defeat, Disaster, and Dedication*, pp. 71-72; Edgar, *Campaign of 1776*, p. 320.

17. Slagle, "The Von Lossberg Regiment," AU, p. 85; *Pennsylvania Evening Post*, July 26, 1777; Neider, ed., *George Washington*, p. 333; Stephenson, *Patriot Battles*, p. 255; Fischer, *Washington's Crossing*, pp. 204, 231-232, 240; Smith, *The Battle of Trenton*, pp. 27-28; Stryker, *TheBattles of Trenton and Princeton*, pp. 115-116, 121-122.; Edgar, *Campaign of 1776*, p. 324; Chernow, *Washington*, p. 275.

18. Robert B. Asprey, *Frederick the Great, The Magnificent Enigma*, (New York: History Book Club, 1986), pp. xiii-629; Telford Taylor, *Sword and Swastika, Generals and Nazis in the Third Reich*, (Chicago: Quadrangle Paperbacks, Ltd., 1960), pp. 15-18; Bill, *The Campaign of Princeton*, p. 41; Fischer, *Washington's Crossing*, p. 55; Chastellux, *Travels in North America*, p. 163; Cox, *A Proper Sense of Honor*, p. 44.

19. Von Hagen, *The Germanic People in America*, p. 156; Fischer, *Washington's Crossing*, pp. 52.

20. *Pennsylvania Evening Post,* July 26, 1777; Fischer, *Washington's Crossing,* pp. 55-57; Stephenson, *Patriot Battles,* p. 254; Troiani and Kochan, *Don Troiani's Soldiers of the American Revolution,* pp. 61-73; Burgoyne, *Defeat, Disaster, and Dedication,* pp. i-iii; Smith, *The Battle of Trenton,* p. 31; Burgoyne, *Defeat, Disaster, and Dedication,* p. 20; Urban, *Fusiliers,* p. 76; Savas and Dameron, *The New American Revolution Handbook,* p. 37.

21. Anderson, *The Command of the Howe Brothers,* pp. 203, 206-207, 212; Ferling, *Almost A Miracle,* p. 162; Boatner, *Encyclopedia of the American Revolution,* p. 285; Stryker, *Battles of Trenton and Princeton,* pp. 115-116; Edgar, *Campaign of 1776,* p. 324.

22. Fischer, *Washington's Crossing,* p. 184; Lengel, *General George Washington,* p. 185; Anderson, *The Command of the Howe Brothers,* p. 208; Buchanan, *The Road to Valley Forge,* p. 160; Mitnick, ed., *New Jersey in the American Revolution,* pp. 48-49; Bill, *The Campaign of Princeton,* p. 27; Smith, *The Battle of Trenton,* p. 14; Chernow, *Washington,* p. 275.

23. Slagle, "The Von Lossberg Regiment," AU, pp. 179-196; *Pennsylvania Evening Post,* July 26, 1777; Dwyer, *The Day Is Ours!,* pp. 216-218; Hunt, *The Irish and the American Revolution,* p. 24; Buchanan, *The Road to Valley Forge,* p. 150; Bill, *The Campaign of Princeton,* p. 37; Smith, *The Battle of Trenton,* pp. 28, 31; Stryker, *The Battles of Trenton and Princeton,* pp. 51, 74; Chernow, *Washington,* pp. 267, 275; Samuel Griffin, Wikipedia; Fischer, *Washington's Crossing,* pp. 55-57.

24. Boatner, *Encyclopedia of the American Revolution,* pp. 426, 494, 911; Bonk, *Trenton and Princeton 1776-77,* p.19; Trussell, *The Pennsylvania Line,* pp. 222-226; Von Hagen, *TheGermanic People in America,* p. 162; Retzer, *The German Regiment of Maryland and Pennsylvania,* pp. v-141; Henry Melchier and Muhlenberg Richards, *The Pennsylvania-German in the Revolutionary War, 1775-1783,* (General Books, 2010), p. 399; H. G. Wells, *TheOutline of History, The Whole Story of Man,* (2 vols., New York: Garden City Books, 1956), vol. 2, p. 705; Cox, *A Proper Sense of Honor,* pp. 29-30, 44; Fischer, *Washington's Crossing,* pp. 364, 391; Styker, *The Battles of Trenton and Princeton,* pp. 19, 42.

25. Retzer, *The German Regiment of Maryland and Pennsylvania,* pp. 6, 131-133, 141-142.

26. Trussell, *The Pennsylvania Line,* pp. 225-226; Bonk, *Trenton and Princeton 1776-77,* p. 19; Fischer, *Liberty and Freedom,* pp. 90-93; Retzer, *The German Regiment ofMaryland and Pennsylvania,* pp. 6-7, 66; Fischer, *Washington's Crossing,* p. 391.

27. Retzer, *The German Regiment of Maryland and Pennsylvania,* pp. v-141; Melchier and Richards, *The Pennsylvania-German in the Revolutionary War,* p. 403; Conrad Weiser Homestead Archives, Womelsdorf, Pennsylvania; Fischer, *Washington's Crossing,* p. 391.

28. Retzer, *The German Regiment of Maryland and Pennsylvania,* p. 136.

29. Retzer, *The German Regiment of Maryland and Pennsylvania,* p. 134.

30. Bonk, *Trenton and Princeton 1776-77,* p. 19.

31. Samuel John Atlee Journal on the Battle of Long Island, 1776-1776, Brooklyn Historical Society, Brooklyn, New York; Newland, *The Pennsylvania Militia,* p. 134.

32. Trussell, *The Pennsylvania Line,* pp. 178-182; Smith, *The Battle of Trenton,* p. 20.

33. Stone, *Letters of Brunswick and Hessian Officers During the American Revolution*, p. 133, note; Bonk, *Trenton and Princeton 1776-77*, p. 20.

34. Stone, *Letters of Brunswick and Hessian Officers During the American Revolution*; Fischer, *Liberty and Freedom*, pp. 90-93; Trussell, *The Pennsylvania Line*, 222-226; Retzer, *The German Regiment of Pennsylvania and Maryland*, pp. 73, 152; Von Hagen, *The Germanic People in America*, p. 191.

35. Retzer, *The German Regiment of Pennsylvania and Maryland*, pp. 72-80, 148; Richard Wheeler, *Voices of 1776*, (Greenwich: Fawcett Publications, 1972), p. 208; Fischer, *Washington's Crossing*, pp. 52-57, 60; Stryker, *The Battles of Trenton and Princeton*, pp. 110-111; Edgar, *Campaign of 1776*, pp. 253, 266; Fischer, *Washington's Crossing*, pp. 55-65.

36. Retzer, *The German Regiment of Pennsylvania and Maryland*, pp. 7-8, 48-49, 74-75; Melchier and Richards, *The Pennsylvania-German in the Revolutionary War*, p. 399.

37. Davis, *The Trial of Lt. Colonel Abraham Hunt*, pp. 176-178; *New York Times*, December 24, 1895; Bill, *The Campaign of Princeton*, p. 53; Ketchum, *The Winter Soldiers*, pp. 76, 238; Fischer, *Washington's Crossing*, pp. 170-171; Faro, Wikipedia, internet; Hanser, *The Glorious Hour of Lt. Monroe*, p. 147; Stryker, *The Battles of Trenton and Princeton*, p. 110; Davis, *100Decisive Battles*, p. 251.

38. *Maryland Gazette*, February 27, 1777; *Pennsylvania Evening Post*, July 26, 1777; Stephenson, *Patriot Battles*, pp. 254-255; Mark Urban, *Fusiliers, The Saga of a British Redcoat Regiment in the American Revolution*, (New York: John Walker and Company, 2007), p. xiii; Lengel, *General George Washington*, pp. 181, 185; Flood, *Rise, And Fight Again*, p. 99; Fleming, *1776*, p. 345; Stephen Tanner, *Epic Retreats, From 1776 to the Evacuation of Saigon*, (Edison: Castle Books, 2002), p. 45; Paul K. Davis, *100 Decisive Battles, From Ancient Times to the Present, The World's Most Decisive Battles and How They Shaped History*, (New York: Oxford University Press, 1999), p. 253; Bill, *The Campaign of Princeton*, p. 43; Atwood, *The Hessians*, p. 36; Fischer, *Washington'sCrossing*, pp. 54, 204-205, 231-232, 240, 344; Dwyer, *"The Day Is Ours!,"* p. 247; Hanser, *TheGlorious Hour of Lt. Monroe*, pp. 147-148; Smith, *The Battle of Trenton*, pp. 17, 27; Burgoyne, *Defeat, Disaster, and Dedication*, pp. 7, 11; Edgar, *Campaign of 1776*, p. 324; Lengel, *InventingGeorge Washington*, p. 200; Chernow, *Washington*, p. 273.

39. *New York Times*, December 24, 1895; Lengel, *Inventing George Washington*, p. 200; Fischer, *Washington's Crossing*, p. 240.

40. Stryker, *The Battles of Trenton and Princeton*. p. 361; Fischer, *Washington's Crossing*, pp. 204-205; Joseph M. Malit interview with author, July 9, 2010; Lengel, *Inventing George Washington*, p. 200; Davis, *100 Decisive Battles*, p. 253.

41. Chandler, *The Campaigns of Napoleon*, pp. 141-142.

42. *Pennsylvania Evening Post*, July 26, 1777; Stephenson, *Patriot Battles*, pp. 254-255; Lengel, *General George Washington*, pp. 173, 178-179; Atwood, *The Hessians*, pp. 43, 64, 77-79; Burrows, *Forgotten Patriots*, p. 34; Smith, *The Battle of Trenton*, pp. 11, 13-14, 26; Fischer, *Washington's Crossing*, p. 204-205; Burgoyne, *Defeat, Disaster, and Dedication*, p. 71.

43. Slage, "The Von Lossberg Regiment," AU, p. 71; *Pennsylvania Evening Post*, July 26, 1777; Anderson, *The Command of the Howe Brothers*, p. 206; Dwyer, *This Day is Ours!*,

pp. 9-10, 14-16, 151-152, 166-168; Von Hagen, *The Germanic People in America*, p. 161; Stephenson, *Patriot Battles*, pp. 254-255; Lengel, *General George Washington*, p. 185; Buchanan, *The Road to Valley Forge*, p. 160; Bill, *The Campaign of Princeton*, p. 39; Atwood, *The Hessians*, pp. 86-88, 91-92; Fischer, *Washington's Crossing*, pp. 57, 60; Smith, *The Battle of Trenton*, pp. 7-8, 13-15, 26-27; Smith, *The Battle of Trenton*, pp. 17, 27; Stryker, *Battles of Trenton and Princeton*, pp. 42, 66, 94.

44. Buchanan, *The Road to Valley Forge*, p. 160; Bill, *The Campaign of Princeton*, p. 37; Atwood, *The Hessians*, pp. 91-92; Fischer, *Washington's Crossing*, pp. 183-184; Smith, *TheBattle of Trenton*, pp. 13-14, 27.

45. Edwin G. Burrows, *Forgotten Patriots: The Untold Story of American Prisoners During the Revolutionary War*, (New York: Perseus Books Group, 2008), p. 2.

46. Cox, *A Proper Sense of Honor*, 39.

47. Edwin Nott Hopson, *Captain Daniel Neil*, (Paterson: Braen-Heusser Printing Company, 1927), p. 18; Brochure, "Military Hospital at the Thompson-Neely House," Washington Crossing State Park, PHPMC; Fischer, *Washington's Crossing*, pp. 224, 227-228; Lawrence S. Kaplan, *Alexander Hamilton, Ambivalent Anglophile*, (Wilmington: Scholarly Resources, 2002), pp. 2, 24-26.

48. Elisha Bostwick Memoir, YUL; Stryker, *The Battles of Trenton and Princeton*, p. 58, note 1; Chernow, *Washington*, pp. 274-275.

49. Bellamy, *The Private Life of George Washington*, pp. 109-110.

50. *Maryland Gazette*, January 2, 1777; Buchanan, *The Road to Valley Forge*, p. 161; Wood, *Battles of the Revolutionary War*, p. 72; Fleming, *1776*, p. 457; Ketchum, *The Winter Soldiers*, pp. 27, 253-254; Bellamy, *The Private Life of George Washington*, pp. 109, 149; Fischer, *Washington's Crossing*, p. 231, 234; *A Young Patriot in the American Revolution*, p. 81; Smith, *The Battle of Trenton*, p. 20; Hanser, *The Glorious Hour of Lt. Monroe*, p. 143; Stryker, *The Battles of Trenton and Princeton*, p. 144; Elisha Bostwick Memoir, YUL; Chernow, *Washington*, pp. 274-275; Bunch-of-Grapes, Wikipedia; Rappleye, *Sons of Providence*, p. 175; Marble, *James Monroe*, p. 42; Michael McNally, *Teutoburg Forest AD 9*, (Oxford: Osprey Publishing, 2011), pp. 5-85.

51. Dwyer, "*The Day is Ours!*," pp. 33, 129, 132; Fleming, *1776*, p. 457; Lengel, *This Glorious Struggle*, pp. 87, 89; Gragg, *In the Hand of Providence*, p. 27.

52. Griffin, *Catholics and the American Revolution*, vol. 2, p. 273; Ketchum, *The Winter Soldiers*, p. 254.

53. Stryker, *The Battles of Trenton and Princeton*, p. 366; Dwyer, "*The Day is Ours!*," p. 38; Lengel, *General George Washington*, pp. 57, 59, 181; Ketchum, *The Winter Soldiers*, p. 250; *AYoung Patriot in the American Revolution*, p. 81; Ward, *Major General Adam Stephens and the Cause of American Liberty*, pp. 110-111, 113, 148; Burgoyne, *Death, Disaster, and Dedication*, p. 71; Chernow, *Washington*, pp. 275-276.

54. Ward, *Major General Adam Stephens and the Cause of American Liberty*, pp. 114-115.

55. Cecere, *They Behaved Like Soldiers*, p. 15.

56. Dwyer, "*The Day is Ours!*," p. 165.

57. Boatner, *Encyclopedia of the American Revolution*, p. 1205; Wheeler, *Voices of 1776*, p. 208; Stryker, *The Battles of Trenton and Princeton*, p. 143; Elisha Bostwick Memoir,

YUL; Linklater, *An Artist in Treason*, pp. 5-328; Chernow, *Washington*, pp. 274-275, 279.

58. Lengel, *General George Washington*, p. 179; Fleming, *1776*, pp. 274-279.

59. Gragg, *By the Hand of Providence*, pp. 95-96.

60. Lengel, *General George Washington*, p. 87.

61. Slagle, "The Von Lossberg Regiment," AU, pp. 73-74; Fleming, *1776*, pp. 440-441, 457-458; Buchanan, *The Road to Valley Forge*, p. 162; Smith, *The Battle of Trenton*, pp. 11, 13, 20, 23; Elisha Bostwick Memoir, YUL; Stryker, *The Battles of Trenton and Princeton*, p. 143; Zondervan, NIV Study Bible, pp. 379-404; Ward, *The War of the Revolution*, p. 296; Chernow, *Washington*, pp. 275-276; Rappleye, *Sons of Providence*, p. 175.

62. *A Young Patriot in the American Revolution*, p. 81; Lengel, *This Glorious Struggle*, p. 87.

63. Slagle, "The Von Lossberg Regiment," AU, p. 86, note 37; Fischer, *Washington's Crossing*, pp. 231-234, 264; Hanser, *The Glorious Hour of Lt. Monroe*, pp. 143-144; Royster, *Light-Horse Harry Lee*, p. 201; Chastellux, *Travels in North-America*, p. 126.

64. *Pennsylvania Evening Post*, July 26, 1777; Stephenson, *Patriot Battles*, pp. 254-255; Anderson, *The Command of the Howe Brothers*, pp. 201-203; Burgoyne, *Defeat, Disaster, and Dedication*, p. 71; Lengel, *This Glorious Struggle*, p. 87.

65. Stryker, *The Battles of Trenton and Princeton*, pp. 114, 139, 143, 360-361; Liell, *46 Pages*, pp. 143-144; Lengel, *This Glorious Struggle*, p. 87; Fischer, *Washington's Crossing*, p. 209.

66. Gragg, *In the Hand of Providence*, p. 79; Ward, *The War of the Revolution*, p. 295.

67. Buchanan, *The Road to Valley Forge*, p. 163; Atwood, *The Hessians*, pp. 46, 49, 166; Ketchum, *The Winter Soldiers*, p. 253; Fischer, *Washington's Crossing*, pp. 225, 231, 234-235; Smith, *The Battle of Trenton*, p. 20; Hanser, *The Glorious Hour of Lt. Monroe*, pp. 148-149; Stryker, *The Battles of Trenton and Princeton*, p. 147; Lengel, *This Glorious Struggle*, p. 87. Maureen O'Connor Leach to author, November 29, 2013.

68. Slagle, "The Von Lossberg Regiment," AU, pp. 90-91; Stryker, *The Battles of Trenton and Princeton*, pp. 141, 147-148, 361-362; Bonk, *Trenton and Princeton 1776-1777*, p. 53; Wheeler, *Voices of 1776*, p. 205; *New York Times*, December 25, 1876; Fleming, *1776*, p. 459; Buchanan, *The Road to Valley Forge*, p. 158; Bill, *The Campaign of Princeton*, p. 52; Atwood, *TheHessians*, pp. 74-75; Clark, *All Cloudless Glory*, p. 304; Ketchum, *The Winter Soldiers*, pp. 254-255; Fischer, *Washington'sCrossing*, pp. 58, 170, 204-205, 231-232, 235, 391; Dwyer, *The Day Is Ours!*, p. 264; Smith, *The Battle ofTrenton*, pp. 12, 20; Hanser, *The Glorious Hour of Lt. Monroe*, pp. 148-150; Burgoyne, *Defeat, Disaster, and Dedication*, pp. 66-69, 74, 94-95; Edgar, *Campaign of 1776*, pp. 253, 263-264; Chernow, *Washington*, p. 276; Lengel, *This Glorious Struggle*, p. 87; Weller, "Guns of Destiny," MA, p. 8; Barbara Ehrenreich, *Blood Rites, Origins and History of the Passions of War*, (New York: Henry Holt and Company, 1997), p. 9.

69. Burgoyne, *Defeat, Disaster, and Dedication*, p. 74; Buchanan, *The Road to Valley Forge*, p. 157; Smith, *The Battle of Trenton*, p. 20; Stryker, *The Battles of Trenton and Princeton*, p. 147.

70. Slagle, "The Von Lossberg Regiment," AU, pp. 56-58, 214-215; *Maryland Gazette*, January 2, 1777; Stryker, *The Battles of Trenton and Princeton*, pp. 144, 147-148, 362-363,

391; Marble, *James Monroe*, pp. 24, 46; Fischer, *Washington's Crossing*, pp. 204-205, 221-22, 231, 237, 240; Bill, *The Campaign of Trenton*, p. 52; Atwood, *The Hessians*, p. 89-90, 92-93; Ketchum, *The Winter Soldiers*, p. 255; Dwyer, *"The Day Is Ours!,"* p. 264; Hanser, *The Glorious Hour of Lt. Monroe*, pp. 60, 143; Cecere, *They Behaved Like Soldiers*, p. 15; Smith, *The Battle of Trenton*, p. 20; Burgoyne, *Defeat, Disaster, and Dedication*, pp. 19, 74.

71. *Maryland Gazette*, January 2, 1777; Ketchum, *The Winter Soldiers*, p. 255; Fischer, *Washington's Crossing*, pp. 237-238; Dwyer, *The Day Is Ours!*, p. 264; Smith, *The Battle of Trenton*, p. 20; Hanser, *The Glorious Hour of Lt. Monroe*, pp. 148-149; Burgoyne, *Defeat,Disaster, and Dedication*, p. 74.

72. Burgoyne, *Defeat, Disaster, and Dedication*, p. 74; Marble, *James Monroe*, p. 46; Fischer, *Washington's Crossing*, pp. 221, 237; Atwood, *The Hessians*, p. 93

73. Slagle, "The Von Lossberg Regiment," AU, pp. 91, 214; Stryker, *The Battles of Trenton and Princeton*, p. 353; Lengel, *General George Washington*, p. 186; Atwood, *The Hessians*, pp. 92-93; Smith, *The Battle of Trenton*, p. 20.

74. Lengel, *General George Washington*, p. 186; Atwood, *The Hessians*, pp. 89-90, 92-93; Fischer, *Washington's Crossing*, 204-205, 237-238; Hanser, *The Glorious Hour of Lt. Monroe*, p. 70; Smith, *The Battle of Trenton*, p. 20; Edgar, *Campaign of 1776*, p. 277.

75. Fischer, *Washington's Crossing*, p. 241.

76. Burgoyne, *Defeat, Disaster, and Dedication*, p. 74.

77. Burgoyne, *Defeat Disaster, and Dedication*, p. 74.

78. Slagle, "The Von Lossberg Regiment," AU, pp. 91, 216;Von Hagen, *The Germanic People in America*, p. 162; Stryker, *The Battles of Trenton and Princeton*, pp. 149, 371; Boatner, *Encyclopedia of the American Revolution*, p. 1169; Marble, *James Monroe*, p. 46; Dwyer, *"The Day Is Ours,"* pp. 252, 263, 265; Fischer, *Washington's Crossing*, p. 405.

79. Hanser, *The Glorious Hour of Lt. Monroe*, pp. 149-150; Dwyer, *"The Day Is Ours!,"* p. 252.

80. Slagle, "The Von Lossberg Regiment," AU, p. 91; Dwyer, *"The Day Is Ours!,"* pp. 252, 263; Stryker, *The Battles of Trenton and Princeton*, pp. 149-150, 358, 392; Haltigan, *The Irish in the American Revolution and their Early Influence in the Colonies*, p. 400; Troianai and Kochan, *Don Troiani's Soldiers of the American Revolution*, p. 109; "Morris, Samuel-Capt." Ancestralheroes.com, internet; Edgar, *Campaign of 1776*, p. 337.

81. Burgoyne, *Defeat, Disaster, and Dedication*, pp. 73-74; Dwyer, *"The Day Is Ours!,"* p. 265; Fischer, *Washington's Crossing*, p. 238.

82. Slagle, "The Von Lossberg Regiment," AU, p. 91; Randall, *George Washington*, p. 324; Stryker, *The Battles of Trenton and Princeton*, pp. 152-153; Smith, *The Battle of Trenton*, p. 20; Burgoyne, *Defeat, Disaster, and Dedication*, p. 74; Fischer, *Washington's Crossing*, p. 238.

83. Burgoyne, *Defeat, Disaster, and Dedication*, p. 74; Dwyer, *"The Day Is Ours!,"* p. 265; Smith, *The Battle of Trenton*, p. 20.

84. Burgoyne, *Defeat, Disaster, and Dedication*, p. 78.

85 .Christopher Hibbert, *Redcoats and Rebels, The American Revolution Through British Eyes*, (New York: W. W. Norton, 2002), p. 148; Von Hagen, *The Germanic People in*

America, p. 162; John E. Rodes, *Germany: A History*, (New York: Holt, Rinehart and Winston, 1964), pp. 42, 48, 52-55, 110, 134.

86. Howard Zinn, *A People's History of the American Revolution, How Common People Shaped the Fight for Independence*, (New York: Harper Collins Publishers, Inc., 2002), p. 91; Boatner, *Encyclopedia of the American Revolution*, p. 911; Moran, "Colonel Johann Gottlieb Rall," *TLTN*; Smith, *The Battle of Trenton*, p. 31; Chandler, *The Campaigns of Napoleon*, p. 135, 141.

87. Clark, *All Cloudless Glory*, pp. 298-299; Fischer, *Washington's Crossing*, pp. 191, 235, 240; Boatner, *Encyclopedia of the American Revolution*, pp. 918-919; Lengel, *Inventing George Washington*, p. 200.

88. Chadwick, *George Washington's War*, p. 17.

89. Clark, *All Cloudless Glory*, p. 304.

90. Ibid; Stryker, *The Battles of Trenton and Princeton*, pp. 97, 102, 145-146, 151-152, 168, 218, 357, 363; Fisher, *Washington's Crossing*, pp. 201, 222-223, 235; Randall, *Alexander Hamilton*, p. 117; *New York Times*, January 24, 1932; Buchanan, *The Road to Valley Forge*, p. 158; Wood, *Battles of the Revolutionary War*, p. 71; Ketchum, *The Winter Soldiers*, pp. 255-256; Fischer, *Washington's Crossing*, pp. 235, 238, 393; Boatner, *Encyclopedia of the American Revolution*, pp. 330-332; Dwyer, *"The Day Is Ours!,"* p. 251; Smith, *The Battle of Trenton*, pp. 13-14, 20-22; Michael Pearson, *Those Damned Rebels, The American Revolution as Seen Through British Eyes*, (New York: Da Capo Press, 2000), pp. 217-218; Egerton, *Death or Liberty*, pp. 74, 76; Troiani and Kochan, *Don Troiani's Soldiers of the American Revolution*, p. 95; Gragg, *By the Hand of Providence*, p. 69; Weller, "Guns of Destiny," *MA*, p. 8.

91. Stryker, *The Battles of Trenton and Princeton*, p. 371.

92. Elisha Bostwick, YUL; Smith, *The Battle of Trenton*, p. 20; Clark, *All Cloudless Glory*, p. 304.

93. Dwyer, *"The Day Is Ours!,"* p. 251.

94. Buchanan, *The Road to Valley Forge*, p. 163; Fischer, *Washington's Crossing*, p. 235.

95. Fischer, *Washington's Crossing*, p. 235; Michael E. Haskew, editor, *Great Military Disasters*, (Bath: Parragon Books, Ltd., 2009), pp. 11-17; Hart, *Strategy*, pp. 48-49; Clark, *All Cloudless Glory*, p. 304.

96. Ketchum, *The Winter Soldiers*, p. 258; Wheeler, *Voices of 1776*, p. 206; Boatner, *Encyclopedia of the American Revolution*, pp. 1205-1206; Linklater, *An Artist in Treason*, pp. 18-28.

97. Stryker, *The Battles of Trenton and Princeton*, p. 363; Fischer, *Washington's Crossing*, pp. 204-205, 240, 244; Crown and Rogers, *Image of America, Trenton*, 17.

98. Hanser, *The Glorious Hour of Lt. Monroe*, p. 145; Fischer, *Washington's Crossing*, pp. 204-205, 240, 244; Burgoyne, *Defeat, Disaster, and Dedication*, p. v.

99. Lengel, *General George Washington*, pp. 39-47; Atwood, *The Hessians*, p. 89; Fischer, *Washington's Crossing*, p. 235; Clark, *All Cloudless Glory*, p. 304.

100. William A. Hunter, "Victory at Kittanning," *Pennsylvania History*, vol. 23, (July 1956), pp. 376-407; Fischer, *Washington's Crossing*, p. 240.

101. Hanser, *The Glorious Hour of Lt. Monroe*, pp. 149-150.

102. Fischer, *Washington's Crossing*, pp. 60, 240; Wheeler, *Voices of 1776*, pp. 203-204; Rose, *Washington's War*, p. 83; Trenton, New Jersey, Wikipedia, internet; Mitnick, ed., *New Jersey and the American Revolution*, p. 167; Bill, *The Campaign of Princeton*, p. 38; Kochan, *DonTroiani's Soldiers of the American Revolution*, pp. 66-67; *New York Times*, Decembe 27, 1880; Atwood, *The Hessians*, p. 45; Ketchum, *The Winter Soldiers*, pp. 202-203; Ketchum, *The Winter Soldiers*, p. 234; Smith, *The Battle of Trenton*, pp. 13, 26; Crown and Rogers, *Images of America, Trenton*, pp. 9-10; Edgar, *Campaign of 1776*, pp. 144-145, 276, 298-299.

103. Lengel, *General George Washington*, pp. 39-47.

104. Slagle, "The Von Lossberg Regiment," AU, pp. 98-99; *Pennsylvania Evening Post*, July 26, 1777; Von Hagen, *The Germanic People in America*, p. 162; Stephenson, *Patriot Battles*, pp. 254-255; Bill, *The Campaign of Princeton*, p. 39; Atwood, *The Hessians*, pp. 88-90, 92; Smith, *The Battle of Trenton*, pp. 11, 13-14, 27; Fischer, *Washington's Crossing*, pp. 204-205, 240; Chandler, *The Campaigns of Napoleon*, pp. 356-360; Weller, "Guns of Destiny," *MA*, p. 4; Stryker, *The Battles of Trenton and Princeton*, p. 147; Smith, *The Battle of Trenton*, p. 17.

105. Neider, ed., *George Washington*, p. 338; Fischer, *Washington's Crossing*, p. 190; Atwood, *The Hessians*, p. 90; Smith, *The Battle of Trenton*, p. 15.

106. Lengel, *General George Washington*, p. 185; Atwood, *The Hessians*, pp. 91-97; Ketchum, *The Winter Soldiers*, p. 235; Smith, *The Battle of Trenton*, p. 14.

107. Bill, *The Campaign of Princeton*, p. 39; Atwood, *The Hessians*, p. 88; Slagle, "The Von Lossberg Regiment," AU, pp. 94, 98-99; Smith, *The Battle of Trenton*, pp. 17, 27; Weller, "Guns of Destiny," *MA*, p. 4; Stryker, *The Battles of Trenton and Princeton*, pp. 128,147; Fischer, *Washington's Crossing*, p. 250.

108. *Pennsylvania Evening Post*, July 26, 1777; Burgoyne, *Defeat, Disaster, and Dedication*, p. 71.

109. Burgoyne, *Defeat, Disaster, and Dedication*, p. 73.

110. Ephraim Kam, *Surprise Attack, The Victim's Perspective*, (Cambridge: Harvard University Press, 2004), pp. xiii-233; Samuel Griffin, Wikipedia; Smith, *The Battle of Trenton*, p. 15; Fischer, *Washington's Crossing*, pp. 201-235.

Chapter IV

1. Elisha Bostwick Memoir, YUL: Stryker, *The Battles of Trenton and Princeton*, p. 115.

2. Fischer, *Washington's Crossing*, p. 241; Biddle Family Papers, 1766-1943, Special Collections, University of Delaware Library, University of Delaware, Newark, Delaware; Crown and Rogers, *Images of America, Trenton*, p. 7; Man Full of Trouble Tavern, "Now is the Time for Drinking," (Horace), USHistory. Org., internet; Gragg, *By the Hand of Providence*, pp. 11-13..

3. Slagle, "The Von Lossberg Regiment," AU, pp. 10, 29; Flood, *Rise, and Fight Again*, pp. 94-149; Bill, *The Campaign of Princeton*, p. 47; Biddle Family Papers, 1766-1943,

UDL; Keane, *Tom Paine*, pp. 16-22; Edgar, *Campaign of 1776*, p. 155; Gragg, *By the Hands of Providence*, p. 69.

4. Valentine, *Lord Stirling*, p. 171; Stryker, *The Battles of Trenton and Princeton*, p. 361; Fischer, *Washington's Crossing*, p. 235; Crown and Rogers, *Images of America, Trenton*, pp . 7, 9-10; Literature, "Meet William Trent,: WTHM; Smith, *The Battle of Trenton*, pp. 6, 26; Fischer, *Liberty and Freedom*, p. 148.

5. Dwyer, *"The Day is Ours!,"* p. 101; Keane, *Tom Paine*, pp. xx-xxi, 104-145.

6. Stryker, *The Battles of Trenton and Princeton*, p. 371.

7. Buchanan, *The Road to Valley Forge*, p. 160.

8. Cecere, *They Behaved Like Soldiers*, pp. 14-15, 18-19, 21; Fischer, *Washington's Crossing*, pp. 158-159; Edgar, *Campaign of 1776*, pp. 157-159, 180-183, 328.

9. Dwyer, *The Day Is Ours!*, p. 249; Weller, "Guns of Destiny," *MA*, p. 8.

10. William J. Bennett, *America, The Last Best Hope, From the Age of Discovery To a World at War 1492-1914*, volume I, (New York: Nelson Current, 2006), p. 89; Ketchum, *The WinterSoldiers*, p. 243; Fischer, *Washington's Crossing*, pp. 57, 60, 364; Stryker, *The Battles of Trenton and Princeton*, p. 281.

11. Gragg, *In the Hand of Providence*, p. 79.

12. Richard Kluger, *Seizing Destiny*, (New York: Vintage Books, 2007), pp. 84-85; Smith, *The Battle of Trenton*, p. 32.

13. Stryker, *The Battles of Trenton and Princeton*, p. 54.

14. Ward, *Major General Adam Stephens and the Cause of American Liberty*, p. 152; Bonk, *Trenton and Princeton 1776-1777*, p. 53; Trussell, *The Pennsylvania Line*, p. 226; Lengel, *General George Washington*, p. 186; Buchanan, *The Road to Valley Forge*, p. 158; Wood, *Battles of the Revolutionary War*, p. 69; Bill, *The Campaign of Princeton*, p. 48; Fleming, *1776*, pp. 443-456; Ketchum, *The Winter Soldiers*, p. 201; Fischer, *Washington's Crossing*, pp. 235, 244, 364, 391; English, *General Hugh Mercer*, pp. 69, 75; Joseph M. Waterman, *With Sword and Lancet, The Life of Hugh Mercer*, (Richmond: Garrett and Massie, 1947), pp. 133-134, 136-137; Stryker, *The Battles of Trenton and Princeton*, p. 370; Weller, "Guns of Destiny," *MA*, pp. 4, 8, 14; Smith, *The Battle of Trenton*, p. 22.

15. Buchanan, *The Road to Valley Forge*, p. 158; Boatner, *Encyclopedia of the American Revolution*, p. 366; Stryer, *The Battles of Trenton and Princeton*, p. 168; Smith, *The Battle of Trenton*, p. 20.

16. *Maryland Gazette*, January 2, 1777; Stryker, *The Battles of Trenton and Princeton*, pp. 163-164;168, 357, 363, 367, 370; Bonk, *Trenton and Princeton 1776-1777*, pp. 20, 55, 58; Neider, ed., *George Washington*, pp. 333-334; Wright, *The Continental Army*, p. 103; Lengel, *General George Washington*, pp. 185-186; Billias, *General John Glover and His Marblehead Mariners*, p. 11; Tagney, *The World Turned Upside Down*, p. 285; Hopson, *Captain Daniel Neil*, pp. 14-15, 29; Buchanan, *The Road to Valley Forge*, pp. 152, 158; Farling, *Almost A Miracle*, p. 177; Bill, *The Campaign of Princeton*, pp. 52-53; Ketchum, *The Winter Soldiers*, pp. 256, 258; McNab, *Armies of the Napoleonic Wars*, pp. 74-78; Fischer, *Washington's Crossing*, pp. 153, 244; Nead, "A Sketch of General Thomas Procter," *PMHM*, pp. 454-470; Dwyer, *The Day Is Ours!*, pp. 252-253.; Smith,

The Battle of Trenton, pp. 20, 22, 24; Christopher Herold, *The Battle of Waterloo*, (New York: American Heritage Publishing Company, 1967), pp. 73, 89; Ward, *Major General Adam Stephen and the Cause of American Liberty*, p. 152; Edgar, *Campaign of 1776*, p. 328; Stephen Pope, *Dictionary of the Napoleonic Wars*, (New York: Facts On File, Inc., 1999), pp. 70-71; *Daughters of the American Revolution Magazine*, vol. XLIV, no. 1, (January 1914), p. 7; Bevin Alexander, *How Hitler Could Have Won World War II*, (Old Saybrook: Konecky & Konecky, 2000), p. 83; Chandler, *The Campaigns of Napoleon*, pp. 82, 356, 360, 363-364; Weller, "Guns of Destiny," *MA*, pp. 7-9; Owen Connelly, *On War and Leadership, The Words of Combat Commanders from Frederick the Great to Norman Schwarzkopf*, (Princeton: Princeton University Press, 2002), p. 11.

17. Chandler, *The Military Maxims of Napoleon*, p. 62; Stryker, *The Battles of Trenton and Princeton*, p. 370

18. *Maryland Gazette*, January 2, 1777; Stryker, *The Battles of Trenton and Princeton*, pp. 367, 370, 373; Wheeler, *Voices of 1776*, p. 206; Bennett, *America*, vol. I, p. 89; Wood, *Battles of the Revolutionary War*, p. 69; Nead, "A Sketch of General Thomas Proctor," *PMHB*, pp. 454-470; Fischer, *Washington's Crossing*, p. 244; Dwyer, *The Day Is Ours!*, pp. 252-253; Fischer, *Libertyand Freedom*, pp. 135-136; Weller, "Guns of Destiny," *MA*, pp. 7-8.

19. Wheeler, *Voices of 1776*, p. 206; Ketchum, *The Winter Soldiers*, p. 258.

20. Stryker, *The Battles of Trenton and Princeton*, pp. 166-167, 170; Weller, "Guns of Destiny," *MA*, pp. 4, 8, 14.

21. *Maryland Gazette*, January 2, 1777; *New York Times*, April 9, 1876; Brendan Morrissey, *Monmouth Courthouse 1778, The last great battle in the North*, (Oxford: Osprey Publishing, Ltd., 2004), p. 20; Crown and Rogers, *Images of America, Trenton*, p. 12.

22. Nead, "A Sketch of General Thomas Proctor," *PMHB*, pp. 454-470; Neider, ed., *GeorgeWashington*, p. 334; Bonk, Trenton and Princeton 1776-1777, p. 55; Randall, *Alexander Hamilton*, pp. 114-117; Stryker, *The Battles of Trenton and Princeton*, pp. 158-159, 357, 367, 389; Buchanan, *The Road to Valley Forge*, pp. 152, 158; Wood, *Battles of the Revolutionary War*, p. 69; Bill, *The Campaign of Princeton*, p. 50; Burgoyne, *Defeat, Disaster, and Dedication*, p. 74; Fischer, *Washington'sCrossing*, p. 130; Edgar, *Campaign of 1776*, pp. 255, 344-345; Chernow, *Washington*, pp. 786-789; Weller, "Guns of Destiny," *MA*, pp. 4, 8; Richard Brookhiser, *Alexander Hamilton, American*, (New York: Touchstone, 2000), pp. 1-2

23. John C. Hamilton, *The Life of Alexander Hamiton by his son*, (2 vols: New York: Halstel and Voorhies, 1834), pp. 1-38, 44-67; Randall, *Alexander Hamilton*, pp. 6-117, 123-124; Miller, *Alexander Hamilton*, pp. 3-21; Bill, *The Campaign of Princeton*, p. 50; Burgoyne, *Defeat, Disaster, and Dedication*, p. 71; Stryker, *The Battles of Trenton and Princeton*, pp. 16, 158-159; Kaplan, *Alexander Hamilton*, pp. 23-26; Brookhiser, *Alexander Hamilton*, pp. 1-3, 13-28.

24. Hamilton, *The Life of Alexander Hamilton*, vol. 1, pp. 35, 65-67.

25. Brookhiser, *Alexander Hamilton*, p. 10.

26. Tilghman, *Memoir of Lieutenant Colonel Tench Tilghman*, p. 173; Weller, "Guns of Destiny," *MA*, p. 8; Cox, *A Proper Sense of Honor*, p. 56.

27. Dwyer, *This Day is Ours!*, p. 166.

28. Miller, *Alexander Hamilton*, p. 20.

29. Neider, ed., *George Washington*, p. 334; Bonk, *Trenton and Princeton 1776-1777*, pp. 20, 55; Wright, *The Continental Army*, pp. 62, 102; Stryker, *The Battles of Trenton and Princeton*, p. 367; Bennett, *America*, vol. I, p. 89; Buchanan, *The Road to Valley Forge*, p. 158; Bill, *TheCampaign of Princeton*, pp. 62-53; Miller, *Alexander Hamilton*, p. 20; *Edgar, Campaign of 1776*, p. 255; Weller, "Guns of Destiny," *MA*, pp. 8-9.

30. Chastellux, *Travels in North-America*, p. 70.

31. Urban, *Fusiliers*, p. 83;Valentine, *Lord Stirling*, pp. 180-196; Stryker, *The Battles of Trenton and Princeton*, pp. 27, 267, 370; Stephenson, *Patriot Battles*, p. 239; Tucker, *The Important Role of the Irish in the American Revolution*, pp. 32-64; Smith, *New York 1776*, pp. 50-54; Bill, *The Campaign of Princeton*, p. 48; Fischer, *Washington's Crossing*, p. 244; Ward, *Major General Adam Stephen and the Cause of American Liberty*, p. 152; Edgar, *Campaign of 1776*, pp. 149-151; John C. Conradis, "'The Red and Buff': Setting the Record Straight On the Military Dress of Smallwood's Battalion of Maryland Regular Troops, 1776," *Military Collector & Historian*, vol. 60, no. 4, (Winter 2008), pp. 274-276.

32. Valentine, *Lord Stirling*, p. 198.

33. *Virginia Gazette*, Williamsburg, Virginia, October 21, 1775 and January 24, 1777; Cox, *A Proper Sense of Honor*, pp. 1-2; Bonk, *Trenton and Princeton 1776-77*, p. 19; Ennion Williams Painting by Charles Willson Peale, The Metropolitan Museum, New York, New York; Stryker, *The Battles of Trenton and Princeton*, pp. 27, 292; Kwasny, *Washington's Partisan War*, p. 61; "Fleming Family," *The William and Mary Quarterly*, vol. 12, no. 1, (July 1903), pp. 45, 47; Samuel Harzard, *Pennsylvania Archives*, vol. 5, (Philadelphia: Joseph Severns and Company, 1853), p. 105; Urban, *Fusiliers*, p. 83.

34. Bonk, *Trenton and Princeton 1776-1777*, pp. 19, 53, 58; Stryker, *The Battles of Trenton and Princeton*, p. 367; Ward, *Major General Adam Stephen and the Cause of American Liberty*, p. 152.

35. Lengel, *General George Washington*, pp. 57, 59, 181; Bonk, *Trenton and Princeton 1776-77*, p. 19; Boatner, *Encyclopedia of the American Revolution*, p. 1055; Bill, *The Campaign of Princeton*, p. 48; Fischer, *Washington's Crossing*, p. 232; Ward, *Major General Adam Stephen and the Cause of American Liberty*, pp. ix-245.

36. Ward, *Major General Adam Stephen and the Cause of American Liberty*, p. 148.

37. Farling, *Almost A Miracle*, p. 176; Wright, *The Continental Army*, p. p. 286; Bill, *TheCampaign of Princeton*, pp. 48, 51; Fischer, *Washington's Crossing*, pp. 231-232.

38. Bonk, *Trenton and Princeton 1776-1777*, p. 53.

39. Buchanan, *The Road to Valley Forge*, p. 157; *Maryland Gazette*, May 1, 1777.

40. Buchanan, *The Road to Valley Forge*, p. 157; Chandler, *The Campaigns of Napoleon*, pp. 362-364; William G. Robertson, General Editor, and Lawrence A. Yates, Managing Editor, *Block by Block, The Challenges of Urban Operations*, (Fort Leavenworth: U. S. Army Command and General Staff College, 2003), pp. 1-8.

41. Newland, *The Pennsylvania Militia*, p. 144.

42. Robertson and Yates, editors, *Block by Block*, pp. 20-21.

43. Stryker, *The Battles of Trenton and Princeton*, p. 372; Wheeler, *Voices of 1776*, p. 206; Bill, *The Campaign of Princeton*, p. 53; Fischer, *Washington's Crossing*, pp. 240, 244-245; Hanser, *The Glorious Hour of Lt. Monroe*, p. 145.

44. Stryker, *The Battles of Trenton and Princeton*, p. 363; Weller, "Guns of Destiny," *MA*, p. 8.

45. Stephenson, *Patriot Battles*, pp. 252, 258; Bonk, *Trenton and Princeton 1776-77*, p. 20; Robert A. Mayers, *The War Man, A True Story of a Citizen-Soldier Who Fought from Quebec to Yorktown*, (Yardley: Westholme Publishing, 2009), p. 25; Dwyer, *"The Day Is Ours!,"* p. 254; Weller, "Guns of Destiny," *MA*, pp. 7-9; Stryker, *The Battles of Trenton and Princeton*, p. 357.

46. Stone, *Letters of Brunswick and Hessian Officers during the American Revolution*, p. 133, note.

47. Wood, *Battles of the Revolutionary War*, p. 69; Ketchum, *The Winter Soldiers*, p. 258; Fischer, *Washington's Crossing*, p. 244; Biography of Colonel John Durkee, Ancestry. com Family Tree, internet.

48. Fleming, *1776*, p. 449; Edgar, *Campaign of 1776*, p. 300.

Chapter V

1. Slagle, "The Von Lossberg Regiment," AU, pp. 40, 74; Stryker, *The Battles of Trenton and Princeton*, pp. 103, 147, 153-154, 170, 392; Smith, *The Battle of Trenton*, p. 17; Clark, *AllCloudless Glory*, p. 304.

2. Stryker, *The Battles of Trenton and Princeton*, pp. 153-154; Smith, *The Battle of Trenton*, p. 22; Fischer, *Washington's Crossing*, p. 240; Clark, *All Cloudless Glory*, p. 304; Ward, *The War of the Revolution*, p. 298.

3. *Pennsylvania Evening Post*, July 26, 1777; Stryker, *The Battles of Trenton and Princeton*, pp. 153-154, 389, 392; Slagle, "The Von Lossberg Regiment," AU, pp. 34, 73-74.

4. Slagle, "The Von Lossberg Regiment," AU, pp. 10-64, 74, 86, 88, 92, 99, 127; *PennsylvaniaEvening Post*, July 26, 1777; Wood, *Battles of the Revolutionary War*, p. 70; Bill, *The Campaign of Princeton*, p. 53; Atwood, *The Hessians*, p. 93; Fischer, *Washington'sCrossing*, pp. 240-241, 244; Stryker, *The Battles of Trenton and Princeton*, pp. 91, 94-95, 97, 145, 147, 153-156, 158, 160-161, 372, 376, 393; Dwyer, *"The Day Is Ours!,"* p. 265; Fischer, *Washington's Crossing*, pp. 204-205; Hanser, *The Glorious Hour of Lt. Monroe*, p. 146; Smith, *The Battle of Trenton*, pp. 17, 22, 27; Burgoyne, *Defeat, Disaster, and Dedication*, pp. 18; Don Troiani, Historical Art Prints, Norwich, Connecticut, email to author, June 28, 2010; Edgar, *Campaignof 1776*, pp. 144, 255, 325; Joseph M. Malit email to author, July 20 and 21, 2010; Weller, "Guns of Destiny," *MA*, p. 8

5. Slagle, "The Von Lossberg Regiment," AU, p. 74; Farling, *Almost A Miracle*, p. 177; Wood, *Battles of the Revolutionary War*, p. 70; Bill, *The Campaign of Princeton*, pp. 39, 53; Atwood, *The Hessians*, pp. 90, 92-93; Ketchum, *The Winter Soldiers*, pp. 258-259; Fischer, *Washington's Crossing*, pp. 243-244; Stryker, *The Battles of Trenton and*

Princeton, pp. 97, 145, 147, 154, 159-160; Dwyer, *"The Day Is Ours!,"* pp. 265-266; Smith, *The Battle of Trenton*, pp. 17, 22; Edgar, *Campaign of 1776*, pp. 255, 337, 339.

6. Slagle, "The Von Lossberg Regiment," AU, pp. 16-17; Fischer, *Washington's Crossing*, pp. 240, 244; Bonk, *Trenton and Princeton 1776-77*, p. 19; Wallace, *An Appeal to Arms*, p. 130; Wood, *Battles of the Revolutionary War*, p. 69; Atwood, *The Hessians*, pp. 89-90, 92; Atwood, *The Hessians*, p. 96; Ketchum, *The Winter Soldiers*, pp. 258-259; Stryker, *The Battles of Trenton and Princeton*, pp. 156, 158, 391; Dwyer, *"The Day Is Ours!,"* pp. 265-267; Smith, *The Battle of Trenton*, pp. 22, 24; Burgoyne, *Defeat, Disaster, and Dedication*, p. 71; Ward, *The War of the Revolution*, p. 300; Edgar, *Campaign of 1776*, p. 325.

7. Chastellux, *Travels in North-America*, p. 157.

8. Ehrenreich, *Blood Rites*, p. 186.

9. Farling, *Almost A Miracle*, p. 178; Wood, *Battles of the Revolutionary War*, p. 70; Chadwick, *George Washington's War*, p. 18; Fischer, *Washington's Crossing*, p. 240; Stryker, *The Battles of Trenton and Princeton*, p. 156; Dwyer, *"The Day Is Ours!,"* p. 265; Smith, *TheBattle of Trenton*, p. 17.

10. Slagle, "The Von Lossberg Regiment," AU, p. 106; *New York Times*, April 9, 1876; Atwood, *The Hessians*, pp. 89-91, 93; Stryker, *The Battles of Trenton and Princeton*, pp. 155-156, 391, 394; Smith, *The Battle of Trenton*, p. 26; Robertson and Yates, eds., *Block by Block*, pp. 20-21; Fischer, *Washington's Crossing*, p. 240.

11. Fischer, *Washington's Crossing*, p. 244; Keane, *Tom Paine*, p. 145; Stryker, *The Battles of Trenton and Princeton*, pp. 159-160; Edgar, *Campaign of 1776*, p. 339.

12. Stryker, *The Battles of Trenton and Princeton*, p. 371; Chastellux, *Travels in North-America*, p. 70; Fischer, *Washington's Crossing*, p. 153.

13. Chastellux, *Travels in North-America*, p. 163.

14. Slagle, "The Von Lossberg Regiment," AU, pp. 92-95; Atwood, *Hessians*, pp. 92-94, 95-97, 240; Todish and Todish, *Alamo Sourcebook 1836*, p. 160; Zaboly, *AmericanColonial Rangers*, pp. 4, H; Bill, *The Campaign of Princeton*, pp. 28, 40, 42; Newland, *The Pennsylvania Militia*, p. 135; Fischer, *Washington'sCrossing*, pp. 204-205, 240-241, 244; Bonk, *Trenton and Princeton, 1776-77*, p. 19; Stryker, *TheBattles of Trenton and Princeton*, pp. 96, 99, 155-156, 158, 170; Crown and Rogers, *Images of America, Trenton*, p. 12; Chris Kyle, *American Gun, A History of the U. S. in Ten Firearms*, (New York: William Morrow, 2013), pp. 3, 5;Burgoyne, *Defeat, Disaster, and Dedication*, pp. 71, 74; Smith, *TheBattle of Trenton*, pp. 17, 26; Edgar, *Campaign of 1776*, 144-145, 263; Ehrenreich, *Blood Rites*, pp. 185-186; Chandler, *The Campaigns of Napoleon*, p. 454.

15. Kyle, *American Gun*, pp. 3-10

16. Trussell, *The Pennsylvania Line*, pp. 31-32; Wright, *The Continental Army*, p. 259; David Sisca, "Standard of the First Regiment of the Continental Line of the United States of America," Home of the National Tactical Invitational site, internet; Troiani and Kochan, *Don Troiani's Soldiers of the American Revolution*, pp. 91-92; Edgar, *Campaign of 1776*, pp. 159, 161; Michel Williams Craig, *General Edward Hand, Winter's Doctor,*

(Lancaster: Rock Ford Foundation, 1984), pp. 1-43; Boatner, *Encyclopedia of the American Revolution*, p. 1098.

17. Slagle, "The Von Lossberg Regiment," AU, pp. 73-74, 95; Atwood, *Hessians*, pp. 95-96; Wood, *Battles of the Revolutionary War*, p. 72; Stryker, *The Battles of Trenton and Princeton*, p. 140; Burgoyne, *Defeat, Disaster, and Dedication*, p. 71; Ward, *The War of the Revolution*, p. 300.

18. Atwood, *Hessians*, pp. 95-96; Wood, *Battles of the Revolutionary War*, p. 72.

19. Slagle, "The Von Lossberg Regiment," AU, pp. 74, 98-99; Hopson, *Captain Daniel Neil*, pp. 14-15; Wood, *Battles of the American Revolution*, p. 70; Fischer, *Washington's Crossing*, pp. 243-244; Stryker, *The Battles of Trenton and Princeton*, p. 156; Smith, *The Battle of Trenton*, pp. 17, 27; Weller, "Guns of Destiny," *MA*, p. 4.

Chapter VI

1. Chandler, *The Military Maxims of Napoleon*, p. 63; Joseph M. Malit to author, July 21, 2010.

2. Slagle, "The Von Lossberg Regiment," AU, pp. 17, 19, 92-93; Nead, "A Sketch of General Thomas Proctor," *PMHB*, pp. 454-470; Randall, *George Washington*, pp. 324-325; Wright, *The Continental Army*, p. 335; Stryker, *The Battles of Trenton and Princeton*, pp. 95,156, 158-161, 244, 370, 391, 478-479; Wood, *Battles of the American Revolution*, p. 70; diss, p. 92; Atwood, *The Hessians*, p. 93; Ketchum, *The Winter Soldiers*, p. 259; Laffin, *Jackboot*, p. 13; Troiani and Kochan, *Don Troiani's Soldiers of the American Revolution*, pp. 21, 68, 73; Fischer, *Washington's Crossing*, pp. 153, 204-205, 223-225, 243-245; Hanser, *The Glorious Hour of Lt. Monroe*, pp. 151-152; Smith, *The Battle of Trenton*, pp. 22, 26; Edgar, *Campaign of 1776*, p. 339; Joseph M. Malit email to author, July 21, 2010; Chandler, *The Campaigns of Napoleon*, pp. 438, 454; Weller, "Guns of Destiny," *MA,* pp. 4-5, 8; Ward, *The War of the Revolution*, p. 300.

3. Ward, *Charles Scott and the "Spirit of '76,'* pp. 27, 29, 152; Ward, *Major General Adam Stephen and the Cause of American Liberty*, pp. 146, 152; Lengel, *General George Washington*, p. 186.

4. Ward, *Charles Scott and the "Spirit of '76,'* p. 29.

5. Slagle, "The Von Lossberg Regiment," AU, pp. 17, 19, 92-93, 95, 99, 215; Farling, *AlmostA Miracle*, p. 185; Bonk, *Trenton and Princeton 1776-77*, p. 19; Randall, *George Washington*, pp. 324-325; Ketchum, *The Winter Soldiers*, pp. 233, 259-260; Wood, *Battles of the American Revolution*, pp. 70, 72; Bill, *The Campaign of Princeton*, p. 105; Atwood, *The Hessians*, p. 93; Stryker, *The Battles of Trenton and Princeton*, pp. 95, 97, 136, 154-158, 160-162, 244, 370, 372, 381, 389-390; Fischer, *Washington's Crossing*, p. 245; *A Young Patriot in the American Revolution*, p. 51; Troiani and Kochan, *Don Troiani's Soldiers of the American Revolution*, p. 73; Charles Grant, *FootGrenadiers of the Imperial Guard*, (Reading: Osprey Publishing Limited, 1971), p. 5; Hanser, *The Glorious Hour of Lt. Monroe*, pp. 150-152; J. Burgoyne to author, June 18, 2010; Kochan, *Don Troiani's Soldiers of the American Revolution*, p. 104; Smith, *The Battle*

of Trenton, pp. 22, 26; Edgar, *Campaign of 1776*, p. 234, 263-264, 267, 340, 382; Wheeler, *Voices of 1776*, p. 206; Lengel, *Inventing George Washington*, p. 123; Boatner, *Encyclopedia of the American Revolution*, p. 448; John R. Elting, *Swords Around A Throne, Napoleon's Grande Armee*, (New York: Da Capo Press, 1988), p. 443; Weller, "Guns of Destiny," *MA*, pp. 4, 8; Puls, *Henry Knox*, pp. 73, 76; Needleman, *The American Soul*, p. 85; Ferling, *The Ascent of George Washington*, pp. 22, 29, 86.

6. Wood, *Battles of the Revolutionary War*, p. 70; Ketchum, *The Winter Soldiers*, p. 260; Chadwick, *George Washington's War*, pp. 13-14; Atwood, *The Hessians*, p. 93; Stryker, *The Battles of Trenton and Princeton*, pp. 157-158, 162, 391; Smith, *The Battle of Trenton*, pp. 22-24; Hanser, *The Glorious Hour of Lt. Monroe*, p. 152; Chastellux, *Travels to North-America*, p. 70; Edgar, *Campaign of 1776*, pp. 195-196, 340; Royster, *Light-Horse Harry Lee*, p. 201; Chandler, *The Campaigns of Napoleon*, pp. 362-364, 504-505, 708, 734; Weller, "Guns of Destiny," *MA*, pp. 4-5.

7. Hanser, *The Glorious Hour of Lt. Monroe*, pp. 151-152; Weller, "Guns of Destiny," *MA*, p. 4; Ward, *The War of the Revolution*, p. 282.

8. Slagle, "The Von Lossberg Regiment," AU, pp. 34-35, 92; Fred B. Walters, *John Haslet, AUseful One* (private printing, 2005), pp. v-vi, 4, 6, 9, 11-22, 163, 192-207, 269, 278, 281, 291-360; Ferling, *Almost A Miracle*, p. 185; Wright, *TheContinental Army*, pp. 273, 285; Scheer and Franklin, *Rebels and Redcoats*, p. 233; Dawson, *Westchester-County, New York, during the American Revolution*, pp. 263, 267; Wood, *Battles of the Revolutionary War*, p. 70; Ketchum, *The Winter Soldiers*, pp. 196-197, 201; Fischer, *Washington's Crossing*, p. 221; Hanser, *The Glorious Hour of Lt. Monroe*, pp. 109-110, 152-153; Hunt, *The Irish and the American Revolution*, pp. 24-28; Ross, *War on the Run*, p. 444; Stryker, *The Battles of Trenton and Princeton*, pp. 157-158, 453; Edgar, *Campaign of 1776*, pp. 141, 148, 228-229, 285; Smith, *The Battle of Trenton*, p. 24; Troiani and Kochan, *Don Troiani's Soldiers of the American Revolution*, p. 57; Chastellux, *Travels in North-America*, p. 292, note; Jim Piecuch, *The Battle of Camden, A Documentary History*, (Charleston: The History Press, 2006), p. 71.

9. Fleming, *1776*, p. 431; Atwood, *The Hessians*, pp. 73-75; Edgar, *Campaign of 1776*, pp. 236-237, 304; Chernow, *Washington*, p. 269.

10. Stryker, *The Battles of Trenton and Princeton*, pp. 157-158, 479; Wright, *The Continental Army*, p. 335; Randall, *George Washington*, p. 325; Wood, *Battles of the Revolutionary War*, p. 70; McNab, *Armies of the Napoleonic War*, p. 69; "The Good Soldier White," *AmericanHeritage*, (June 1956), p. 74; Savas and Dameron, *The New American Revolution Handbook*, p. 20; Weller, "Guns of Destiny," *MA*, p. 9.

11. Stryker, *The Battles of Trenton and Princeton*, p. 479; Wright, *The Continental Army*, p. 335; Ketchum, *The Winter Soldiers*, p. 355, note; "The Good Soldier White," *AmericanHeritage*, p. 77; Weller, "Guns of Destiny," *MA*, p. 9

12. Fischer, *Washington's Crossing*, p. 247; Stryker, *The Battles of Trenton and Princeton*, p. 479; Ketchum, *The Winter Soldiers*, p. 355, note; Dwyer, *"The Day Is Ours!,"* p. 256; Edgar, *Campaign of 1776*, p. 340; "The Good Soldier White," *American Heritage*, pp. 74-77; Savas and Dameron, *The New American Revolution Handbook*, p. 20; Weller, "Guns of Destiny," *MA*, p. 9.

13. Weller, "Guns of Destiny," *MA*, p. 9; Stryker, *The Battles of Trenton and Princeton*, p. 479; Wood, *Battles of the American Revolution*, p. 70.

14. Hanser, *The Glorious Hour of Lt. Monroe*, pp. 151-153; Fischer, *Washington's Crossing*, p. 243; Stryker, *The Battles of Trenton and Princeton*, pp. 162, 281; Edgar, *Campaign of 1776*, p. 340.

15. Boatner, *Encyclopedia of the American Revolution*, p. 1169; Stuart Gerry Brown, *TheAutobiography of James Monroe*, (Syracuse: Syracuse University Press, 1959), pp. 3, 15, 21-22, 25; Ammon, *James Monroe*, pp. 7-13; Styker, *The Battles of Trenton and Princeton*, pp. 162, 157-158, 366; Wheeler, *Voices of 1776*, p. 206; St. Michael's Church, Trenton, New Jersey, Wikipedia, internet; St. Michael's Church History, Ministry. com, internet; Wright, *TheContinental Army*, p. 285; Randall, *George Washington*, pp. 324-325; Walters, *John Haslet*, p. 360; Wood, *Battles of the Revolutionary War*, p. 70; Fischer, *Washington's Crossing*, p. 245; dis, p. 92; Fleming, *1776*, p. 461; Ketchum, *TheWinter Soldiers*, p. 260; Dwyer, *"The Day Is Ours!,"* p. 246; Ward, *Major General Adam Stephen and the Cause of American Liberty*, pp. 146, 152; Hanser, *The Glorious Hour of Lt. Monroe*, pp. 4,9, 14-16, 18, 36-37, 151-153; Lengel, *General George Washington*, p. 186; Edgar, *Campaign of 1776*, pp. 263-264, 267, 340, 382; Weller, "Guns of Destiny," *MA*, pp. 5-6.

16. Ward, *Major General Adam Stephen and the Cause of American Liberty*, pp. 146, 152; Smith, *The Battle of Trenton*, pp. 22-23; Stryker, *The Battles of Trenton and Princeton*, pp. 163-164; Lengel, *General George Washington*, p. 186.

17. Stryker, *The Battles of Trenton and Princeton*, p. 363; Ward, *Major General Adam Stephen and the Cause of American Liberty*, p. 152; Lengel, *General George Washington*, p. 186.

18. Weller, "Guns of Destiny," *MA*, p. 9; Fischer, *Washington's Crossing*, p. 245; Smith, *TheBattle of Trenton*, pp. 22-23; Stryker, *The Battles of Trenton and Princeton*, pp. 163-164, 479; "The Good Soldier White," *American Heritage*, pp. 74, 76-77; Weymouth, Massachusetts, Wikipedia, internet.

19. Ward, *Major General Adam Stephen and the Cause of American Liberty*, p. 152.

20. Arthur S. Lefkowitz, *George Washington's Indispensable Men, The 32 Aides-de-Camps Who Helped Win American Independence*, (Mechanicville: Stackpole Books, 2003), p. 90.

21. Lengel, *General George Washington*, p. 186; Wright, *The Continental Army*, p. 286; Ward, *Major General Adam Stephens and the Cause of American Liberty*, p. 152.

22. Slagle, "The Von Lossberg Regiment," *AU*, p. 93; Liell, *46 Pages*, pp143-144; Wheeler, *Voices of 1776*, p. 206; Wood, *Battles of the Revolutionary War*, p. 71; Smith, *The Battle of Trenton*, pp. 23-24; Ward, *Major General Stephen and the Cause of American Liberty*, p. 152; Lengel, *General George Washington*, p. 186; Hanser, *The Glorious Hour of Lt. Monroe*, p. 153; Edgar, *Campaign of 1776*, pp. 340, 392.

23. Slagle, "The Von Lossberg Regiment," *AU*, p. 93; Brown, *The Autobiography of James Monroe*, pp. 25-26; Ammon, *James Monroe*, pp. 7-8, 13-14; Marble, *James Monroe*, p. 46; Stryker, *The Battles of Trenton and Princeton*, pp. 162, 368, 370; Wheeler, *Voices of 1776*, p. 206; *New York Times*, December 26, 1876; Rose, *Washington's War*, p. 82;

Wood, *Battles of the Revolutionary War*, pp. 70-71; Fischer, *Washington's Crossing*, p. 247; Smith, *The Battle of Trenton*, p. 23; Hanser, *The Glorious Hour of Lt. Monroe*, pp. 106, 155; Walter R. Borneman, *1812, The War That Forged a Nation*, (New York: Harper Perennial, 2004), pp. 226-227.

24. Rodney, *Diary of Captain Thomas Rodney*, p. 51; Stryker, *The Battles of Trenton and Princeton*, p. 366; Wheeler, *Voices of 1776*, p. 206; Hanser, *The Glorious Hour of Lt. Monroe*, pp. 153-154.

25. Rodney, *Diary of Captain Thomas Rodney*, p. 51; Boatner, *Encyclopedia of the American Revolution*, p. 941; Ferling, *The Ascent of George Washington*, p. 120.

26. Hanser, *The Glorious Hour of Lt. Monroe*, pp. 153-154.

27. Elisha Bostwick Memoir, YUL; Slagle, "The Von Lossberg Regiment," AU, p. 98; Buchanan, *The Road to Valley Forge*, p. 165; Hanser, *The Glorious Hour of Lt. Monroe*, pp. 153-154; Edgar, *Campaign of 1776*, p. 144.

28. Slagle, "The Von Lossberg Regiment," AU, p. 98; Buchanan, *The Road to Valley Forge*, p. 165; Fischer, *Washington's Crossing*, pp. 244-245; Weller, "Guns of Destiny," *MA*, p. 8; Neier, ed., *George Washington, A Biography by Washington Irving*, p. 330

29. "The Good Soldier White," *American Heritage*, p. 77; Weller, "Guns of Destiny," *MA*, p. 9; Puls, *Henry Knox*, pp. 73, 76.

30. Stryker, *The Battles of Trenton and Princeton*, pp. 163-164; Ward, *Major General Adam Stephens and the Cause of American Liberty*, p. 152; Lengel, *General George Washington*, p. 186.

31. Slagle, "The Von Lossberg Regiment," AU, pp. 93, 98-99; Stryker, *The Battles of Trenton and Princeton*, pp. 161-162, 170; Smith, *The Battle of Trenton*, p. 23.

32. Stryker, *The Battles of Trenton and Princeton*, pp. 162-163, 166-168, 378; Edgar, *Campaign of 1776*, pp. 342-243; Ward, *The War of the Revolution*, p. 301.

33. Slagle, "The Von Lossberg Regiment," AU, pp. 95, 99; Wright, *The Continental Army*, p. 203; *A Young Patriot in the American Revolution*, pp. 82-83; Stryker, *The Battles of Trenton and Princeton*, pp. 97, 101, 168; Thomas Egleston, *The Life of John Paterson: Major General in the Revolutionary Army*, (New York: G. P. Putnam's Sons, 1894), pp. 50, 60-57; "The Good Soldier White," *American Heritage*, p. 77; Smith, *The Battle of Trenton*, p. 20; Weller, "Guns of Destiny," *MA*, pp. 8-9.

34. Burgoyne, *Defeat, Disaster, and Dedication*, pp. 74-75; Smith, *The Battle of Trenton*, pp. 22-24; Stryker, *The Battles of Trenton and Princeton*, pp. 161-162, 165; Weller, "Guns of Destiny," *MA*, p. 8; Ward, *War of the Revolution*, p. 301.

35. Slagle, "The Von Lossberg Regiment," AU, pp. 93, 215; Ketchum, *The Winter Soldiers*, p. 260; Wood, *Battles of the Revolutionary War*, pp. 72-73; Fischer, *Washington's Crossing*, p. 245; Smith, *The Battle of Trenton*, pp. 22-24; Stryker, *The Battles of Trenton and Princeton*, pp. 163, 391, 407; Historic plague, Quaker Meeting House, Trenton, New Jersey.

36. Slagle, "The Von Lossberg Regiment," AU, pp. 17-10, 92-93, 214, 217, 219-220; Wood, *Battles of the Revolutionary War*, pp. 72-73; Bill, *The Campaign of Princeton*, pp. 53-54; Stryker, *The Battles of Trenton and Princeton*, pp. 165-166, 392, 478-479, 520, note 58; Smith, *The Battle of Trenton*, pp. 23-24, 26-27; Edgar, *Campaign*

of 1776, p. 264; Joseph M. Malit to author, July 20 and 21, 2010; Kochan, *Don Troiani's Soldiers of the American Revolution*, p. 68; "The Good Soldier White," *American Heritage*, p. 77; Ward, *The War of the Revolution*, p. 301; Weller, "Guns of Destiny," *MA*, pp. 8-9.

37. Slagle, "The Von Lossberg Regiment," AU, p. 94; Stryker, *The Battles of Trenton and Princeton*, p. 166; Haskew, ed., *Great Military Disasters*, pp. 11-17; Ward, *The War of the Revolution*, p. 301; Hart, *Strategy*, pp. 48-49.

38. Slagle, "The Von Lossberg Regiment," AU, pp. 17, 98; Stryker, *The Battles of Trenton and Princeton*, pp. 124, 128, 147, 166, 162-163, 394; Smith, *The Battle of Trenton*, p. 24; Weller, "Guns of Destiny," *MA*, p. 8.

Chapter VII

1. John Sullivan Papers, Library of Congress, Washington, D.C.; Chastellux, *Travels in North-America*, p. 347, note.

2. Elisha Bostwick, YUL; Smith, *The Battle of Trenton*, p. 23; Stryker, *The Battles of Trenton and Princeton*, p. 166; Hart, *Strategy*, pp. 48-49.

3. Heath, *Memoirs of Major-General William Heath by Himself*, p. 86; Wood, *Battles of the Revolutionary War*, pp. 71; Stryker, *The Battles of Trenton and Princeton*, pp. 166-168; Smith, *The Battle of Trenton*, p. 24; Edgar, *Campaign of 1776*, p. 151.

4. Rose, *John Stark*, pp. 96-97; Smith, *The Battle of Trenton*, pp. 20, 24-25; Stryker, *The Battles of Trenton and Princeton*, pp. 166-168; Edgar, *Campaign o f 1776*, pp. 152, 192, 328; Weller, "Guns of Destiny," *MA*, p. 8.

5. Edgar, *Campaign of 1776*, p. 328.

6. Stryker, *The Battles of Trenton and Princeton*, pp. 92, 152, 168, 170; Slagle, "The Von Lossberg Regiment," AU, p. 74; Edgar, *Campaign of 1776*, p. 276; Smith, *The Battle of Trenton*, p. 9; Randall, *George Washington*, p. 324; Crown and Rogers, *Images of America, Trenton*, p. 13; History Files, Old Barracks Museum, Trenton, New Jersey.

7. Slagle, "The Von Lossberg Regiment," AU, p. 74; Boatner, *The Dictionary of the American Revolution*, p. 428; Stryker, *The Battles of Trenton and Princeton*, pp. 97, 152, 166-168, 170; Crown and Rogers, *Images of America, Trenton*, p. 13; Ketchum, *The Winter Soldiers*, pp. 233-234; Smith, *The Battle of Trenton*, p. 9; History Files, Old Barracks Museum; Edgar, *Campaign of 1776*, p. 270.

8. Arthur St. Clair Papers, Library of Congress, Washington, D.C.: Slagle, "The Von Lossberg Regiment," AU, p. 95; Fischer, *Washington's Crossing*, pp. 239-240, 244; Rose, *John Stark*, pp. 95-96, 117, 156, 159; Bonk, *Trenton and Princeton 1776-77*, pp. 20, 52, 57; Wright, *TheContinental Army*, pp. 198; *The Washington Post*, September 28, 1902; Irving, *GeorgeWashington*, p. 335; Atwood, *The Hessians*, p. 93; Smith, *The Battle of Trenton*, p. 20; Stryker, *The Battles of Trenton and Princeton*, pp. 152, 166-168, 170; Captain Ebenezer Frye Biographical information, internet.

9. Chastellux, *Travels in North-America*, p. 76.

10. Stephen Brumwell, *White Devil, A True Story of War, Savagery, and Vengeance in Colonial America*, (New York: Da Capo Press, 2004), p. 106; Ross, *War on the Run*, pp. 127-130, 137-138.

11. Rose, *John Stark*, pp. xiii, 9-11, 23-38, 95-97, 152; Stryker, *The Battles of Trenton and Princeton*, p. 350; Edgar, *Campaign of 1776*, p. 328; Ross, *War on the Run*, pp. 127-130, 137-138.

12. Slagle, "The Von Lossberg Regiment," AU, p. 95; Rose, *John Stark*, p. 97; Wood, *Battles of the Revolutionary War*, p. 71; Atwood, *The Hessians*, p. 93; Fischer, *Washington's Crossing*, p. 244; Dwyer, *The Day Is Ours!*, p. 257; Boatner, *Encyclopedia of the American Revolution*, p. 1206; Stryker, *The Battles of Trenton and Princeton*, pp. 94, 166-168, 170; Smith, *The Battle of Trenton*, pp. 20, 24; Bonk, *Trenton and Princeton 1776-77*, p. 57; Edgar, *Campaign of 1776*, p. 338; Weller, "Guns of Destiny," *MA*, p. 8.

13. *New York Daily Times*, New York, New York, August 24, 1854;Rose, *John Stark*, pp. xi-160; Bonk, *Trenton and Princeton 1776-77*, p. 20; Wood, *Battles of the Revolutionary War*, p. 71; Stryker, *The Battles of Trenton and Princeton*, p. 166-168.

14. Rose, *John Stark*, pp. 96-97,100; Styker, *The Battles of Trenton and Princeton*, pp. 166-168.

15. Savas and Dameron, *The New American Revolution Handbook*, p. 3.

16. Dwyer, "*The Day Is Ours!*," p. 257; Wood, *Battles of the Revolutionary War*, p. 71; Stryker, *The Battles of Trenton and Princeton*, pp. 166-168.

17. Stryker, *The Battles of Trenton and Princeton*, pp. 166-168; Smith, *The Battle of Trenton*, p. 20.

18. Slagle, "The Von Lossberg Regiment," p. 95; Fischer, *Washington's Crossing*, pp. 240, 244; Dwyer, "*The Day Is Ours!*," p. 257; Stryker, *The Battles of Trenton and Princeton*, pp. 168, 170; Smith, *The Battle of Trenton*, p. 20.

19. Rose, *John Stark*, p. 100; Fischer, *Washington's Crossing*, p. 251; Dwyer, "*The Day Is Ours!*," p. 257; Stryker, *The Battles of Trenton and Princeton*, pp. 168, 170, 406.

20. Stryker, *The Battles of Trenton and Princeton*, pp. 164-168, 170-171, 392; Wood, *Battlesof the Revolutionary War*, p. 72-73; Ketchum, *The Winter Soldiers*, p. 260; Edgar, *Campaign of 1776*, p. 279.

21. Flexner, *Washington*, pp. 96-97; Lengel, *General George Washington*, pp. 164-168; Hanser, *The Glorious Hour of Lt. Monroe*, pp. 155-156; Stryker, *The Battles of Trenton and Princeton*, p. 152; Edgar, *Campaign of 1776*, pp. 342-343; Kyle, *American Gun*, pp. 2, 10; Ward, *The War of the Revolution*, p. 301.

22. Stryker, *The Battles of Trenton and Princeton*, p. 166; Golway, *Washington's General*, p. 111; Langguth, *Patriots*, pp. 408, 415-416; Ketchum, *The Winter Soldiers*, pp. 260-261; Monroe, *The Glorious Hour of Lt. Monroe*, pp. 155-156; Edgar, *Campaign of 1776*, pp. 343, 382; Kochan, *Don Troiani's Soldiers of the American Revolution*, p. 12; Craig, *General Edward Hand*, p. 12; Ward, *The War of the Revolution*, p. 301; Robertson and Yates, eds., *Block by Block*, pp. 7-8.

23. Langguth, *Patriots*, p. 416; Keane, *Tom Paine*, p. 140; Stryker, *The Battles of Trenton and Princeton*, pp. 167-168, 170; Weller, "Guns of Destiny," *MA*, p. 8.

24. Slagle, "The Von Lossberg Regiment," p. 74; Billias, *General John Glover and his Marblehead Mariners*, pp. 10-11, 70; Bonk, *Trenton and Princeton 1776-77*, pp. 19-20, 52, 54; Tagney, *The World Turned Upside Down*, p. 285; Wood, *Battles of the Revolutionary War*, p. 71; Bill, *The Campaign of Princeton*, p. 105; Fischer, *Washington's Crossing*, p. 242, map; *A Young Patriot in the American Revolution*, pp. 82-83; Rose, *John Stark*, pp. 96-97; Stryker, *The Battles of Trenton and Princeton*, pp. 167-168, 170.; Smith, *The Battle of Trenton*, p. 20

25. "Triggers, Weapons that Changed the World, Combat Shotguns," Military Channel, May 8, 2013; Staff Writer, Blunderbuss Short-Ranged Musket (1720), internet; Larry Sands, 14th Massachusetts Continental Regiment re-enactor, emails to author, May 9 and 10, 2013.

26. Lord and Gamage, *Marblehead*, p. 123.

27. Billias, *General John Glover and his Marblehead Mariners*, pp. 110-123.

28. Billias, *General John Glover and his Marblehead Mariners*, pp. 10-11; Bonk, *Trenton and Princeton 1776-77*, p. 19.

29. Baldwin to wife, December 19, 1776, HU; Boatner, *Encyclopedia of the American Revolution*, pp. 55-56; William Baldwin Biographical Sketch, Wikipedia, internet.

30. Tagney, *The World Turned Upside Down*, p. 285; Billias, *General John Glover and his Marblehead Mariners*, p. 12; Wood, *Battles of the Revolutionary War*, p. 71; Atwood, *TheHessians*, pp. 72-73; Bill, *The Campaign of Princeton*, p. 29; Fischer, *Washington's Crossing*, p. 242; Stryker, *The Battles of Trenton and Princeton*, pp. 168, 170; Edgar, *Campaign of 1776*, pp. 224-227; Smith, *The Battle of Trenton*, p. 20; Sands emails to author, May 9 and 10, 2013; "Combat Shotgun," MC.

31. Upham, *A Memoir of General John Glover*, pp. 21, 23, 26; Wood, *Battles of the Revolutionary War*, p. 72.

32. Billias, *General John Glover and his Marblehead Mariners*, pp. 12-13; Wood, *Battles of the Revolutionary War*, p. 71: Fischer, *Washington's Crossing*, p. 251; Stryker, *The Battles of Trenton and Princeton*, p. 158; Edgar, *Campaign of 1776*, pp. 343, 341; Lengel, *General George Washington*, p. 88; Smith, *The Battle of Trenton*, p. 20.

33. Slagle, "The Von Lossberg Regiment," AU, p. 95; Atwood, *The Hessians*, pp. 49, 92-93, 95; Fischer, *Washington's Crossing*, pp. 240, 251-252; Smith, *The Battle of Trenton*, p. 27; Burgoyne, *Defeat, Disaster, and Dedication*, p. v; Stryker, *The Battles of Trenton and Princeton*, pp. 165, 170, 406; Edgar, *Campaign of 1776*, pp. 325.

34. Chandler, *The Campaigns of Napoleon*, p. 135; Puls, *Henry Knox*, p. 78.

35. Puls, *Henry Knox*, pp. 75, 78; Paul Johnson, *Napoleon, A Life*, (New York: Penguin Books, 2002), pp. 20-22, 56; Wood, *Battles of the Revolutionary War*, pp. 62. 72; Chandler, *TheCampaigns of Napoleon*, p. 8.

36. Wheeler, *Voices of 1776*, p. 206; Stryker, *The Battles of Trenton and Princeton*, p. 370; Griffin, *Catholics and the American Revolution*, vol. 2, p. 202; Puls, *Henry Knox*, p. 78; Philip Haythornthwaite, *Napoleon's Specialist Troops*, (London: Osprey Publishing Limited, 1989), p. 3.

37. Griffin, *Catholics and the American Revolution*, vol. 2, pp. 201-202; Wheeler, *Voices of 1776*, p. 206; Stryker, *The Battles of Trenton and Princeton*, p. 370.

38. Stryker, *The Battles of Trenton and Princeton*, p. 370; Weller, "Guns of Destiny," *MA*, p. 8.

39. "The Good Soldier White," *American Heritage*, p. 77; Stryker, *The Battles of Trenton and Princeton*, p. 479; Kukla, *Mr. Jefferson's Women*, p. 186; Weller, "Guns of Destiny," *MA*, pp. 8-9; Puls, *Henry Knox*, pp. 73, 76.

40. Wood, *Battles of the Revolutionary War*, p. 73; Ball, *The Campaign of Princeton*, p. 45; Ketchum, *The Winter Soldiers*, pp. 260-261; Stryker, *The Battles of Trenton and Princeton*, pp. 166-168; Smith, *The Battle of Trenton*, p. 24; Bonk, *Trenton and Princeton 1776-77*, p. 57; "The Good Soldier White," *American Heritage*, p. 77; Weller, "Guns of Destiny," *MA*, pp. 4, 8-9, 13; Puls, *Henry Knox*, pp. 73, 76.

41. Dwyer, *"The Day Is Ours!,"* p. 257; Paul Dudley Sargent, Virtual American Biographies, internet; Wright, *The Continental Army*, p. 15; Bonk, *Trenton and Princeton 1776-77*, p. 19; Fischer, *Washington's Crossing*, p. 252; Stryker, *The Battles of Trenton and Princeton*, p. 168; Edgar, *Campaign of 1776*, p. 264.

42. Slagle, "The von Lossberg Regiment," *AU*, p. 17; Bill, *The Campaign of Princeton*, p. 54; Ketchum, *The Winter Soldiers*, pp. 261-262; Stryker, *The Battles of Trenton and Princeton*, p. 168.

43. Bonk, *The Battles of Trenton and Princeton*, p. 20; Wright, *The Continental Army*, p. 198; Kochan, *Don Troiani's Soldiers of the American Revolution*, p. 113; *Sherman Family Tree*, internet; *Genealogical and Family History of the State of Maine*, (New York: Lewis Publishing Company, 1909), biographical sketches; Edgar, *Campaign of 1776*, p. 192; Craig, *GeneralEdward Hand*, p. 13.

44. Fischer, *Washington's Crossing*, p. 252; Billas, *General John Glover and his Marblehead Mariners*, pp. 12-14.

45. Tagney, *The World Turned Upside Down*, p. 286; Fischer, *Washington's Crossing*, pp. 154, 252-254; Smith, *The Battle of Trenton*, pp. 12, 26; Weller, "Guns of Destiny," *MA*, p. 8; Stryker, *The Battles of Trenton and Princeton*, pp. 170, 394; Sands emails to author, May 9 and 10, 2013; "Combat Shotguns," *MC*.

46. Gamage and Lord, *The Lure of Marblehead*, pp. 2-3.

47. Zaboly, *American Colonial Rangers*, pp. 5, 10-11, 28-29, 44, 48-49; Brumwell, *WhiteDevil*, pp. 72, 83-85,

48. Ketchum, *The Winter Soldiers*, pp. 260-261;Wood, *Battles of the Revolutionary War*, p. 73; Fischer, *Washington's Crossing*, p. 252; Weller, "Guns of Destiny," *MA*, p. 8; Stryker, *TheBattles of Trenton and Princeton*, p. 392.

49. Smith, *The Battle of Trenton*, pp. 23, 26; Fischer, *Washington's Crossing*, pp. 245-246, 251; Stephenson, *Patriot Battles*, p. 258; Ketchum, *The Winter Soldiers*, p. 261; Burgoyne, *Defeat, Disaster, and Dedication*, pp. 74-75; Stryker, *The Battles of Trenton and Princeton*, pp. 161,165-169, 215, 389; Ward, *War of the Revolution*, p. 301.

50. Burgoyne, *Defeat, Disaster, and Dedication*, p. 75.

51. Stryker, *The Battles of Trenton and Princeton*, p. 372.

52. Hanser, *The Glorious Hour of Lt. Monroe*, p. 157.

53. Smith, *The Battle of Trenton*, p. 23; Stephenson, *Patriot Battles*, p. 258; Lengel, *ThisGlorious Struggle*, pp. 88.

54. Smith, *The Battle of Trenton*, p. 23; Bonk, *Trenton and Princeton 1776-77*, pp. 19-20; Trussell, *The Pennsylvania Line*, p. 226; Stephenson, *Patriot Battles*, p. 258; Ketchum, *TheWinter Soldiers*, pp. 261-262; Fischer, *Washington's Crossing*, pp. 246, 391; Dwyer, *"The Day Is Ours!,"* p. 258; Stryker, *The Battles of Trenton and Princeton*, pp. 102, 168; Lengel, *This Glorious Struggle*, p. 88.

55. Retzer, *The German Regiment of Maryland and Pennsylvania*, pp. 74, 87, 123, 148, 154; Fischer, *Washington's Crossing*, p. 246.

56. Retzer, *The German Regiment of Maryland and Pennsylvania*, pp. 78-79; John Stricker, Maryland Online Encyclopedia, internet; Stephenson, *Patriot Battles*, p. 239; Tucker, *TheImportant Role of the Irish in the American Revolution*, pp. 32-64.

57. Trussell, *The Pennsylvania Line*, p. 225; Von Hagen, *The Germanic People in America*, p. 162; Fischer, *Washington's Crossing*, p. 246.

58. Smith, *The Battle of Trenton*, p. 23; Lengel, *The Glorious Struggle*, p. 88; Puls, *HenryKnox*, pp. 73, 76.

Chapter VIII

1. Slagle, "The Von Lossberg Regiment," AU, p. 100; Johannes Reuber Journal, December 25 [26], Special Collections and University Archives, Rutgers University, New Brunswick, New Jersey; Bill, *The Campaign of Princeton*, p. 56; Stephenson, *Patriot Battles*, p. 258; Ketchum, *The Winter Soldiers*, p. 262; Fischer, *Washington's Crossing*, pp. 246, 519 note 38; Dwyer, *TheDay Is Ours!*, p. 259; Smith, *The Battle of Trenton*, pp. 23-24; Burgoyne, *Defeat, Disaster, and Dedication*, pp. 74-76; Stryker, *The Battles of Trenton and Princeton*, pp. 166, 168-170, 215; Connelly, *Blundering to Glory, Napoleon's Military Campaigns*, pp. 66-68; Lengel, *This Glorious Struggle*, p. 88; Chandler, *TheCampaigns of Napoleon*, pp. 287-296; The Good Soldier White," *American Heritage*, p. 77; Weller, "Guns of Destiny," *MA*, p. 9; Puls, *Henry Knox*, pp. 73, 76.

2. Reuber Journal, RU; Fischer, *Washington's Crossing*, p. 519, note 38; Chandler, *TheMilitary Maxims of Napoleon*, p. 61; Stryker, *The Battles of Trenton and Princeton*, p. 170.

3. Reuber Journal, RU; Fischer, *Washington's Crossing*, p. 519, note 38; Smith, *The Battle of Trenton*, p. 24; Stryker, *The Battles of Trenton and Princeton*, pp. 168-169; Edgar, *Campaign of 1776*, p. 343; Weller, "Guns of Destiny," *MA*, p. 8

4. Reuber Journal, RU; Fischer, *Washington's Crossing*, p. 519, note 38; Stryker, *The Battles of Trenton and Princeton*, pp. 169, 366, 392; Smith, *The Battle of Trenton*, p. 24.

5. Stryker, *The Battles of Trenton and Princeton*, pp. 390-391.

6. Reuber Journal, RU; Burgoyne, *Defeat, Disaster, and Dedication*, p. 76; Smith, *The Battle of Trenton*, pp. 23-24; Stephenson, *Patriot Battles*, p. 258; *The Washington Post*, September 28, 1902; Bill, *The Campaign of Princeton*, p. 56; Ketchum, *The Winter Soldiers*, p. 262; Boatner, *Encyclopedia of the American Revolution*, p. 1217; Fischer, *Washington's Crossing*, pp. 246-247, p. 519, note 38; Dwyer, *"The Day Is Ours!,"* pp.

259, 267; Stryker, *The Battles of Trenton and Princeton*, pp. 169-170, 370, 389, 393-394; *A Young Patriot in the American Revolution*, pp. 82-83; Edgar, *Campaign of 1776*, p. 343; "The Good Soldier White," *American Heritage*, p. 77; Weller, "Guns of Destiny," *MA*, pp. 8-9; Robert Bray and Paul Bushnell, editors, *Diary of a Common Soldier in the American Revolution, 1775-1783, An Annotated Edition of the Military Journal of Jeremiah Greenwood*, (DeKalb: Northern Illinois University Press), p. 178; Puls, *Henry Knox*, pp. 73, 76.

7. Reuber Journal, RU; Slagle, "The Von Lossberg Regiment," AU, pp. 17, 94-95; Stryker, *The Battles of Trenton and Princeton*, pp. 170-171, 368, 392; Ketchum, *The Winter Soldiers*, p. 262; Fischer, *Washington's Crossing*, pp. 246-247, 519, note 38; *A Young Patriot in the American Revolution*, pp. 82-83; Smith, *The Battle of Trenton*, p. 24; Dwyer, *"The Day Is Ours!,"* p. 257; Edgar, *Campaign of 1776*, p. 343; John Paterson, Virtual American Biographies, internet.

8. Smith, *The Battle of Trenton*, p. 24; Stryker, *The Battles of Trenton and Princeton*, pp. 171, 392.

9. Slagle, "The Von Lossberg Regiment," AU, p. 95, 215; Stryker, *The Battles of Trenton and Princeton*, pp. 171, 391; Ward, *The War of the Revolution*, p. 301.

10. Slagle, "The Von Lossberg Regiment," AU, pp. 95, 215; Dwyer, *"The Day Is Ours!,"* p. 259; Fischer, *Washington's Crossing*, pp. 249, 405; Smith, *The Battle of Trenton*, p. 27; Burgoyne, *Defeat, Disaster, and Dedication*, p. 2; Stryker, *The Battles of Trenton and Princeton*, pp. 170-172, 391-392; Weller, "Guns of Destiny," *MA*, p. 8.

11. Slagle, "The Von Lossberg Regiment," AU, pp. 95, 215, 217; Stryker, *The Battles of Trenton and Princeton*, pp. 172, 392.

12. Reuber Journal, RU; Stryker, *The Battles of Trenton and Princeton*, p. 172; Bill, *TheCampaign of Princeton*, p. 56; Fischer, *Washington's Crossing*, pp. 246-248, 519, note 38; Ketchum, *The Winter Soldiers*, pp. 262-263; Tagney, *The World Turned Upside Down*, p. 286; Dwyer, *"The Day Is Our!,"* pp. 257-259; *A Young Patriot in the American Revolution*, pp. 83-84; Puls, *Henry Knox*, pp. 73, 76.

13. Reuber Journal, RU; Fischer, *Washington's Crossing*, p. 519, note 38; *A Young Patriot in the American Revolution*, pp. 82-83; Smith, *The Battle of Trenton*, pp. 23-24; Egleston, *The Life of John Paterson*, pp. 1-69, 225-226, 256-260, 834-835; Bonk, *Trenton and Princeton 1776-77*, p. 20; Dwyer, *"The Day Is Ours!,"* p. 257.

14. Reuber Journal, RU; Fischer, *Washington's Crossing*, p. 519, note 38; Slagle, "The Von Lossberg Regment," AU, pp. 95, 216; Stryker, *The Battles of Trenton and Princeton*, pp. 172, 391-392.

15. Reuber Journal, RU; Fischer, *Washington's Crossing*, p. 519, note 38; *A Young Patriot in the American Revolution*, pp. 82-83; Dwyer, *"The Day Is Ours!,"* p. 257.

16. Reuber Journal, RU; Slagle, "The Von Lossberg Regiment," AU, p. 17; Stryker, *The Battles of Trenton and Princeton*, pp. 66, 83, 172, 178-179; Fischer, *Washington's Crossing*, p. 519, note 38; Weller, "Guns of Destiny," *MA*, p. 8.

17. Reuber Journal, RU; Slagle, "The Vonn Lossberg Regiment," AU, p. 95; *A Young Patriot in the American Revolution*, pp. 83-84; Ketchum, *The Winter Soldiers*, pp. 262-263; Tagney, *TheWorld Turned Upside Down*, p. 286; Dwyer, *The Day Is Ours!*, pp. 257,

259; Stryker, *The* Battles *of Trenton and Princeton*, p. 172; Edgar, *Campaign of 1776*, p. 301; Fischer, *Washington's Crossing*, p. 519, note 38; Weller, "Guns of Destiny," *MA*, p. 8.

18. Reuber Journal, RU; Slagle, "The Von Lossberg Regiment," AU, pp. 94-96, 215-217; Tagney, *The World Turned Upside Down*, p. 286; Bill, *The Campaign of Princeton*, p. 56; Ketchum, *The Winter Soldiers*, pp. 262-263; Fischer, *Washington's Crossing*, pp. 247-248, 252, 519, note 38; Dwyer, *"The Day Is Ours!,"* pp. 257-259; Stryker, *The Battles of Trenton and Princeton*, pp. 168, 172-174, 358, 392; *A Young Patriot in the American Revolution*, pp. 82-83; Weller, "Guns of Destiny," *MA*, pp. 8-9.

19. Jacob Francis Biographical Sketch, African American Life in New Jersey, internet; Dwyer, *"The Day Is Ours!,"* p. 257; Bonk, *Trenton and Princeton 1776-77*, p. 19; Billias, *General John Glover and His Marblehead Mariners*, pp. 68-69

20. Reuber Journal, RU; Slagle, "The Von Lossberg Regiment," AU, pp. 94, 96; Ketchum, *The Winter Soldiers*, p. 263; Wood, *Battles of the Revolutionary War*, p. 73; Fischer, *Washington's Crossing*, pp. 248, 519, note 38; Dwyer, *"The Day Is Ours!,"* pp. 257-259; Smith, *The Battle of Trenton*, p. 24; Stryker, *The Battles of Trenton and Princeton*, pp. 141, 170, 172-173; *A Young Patriot in the American Revolution*, pp. 83-84.

21. Reuber Journal, RU; *New York Times*, April 9, 1876; Fischer, *Washington's Crossing*, pp. 248-249, 519, note 38; Dwyer, *"The Day Is Ours!,"* pp. 257, 267; *A Young Patriot in the American Revolution*, pp. 83-84; Edgar, *Campaign of 1776*, p. 343; Stryker, *The Battles of Trenton and Princeton*, p. 170.

22. Reuber Journal, RU; Burgoyne, *Defeat, Disaster, and Dedication*, p. 75; Fischer, *Washington's Crossing*, p. 519, note 38.

23. Reuber Journal, RU; Slagle, "The Von Lossberg Regiment," AU, pp. 94-96; Fischer, *Washington's Crossing*, pp. 248, 519, note 38; Bonk, *Trenton and Princeton, 1776-77*, p. 19; Patterson, *Washington and Cornwallis*, p. 89; Wood, *Battles of the Revolutionary War*, p. 73; Ketchum, *The Winter Soldiers*, p. 121; Dwyer, *"The Day Is Ours!,"* p. 259; Edgar, *Campaign of 1776*, pp. 145, 161, 263-266, 343; Ward, *The War of the Revolution*, pp. 300-301; Stryker, *The Battles of Trenton and Princeton*, p. 174.

24. Wheeler, *Voices of 1776*, p. 206; Stryker, *The Battles of Trenton and Princeton*, p. 174.

25. Stryker, *The Battles of Trenton and Princeton*, p. 372.

26. Reuber Journal, RU; Slagle, "The Von Lossberg Regiment," AU, p. 96; Dwyer, *"The Day Is Ours!,"* p. 263; Fischer, *Washington's Crossing*, pp. 248, 519, note 38; Stryker, *The Battles of Trenton and Princeton*, pp. 174-175, 392.

27. Stryker, *The Battles of Trenton and Princeton*, p. 372.

28. Reuber Journal, RU; Smith, *The Battle of Trenton*, p. 24; Fischer, *Washington's Crossing*, pp. 248-249, 519, note 38; Dwyer, *"The Day Is Ours!,"* p. 267; Stryker, *The Battles of Trenton and Princeton*, p. 91; Slagle, "The Von Lossberg Regiment," AU, p. 95.

29. Wheeler, *Voices of 1776*, p. 206; Fischer, *Washington's Crossing*, pp. 248-249.

30. Slagle "The Von Lossberg Regiment," AU, p. 99; Smith, *The Battle of Trenton*, p. 24; Dwyer, *"The Day Is Ours!,"* p. 259; Fischer, *Washington's Crossing*, p. 249; Burgoyne, *Defeat, Disaster, and Dedication*, p. 20.

31. *A Young Patriot in the American Revolution*, pp. 82-84; Smith, *The Battle of Trenton*, pp. 24, 27; Burgoyne, *Defeat, Disaster, and Dedication*, p. 20; Dwyer, *"The Day Is Ours!,"* p. 257.

32. Dwyer, *"The Day Is Ours!,"* pp. 257, 260-261; Smith, *The Battle of Trenton*, p. 24.

33. Stryker, *The Battle of Trenton and Princeton*, p. 372,

34. Slagle, "The Von Lossberg Regiment," AU, pp. 17, 96; Dwyer, *"The Day Is Ours!,"* p. 259; Fischer, *Washington's Crossing*, p. 249; Smith, *The Battle of Trenton*, p. 24.

35. Chandler, *The Campaigns of Napoleon*, p. 135.

36. Slagle, "The Von Lossberg Regiment," AU, p. 96; Trussell, *The Pennsylvania Line*, p. 33; Retzer, *The German Regiment of Maryland and Pennsylvania*, p. 8; Smith, *The Battle of Trenton*, p. 24; Craig, *General Edward Hand*, pp. 48-49.

37. Retzer, *The German Regiment of Maryland and Pennsylvania*, p. 8, Wheeler, *Voices of 1776*, p. 206; Bill, *The Campaign of Princeton*, p. 48; Craig, *General Edward Hand*, pp. 48-49.

38. Slagle, "The Von Lossberg Regiment," AU, p. 96; Wood, *Battles of the American Revolution*, pp. 73-74; Smith, *The Battle of Trenton*, p. 24.

39. Billias, *General John Glover and his Marblehead Mariners*, pp. 11-14; Bill, *The Campaign of Princeton*, p. 56; Fischer, *Washington's Crossing*, pp. 154, 251-252; Ketchum, *The Winter Soldiers*, pp. 261-262; Stryker, *The Battles of Trenton and Princeton*, p. 168; Weller, "Guns of Destiny," *MA*, p. 8.

40. Ketchum, *The Winter Soldiers*, pp. 262-263; Stryker, *The Battles of Trenton and Princeton*, p. 172; Edgar, *Campaign of 1776*, p. 301; Dwyer, *"The Day Is Ours!,"* pp. 257, 267; Tagney, *The World Turned Upside Down*, p. 286; Bill, *The Campaign for Princeton*, p. 56; Edgar, *Campaign of 1776*, p. 343; Weller, "Guns of Destiny," *MA*, pp. 4,8, 13.

41. Stryker, *The Battles fo Trenton and Princeton*, p. 372.

42. Ibid.

43. Slagle, "The Von Lossberg Regiment," AU, pp. 95-96, 215; Ketchum, *The Winter Soldiers*, p. 263; Wood, *Battles of the Revolutionary War*, pp. 73-74; Fischer, *Washington's Crossing*, pp. 248, 251; Smith, *The Battle of Trenton*, p. 24; Burgoyne, *Defeat, Disaster, and Dedication*, pp. 20, 103; Stryker, *The Battles of Trenton and Princeton*, pp. 109-110, 372, 390; Edgar, *Campaign of 1776*, p. 343; Weller, "Guns of Destiny," *MA*, pp. 4, 8, 13

44. Slagle, "The Von Lossberg Regiment," AU, p. 96; Smith, *The Battle of Trenton*, p. 24; Edgar, *Campaign of 1776*, p. 343.

45. Wheeler, *Voices of 1776*, p. 206; Fischer, *Washington's Crossing*, pp. 248-249.

46. Craig, *General Edward Hand*, pp. 1-43; Weller, "Guns of Destiny," *MA*, p. 10.

47. Slagle, "The Von Lossberg Regiment," AU, pp. 17, 96, 100; Retzer, *The German Regiment of Maryland and Pennsylvania*, pp. 8-10; Wright, *The Continental Army*, p. 259; Trussell, *The Pennsylvania Line*, pp. 33, 223, 225-226; Ketchum, *The Winter Soldiers*, p. 263; Fischer, *Washington's Crossing*, pp. 249, 251; Smith, *The Battle of Trenton*, p. 24; Wheeler, *Voices of 1776*, p. 206; Craig, *General Edward Hand*, pp. 1-48; Edgar, *Campaign of 1776*, p. 343; Chandler, *The Campaigns of Napoleon*, p. 179;

Weller, "Guns of Destiny," *MA*, p. 8; Stryker, *The Battles of Trenton and Princeton*, pp. 372, 405.

48. Slagle, "The Von Lossberg Regiment," AU, pp. 96, 99; Fischer, *Washington's Crossing*, p. 251;Retzer, *The German Regiment of Maryland and Pennsylvania*, pp. 8-10; Smith, *The Battle of Trenton*, p. 24.

49. Slagle, "The Von Lossberg Regiment," AU, p. 96; Steven V. Roberts, "Taking up arms– and assimilation" book review, *Washington Post*, April 11, 2010; Smith, *The Battle of Trenton*, p. 24; Fischer, *Washington's Crossing*, pp. 375-379.

50. Craig, *General Edward Hand*, p. 37.

Chapter IX

1. *Maryland Gazette*, May 1, 1777; Burrows, *Forgotten Patriots*, p. 6; Edgar, *Campaign of 1776*, p. 146; Craig, *General Edward Hand*, pp. 27-28; Fischer, *Washington's Crossing*, p. 391.

2. Lengel, *General George Washington*, pp. 167-168, 188; Dwyer, *"The Day Is Ours!,"* pp. 12-13.

3. Stryker, *The Battles of Trenton and Princeton*, p. 375.

4. Slagle, "The Von Lossberg Regiment," AU, p. 96; Dwyer, *"The Day Is Ours!,"* p. 259; Ferran's Limerick Directory 1769, internet; "Havens and Hideaways, Seaside Charm in West Cork," internet; George Washington letter to Apollos Morris, January 29, 1777, Gilder Lehrman Collection, New York Historical Society, New York City; Smith, *The Battle of Trenton*, p. 24.

5. Stryker, *The Battles of Trenton and Princeton*, p. 366; Fischer, *Washington's Crossing*, p. 247.

6. Stryker, *The Battles of Trenton and Princeton*, p. 368; Valentine, *Lord Stirling*, p. 197; Weller, "Guns of Destiny," *MA*, p. 10.

7. Slagle, "The Von Lossberg Regiment," AU, pp. 17-18, 93, 96, 214-215; Retzer, *TheGerman Regiment of Maryland and Pennsylvania*, p. 8; Trussel, *The Pennsylvania Line*, p. 33; Atwood, *The Hessians*, pp. 74-75; Smith, *The Battle of Trenton*, pp. 24-25; Ketchum, *The Winter Soldiers*, p. 263; Boatner, *Encyclopedia of the American Revolution*, pp. 64, 245; Cox, *A Proper Sense of Honor*, p. 30; Brookhiser, *Alexander Hamilton*, p. 29; Fischer, *Washington's Crossing*, pp. 247, 251; Hanser, *The Glorious Hours of Lt. Monroe*, p. 155; Joseph M. Malit email to author, July 21, 2010; Edgar, *Campaign of 1776*, p. 144; Bill and Marjorie K. Walraven, *The Magnificent Barbarians, Little Told Tales of the Texas Revolution*, (Austin: Eakin Press, 1993), p. 171; Weller, "Guns of Destiny," *MA*, p. 8; Stryker, *The Battles of Trenton and Princeton*, p. 175; Clark, *All Cloudless Glory*, p. 240; Marble, *James Monroe*, pp. 46-47.

8. Stryker, *The Battles of Trenton and Princeton*, p. 372.

9. Ibid., p. 375.

10. Ibid., p. 376; Kochan, *Don Troiani's Soldiers of the American Revolution*, pp. 61-73; Kyle, *American Gun*, pp. 3-6.

11. Griffin, *Catholics and the American Revolution*, vol. 2, pp. 371, 374, 383; Wheeler, *Voices of 1776*, p. 207; Fischer, *Washington's Crossing*, p. 251; Smith, *The Battle of Trenton*, p. 24.

12. Weller, "Guns of Destiny," *MA*, p. 8; Wheeler, *Voices of 1776*, p. 207; Irving, *George Washington*, p. 336.

13. Heath, *Memoirs of Major-General William Heath*, p. 95; Erza Stiles, *The Literary Diary of Erza Stiles, D. D., LL. D.*, (2 vols., New York: Charles Scribner's Sons, 1901), vol. 2, p. 109; Fischer, *Washington's Crossing*, p. 251; Smith, *The Battle of Trenton*, p. 24.

14. Ward, *The War of the Revolution*, p. 301.

15. Stryker, *The Battles of Trenton and Princeton*, pp. 375-376.

16. Ibid., pp. 480-481.

17. Elisha Bostwick Memoir, YUL; Smith, *The Battle of Trenton*, pp. 23-24.

18. Trussell, *The Pennsylvania Line*, p. 33; Smith, *The Battle of Trenton*, p. 23; Fischer, *Washington's Crossing*, p. 251; Edgar, *Campaign of 1776*, p. 382; Fischer, *Liberty and Freedom*, p. 146.

19. Puls, *Henry Knox*, p. 77.

20. Valentine, *Lord Stirling*, p. 197; Mitnick, ed., *New Jersey and the American Revolution*, pp. 4, 17; Rodney, *Diary of Captain Thomas Rodney*, p. 51.

21. Valentine, *Lord Stirling*, p. 197; Walters, *John Haslet*, p. 369.

22. Valentine, *Lord Stirling*, p. 198; Mitnick, ed., *New Jersey in the American Revolution*, pp. 142-143,

23. *Maryland Gazette*, May 1, 1777; Peckham, *The War of Independence*, p. 42; Mitnick, ed., *New Jersey and the American Revolution*, p. 182; *New York Times*, December 27, 1880; Smith, *New York 1776*, pp. 50-54.

24. Lengel, *General George Washington*, p. 209; Boatner, *Encyclopedia of the American Revolution*, p. 16.

25. Stryker, *The Battles of Trenton and Princeton*, p. 376.

26. Walters, *John Haslet*, p. 369.

27. Slagle, "The Von Lossberg Regiment," AU, pp. 36, 110; Smith, *New York 1776*, p. 54; *New York Times*, December 27, 1880; Boatner, *Encyclopedia of the American Revolution*, p. 499; Burrows, *Forgotten Patriots*, pp. 6, 30; Edgar, *Campaign of 1776*, p. 151.

28. Slagle, "The Von Lossberg Regiment," AU, pp. 38, 215; Irving, *George Washington*, p. 336.

29. Farling, *Almost A Miracle*, p. 178; Hanser, *The Glorious Hour of Lt. Monroe*, p. 161; Edgar, *Campaign of 1776*, pp. 344, 392.

Chapter X

1. Slagle, "The Von Lossberg Regiment," AU, p. 98; Billias, *General John Glover and his Marblehead Mariners*, p. 14; Bill, *The Campaign of Princeton*, p. 56; Ketchum, *The Winter Soldiers*, pp. 263-264; Fischer, *Washington's Crossing*, p. 252; Dwyer, *"The Day Is Ours!,"* pp. 259-260; Smith, *The Battle of Trenton*, pp. 24-25; Burgoyne, *Defeat,*

Disaster, and Dedication, p. 76; Weller, "Guns of Destiny," *MA*, p. 8; Ward, *The War of the Revolution*, p. 301

2. Dwyer, *The Day Is Ours!*, p. 260; Smith, *The Battle of Trenton*, p. 25; Weller, "Guns of Destiny," *MA*, p. 10.

3. Slagle, "The Von Lossberg Regiment," AU, p. 58; Randall, *George Washington*, p. 325; Bill, *The Campaign of Princeton*, p. 57; Ketchum, *The Winter Soldiers*, pp. 264-265; Fischer, *Washington's Crossing*, pp. 251-252, 254, 405; Dwyer, *"The Day Is Ours!*," p. 268; Smith, *TheBattle of Trenton*, pp. 22, 25; Linklater, *An Artist in Treason*, p. 28; Burgoyne, *Defeat, Disaster, and Dedication*, pp. 66-67, Stryker, *The Battles of Trenton and Princeton*, pp. 227, 357, 389, 392-393; Weller, "Guns of Destiny," *MA*, pp. 4, 8, 13.

4. Burgoyne, *Defeat, Disaster, and Dedication*, p. 76; Bill, *The Campaign of Princeton*, p. 57; Smith, *The Battle of Trenton*, p. 25; Edgar, *Campaign of 1776*, p. 344; Dwyer, *"The Day Is Ours!*," pp. 268-269; Stryker, *The Battles of Trenton and Princeton*, p. 168.

5. Troiani and Kochan, *Don Troiani's Soldiers of the American Revolution*, p. 62; Ketchum, *The Winter Soldiers*, pp. 264-265; Fischer, *Washington's Crossing*, p. 252; Dwyer, *"The Day Is Ours!*," pp. 268, 273; Burgoyne, *Defeat, Disaster, and Dedication*, p. 76.

6. Burgoyne, *Defeat, Disaster, and Dedication*, p. 76; Edgar, *Campaign of 1776*, pp. 345-347.

7. Fischer, *Washington's Crossing*, p. 252; Dwyer, *"The Day Is Ours!*," p. 257; John Keane, *TomPaine, A Political Life*, (New York: Little, Brown and Company, 1995), pp. 16-22, 192-196; Crown and Rogers, *Images of America, Trenton*, p. 7.

8. Ketchum, *The Winter Soldiers*, p. 265; Fischer, *Washington's Crossing*, pp. 253, 405; Linklater, *An Artist in Treason*, pp. 7, 19, 28-328; Smith, *The Battle of Trenton*, p. 25; Stryker, *The Battles of Trenton and Princeton*, p. 393.

9. A *Young Patriot in the American Revolution*, pp. 83-85.

10. Dwyer, *"The Day Is Ours!*," p. 269; Hanser, *The Glorious Hour of Lt. Monroe*, p. 161; Smith, *The Battle of Trenton*, pp. 25-26.

11. Ward, *The War of the Revolution*, p. 303.

12. Elisha Bostwick Memoir, YUL.

13. Tagney, *The World Turned Upside Down*, p. 286.

14. Ward, *Major General Adam Stephen and the Cause of American Liberty*, p. 152.

15. Stryker, *The Battles of Trenton and Princeton*, p. 376.

16. "The Good Soldier White," *American Heritage*, p. 77; Fischer, *Washington's Crossing*, pp. 249, 254, 405; Dwyer, *"The Day Is Ours!*," pp. 259, 261.

17. Griffin, *Catholics in the American Revolution*, vol. 2, p. 388; Brian Lalor, editor, *TheEncyclopedia of Ireland*, (New Haven: Yale University Press, 2003), p. 393.

18. Tilghman, *Memoir of Lieutenant Colonel Tench Tilghman*, pp. 10, 15,149.

19. Smith, *The Battle of Trenton*, pp. 25-26; Edgar, *Campaign of 1776*, pp. 349, 362.

20. Washington letter to Morris, January 29, 1777; Lehrman Collection, NYHS; Ferran's Limerick Directory 1769, internet; Dwyer, *"The Day Is Ours!*," p. 259.

21. Elisha Bostwick Memoir, YUL; Fischer, *Washington's Crossing*, p. 251.

22. Hamilton, *The Life of Alexander Hamilton by his son*, vol. 1, p. 57.

23. Cox, *A Proper Sense of Honor*, pp. 58-59.

24. Troiani and Kochan, *Don Troiani's Soldiers of the American Revolution*, p. 68; Dwyer, *The Day Is Ours!*, p. 382.

25. Upham, *A Memoir of General John Glover*, p. 60; Burgoyne, *Defeat, Disaster, and Dedication*, pp. 10-11; Stryker, *The Battles of Trenton and Princeton*, p. 356; Chastellux, *Travelsin North America*, p. 69

26. Stone, *Letters of Brunswick and Hessian Officers During the American Revolution*, pp. 128-129.

27. *A Young Patriot in the American Revolution*, pp. 82, 85-86.

28. *A Young Patriot in the American Revolution*, p. 85.

29. Burgoyne, *Defeat, Disaster, and Dedication*, p. 21.

30. Burgoyne, *Defeat, Disaster, and Dedication*, pp. 77-78, 86-87, 94-95.

31. Burgoyne, *Defeat, Disaster, and Dedication*, p. 76.

32. "The Good Soldier White," *American Heritage*, pp. 74-77.

33. Slagle, "The Von Lossberg Regiment," AU, p. 95; Burgoyne, *Defeat, Disaster, and Dedication*, p. 21.

34. *Maryland Gazette*, May 1, 1777; Craig, *General Edward Hand*, pp. 1, 35-36; Alderman, *Colonists For Sale*, p. 170.

35. *Annual Register*, London, England, 20, 1777.

36. Robert Leckie, *George Washington's War, The Saga of the American Revolution*, (New York: HarperCollins Publishers, 1993), p. 322.

37. David McCulloch, *1776*, (New York: Simon and Schuster, 2005), p. 284.

38. *A Young Patriot in the American Revolution*, p. 82; Weller, "Guns of Destiny," *MA*, p. 10.

39. Stephenson, *Patriot Battles*, pp. 252, 257, 258-259; Valentine, *Lord Stirling*, p. 197; Buchanan, *The Road to Valley Forge*, p. 165; Atwood, *The Hessians*, p. 96; Dwyer, *"The Day Is Ours!*," p. 268; Edgar, *Campaign of 1776*, p. 343.

40. Slagle, "The Von Lossberg Regiment," AU, p. 216; Fischer, *Washington's Crossing*, p. 249; Dwyer, *"The Day Is Ours!*," pp. 267-268.

41. Von Hagen, *The Germanic People in America*, p. 162; Wheeler, *Voices of 1776*, p. 203; Irving, *George Washington*, p. 336.

42. Stryker, *The Battles of Trenton and Princeton*, pp. 263-264; Retzer, *The German Regiment of Maryland and Pennsylvania*, pp. 7-10, 48-49.

43. *New York Times*, December 27, 1880.

44. Stone, *Letters of Brunswick and Hessian Officers During the American Revolution*, p. 131; Flood, *Fight, And Rise Again*, pp. 105, 131-132.

45. Slagle, "The Von Lossberg Regiment," AU, p. 9; Rodes, *Germany*, pp. 248-250; Smith, *The Battle of Trenton*, pp. 27-28, 31; Fischer, *Washington's Crossing*, pp. 60, 62-63.

46. *Maryland Gazette*, February 20, 1777; Atwood, *The Hessians*, p. 186; Burgoyne, *Defeat, Disaster, and Dedication*, p. 76; Fischer, *Washington's Crossing*, p. 62.

47. Henry Steele Commanger and Richard B. Morris, eds., *The Spirit of Seventy-Six, The Story of the American Revolution as Told by its Participants* (New York: Da Capo Press, 1968), pp. 268-269.

48. Atwood, *The Hessians*, pp. 186, 195; Burgoyne, *Defeat, Disaster, and Dedication*, pp. 99-101, 104.

Chapter XI

1. Needleman, *The American Soul*, pp. 86-87; Lengel, *This Glorious Struggle*, p. 89; Chandler, *The Campaigns of Napoleon*, pp. 126-130, 135-136, 141.

2. Needleman, *The American Soul*, pp. 86-87; Edgar, *Campaign of 1776*, p. 183.

3. *Maryland Gazette*, January 23, 1777; Kwasny, *Washington's Partisan War*, pp. 95-99, 109-112; Fleming, *1776*, pp. 462, 464; Smith, *The Battle of Trenton*, pp. 13-14.

4. *Maryland Gazette*, July 3, 1777.

5. *Maryland Gazette*, January 2, 1777; Leckie, *George Washington's War*, p. 317; Dwyer, *"The Day Is Ours!,"* p. 266; Crown and Rogers, *Images of America, Trenton*, p. 12; Smith, *The Battle of Trenton*, p. 26.

6. *Maryland Gazette*, May 29, 1777.

7. Bill, *The Campaign of Trenton*, p. 42; Atwood, *The Hessians*, pp. 8-20, 153, 171-183; Dwyer, *"The Day Is Ours!,"* p. 268; Smith, *The Battle of Trenton*, pp. 17, 27; Burgoyne, *Defeat, Disaster, and Dedication*, p. 75; Edgar, *Campaign of 1776*, p. 345; Fischer, *Washington's Crossing*, pp. 239-240; Stryker, *The Battles of Trenton and Princeton*, p. 402.

8. Slagle, "The Von Lossberg Regiment," AU, pp. 70-71; *Pennsylvania Evening Post*, July 26, 1777; Anderson, *The Command of the Howe Brothers*, pp. 202-203; Leckie, *George Washington's War*, p. 317; Ferling, *Almost A Miracle*, p. 173; Mitnick, ed., *New Jersey in the American Revolution*, pp. 48-49; Smith, *The Battle of Trenton*, p. 14; Fischer, *Washington's Crossing*, pp. 204-205; Burgoyne, *Defeat, Disaster, and Dedication*, p. 71.

9. Slagle, "The Von Lossberg Regiment," AU, pp. 92, 99, 106. 108; *Pennsylvania Post*, July 26, 1777; Atwood, *The Hessians*, pp. 36, 40, 68-69, note 44, page 68, 82, 89-90, 92; Dwyer, *"The Day Is Ours!,"* p. 267; Fischer, *Washington's Crossing*, pp. 55-57, 260; Stryker, *The Battles of Trenton and Princeton*, pp. 170, 391-393, 398-422; Edgar, *Campaign of 1776*, p. 325; *A Young Patriot in the American Revolution*, pp. 82-83.

10. Slagle, "The Von Lossberg Regiment," AU, p. 106; Atwood, *The Hessians*, pp. 43-44, 89; Smith, *The Battle of Trenton*, pp. 25-26; *A Young Patriot in the American Revolution*, pp. 82-83.

11. Slagle, "The Von Lossberg Regiment," AU, p. 89; Troiani and Kochan, *Don Troiani's Soldiers of the American Revolution*, p. 73; Atwood, *The Hessians*, p. 81; Burgoyne, *Defeat, Disaster, and Dedication*, p. 71; Stryker, *The Battles of Trenton and Princeton*, p. 99.

12. Slagle, "The Von Lossberg Regiment," AU, p. 89; Bill, *The Campaign of Princeton*, p. 40; Atwood, *The Hessians*, pp. 89-90, 92; Smith, *The Battle of Trenton*, p. 18; Burgoyne, *Defeat, Disaster, and Dedication*, p. 71; Bill, *The Campaign of Princeton*, p. 13; Weller, "Guns of Destiny," *MA*, pp. 10, 15.

13. Stryker, *The Battles of Trenton and Princeton*, p. 372.

14. Weller, "Guns of Destiny," *MA*, pp. 1-10; Chandler, *The Campaigns of Napoleon*, pp. 504-505, 734; Haythornthwaite, *Napoleon's Specialist Troops*, p. 4.

15. Chandler, *The Campaigns of Napoleon*, pp. 28, 504-505, 708, 734; Weller, "Guns of Destiny," *MA*, p. 10.

16. Lengel, *General George Washington*, p. 186; Chandler, *The Campaigns of Napoleon*, pp. 504-505, 708, 734; Weller, "Guns of Destiny," *MA*, p. 10.

17. Slagle, "The Von Lossberg Regiment," AU, pp. 101, 104; Griffin, *Catholics and the American Revolution*, vol. 2, pp. 202-203; Stryker, *The Battles of Trenton and Princeton*, pp. 281, 370, 478-479; Edgar, *Campaign of 1776*, pp. 382-383; "The Good Soldier White," *American Heritage*, pp. 75-77; Weller, "Guns of Destiny," *MA*, pp. 1-10; Fischer, *Washington's Crossing*, pp. 247-248

18. Chadwick, *George Washington's War*, p. 19; Buchanan, *The Road to Valley Forge*, p. 152; Edgar, *Campaign of 1776*, p. 343; Stryker, *The Battles of Trenton and Princeton*, pp. 370, 479; Chandler, *The Campaigns of Napoleon*, p. 179; Weller, "Guns of Destiny," *MA*, pp. 1-10; Haythornwaite, *Napoleon's Specialist Troops*, p. 4.

19. Buchanan, *The Road to Valley Forge*, pp.164-166; Chandler, *The Campaigns of Napoleon*, pp. 708, 734; Weller, "Guns of Destiny," *MA*, pp. 1-10.

20. Puls, *Henry Knox*, pp. 2, 76; Stryker, *The Battles of Trenton and Princeton*, pp. 370, 479; McCulloch, *1776*, p. 270; Fischer, *Washington's Crossing*, p. 153; Edgar, *Campaign of 1776*, p. 343; "The Good Soldier White," *American Heritage*, pp. 75-77; Weller, "Guns of Destiny," *MA*, pp. 1-10.

21. Puls, *Henry Knox*, pp. 75, 78; Johnson, *Napoleon*, pp. 56-57; Wood, *Battles of the Revolutionary War*, p. 72; Fischer, *Washington's Crossing*, p. 374; Stryker, *The Battles of Trenton and Princeton*, p. 370; "The Good Soldier White," *American Heritage*, pp. 76-77; Chandler, *The Campaigns of Napoleon*, pp. 179, 504-505, 708, 734; Weller, "Guns of Destiny," *MA*, pp. 1-10; Haythornwaite, *Napoleon's Specialist Troops*, p. 4.

22. Bill, *The Campaign of Princeton*, p. 46; Smith, *The Battle of Trenton*, pp. 13-14.

23. Weller, "Guns of Destiny," *MA*, pp. 10, 15.

24. Puls, *Henry Knox*, p. 78.

25. Fischer, *Washington's Crossing*, p. 254; Edgar, *Campaign of 1776*, p. 343.

26. Stryker, *The Battles of Trenton and Princeton*, p. 372.

27. Ibid., pp. 372, 436.

28. Ibid., p. 364.

29. Slagle, "The Von Lossberg Regiment," AU, pp. 102-103; Edgar, *Campaign of 1776*, p. 343; Stryker, *The Battles of Trenton and Princeton*, p. 370; "The Good Soldier White," *American Heritage*, pp. 76-77; Weller, "Guns of Destiny," *MA*, pp. 1-10; Fischer, *Washington's Crossing*, pp. 201-235; Smith, *The Battle of Trenton*, pp. 15-26.

30. Burgoyne, *Defeat, Disaster, and Dedication*, p. 77.

31. Von Hagen, *The German People in America*, p. 157; Fischer, *Washington's Crossing*, pp. 259-260.

32. *Maryland Gazette*, January 23, 1777.

33. Slagle, "The Von Lossberg Regiment," AU, p. 103; James C. Corbett, compiler, *German General Officers Serving in the American Revolution, 1776-1784*, (Oldwick: The King's Arms Press & Bindery, 1978), pp. 4-5; Boatner, *Encyclopedia of the American Revolution*, p. 499; *New York Times*, December 27, 1880; Valentine, *Lord Stirling*, pp. 186-187, 197.

34. Slagle, "The Von Lossberg Regiment," AU, pp. 96,108, 214-217; Fischer, *Washington'sCrossing*, pp. 252, 405-406; Dwyer, *"The Day Is Ours!,"* p. 263; Smith, *The Battle of Trenton*, p. 27; Burgoyne, *Defeat, Disaster, and Dedication*, pp. 42-43, 70, 76-77.

35. Stryker, *The Battles of Trenton and Princeton*, p. 195; Slagle, "The Von Lossberg Regiment," AU, p. 99.

36. Fischer, *Washington's Crossing*, p. 88.

37. Ketchum, *The Winter Soldiers*, pp. 265; Edgar, *Campaign of 1776*, p. 345; Raphael, *Founders*, p. 286.

38. Stryker, *The Battles of Trenton and Princeton*, p. 376.

39. Valentine, *Lord Stirling*, p. 198.

40. Ibid; Fischer, *Washington's Crossing*, pp. 247, 254; Boatner, *Encyclopedia of the American Revolution*, p. 1100; Farling, *Almost A Miracle*, p. 631.

41. Smith, *The Battle of Trenton*, p. 27; Fischer, *Washington's Crossing*, p. 406.

42. Angell, *Diary of Colonel Israel Angell*, pp. 28-29, note 4.

43. Charles Anderson File, Register of the California Society of the Sons of the American Revolution, Sons of the American Revolution, internet; Stryker, *The Battles of Trenton and Princeton*, p. 121; Robert Anderson, *An Artillery Officer in the Mexican War, 1846-47*, (New York: G. P. Putnam's Sons, 1911), pp. xii-xiii; Fischer, *Washington's Crossing*, p. 406; Dwyer, *"The Day is Ours!,"* pp. 249-250; Richard N. Current, *Lincoln and the First Shot*, (New York: J. B. Lippincott Company, 1963), pp. 124-125.

44. Tagney, *The World Turned Upside Down*, p. 280; Edgar, *Campaign of 1776*, p. 343.

45. Farling, *Almost A Miracle*, p. 631; Fischer, *Washington's Crossing*, pp. 254-255.

46. Cox, *A Proper Sense of Honor*, pp. 191-192.

47. Edgar, *Campaign of 1776*, p. 343; Irving, *George Washington*, p. 338; Ketchum, *TheWinter Soldiers*. p. 270; Fischer, *Washington's Crossing*, p. 255; Dwyer, *"The Day Is Ours!,"* p. 263; Smith, *The Battle of Trenton*, pp. 27, 31; Burial Records, First Presbyterian Church Archives, Trenton, New Jersey.

48. Burgoyne, *Defeat, Disaster, and Dedication*, p. 76; Ketchum, *The Winter Soldiers*, p. 270; Dwyer, *The Day Is Ours!*, p. 261.

49. Burgoyne, *Defeat, Disaster, and Dedication*, p. 76; Fischer, *Washington's Crossing*, p. 58.

50. Burgoyne, *Defeat, Disaster, and Dedication*, p. 20.

51. Slagle, "The Von Lossberg Regiment," AU, p. 216; Dwyer, *"The Day Is Ours!,"* p. 261; Fischer, *Washington's Crossing*, p. 405; Crown and Rogers, *Images of American, Trenton*, p. 17; Smith, *The Battle of Trenton*, p. 27; Burgoyne, *Defeat, Disaster, and Dedication*, p. 2.

52. Pastor John R. Allen, First Presbyterian Church, Trenton, New Jersey, to author, June 24, 2010.

53. Research of Joseph Keller, Waldorf, Maryland, and interview with author, July 31, 2010.

54. Adi-Kent Thomas Jeffrey, *Ghosts in the Valley*, (New Hope: New Hope Art Shop, 1972), p. 20.

55. Slagle, "The Von Lossberg Regiment," AU, pp. 179-196; Edgar, *Campaign of 1776*, p. 345; Stryker, *The Battles of Trenton and Princeton*, pp. 226-231, 402.

56. Stryker, *The Battles of Trenton and Princeton*, p. 227.

57. Scott G. Rall, Waldorf, Maryland, to author, July 22, 2010.

58. Slagle, "The Von Lossberg Regiment," AU, p. 182; *New York Times*, April 9, 1876; Fischer, *Washington's Crossing*, p. 260; Stryker, *The Battles of Trenton and Princeton*, pp. 229-231.

59. Flood, *Rise, And Fight Again*, p. 100; Slagle, "The Von Lossberg Regiment," AU, p. 108.

60. Stryker, *The Battles of Trenton and Princeton*, pp. 199, 226-231, 402.

61. Zaboly, *American Colonial Ranger*, p. 21; English, *General Hugh Mercer*, p. 78-79, 81; Goolrick, *The Life of General Hugh Mercer*, p. 49; Middlekauff, *The Glorious Cause*, pp. 340-341; Fleming, *1776*, pp. 176, 294; Fischer, *Washington's Crossing*, pp. 370-373; Raphael, *Founders*, p. 290.

62. Raphael, *Founders*, p. 290; Fischer, *Washington's Crossing*, pp. 370-375.

63. Kwanwy, *Washington's Partisan War*, pp. xiv, 111-113, 337-339; Fischer, *Washington'sCrossing*, p. 256; Raphael, *Founders*, p. 287; Ward, *The War of the Revolution*, p. 302..

64. Clark, *All Cloudless Glory*, p. 307.

65. *Maryland Gazette*, January 23, 1777; Stryker, *The Battles of Trenton and Princeton*, pp. 281-282; Reid, *Culloden Moor 1746*, pp. 85, 87; Hopson, *Captain Daniel Neil*, pp. 19-20; Buchanan, *The Road to Valley Forge*, pp. 175-178; Randall, *George Washington*, pp. 328-329; Alden, *A History of the American Revolution*, pp. 276-277, 282-283; Hugh Mercer Will, March 20, 1776, Mss2 M5346 a 1, Virginia Historical Society, Richmond, Virginia; Bill, *The Campaign of Princeton*, pp. 104-105; Fischer, *Washington's Crossing*, p. 333; Dwyer, *"The Day Is Ours!,"* pp. 313, 345; Waterman, *With Sword and Lancet*, p. 155; Weller, "Guns of Destiny," *MA*, p. 8; Raphael, *Founders*, pp. 288-289.

66. *Maryland Gazette*, January 23, 1777; Fischer, *The Crossing*, p. 415, note 10; James Potter biography, Wikipedia, internet; Dwyer, *"The Day Is Ours!,"* pp. 358-359; Hopson, *Captain Daniel Neil*, p. 24.

67. *Maryland Gazette*, February 13, 1777; Irving, *George Washington*, p. 340; Hopson, *CaptainDaniel Neil*, p. 24; Bill, *The Campaign of Princeton*, pp. 104-105; Fischer, *Washington'sCrossing*, p. 255.

68. *Maryland Gazette*, February 13, 1777; Walters, *John Haslet*, pp. vii, 3-5, 24, 381, 383; Lalor, ed., *The Encyclopedia of Ireland*, pp. 257-258, 831-833.

69. *Maryland Gazette*, January 23, 1777; Buchanan, *The Road to Valley Forge*, p. 178; Goolrick, *The Life of General Hugh Mercer*, p. 49; English, *General Hugh Mercer*, pp. 78-79, 81; Dwyer, *"The Day Is Ours!,"* p. 353.

70. Goolrick, *The Life of General Hugh Mercer*, pp. 28-29, 31, 39

71. *Maryland Gazette*, March 13, 1777; *Virginia Gazette*, October 21, 1775 and January 24, 1777; Stryker, *The Battles of Trenton and Princeton*, pp. 284, 292, note 2; Collins, *A Brief Narrative of The Ravages of the British and Hessians at Princeton In 1776-1777*,

pp. 43-44; James Potter Biography, Wikipedia, internet; Dwyer, *"The Day Is Ours!,"* pp. 345, 358-359; Hopson, *Captain Daniel Neil,* p. 24; Bill, *The Campaign of Princeton,* p. 106; ""Fleming Family," *WMQ,* pp. 45, 47.

72. Hopson, *Captain Daniel Neil,* p. 25; Bill, *The Campaign of Princeton,* p. 106; Dwyer, *"TheDay Is Ours!,"* p. 345; Weller, "Guns of Destiny," *MA,* p. 8.

73. Golway, *Washington's General,* p. 117; Bill, *The Campaign of Princeton, 1776-1777,* p. 41; Dwyer, *"The Day Is Ours!,"* p. 345; English, *General Hugh Mercer,* p. 100; Stryker, *The Battles of Trenton and Princeton,* p. 393.

74. *Maryland Gazette,* January 23, 1777; Boatner, *Encyclopedia of the American Revolution,* p. 1217; Barbara Pratt Willis, *Handbook of Historic Fredericksburg, Virginia,* (Fredericksburg, Va.: Historic Fredericksburg Foundation, Inc., 1993), p. 16; Goolrick, *TheLife of General Hugh Mercer,* pp. 105-106.

75. Slagle, "The Von Lossberg Regiment," *AU,* pp. 17-18, Kochan, *Don Troiani's Soldiers of the American Revolution,* p. 71; Boatner, *Encyclopedia of the American Revolution,* p. 64; Joseph M. Malit to author, July 21, 2010; Stryker, *The Battles of Trenton and Princeton,* p. 401.

76. Chadwick, *George Washington's War,* p. 31.

77. Walter Millis, *Arms and Men, A Study of American Military History,* (New York: Mentor Books, 1956), pp. 12-30; Zinn, *A People's History of the American Revolution,* pp. 398-399; Fischer, *Washington's Crossing,* pp. 261, 363; Chandler, *The Campaigns of Napoleon,* pp. 126-129, 135.

78. *New York Times,* April 9, 1876; Boatner, *Encyclopedia of the American Revolution,* p. 610.

79. Lengel, *General George Washington,* p. 209; Ketchum, *The Winter Soldiers,* p. 145; Ward, *Major General Adam Stephen and the Cause of American Liberty,* pp. 198-199.

80. Flexner, *Washington,* p. 98.

81. Rose, *Washington's War,* pp. 10-24, 198-200; Peckham, *The War of Independence,* p. 56; Barbara W. Tuchman, *The March of Folly, From Troy to Vietnam,* (New York: Alfred A. Knopf, 1984), pp. 128-231; Fischer, *Washington's Crossing,* pp. 344-345.

82. Baker, *George Washington's War,* pp. 85, 154.

83. Stryker, *The Battles of Trenton and Princeton,* p. 373.

84. Wallace, *Appeal to Arms,* p. 133; Atwood, *The Hessians,* pp. 103, 106-107; Fischer, *Washington's Crossing,* p. 260.

85. *Maryland Gazette,* January 23, 1777; Fischer, *Washington's Crossing,* p. 367; Edgar, *Campaign of 1776,* p. 345.

86. Stryker, *The Battles of Trenton and Princeton,* p. 372.

87. Ibid., p. 226.

88. Ibid., p. 427.

Epilogue

1. *Maryland Gazette,* March 20, 1777.

2. David L. Jacobson, *Essays on the American Revolution*, (New York: Holt, Rhinehart and Winston, Inc., 1970), p. 176; Anderson, *The Command of the Howe Brothers*, pp. 200-212; Stryker, *The Battles of Trenton and Princeton*, p. 310; James Kirby Martin and Mark Edward Lender, *A Respectable Army, The Military Origins of the Republic 1763-1789*, (Arlington Heights: Harlin Davidson, Inc., 1982), p. 50; Tuchman, *The March of Folly*, p. 213; Fleming, *Washington's Secret War*, pp. 7-8; Ferling, *The Ascent of George Washington*, pp. 102, 108, 111.

3. Ferling, *The Ascent of George Washington*, p. 121; Pearson, *Those Damned Rebels*, pp. 220-221; Fleming, *Washington's Secret War*, pp. 7-8.

4. Rose, *Washington's War*, pp. 83, 94; Farling, *Almost A Miracle*, p. 179; Ketchum, *The Winter Soldiers*, p. 211; Alfred Hoyt Bill, *Valley Forge, The Making of An Army*, (New York: Harper and Brothers, 1952), pp. 3-6; Person, *Those Damned Rebels*, pp.221-225; Troiani and Kochan, *Don Troiani's Soldiers of the American Revolution*, p. 167; William C. Stinchcombe, *The American Revolution and the French Alliance*, (Syracuse: Syracuse University Press, 1969), pp. 9-10; Ferling, *The Ascent of George Washington*, pp. 102, 108, 111.

5. Stiles, *The Literary Diary of Erza Stiles*, vol. 2, p. 113.

6. Piers Mackesy, *The War for America 1775-1783*, (Lincoln: University of Nebraska Press, 1992), p. xxiv.

7. Chadwick, *George Washington's War*, p. 36.

8. Fischer, *Washington's Crossing*, p. 345.

9. Raphael, *Founders*, pp. 281-284, 287.

10. Hanser, *The Glorious Hour of Lt. Monroe*, p. 162.

11. Davis, *100 Decisive Battles*, p. xi.

12. Bellamy, *The Private Life of George Washington*, p. 20.

13. Commager and Morris, eds., *The Spirit of Seventy-Six*, pp. 269-270.

14. Davis, *100 Decisive Battles*, pp. 253.

15. Hopson, *Captain Daniel Neil*, pp. 3-5, 25-26, 29; Stryker, *The Battles of Trenton and Princeton*, p. 453.

16. Hopson, *Captain Daniel Neil*, p. 28.

17. Ibid., p. 28.

18. Ibid., p. 29.

19. Stryker, *The Battles of Trenton and Princeton*, p. 453.

20. Hopson, *Captain Daniel Neil*, pp. 29-30.

21. Ibid; Ketchum, *The Winter Soldiers*, pp. 250-251; English, *General Hugh Mercer*, pp. 79, 81; Goolrick, *The Life of General Hugh Mercer*, pp. 13-21, 49; Atwood, *The Hessians*, pp. 40, 49; Fischer, *Washington's Crossing*, p.154; Stryker, *The Battles of Trenton and Princeton*, pp. 390-394; Ellis, *American Creation*, pp. 15, 35-36; Ferling, *The Ascent of George Washington*, pp. 122-123

22. Angelo Codevilla and Paul Seabury, *War, Ends and Means*, (Washington, D.C.: Potomac Books, 2006), p. 2.

23. Needleman, *The American Soul*, p. 83; Fleming, *1776*, pp. 441, 462; Ketchum, *The Winter Soldiers*, pp. 249-251; Bill, *The Campaign of Princeton*, p.47; Bill, *Valley Forge,*

p. 6; Chandler, *The Campaigns of Napoleon*, pp. 129, 130, 135; Stryker, *The Battles of Trenton and Princeton*, pp. 452-455; Raphael, *Founders*, pp. 267, 285, 290; Ferling, *The Ascent of George Washington*, pp. 119-123.

24. Ferling, *The Ascent of George Washington*, pp. 119-123; 365-366; Chadwick, *George Washington's War*, pp. 499-500; Goolrick, *The Life of General Hugh Mercer*, pp. 13-21, 49; English, *General Hugh Mercer*, pp. x-81; Tony Perrottet, *Napoleon's Privates, 2,500 Years of History Unzipped*, (New York: MJF Books, 2008), p. 207; Atwood, *The Hessians*, pp. 204-205; von Hagen, *The Germanic People in America*, pp. 158, 338; Codevilla and Seabury, *War,*. Pp. 95-97

25. Ferling, *The Ascent of George Washington*, pp. 120-123, 365-366; Stryker, *The Battles of Trenton and Princeton*, p. 310.

26. Clark, *All Cloudless Glory*, p. 529.

27. Giles, trans., *The Art of War, Sun Tzu*, pp. 62-63; Goolrick, *The Life of General Hugh Mercer*, pp. 13-21,49; English, *General Hugh Mercer*, pp. x-81; Raphael, *Founders*, p. 290; Ferling, *The Ascent of George Washington*, pp. 119-123.

28. *Pennsylvania Evening Post*, January 21, 1777; Raphael, *Founders*, pp. 287; Ferling, *The Ascent of George Washington*, pp. 119-123.

29. Stryker, *The Battles of Trenton and Princeton*, p. 1; Needleman, *The American Soul*, p. 83; Ferling, *The Ascent of George Washington*, pp. 119-123,.

30. Upham, *A Memoir of General John Glover*, pp. 34-35; Billias, *General John Glover and his Marblehead Mariners*, pp. 177, 183-191; Ferling, *The Ascent of George Washington*, pp. 119-123.

31. Billias, *General John Glover and his Marblehead Mariners*, pp. 183-187; Gamage and Lord, *The Lure of Marblehead*, pp. 33-34.

32. *Maryland Gazette*, March 20, 1777; Fischer, *Washington's Crossing*, pp. 254-255.

33. *Maryland Gazette*, March 20, 1777; Stryker, *The Battles of Trenton and Princeton*, p. 194.

34. Valentine, *Lord Stirling*, p. 199.

35. Ferling, *The Ascent of George Washington*, p. 122.

36. Stone, *Letters of Brunswick and Hessian Officers During the American Revolution*, p. 214.

37. Ibid., pp. 208; Dwyer, *The Day Is Ours!*, pp. 382-383.

38. Ferling, *The Ascent of George Washington*, pp. 108, 111; Russell Banks, *Dreaming Up America*, (New York: Seven Stories Press, 2008), pp. 1-98.

39. Banks, *Dreaming Up America*, pp. 1-98; Walter A. McDougall, *Promised Land, Crusader State, The American Encounter with the World Since 1776*, (New York: Houghton Mifflin Company, 1997), pp. 4-5, 15-17; Needleman, *TheAmerican Soul*, pp. 5, 34-35.

40. Fischer, *Washington's Crossing*, pp. 6, 10-16; Gelb, *Less Than Glory*, p. 13; Keane, *TomPaine*, pp. 106-145; Needleman, *The American Soul*, pp. 5, 34-35, 39, 41.

41. *New York Times*, February 22, 1861; McCulloch, *1776*, p. 273; Kennenth M. Stampp, "One Alone? The United States and National Self-Determination," in Gabor S. Boritt, *Lincoln, The War President, The Gettysburg Lectures*, (New York: Oxford University Press, 1992), pp. 188-189; Fred Kaplan, *Lincoln, The Biography of a Writer*, (New York: HarperCollins Publishers, 2008), pp. 78-79, 118-119, 320-324.

42. James M. McPherson, *Tried by War, Abraham Lincoln as Commander in Chief*, (New York: Penguin Press, 2008), pp. 1-2; Eric Foner, *The Fiery Trial, Abraham Lincoln and American Slavery,* (New York: W. W. Norton and Company, 2010), pp. 69-70.

43. Boritt, *Lincoln*, p. 189.

44. Keane, *Tom Paine*, pp. 108-145; Fischer, *Washington's Crossing*, pp. 138-143; Liell, *46Pages*, pp. 143-144; Ellis, *American Creation*, pp. 41-44

45. Keane, *Tom Paine*, pp. xx, 106-145; Needleman, *The American Soul*, p. 39; Ferling, *TheAscent of George Washington*, pp. 119-123.

46. Slagle,, "The Von Lossberg Regiment," AU, pp. 214, 216; *New York Times*, June 15, 1863; Fischer, *Washington's Crossing*, p. 3; Bruce Quarrie, *Hitler's Teutonic Knights, SS Pansers in action*, (Wellingborough: Thorsons Publishing Group, 1986), p. 78; Brochure, "Washington Crossing the Delaware (1851) by Emanuel Leutze, Washington Crossing Historic Park, Pennsylvania; John W. Stevens, *Reminiscences of the Civil War*, (Hillsboro: Hillsboro Mirror Print, 1902), p. 41.

47. Lengel, *General George Washington*, p. 87; Fischer, *Washington's Crossing*, p. ix; Ferling, *The Ascent of George Washington*, pp. 119-123.

48 .Chernow, *Washington*, p. 283; Asprey, *Frederick the Great*, pp. xiii-xxv; Robert Asprey, *The Reign of Napoleon Bonaparte*, (New York: Basic Books, 2001), p. 37; Ferling, *The Ascent of George Washington*, pp. 119-123.

49. Needleman, *The American Soul*, pp. 79, 83; Stryker, *The Battles of Trenton and Princeton*, p. 372; *New York Times*, February 22, 1861; McPherson, *Tried by War*, pp. 1-2; Foner, *TheFiery Trial*, p. 31; Ferling, *The Ascent of George Washington*, pp. 119-123; Bellamy, *The Private Life of George Washington*, pp. 109, 149

50. Stryker, *The Battles of Trenton and Princeton*, p. 452.

51. Gragg, *By the Hand of Providence*, p. 95; Bellamy, *The Private Life of George Washington*, p. 149.

52. Needleman, *The American Soul*, p. 22; Ferling, *The Ascent of George Washington*, pp. 119-123; Gragg, *By the Hands of Providence*, p. 87.

53. Stryker, *The Battles of Trenton and Princeton*, p. 376.

54. Ferling, *The Ascent of George Washington*, pp. 119-123; Fleming, *Liberty*, pp. 210-381; Golway, *Washington's General*, p. 106; Stryker, *The Battles of Trenton and Princeton*, p. 372.

55. Needleman, *The American Soul*, pp. 3-10, 64, 256; Ellis, *American Creation*, pp. 3-9, 56-57; Ferling, *The Ascent of George Washington*, pp. 119-123.

56. Stryker, *The Battles of Trenton and Princeton*, p. 376; Valentine, *Lord Stirling*, p. 171; Ferling, *The Ascent of George Washington*, pp. 119-123.

57. *Maryland Gazette*, November 29, 1781.

Index